EDUCATING
EXCEPTIONAL
CHILDREN

HOUGHTON MIFFLIN COMPANY · BOSTON

DALLAS · GENEVA, ILLINOIS · HOPEWELL, NEW JERSEY
PALO ALTO · LONDON

SAMUEL A. KIRK   UNIVERSITY OF ARIZONA

JAMES J. GALLAGHER   UNIVERSITY OF NORTH CAROLINA

THIRD EDITION

EDUCATING · EXCEPTIONAL · CHILDREN

Library of Congress Catalog Card Number: 78-69609

ISBN: 0-395-26526-6

PHOTO CREDITS

page 2, Frank Wing/Stock, Boston; page 26, Anestis Diakopoulos/Stock, Boston; page 58, Julie O'Neil; page 102, Burk Uzzle/Magnum Photos; page 134, Burk Uzzle/ Magnum Photos; page 180, Michael Philip Manheim/Photo Researchers; page 236, John B. Hey/Stock, Boston; page 280, John B. Hey/Stock, Boston; page 314, Charles Harbutt/Magnum Photos; page 348, Julie O'Neil/Lesley College Compass Summer Program, Cambridge, Mass. Dr. Jerome Schultz, Director, Shawn Turner; page 388, Burk Uzzle/Magnum Photos, page 432, Hella Hammid from Rapho/Photo Researchers; page 466, Cary Wolinsky/Stock, Boston

CONTENTS

1
THE EXCEPTIONAL CHILD AND SPECIAL EDUCATION 3

2
INDIVIDUAL DIFFERENCES 27

3
CHILDREN WITH INTELLECTUAL SUPERIORITY AND TALENTS 59

4
CHILDREN WITH LOW INTELLIGENCE 103

5
EDUCATING CHILDREN WITH LOW INTELLIGENCE 135

v

LIST OF FIGURES

LIST OF TABLES

FOREWORD

The impetus for writing *Educating Exceptional Children* was my experience, thirty years ago, with using multiple authors to prepare the Forty-ninth Yearbook of the National Society for the Study of Education. The multiple-author approach had the advantage of utilizing experts in each field. But the difficulties of coordinating different styles and philosophies, and often overlapping content, convinced me of the importance of an approach emphasizing continuity of style and philosophy—particularly for beginning students. Thus, in 1962, I chose to personally compile material from the many areas of special education into a unified introductory textbook. In 1972, I prepared the second edition in the same way, with suggestions and criticisms from many of my professional colleagues.

For this third edition, however, I have been fortunate enough to secure the partnership of my colleague and personal friend of long standing, Dr. James Gallagher. Dr. Gallagher has devoted his professional career to the study of exceptional children and the development of practical programs and research in various aspects of the field. As the first director of the Bureau of Education for Handicapped Children in the U.S. Office of Education, he provided the national leadership that this country needed.

In writing this third edition, Dr. Gallagher and I hope we have retained a unified approach and a style that presents complex information simply but without compromising scholarship.

As was noted in earlier editions of *Educating Exceptional Children*, our democratic philosophy is based on the belief that " 'all men are created equal'—equal before the law'—so it involves equality of opportunity. This implies educational opportunity for all children—the right of each child to receive help in learning to the limits of his capacity whether that capacity be small or great." It is ironic that it took nearly two hundred years for this philosophy to be enacted into law. The intent of PL 94–142, ''The Education of All Handicapped Children,'' enacted by the U.S. Congress in 1975, matches that of the Declaration of Independence, the cornerstone of our democratic society. I have paraphrased the intent of the new law in the words of the time-honored Declaration as follows:

We hold these truths to be self-evident, that all children, handicapped and nonhandicapped, are created equal; that they are endowed by their creator with certain inalienable rights, among these are the right to equal education to the maximum of each child's capability. To secure these rights, Public Law 94–142 was established. We, the people of these United States, solemnly declare that all exceptional children shall be educated at public expense, and that their education will be in the least restrictive environment.

To help realize this prodigious goal is the aim of *Educating Exceptional Children.*

Samuel A. Kirk

PREFACE

Educating Exceptional Children, third edition, is an introductory text for those who will work with exceptional children: prospective special educators, regular elementary and secondary school teachers, school counselors, school psychologists, and inservice educators. As a result of recent federal and state laws that mandate free appropriate education for all children in the least restrictive environment, special education is no longer the particular province of special educators. Handicapped children are increasingly integrated into public schools and regular classrooms. Commensurately, more professionals—both pre- and inservice—need basic training. Customarily, students reading this text will have had introductory courses in psychology, education, and child development. An attempt is made herein to avoid extensive content that would overlap other courses and to include only information that is germane to introducing exceptional children to a broadening audience.

During the latter part of the 1960s and especially during the 1970s, increased attention was given to the educational needs of exceptional children, especially the handicapped. New philosophies developed and new practices were tried. The effects of labeling children; the use of categories; the relative values of self-contained classes, resource rooms, and itinerant teachers; eligibility for services; mainstreaming and other efforts to integrate exceptional children with average children—these and many other issues have been the subjects of heated controversies. But despite the intensity of doctrinaire differences, all special educators agree on the need to provide special help for exceptional children, though they may disagree on the nature of that help. While we recognize the reality and the importance of many current controversies, we believe that our first task, as authors of a beginning text, is to present the characteristics and problems of each of the different clusters of atypical children, using here the categorical terminology necessary for purposes of communication. The organization of this book is intended to allow students to go further more easily—to be sensitive and effective teachers, who meet the exceptional child's needs: cognitive, social, and personal, among them.

Knowing full well that each child is unique, we stress individual differences—interindividual and intraindividual. As a theme that permeates the book, this emphasis not only helps mitigate against the misuse of labels, it also contributes to a unified and integrated presentation. We rely heavily on the concept of *intraindividual differences* in growth within each exceptional child and apply this concept to the various clusters of deviating children. We thus attempt to supply an integrating element that gives meaning to both the differences and similarities among children and the suitable modifications of educational practices.

Bearing in mind the characteristics and the distinctive problems of different learners, each chapter in this new edition is organized around three concepts:

1. the learner, that is, the exceptional child
2. curricular and instructional adaptations
3. the environment of the learner

This organization extends the basic format of earlier editions by applying knowledge about the exceptional child to teaching.

To help students better evaluate the pros and cons of concepts and practices, the discussion of current issues is deliberately placed in a separate, final chapter of the book. This chapter extensively treats such significant topics as the changing role of parents, mainstreaming and least restrictive alternatives, labeling and categorizing, the role of the courts, the impact of federal legislation, and early education for the handicapped.

This new edition retains the salient features of *Educating Exceptional Children*: the integrated approach, emphasizing intraindividual differences, the basic level promoted by format and style, and factual coverage. Yet this book is a thoroughgoing revision. Each chapter has been rewritten. New opening and closing chapters have been added; coverage of specific learning disabilities has been expanded into two chapters; and chapters on children with low intelligence, the gifted, communication disorders, and children with behavioral and emotional differences have undergone considerable change.

In preparing this revised text, we have sought professional advice from various sources. Each chapter was submitted to specialists for criticisms and suggestions. Our colleagues have been most gracious in critically evaluating the chapters and in making constructive suggestions for improvement. We are greatly indebted in particular to Drs. Nettie Bartel, Daniel Boone, Herbert Goldstein, William Healey, Cloyzelle Jones, Evelyn Deno, Philip Hatlen, Anita Hermann, Janet Lerner, Leonard Lucito, Joseph Renzulli, Melvyn Semmel, Richard Umstead, Frank Wood, Donald Moores, Phillip Schmitt, Edward Sontag, John Umbreit, Rollie Van Hattum, and Jeanne McCarthy.

Appreciation is also due to Winifred D. Kirk, wife of the senior author. As in the preparation of the two previous editions, her professional and technical astuteness has been most valuable.

We wish also to acknowledge the meticulous and ingenious care with which Ms. Judith Wesley prepared the manuscript for publication.

Samuel A. Kirk

James J. Gallagher

EDUCATING
EXCEPTIONAL
CHILDREN

1

Education in any society tends to reflect the political philosophy of that society. Under a democracy as practiced in the United States, where the state is believed to exist for the welfare of the individual, education must be organized primarily to achieve that end. "All men are created equal" has become trite, but it still has important meaning for education in a democratic society. Although it was used by the founders to denote equality before the law, it has also been interpreted to mean equality of opportunity. That concept implies educational opportunity for all children—the right of each child to receive help in learning to the limits of his or her capacity, whether that capacity be small or great. Recent court decisions have confirmed the right of all children—handicapped or not—to an appropriate education. Those legal decisions have mandated that the public schools take whatever action necessary to provide that education to handicapped children (Gilhool, 1973).

Those legal decisions are consistent with a democratic philosophy that all children be given the opportunity to learn, whether they are average, bright, dull, retarded, blind, deaf, crippled, delinquent, emotionally disturbed, or otherwise limited in their capacities to learn. American schools have evolved numerous modifications of regular school programs to adapt instruction to children who deviate from the average and who cannot profit substantially from the regular program. Those modified programs have been designated programs for exceptional children.

Who is the exceptional child?

There have been various attempts to define the term *exceptional child,* and all need considerable elaboration before they can be understood. Some use it when referring to the particularly bright child or the child with unusual talent. Others use it when referring to any atypical or deviant child. The term has been generally accepted, however, to include both the handicapped and the gifted child. For the present purposes the exceptional child is defined as *the child who deviates from the average or normal child (1) in mental characteristics, (2) in sensory abilities, (3) in neuromotor or physical characteristics, (4) in social behavior, (5) in communication abilities, or (6) in multiple handicaps. Such deviation must be of such an extent that the child requires a modification of school practices, or special educational services, to develop to maximum capacity.*

But that is a very general definition and raises many questions. "What is average or normal?" "How extensive must the deviation be to require special education?" "What is special education?"

To complicate the picture further, the exceptional or deviating child has been studied by various disciplines—psychology, sociology, physiology, medicine, and education—and thus from varying points of view. If we define an exceptional child as one who deviates from the norm of his or her group, then we have many kinds of exceptionalities. A redheaded child in a class would be an exceptional child if he or she differed from the norm of the group. A child with a defective or missing thumb would be exceptional. Actually, such deviations, although of possible importance to physicians, psychologists, geneticists, and others, are of little concern to the teacher. A redhead is not an exceptional child educationally speaking because the educational program of the class does not have to be modified to serve his or her needs. Children are considered educationally exceptional only when it is necessary to alter the educational program to meet their needs. Hence the use of *exceptional children* in education may differ from its use in biology, in psychology, and in other disciplines and professions. A child is educationally exceptional if the educational development deviates in kind and degree to such an extent that it requires educational provisions not needed by most children for maximum development.

Although we group children of like characteristics for instructional purposes (6-year-olds in the first grade), it is sometimes necessary to group exceptional children for communication purposes. The following groupings may be helpful.

1. mental deviations, including children who are (a) intellectually superior and (b) slow in learning ability—mentally retarded
2. sensory handicaps, including children with (a) auditory impairments and (b) visual impairments
3. communication disorders, including children with (a) learning disabilities and (b) speech and language impairments
4. behavior disorders, including (a) emotional disturbance and (b) social maladjustment
5. multiple and severe handicaps, including various combinations of impairments: cerebral palsy and mental retardation, deaf-blind, severe physical and intellectual disabilities, and so forth

History of the education of exceptional children

As we look back into history, we find that the entire concept of educating each child to the limits of his or her ability is relatively new. The current use of the term *exceptional* is itself a reflection of radical changes in society's view of those who deviate. We have come a long way from the Spartans' practice of killing the deviant or malformed infant, but the journey was by slow stages. Exploitation of the handicapped in the role of court jesters several hundred years ago can still be found in today's circus side shows. But certainly, on the whole, tremendous changes have taken place in society's attitude toward the exceptional person.

Historically, four stages in the development of attitudes toward the handicapped child can be recognized. First, during the pre-Christian era the handicapped tended to be neglected and mistreated. Second, during the spread of Christianity they were protected and pitied. Third, in the eighteenth and nineteenth centuries institutions were established to provide separate education. Fourth, in the latter part of the twentieth century there has been a movement toward accepting the handicapped and integrating them into society to the fullest extent possible.

In the early years of our Republic there were no public provisions for the handicapped. Such individuals were "stored away" in poorhouses and other charitable centers or remained at home without educational provisions. It was estimated that, as late as 1850, 60 percent of the inmates of the poorhouses consisted of the deaf, the blind, the insane, and "idiots" (National Advisory Committee on the Handicapped, 1976).

Beginning in 1817, a residential institution for the deaf was established in Hartford, Connecticut, and named the American Asylum for the Education and Instruction of the Deaf. It is now the American School for the Deaf. In 1829 a residential school for the blind was organized in Watertown, Massachusetts, and named the New England Asylum for the Blind, subsequently named the Perkins Institution for the Blind. In 1859 a residential school for the mentally retarded was established in South Boston, Massachusetts, and called the Massachusetts School for Idiotic and Feebleminded Youth. During the period from 1817 to the beginning of the Civil War, a period of nearly fifty years, many states established residential schools for the deaf, the blind, the mentally retarded, the orphaned, and others, as was being done in Europe. Thus, the leaders and reformers of that period (Horace Mann, Samuel Gridley Howe, Dorothea Dix, and others) gave impetus to our second stage, the establishment of residential schools. Those institutions offered training, but equally important was the protective environment, often covering the life span of the individual.

The third stage in the development of provisions for the handicapped in America was the establishment of special classes in the public schools. The first day class that was created was one for the deaf in Boston in 1869. It was not until 1896 that the first special class for the mentally retarded was organized in Providence, Rhode Island. It was followed by a class for the crippled in 1899 and by a class for the blind in 1900 in Chicago. Since 1900 special classes have been organized in many public schools throughout the nation.

American history thus shows a repetition of the stages seen in Europe. The first fifty years, after 1776, were ones of general neglect of the handicapped. The second stage for the following fifty years (after 1817) was the organization of residential schools, while the third stage was the development of special classes within the public schools (in addition to residential schools).

The fourth stage of development is difficult to analyze at this time. We know that during the first one-half of the next fifty years,

TABLE 1.1

Significant ideas influencing American special education

Initiator	Dates	Nationality	Major idea
Jean Marc Gaspard Itard	1775–1838	French	Single-subject research can be used to develop training methods for the mentally retarded
Samuel Gridley Howe	1801–1876	American	Handicapped children can learn and should have an organized education, not just compassionate care
Edward Seguin	1812–1880	French	Mentally retarded children can learn if taught through specific sensory-motor exercises
Francis Galton	1822–1911	English	Genius tends to run in families, and its origin can be determined
Alfred Binet	1857–1911	French	Intelligence can be measured, and it is amenable to improvement through education
Louis Braille	1809–1852	French	The blind can learn through an alternative system of communication based on a code of raised dots
Thomas Hopkins Gallaudet	1787–1851	American	Deaf children can learn to communicate by spelling and gesturing with their fingers
Alexander Graham Bell	1847–1922	American	Hearing-handicapped children can learn to speak and can use their limited hearing if it is amplified
Maria Montessori	1870–1952	Italian	Children can learn at very early ages, using concrete experiences designed around special instructional materials
Anna Freud	1895–	Austrian	The techniques of psychoanalysis can be applied to children to help their emotional problems
Lewis Terman	1877–1956	American	Intelligence tests can be used to identify gifted children who tend to maintain superiority throughout life
Alfred Strauss	1897–1957	German	Some children show unique patterns of learning disabilities that require special training and are probably due to brain injury

1950 to 1975, there was an explosion of provisions for the handicapped, spearheaded by state and federal legislation and appropriations. The next 25 years (1975–2000) will see further developments, especially in a trend toward educating the exceptional child with his or her normal peers to whatever extent is compatible with potential for the fullest development. The 1975 federal law PL 94-142, entitled Education for All Handicapped Children Act, will help determine the future. This act is explained in Chapter 13.

Current American practices and organizations that try to provide an optimum education for exceptional children have been influenced by major ideas and concepts from a number of pioneers who were active in the last part of the nineteenth century and at the beginning of the twentieth century.

Sir Isaac Newton once remarked, "If I see farther than others, it is because I stand on the shoulders of giants." Every profession and professional person is dependent, whether recognized or not, on the past contributions of pioneers. The current generation of special educators owes much to a group of creative innovators, some of the most notable of which are listed in Table 1.1. Those creative persons are very diverse in background, but they had in common an attitude of optimism, of seeking to draw forth a better understanding of the exceptionality and to discover a variety of techniques for maximizing the remaining abilities of the exceptional child.

Their contributions remind us that we have been traditionally too pessimistic about exceptional children and consequently find ourselves continually being surprised at what they can do if we are imaginative enough to find better methods and procedures by which to stimulate them.

Prevalence of exceptional children

Various attempts have been made to determine the prevalence of handicapped and gifted children in the population. Those attempts have yielded such diverse results that investigators hesitate to give a definite figure for each type of exceptional child. Much of this difficulty stems from the fact that the line of demarcation between a normal and an exceptional child is not agreed on. For example, some may define a gifted child as one obtaining an IQ of 120 and above on an individual intelligence test. Others might use as a criterion an IQ of 135 and above, or 140 and above. Still others use an achievement criterion or leadership ratings in addition to an intelligence test. In this case the child must have an IQ of 130 and be accelerated in school achievement by two or more years. It is obvious that with such differing criteria there will be different percentage figures. For children with learning disabilities the estimates vary from 2 percent to 20 percent, depending on what is meant by a learning disability. In addition to differences in criteria, communities themselves differ. For example, a national figure of 2 percent mentally retarded does not apply to all communities. Some areas may have 3 or 4 percent and others less than 2 percent, even though they all use the same criteria.

Despite these difficulties in determining the prevalence of exceptional children in school, various writers have been able to hazard guesses based on different studies. The U.S. Office of Education has from time to time issued estimates of the frequency of exceptional children in the school population. In 1944 it estimated that 12.4 percent of all schoolchildren (or four million) required special services (Martens, 1944). In a later report from the U.S. Office of Education, Mackie and Dunn (1954) estimated that the percentage of exceptional children in the schools of the United States stood at 12.7, roughly the same as the earlier estimate.

Because of federal legislation enacted since 1964 and the creation in 1967 of the Bureau of Education for the Handicapped within the

TABLE 1.2

Estimated number of handicapped children served and unserved by type of handicap (USOE/BEH/ASB)

	1975–1976 served (projected)	1975–1976 unserved	Total handicapped children served and unserved	% served	% unserved
Total age 0–19	4,310,000	3,577,000	7,887,000	55	45
Total age 6–19	3,860,000	2,840,000	6,700,000	58	42
Total age 0–5	450,000	737,000	1,187,000	38	62
Speech impaired	2,020,000	273,000	2,293,000	88	12
Mentally retarded	1,350,000	157,000	1,507,000	90	10
Learning disabilities	260,000	1,706,000	1,966,000	13	87
Emotionally disturbed	255,000	1,055,000	1,310,000	19	81
Crippled and other health impaired	255,000	73,000	328,000	78	22
Deaf	45,000	4,000	49,000	92	8
Hard of hearing	66,000	262,000	328,000	20	80
Visually handicapped	43,000	23,000	66,000	65	35
Deaf-blind and other multihandicapped	16,000	24,000	40,000	40	60

Source: National Advisory Committee on the Handicapped, 1976, p. 2.

Office of Education, new approaches to the acquisition of prevalence figures have been used. To obtain state funds under federal regulations, each state has been required to submit a report of the number of handicapped children in the state and a statement of the number being served. In many instances the number of children not being served is a "guesstimate" based on a general percentage of prevalence. For example, if there are 500,000 children of school age in a state and that state accepts a 3 percent prevalence figure for mental retardation, they report $.03 \times 500,000$ or 15,000 mentally retarded in the state. It is cautioned that those methods must be considered in evaluating Table 1.2.

Table 1.2 shows the total number of handicapped children reported who are and who are not receiving special education services in the public schools for the school year 1975–1976.

1. For the total age group of 0–19 we can note that over four million children are receiving special services but that almost the same number is not.

2. As might be expected, the percentage served in the age group 0–5 is less than that for the school-age group. Still, 38 percent of the children are receiving service in that age range. That figure reflects a major effort to try to bring services to exceptional children very early in their lives.

3. The largest number of exceptional children is found in the exceptionalities of speech impairment, mental retardation, learning disabilities, and emotional disturbances.

4. Children with serious sensory problems such as the visually impaired and auditorily handicapped make up a much smaller group.

5. Over 80 percent of the mentally retarded, deaf, and speech-impaired children were reported to be receiving special services, while less than 20 percent of the learning-disabled and emotionally disturbed children were reported to be receiving special help. Such figures reflect the recency of special education interest in the latter categories, with learning disabilities considered a major category only since the late 1960s and with the emotionally disturbed child seen as an educational responsibility at about the same time.

Growth in enrollment

Table 1.3 presents the enrollment figures for special schools and classes in public school systems for 1922–1975. Great care should be taken in drawing conclusions from the table. The 1969 and 1975 figures include enrollment in both public and private schools and also in residential institutions, whereas the earlier figures did not consistently include children in private schools and residential institutions. It should also be borne in mind that the figures for the period 1922–1958 are not necessarily complete because the information was obtained from questionnaires to local school systems and because the return of questionnaires is notoriously inadequate. Note should also be made of figures being influenced from period to period by changing definitions, changing conditions, and changing cutoff points.

Some conclusions, however tentative, may be drawn from the data in Table 1.3, for the figures seem to reflect certain historical facts.

1. Although there were marked increases in children served in most categories from 1932 to 1940, it will be noted that the period from 1940 to 1948 showed little increase in enrollment and even decreases for some of the groups of exceptional children. Those figures may reflect a lack of emphasis on the education of exceptional children during World War II, as well as the shortage of teachers, facilities, and funds at that time.

TABLE 1.3

Enrollments in public special schools and classes, 1922–1975

Type	1922[a]	1932[a]	1940[a]	1948[b]	1952[c]	1958[c]	1969[d]	1975[e]
Mentally retarded	23,252	75,099	98,416	87,030	113,565	213,402	703,800	1,350,000
Speech defective	No data	22,735	126,146	182,308	306,747	474,643	1,122,200	2,020,000
Crippled	No data	16,166	25,784	14,510	17,813	28,355	109,000	255,000
Deaf and hard of hearing	2,911	4,434	13,478	13,959	15,867	19,199	65,200	111,000
Blind and partially seeing	No data	5,308	8,875	8,185	8,853	11,008	22,700	43,000
Special health problems	No data	24,020	27,291	19,579	11,455	21,714	Under Crippled	Under Crippled
Gifted	No data	1,834	3,255	20,712	22,916	52,005	No data	No data
Socially maladjusted	No data	14,354	10,477	15,340	No data	27,447	99,400	255,000
Learning disabilities	No data	No data	No data	No data	No data	No data	120,000	260,000

Sources: [a] *Statistics of Special Schools and Classes for Exceptional Children,* Biennial Survey of Education in the United States, 1946–1948 (Washington, D.C.: Federal Security Agency, U.S. Office of Education, 1948), p. 10.
[b] *Statistics of Special Education for Exceptional Children,* Biennial Survey of Education in the United States, 1952–1954 (Washington, D.C.: Department of Health, Education, and Welfare, U.S. Office of Education, 1954), p. 15.
[c] Romaine P. Mackie and Patricia P. Robbins, "Exceptional Children in Local Public Schools," *School Life* 43 (November 1960), p. 15.
[d] *Handicapped Children in the United States and Special Education Personnel Required,* 1968–1969 (est.) (Washington, D.C.: Bureau of Education for the Handicapped, U.S. Office of Education, 1970).
[e] Bureau of Education for the Handicapped, U.S. Office of Education, 1976.

2. Beginning with the 1940 figures, the largest number of exceptional children served has been in the area of speech impairment. Those children are generally being educated in the regular classes, receiving speech remediation two or three times a week for short periods. In some schools one speech clinician may carry a load of up to one hundred children. The last thirty-five years have seen a very rapid rise in the services offered speech-impaired children.

3. In programs for the mentally retarded there has also been a marked increase in enrollment, the number receiving special help being second only to the number of speech-impaired children being served. That increase probably reflects the increased awareness of the problem of mental retardation in our society resulting partly from the organization of state and national parents' groups, which have vigorously brought the problem to the attention of the general public, school administrators, and legislators. It will be noted that the most rapid rate of increase has been since 1952 when the efforts of parents' groups were just beginning to materialize. It should also be noted that the recent increase in services for the mentally retarded includes the addition of children in classes for the trainable mentally retarded—classes that were rare in the 1930s and 1940s.

4. Classes for the hearing impaired made a rapid increase before 1940 but only a gradual gain in enrollment since then. The higher figures indicated in 1969 and 1975 reflect the inclusion of children in private schools and institutions.

5. There is historical significance in the sequence of figures for children in classes for the blind and visually impaired. The enrollment here remained fairly constant up to 1958 when there was a sudden jump in enrollment. In large part this increase can be explained by (a) the influx of six-year-old children suffering from an eye malady known as retrolental fibroplasia (which will be discussed in Chapter 7) and (b) an increase in visual impairments due to the rubella epidemic in the 1960s.

Another index of growth in special education programs during the last few years is the increasing amount of funds allocated by local and state education sources to programs for exceptional children. Figure 1.1 shows the amounts spent on programs supported by local and state funds. There has been an increase of almost 300 percent in the amount of money spent over the six-year period represented in the graph. The total of those funds had risen to a level of $2 billion in 1972 and is expected to reach $3 to $4 billion by 1980. Those gains represent a fuller acceptance of the proposition that every child has a right to an education appropriate to his or her needs in the American society.

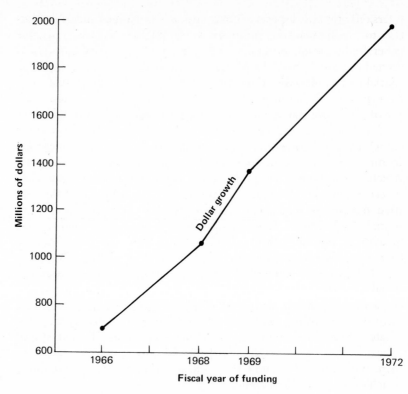

FIGURE 1.1
*Nonfederal expenditures for
handicapped children in public
school programs*

Source: J. Gallagher, P. Forsythe, F. Weintraub, and D. Ringelheim, 1975, p. 442.

Special education—its meaning and practices

The term *special education* has been used to denote those aspects of education that are applied to handicapped and gifted children but are not usually used with the majority of average children. *Special* is defined by Webster as "distinguished by some unusual quality; uncommon; noteworthy; extraordinary; additional to the regular; extra; utilized or employed for a certain purpose in addition to the ordinary." Those definitions are certainly applicable to special education, which consists of the modifications of, or additions to, school practices intended for the ordinary child—practices that are unique, uncommon, of unusual quality, and in particular in addition to the organization and instructional procedures used with the majority of children.

It should be pointed out that special education is not a total program entirely different from the education of the ordinary child. It refs only to those aspects of education that are unique and/or in addition to the instructional program for all children. For example, the general educational program for a child with a speech handicap is carried out in all phases by his or her regular classroom teacher. The special part of that education is the remediation of speech impairment by a speech clinician. It may be carried on for only two hours a week out of a possible thirty hours in the regular classroom. On the other hand, a deaf child is usually assigned to a special class for the deaf for the whole day. The teacher for the regular portions of his or her education is the same teacher who ministers to the child's special needs, which in the case of the deaf are speech reading, speech development, special techniques of language training, and so forth. What the deaf child receives as special education is, of course, a great deal more special than that received by a child with a minor speech handicap. As the child learns and matures, increasingly greater placement with the peer group of hearing children is possible.

The amount and kind of special education needed by an exceptional child depend on many factors, among them the degree of discrepancy between the atypical child's development and the development of the ordinary child (the greater the degree of discrepancy, the greater the extent to which special education is needed). The special education needed is also dependent on the discrepancies in development within the child and the effects of the disability on other areas of achievement. Various areas of special education will be described in subsequent chapters. It suffices to say at this point that special education—its quality, kind, and amount—is dependent on the growth patterns of the children in relation to their peers and on the discrepancies in growth within each. That concept is explained further in Chapter 2.

The need for special education can be recognized in the problems faced by a regular teacher. In many schools a teacher has a class of thirty-five children, one of whom is gifted and one of whom is mentally retarded. The teacher also has one child who stutters and one who is a behavior problem. Asked to organize an educational program for a fifth-grade class, the teacher must adapt instruction for the mentally retarded child who reads at barely the second-grade level, for the gifted child who reads at nearly the eighth-grade level, for the speech impaired, for the problem child, and for the other thirty-one children in the class, who also deviate but not to the extent of those mentioned. Because of the difficulty of this task for the regular teacher, special education programs have evolved in the form of special classes or some form of assistance to the regular teacher who retains the child in the class for most of the day.

It is said that education often begins where medicine stops. For example, fitting a visually impaired child with glasses or a hard-of-hearing youngster with a hearing aid is a medical concern. But teaching the child to use the available vision and hearing most effectively and to use other senses compensatorily is a special education function.

If a hearing loss, for example, can be corrected, the problem is solely a medical, not an educational, concern. If it cannot be corrected, it must be ameliorated to whatever extent is possible by decreasing its effects. Hearing aids, auditory training, and speech reading are directly geared to strengthening the ability to function auditorily and are considered amelioration, not cure.

The general aims of special education are first to ameliorate the deficit by medicine, training, or whatever means are feasible and then to compensate for the residual deficit by strengthening other abilities and providing specially adapted materials.

Professionals and scientists in many different fields have become involved with the problems of the exceptional child especially at the following stages of concern.

Origins of exceptionality. Many scientists from the fields of biology, neurology, physiology, psychology, and others are seeking to find the origins or conditions leading to exceptionality.

Identification of exceptionality. Another group of professionals who are in clinical practice are particularly helpful in the initial identification of the child as exceptional. Pediatricians, social workers, clinical psychologists, and audiologists are often active in the phase of discovery and initial diagnosis.

Treatment-enhancing capabilities. A variety of devices have been discovered and developed that can help the exceptional child to respond better to his or her environment: a hearing aid for the hard of hearing, drug therapy for the hyperactive child, motorized wheelchairs for the orthopedically handicapped, and a molded palate for a cleft-palate child. The clinician who originally discovered the problem may prescribe treatment but may be joined by otolaryngologists, rehabilitation counselors, audiologists, or other professionals.

Continuous special programming. Once the assessment has been completed along with the prescription for whatever devices are appropriate, there comes the necessity of carrying out the day-by-day special program for the child. At this point the special educator, speech pathologist, and other intervention personnel may play a more important role.

It is not unusual for the parent of a handicapped child to come into contact with professionals from six or seven different disciplines. Those contacts can be both reassuring and bewildering because of the different perspectives from which each professional approaches the exceptional child.

Alternate learning environments

In addition to instructional adaptations, content changes, and special skills training, there are also environmental changes necessary to accomplish the goals of special education. It is often necessary to modify the setting in which such education takes place. The settings or environmental changes are: (1) consultant service in the regular grades, (2) itinerant personnel, (3) resource rooms, (4) part-time special classes, (5) self-contained special classes, (6) special day schools, (7) residential schools, and (8) hospital and homebound teaching.

The current philosophy of educating exceptional children maintains that children should be placed in the least restrictive environment; that is, they should be given an environment as nearly as possible like that of the main body of children. Reynolds (1973) has presented graphically the hierarchy of services for exceptional children. An adaptation of Reynolds's hierarchy is presented in Figure 1.2. The highest three sections constitute the largest number of children and the milder forms of exceptionality. Those children are assigned to the regular grades and through such *mainstreaming* are the primary responsibility of the regular teacher with supporting help from (1) consultants, (2) itinerant personnel, and (3) resource teachers. The lower five levels in the figure constitute more severe handicaps requiring more restrictive environments. Those fewer children are the primary responsibility of special education personnel. A more detailed explanation of the special services for exceptional children follows.

CONSULTANT SERVICES

To facilitate the education of handicapped children remaining in the regular grades under the *mainstream* philosophy, school systems may provide consultant services to regular teachers in the form of special teachers, psychologists, social workers, and medical personnel. The consultants are available to regular teachers when they have questions about a child or when they need advice concerning special materials and methods of instruction.

ITINERANT PERSONNEL

Speech clinicians, social workers, school psychologists, remedial reading teachers, learning disability specialists, and other special educational personnel may deal with exceptional children on an itinerant basis. They may serve several schools and travel over a considerable area, visiting the exceptional children and their teachers at regular intervals or whenever necessary. Thus, the youngster spends the most time in the regular classroom and is taken out of the room only for short periods for tutorial help. A speech clinician, for example, may work with the speech-impaired child several times a week for short periods, while an itinerant teacher for the visually impaired child might visit only once a week to bring special materials and to consult with the regular teacher in the use of the materials. In both cases the primary responsibility for the general education of the exceptional child rests with the regular classroom teacher.

The school social worker and psychologist may interview and confer with a child, the parents, and the teacher and may generally assist in the adjustment of the behaviorally disturbed child in the home and school. They may counsel a child consistently over an extended period of time or only occasionally.

The itinerant special-teacher program is particularly valuable in rural areas where exceptional children are few and scattered over a wide area. Thus one teacher may serve several schools. That program is also well suited to certain types of exceptionality such as defective speech or partial vision, which require limited services or materials. Often one of the itinerant teacher's primary roles will be that of a consultant or resource person for the classroom teacher. Itinerant teachers also provide homebound and hospital services, as described later.

RESOURCE ROOMS

Wiederholt, Hammill, and Brown (1978) define a *resource room* as "any instructional setting to which a child comes for specified periods of time, usually on a regularly scheduled basis" (p. 13). The usual setting for a resource room is a small classroom to which a special teacher is assigned and to which the children come during the day for brief periods of special remedial work. The resource room teacher also consults with the regular teacher, and together they develop a program that is intended to eliminate the eventual need for resource room assistance.

PART-TIME SPECIAL CLASSES

The part-time special class accepts children who require more special instruction than the short period in the resource room. The programs for the children in those classes are the responsibility of the special class teacher. Children in such classes may spend a half-day in the special class and are assigned to regular grades or classes in areas in which they can contend. In junior and senior high schools this practice is common for some kinds of exceptional children.

SELF-CONTAINED SPECIAL CLASSES

It is sometimes advisable to assign the more severely handicapped children to self-contained special classes where the special teacher assumes the major responsibility for their programs. In the past this kind of class was the most common for all degrees of mental handicaps. It has been replaced, especially for the more mildly handicapped, with resource rooms, itinerant teachers, and part-time special classes.

SPECIAL DAY SCHOOLS

Some school systems have organized special day schools for different kinds of exceptional children, especially the emotionally disturbed, crippled, trainable mentally retarded, and multiply handicapped. In general there is a trend toward reducing the number of special schools, at least for certain types of handicapping conditions. Physically handicapped and mentally retarded children can make appreciable adjustment with normal children. It is also felt that contact with average children provides atypical children with a better preparation for future life. There are still a substantial number of special day schools, particularly for the child with severe behavior disorders, for the severely mentally retarded, and for the severely multiply handicapped.

RESIDENTIAL SCHOOLS

All the states of the Union have residential schools or institutions for various types of handicapped children, including the mentally retarded, delinquent, blind, deaf, crippled, and emotionally disturbed. Such institutions are sometimes privately administered, but they are usually administered by a state agency. Historically, residential schools are the oldest educational provision for exceptional children. They tended to be built away from population centers and too often became segregated, sheltered asylums with little community contact. In recent years those faults have been recognized and to an extent remedied.

Disadvantages of a residential school include removal of the child from home and neighborhood, emphasis on the handicap, and the rigidity of institutional life. This is not to say that such a program no longer meets the needs of certain exceptional children, for it does indeed. In a sparsely populated area no other provision may be feasible, especially for a condition like deafness, which requires extensive equipment and special training on the part of the teacher. In some cases the condition itself demands professional attention for more than a few hours a day. Often with young deaf-blind children specialized treatment, stimulation, and education are carried out in the dormitory or cottage of the residential school during the children's waking hours. Situations within the child's home may require that for the welfare of the family, he or she be placed in a residential school, at least for a time.

There is no reason to believe that any of the types of programs discussed will disappear in the immediate future; they will continue to supplement each other. A changing role may, however, be seen for many residential schools. As special education programs in public schools expand and enroll more exceptional children, the residential schools may emphasize programs for the severely and multiply handicapped children.

HOSPITAL AND HOMEBOUND SERVICES

Sometimes physically handicapped children are confined to hospitals or to their homes for long periods of time. To avoid educational retardation, itinerant teachers specially prepared to teach the homebound go to the hospital or home and tutor those children during their convalescence. Usually the local school system assigns the teachers of the homebound to help such children for an hour or more a day if the youngster's condition permits. The teacher's case load varies according to the type of disabilities and the amount of academic help needed. In larger children's hospitals such classes are taught by full-time teachers.

In some cities two-way telephone communication can be established between the child's home and the classroom so that the child can listen in on the class discussion and make a contribution.

It has been one of the common philosophical positions for special educators that the environment should be kept as close to the normal or average educational environment as is possible. In 1945 a slogan in Illinois was "Special education is *a part of,* not *apart from,* regular education." It has been referred to as the philosophy of the *least restrictive environment* and is included in the 1975 federal law Education for All Handicapped Children Act. That means that the child should be taken from the regular classroom only when it is not possible to deliver the needed service within the regular classroom, that a special class should be established only when it becomes obvious that a part-time resource room or itinerant teacher program is not adequate to do the job, and that the child should be institutionalized only when all other efforts to provide good education within the framework of the local school system have failed. We are always trying to move to the bottom of the model shown in Figure 1.2.

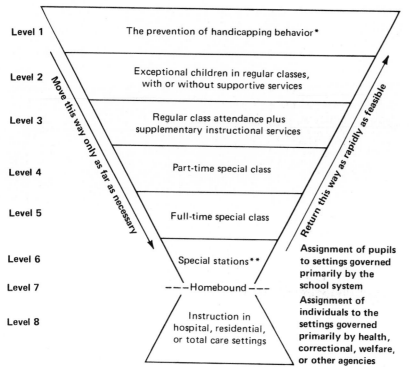

Level 1 — The prevention of handicapping behavior*

Level 2 — Exceptional children in regular classes, with or without supportive services

Level 3 — Regular class attendance plus supplementary instructional services

Level 4 — Part-time special class

Level 5 — Full-time special class

Level 6 — Special stations**

Level 7 — ———Homebound———

Level 8 — Instruction in hospital, residential, or total care settings

Move this way only as far as necessary

Return this way as rapidly as feasible

Assignment of pupils to settings governed primarily by the school system

Assignment of individuals to the settings governed primarily by health, correctional, welfare, or other agencies

FIGURE 1.2
The cascade system of special education services

Source: Reprinted from Deno, E. Cited in Maynard Reynolds, "Two Policy Statements Approved by CEC Delegate Assembly." *Exceptional Children,* September 1973, p. 71, by permission of the Council for Exceptional Children. Copyright 1973 by the Council for Exceptional Children.

*This means the development of positive cognitive, affective, and psychomotor skills in all pupils that will reduce or prevent the frequency of handicapping behavior.

**Special schools in public school systems.

The emphasis on individual differences in this book

The major focus of this book is on individual differences and the strategies for adapting educational programs to educationally different clusters of children. It is recognized that every child is unique and that all children differ from each other (interindividual differences), but also that they have differences in abilities and disabilities within themselves (intraindividual differences). (See Chapter 2.)

The degree of deviation and the constellation of differences differ with each child. Even within a group of so-called normal or average children, no two children have the same constellation of differences. But there are minor differences that are accepted in the rubric of "normal" because a high percentage of the population differs to that extent. Outside that larger group of children we find clusters of children who differ from the majority in one or more learning characteristics. Those children have similarities of characteristics such as are found in clusters of auditorily or visually impaired children, in other clusters of children with problems in interacting with their peers, or in those with significantly slower learning ability. The similarities *within* each cluster do not eliminate individual differences.

In any book on education the focus or organization of the text can be centered around one of three major dimensions of the education process: (1) the learner, (2) the teacher-learner interaction (that is, instruction), or (3) the learning environment.

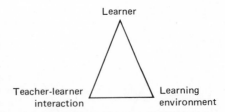

If we focus on the *learner,* then we will discuss and describe individual children or clusters of children. If we focus on the *teacher-learner interaction,* then we must organize the book around various teaching techniques such as the stimulation of language development and behavior modification. If we focus on the *environment,* then the book would be organized around various environmental modifications such as special classes, resource rooms, and itinerant teacher programs.

We, the authors, have chosen the first of those three approaches—the exceptional child as a learner—as a way of organizing this book. It is important to give a portrait of the exceptional child as a human being. From the vantage point of the individual child it is easier to select the most suitable learning environment and the most suitable teacher-learner interaction strategies.

Despite the obvious fact that no one child or adult is the same as another, we daily group or cluster people together as a convenient form of reference. Mothers, quarterbacks, bankers, carpenters, and friends are all terms that allow us to consider how an individual relates to large numbers of other individuals with similar characteristics or functions. So it is with exceptional children. Those children are grouped together in various categories through classification to allow for the organization of special remedial programs.

That we have chosen to study and discuss exceptional children divided into subgroups or clusters does not indicate that we would keep them separated from other children in all areas of instruction or in daily living.

Educational authorities have long recognized that exceptional children do not always fit into neat, well-defined categories with uniform characteristics. They have recognized that mentally retarded children, even with a narrow IQ range, are not homogeneous in characteristics and that not all deaf children learn at the same rate. One deaf child might learn speech reading, while another unfortunately does not. One child may be classified as cerebral palsied but may also be mentally retarded, while another cerebral-palsied child may learn adequately in school or may even be gifted.

To classify or not to classify

One of the current controversies (to be discussed in greater detail in Chapter 13) is whether or not to classify or categorize exceptional children into subgroups (that is, the mentally retarded, emotionally disturbed, and others). Some feel: (1) that classification leads to misclassification and mislabeling, particularly in low-income families, (2) that categories do not lead to educationally relevant programs, and (3) that categories and labels are detrimental to the self-concept of children so labeled.

Those who advocate the use of classification systems state: (1) that the purpose of classification is to bring the child with special needs into contact with specially trained personnel who will provide a special educational program in a special learning environment; (2) that categories have aided in focusing the attention of lawmakers on the problems of exceptional children, thereby aiding in obtaining legislation to support special programs; (3) that categories allow us to pursue the causes of the handicapping conditions; and (4) that categories, when used properly, aid in communication.

In 1972 the question of "to label or not to label" became acute. The then Secretary of Health, Education, and Welfare (Elliot Richardson) requested a task force to study that question and selected Nicholas Hobbs of Vanderbilt University to serve as its chairman. The task force studied and analyzed the benefits of classification and labeling as well as the harmful effects. Hobbs (1975) summarized the conclusions and recommendations of the task force by stating that there are both detrimental and beneficial effects from labeling. His task force registered its concern for the negative effects of labeling but noted its useful elements as well. Special educators are currently seeking ways for minimizing labels while retaining the beneficial results.

The concern over labels and categories is not confined to the United States. In 1973 the British Parliament appointed the Warnock Committee to review the educational provisions for handicapped children and youth in England, Scotland, and Wales. The 1978 report of this committee gives considerable attention to the pros and cons of using existing labels, such as *educationally subnormal* (or, as in Scotland, *mentally handicapped*), maladjusted, and other categorization of handicapped pupils. The members of the committee accept the use of existing forms of description for children with physical and sensory disabilities but recommend that "the term *children with learning difficulties* should be used in the future to describe both those children who are currently categorized as educationally subnormal and those with educational difficulties who are often at present the concern of remedial services." They defend this substitution of one label for another as being less likely to stigmatize the child. They also recommend the retention of the term *maladjusted* as being "a serviceable form of description" (Warnock, 1978, p. 43).

Action stages

The usual procedures in classification and program implementation are outlined as follows. The procedures are dependent on the adequate identification of the child and on what aspect of assistance is being discussed—that is, instituting prevention, diagnosis, prescriptions, special placement, program implementation, or funding.

I. Prevention	Identification of the exceptionality is a first step toward discovering its causes and finding possible preventive and helpful agents.
II. Identification and diagnosis	The exceptional child must be found and then the exceptionality distinguished from other possible conditions (autism from hearing impairment, retardation from delayed speech) in preparation for differential education.
III. Prescription and prosthesis	Once the exceptionality is correctly identified there exists the possibility that various devices can be introduced to lessen the impact of the exceptionality (that is, hearing aids, special glasses, mobility aids, and so forth).
IV. Special placement	The classification of exceptional children often has the result of placing them in a special learning environment and into interaction with specially trained personnel.
V. Program implementation	A continuous program of instruction and remediation can be instituted, which will be based on the individual characteristics of the exceptional child.
VI. Financing	The accurate classification of various types of exceptional children enables schools and agencies to apply and qualify for state and federal funds.

Summary

Inherent in the philosophy of a democracy is the right of all children to develop to their maximum potential. That philosophy has led to the organization of programs for exceptional children. We have considered the following concepts:

1. *Exceptional children* have been defined as those children who deviate from the average in (a) mental, (b) physical and neuromotor,

(c) sensory, (d) behavior, (e) communication, or (f) multiple handicapping characteristics such that they require a modification of school practices and services to develop to their maximum.

2. Special education has been defined as those additional services, over and above the regular school program, that are provided for exceptional children to assist in the development of their potentialities and/or the amelioration of their disabilities.

3. During the two centuries of our Republic, we have moved from (a) neglect of the handicapped to (b) the establishment of residential institutions to (c) the development of special classes in public schools to (d) normalization and mainstreaming when feasible.

4. About eight million children in the United States have been identified as exceptional children. They constitute approximately 15 percent of schoolchildren. Despite recent major increases in services, almost one-third of those children still do not receive adequate special services.

5. There has been a continuing increase in the financial resources and in the special programs for exceptional children during the past fifty years with a marked acceleration in the past two decades.

6. Special educational programs developed for exceptional children include mainstreaming, consultant service, itinerant personnel, resource rooms, part-time special classes, self-contained classes, day schools, residential schools, and services for hospitalized and homebound children.

7. The trend in the education of exceptional children has been toward the organization of programs that will result in the least restrictive environment.

8. This book is organized with a focus on the subcategories of exceptional children (the learner) with discussions of appropriate special learning environments and teacher-learner interactions in each section.

References

GALLAGHER, J., P. FORSYTHE, F. WEINTRAUB, AND D. RINGELHEIM. 1975. "Funding Patterns and Labeling." In N. Hobbs, ed., *Issues in the Classification of Children.* San Francisco: Jossey-Bass. P. 442.

GILHOOL, T. K. 1973. "Education: An Inalienable Right." *Exceptional Children* 39 (May): 597–610.

HOBBS, N. 1975. *The Futures of Children: Categories, Labels, and Their Consequences.* San Francisco: Jossey-Bass.

KIRK, S. A. 1972. *Educating Exceptional Children,* 2nd ed. Boston: Houghton Mifflin.

MACKIE, R. P., AND L. M. DUNN. 1954. *College and University Programs for the Preparation of Teachers of Exceptional Children.* U.S. Office of Education, Bulletin No. 13. Washington, D.C.: U.S. Government Printing Office.

MARTENS, ELISE H. 1944. *Needs of Exceptional Children.* U.S. Office of Education, Leaflet No. 74. Washington, D.C.: U.S. Government Printing Office.

NATIONAL ADVISORY COMMITTEE ON THE HANDICAPPED. 1976. *The Unfinished Revolution: Education for the Handicapped, 1976 Annual Report.* Department of Health, Education, and Welfare, U.S. Office of Education. Washington, D.C.: U.S. Government Printing Office.

REYNOLDS, M. C. 1973. "Two Policy Statements Approved by CEC Delegate Assembly." *Exceptional Children* 40 (September): 71.

WARNOCK, H. M. 1978. *Special Educational Needs: Report of the Committee of Enquiry into the Education of Handicapped Children and Young People.* London: Her Majesty's Stationery Office.

WIEDERHOLT, L., D. HAMMILL, AND V. BROWN. 1978. *The Resource Teacher: A Guide to Effective Practices.* Boston: Allyn and Bacon.

2

The ringing sentence in the Declaration of Independence that "all men are created equal" is familiar to all Americans. Its meaning is legal, rather than biological, since the statement refers to equality before the law or equality in rights regardless of biological, racial, genetic, sex, or other diversities.

Society has not always been concerned with individual differences among children and with the adaptation of educational programs to meet their needs. Wundt, who is considered the father of modern psychology, established the first laboratory of psychology in Leipzig in 1879. In his studies he ruled out individual differences as a legitimate field of interest for psychologists, since he felt that psychology ought to be concerned with the "generalized human mind." Thus children, psychotics, and animals were excluded from psychology, as was the study of individual differences. Only with the advent of the mental testing movement in the early 1900s did refined techniques for assessing individual differences in areas other than the physical begin to be developed. With those diagnostic methods came ideas and concepts that made possible the modern programs of education for exceptional children.

The introduction of compulsory education laws in the latter part of the nineteenth century in the United States was a prime factor in directing the attention of schools to individual differences among children. They found that not all children learn at the same rate, move at the same rate, react emotionally in the same way, and see and hear equally well. Prior to compulsory education, handicapped children dropped out of school since they could not compete with normals and the schools were not organized for them. Today in the United States, as well as in Western European countries and the Soviet Union, provisions for the education of exceptional children are almost universal. Virtually all countries that have established universal and compulsory education have found that general programs for the ordinary child are not suitable for the exceptional child.

In any complex subject, as the study of exceptional children and special education certainly is, it is easy to be overwhelmed by the wide range of apparently unrelated facts about each type of child and the many educational options that are available. We, the authors, wish to propose two broad concepts to aid the student in integrating that information into a more coherent whole. The first of these concepts encompasses the uneven development—or "split growth"—within the exceptional child, a concept we shall speak of as intraindividual differences. This concept portrays the pattern of development or the product of the exceptionality.

The second concept is a system designed to show what parts of information processing, which we all use to receive and analyze

INDIVIDUAL DIFFERENCES

information and to communicate it to others, are most affected by each of the various types of exceptionalities. The system provides an explanation of the process by which the pattern of skills develops unevenly over time in each type of exceptionality.

This chapter deals with diversities in abilities and achievements among children and will discuss (1) interindividual differences, (2) intraindividual differences, and (3) how different types of exceptional children process information differently.

Interindividual differences

One concept of individual differences, and the one most commonly used, is interindividual differences, that is, the differences between people—the variability among and between members of a group. To say "Johnny is shorter than Billy" tells about an interindividual difference between Johnny and Billy.

Whenever we measure a group of children, we find that children, like all biological organisms, group themselves along what is known as the Gaussian curve, or normal distribution, for most characteristics. When a large sample of the population is examined on almost any common characteristic, we find most members of the group clustering near the average with fewer and fewer members spread out to the extremes. Figure 2.1 shows the distribution of IQs and illustrates the normal dispersion.

From Figure 2.1 the following facts will be noted:

1. Sixty-eight percent (68.26 percent) of the children fall into the range of -1σ IQ points (minus one standard deviation) to $+1\sigma$ IQ points (plus one standard deviation). That means, in terms of the Wechsler scale IQ, that 68.26 percent of the children fall between an IQ of 85 and an IQ of 115. Children in that range are considered normal or average.

2. Nearly 14 percent of the children are in the -2σ to -1σ IQ point range, or between Wechsler IQs of 70 and 85. Likewise, 13.59 percent of the children are between $+1\sigma$ and $+2\sigma$, or between IQs of 115 and 130.

3. Approximately 2 percent (2.14 percent) are between -3σ and -2σ, or between IQs of 55 and 70, and approximately 2 percent (2.14 percent) are between $+2\sigma$ and $+3\sigma$, or between IQs of 130 and 145.

4. A very small percentage of children, 0.13 percent, are below an IQ of 55, and 0.13 percent are above an IQ of 145.

Those distributions represent a theoretical curve of the ranges of

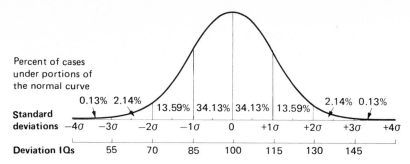

Percent of cases
under portions of
the normal curve

0.13% 2.14% 13.59% | 34.13% | 34.13% | 13.59% 2.14% 0.13%

Standard
deviations −4σ −3σ −2σ −1σ 0 +1σ +2σ +3σ +4σ

Deviation IQs 55 70 85 100 115 130 145

FIGURE 2.1

The distribution of IQs

Source: From Test Service Bulletin No. 48 published by the Psychological Corporation.

intelligence among children based on an intelligence test. When we measure reading, writing, spelling, height and weight, or even the length of the little finger, we find that the distribution follows approximately the theoretical normal curve shown on intelligence scores.

The intelligence test, which purports to measure how fast the child is developing intellectually, has come under severe attack in recent years. The attack stems from strong disagreement as to what the IQ actually means. It has been used in the past

1. to indicate innate intellectual potential
2. to predict future academic performance
3. to indicate present rate of mental development of this child compared to others of the same age

It is the first of those uses that has brought intelligence tests under severest attack. Extensive discussions in recent years leave little doubt that intelligence tests should never be used to buttress simplified discussions of whether one or another ethnic or racial group is innately superior to others. The tests are clearly not measures of genetic potential. However, the predictive value of the intelligence test and its ability to fix the current rate of mental development remain powerful; the test is still used professionally for the latter purpose.

Most of the tests that have been developed in psychology and education (intelligence, reading, spelling, arithmetic, and so forth) are tests developed to measure interindividual differences. They are used primarily for classification of children and for placement purposes. Teachers use educational tests and ratings to group children in clusters with similar achievements. Likewise, children with low IQs will often be placed or grouped for instructional purposes in a group different from that of those who have very high IQs.

The main purpose of tests that measure achievement level or global scores of intelligence is to help place the child in the group in which he or she will most likely get appropriate instruction. Such tests are limited to placement purposes and do not tell the teacher what specific program each child needs.

Intraindividual differences

Another meaning for individual differences, and the one that is dominant in special education, is the concept of intraindividual differences; namely, the differences in abilities within a particular child. This comparison, rather than a comparison with other children, determines intraindividual differences and provides information to help develop a program of instruction for an individual child.

Exceptional children differ from nonexceptional children in many characteristics. They may be intellectually superior, they may not see or hear as well, they may not have the mobility of the average child, they may not have the facility or skill in language or speech of the average child, or they may be deviant in interpersonal relationships. To a teacher it is more important to know a child's unique pattern of assets and deficits than to know how those average out in comparison with other children. The teacher needs to know how to organize a program for that particular child. What are his or her discrepancies in development? What can the child do and what is difficult to do? Does the child read at the first-grade level and do arithmetic at the third-grade level, showing a discrepancy in achievement? Such variance has led many to say that the exceptional child is a normal child who has exceptionalities or deviations only in some characteristics. In other words, they feel that the similarities in characteristics of the exceptional child and the average child far exceed the differences.

In general, the concept of *interindividual* differences is used for classification and for grouping children in special classes or ability groups. The concept of *intraindividual* differences, on the other hand, is used to organize an instructional program for a particular child in conformity with abilities and disabilities, without regard to how he or she compares with other children.

To illustrate (1) how the exceptional child differs from the average and (2) how the exceptional child grows unevenly, the following discussion will present the major types of exceptional children in the form of profiles as well as descriptive material. In subsequent chapters each of those types of exceptional children will be discussed in greater detail with suggested educational programs adapted to the discrepancies in growth. This chapter gives a very brief overview of discrepancies in each area of deviation.

MENTAL DEVIATES—THE INTELLECTUALLY
GIFTED AND RETARDED

Intellectually gifted and intellectually retarded (mentally retarded) children represent the upper and lower groups on the intelligence scale. Figure 2.1 shows that children with an IQ below 70 (-2 standard deviations) constitute 2.14 percent of the population studied and represent the group generally labeled mentally retarded or mentally deficient. The right-hand portion of the curve shows children with IQs above 130 ($+2$ standard deviations) and represents 2.14 percent of the population. Those children are generally labeled very superior or gifted.

It is with the two extreme groups, the intellectually accelerated and the intellectually retarded, that we are concerned at present. Their unique characteristics and educational programs will be discussed in later chapters. Here it is well to take a look at a picture of the development of those two kinds of exceptional children to see how they deviate in growth from the normal (interindividual differences) and how they are affected by deviations within themselves (intraindividual differences).

Figure 2.2 shows the discrepancies in growth of an *intellectually gifted child* and of an *intellectually retarded child*. Both children are ten years of age; both are in a fifth-grade class; both have normal hearing and vision. But the similarities stop there. They differ markedly from the average child in many characteristics and, in addition, have variations in growth within themselves. The history and status of those two children, typical of their types of exceptionality, can best be illustrated by a description of their characteristics and development and by the profile in Figure 2.2.

John, the gifted child, was the older of two children. His father was employed as a teacher in the local high school. John's developmental history showed that he learned to talk at an earlier age than most children and that he walked at the age of 10 months. He became interested in books and at the age of 5½ was reading some books and simple picture stories.

On entering school at the age of 6, he quickly learned to read, and by the end of the year he was a fluent reader in third-grade material. He was not allowed to advance in school beyond his age group,

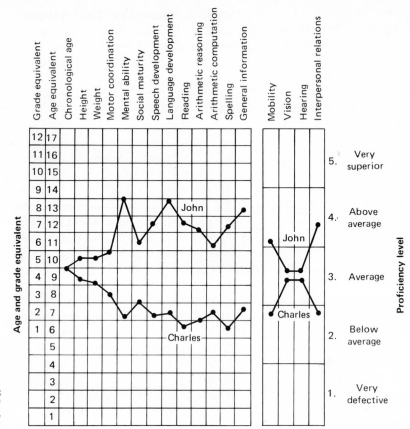

FIGURE 2.2

*Profiles of a gifted and a retarded
child*

and by the age of 10 he was in the fifth grade. At that time a series of examinations was administered to him.

Test results are given in various forms. For example, John had an IQ score of 140 and a mental age of 14 years. His height age was 10–8, meaning that his height was similar to that of an average boy of 10 years, 8 months, even though John was only 10 years of age (10–0). On a reading test his score was Grade 7–7, meaning that his reading level was similar to the average of children in the seventh month of the seventh grade, even though John was in the fifth grade. His reading score, when translated into an age score, was 12 years, 7 months (12–7).

There are other characteristics of an individual that cannot be stated in terms of precise age. For example, vision and hearing are either normal or defective. John's vision and hearing were normal. Interpersonal relations do not necessarily increase with age; hence there are no age norms. In the profile those characteristics are represented on a five-point scale: (1) very superior, (2) above average, (3) average, (4) below average, and (5) very defective.

On the various tests given to John, the scores were translated into ages or points on a scale so that they could be readily compared. His scores were as follows:

Chronological age	10–0
Height age	10–8
Weight age	10–8
Motor coordination age	10–11
Mental age	14–0
Social age	11–6
Speech development age	12–8
Language age	13–10
Reading age	12–7
Arithmetic reasoning age	12–2
Arithmetic computation age	11–4
Spelling age	12–4
General information age	13–2
Mobility	above average
Vision	average
Hearing	average
Interpersonal relations	above average

Figure 2.2 shows John's growth patterns at the life age of 10. Note that there are some points on the profile showing John to be like other children of his age. In vision and hearing he is like other children with normal sense organs, neither superior nor inferior. His height, weight, and motor coordination are slightly superior to those of most children, but not abnormally so. His mental age, however, deviates very markedly from the average of other 10-year-olds and is four years beyond his age and grade placement. His social age is not as advanced as his mental age, being only a year and one-half accelerated. His achievements in school vary but in general are more accelerated than the physical factors, though not as far as is the mental-age level. Note that general information, language, speech, and reading are more advanced than arithmetic computation. Such is a quite common finding among intellectually advanced children.

On the scaled portion of the profile, John shows above average mobility, average hearing and vision, and above average interpersonal relations. He presents a developmental picture different from that of a child who is average in all respects. On that scale an average child would show only minor deviations from a straight line.

Not only does John differ from the average child in many characteristics, but he also varies within himself in some characteristics. In this respect he is said to have *discrepancies in growth* or, more precisely, *intraindividual differences*. Because of those deviations, he will require certain adaptations of educational practices—to be described in later chapters.

Charles, the intellectually retarded child in Figure 2.2, shows a profile markedly different from that of John, the gifted child. The profiles are very nearly mirror counterparts of each other. Charles was the second child in a family of four children. His father worked as a machinist. During infancy Charles was a sickly child and at the age of 1 year had a very high fever, diagnosed as encephalitis and later assumed to have had neurologic effects fundamental to his slow mental development. Charles developed at a slower rate than the other children. He walked at 16 months but did not talk in sentences until he was 3 years of age. (On the average, children begin to talk in sentences at 2 years of age.) He was admitted to the first grade at the age of 6 and in spite of his inability to learn was promoted year by year until at the age of 10 he, like John, was in the fifth grade. The school system in which he was enrolled believed that children should be neither held back in school nor accelerated. The philosophy of the school held that the teacher should adapt instruction to wide individual differences among children.

In the fifth grade Charles was given a series of examinations. He obtained the following ratings:

Chronological age	10–0
Height age	9–2
Weight age	9–1
Motor coordination age	8–5
Mental age	7–2
Social age	8–0
Speech development age	7–3
Language age	7–4
Reading age	6–8
Arithmetic reasoning age	7–0
Arithmetic computation age	7–5
Spelling age	6–6
General information age	7–6
Mobility	below average
Vision	average
Hearing	average
Interpersonal relations	below average

When those age scores and ratings are plotted in Figure 2.2, we find that Charles, with an IQ score of 72, presents a reversal of the picture shown by John. Although both boys are 10 years old and have normal hearing and vision, their growth patterns in other characteristics are very different.

As with most intellectually retarded children, Charles's profile indicates that he can be considered normal or near normal in height, weight, mobility, motor coordination, and in vision and hearing. But he is exceptional in other areas of development. He differs from the average child in social, mental, and educational characteristics. His mental age is 7–2, and in the academic subjects of reading, spelling, and arithmetic, he tests at educational ages of 6–8, 6–6, 7–0, and 7–5; that is, after four years in school his educational accomplishments are at the first- and beginning second-grade level. His deviation from the majority of children in the fifth grade in mental, social, and academic abilities, in spite of his similarity to the other children in physical characteristics, again requires a special adaptation of school practices, which will be discussed in later chapters.

THE CHILD WITH AUDITORY IMPAIRMENTS

Figure 2.3 shows the developmental pattern of Tony, a 10-year-old deaf child. Auditorily impaired children may be totally deaf or only hard of hearing. They may have been born deaf or they may have acquired deafness after learning language and speech. Tony was born deaf. He does not have sufficient hearing even with the use of a hearing aid to develop language and speech through the sense of hearing.

Tony's profile shows that he is average in height, weight, and vision. He is slightly below other 10-year-olds in mobility, motor coordination, and mental age but is considered within the average range in those characteristics. The lowest point is, of course, his hearing, which is rated as very defective. In Tony's case this defect is irremediable. He will have to live with it all his life. The question here is how deafness affects his other traits. First of all, we notice that it affects speech development most. Even with special instruction his speech is no better than that of a 2-year-old child. His next lowest points are in language, reading, and spelling. Although he is average in mental development, his achievement in language, reading, and spelling is similar to that of a first-grade child. The hearing defect has interfered with his development in those areas. Furthermore, his difficulty with communication skills has created problems in interpersonal relations and prevented normal social maturity.

Thus Tony, who is normal in many ways, differs from the

average child in his response to the usual school program. He has greater discrepancies in growth; he differs within himself in many characteristics. An educational program must take into consideration his deviations from the average and the deviations within himself. It must organize instruction so as to circumvent the irremediable deafness. For Tony's adequate development, special education must use channels of communication other than hearing.

The hard-of-hearing child is not as retarded as the deaf child in speech, language, and school subjects. The less the disability, the less special education is usually needed. But whether such a child is mildly or severely hard of hearing, retardation below average children and below his or her other abilities is considerably less than that of a deaf child. In most instances the child remains in the regular classroom but receives special instruction in speech and auditory training to assist him or her in coping with the regular school curriculum. While the deaf child requires a great deal of teaching in a special

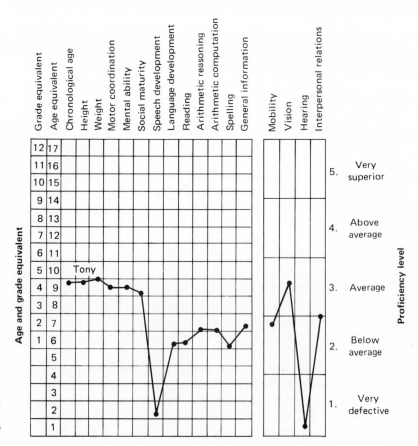

FIGURE 2.3
Profile of an auditorily handicapped child

class and by a skilled teacher, the hard-of-hearing child requires only extra consideration and some specialized education. How much of the latter is needed depends on discrepancies in growth. This total program will be discussed in greater detail in later chapters.

THE CHILD WITH VISUAL IMPAIRMENTS

Children with visual impairments fall into several categories for educational purposes. In the first group are those whose visual defects can be corrected through medical treatment or optical aids. Such children are not regarded as exceptional since with corrective devices they are considered normal and can be educated without modification of school practices.

In the second group are children whose vision is quite defective even after correction. They have difficulty in the regular grades and need instructional compensations for their defects. They utilize their eyes in learning, but to a lesser degree than does the average child. They are referred to as *visually impaired children*. Since they can use their residual vision in learning, they are not considered blind.

In the third group are the blind. They, like the deaf, require instruction primarily through other senses.

Figure 2.4 shows the developmental pattern of Sarah, a blind 10-year-old girl. Vision is her lowest point on the profile. Associated with blindness are retarded mobility, restricted interpersonal relations, and lowered school achievement. Because Sarah cannot see to learn to read, she learns reading through the tactile sense by means of Braille. The process is generally more time consuming than learning to read through the use of the eyes, and for that reason Sarah is slightly retarded educationally.

Another profile could show the growth patterns of a visually impaired child. In general, the educational retardation would not be as great as in the blind. The differences between the average child and the visually impaired child are fewer. The discrepancies in growth within the child are also fewer. Hence, the modifications of school practice and the adaptations of instructional material are not as radical or as great as they are for the blind child.

THE CHILD WITH SPEECH IMPAIRMENTS

Speech is one of the major characteristics differentiating humans from the lower animals. Much communication among people is dependent

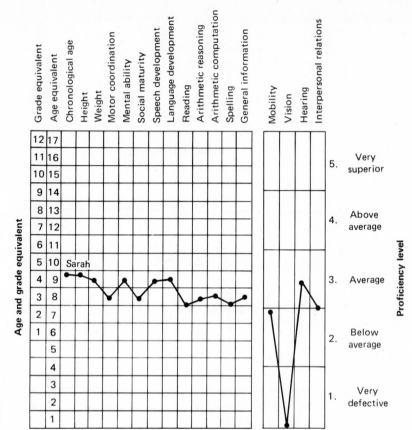

on their ability to speak and to understand the spoken word. Any defect in one's speaking ability is likely to interfere with his or her interpersonal relations.

There are many forms of speech disorders, ranging from complete inability to speak to minor language disabilities and impairments involving articulation and voice, among others. There are also many causes for speech difficulties. The deviation is sometimes associated with other handicapping conditions, such as deafness, mental retardation, and cerebral palsy, as will be discussed in subsequent chapters.

Figure 2.5 shows the developmental pattern of a speech-impaired child of 10 years of age. Betty's profile differs markedly from that of the gifted, mentally retarded, or deaf child. She is, for educational purposes, normal except that speech and to a lesser extent language development are below average. No very extensive educational adaptations have to be made for her in the regular grades. Special classes are not usually organized for this type of child. Betty was left in the

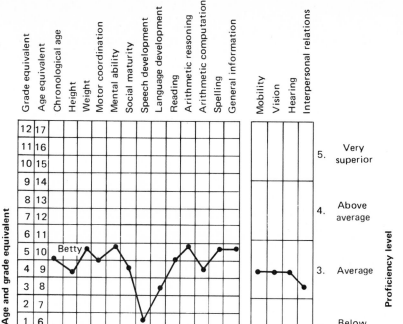

FIGURE 2.5
Profile of a speech-impaired child

regular grades with other children, but an itinerant speech clinician gives Betty corrective lessons several times a week. With such help and that of the regular classroom teacher, Betty's difficulties can probably be removed.

Thus the speech-impaired child with an otherwise average developmental pattern does not differ from the normal, nor does the child differ within himself or herself except for the one specific difficulty, speech. Such a child does not necessarily have widely varying discrepancies in growth. The educational program provided is like that of other children. Special education is provided on a part-time basis by an itinerant speech clinician while the child is being educated in the regular grades.

As will be discussed in Chapter 10, those children may, of course, have other handicaps. A cerebral-palsied child may have a motor handicap, speech handicap, and visual handicap. In such cases a special class instead of only an itinerant teacher may be required.

THE CHILD WITH ORTHOPEDIC OR MULTIPLE IMPAIRMENTS

The orthopedically handicapped child is one who is disabled in motor abilities. A simple example is a child who, through an accident, had lost the use of both legs and is obliged to use a wheelchair. The growth pattern of such a child, according to the profile of Mark (Figure 2.6), shows deficiencies in mobility, motor coordination, social age, and interpersonal relations. There is no retardation in educational subjects. The motor disability does not affect his educational achievements in school although consequent emotional problems may. He learns to read, write, and spell by the same methods as do other children in the class. The school adapts to his disability primarily by providing the physical facilities that he needs because of the use of the wheelchair. His lack of mobility tends to interfere with his social development and his interpersonal relations.

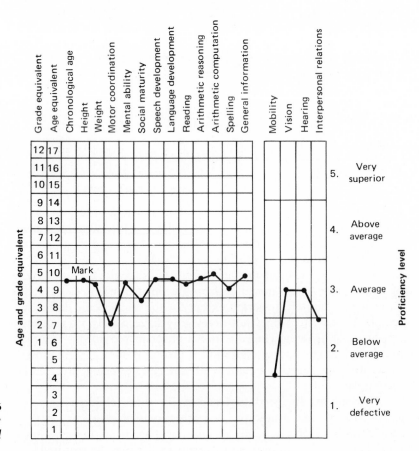

FIGURE 2.6
*Profile of an orthopedically
handicapped child*

Not all orthopedically handicapped children show similar profiles. Motor handicaps can result from brain injuries, such as those found in cerebral-palsied children, in which case they are often associated with speech defects, mental retardation, other handicapping conditions, or combinations of all three. Those conditions, of course, complicate the educational picture, for the more disabling the mental and physical circumstance, the more necessary special education is. The cerebral-palsied child is discussed in greater detail in Chapter 12, but no profile is given here because the individuals show no consistent pattern.

In many instances we find *multiple handicaps* (Wolf and Anderson, 1969) or other combinations of divergences from the normal. A crippled child may be gifted. A deaf child may be blind. A cerebral-palsied child may have many deviations and may be visually impaired, hard of hearing, mentally retarded (or gifted), and defective in speech. Sometimes two handicaps are so severe that the child cannot adapt to a special class for either one. In such cases other arrangements must be made, using itinerant teachers, homebound education, or more specifically adapted special classes. In such cases a special program must be designed for each individual child.

THE CHILD WITH BEHAVIOR PROBLEMS

Behavior problems may take a variety of forms and stem from a variety of causes. There may be hostility and aggression or withdrawal and restraint. There may be a high or low IQ. There may or may not be physical concomitants. There may be academic success but more often failure in at least some school subjects. The category of those with behavior disorders may include psychotic and neurotic children, children with lesser emotional difficulties, and delinquent children.

The child represented in Figure 2.7 was a rebellious truant 10 years old. As can be seen by reading his profile, Steve was normal mentally and physically, but in addition to his low scores in interpersonal relations and social adjustment, he showed retardation of a year or two in most school subjects. A series of unfortunate family experiences had left Steve with hostile attitudes and no interest in school. With many absences and much failure he had no motivation to succeed and was dropping further and further behind in his academic subjects.

Such a child needs specific help in alleviating some of the underlying causes of his maladjustment, including counseling and guidance by professional workers at home and at school. In addition,

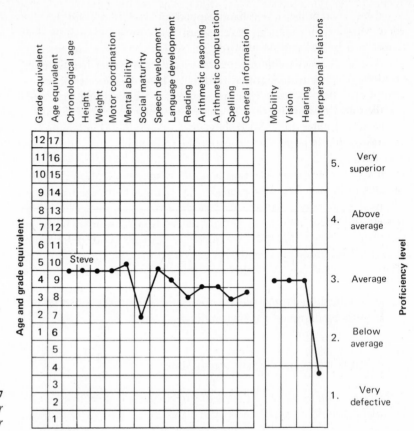

FIGURE 2.7
*Profile of a child with a behavior
disorder*

there will have to be some adaptation of the school program. Steve, for example, may need some individual tutoring and certainly modified materials since he is educationally unable to function at a fourth-grade level. Only for more extreme cases are there special classes or special schools. If Steve's problems bring him into too great a conflict with society, he may even require institutionalization.

THE CHILD WITH SPECIFIC LEARNING DISABILITIES

Specific learning disabilities is a relatively new category in the education of exceptional children. Its gradual evolvement resulted from the recognition that handicapped children do not always fit into neat, well-defined categories with uniform characteristics. Special educators have found that there are a number of children who are not deaf but cannot understand language; who are not blind but cannot perceive visually; or who are not mentally retarded but cannot learn under ordinary school instruction.

Children listed under the caption *specific learning disabilities* are children who cannot be grouped under the traditional categories of exceptional children, but who show significant retardation in learning to talk, or who do not develop normal visual or auditory perception, or who have great difficulty in learning to read, to spell, to write, or to make arithmetic calculations.

Although those children form a heterogeneous group and fail to learn for diverse reasons, they have one thing in common; namely, developmental discrepancies (intraindividual differences in growth). Figure 2.8 presents the profile of Julius at the age of 10–0. He was the first-born child of parents who were both teachers. His development was normal physically and mentally, he had no motor problems, and

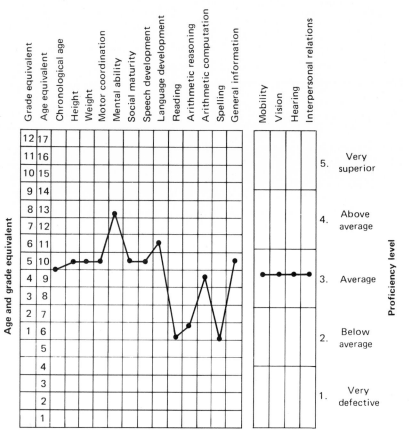

FIGURE 2.8
Profile of a child with a specific learning disability

his visual and hearing acuities were normal. On the Wechsler Intelligence Scale for Children he obtained a total IQ of 130, with no marked discrepancies between his verbal or performance IQ. Yet, after four years of school he was unable to learn to read. Because of his general knowledge and his ability in arithmetic he had been socially promoted to the fourth grade. It will be noted from the profile that in his case discrepancies in growth are quite marked. He is unable to read or spell in spite of regular school attendance, adequate instruction, and adequate family background. His retardation in reading and spelling cannot be accounted for as a result of mental retardation, sensory handicap, emotional disturbance, or environmental deprivation. He has a specific learning disability in the form of severe retardation in reading and spelling.

OTHER HANDICAPPING CONDITIONS

There are other types of handicapping conditions that make modification of school practices necessary. Most of them are health problems. A tuberculous child, for example, needs an opportunity for rest during the school day. Children with cardiac disabilities may find the regular class too strenuous. For many of those children, however, the educational program is not altered. Only the physical arrangements are varied from those for the average child.

The preceding profiles representing discrepancies in growth of different kinds of exceptional children were specific to the conditions discussed. For any particular child, such discrepancies may be less or greater than the ones represented. In all of those cases, however, educational adaptations are needed for the maximum development of the child. The differences in growth and development will be discussed in greater detail in the subsequent chapters that deal separately with each kind of exceptional child.

Information processing in children

Why and how does one child receive information and use it effectively while another child does not? How can we account for interindividual and intraindividual differences? To understand the differences between the exceptional and the average child, one must first understand normal child performance. With the exception of the gifted in whom certain abilities are enhanced, the differences of exceptionality represent malfunctions in the child's (1) perception, (2) mental operations in dealing with what is perceived (such as memory and seeing relationships), (3) ability to express oneself, and (4) decision making. Just as one has to know the normal workings of an automobile before one can understand its breakdowns, so one must analyze the normal systems by which the average child processes information.

To help the student in the quest for such an understanding, we, the authors, present an information-processing model to give a general portrait of normal functioning. We will then describe what happens to individuals representative of each exceptionality. The model presented here is only one version of many similar ones that have been developed as educators and scientists try to bring into focus various cognitive steps in the remarkable feat of learning, which adults often take so much for granted. While such models as the one presented here are not universally accepted, they provide a way of thinking about exceptional children that many have found useful. For example:

> Helen mounts a tricycle that she has not seen for a couple of months. Shortly—very shortly—she is riding with all the skill displayed in her earlier use of the toy.

Where did the child keep those complex visual-motor coordination skills during the elapsed time? How was she able to bring them forth as good as those displayed earlier? Remarkable? We should think so!

> A preschool boy runs up to his mother, shouting excitedly, "Mommie, Mommie, Sally *goed* across the street again!"
> Mother responds, "She went across the street?"
> "Yes, yes, yes!" cries Billy. "She *goed* across the street!"

Where did Billy learn the word *goed*? Not from imitation of his mother or other adults. No, he has learned a rule that you put *ed* on most verbs to represent past tense. That he applied the rule incorrectly makes his statement mildly amusing, but what we should be in awe of is that *he has incorporated a complex linguistic rule into his speech* at such a young age. The average child has, by the age of 3, independently discovered so many linguistic rules that it challenges a master psycholinguist to trace and track them all. Amazing? Yes, indeed!

The means by which children acquire information is a more complex chain of events than we ordinarily imagine. Whenever there are difficulties in any link of that chain, the ability of the child to process information adequately is disturbed. Figure 2.9 shows a schematic diagram of the sequence of steps by which we process information.

1. Stimuli are received from the environment (including one's body) and taken note of, that is, *perceived.* Perception can occur through a number of avenues, including visual, auditory, gustatory, haptic, kinesthetic, and olfactory ones.

2. Those perceptions are then acted on by various *mental operations* so that proper interpretation and use may be made of them. Interpretation may be made by using such mental operations as memory, association, reasoning, extrapolation, and evaluation.

3. The individual may then proceed to give *expression* by speaking or acting through vocal or motor avenues.

4. Through *feedback,* or monitoring the results of his or her own action, the individual makes further interpretation (mental operations) and utilizes the *decision-making* function to determine what he or she should do next. Decision making can result in attention to new perceptions, in application of specific thinking strategies, and in varieties of expression.

To trace the process of information through the system, assume, for example, that the *stimulus* of a barking dog confronts a young child, Mary, whose information-processing system goes into action. Mary receives the stimulus through a number of different channels— the visual, the auditory, the haptic (if the dog jumps up on her), and others.

FIGURE 2.9
Information-processing model

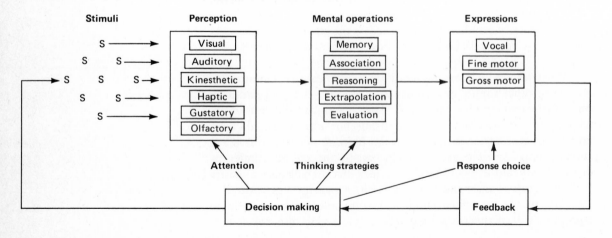

Mary perceives the stimulus. That information is then fed into her *mental operations* system for more analysis. From her analysis of past experience, the child may now know that the dog is Rover, the neighbor's dog, that Rover barks often when excited, and that his bark does not mean he is angry, especially if his tail is wagging (retrieval of prior information from Mary's mother and father).

Mary acts on that interpretation of the information by inhibiting the temptation to run away, backing away instead, and saying, "Go away, Rover, you are a naughty dog," using her *expression* capabilities.

Mary now gets additional information on the effect of her actions (*feedback*) by noting that Rover has run off down the street. She catalogues the experience in her memory, together with the hundreds of other experiences she will have that day, for future reference and use.

But suppose Mary could not see and therefore could not get the visual image of the dog cavorting in front of her, or could not hear so that the dog's barking went unperceived, or was unable to draw easily on past information and reason through to a proper course of action. Or suppose Mary could not speak and so could not shout at the dog, or was crippled so that she could not move away. A deficit in any of those areas creates special problems that become important in the ability to react competently.

Each of the major segments of the information-processing model in Figure 2.9 will be briefly discussed to elaborate on those elements involved in the normal and the exceptional child's growing ability to respond to his or her world.

PERCEPTION

The first major component in the information-processing system is *perception,* which deals with incoming stimuli, as shown in the model. It is not, however, a simple transmission of stimulus to awareness but is a complex synthesizing system that adds something of the individual's past experience to each piece of incoming information. If you have ever taken an inkblot test in which random splotches of ink can turn into perceived flower gardens or galloping animals or frightening masks, you can see how all of us add something of ourselves and our own past experience to the stimuli to which we attend.

We have all observed young children in bed at night who become terrified as the shadows in the darkened room turn, in their perception, into monsters and goblins. If that perceptual link in the information chain is broken or distorted—as may occur with brain-damaged children and with children who have sensory defects—it is obvious that the child will not be able to utilize adequately all his or her perceptions in later processing steps. The cumulative effect of such problems on handicapped children day after day, year after year, challenges educators in helping those children to reach their maximum potential.

MENTAL OPERATIONS

A variety of *mental operations* interpret the perceptions as a prelude to effective action. Those mental operations become progressively more complex as the child grows older. As indicated in the model, they include *memory, association, reasoning, extrapolation,* and *evaluation.*

Memory is one of the most spectacular skills of the central nervous system, and few other skills can match the ability of an individual to reconstruct past experiences. The ability to draw on past experiences and stored knowledge is so fundamental to any serious intellectual activity that it is hard to imagine anyone learning if that function were made inoperative. In aphasia, for example, a lack of memory may hinder the use of language and have catastrophic effects on other learning. Many children show minor deficits in memory, and those, too, cause manifest but less serious problems.

The most common analogy that can help us understand the memory process is that of a computer. We can place information in the storage bank (the computer's memory) where it is pigeonholed or coded to be withdrawn at some later time. Sometimes defects in memory appear to be due to poor coding, which makes retrieval of the information difficult. It is as if a book in a library is filed on the wrong shelf. If children file memories "on the wrong shelf," the experiences they have had will be of little use to them in later circumstances. Emotionally disturbed children sometimes bring forth different and, to us, bizarre reactions because some past experience was perceived abnormally and filed away with their fears instead of with meaningful relationships.

Association is a significant skill possessed by most human beings and is essential to their adaptability. The ability to link one idea or action to another—to associate ideas—is central to adaptability since associations can be organized, combined, and recombined in a variety of ways that expand the child's knowledge base. The more varied and detailed those conceptual bundles are, the more likely the child will be to respond to his or her environment effectively. Even at the preschool age children begin to cluster events and experiences into conceptual categories or classes. They may be simple classes such as "all things that are red" or more discrete classes such as "all things that are brown and soft and alive." Each child will have a unique set of such conceptual bundles formed, in part, by unique experiences. The gifted child will have more, and more complex, organizations of concepts than the normal child, who in turn will have more than the retarded child.

Association and classification help organize the child's world. *Reasoning* provides the child with the power to add to it by generating *new* information from the data already available. Consider the following:

> Joe is taller than Pete.
> Pete is taller than Carlos.

Using those bits of information, the child is able to know a new fact about Joe and Carlos that he or she did not know before (that is, Joe is taller than Carlos). It is this ability, multiplied in thousands of separate instances, that enables developing children to increase rapidly their storehouses of knowledge.

Extrapolation, which is a variation on the reasoning process, is the child's ability to project his or her knowledge into hypothetical situations. For example, "What are all of the things that might happen if we ran out of oil?" In that instance, the child is asked to scan his past knowledge and pick a large number of possible results—still using the basic reasoning operations.

The final mental operation of importance in the human repertoire of information processing is *evaluation,* the ability to weigh one idea against another or to judge one's own idea against some criteria. For instance, the answer to "Does this novel have a well-constructed story?" depends on the meaning of "well-constructed."

If Mary is asked to react to another animal, a little black animal with a white stripe down its back, she needs to have both a criterion for proper action (don't hurt harmless animals) and some knowledge of the animal in question (he squirts awful stuff) in order to make a sound judgment.

If we were asked to evaluate the relative importance of the wombat and the kangaroo to Australian society, most of us would be stumped for a good decision. Many children exhibit "bad judgment" or poor evaluation not because there is a defect in their evaluation process but merely because they lack relevant information on which to make the decision. A rich linguistic and conceptual background will obviously enhance the effective use of such mental operations and place the child several giant steps ahead in ability to survive and prosper. Gifted children are characterized by their superior ability to perform such mental operations. Children who have a limited capacity to carry out those mental operations (for example, the mentally retarded) obviously are going to have great difficulty in adapting to the educational setting and to life.

EXPRESSION

Another key element in the total information-processing system is the *expressive ability* that allows the child to communicate ideas and feelings to others. The model presented in Figure 2.9 divides the expressive domain into two major categories, vocal and motor skills.

Vocal expression is one of the skills that differentiate human beings from other species of animal life. As the child matures, speech allows him or her to project increasingly more complex and subtle messages that emerge from the mental operations, messages that can hardly be projected in any other way.

Since speech and language are among the most complex functions, they can be adversely affected by a wide variety of other difficulties ranging from hearing impairment to mental retardation to brain injury to emotional disturbance. The failure of the child to communicate may be a simple matter of limited experience, or it may be a symptom of a wide variety of other disorders. Whatever the cause, failure to use speech and language will result in many social and communication problems.

The young child normally develops an extraordinary ability to coordinate relatively limited sets of muscle groups in order to perform complex skills. Writing with a pen, dialing a telephone, smiling engagingly, and knitting a sweater are examples of the use of *fine motor skills*.

Young children show relatively slow maturation in fine motor skills as opposed to gross motor skills. One of the specialized uses of fine motor skills in special education is the deaf child's learning to finger-spell, that is, to shape the fingers to represent each letter of the alphabet.

Failure to develop in the fine motor area can preclude a major channel of communication—writing. The motor deficits in cerebral palsy not only limit mobility but also limit such channels of communication as writing and speaking.

The term *gross motor skills* refers to the use of large muscle groups to achieve a variety of tasks such as running, dancing, riding a bicycle, and swimming. Such skills can also communicate feelings of anger, despair, and joy, for example, as many interpretative dancers and pantomimists can demonstrate. Failure in the use of skills in this area can result in limited mobility for the child and consequently a more limited range of communication.

DECISION MAKING

No information-processing model would be complete without the addition of a major function that, in fact, influences and directs all the other processes. No one can observe human beings for very long without noting the wide variety of decisions that they make every day. In the model (Figure 2.9) this operation is referred to as the *decision-making* function.

The decision-making function can be described in terms of four rather distinctive processes and the elements involved in them: (1) the stimuli and perceptions to which attention should be given, (2) the mental operations that should be applied to a given problem, (3) the mode of expression that should be used, and (4) the use that is made of the feedback of information about one's own performance.

It is not necessary to portray a little green man sitting at a computer console at the base of the brain, pushing switches, and turning knobs in order to think of decision making. Instead, one can think of the accumulated past experience. If in the past it had been important for the individual to respond to a certain kind of stimulus (for example, mother's vocal tone), then that stimulus will be given special attention when it occurs again. If in the past visual signals had been more important than auditory signals, then the visual component of a stimulus may get more attention than the auditory portion (for example, the TV picture may register on the child, whereas the accompanying TV sound may not). If in the past reasoning ability had helped the person solve problems, then it will more likely be called on in the future as a strategy for dealing with problems facing the person. Following are some of the strategies that may be utilized.

ATTENTIONAL STRATEGIES. Children swim in a sea of competing stimuli: sights, sounds, smells, and tastes. They must be able to sort out those stimuli that are important or relevant, to shine a mental spotlight on certain stimuli. If we have developed normally, we can pull the relevant stimuli into our attentional foreground (the voice on the radio), while other less important stimuli (the fan on the furnace, the car passing by outside, the water running in the bathtub) get pushed into the background.

We do not know exactly how this mental process of attention works, except that there are sections of the central nervous system that can operate either to enhance or to dampen the power or intensity of stimuli as they arrive at the cortex. If that attentional system is not working, one may refer to the child as "distractible" or "not task oriented." Some children with identifiable damage to the central nervous system seem unable to focus their attention under ordinary conditions, thus experiencing predictable learning problems.

THINKING STRATEGIES. One of the commonplace but important decisions made by children and adults is whether to call into action their full range of intellectual skills or to respond at a routine or habit level. A child might be walking in the woods, not thinking about much of anything, and suddenly find himself or herself lost. A heightened sense of awareness might be noted as the child seeks to find any clues as to direction or location.

The child may adopt a strategy of mentally reviewing how he or she arrived at the present point or of estimating the distance covered during the elapsed time. The child may review alternatives of action before proceeding farther. In short, he or she would be using the decision-making function to apply a number of already available thinking strategies to the problem at hand.

RESPONSE CHOICE. To follow the adventures of our lost child further, he or she has some variety of possible expressive strategies that can be used. The child could call for help, could utilize gross motor skills to travel in gradually widening circles, trying to find a clue to a way out, or could use fine motor skills to write a note and pin it to a tree.

FEEDBACK UTILIZATION. The fourth major part of the decision-making function is the utilization of the reaction of the environment to our own actions. If a child laughs at the misfortunes of another child while other children are sympathizing, then the laughing child needs to be sensitive to the harsh looks the laughter brought, or risk some social censure. If a child is not sensitive to how the teacher is reacting to noisy antics, then there can be many social consequences of that as well. Many children can hear a subtle change in the teacher's voice quality that means he or she may be about to become angry, or they can tell whether an older brother is in the mood to lend his bicycle by the way he says "hello." Much of what we refer to as "social sensitivity" is the ability to pick up subtle cues as to how the social environment is reacting to us. The ability to use information about how the world is reacting to us is crucial to our social adjustment, and it is the skill that is most obviously awry in children we call "emotionally disturbed."

Any substantial deviation from normal development in any of the components of the information processing presented in the model in Figure 2.9 can have serious consequences for the developing child.

Process leading to product

The differential characteristics and achievements of the typical child of each exceptionality may be due, at least in part, to differential problems in information processing. How do difficulties in processing information lead to the differing profiles shown earlier in this chapter? Some examples follow.

CHANGES IN MENTAL OPERATIONS

The two areas of exceptionality that are most obviously differentiated by changes in the mental operations dimension are those of the mentally retarded and the gifted. The profiles of a gifted and a retarded child, shown in Figure 2.2, turn out to be mirror images of one another.

In the retarded child, the limited ability to remember, associate, reason, extrapolate, and evaluate ideas will negatively affect academic performance. Such a defect in mental operations reverberates throughout the information-processing system and progressively affects other parts of the system such as perception and expression. The low performance of the mentally retarded child is shown on the profile (Figure 2.2) in reading, speech development, arithmetic reasoning, and other areas, all consequences of limited capabilities in mental operations.

Since mentally retarded children have less knowledge, their expression appears impaired as well. Failure is a natural consequence of limited mental performance, and the child is less likely to pay attention or develop new problem-solving strategies through the decision-making function. Thus a defect in the mental operations eventually impairs all the other components of the system.

In contrast, the mental operations of the gifted child are functioning in a superior and advanced fashion, so the profile (Figure 2.2) reveals superior reading, speech development, and reasoning. The gifted child associates ideas better, remembers more, and reasons, evaluates, and extrapolates ideas at a superior level. Superior mental operations lead to superior expression, which lead to academic success. Success then leads to better attention, greater enthusiasm for learning, and a heightened perception and interest in the surrounding world. The richer store of knowledge increases the probability that the gifted child will be an effective problem solver.

CHANGES IN PERCEPTION

The loss of hearing does not at first glance seem as serious educationally as it turns out to be. Yet the profile in Figure 2.3 reveals major delays in speech and language development. The development of language in young children relies on certain parts of the information-processing system in order to function properly. Children must be able to hear in order to perceive the speech and language of others. They must be able to hear themselves speak through the feedback mechanism in order to correct their own imperfect first efforts at speech. If they can hear neither their own speech nor the speech of others, the symbolic system of oral and aural language is closed to them.

Without language symbols short-cut mental operations become progressively impaired. Thus the hearing-impaired child has serious problems at all levels of academic performance as shown in Figure 2.3, often being three and a half years behind his or her chronological age. That problem presents a major challenge to special education.

In contrast to the serious academic problems of the auditorily impaired child, those of the youngster with a visual handicap whose development is profiled in Figure 2.4 do not seem such an educational difficulty. The impact of not being able to see is a problem easy for us to understand. We readily perceive some of that impact on other parts of the information-processing system. Children with visual impairments will have certain association problems in understanding "he is wearing a red- and black-striped shirt" and "it is as big as a football field." However, many of the mental operations remain relatively unaffected. A secondary consequence of the visual handicap is reduced mobility, which can further limit the available field of experience.

With those children, however, there is a crucial language cycle in information processing that is unbroken. Hearing others speak, being able to hear oneself speak, and being able to store the knowledge gained from auditory sources result in a profile showing that the visually impaired child is only slightly retarded in academic skills.

CHANGES IN EXPRESSION

Children who have specific deficits in the area of expression but not in the other dimensions of the information-processing system do not have as serious an educational problem as do children with defects in other parts of the model. The fundamental reason for this is that the information input and operations by which the youngster learns have not been altered. The basic problem in speech expression can cause the youngster some consequent social problems but does not necessarily deter academic progress.

If the development of motor skills has been impaired, then the child may be limited in mobility. Limitation in mobility results in more limited experience for the youngster and may be a deterrent for social adaptability. Still, unless the handicap also involves other parts of the information-processing system, it is unlikely that serious educational consequences will result since the information input and operations are essentially unaffected.

In many instances expressive disorders accompany disorders in other domains. Thus a cerebral-palsied youngster may also have deficits in the domain of mental operations. The speech-handicapped youngster may have problems in auditory perception. In those instances youngsters may be referred to as "multiply handicapped."

CHANGES IN DECISION MAKING

If the child has substantial deficits in the decision-making function, then the ability to attend to the appropriate perceptions and to adopt the proper strategies in problem solving and in making appropriate expression will be impaired. Such youngsters may be learning disabled or emotionally disturbed, depending on the particular nature of the deficit. Since decision making depends on appropriate data intake and past experience, the youngsters with severe mental retardation or perceptual difficulties that prevent their gaining proper experience may also appear impaired in decision making.

The information-processing system has been described through each of its component parts for purposes of explanation and description. The essential concept of the developing human being is that those parts are always interrelated; influences in one area are bound to have consequences in other areas as well. Just as in the physical systems of the body where a defect in the circulation system will result in problems in other parts of the organism, so defects in one part of the information-processing system result in difficulties and problems in other parts as well. As different groups of exceptional children are reviewed in each of the subsequent chapters, the student should ask the question: What part or parts of the information-processing system are affected, and how does the special program described ameliorate or compensate for the interference in normal development?

Summary

1. Adaptation of instruction to individual differences in children became a requirement when compulsory education was mandated in the early part of the nineteenth century.

2. The concept of interindividual differences has been used to compare one child with another and to classify children into subgroups according to their deviations from the average.

3. The concept of intraindividual differences has been introduced to compare abilities and disabilities of a child with himself or herself, rather than with other children. Adaptation of instruction to an individual child's uneven growth is the essence of special education.

4. Profiles of "split growth" or intraindividual differences have been presented to show the discrepancies in development for each type of exceptional child.

5. An information-processing system has been presented to show what parts of the process are affected in each of the various types of exceptional children.

References

KIRK, S. A. 1972. *Educating Exceptional Children,* 2nd ed. Boston: Houghton Mifflin.

WOLF, J. M., AND R. M. ANDERSON, EDS. 1969. *The Multiply Handicapped Child.* Springfield, Ill.: Charles C Thomas.

3

Society has a special interest in gifted and talented children both as individuals and as potential contributors to the society's well-being. As individuals they have the same right to opportunities for full development as do all children. In addition that group of children will likely produce many of the leaders and molders of the next generation, and few societies can long afford to ignore or scorn that potential.

Children of all of the other groups described under the label "exceptional" are children with a deficit in one or more parts of the information-processing system. The gifted are the only group that has a surplus of abilities or talent. In the gifted child the central processing functions (see Chapter 2) of memory, association, reasoning, extrapolation, and evaluation are enhanced, and such advanced development influences positively the other major components of information processing.

As this chapter will show, there is little question that the very surplus of abilities creates some distinctive educational problems for the typical school system.

CHILDREN WITH INTELLECTUAL SUPERIORITY AND TALENTS

Historical perspective

In ancient Greece, over two thousand years ago, Plato advocated that children with superior intellect be selected at an early age and offered a specialized form of instruction in science, philosophy, and metaphysics. The most intelligent and knowledgeable would then become the leaders of the state. Plato felt that the survival of Greek democracy was contingent upon its ability to educate superior citizens for leadership positions in that society.

In the sixteenth century Suleiman the Magnificent made special efforts to identify the gifted Christian youth throughout the Turkish Empire and provide them with education in the Moslem faith and in war, art, science, and philosophy (Sumption and Luecking, 1960). His talent scouts, who surveyed the population at regular intervals, were able to select and educate a large group of superior individuals. Thus, within a generation after that system of education began, the Ottoman Empire became a great power in art, science, culture, and war and even attempted to conquer the whole of Europe.

During the nineteenth and twentieth centuries little organized effort was made in Europe to select gifted children or to offer them special education. It was not felt to be necessary since secondary schools and universities were in general keyed to the education of those in the higher social strata, from which it was believed the more intelligent leadership would come. Supposedly, selection was made according to the interests and academic achievement of the child. In many countries in Europe a small proportion of the population of children is selected at the fourth or sixth grade and assigned to academic secondary schools, while the masses continue in the common schools and learn a trade. The percentage of those who attend secondary schools or universities is smaller in most European countries than the percentage who attend such schools in the United States.

In the United States the concentration of effort in public education has been on the education of "all of the children of all of the people." With a few exceptions opportunities for education under public auspices have been offered all children without differentiation. It is as if we had implicit faith that all men are created with equal potential, as well as equal rights, and that education is the avenue through which this equality could express itself. A noted behavioral psychologist, John B. Watson, bolstered this point of view when he stated that he could take any well-formed, healthy baby and make of it what he pleased—"rich man, poor man, beggar man, thief."

Interest in the gifted and talented waxes and wanes in American society. In the decade 1955–1964 there was an intensified interest in the education of gifted children, stimulated in large measure by the perceived competitive threat to our society by the Soviet Union. The launching of the first Russian satellite *Sputnik* sent a collective shock wave through the American society that had long prided itself on its scientific and technological superiority in the world. A number of states started special programs for gifted students; The National Defense Education Act provided student fellowships; and The National Science Foundation supported major curriculum reforms in science and mathematics.

The following decade showed a marked decline in interest and special efforts for the gifted and talented as the emphasis shifted to the problems of minority-group, low-income children. Concern for the gifted, like that for many other exceptional children, arises from the needs and the social and political philosophy of the times.

In this chapter we will discuss, from the standpoint of the American culture, who are the gifted, their characteristics, and the variety of strategies undertaken to meet their educational and special needs.

Who are the gifted?

Each culture defines giftedness in its own image and fixes the nature of the gifted person in the culture. From that definition we learn something about the values and lifestyles of that culture. The person called gifted in a primitive society may be very different from one so honored in an advanced technological society. Ancient Greece honored the orator, while Rome valued the engineer and the soldier.

The earliest definition of the gifted in the United States was tied to the figure of an IQ and particularly to the Stanford-Binet IQ that was developed by Terman shortly after World War I. Those children who scored above a certain point, an IQ of 130 or 140 or whatever was agreed on, were declared to be gifted.

In an attempt to broaden the concept, various educators proposed a more general definition in the late 1950s. "The gifted or talented child is one who shows consistently remarkable performance in any worthwhile line of endeavor" (Henry, 1958, p. 19).

Newland (1976) pointed out that such a definition has at least two major flaws. First, the child has to demonstrate his or her giftedness by performance, ruling out early identification, and second, what does "any worthwhile line of endeavor" really mean?

No definition is worth very much unless its broad, general statements can be translated into some measurable characteristic. That is why the IQ remains an important part of any operational definition of *gifted* despite the recent criticisms of intelligence tests.

The definition currently in vogue was reported by Marland (1972) who, as U.S. Commissioner of Education, rekindled interest in the field of the gifted and talented student:

> Gifted and talented children are those identified by professionally qualified persons who by virtue of outstanding abilities are capable of high performance. These are children who require differentiated educational programs and services beyond those normally provided by the regular program in order to realize their contribution to self and society.
>
> Children capable of high performance include those with demonstrated achievement and/or potential ability in any of the following areas.
> 1. General intellectual ability
> 2. Specific academic aptitude
> 3. Creative or productive thinking
> 4. Leadership ability
> 5. Visual and performing arts
> 6. Psychomotor ability (p. 10)

The purpose of such a definition was to recognize youngsters who possessed a diversity of talents, rather than to restrict the definition to the more linguistically facile child, as had been done in the past.

Despite that effort to go beyond the strictly cognitive domain, there still remains a strong emphasis on intelligence tests for identification because (1) they are well-developed and proven instruments and (2) they tap the memory, association, reasoning, and information processing abilities so crucial to high performance in school-related activities.

When the term *talented* is used, it generally refers to a specific dimension of skill (that is, musical or artistic talent) that may not be matched by the child's more general abilities. In most children there is a substantially positive relationship between intellectual giftedness and talented performance. There are occasional cases in which a child may have an unusual talent in one area and have limited abilities in other areas.

The intellectually gifted are often socially talented; the musically talented may also be intellectually and mathematically gifted. The academically talented are usually intellectually gifted, although not all intellectually gifted children are academically talented.

The direction in which a gifted intellect goes is dependent on many other factors such as experience, motivation, interest, emotional stability, hero worship, parental urgings, and even chance. Many intellectually gifted individuals might also have been successful in another area had their interests and training been in that direction.

Even though we admit that superior intelligence is only one factor in determining success, achievement, or contribution to society, it still remains a basic ingredient of giftedness. Trying to include in a definition of giftedness factors other than cognitive, such as social leadership, is commendable, but it confuses the concept of giftedness with our goals for gifted children. We do have gifted children who are not outstanding in creativity; we do have gifted children who are using their talents in socially unacceptable ways. But the common denominator is intellectual superiority!

LEADERSHIP AND GIFTEDNESS

The inclusion of *leadership* in the roster of characteristics identifying gifted individuals raises a series of important questions. Is there such a common trait in the first place? Is leadership the same whether it is manifested by the football captain, the debate team leader, or the student protest leader?

Everyone is intrigued by the characteristics of good leadership since it always seems to be in short supply. But what are the traits of leadership that cause others to follow and submerge their own interests in a particular cause? Stogdill (1974) presented two classic leadership theories.

> *The Great Man Theory* which holds that particular individuals are endowed with an abundance of characteristics that cause them to stand out from the many and permit them to guide, direct, and lead the majority.

The Times Theory which views leadership as a function of a given set of social characteristics and situations. At any particular time, groups of people have certain needs which require the services of an individual to assist them in meeting those needs. The individual in this view comes to play the role of leader by being at the right place at the right time.

Most syntheses of the data on leadership suggest that some combination of the two theories seems most correct.

Another point of great interest to educators is whether this leadership trait can be trained or further developed in those individuals who show evidences of leadership. On this point there seems to be little doubt that intensive leadership training of adults can be effective. Stogdill concluded that "results of research suggest that direct training and techniques of leadership result in improved effectiveness as a leader."

The characteristics most often identified as being possessed by leaders in a variety of situations are: (1) a strong drive for responsibility and task completion, (2) vigor and persistence in the pursuit of goals, (3) venturesomeness and originality in problem solving, (4) self-confidence and sense of personal identity, (5) the willingness to absorb interpersonal stress, (6) the willingness to tolerate frustration and delay, (7) the ability to influence other persons' behavior, and (8) the capacity to structure social interaction systems to the purpose at hand (Arnold, 1976).

In leadership it is clear that we are not simply describing inborn characteristics but instead the cumulative capabilities that youngsters demonstrate as a result of some intermix of constitutional ability and experience.

Finding gifted children

Before gifted children can be engaged in special educational opportunities, they first have to be found. That task is often more difficult than the average citizen supposes. In every generation many gifted children pass through school unidentified, their talents uncultivated. Prominent among those undiscovered are children from low socioeconomic backgrounds or subcultures that place less stress on such characteristics as verbal ability. There are, in addition, those who have to drop out of school for economic reasons and those whose emotional problems disguise their intellectual abilities.

There is a general expectation that the teacher will spot those children and do something for them, but various studies have shown that teachers are not effective in recognizing the gifted child; in fact they may fail to identify from 10 to 50 percent of their gifted children. For example, Pegnato and Birch (1959), in evaluating various methods of identifying gifted children, found that teachers were not able to select them with sufficient accuracy. They selected many children (31.4 percent) who were not gifted and missed more than half of the truly gifted ones as measured by standard intelligence tests.

At the kindergarten level the failure of teachers to find gifted children is even more disturbing. W. D. Kirk (1966) found that kindergarten teachers failed to take chronological age (CA) into account and tended to select older children as being bright. Seventy percent of the children selected as bright were mistakenly identified and had a mean IQ of only 102.5. The teachers failed to identify 68 percent of the children with IQs of 116 and above.

When the teachers were given guidelines for selection and an adjustment was made for CA differences, twice as many correct identifications were made, and the teachers missed only 30 percent of the eligible children.

On the basis of those and other studies on identification, it is

TABLE 3.1

Sample scale items: behavioral characteristics of superior students

Part I: Learning characteristics	1. Has unusually advanced vocabulary for age or grade level; uses terms in a meaningful way; has verbal behavior characterized by "richness" of expression, elaboration, and fluency.
	2. Is a keen and alert observer; usually "sees more" or "gets more out of" a story, film, poem, etc., than others.
Part II: Motivational characteristics	1. Strives toward perfection; is self-critical; is not easily satisfied with own speed or products.
	2. Is quite concerned with right and wrong, good and bad; often evaluates and passes judgment on events, people, and things.
Part III: Creativity characteristics	1. Displays a great deal of curiosity about many things; is constantly asking questions about anything and everything.
	2. Displays a keen sense of humor and sees humor in situations that may not appear to be humorous to others.
Part IV: Leadership characteristics	1. Is self-confident with children his own age as well as adults; seems comfortable when asked to show work to the class.
	2. Tends to dominate others when they are around; generally directs the activity in which he is involved.

Source: J. Renzulli and R. Hartman, "Scale for Rating Behavioral Characteristics of Superior Students," *Exceptional Children* 38 (November 1971): 243–248.

clear that subjective evaluation, such as teacher judgment and parent referral, needs to be checked by more objective measures of ability such as standardized tests. Any program for identifying the gifted children in a school system should include both subjective and objective methods of evaluation. Some types of behavior are best observed informally, some by more controlled methods.

Classroom behavior, for example, may point up children's ability to organize and utilize material and reveal their potential for processing information better than a test can. However, the classroom seldom challenges a gifted child to the limit of his or her ability, as can be done in a test situation. Many aspects of creativity and verbal fluency are also best observed in a classroom or in informal experiences.

Table 3.1 provides some sample items from an observational check list that teachers find useful and convenient in identifying gifted children. Through later, more careful testing, children who achieve high ratings on such an observational check list are often shown to be gifted. Such a scale, however, cannot protect against teacher bias or just plain dislike of certain children and a subsequent downgrading of them.

Most schools have test scores available from group intelligence tests or group achievement tests. Those can serve as a starting point in selecting candidates for a special program. Certain pitfalls are widely recognized in utilizing that material:

1. Group intelligence tests are not as reliable as individual tests.
2. They seldom differentiate abilities at the upper limits.
3. Some children do not function adequately in a timed test situation.

Group intelligence tests, however, are practical for screening purposes since it is financially prohibitive to give all children individual examinations. Those children who are near the cutoff point or for whom it is felt that the group test is not representative can be given individual examinations.

Achievement tests are even less discriminating; the same criticisms hold for them as for the intelligence tests. In addition they will detect only children who are achieving well academically. Emotional disturbance, family problems, peer-group standards of mediocrity, poor study habits, a foreign language background, and many other factors may affect a child's ability to perform academically. There are some children who, because of family pressures, good study habits, or intense motivation, achieve at a higher educational level than is consistent with their other abilities or their apparent mental level.

TABLE 3.2

Major procedures used and recommended in the identification of gifted students

Major identification procedures	Percent using	Percent recommending
Teacher observation and nomination	93	75
Group achievement test scores	87	74
Group intelligence tests	87	65
Previously demonstrated accomplishments (including school grades)	56	78
Individual intelligence tests	23	90
Creativity test scores	14	74

Table 3.2 shows a survey of experts in gifted education regarding the desirable and the actual procedures used in identification of gifted students. The experts preferred the individual intelligence test despite its high cost. In actual practice, as Table 3.2 shows, tests or other scales that are easy to administer or collect information readily (that is, teacher observation scales and group tests) tend to be most often used.

So much attention has been focused on the process of identification of gifted students that it seems almost to become a goal in its own right. Martinson (1972) places a needed perspective on such activity.

> Identification per se does not improve learning. Children who are identified and placed in regular programs show no change. . . . Identification cannot reduce the impact of malnutrition, restricted learning opportunities, poor parent-child relationships, lack of interpersonal relationships, and other negative factors. But if a well-planned program reduces these or other defects, performance and achievement of a gifted child will considerably improve. (p. 135)

Profiles of intellectually gifted children

The special educational needs of a gifted child are best understood through an individual study. Educational programs are organized on the basis of averages derived from the study of groups. The application of such averages to an individual is sometimes erroneous since it does not always follow that what is true in a group is true in a particular individual. There are, for example, marked differences among children who have been classified as intellectually gifted.

The profiles of George and Ignatius follow. A series of examinations given to those boys at the age of 10 when they were in the fifth grade yields the results shown.

	George	*Ignatius*
Chronological age	10–4	10–5
Height age	11–9	9–6
Weight age	11–7	9–3
Motor coordination age	12–1	9–4
Mental age	13–11	13–9
Social maturity age	11–5	9–8
Speech development age	13–0	12–0
Language development age	12–7	12–2
Reading age	12–8	12–7
Arithmetic reasoning age	12–1	11–7
Arithmetic computation age	11–5	11–6
Spelling age	11–6	12–0
General information age	11–10	11–6
Mobility	above average	average
Vision	normal	normal
Hearing	normal	normal
Interpersonal relations	above average	average

The test results on George and Ignatius and the corresponding profiles in Figure 3.1 show two boys who can be classified as intellectually gifted but whose growth patterns are markedly different. George's IQ on the Stanford-Binet scale is 135; Ignatius's IQ is 132. Both boys are in the fifth grade. George's age is 10–4, and Ignatius's is 10–5. Physically George is accelerated since his height, weight, motor coordination, and mobility are similar to those of 11-year-old boys in the sixth grade. He is likewise accelerated in social maturity, interpersonal relations, and school achievement. Actually, with the exception of the accident of birth ten years and four months previous to the examination, George is more like 11- and 12-year-old children. The discrepancies between his physical, social, mental, and achievement levels are really not very great. He is above his chronological age group in all areas of development. He does not have wide discrepancies in development within himself. Educationally, George could be accelerated to the sixth or seventh grade since he is more similar to that group than to the 10-year-olds with whom he is placed under his school's policy of year-by-year promotion.

Ignatius scores about as high as George in mental ability and in educational achievement. But Ignatius has wide discrepancies in development among his physical, social, mental, and educational abilities. He is more like 9-year-old children in height, weight, motor coordination, and social maturity. His mobility and interpersonal relations are not superior to those of other children in his grade. His only areas of acceleration are his mental ability and his achievements in speech, language, and academic areas. From an educational point of view, this child should not be accelerated to be with older children. The marked unevenness in his physical, social, and mental development presents educational problems different from those presented by George.

Those two cases demonstrate why no single program suggestion can be accepted as adequate for all gifted children. A diversity of programs is required.

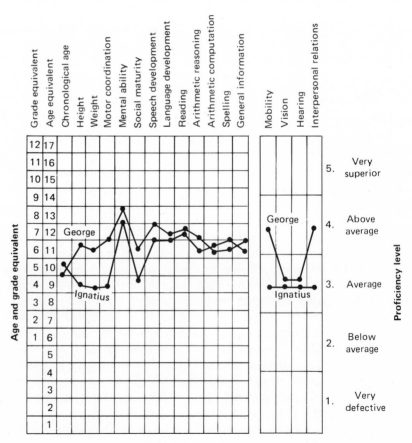

FIGURE 3.1

Profiles of two intellectually gifted children

Histories of great persons

The term *genius* has been applied to outstanding individuals who have attained eminence in some field of intellectual or creative endeavor. Sometimes the individuals are recognized as child prodigies at a young age; sometimes they are not recognized as "great" until they have become known for a unique contribution at a later stage of their lives or, in some instances, after their death.

JOHN STUART MILL (1806–1873)

John Stuart Mill is considered one of the greatest philosophers of the nineteenth century. He was the son of an English author and philosopher who had himself been self-educated. According to Mill's own report, "My father's scheme of education could not have been accomplished if he had not carefully kept me from having any great amount of intercourse with other boys" (1924, p. 36). His father kept him out of school and away from other children to avoid the "contagion of vulgar modes and thought and feeling." He educated John Stuart at home until the boy was 14 years of age. John Stuart began the study of Greek at the age of 3 and geometry and algebra at the age of 8. When he was 12, he began to study philosophy and logic. It is reported that he wrote a history of Rome at the age of 6½. His productive professional career began at age 17. Cox (1926) estimated his IQ to be between 190 and 200.

The degree of Mill's accelerated development may be judged by this passage from a history of Rome that he began at age 6!

> We know not any part, says Dionysius of Halicarnassus, of the history of Rome till the Sicilian invasions. Before that time, the country had not been entered by any foreign invader. . . . The Rutuli, a people living near the sea, and extending along the Numicius up to Livinium, opposed him. However, Turnus their king was defeated and killed by Aeneas. Aeneas was killed soon after this. The war continued to be carried on chiefly against the Rutuli, to the time of Romulus, the first king of Rome. By him it was that Rome was built. (Cox, 1926)

The reactions of John Stuart Mill to his education by the tutorial system of his father (out of school and with little influence of a society of his peers) can best be expressed by direct quotations from his own writings. "I consequently remained long, and in a less degree have always remained, inexpert in anything requiring manual dexterity. . . . The education which my father gave me, was in itself much more fitted for training me to *know* than to *do*" (pp. 36–37).

CHARLOTTE BRONTË (1816–1855)

Charlotte Brontë achieved fame and distinction as a novelist during an age when being a "woman of letters" was a remarkable achievement. Her father was an Irish peasant who became a schoolmaster and then put himself through Cambridge, later becoming a clergyman. Her mother was an intelligent woman who came from a "good family" and who did some writing of her own.

Charlotte and her sisters were strictly reared by their father who provided most of their early education through his own tutorial efforts. Charlotte had only one year of formal school prior to the age of 14 but had followed a regular lesson schedule under her father's direction from an early age. The family environment was clearly conducive to intellectual development with all the children reading omnivorously. As soon as the Brontë children could read and write, they invented and acted out little plays of their own.

Before she was 13, Charlotte wrote a detailed account of family and intellectual activities in "The History of the Year 1829." She composed poems and stories and devised a list of painters whose works she wished to see. She prepared a "Catalogue of My Books up to August 3, 1830," which revealed the production of twenty-two volumes, all written within a period of fifteen months and each containing 60 to 110 pages. They included adventure tales, books of rhymes, and a drama. Despite the lack of formal education, Charlotte soon rose to first place in her class when she entered school at age 14. She was described as "head of the school in all intellectual pursuits" and, at the close of the first half-year, had won prizes for academic performance and good decorum.

After two years of schooling, Charlotte returned home and spent three years assisting in the education of her younger sisters and devoting her leisure hours to reading and writing. Throughout her productive writing years her health was poor, and she died at 39, an early age from the standpoint of potential accomplishments.

Because of the lack of public schooling in that era, the type of tutorial and private schooling that both Charlotte Brontë and John Stuart Mill received was not unusual. The total climate of intellectual activity in Charlotte's unusual family created motivation and practice in reading and writing that allowed her to make up quickly for technical deficiencies in her earlier instruction.

ALBERT EINSTEIN (1879–1955)

The education and early history of Albert Einstein differ markedly from the early education of Mill and Brontë. Reiser (1930) reported that Einstein was retiring in personality and slow in learning to talk and that his parents believed him retarded in development. The father was a merchant conducting an electrical business in Munich, Germany. He was without theoretical training but had abilities in technical matters. Albert's school experiences were not happy ones and did not necessarily contribute to his basic interest in physics and mathematics. Actually he attended the Luifold Gymnasium in Munich, where the basic studies were in the humanities—Latin, Greek, and ancient history. He was bored with school and recalled only one instructor who inspired interest in the classical world.

Einstein's interest in mathematics was aroused by his uncle, his father's partner in the factory. After he had learned the essentials of algebra and heard about the Pythagorean theorem, he studied mathematics on his own and outside of school. At the age of 14 he had mastered the essentials of higher mathematics, which his school did not teach. He continued to be mediocre in school as a language student.

At the age of 15 he left school to go to his parents, who had moved to Milan. Later he failed the entrance examination of the Polytechnic Academy at Zurich. He returned to the secondary school and later was admitted to the Zurich Technical Academy. He became interested in physics, but even here school was not inspiring. He missed classes to read in a wide range of fields, including physics. He completed his work at the University of Zurich and then obtained positions, once as a teacher and once in a patent office. In 1909 he procured a professorship at Zurich. He later held professorships in Austria and finally became Director of the Kaiser Wilhelm Institute for Theoretical Physics in Berlin. Einstein's theory of relativity became famous after World War I when its implications began to be understood by the scientists of the world. His life after 1933 was spent at Princeton University in the Institute for Advanced Study.

The story of Einstein indicates that he did not show precocity at an early age, that he did not come from a family of high educational attainments, and that his early school years did not contribute materially to his later accomplishments in physics and mathematics.

THOMAS A. EDISON (1847–1931)

Thomas Edison is considered one of the great inventors of the nineteenth and twentieth centuries because of his inventions of the phonograph (1877), the incandescent electric lamp (1879), the motion-picture camera (1891), the magnetic ore separator (1908), and many other mechanical devices (Dyer and Martin, 1929).

Edison was raised in an average midwestern American family of his time, his father having been engaged in small business enterprises. His mother, who later educated Thomas, was a former schoolteacher. Throughout his career he attended public school for only three months. During that time, at the age of 7, he was always at the foot of his class. Furthermore, his teacher reported to the local school inspector in Port Huron, Michigan, that the boy was "addled" and should be kept out of school. His mother became incensed at this recommendation, withdrew Thomas from school, and taught him at home, never again admitting him to school.

By the age of 12 he had read such books as Gibbon's *Decline and Fall of the Roman Empire* and Hume's *History of England*. He was, however, unable to master mathematics. At the age of 15 he became editor of his own paper, "The Weekly Herald."

The history of Edison shows a creative mind in the development of mechanical and electrical devices. Although he did not contribute greatly to theoretical knowledge, he is considered creative in a practical sense. It is of note, however, that his education was acquired on a tutorial basis, and his achievements were accomplished without the stimulus of formal schooling.

Characteristics of intellectually gifted children

Gifted children have been the object of interest of numerous investigators. Many of the studies on the characteristics of gifted children, however, are short-term ones and tend to confirm the results of one major longitudinal study covering a period of a third of a century by Lewis M. Terman. Since Terman's research is considered the magnum opus of all such studies of the characteristics of the intellectually gifted, it is reviewed here.

THE TERMAN LONGITUDINAL STUDY

Following his revision and publication of the Binet-Simon tests of intelligence in 1916, Lewis M. Terman, a distinguished professor of psychology at Stanford University, became interested in gifted children. He devoted much of the rest of his life to the study of 1,528 gifted children whom he had identified in 1920. He followed the group for thirty-five years, until his death in 1956. During that period he was instrumental in designing and supervising the research that led to a set of five volumes entitled *Genetic Studies of Genius* (1925–1959).

Terman's search for gifted children was conducted in the public schools of California. Teacher nominations and group intelligence tests were used as screening procedures. (That procedure is now considered to limit the findings since it tends to eliminate gifted children who underachieve or whose behavior teachers may find obnoxious.) The final selection of most subjects was based on an IQ of 140 or above on the 1916 Stanford-Binet Intelligence Scale. Terman estimated that that method identified 90 percent of the eligible students. The average IQ for the more than one thousand children selected by the Binet test was 151. For the total group of 1,528 gifted children, the ratio of boys to girls was 116 to 100. Terman believed that sex difference was due to a greater genetic variability in intelligence among males.

Those gifted children came from homes that were notably in the higher socioeconomic levels. Their parents averaged four to five years more schooling than the average for the United States, and the median family income was more than twice the California average. There was a low incidence of broken homes. It may be that some of the differences that Terman found between the gifted children and the companion groups were due to their superior homes as much as to their high intelligence.

PHYSICAL CHARACTERISTICS. In physique and general health the high-IQ children surpassed the best standards for American children. At birth they averaged three-quarters of a pound heavier than is normal. Height and strength were also superior. They learned to walk a month earlier than the average child and talked three and a half months earlier. Medical examinations revealed that the incidence of sensory defects, dental caries, poor posture, malnutrition, and so forth was below that usually reported by school doctors in the best medical surveys of school populations in the United States. Such physical superiority of the gifted has been maintained throughout the years. At the average age of 44 their mortality rate was four-fifths that of the general population.

INTELLECTUAL AND EDUCATIONAL CHARACTERISTICS. The intellectual superiority of Terman's subjects was established when they were children. In 1940 they were retested on a difficult adult intelligence test to determine whether superiority of intelligence had been maintained. At that time no subject had regressed to the intelligence level of the average adult, and no more than 10 percent were below the 85th percentile rank. Terman concluded that the group as a whole remained intellectually superior, although some bright children did not maintain their degree of superiority. As a rule, he said, the bright child remains bright.

While the gifted children entered school at the usual age (6¼ years), nearly one-half had learned to read before the age of 6. Concerning their academic advancement during their school years, Terman and Oden (1947) stated, "It is a conservative estimate that more than half . . . had already mastered the school curriculum to a point two full grades beyond the one in which they were enrolled, and some of them as much as three or four grades beyond" (p. 28). Those children tended to be advanced in all areas of schoolwork, showing no more variation among subjects than did unselected children.

The rates of college attendance (90 percent for men and 86 percent for women) were eight times those of the general population in California. Although they were graduated a year younger than the average, this superior group participated in extracurricular activities to a greater than average extent. Surprisingly, however, 8 percent of the men and 2 percent of the women "flunked out" of college (although half of those re-entered and graduated).

INTERESTS AND PREOCCUPATIONS. In scholastic areas the gifted children were more interested than those of the comparison groups in abstract subjects such as literature, debate, and ancient history; they were less interested in "practical" subjects such as penmanship and manual training. Gifted and comparison children were equally interested in games and sports.

The gifted appeared less sociable in their interests. They showed a stronger liking for playing with just *one* other person than did the controls. On a scale of sociability of play interest, almost half of the gifted fell in the lowest quartile of control-group scores.

CHARACTER TESTS AND TRAIT RATINGS. A battery of seven character tests showed gifted children above average on every rating. They were less prone to make overstatements and to cheat. Their choice of books and character preferences were judged more wholesome and mature, and they scored above average on an emotional stability test. On all seven tests combined, 86 percent of the gifted boys and 84 percent of the girls scored above the mean for the comparison groups.

Two facts stood out in the study of character tests and trait ratings of gifted children: (1) desirable traits tended to be positively correlated with each other and (2) the upward deviation was not the same in all traits; that is, gifted children were more outstanding in some traits than in others.

MENTAL HEALTH AND GENERAL ADJUSTMENT. One of the areas investigated in the 1947 follow-up report was mental health and adjustment. At that time approximately 80 percent showed "satisfactory adjustment," about 15 percent had "some maladjustment," and 5 percent had "serious maladjustment." The rate is slightly lower than the national expectancy for serious maladjustment. The delinquency rate was far below that of the general population. Alcoholism was found in 1.5 percent of the men and in 0.9 percent of the women; that compares favorably with the general population. Terman concluded that the superior emotional adjustment seen in childhood was maintained in adulthood.

MARRIAGE, DIVORCE, FERTILITY. The marriage rate for the gifted group as adults was about the same as that for the general population (84 percent) and higher than was found for college graduates as a group. The divorce rate to 1955 was somewhat less than that for the general population.

A total of 1,525 offspring of the gifted group have been tested. The mean IQ is 132.7. About one-third test above 140 and only 2 percent below 100.

In general, the gifted group tended slightly toward more and happier marriages, fewer divorces, and fewer offspring. However, it is still too soon for those trends to be considered definite.

VOCATIONAL AND OCCUPATIONAL STATUS. The occupational status of the gifted men reported in 1955 showed about eight times as many men in the professions as was true for the general population. About 80 percent of gifted men were in the two highest occupational groups—Group I, the professional, and Group II, semiprofessional and business. In the entire population only 14 percent were found in those two groups. The incomes for the gifted group were considerably higher than the national average. The most successful gifted men were compared with the least successful gifted, and many striking differences were found. Terman and Oden (1951) state, "Everything considered, there is nothing in which the A [most successful] and C [least successful] groups present a greater contrast than in drive to achieve and in all-round social adjustment" (p. 37). Success for the gifted was associated with well-balanced temperament and freedom from excessive frustration.

Oden (1968), in the last available report on this remarkable project, concluded: "All the evidence indicates with few exceptions the superior child becomes the superior adult. . . . Two-thirds of the men and almost as large a proportion of the women consider that they have lived up to their intellectual abilities fully or reasonably well" (pp. 50–51).

The Stanford *Genetic Studies of Genius,* under the direction of Lewis Terman, stands as a monumental investigation of one kind of exceptional child and thus far is unsurpassed by any other study in the field. It will remain as a monument to its brilliant author, who contributed so much to our knowledge of intelligence.

SPECIAL GROUPS

While the general findings of Terman are still valid for most of the upper-middle-class suburban children with high IQs, there has been growing interest in various subgroups that differ in important ways from this positive portrait. They include the gifted underachiever, culturally different gifted, children of excessively high intellect, and gifted women.

THE UNDERACHIEVING GIFTED. One of the many myths surrounding the gifted has been referred to as the Cannonball Theory. The idea, simply put, is that a gifted child can no more be stopped from achieving his or her potential than a cannonball can be diverted from its path once it has been fired. Like most simplistic ideas regarding human beings, the notion turns out to be incorrect. Its popularity in the face of contrary evidence may be accounted for on the basis that if it were true, we would be relieved of any special responsibility for those children.

The fact is that there is a substantial proportion of gifted children, perhaps as many as 15 to 20 percent, who never achieve the level of performance that their high scores on intelligence tests would seem to predict for them. The longitudinal study by Terman and Oden (1947) uncovered very interesting data on those underachievers. In the study a group of men were identified who had not achieved to the level of their apparent ability. The men were compared with other men who had done well. In their own self-ratings and in ratings by their wives, four major characteristics separated the underachievers from the achievers. The underachievers had *more feelings of inferiority, less self-confidence, less perseverance,* and *less of a sense of their life goals.* Even more striking was an examination of teacher ratings made on those men twenty years earlier while they were in school. Even at that time, teachers were rating the underachieving men as lacking in self-confidence, foresight, and desire to excel.

Later studies by Shaw and McCuen (1960) have confirmed that it was possible to identify underachieving boys as early as the third grade and underachieving girls by the sixth grade. So, underachievement is a condition that is fairly permanent and not significantly influenced by any temporary set of environmental circumstances. Those facts answer one of the major questions about underachievers: Does the problem exist mainly within the child or is it a product of a poor educational system? While poor schooling can always be a contributing factor, there is such a common set of findings related to the attitude and personality of the underachiever that there is little doubt that certain behavior patterns seem to predispose some gifted children to school underachievement.

One factor that predicts underachievement is substantial family conflict, often between father and son in the life of the underachieving boy. It is not certain whether it is part of the cause of the child's problems or merely a secondary result of the child's chronic poor performance, far below the standards of the parents.

Perkins (1965) studied the actual classroom behavior of some underachievers and found that the most prominent feature of their behavior was the characteristic of withdrawal. The underachievers were observed more often than the achievers to be working in another academic area than the one they were supposed to be attending to and to be engaged in nonacademic behavior of a variety of sorts.

In short, the day-to-day classroom behavior of the underachiever more or less guaranteed a continuation of the problem condition. Gallagher (1975) summarizes the situation in this fashion.

> One way to look at the underachiever is that he is in the middle of a circle of barbed wire . . . and all of his environment has contributed to the building of that wire circle—his family, his friends, his school, and, most important, himself. Any movements that he attempts to get out of the barbed wire are going to be painful to him. Sometimes it is more comfortable to sit quietly in the middle of his trap and bemoan his fate than to risk getting scratched trying to get out. (p. 353)

There are two major ways out of that barbed wire. One is counseling, which will allow the underachiever to explore his attitudes toward self and others with a sympathetic and skilled listener and then to reorganize those attitudes that cause continued difficulty for the underachiever in the school setting.

An alternative strategy for educators is to provide some systematic modifications in the classroom environment that might cause the underachiever to modify his characteristic patterns. One such strategy would be deliberately to place the child with a warm, accepting, and flexible teacher who would provide a sympathetic source of identification (Raph, Goldberg, and Passow, 1966). Another special program (Karnes et al., 1963) placed small numbers of underachievers in programs with more efficient gifted children, hoping that the example of the better achievers would carry the underachievers along. All of those methods have shown modest positive results, but none of them have resulted in dramatic changes for the better.

The finding of limited effect of remedial programs seems to confirm the hypothesis that chronic underachievement is a total lifestyle and one that can be modified only under the most persistent, intensive, and early type of educational and personal attention.

THE CULTURALLY DIFFERENT GIFTED. Another special area of interest is that of gifted and talented students who come from subcultures different from the standard American culture. For many years evidence has been accumulating regarding the difference in incidence of measured giftedness in various racial and ethnic groups.

There are two important pieces of information available from past research. The first is that high-level intellectual ability can be found in every ethnic and racial group (Adler, 1963; Jenkins, 1948; Martinson, 1972; Terman and Oden, 1947). The second is that there are demonstrable differences in the percentages of children from various racial and ethnic groups who fall into the category of gifted (Adler, 1967; Barbe, 1955). Those differences clearly show superiority in northern European ethnic groups as opposed to southern European ethnic groups and racial minorities.

While those differences are clear, the reason for them is not at all evident. A possibility remains that some polygenic hereditary combinations are more favorable than others, but social scientists generally reject that view in favor of another alternative. They believe that certain cultural advantages accrue to the favored groups, advantages that allow the gifted among them to maximize their cognitive development, particularly when the intelligence tests that are used favor the kinds of talent and background of the standard American culture.

Boys are consistently found in greater numbers at the highest level of intellectual ability than are girls (Barbe, 1955). The explanation most often accepted for that finding is that boys, in the past history of culture, have received greater encouragement to use fully their intellectual gifts. However, there appears to be a greater proportion of black girls than black boys in the measured gifted range. That finding may mirror the cultural phenomenon that black men have traditionally been discouraged from intellectual attainment and more commonly urged to achieve in physical areas in which the chance of excelling is greater. Black women, on the other hand, have taken on the role of family management in the subculture and have received proportionately greater maternal attention and educational encouragement.

The notion that certain value systems seem more inclined to maximize intellectual talents than others do is given further support by the generally high proportion of gifted children from Jewish (Terman and Oden, 1947) and Oriental families (Coleman et al., 1966). Both cultures encourage the pursuit of intellectual activities and honor the role of "scholar" in the family and community.

Special programs for the culturally different gifted focus on two major problem areas: first, how to identify effectively the culturally different gifted youngsters and, second, how to design special programs that would seem particularly relevant. On the first of those issues, Bruch (1970) proposed identification criteria different from those used to identify youngsters from the standard culture.

1. The primary identification criterion should be that a child exhibits outstanding powers in one or more abilities valued by his or her culture.
2. A child should measure on national norms at the bright average level or better on both ability and achievement.
3. Special consideration should be given to those children with demonstrated creativity.
4. Children who show potential for social leadership should be given special consideration.

In other words, consideration needs to be given to the different values of the cultural backgrounds in making judgments as to whether those youngsters fit into the gifted group, although a measure of intellectual capability relative to their peers is also needed.

In terms of program adjustment Riessman (1973) made a number of specific suggestions; namely, that attention should be given to the fact that youngsters from culturally different groups tend to focus on visual rather than auditory material, are externally oriented rather than introspective, and tend to be problem centered rather than abstract centered. He further suggested the need for structure and control beyond that which the ordinary middle-class gifted student receives.

A recent conference (Gallagher and Kinney, 1974) brought together representatives from various minority subcultures in the American society to make some specific recommendations with regard to needed changes in the American educational system in order better to meet the needs of gifted youngsters from those subgroups. The major recommendations from this report were as follows:

1. The need for the dominant culture to show more respect for cultural pluralism in the educational program. The American culture

has been enriched by contributions from many different ethnic and racial groups. A school program presenting only a portrait of northern European culture is inappropriate in that it narrows the view of our society and discourages children of different backgrounds from making a full contribution.

2. The need of schools to make fuller use of the resources of the total community by bringing in persons who may not have had formal education but who have outstanding talent. They could inspire and motivate gifted children of their own cultural backgrounds.

3. A need to recruit and train persons who could apply understanding and knowledge of cultural pluralism for special programs. It is necessary to use more effectively the special talents of culturally different youngsters. Their talents are more often hidden by different attitudes and behavior patterns than are those found among the middle-class gifted.

4. There was an identified need to use political influence in an organized fashion to get the special needs of minority groups before the general public.

Clearly we are still in the initial stages of finding constructive answers to the educational problems of the culturally different gifted child.

VERY HIGH ABILITY (1 IN 100,000). It is now generally accepted that superior intellectual ability predicts a good academic future and superior personal adjustment, but doubts linger about those youngsters of extraordinary ability—the 1 in 100,000 level of a von Braun or Einstein. There have been some spectacular failures, such as William Sidis who showed early brilliant performance in mathematics as a teen-ager, only to end up as an anonymous accountant. Much more likely, however, is the result described by Montour (1977) who reports on a brilliant student, identified early, who has already accomplished much and still has much of his career ahead of him.

> Dr. Charles L. Fefferman, the first recipient of the National Science Foundation's Alan T. Waterman Award at 27, is a precocious professional on the order of mathematicians like Lagrange and Hamilton. At the University of Chicago in 1971, as a 22-year-old, Fefferman became the youngest college professor in the United States and became the youngest full professor in Princeton University's history when he was named a professor of mathematics there in 1974. . . . He began showing an interest in mathematics by the age of 9 and was already taking a course at a University of Maryland campus near his home at 12. He was 14 when he became a full-time student at Maryland and graduated there in 1966 at 17. (p. 277)

Hollingworth (1942), who studied twelve youngsters with IQs over 180 (one in a million students), found them to have some adjustment problems and pointed out the following five major problems to overcome:

1. to find enough hard and interesting work at school
2. to suffer fools gladly
3. to keep from becoming negativistic toward authority
4. to keep from becoming hermits
5. to avoid the formation of habits of extreme chicanery (p. 299)

It is unrealistic to think that any educational system is going to reorganize its program to fit children like those who may appear once in a lifetime. Nevertheless, the potential impact of such children on society is so great that some degree of attention, such as individualized tutoring and apprenticeship to other talented individuals, may be called for.

GIFTED WOMEN. The "consciousness raising" of the women's movement has caused educators to pay special attention to that subgroup. Gifted girls and women have characteristically differed from gifted boys and men in a number of dimensions that appear related to the expected passive role of women in our society. Two major elements of that traditional "women's role" have been that women were expected to take fewer risks than men and that there were certain areas of interest (for example, athletics and mathematics) that they were expected to avoid, for those areas were clearly marked for males only. The research literature has confirmed that many gifted and talented girls learned their "social lessons" well. For example:

1. In a secondary physics program girls were more conforming, docile, uninterested in risk taking, and intellectually unassertive (Walberg, 1969).
2. In classroom interaction in twelve classes of gifted students, across a variety of content fields, girls were eight times less likely to quarrel with the opinions of their peers or with the teacher as were boys (Gallagher, Aschner, and Jenne, 1967).
3. Girls who were creative or who had ideas off the beaten track were less well accepted by their peers than were boys with similar characteristics (Torrance, 1959).
4. In six biology classes of talented students, boys were observed to talk significantly more in class despite evidence of the girls' having relatively equal intellectual ability (Gallagher, 1967).

What has the emphasis on traditional sex roles done to hinder the gifted girl and woman?

1. In junior high school girls do less well in mathematics and science and perform better in artistic and social subjects, paralleling the expected role for them in society (Astin, 1972).
2. Girls begin to reject toys with masculine identifications, such as fire engines and doctor kits, even before school age (Torrance, 1959).
3. Girls choose occupations in the area of nurturance, such as nursing and teaching, while only a few choose science (Gowan and Groth, 1972).
4. In a talent search for extraordinarily talented students in mathematics, boys appeared with much greater frequency than girls. The top forty-three students, as measured by tests of mathematical aptitude, were all boys (Keating, 1974).

The revolution in thinking about the appropriate role or roles of women in a modern society is probably changing many of those findings in favor of a freer and more productive intellectual life for gifted women. While some outstanding women have overcome the prejudices and restrictions of the earlier culture, there is little doubt that the old order has taken its toll on many.

The barriers that need to be stripped away in order that gifted girls receive full opportunity to develop in mathematics and science have been described by Fox (1977):

1. Sex role stereotypes held by parents that lead them to have different expectations and aspirations for daughters than for sons. This is most noticeable in the area of mathematics achievement and professional goals;
2. Sex role stereotypes held by educators that lead them to discourage rather than encourage intellectual risk taking and the taking of advanced courses in mathematics and science;
3. Sex role stereotypes held by the adolescent peer culture, particularly males, that discourage female creativity, intellectual risk taking, and achievement, particularly in mathematics and science;
4. Sex role stereotypes reinforced by the media and in textbooks that portray females as passive and engaged in nonintellectual pursuits, reinforcing the idea of mathematical and scientific pursuits as masculine and social and nurturing activities as feminine. (pp. 11–12)

One encouraging note is that despite such barriers to be overcome, a number of gifted women have done well. Sears and Barbee (1977) have reported on the career and life satisfactions among Terman's gifted women. Many of the women used their superior intellectual ability to cope successfully with the task of living independently because of being divorced, widowed, or unmarried. Those women appeared to get much satisfaction from their chosen employment, which their high intellectual ability allowed them to attain and maintain.

Educational program adaptations for the gifted

The basic question facing special education for the gifted is what major changes or modifications in the school program will meet their special needs. The three basic dimensions in the educational system that can be changed for the gifted are: (1) content, (2) skills or processes, and (3) learning environment. Each of those program modifications will be reviewed in turn.

CONTENT

Since the gifted child understands ideas and abstract concepts at an advanced level well beyond his or her classmates, it makes sense to design special content experiences that allow the child fully to exercise that ability.

When educators say they are "enriching" the curriculum for gifted children, *that* is what they generally mean. The child is being presented ideas and concepts at his or her level of intellectual understanding, not several levels below it. However, unless the administrators and teachers have a clear vision of what their objectives are, enrichment turns out to be merely a piling on of more and more facts, rather than more and more organization and unification of complex ideas.

Table 3.3 shows some suggested modifications of standard curricula based on the ability level of students. In the area of history, the slow-learning youngsters who learn best through direct experience with the topic under discussion would seem to respond better to specific discussions on how their local government works and how it influences their daily lives. Local affairs are of lesser complexity than

Ability level	History	Nutrition
Bright	Patterns of governing in cultures across time and national boundaries	The biochemistry of food and the translation of food into energy
Average	The beginnings of American government—our historical heritage	Understanding of nutrition; classification of carbohydrates, proteins, fats, etc.
Slow	How local government works and influences me	Kinds of nutritious foods to buy; samples of balanced meals

Source: J. Gallagher, 1975, p. 78.

TABLE 3.3

Curricular levels of abstraction by ability levels

descriptions of the abstract nature of government at the state and federal levels. Such specific discussions also have the advantage of dealing in the present rather than in the historical past, which is an abstraction level difficult for many slow-learning youngsters to handle.

On the other hand, average youngsters at about the middle grade or junior high school level are fully ready to begin understanding the nature of our government and the way in which decisions that affect them are made. They should learn the nature of our country's heritage.

However, the bright or gifted youngster is able to climb higher on the abstract conceptual ladder and to begin considering historical patterns of governance across time and across space. Such a child is able to link together important ideas that stretch across physical space and historical eras. Those abilities allow such children the chance to use their superior talents to link together complex ideas.

Similarly in the field of nutrition (Table 3.3), while slow-learning youngsters seem best able to grasp the concept of a good diet for themselves and their families, the average youngster is able to understand the broader and more abstract concepts such as the building blocks of nutrition—carbohydrates, proteins, fats, and so on. The bright youngster is able not only to understand those concepts but to tie them together in interrelating the system of nutrition with the body's ability to transform food into energy. They may even grasp the complex agricultural system that exists to bring adequate supplies of various foods to the public. Placing the slow-learning child in a curriculum program designed for the bright youngster can be a disaster, but so is placing a bright youngster in a program that is too simple for his or her own advanced intellectual level. Such a placement can cause the gifted child to develop long-lasting bad habits based on the lack of intellectual challenge.

Some of the ways in which curriculum content can be expanded for the gifted include the following: (1) emphasizing the structure of the concepts and basic principles of subject matter fields rather than memorizing individual facts, (2) placing emphasis on *how* information is derived instead of on *what* is derived, and (3) expanding the curriculum in breadth and depth.

1. Emphasizing the structure of concepts and basic ideas of subject matter fields. With the intensity of the knowledge explosion of the last few decades and the prospects for continued expansion of knowledge, curriculum experts have realized that they must do something more than merely cram more and more information into the traditional format of textbooks and classrooms. Instead of piling fact upon fact, a new approach was needed.

In the mid-1950s experts in the fields of physical sciences and mathematics, and soon thereafter those in the social sciences, English, and the humanities, began to develop more basic curricula in which individual facts became less important than the structure or the basic principles and theories underlying each content field. Once they have understood those basic principles, the gifted children, with their readiness to absorb new knowledge and see relationships, can more easily grasp the specifics of the field.

The Physical Science Study Committee (1957), for example, selected certain core concepts to be disseminated. Those theoretical concepts receive the emphasis while the facts of everyday applications are used as examples. Instead of showing that a stick looks bent when partly submerged in water, the basic principles of optics and refraction can be studied with the bent stick merely an example. Instead of emphasizing the mechanics of an automobile engine, the instructional objectives might center on the principles of kinetic energy.

Similar developments have occurred in other fields—mathematics, biological sciences, and social sciences.

2. *Placing emphasis on how information is derived instead of on what information is derived.* The curricular developments in subject matter fields have stressed method rather than product. In science, mathematics, and social sciences, in particular, an effort has been made to help the child learn how to think, utilizing the same procedures and processes as the scientist and the scholar. That is done by creating problems and systematic activities in which the child must follow some method to solve the problem. Rather than being told facts and figures, gifted children are asked to derive the information themselves, to delve for themselves, and to act like scientists. They are thereby not only learning facts but are learning how to acquire facts—how to fit facts together to derive more fundamental generalizations.

3. *Expanding the curriculum in breadth and depth.* Gallagher (1976) has suggested that more use could be made in gifted education of such TV series as "Civilization" and "The Ascent of Man." In both of those series there is a deliberate attempt to focus on major principles and generalizations and to illustrate them liberally. Two examples of such principles easily grasped by preadolescent gifted students were presented by Bronowski (1973):

> War, organized war, is not a human instinct. It is a highly planned and cooperative theft. And that form of theft began ten thousand years ago when the harvesters of wheat accumulated a surplus and the nomads rose out of the desert to rob them of what they themselves could not provide. (p. 88)

> The horse and the rider have many anatomical features in common. But it is the human creature who rides the horse, and not the other way

about. There is no wiring inside the brain that makes us horse riders. Riding a horse is a comparatively recent invention, less than five thousand years old. And yet it has had an immense influence, for instance, on our social structure. Plasticity of human behavior is what makes that possible. That is what characterizes us in our social institutions, of course, and above all, in our books, because they are the permanent products of the total interest of the human mind. (p. 412)

SKILLS IN PRODUCTIVE THINKING

As we have seen, it is not just the accumulation of knowledge that is important but also how that knowledge is used. Gallagher (1975) stated:

> The ability to generate new information through the internal processing of available information is one of the most impressive and valuable skills of mankind. . . . It is the ability to recombine the bits of this information into new meanings that sets mankind apart from the animals. It is the ability to perform these thinking processes well that sets the gifted student apart from the student with average ability. (p. 201)

Another major instructional goal for the educator of the gifted therefore, is to enhance those thinking skills that allow the child to be creative, that is, to produce a unique product (from the child's point of view) from the available data or information. One manifest special education goal is to help the gifted children develop those skills that will eventually make them autonomous thinkers, not dependent on adults or teachers but possessing the tools and ability to seek knowledge on their own.

Over the past two decades the field of the gifted has been influenced greatly by the thinking of J. P. Guilford, who devised a model of thinking processes (Figure 3.2) called the *structure of intellect* (Guilford, 1967). Guilford was able to divide human abilities into three major dimensions: *content, product,* and *operation.* Productive thinking requires the use of many if not all of these intellectual operations, products, and content in the Guilford system. The full model is too complex to be dealt with here. It is important for educators of the gifted because it focuses attention on two thinking processes not often measured in standard intelligence tests: *divergent production* and *evaluation.* Divergent thinking (the ability to produce many different answers to propositions such as "What would happen if everybody was born with three fingers and no thumb?") was supposed to be linked to creative abilities and thus was a legitimate skill to encourage with specific educational exercises.

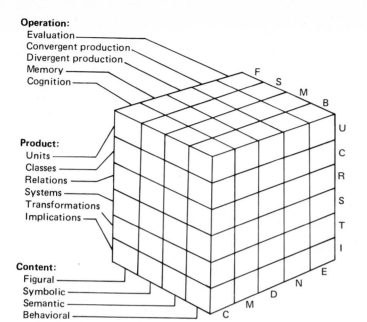

Operation:
Evaluation
Convergent production
Divergent production
Memory
Cognition

Product:
Units
Classes
Relations
Systems
Transformations
Implications

Content:
Figural
Symbolic
Semantic
Behavioral

FIGURE 3.2
Structure of the intellect model

Source: From *The Nature of Human Intelligence* by J. P. Guilford. Copyright © 1967 McGraw-Hill Book Company. Used with permission of McGraw-Hill Book Company.

Extensive analysis of classroom recordings suggests that divergent and evaluative thinking questions by teachers are rare compared with memory and convergent thinking questions (Gallagher, Aschner, and Jenne, 1967). Table 3.4 shows how different thinking processes can be stimulated by varying the types of questions asked in a discussion of *Hamlet*. Any topic can be explored in a similar fashion.

One of the more common devices used to increase *fluency*, or the number of responses that a child or adult can give to a problem, is *brainstorming* (Parnes, 1966). Using that technique a group of people or a whole class discuss a particular problem (for example, how to

Operation	Example
Memory	Whom did Hamlet kill by mistake?
Convergent thinking	Explain why Hamlet rejected Ophelia
Divergent thinking	Name some other ways Hamlet might have accomplished his goals
Evaluative thinking	Was Hamlet justified in killing his uncle?

TABLE 3.4

Guilford system by intellectual operations

Source: J. Gallagher, 1975, p. 238.

improve local government), trying to suggest as many answers as possible. There are important ground rules that they must follow:

1. No criticism allowed. Nothing smothers the free flow of ideas like the sharp, critical remark—or an even sharper guffaw of scorn—of a peer or of a teacher. The temptation to point out faults in an answer is very strong and needs to be quickly checked. The students need to know in advance that no critical comments will be entertained for the moment. Evaluation comes later.

2. The more the better. The students can accept the proposition that the greater the number of ideas presented, the more likely the chances that a good one will be among them. A premium could be placed on unusual or unique ideas.

3. Integration and combinations of ideas welcomed. The students can be alerted to the possibility of combining or adding to previous ideas.

4. Evaluation after all ideas have been presented. The teacher can judge when the fluency or inventiveness of the class is lagging. At that point evaluative thinking should be encouraged on the part of the students.

After all the ideas are produced, the group can pick those that seem most likely to help solve the problem. Thus the "storming" part requires different thinking, while the judgment part is more evaluative.

Another example stressing complex thinking processes comes from a large collection of exercises by Williams (1970).

> The class was asked to use their imaginations and think ahead to the year 2000, to think of how old they will be then, and to try to predict as many changes as they can that will have come about by then. They were asked to discuss in detail how their lives would be affected by changes in food, clothing, automobiles, transportation, places to live, work, leisure activities, etc. After they had made their predictions, they were to test these against the facts by establishing some basis or evidence for their predictions. (p. 107)

One of the other organized efforts to develop thinking skills in students has been referred to as the *discovery method.* That approach was an outcome of some of the National Science Foundation curriculum projects that had, as one goal, a student's learning to *think* and *act* like a scientist, as well as learning specific information. The basic idea was to present the student with a series of problems or facts and ask him or her to generate a broad principle, to explain a phenomenon (for example, a bimetallic strip bending *up* when heated), or to apply principles (for example, describing the social structure of a primitive tribe when given a diagram and description of what was found where in an anthropological excavation).

To use the discovery method, the teacher must know the principle to be "discovered," and be able to organize the material in order to maximize the chances for discovery. If teachers have only a superficial understanding of the content involved, then chances are good that this approach will not be used well.

Kagan (1965) presents psychological reasons for using the discovery method.

1. Studies of both animals and young children indicate that the more active involvement required of the organism the greater the likelihood of learning. . . . A major advantage of the discovery strategy is that it creates arousal and as a result maximal attention.
2. Because the discovery approach requires extra intellectual effort, the value of the task is increased. . . . It is reasonable to assume that activities become valuable to the degree to which effort is expended in their mastery.
3. The inferential or discovery approach is likely to increase the child's expectancy that he is able to solve different problems autonomously. . . .
4. The discovery approach gives the child more latitude and freedom and removes him from the submissive posture ordinarily maintained between teacher and child. (p. 560)

The true value of those thinking exercises may be in creating a more receptive learning atmosphere for intellectual risk taking and for uncommon and unconventional ideas. Studies of creative persons (Barron, 1969) clearly suggest that the more creative persons in our society are ones with a strong self-concept who are not swayed by the crowd and seem strongly motivated to produce their own unique ideas regardless of the opinions of others.

LEARNING ENVIRONMENT

The third possible major change in the traditional school program involves modifications of the *learning environment*. The first two broad areas of program modification, *content* and *skills,* involve changes in the teachers' approach to the child. Changes in the learning environment require administrative decisions, which are usually made by the school system or at a higher level in the educational hierarchy.

The basic reason for changes in the learning environment for gifted students is that some modification of the environment is necessary to accomplish the instructional goals of differential content and skills development. Environmental modifications such as special classes and resource rooms allow any special education program to be more easily applied. When the gifted students are clustered together for part or all of a day, specially trained teachers can be assigned to the program, rather than expecting the classroom teacher to stimulate those children. It may be a problem for the regular teacher to direct the regular program for average children as well as to face the time-consuming problem of dealing with students who need remediation.

Martinson (1972) reported one of the reasons why special educational provisions for gifted children are important.

> In a statewide study which included more than 1,000 gifted children at all grade levels, the kindergarten group on the average performed at a level comparable to second-grade children . . . the average for fourth- and fifth-grade gifted children in all curriculum areas was beyond that of seventh-grade pupils . . . three-fourths of the tenth- and eleventh-grade students exceeded the average of college sophomores . . . a representative group of gifted high school seniors took the Graduate Record Examination and made an average group score which surpassed the average for college seniors. (pp. A2–A3)

SPECIAL GROUPING

To adapt and enrich the curriculum for gifted children in the regular school, various forms of grouping have been used. They include: (1) grouping the children within a regular class in the elementary school, (2) organizing special sections in the subject matters (for example, English, science, mathematics, and social studies) in the upper elementary school and in the secondary school, (3) offering advanced courses for superior students in secondary schools, and (4) offering honors courses for superior students in college.

The preceding groupings are rather generally accepted; more controversial is the establishment of special schools for gifted children or self-contained special classes within the regular schools. Four forms of such organization have been used: (1) resource room and itinerant teacher, (2) special classes, (3) special schools, and (4) out-of-school programs.

RESOURCE ROOM AND ITINERANT TEACHER PROGRAMS. The resource room allows the gifted and talented children to be removed from their regular classes and their age-mates for a portion of the day in order to engage in special activities focused on their talents. Sometimes the program is content related (for example, accelerated mathematics), and sometimes it is a broad general program. That approach, a type of mini–special class, tries to keep the child with his or her social peers for much of the day, but it still gives some degree of special stimulation.

A variation on that theme is the itinerant teacher who works with the gifted children individually, or in small groups, in the regular classroom and who also gives guidance to the regular teacher on how to plan more effectively for the gifted in the regular program. Both of those approaches depend heavily on the quality of the special teachers and their training.

SPECIAL CLASSES. The grouping of gifted children into special classes is practiced in a few city school systems. The children are grouped in grades and progress from one grade to another in a curriculum adapted to their interests and abilities. An example of such classes is found in the major work classes in Cleveland, Ohio, which have been in operation as a part of the Cleveland public school system since 1921. They admit children with measured IQs of 125 and above. The purpose of those classes in the elementary school is to enrich the program but not to accelerate the child. Gifted children graduate from the elementary school at the same age as do other children. Here the gifted learn with other gifted children but participate with all children in such school activities as safety patrol and physical education and in other general school programs. At the secondary level there are "college bound" sections and honors courses that accomplish the same goal.

SPECIAL SCHOOLS. There are only a few special public elementary schools for gifted children. The Hunter College Elementary School is a special school admitting only gifted children, ages 3 to 11. In that school, children are grouped by chronological age and work independently but participate in unit topics and study themes. In addition to special schools, there are some neighborhoods in which the majority of children in the school are gifted. They constitute a natural, more homogeneous group of superior children. In some such schools and classes, as in the specially selected class or school, the average IQ may be 120 or 125.

At the secondary school level there are a few schools devoted entirely to the education of superior students. At the college level there are universities with very high selection standards, admitting only those students with superior aptitudes and superior grades.

OUT-OF-SCHOOL PROGRAMS. One of the troublesome problems facing educators trying to plan for gifted children is what to do with highly talented and competent secondary school students. In many instances those gifted youths may have exhausted the intellectual and academic resources of their high school by the time they are sophomores or juniors, and have nothing of academic consequence to look forward to until they attend college. For such youngsters a *mentor program* has been suggested in which the student spends a part of the time in the community, being tutored by an outstanding adult in some area of interest to the student, whether it be art or science or commerce.

Hirsch (1976) has described a program of *executive high school internships* whereby gifted high schoolers can take a full-semester sabbatical to work with business executives and managers, television producers, hospital administrators, judges, and others, earning a full range of academic credit in the process. The interns work Monday through Thursday in their job placements and attend Friday seminars on management, administration, and decision making based on the Harvard Business School case study approach.

ACCELERATION

The second major concern that stimulates the recommendations of changes in learning environment is the length of the educational program itself. As more and more must be learned at the highest levels of the professions, talented and gifted students find themselves in school almost until the age of 30. Whereas a skilled worker may have begun earning a living and starting a family ten to twelve years earlier, the gifted student has been in a role of semidependence for a good deal of his or her active adult life. The procedure of *acceleration,* or methods to shorten the time that the student spends in the total educational program, is therefore a clear educational objective related to gifted children.

Acceleration of gifted pupils has been practiced in various forms for many years. It refers to (1) admitting gifted children to kindergarten or first grade according to mental age rather than chronological age, (2) skipping grades, (3) telescoping grades, (4) early admission to secondary schools or colleges, and (5) other methods such as passing courses in high school and college by examination. All of these administrative procedures are designed to cut down the time a person must remain in school.

EARLY SCHOOL ADMISSION. Age of admission to kindergarten or first grade is a matter of law in most states. The age is generally set at 5 years for kindergarten and 6 years for first grade, with a few months' leeway for each. In some states the child's sixth birthday must come by a certain date if he or she is to be eligible for enrollment in the first grade in September. A child born one day after that arbitrary date would have to wait until the following September for admission. In programs of early school admission, the gifted child who is socially and intellectually mature may be allowed to enter in advance of the normal age.

SKIPPING GRADES. Skipping grades, another form of acceleration, refers to completely eliminating one grade or one semester in school. Contrary to current belief, and as evidenced by the Terman study and others already cited, children who have skipped grades have shown social, educational, and vocational adjustment superior to, or comparable to, that of equally intelligent nonaccelerates. Nevertheless, skipping grades is an unpopular and decreasingly used form of acceleration because of its potential for creating temporary adjustment problems for the gifted student.

TELESCOPING GRADES. Since skipping a grade sometimes leaves a gap in a child's experiences, some school systems have established programs that enable a child to cover the same material that is offered in the regular curriculum but in a shorter period. The *ungraded primary* program is a good example. In that program children may progress through the first three grades as rapidly as they are able. Some may finish in two years, some may take four years, and a few even finish three grades in one year. Occasionally seventh and eighth grades are combined in order to accelerate a group of capable students at that level. Another type of telescoping is sometimes done on an individual basis in high school. By carrying extra courses each term, certain students go through high school in three years instead of four.

ADVANCED PLACEMENT AND EARLY COLLEGE ADMISSION. One of the more popularly used devices for acceleration, requiring little administrative change in the school, is the advanced placement program. In that program students will take courses in high school for which they will receive college credit. As much as a half-year of college courses can be obtained by talented students in many high schools, thus reducing the length of their college careers. Other programs have allowed gifted youngsters to enter colleges and universities at the age of 16 or 17 with little observable negative effect when the students are properly screened for social and emotional adjustment as well as for academic talent.

A recent program of more radical acceleration in mathematics and science has been carried out by Stanley (1973). He found some children who were remarkably precocious in mathematics, and enrolled them at the age of 13–15 in Johns Hopkins University. All of these students appear to be adjusting quite well, socially and intellectually performing at an honors level in their college classes. Stanley proposes to continue the procedure with five or six children a year.

EVALUATION OF ACCELERATION EFFECTS. Plowman and Rice (1967) reported on the results of the acceleration of more than five hundred pupils in ten separate programs in Project Talent, a state program for the gifted in California. Those students had high ability, high achievement, and advanced physical and social adjustment. Only nine of the children were reported to have serious problems, and they were doubtful participants in the first place.

Those findings continue an unbroken string of positive results reported in the educational literature. From early admission to school (Braga, 1971; Reynolds, 1962) to early admission to college (Terman and Oden, 1947), the research studies invariably report those children who were accelerated made adjustments as good or better than those of the comparison children of similar ability. Despite the favorable findings, there continue to be strong negative feelings among parents and teachers against the practice, while educational administrators dislike the awkwardness of dealing with those children as special cases. The result is that many gifted youths have been resigned to spending the greater part of their first three decades of life encased in an educational system in a relatively unproductive role, to the detriment of themselves and their society.

The major objection to the acceleration of students, whether by early admission, skipping, or telescoping, has been a fear that acceleration displaces the gifted child from his social and emotional peers and thus affects his subsequent social adjustment. That concern has persisted in spite of the evidence that no serious detriment to social and emotional adjustment appears to result from acceleration. The studies submitting such evidence, however, have dealt primarily with acceleration of one or two years. There is little information on the effects of acceleration of four or five years.

EVALUATION OF SPECIAL PROGRAMS

Do special programs result in positive change? Do they also result in unfavorable side effects? Those are questions to which parents and the general public want answers. While full-scale and careful evaluation of programs is limited, there is some evidence supporting the usefulness of special groupings, *whenever the program includes content and skills changes,* as well as administrative modifications. Robeck (1967) reported on the impact of special programs for gifted students in California that were in the major California Project Talent program. In those situations the children attending Saturday special classes, and fulltime special class programs where special program changes were stressed, showed significant gains on standard achievement tests over the comparison groups of talented students not in such programs.

Martinson (1972) addressed herself to the issue of possible side effects of special programs. She summarized a wide variety of evaluation studies in Ohio, New York, California, and Illinois and reached the following conclusion:

> Conclusions drawn from these studies generally agree that participants did not develop personality or social problems, did not become conceited, or did not suffer health problems because of pressures; rather, participants showed improvement not only in academic areas but in their social and emotional development as well. (p. A47).

House, Kerins, and Steele (1969) observed in classes for gifted and average students in Illinois and reported classroom evidence that a wider range of thinking processes occurs in classes for the gifted than in ordinary classes. In the programs in which students are grouped for ability in language arts, for example, there is a greater freedom to encourage creative and reflective thinking on the part of the students.

Goldberg (1965) cautions, however, that merely grouping children by ability is no guarantee that good things are going to happen. The curriculum or learning processes must be expanded on a systematic and planned basis.

WHICH PROGRAM SHOULD A GIFTED CHILD BE IN?

It is obvious that there is no single plan appropriate for the education of *all* gifted children. Each gifted child is a unique individual, and gifted children cannot be organized as a group under a single plan of education. Efforts to educate properly all those children by only one specific plan, such as acceleration, special classes, or enrichment in the regular grades, will be inadequate for some of them.

The decision on where to place a gifted child, how to organize his or her education, and what teaching techniques and materials to use depends largely on the pattern of development of that particular child and on the provisions for all children in the school system. It is therefore necessary that a gifted child be evaluated in terms of abilities, interests, habits, home environment, and community values. The educational program for the child can be better determined on the basis of that evaluation than by setting up a special educational program and trying to fit all gifted children into it.

Some of the adaptations and adjustments that should be taken into consideration are the following:

1. When a child's patterns of growth in physical, social, mental, and educational areas are all accelerated beyond the chronological age, as indicated by George in Figure 3.1, acceleration in grade placement should be considered.

2. When the physical, social, and emotional areas are equal to the chronological age, but the educational achievement is advanced, a special class or resource room can be considered.

3. When the school system is too small (not providing sufficient numbers of gifted children of a particular kind for a special class), enrichment, tutoring, or itinerant teachers for the gifted children in the regular classroom may be necessary.

4. When the class in which a gifted child is placed contains a preponderance of children of superior intelligence, even though it is not designated as a class for the gifted, enrichment of the program is probably more desirable than special classes or acceleration, neither of which may be necessary.

5. When the child is gifted but underachieving, special attention to social and emotional problems or to possible areas of weakness is called for. Intensive counseling and parent education or even remedial instruction may be more important for the child than classroom placement.

6. When inner discrepancies in growth are quite marked, as we often find in children with extremely high IQs, a tutorial or individualized method of instruction may be necessary, especially when the child is found to be unable to adjust to existing educational situations.

7. When school systems feel that enrichment in the regular grades is the most feasible plan, a special teacher or coordinator for gifted children is advisable. Many feel that it is unrealistic to expect every teacher to furnish enrichment in the regular grades. Teachers need the help of a specialist or consultant.

SOCIETAL VALUES INFLUENCE GIFTED PROGRAMS

What each community and the collective American society decide to do about providing special educational experiences for gifted children probably depends more on societal attitudes and values than on educational evaluations. Gallagher (1976) identified four such broad forces that have influenced action in the past.

1. Egalitarianism. There is a strong belief in the need to give all citizens equal treatment and equal opportunity and a determination that there be no special privileges for special people. Such attitudes, narrowly applied, can hinder special provisions for gifted children, especially since "equal education" often gets translated into "identical education."

2. Universal education. The commitment of the United States to full education for all children through high school has retained many children of limited ability in school. That situation has created a range of talents and achievement at junior and senior high school ages that is difficult to manage within a single classroom. Much of the pressure for special provisions for the gifted is a recognition of extraordinary student diversity and the problems it creates for the conscientious teacher.

3. Decentralization of educational decision making. When each separate school district makes its own major educational decisions, the need for special education for the gifted does not seem as pressing as other more immediate needs. At the state and federal levels there is greater opportunity for taking a longer-range perspective. The program stimulus for the gifted often comes from those levels.

4. Sense of societal confidence. As long as there is overconfidence in the ability of the United States to conquer any obstacle or solve any problem as it arises—to muddle through if necessary—then the pressure to provide special educational help for the talented is quite low. When some of that overconfidence is lost, then there is increased pressure to build programs that would enhance the education of the most talented students in the society.

Recognition of the social forces that influence or determine our education policies is the first step toward understanding the otherwise curious reluctance of the society to do more for the gifted student.

Summary

1. Gifted children are currently defined as those showing outstanding abilities in a variety of areas, including intellectual ability, academic aptitude, talent in creative thinking, leadership ability, skills in visual and performing arts, and psychomotor ability.

2. The identification of gifted children has traditionally been accomplished through a combination of procedures, including group intelligence tests, past achievement in school, peer referral, teacher identification, and individual intelligence tests. Additional measures of creative and productive thinking are being tried on an experimental basis.

3. The prevalence of gifted children in any community depends on the criteria used to identify them and the socioeconomic status of the community. It could range from 1 percent of the school population to 15 or 20 percent in a community of high socioeconomic level.

4. The studies on gifted children, particularly the longitudinal research of Terman, have indicated that the gifted are:

    a. superior in physical and health characteristics
    b. advanced two to four years beyond average in school subjects

c. able to maintain their intellectual maturity into adulthood

d. superior in mental health adjustment

e. less prone to serious maladjustment and delinquency

f. eight times more prevalent in the professions than in the general population

5. Attention is now being directed to special subgroups of intellectually gifted children who have their own unique sets of characteristics and educational problems. They include the underachiever, the gifted child who is culturally different, children with extremely high IQs, and gifted women.

6. The three major ways to modify the educational program for gifted children involve changes in curriculum content, in the application of learning skills, and in learning environments.

7. Changes in content focus on emphasizing the structure and basic concepts of subject matter fields. Interest has also been shown in adding special areas, such as the teaching of values and ethics.

8. Skills instruction for gifted students emphasizes stimulation of their productive thinking and creative skills. The reasons for that are attempts to develop autonomous thinkers and to encourage maximum productive thinking. Special interest is often placed on the learning processes by which one solves problems, such as the scientific method or the sequence of steps in the creative process itself.

9. Changes in the learning environment may be found to vary from one community to another; they include resource rooms, summer classes, special classes, special schools, and various forms of acceleration when appropriate.

10. Evaluations of special programs for gifted children have generally found positive results.

11. Major social forces in the society have a determining influence on the type and amount of special programs provided for gifted students.

References

ADLER, M. 1963. "A Study of the Effects of Ethnic Origin on Giftedness." *Gifted Child Quarterly* 7: 98–101.

ARNOLD, A. 1976. "Leadership: A Survey of the Literature." In *A New Generation of Leadership.* Los Angeles: National/State Leadership Training Institute on the Gifted and Talented. Pp. 53–85.

ASTIN, H. 1972. "Sex Differences on Mathematical and Scientific Precocity." Paper presented at AAAS meeting. Washington, D.C.

BARBE, W. 1955. "A Study of the Family Background of the Gifted." *Journal of Educational Psychology* 47 (May): 302–309.

BARRON, F. 1969. *Creative Person and Creative Process*. New York: Holt, Rinehart and Winston.

BRAGA, J. 1972. "Early Admission: Opinion vs. Evidence." *Elementary School Journal* 72 (October): 35–46.

BRONOWSKI, J. 1973. *The Ascent of Man*. Boston: Little, Brown.

BRUCH, C. 1970. "A Proposed Rationale for the Identification and Development of the Gifted Disadvantaged." *Gifted Child Newspaper* 12: 40–49.

COLEMAN, J., E. Q. CAMPBELL, C. J. HOBSON, J. MC PARTLAND, A. M. MOOD, F. D. WEINFELD, AND R. L. YORK. 1966. *Equality of Educational Opportunity*. Washington, D.C.: U.S. Government Printing Office.

COX, C. M. 1926. *The Early Mental Traits of Three Hundred Geniuses*. Genetic Studies of Genius, vol. II. Stanford: Stanford University Press.

DYER, F. L. AND T. C. MARTIN. 1929. *Edison: His Life and Inventions,* vols. I, II. New York: Harper & Brothers.

FIEDLER, F. 1971. *Leadership*. New York: General Learning Press.

FOX, L. 1977. "Changing Times and the Education of Gifted Girls." Address given at Second World Conference on Gifted and Talented Children. San Francisco.

GALLAGHER, J. 1976. "Needed: A New Partnership for the Gifted." In J. Gibson and P. Chennels, eds., *Gifted Children: Looking to the Future*. London: Anchor Press.

GALLAGHER, J. 1975. *Teaching the Gifted Child,* 2nd ed. Boston: Allyn and Bacon. P. 238.

GALLAGHER, J. 1967. "Teacher Variation in Concept Presentation in Biological Science Curriculum Study Program." *Biological Science Curriculum Study Newsletter* 30: 8–19.

GALLAGHER, J., M. ASCHNER, AND W. JENNE. 1967. *Productive Thinking of Gifted Children in Classroom Interaction*. CEC Research Monograph Series-B5. Reston, Va.: Council for Exceptional Children.

GALLAGHER, J., AND L. KINNEY, EDS. 1974. *Talent Delayed—Talent Denied: A Conference Report*. Reston, Va.: Foundation for Exceptional Children.

GOLDBERG, M. L. 1965. *Research on the Talented*. New York: Bureau of Publications, Teachers College, Columbia University.

GOWAN, J., AND N. GROTH. 1972. "The Development of Vocational Choice in Gifted Children." In J. Gowan, ed., *The Guidance and Measurement of Intelligence Development and Creativity*. Northridge, Calif.: San Fernando Valley State College.

GUILFORD, J. P. 1967. *The Nature of Human Intelligence*. New York: McGraw-Hill.

HENRY, N. B., ED. 1958. *Education for the Gifted*. The Fifty-seventh Yearbook of the National Society for the Study of Education, Part II. Chicago: University of Chicago Press.

HIRSCH, S. P. 1976. "Executive High School Internships—A Boon for the Gifted and Talented." *Teaching Exceptional Children* 9 (Fall): 22–23.

HOLLINGWORTH, L. 1942. *Children Above 180 IQ.* Yonkers, New York: World Book.

HOUSE, E., T. KERINS, AND J. STEELE. 1969. *Illinois Gifted Program Evaluation.* Urbana: Center for Instructional Research and Curriculum Evaluation, University of Illinois.

JENKINS, M. 1948. "Case Studies of Negro Children of Binet IQ 160 and Above." *Journal of Negro Education* 12 (Spring): 159–166.

KAGAN, J. 1965. "Personality and the Learning Process." *Daedelus* 94 (Summer): 553–563.

KARNES, M., G. M. MC COY, R. R. ZEHRBACH, J. WOLLERSHEIM, AND H. F. CLARIZIO. 1963. "The Efficacy of Two Organizational Plans for Underachieving Intellectually Gifted Children." *Exceptional Children* 29 (May): 438–446.

KEATING, D. 1974. "The Study of Mathematically Precocious Youth." In J. Stanley, D. Keating, and E. Fox, eds., *Mathematical Talent: Discovery, Description, and Development.* Baltimore: Johns Hopkins University Press.

KIRK, W. D. 1966. "A Tentative Screening Procedure for Selecting Bright and Slow Children in Kindergarten." *Exceptional Children* 33 (December): 235–241.

MARLAND, S. 1972. *Education of the Gifted and Talented.* Report to the Subcommittee on Education, Committee on Labor and Public Welfare, U.S. Senate. Washington, D.C.

MARTINSON, R. A. 1972. "An Analysis of Problems and Priorities: Advocate Survey and Statistics Sources." In S. Marland, ed., *Education of the Gifted and Talented.* Report to the Congress of the United States by the U.S. Commissioner of Education. Washington, D.C.: U.S. Government Printing Office.

MILL, J. S. 1873. *Autobiography.* London: Longmans, Green, Reader and Dyer.

MONTOUR, K. 1977. "William James Sidis, The Broken Twig." *American Psychologist* 32 (April): 265–279.

NEWLAND, T. E. 1976. *The Gifted in Socio-Educational Perspective.* Englewood Cliffs, N.J.: Prentice-Hall.

ODEN, M. 1968. "The Fulfillment of Promise: Forty Year Follow-up of the Terman Gifted Group." *Genetic Psychology Monographs* 77 (February): 3–93.

PARNES, S. J. 1966. *Programming Creative Behavior.* Buffalo: State University of New York.

PEGNATO, W., AND J. W. BIRCH. 1959. "Locating Gifted Children in Junior High School." *Exceptional Children* 26 (March): 303–304.

PERKINS, H. V. 1965. "Classroom Behavior and Underachievement." *American Educational Research Journal* 2 (January): 1–12.

Physical Science Study Committee. 1957. *First Annual Report of the Physical Science Study Committee.* Watertown, Mass.

PLOWMAN, P., AND J. RICE. 1967. *California Project Talent, Final Report.* Sacramento: California State Department of Education.

RAPH, J. B., M. L. GOLDBERG, AND A. H. PASSOW. 1966. *Bright Underachievers.* New York: Teachers College Press, Columbia University.

REISER, A. 1930. *Albert Einstein.* New York: Albert and Charles Boni.

RENZULLI, J. S., AND R. K. HARTMAN. 1971. "Scale for Rating Behavioral Characteristics of Superior Students." *Exceptional Children* 38 (November): 243–248.

REYNOLDS, M. C. 1962. "A Framework for Considering Some Issues in Special Education." *Exceptional Children* 29 (March): 147–169.

RIESSMAN, F. 1965. "The Slow Gifted Child." In J. Gallagher, ed., *Teaching Gifted Students: A Book of Readings.* Boston: Allyn and Bacon.

ROBECK, M. 1967. "Special Classes for Intellectually Gifted Students." In P. Plowman and J. Rice, eds., *California Project Talent. Final Report.* Sacramento: California State Department of Education.

SEARS, P., AND A. BARBEE. 1977. "Career and Life Satisfaction Among Terman's Gifted Women." In J. Stanley, W. George, and C. Solano, eds., *The Gifted and the Creative: Fifty Year Perspective.* Baltimore: Johns Hopkins University Press.

SHAW, M. C., AND J. T. MC CUEN. 1960. "The Onset of Academic Underachievement in Bright Children." *Journal of Educational Psychology* 51 (June): 103–108.

STANLEY, J. C. 1973. "Accelerating the Educational Progress of Intellectually Gifted Youths." *Educational Psychologist* 10 (3): 133–146.

STOGDILL, R. M. 1974. *Handbook of Leadership: A Survey of Theory and Research.* New York: The Free Press. P. 412.

SUMPTION, M. R., AND E. M. LUECKING. 1960. *Education of the Gifted.* New York: Ronald Press.

TERMAN, L., AND M. ODEN. 1951. "The Stanford Studies of the Gifted." In P. Witty, ed., *The Gifted Child.* Boston: D. C. Heath.

TERMAN, L., AND M. ODEN. 1947. *The Gifted Child Grows Up.* Genetic Studies of Genius, vol. IV. Stanford: Stanford University Press.

TORRANCE, E. P. 1959. *Explorations in Creative Thinking in the Early School Years. VI: Highly Intelligent and Highly Creative Children in a Laboratory School.* Minneapolis: Bureau of Educational Research, University of Minnesota.

WALBERG, H. 1969. "Physics, Femininity, and Creativity." *Developmental Psychology* 1 (January): 47–54.

WILLIAMS, F. 1970. *Classroom Ideas for Encouraging Thinking and Feeling.* Buffalo, N.Y.: Dissemination of Knowledge Publishers.

YAMAMOTO, K. 1965. "Creativity: A Blind Man's Report on the Elephant." *Journal of Counseling Psychology* 12 (Winter): 428–434.

4

Children whose learning ability and general adaptation to society are below average have been of interest to various workers—physicians, psychologists, educators, sociologists, geneticists, and others—and each area has evolved its own classifications, concepts, and terminology. As a result the beginning student becomes quite confused with such different terms as feeble-minded, mentally retarded, idiot, imbecile, moron, oligophrenia, exogenous, endogenous, educable, trainable, totally dependent, custodial, and many others referring to children with low intelligence. This chapter reviews the different definitions, classifications, causes, and prevalence of children with low intelligence.

CHILDREN WITH LOW INTELLIGENCE

Definitions

There have been numerous attempts to define *mental retardation*. Since the beginning of history, humanity has had to deal with the problems of children with low intelligence. The problems of identification, definition, classification, and etiology have been extensive in view of the fact that many disciplines work with retarded children and each looks at the child from its own perspective. For that reason no one definition of children with low intelligence has been generally accepted by all.

Professional workers and scientists have had a difficult time in finding a satisfactory definition of mental retardation. An analysis of the problem reveals many reasons for that difficulty. Mental retardation is not a disease like tuberculosis or cancer but is a condition that involves many variables. For example, how do we define *small man?* Are small men all those who are less than five feet in height? Suppose some men below five feet weigh more than some men above six feet. Are they still "small men"? Or do we add a weight criterion and say that all men below five feet who weigh less than 120 pounds are considered small men? Would they still be considered small in a tribe of pygmies? Similarly, in defining mental retardation we find ourselves in the same predicament since we must include many criteria. To arrive at a multidimensional definition, we find ourselves with overlapping medical, social, psychological, economic, physical, and educational determinants.

Recent attempts to define mental retardation have shifted significantly in their emphasis from describing a condition that exists solely within the individual to a condition that is an interaction between an individual and a particular environment.

In 1961 the American Association on Mental Deficiency (AAMD) defined *mental retardation* as (1) including subaverage general intellectual functioning (an IQ of 84 and below on an individual intelligence test), (2) existing before the age of 16, and (3) showing impairment in adaptive behavior. All three criteria must be met before a child can be classified as mentally retarded. Dissatisfaction with the IQ criterion and the consequences thereof (discussed in the next section) led to a reformulation of the AAMD definition as follows (Grossman et al., 1973): "Mental retardation refers to significantly subaverage general intellectual functioning existing concurrently with deficits in adaptive behavior, and manifested during the developmental period" (p. 11).

That definition is only slightly changed from the earlier AAMD definition since it includes the words *significantly subaverage,* instead of only *subaverage,* but it defined *significantly* as having a two standard deviation deficit, or an IQ of 68 and below, instead of a one standard deviation, or an IQ of 84 and below. That definition tended to remove from the classification of mental retardation a large proportion of children with IQs of between 68 and 84. Actually, it returned the IQ criterion for mental subnormality to the 1910–1940 concept since Goddard had defined the highest grade of mental retardation as a *moron* with an IQ below 70. In Wisconsin, for example, the regulation (Special Education for Handicapped Children, 1927–1928) for admission to special classes for the mentally retarded in 1927–1928 stated: "The intelligence quotient of children in these classes for whom state aid is drawn shall range between fifty and seventy inclusive" (p. 6).

A further elucidation of the definition follows.

Definition	*Explanation*
Mental retardation refers to significantly subaverage general intellectual functioning	Defined as a score on standard intelligence tests that would be lower than that obtained by 97 to 98 percent of persons of same age.
existing concurrently with deficits in adaptive behavior	Meeting standards of independence and social responsibility expected of age and cultural group (that is, learning basic academic skills, participating in appropriate social group activity).

Definition	*Explanation*
and manifested during the developmental period.	Should be observable during childhood. Problems of a similar nature manifested only in adulthood would likely be mental illness or brain dysfunctioning, not mental retardation.

The key difference between the current AAMD definition and earlier definitions is the greater emphasis on *adaptive behavior* as one of the key elements of the definition. Adaptive behavior depends partly on factors outside the child—the environmental envelope in which the child exists. Contrast that definition with the following one by Edgar Doll (1941), which places the burden squarely on the constitutional nature of the individual. Doll defined *mental deficiency* as (1) social and occupational incompetency with inability to manage affairs at the adult level, (2) mental subnormality, (3) intellectual retardation from birth or early age, (4) retardation at maturity, (5) a result of constitutional origin, through heredity or disease, and (6) essential incurability.

Although the following definition by Tredgold (1937) included adaptation to the normal environment, he implied incurability. He stated: "A state of incomplete development of such a kind and degree that the individual is incapable of adapting himself to the normal environment of his fellows in such a way as to maintain existence independently of supervision, control, or external support" (p. 407).

With the inclusion of *adaptability* in the recent AAMD definition, the condition becomes contingent not only upon the intellectual capacity but also upon the environment or requirements of the environment. If one community's social adaptive requirements are less than another, a person can be mentally retarded in one community and not in another.

Intellectual subnormality refers essentially to the slow development of children's ability to process the information they have received. Memory is less efficient; ability to associate one idea with another is limited for the child's age, as is the ability to use information to reason, extrapolate, and evaluate. Those are the mental operations that are being measured by the traditional intelligence test.

Although there is a controversy about whether or not one can modify the development of intellectual performance, there is universal acceptance of the proposition that through training one can influence adaptive performance of retarded children. Thus it may be possible in some instances to "cure" mental retardation, if not intellectual subnormality, through educational programming.

INTELLECTUAL SUBNORMALITY VERSUS MENTAL RETARDATION

By the current AAMD definition, we can see that some children can be intellectually subnormal without being mentally retarded. It also means that *any* definition of mental retardation is contingent upon the competence of the child within the context of the environment. The classification of mental retardation can be changed by increasing the competence of the child, by decreasing the demands of the community, or by both.

Some believe that the increasingly complex nature of our society may result eventually in an increase in the prevalence of mental retardation. Consider the rural agricultural sector of the society, for example. Fifty years ago the life of the farmer was physically demanding but not as intellectually challenging, especially to a farm hand working as a helper. An intellectually subnormal person who learned to plow, to feed the animals, and to handle simple machinery could perform on the farm of a half-century ago in a reasonably competent fashion.

Consider the situation today. The modern farmer has to cope with farm supports and allotments, involved tax regulations, complex long-term financing of complicated equipment, and so on. Also, much of the hand labor has been eliminated by the use of machinery. The growing technology of the farm has eased the physical burdens of farmers, but it has substantially increased the intellectual demands of the job. In short, accepted community standards have now been raised to the point at which an intellectually subnormal child who previously might have adapted to the farm community may now be unable to do so.

Mercer (1973) has been especially critical of the practice of using intelligence test scores as the sole index of mental retardation (that is, relying only on intellectual subnormality as a criterion of mental retardation), a practice that ignores the concept of social adaptability. That is a particularly serious fault when applied to children emerging from subcultures, such as the urban ghetto and rural Appalachia, that have language patterns different from the majority culture. Table 4.1 summarizes the different attitudes toward mental retardation by contrasting the perspectives of the social role definition with those of the earlier clinical definition.

Mercer pointed out that it is no longer possible under the AAMD definition to anticipate the percentage of children who will be mentally retarded. While we can estimate with substantial accuracy the number of *intellectually subnormal* children in a given population, we cannot know what proportion of them will lack sufficient levels of *adaptability* to allow them to function in average environments.

The President's Committee on Mental Retardation (1970) in one of its reports, *The Six-Hour Retarded Child,* observed that some children are retarded (nonadaptive) only during the hours of 9:00 A.M. to 3:00 P.M., while they are in school. The school's activities, requirements, and expectations create an environment in which the child is retarded, but in family or neighborhood settings the child may be adapting in an adequate fashion and would not be, and is not, considered retarded before 9:00 A.M. or after 3:00 P.M.

Another major difficulty with the IQ (psychometric) criterion for mental retardation is the changing standards of IQ levels. In the first third of the century, the IQ criterion for assignment of school-children to special classes for the mentally retarded was an IQ of 69 and below. In the 1950s and 1960s the IQ level was changed to 75, then to 80, and in some cases to 84 to correspond to the level of minus one standard deviation of the earlier AAMD criterion. The change to an IQ level of 84 resulted in the assignment to special

TABLE 4.1

Social versus clinical definition of retardation

Social system	Clinical
Mental retardation is an achieved status in a social system and is the role played by a person holding that status.	Mental retardation is an individual pathology that can be diagnosed by using the medical-pathological and/or statistical models of "normal."
Mental retardation is specific to the social system. A person may be retarded at one time and not be retarded at another, depending on whether the person is labeled by the system in which he or she is participating.	Mental retardation is an individual characteristic that transcends cultures and sociocultural groupings. A person either *is* or *is not* mentally retarded.
The prevalence rate for mental retardation will be relative to the content focus, level formation, and tolerance limits of the norms of a particular social system, and to the extent to which the status of mental retardate is differentiated within the structure.	The "real" prevalence rate for mental retardation in any social system can be determined without regard for the norms of a particular social system, given adequate research design and instruments.

Source: Adapted from J. Mercer, "The Myth of 3% Prevalence." In R. K. Eyman, C. E. Meyers, and G. Tarjan, eds., *Sociobehavioral Studies in Mental Retardation: Papers in Honor of Harvey F. Dingman.* (Monographs of the American Association on Mental Deficiency, No. 1, 1973). Pp. 1–18.

classes for the mentally retarded of a disproportionate number of minority-group children (who tested 84 and below on tests standardized on white children). When objections to this practice arose, the AAMD reduced the IQ criterion to 68, or two standard deviations below the mean. In other words, some children who were considered mentally retarded in the 1950s and 1960s, based on an IQ criterion, were no longer considered mentally retarded in the 1970s.

Classification

Since the mentally retarded constitute a heterogeneous group of children with varying characteristics, the different disciplines have found it necessary to separate those children into subgroups that are more meaningful in terms of the responsibilities of the disciplines. The following discussion of classification will include subgroupings under (1) the medical-biological classification, (2) the social-psychological classification, and (3) the classification for educational purposes.

THE MEDICAL-BIOLOGICAL CLASSIFICATION

From a medical point of view, mental retardation is regarded as a result of some underlying disease process or defective biological condition. It is natural for a medical classification to be based on etiological (causal) factors. Grossman et al. (1973) list the following etiological categories of disease: (1) infection and intoxication, (2) trauma or physical agents, (3) disorders of metabolism or nutrition, (4) gross brain disease (postnatal conditions), (5) unknown prenatal influences, (6) chromosomal abnormality, (7) gestational disorders, (8) postpsychiatric disorders, (9) environmental influences, and (10) other conditions. That classification of causes includes about one-quarter of those identified as mentally retarded. It is possible that as medical science progresses further, other biological factors will be found to explain the causal factors in some cases now considered "cause unknown."

THE SOCIAL-PSYCHOLOGICAL CLASSIFICATION

The social-psychological classification, referred to as the behavioral classification by AAMD, consists, as indicated earlier, of two major factors: a psychometric criterion and an adaptive behavior criterion.

To be classified as mentally retarded, the individual must manifest deficiencies both in measured intellectual functions and in adaptive behavior.

LEVELS OF RETARDATION ACCORDING TO INTELLIGENCE QUOTIENTS. Grossman et al. (1973) include four levels of mental retardation based on the Wechsler scales.

	Intelligence quotient range
Mild mental retardation	55–69
Moderate mental retardation	40–54
Severe mental retardation	25–39
Profound mental retardation	24 and below

LEVELS OF RETARDATION ACCORDING TO ADAPTIVE BEHAVIOR. The same levels of classification (mild, moderate, severe, and profound) as those demarcated by intelligence quotients are used with adaptive behavior, with the exception that adaptive behavior is not as easily measured as intelligence. The Vineland Social Maturity Scale is one rating scale that renders a social quotient. It has been used to measure some aspects of adaptive behavior. An AAMD adaptive behavior scale has been developed to measure different aspects of adaptive and maladaptive behavior. The adaptive behavior scale includes a section for young children and one for older children and adults. The items for young children include behaviors that indicate self-sufficiency (eating, sleeping, dressing, and others), sensory ability, motor development, language development, and social adaptability. For older children and adults adaptive behavior is measured by ratings of performance in domestic skills, vocational potential, and responsibility. Ratings of maladaptive behavior include emotional problems, attacks of physical violence, self-destruction, and withdrawn behavior, among others. The levels of retardation on this variable are estimated by the judgment of a clinician and do not have as fine a gradation as the demarcation of levels with intelligence quotients.

CLASSIFICATION FOR EDUCATIONAL PURPOSES

For educational placement children with low intelligence are classified for the most part on grounds of the level of intellectual subnormality. Four groups are demarcated for educational attention: (1) the borderline or the slow learner (IQ of 70 to 85), (2) the educable mentally retarded (IQ of 50 to 70 or 75), (3) the trainable mentally retarded (IQ of 30 or 35 to 50 or 55), and (4) the totally dependent or profoundly

mentally retarded (IQ of below 25 or 30). Other factors besides the
IQ are considered for special services, especially in the gray areas between subgroups and in relation to the child's capabilities and needs.
Since educational programs for the mentally retarded deal with (1) the
educable, (2) the trainable, and (3) the profound or totally dependent,
those subgroups will be defined further.

THE EDUCABLE MENTALLY RETARDED CHILD. An educable mentally
retarded child (corresponds to the mildly retarded child in the
AAMD classification) is one who, because of subnormal mental development, is unable to profit sufficiently from the regular program
of the regular elementary school but who is considered to have potentialities for development in three areas: (1) educability in academic
subjects of the school at the primary or advanced elementary grade
levels, (2) educability in social adjustment to a point at which the
child can get along independently in the community, and (3) occupational adequacies to such a degree that the child can later be self-supporting partially or totally at the adult level.

In many instances, during infancy and early childhood the educable retarded child is not known to be retarded. Retardation and
growth in mental and social activities can sometimes be noted, however, if the child is observed closely during the preschool years and in
a definitive environment. Most of the time retardation is not evident

TABLE 4.2

Levels of mental retardation

	Educable	Trainable	Profound or dependent
Etiology	Predominantly considered a combination of genetic and poor social and economic conditions	A wide variety of relatively rare neurologic, glandular, or metabolic defects or disorders that can result in moderate or severe retardation.	
Prevalence	About 10 out of every 1,000 persons	About 2–3 out of every 1,000 persons	About 1 out of every 1,000 persons
School expectations	Will have difficulty in usual school program; need special adaptations for appropriate education	Need major adaptation in educational programs; focus is on self-care or social skills; limited effort on traditional academics	Will need training in self-care skills (feeding, toileting, dressing)
Adult expectations	With training can make productive adjustment at an unskilled or semiskilled level	Can make social and economic adaptation in a sheltered workshop or, in some instances, in a routine task under supervision	Will always need continued custodial care

Source: J. Gallagher, 1976.

because expectations for the child are not heavily weighted with intellectual content during the preschool years. The educable retarded child may be first identified by the school when learning ability becomes an important part of social expectations. In most instances there are no obvious pathological conditions to account for the retardation.

THE TRAINABLE MENTALLY RETARDED CHILD. The trainable mentally retarded child (corresponds to the moderately and severely retarded children in the AAMD classification) is one who is not considered educable in the sense of minimal (first grade) academic achievement, ultimate independent social adjustment in the community, and total occupational adjustment at the adult level. This is what differentiates a trainable mentally retarded child from an educable mentally retarded child. The trainable mentally retarded child, however, has a potential for learning (1) self-help skills, (2) social adjustment in the family and in the neighborhood, and (3) economic usefulness in the home, in a residential school, or in a sheltered workshop. In most instances such children will be known to be retarded during infancy and early childhood. The retardation is generally noted because of known clinical or physical stigmata or deviations or because the children are markedly delayed in talking and walking.

THE PROFOUNDLY OR DEPENDENT MENTALLY RETARDED CHILD. The profoundly mentally retarded child is one who, because of very severe mental retardation, is unable to be trained to a high level of self-care, socialization, and economic usefulness. Such a child requires almost complete care and supervision throughout his or her life because of an inability to survive without help.

Table 4.2 summarizes for educational purposes the essential distinctions between the three levels of mental retardation. Other groups have adopted similar subclassifications of retardation. For example, the World Health Organization and the American Psychiatric Association used the three levels of mild, moderate, and severe subnormality.

Growth patterns of children with low intelligence

Children with varying degrees of low intelligence present different growth patterns. In Figure 4.1 four children of differing degrees of intelligence are represented. Each child is 10 years old. The chronological age is the only point on the profiles that is the same for all four

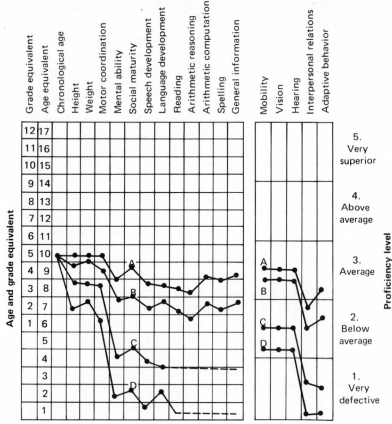

FIGURE 4.1
*Profiles of four children of
differing degrees of mental
retardation*

A = slow learner; B = educable mentally retarded child; C = trainable mentally retarded child; D = dependent mentally retarded child

children. Child A is a slow learner; Child B, an educable mentally retarded child; Child C, a trainable retarded child; and Child D, a profoundly or totally dependent retarded child.

The growth patterns presented for the different subgroups of children with low intelligence are patterns that occur frequently when a group is measured, but do not necessarily apply to an individual child. Sometimes a slow learner has less adaptive behavior than a trainable or educable mentally retarded child. All that the graphs mean is that when we combine a large group of children in the clusters discussed, they average as indicated in the graphs.

It will be noted that the 10-year-old slow-learning child, Child A, is quite a bit like the average 10-year-old in the physical areas of height, weight, and motor coordination. With an IQ of 85 the child is a little more than a year retarded mentally below chronological age, about half a year in social maturity, and between one and two years on all other characteristics. Reading, for example, is at a third-grade level although the child is placed in the fifth grade in school. That child is able to get along in the regular grades even though grade placement is below the level of general educational achievement. In most fifth grades a number of children are doing third-grade and fourth-grade work, and some are doing sixth-grade and even seventh- and eighth-grade work. Thus a fifth grade in the regular school has an achievement range of about two years below to two years above that grade. We expect the regular grade to provide instruction adapted to children within that range of ability. For that reason slow-learning children are not considered mentally retarded and tend to remain in the regular grades with appropriate adaptation of programs for some of them.

The 10-year-old educable mentally retarded child, Child B in Figure 4.1, scored a Binet IQ of 72 and a Wechsler IQ of 68. The child is doing beginning second-grade work in school. The discrepancy between Child B's achievement and that of the average child of that age is quite marked; the retarded child is unable to cope with the regular class program without supportive help. Although a child with third-grade reading and arithmetic may be able to struggle through a fifth-grade program, first- or second-grade achievement leaves too large a gap. The educable mentally retarded child requires some special educational provisions in or outside the regular classroom.

The profile of a trainable mentally retarded child, Child C in Figure 4.1, shows discrepancies in growth much wider than those of the educable child. Here we find an IQ score of 40 and a mental level of four years. Physical development in terms of height and motor coordination also may be considerably retarded, but not as much as mental ability. Speech, language, general information, and adaptive behavior (social maturity) are also close to the four-year level. In reading, spelling, and arithmetic the profile is shown with broken lines, indicating that the child has not begun to achieve in those subjects.

Child D with an IQ of 20 shows still greater discrepancies in growth and a wider difference between his or her development and that of an average child or even an educable or trainable one. That child has not developed to the point of being able to do much of anything for himself or herself. Even as late as 16 or 17 years of age, Child D may not be able to take care of all personal needs. The child must be cared for by others and for that reason is considered a profoundly or dependent mentally retarded child.

The prevalence of children with low intelligence

How many mentally retarded children are there? Numerous surveys to determine the prevalence of children with low intelligence have shown a wide range of estimates. While the figures for the prevalence of profoundly and trainable retarded children agree quite well from one population to another, the figures for the number of educable and mildly mentally retarded vary substantially from place to place. There are a number of reasons why researchers obtain different prevalence figures, among which are:

1. Different IQ cutoff points for intellectual abnormality. For example, Farber (1968) reported on studies by Akkeson in Sweden and Lofthus in Norway. Akkeson used an IQ limit of 70 and found 1.8 percent mentally retarded, while Lofthus used an IQ limit of 75 and obtained 3.8 percent, or twice the number of mentally retarded in the population.

2. Different ways in which the various investigators treat the issue of adaptive behavior. If a number of intellectually subnormal children (IQ below 70) are adapting to their community expectation, then they may or may not be included in the sample of "mentally retarded." A good example of the difference that makes is illustrated by Birch et al. (1970). Those investigators picked Aberdeen, Scotland, as a city for study since the school system there routinely uses intellectual screening for all of its 7-year-olds, thus providing an opportunity to get a count of the entire population at a given age. After screening, the children were examined individually by psychologists and medical officers. They found about 1.3 percent of the children eligible for special class placement. In their study less than half of the children who scored low in IQ were identified by the total clinical process as mentally retarded.

3. Other factors. Various factors tend to influence the judgment of clinicians and others in labeling a child as mentally retarded. They include social class, age, and degree of retardation.

Social class. In the study by Birch et al. (1970), it is reported that the prevalence rate for the educable in the highest social class was 1.1 percent and in the lowest social class 4.3 percent. Heber, Dever, and Conry (1968) reported that white children in one community had a prevalence rate of 0.5 percent in the highest social class and 7.8 percent in the lowest social class.

Age. A number of observers have commented that the prevalence rate of the mildly mentally retarded is related to the age of the group studied as well as to other factors. Tarjan et al. (1973) remarked that the greatest prevalence of mental retardation is found at the school-age level. It is usually low at the preschool age and often declines during late adolescence or young adulthood.

Degree of retardation (trainable children).   In contrast to the wide variation in prevalence figures for the educably retarded, a marked consistency is shown in the number of trainable children. In most studies, 0.2 to 0.4 percent are found to be trainable and occur in the same proportion in different socioeconomic groups.

In reviewing *incidence,* occurrence of condition, and *prevalence,* its existence at a particular time, MacMillan (1977) stated that the best current prevalence estimate is 1 percent.

The best inference we, the authors, can make about the prevalence of mental retardation in the population is that there are approximately 0.25 to 0.50 percent who are trainable and profoundly retarded, and approximately 0.50 to 1 percent who can be classified as educable mentally retarded. The usual figure of 3 percent given in many reports includes slow-learning children and possibly 1 to 2 percent of children who are mentally subnormal but who are not retarded when the adaptive criterion is used.

Causes of mental retardation

The search for the causes of mental retardation is motivated by the desire to prevent mental retardation. If the cause can be discovered, it is possible in some instances to introduce measures that would prevent such occurrences.

That search can take us in a wide variety of directions since any factor that hinders the development of the brain and other parts of the central nervous system can be included in the list. They include chromosomal damage, metabolic imbalances, specific disease entities, and even poor nutrition and inadequate learning environments. Fortunately, most of those factors are extremely rare in occurrence.

The etiologies (causes) of mental retardation are diverse and will be discussed under the following headings: (1) genetic, (2) prenatal, (3) perinatal, (4) postnatal, and (5) sociocultural.

GENETIC CAUSES

For many years a number of conditions associated with mental retardation were recorded as "cause unknown." Recent discoveries in biochemistry and genetics have thrown new light on previously unexplained cases. Special techniques have been developed which have made it possible to study tissue cultures and to identify chromosomes. Discoveries in biochemistry and genetics have led to the delineation of a number of genetic causes of mental retardation previously unknown.

BIOCHEMICAL DISORDERS. Waisman and Gerritsen (1964) state that there are now nearly ninety diseases that can be traced to inborn errors of metabolism and that those diseases are transmitted genetically by means of a heritable trait. They assert:

> This implies a defect in some gene which controls a certain enzyme system necessary for the normal function of a body tissue. Thus, the intimate relationship between genes and enzymes underlines the significance of biochemistry and genetics in those diseases which are associated with mental deficiency. (p. 308)

Biochemists have identified a number of chemical substances (carbohydrates, lipids, and amino acids) through which a number of abnormal genetic conditions can be traced. Two examples of them follow.

Phenylketonuria is a well-known inherited disease causing mental retardation. It is caused by an inherited abnormality in amino acid metabolism: the inability to convert phenylalanine to tryosine due to a deficiency of a specific liver enzyme. The condition was discovered by Folling in Norway in 1934 and was first described in this country by Jervis in 1937. Since then there have been many studies related to the condition. Although phenylketonuria, known as PKU, occurs with a frequency of 4 per 100,000 births (Anderson, 1964) or 1 in 20,000 (Hsia, 1971), its discovery has led to a search for comparable inborn errors of metabolism that could account for other conditions causing mental retardation.

Phenylketonuric children can be diagnosed early by means of urine analysis. A child with this condition is found to have a deficiency in phenylalanine hydroxylase. Waisman and Gerritsen (1964) state that the error in metabolism is transmitted as a recessive trait. If both parents are carriers of the gene, there is a chance that one out of four children may have PKU.

It has been found that if the phenylalanine deficiency is detected at an early age and if the child is given a diet low in phenylalanine, the harmful effects on the brain are prevented, and the child may not become mentally retarded. It is an illustration of current efforts to prevent mental retardation resulting from a genetic cause by intervening in the course of events—in this case by prescribing a phenylalanine-free diet.

Baumeister (1967) has reviewed the effects of starting treatment of phenylketonuria early, placing the newborn on a special low-phenylalanine diet. Baroff (1974) reported that when the diet was initiated at 1 to 13 weeks, the average IQ was 89. When it was started at 14 to 26 weeks, the average IQ was 74; when initiated at 27 to 156 weeks, the average IQ was 50; and when started after 156 weeks, the average IQ was 26. Those results indicate that treatment is effective only when initiated at an early age.

Galactosemia is another example of defective carbohydrate metabolism. It is considered an inherited recessive trait. The child is jaundiced at birth and shows early growth failure, feeding problems, and sometimes early cataracts. This condition, like PKU, can be detected by urine tests and, if detected early, can be reversed. Treatment consists of a special diet that excludes galactose by withholding milk and by using a soybean milk substitute. Symptoms decrease or disappear if the galactose-free diet is initiated early in life.

Those two conditions are examples of inborn errors of metabolism that can be treated successfully if detected early. Others have been discovered, and probably many more will be discovered by biochemists in the near future. Control of genetic deficiencies is currently being explored by many eminent geneticists. Even though the percentage of mental retardation resulting from inborn biochemical abnormalities is quite small, the problem of preventing the resulting mental retardation continues to be most important.

CHROMOSOMAL ABNORMALITIES. Developments in the study of tissue culture and in the identification of chromosomal abnormalities have led to major discoveries in the genetics of mental retardation. The most common chromosomal abnormality is found in *Down's syndrome,* or mongolism. The condition was described by Langdon Down about one hundred years ago. It was originally called Down's disease, but because of the appearance of slanting eyes, it was termed *mongolism,* an unfortunate choice since the only resemblance in any respect to the Mongolian race is the epicanthic fold of the eyelids. The name is currently being changed in professional terminology to Down's syndrome.

The child born with this syndrome is mentally retarded and at a later age can range in IQ between 20 and 60, with the large majority in the IQ range of 30 to 50. Many studies have been made on children with Down's syndrome in an attempt to determine its etiology. No definite cause was discovered, biochemical or otherwise, for about ninety years after it was first described. Not until methods had been perfected for the study of human chromosomes was a definite genetic cause determined. It was then found that in human beings there are 46 chromosomes arranged in 23 pairs. In 1959 Lejeune, Gautier, and

Turpin (1959) discovered that in children with Down's syndrome there are 47 chromosomes and that the chromosome pair number 21 is not a pair but a triplet creating a condition known as *trisomy*. Note the third chromosome in the chromosome pair 21.

$$XX \quad XXX \quad XX$$
$$20 \qquad 21 \qquad 22$$

Another form of chromosomal abnormality causing Down's syndrome results from *translocations;* the child has 46 chromosomes, but a pair of one is broken and the broken part is fused to another chromosome. A third type is called *mosaic Down's syndrome*. The latter two kinds of chromosomal abnormalities account for only 4 to 5 percent of Down's syndrome in children (Lilienfield, 1969). The incidence of Down's syndrome is 1 to 2 births out of 1,000.

Until the last decade the diagnosis of Down's syndrome, as well as a wide variety of other pathological conditions, was not made until the birth of the baby or later. The development of a new diagnostic technique, amniocentesis, has opened the possibility of much earlier diagnosis. Amniocentesis is a procedure for drawing some of the amniotic fluid from the pregnant woman. Since cells from the fetus are found in that fluid, the cells can be analyzed for chromosomal abnormality by a process called "karyotyping." Thus, high-risk parents can know early in a pregnancy that they will or will not have a handicapped child.

The medical procedures described in the preceding have generated a moral issue of major consequences. Should the individual parents have the right to terminate a pregnancy, given the information that they will have a handicapped child? The controversy over that issue has resulted in limited use of the amniocentesis procedure.

PRENATAL CAUSES

In addition to genetic causes of mental retardation, there are many conditions that can affect the developing embryo and cause maldevelopment of the nervous system and consequent mental retardation. That problem raises the question of the effects on the intelligence of the offspring caused by the mother's nutritional, psychological, and physical environment. Answers to many such questions have not been found except in a few specific cases. Examples of some of them will be described briefly.

RUBELLA. In the early 1940s it was discovered (Swan, Fostevin, and Barham-Black, 1946) that German measles (rubella) contracted by the mother during the first three months of pregnancy may cause congenital defects in the child, including mental retardation. Such defects as cataracts, deafness, heart disease, and microcephaly, as well as general mental retardation, have been associated with the disease. Earlier reports indicated a high incidence of children with defects following an attack of rubella by the mother, but later reports by Fraser (1964) show that only 17 to 24 percent of the children are defective and that many mothers who contract rubella during the first trimester of pregnancy do not have defective children. The last epidemic in the United States occurred in 1964 and affected 30,000 children (Cooper, 1968). The virus for rubella has been isolated, and a vaccine has been developed. It is anticipated that in the future mental retardation as a result of rubella will decrease or be eliminated.

THE Rh FACTOR. In 1940 Landsteiner and Wiener (Gates, 1946) reported the study of a condition involving the presence of agglutinin in the blood of rabbits. The condition was produced experimentally by injecting blood from the rhesus monkey, hence the label *Rh*. Among human beings the Rh-positive factor is found in the blood of 86 percent of individuals. The blood of the remaining 14 percent does not contain the Rh factor and is said to be Rh negative. Rh-positive blood and Rh-negative blood are incompatible and, when occurring in the same blood stream, produce agglutinin, which causes blood cells to clump together, thus producing immature blood cells due to their failure to mature in the bone marrow.

Yannet and Lieberman (1944) and Snyder, Schonfeld, and Offerman (1945) have shown a relationship between the presence of Rh-incompatible blood and mental retardation. The writers indicate that when the fetus inherits an Rh factor that is incompatible with that of the mother, the child is apt to be mentally retarded unless treated medically at an early age.

PERINATAL CAUSES

Perinatal causes refer to those conditions that may affect the child during or immediately preceding birth. Primarily they include birth injuries, asphyxia, and prematurity.

The diagnosis of *brain injury* in children is often a retrospective one. It is inferred later in life when the child is found to be mentally retarded. Histories of the birth process relating to prolonged or difficult labor, forceps delivery, breech presentation, and other mechanical causes may lead a diagnostician to a general diagnosis of brain injury without specifying what kind of an injury it is.

A specific cause of injury is *asphyxia,* which is caused by lack of oxygen to the brain during the birth process. Earlier Frederick Schreiber (1939) studied the problem extensively and has presented evidence that mental defects in children are sometimes the result of what he terms *cerebral anoxia.* The brain cannot function without an adequate supply of oxygen. When the oxygen supply to the brain is blocked for more than a few minutes, irreparable damage to the brain cells results. Masland, Sarason, and Gladwin (1958) reviewed the literature concerning the relationship of asphyxia and mental retardation and found that the investigators do not all agree. Some children with anoxia at birth die in infancy, some are defective later, while others develop normally. Anoxia is a condition that could be prevented.

Studies on *prematurely born* children have shown a relationship between prematurity and mental retardation. Alm (1953) studied 999 premature boys and compared them statistically with 1,002 boys who were not born prematurely. He found that there were more epileptics, cerebral palsied, and mentally deficient among the premature boys. Of those who lived, height and weight at age 20 were less for the prematurely born, and more of them had disorders of some kind. Most studies, although not as extensive as Alm's, show similar results. It should be remembered, however, that such defects apply to only a small proportion of premature births, since the large majority of such births show normal development of the children.

Wortis (1961) reported that in the Soviet Union the rate of premature births per 100 population in Kiev was 4.7. In New York at that time the rate was 9.4 per 100, and in the poorer districts, 16 per 100. It appears that the incidence of prematurity is greater in lower socioeconomic areas than in higher ones. That fact can be due to lack of adequate prenatal medical treatment, to poor nutrition, and to other factors.

POSTNATAL CAUSES

In addition to genetic, prenatal, and perinatal conditions that can cause mental retardation, some conditions and diseases can result in mental retardation when they occur in infancy and early childhood. Those conditions are discussed briefly as follows.

INFECTIOUS DISEASES. *Encephalitis* refers to an inflammation of the central nervous system caused by a particular virus. The term *encephalitis* covers a variety of disorders or infections at an early age that produce a high fever and possibly cause destruction of brain cells.

One of the other risks, encountered mainly by poor families, is the danger of children's contracting lead encephalitis or lead poisoning. The condition comes from eating the flakes of lead-based paint found in old and run-down houses. The lead produces a toxic effect on the central nervous system leading to possible severe retardation (Challop, 1971; Lin-Fu, 1972). Although some efforts have been made to pass legislation that would make that situation less possible, it still represents a major unsolved problem in public health.

Meningitis, a condition resulting from bacterial infection and consequent inflammation of the meninges and damage to the central nervous system, has been well known as a potential cause of deafness and blindness but has also been recognized as a possible cause of mental retardation.

NUTRITIONAL PROBLEMS. The role that chronic malnutrition plays in mental development is still a matter of controversy. Poor nutrition can lead to a greater risk of infection and increase the likelihood of disease from other harmful agents (Birch and Cravioto, 1966).

The last trimester of pregnancy and the first eighteen months of infancy have been identified as the period when the brain appears to have a "once only" opportunity to grow properly. Nutritional deficiencies (particularly lack of protein) at that developmental period, even if they are subsequently reversed, can have a permanently negative influence on the intellect of the child (Dobbins, 1974).

The extent of nutritional influence is made more difficult to assess by the simultaneous occurrence of other potentially negative forces in families of the lower socioeconomic class in which poor nutrition is most likely to occur. For example, maternal malnutrition may lead to prematurity with its increased risk of damage to the fetus. The inadequate health care provided poor mothers has its consequences in a greatly increased rate of infant mortality and birth complications with predictably increased numbers of retarded children. The large number of retarded children coming from poor families is often attributed to environmental deficits without considering the potential physical hazards those children run (Passamanick, 1959).

SOCIOCULTURAL FACTORS

The exact role played by the environment in the development of intellectual ability is still not clearly understood, but most psychologists and educators are convinced that it is a significant one. Several lines of evidence are used to reach that conclusion. The first line is the evidence of what can happen under extraordinarily negative conditions, which has been illustrated in the famous case of the "wild boy of Aveyron" (Itard, 1932).

In September, 1799, a boy of 11 or 12, running naked in the woods, subsisting on acorns and roots, was captured by three hunters near Aveyron, France. The task of trying to educate this wild boy, who had no speech, was unresponsive to others, indifferent to everything, and attentive to nothing, was taken on by Jean Itard, a young physician, who was convinced that with sufficient training and attention the boy could become normal.

Itard documented in great detail his five years of efforts with the boy, accomplishing a great deal. In place of the "hideous creature" brought to him, Itard helped the wild boy to become an "almost normal child who could not speak, but who lived like a human being; clean, affectionate, able to read a few words and to understand much that was said to him" (p. xii). Unhappily, Itard was unable to accomplish much beyond that and considered that he had failed. The wild boy died in an institution at the age of 40 without ever approaching the state of a normal human being.

Itard's contribution was in providing one of the first versions of prescriptive teaching by which he arranged the special lessons to fit the special needs of the individual child.

Itard also gave the world a brilliant student, Edward Seguin, who became the acknowledged leader in educating retarded children in the nineteenth century and whose methods clearly stemmed from the instructional patterns established by Itard.

More compelling is the evidence of what can be accomplished through the enrichment of the environment of children in unfavorable circumstances. If major changes can take place under environmental stimulation, then one conclusion would be that the environment played some role in the cause in the first place. If the total influence were hereditary, then modifying the environment should have as little influence as it would have in changing eye color.

The controversy on the effect of early deprivation and early training on intelligence (the nature-nurture controversy) has existed for some time and has been reviewed by many (Clarke and Clarke, 1976; Hunt, 1961). Of concern here are the effects of early training on the development of intelligence in children with low-tested intelligence.

PRESCHOOL INTERVENTION

Skeels and Dye (1939) report a significant study on the effects of earlier environmental intervention. They took thirteen children from an orphanage and placed them in a state institution for the mentally re-tarded. The children were under 3 years of age and had an average IQ of 64, their initial IQ scores ranging from 35 to 89. Each was placed in a different ward of the institution with older patients so that they would receive a great deal of individual attention from older girls and attendants. A year and a half later, their IQs as measured by the Kuhl-mann Test of Mental Development had increased on the average 27.5 IQ points.

As a contrast group Skeels and Dye used twelve babies who were retained in the orphanage. Those twelve children had an average initial IQ score of 87.6, ranging from 50 to 103. After thirty months this group, who remained in the orphanage under a nonstimulating environment, dropped in IQ on the average 26.2 IQ points.

Skeels has made two follow-up studies of those twenty-five chil-dren. One was made three years after the study and the other twenty-one years later. Skeels (1942) found that after three years the experi-mental children had retained their accelerated rate of development in foster homes, while the orphanage children retained their decreased intellectual performance.

In the second study Skeels (1966) followed up on the twenty-five children after a lapse of twenty-one years. Every one of the twenty-five subjects was located, and information was obtained on them. Skeels found:

1. The 13 children in the experimental group were self-support-ing, and none were wards of any institution, public or private.
2. In the contrast group of 12 children, one died in adolescence following residence in an institution for the mentally re-tarded, and four were wards of institutions.
3. The median grade in school completed by the 13 experimen-tal children was twelfth grade. The median grade for the con-trast group was less than third grade.

That study is one of the rare longitudinal studies of children ex-amined at an early age and followed up on when the children had become adults. It demonstrates that differential stimulation at the age of 1 or 2 years displaces the rate of mental development upward or downward with children who do not reveal any abnormality. It also demonstrates that the gains or losses made at an early age can be maintained at later ages.

In a series of studies on young mentally retarded children, Kirk (1958; 1965) found similar trends. In one study on institutionalized children, fifteen were offered preschool education, while twelve chil-dren of similar ages and IQ scores were retained in the wards. Both groups were 4½ years of age at the beginning of the experiment and were last examined three years later at ages 7 and 8 years. The results of that experiment are presented in Figure 4.2.

1. The experimental group gained substantially on the Stanford-Binet scale, the Kuhlmann Test of Mental Development, and the Vineland Social Maturity Scale.
2. The contrast group showed a decrease on all the follow-up tests.
3. Of the fifteen children in the experimental group, six were paroled from the institution, either to their own homes or to foster homes, because of increases in IQs and adjustment. Not one of the contrast group was paroled from the institution during that period.
4. Unlike Skeels's children, approximately one-half of the experimental group had a definite medical diagnosis of disease.

In a similar experiment in the community, twelve children from inadequate homes who attended a special community preschool for the

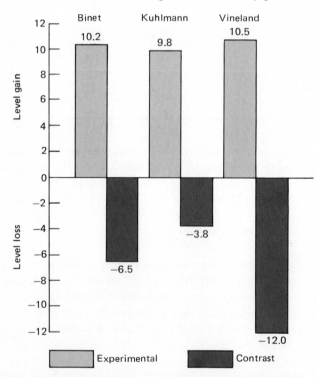

FIGURE 4.2

IQ and SQ change scores of institutionalized retarded children as a function of preschool experience

Source: From S. A. Kirk, "Diagnostic, Cultural, and Remedial Factors in Mental Retardation." In Sonia F. Osler and R. E. Cooke, eds., *The Biosocial Basis of Mental Retardation* (Baltimore: Johns Hopkins Press, 1965), p. 137. Reproduced by permission of the publisher.

mentally retarded were compared with their siblings and twins living in the same home but without the benefits of preschool education. Those two groups were also compared to four children who had been taken out of inadequate homes, placed in foster homes, and also placed in the preschool. The following results were found:

1. The four foster-home children all gained in rate of mental development.
2. Two-thirds of the twelve experimental children who lived in their inadequate homes gained in rate of mental development.
3. Only one-seventh of the twin and sibling controls gained in rate of mental development. The rest either retained their rate of growth or dropped in rate of mental and social growth.

The general conclusions from these data indicate that when intervention is *not* introduced at the preschool level, children from inadequate homes tend to retain their rate of development or drop in rate of development as they grow older. When society offers compensatory education in the form of a preschool or of preschool plus change of home, a reversal of that development is accomplished.

Following the Kirk study of 1958, there has been a series of studies of the effects of preschool education on culturally deprived children and on higher grades of the mentally retarded. Only those dealing with children classified as mentally retarded will be reviewed here.

Guskin and Spicker (1968) reported on an Indiana study. They applied a specialized curriculum to a group of twenty-eight five-year-old, culturally disadvantaged children (white, Appalachian) ranging in IQ scores between 50 and 85. They compared the progress of the children with two other groups, one attending a traditional kindergarten and the other remaining at home. The results of the experiment are presented in Table 4.3. It will be noted in the table that the experimental preschool group of twenty-eight children increased their mean Stanford-Binet IQ score from 75.8 at the kindergarten level to 91.3 after the first grade. The traditional kindergarten group increased their mean IQ scores from 74.1 to 82.9, indicating that

	Size	Kindergarten pretest	Kindergarten posttest	First grade follow-up
Experimental preschool	28	75.8	92.4	91.3
Kindergarten contrast	29	74.1	83.2	82.9
At-home contrast	42	74.0	78.6	86.9

TABLE 4.3

Stanford-Binet IQ means for combined first- and second-year groups, Indiana project

Source: S. L. Guskin and H. H. Spicker, 1968, p. 225.

traditional kindergarten plus first grade has some effect on IQ but not as great an effect as the specialized curriculum. The home group made no progress while at home but began to increase their IQs after their first-grade experience. The results are in harmony with those of Kirk (1958), who found that first-grade experience has some influence on IQ. In other words, schooling is effective whether it is initiated at age 5 or age 6.

One of the most provocative of the existing intervention projects has been designed by Heber and Garber (1975) and by Heber (1977). They have identified families in the census tract in a large urban area that combined many unfavorable social indices, and from that group they picked those families most likely to have retarded children. The criteria used to select the families were established by an earlier study (Heber, Dever, and Conry, 1968), which indicated that, even within an economically deprived area, it was the mothers with IQ scores of less than 80 who accounted for almost four-fifths of the children with IQ scores below 80. That relationship was especially true for those older children. Heber and Garber concluded: "The generally acknowledged statement that slum dwelling children score lower on intelligence tests as they grow older held true only for the offspring of mothers whose IQ's were below 80" (p. 148).

Only babies born to mothers who scored below an IQ of 75 were included in the intervention study. Forty children and their mothers were identified, with half of them assigned to the special program while half remained at home. The program consisted of two major parts: (1) a maternal rehabilitation program that stressed occupational training and strengthening basic academic skills of the mothers and (2) an infant intervention program that consisted of an all-day program in a day-care setting to help the youngsters develop skills in the perceptual, cognitive, language, and socioemotional phases of development.

The direct teaching of the children was done by paraprofessionals with less than usual training as teachers. They were supervised by trained professionals. The program was individualized to each child's needs and often was on a one-to-one basis of child to adult.

The results of that study have startled the field of child development. A major difference in intellectual development began to show itself at 18 months of age and continued to 6 years in favor of the children in the experimental group. Figure 4.3 shows the IQ curves for both groups from age 12 months to 66 months. At age 6 the mean IQ for the experimental group was 124, compared with the control group mean IQ of 94, a difference of 30 points. Intervention was terminated at school entry, but the group was followed up on for four years (Heber, 1977). At age 10 the Wechsler scale IQ for the experimental group was still over 100, while the control group was 20 points lower. In addition to IQs, the experimental and control children were evaluated by many other measures. On other behavioral measures the experimental children were distinctly superior to the controls. Heber (1977) concluded: "Our data to this point in time do nothing to inhibit the hope that it may indeed prove possible to prevent the high frequency of mental retardation among children reared by parents of limited intellectual competence under circumstances of severe economic deprivation" (p. 11).

Gordon (1976) featured parent training as the main focus in a program of intervention on infants from poor southern families. In a follow-up of them at school age, Gordon was able to demonstrate that almost one-fourth of the control or *untreated* group of children coming from that environment were placed in special education programs, while only one or two children whose families received special attention during their first three years were similarly placed.

A similar infant stimulation program conducted with poor rural families in the southeast (Ramey and Campbell, 1977) is emerging

FIGURE 4.3

Mean IQ performance with increasing age for the experimental and control groups

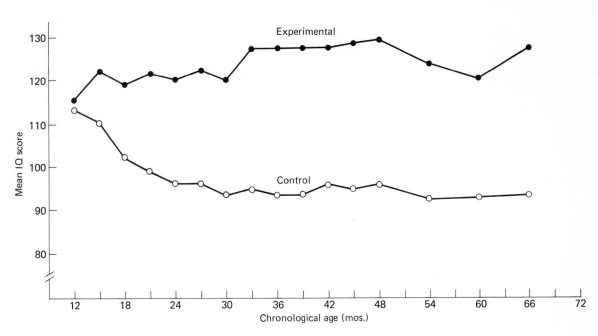

Source: R. Heber et al., 1972, p. 49a.

with parallel results, forcing us to view the developmental period between 6 to 24 months of age as critical for future intellectual development or maldevelopment.

After reviewing the literature on early experience, Clarke and Clarke (1976) came to the conclusion that short and brief intervention periods are not effective: "For the child who is severely deprived, only a massive and lengthy attack upon his problems and those of his family is likely to be rewarding" (p. 227).

From the experiments of Skeels, Kirk, Heber, and others, there is strong evidence that early intervention with psychosocially deprived children will accelerate mental, social, and educational development. The preceding data lend credence to the concept that environmental experiences provide a cultural etiology in mental retardation. The role of experience in development implies that intelligence is not fixed and static but that each individual is born with a range—called the reaction range or norm of reaction by the geneticist Dobzhansky (1955)—on which experience impacts. Poor environment makes the individual function at his lower range of reaction, while a rich experience will develop the individual to a higher functioning level. That concept does not deny the role of heredity but includes the effects of environment on the development of the individual.

Applying our knowledge

The discoveries in the field of mental retardation over the past quarter of a century have resulted in much knowledge with the potential for fruitful application. A recent report of the President's Committee on Mental Retardation (1975) sums up the possibilities for applying our present knowledge as follows:

1. Application of present knowledge of genetics and human reproduction makes it increasingly possible to minimize the birth of defective babies.
2. Application of present knowledge of the environmental hazards to prenatal development and normal birth makes it increasingly possible to avoid the occurrence of maldevelopment and brain damage in the newborn.
3. Application of present knowledge makes it possible to give babies the kind of start in life that stimulates the growth of learning and social adaptation in spite of deprived social environments.
4. Application of present knowledge makes it possible to improve the level of functioning and reduce the dependency of every retarded person regardless of the degree of disability.

5. Application of present knowledge makes life in normal community situations possible for the vast majority of retarded children and adults without imposing undue hardship on their families, their neighbors, or those who care for them.

6. Application of present knowledge of training and habilitation can make it possible for the majority of retarded children to become fully integrated, economically self-sufficient adults, no longer identifiable as retarded. A high proportion of the remainder can, with appropriate support, become partially productive and socially competent. (pp. 7–8)

But that knowledge has not yet been totally implemented. If we applied all we know, we could reduce the incidence and social impact of mental retardation by at least half. If we continue to develop knowledge and apply it to the problem at the rate of the past twenty-five years, the frequency and impact of mental retardation may be a diminishing condition by the end of this century.

Summary

1. The current definition of mental retardation includes two major components: intellectual subnormality and adaptive behavior. A definition of *mentally retarded* depends, in part, on the characteristics of the child and, in part, on the expectations of the social environment.

2. Children with low intelligence, characterized by a limited ability to associate ideas and events, have been classified for educational purposes as (a) slow learners, (b) educable mentally retarded, (c) trainable mentally retarded, and (d) profound or dependent mentally retarded.

3. Estimates on the prevalence of educable mentally retarded vary widely. A conservative estimate of prevalence according to current concepts and definitions of mental retardation is approximately 1.0 to 1.5 percent of the child population.

4. The causes of the condition of mental retardation are many and varied. They include factors within the general categories of (a) genetic, (b) prenatal, (c) perinatal, (d) postnatal, and (e) sociocultural.

5. Environmental deprivation has been isolated as one of the causes of mild mental retardation. Studies show that early intervention through preschool education appears to be effective in preventing mental retardation.

6. Much useful knowledge about the prevention and amelioration of the condition of mental retardation has still not been put into

action. As a consequence the problem of mental retardation remains a large and serious one in the United States today.

References

ALM, I. 1953. "The Long-Term Prognosis for Prematurely Born Children: A Follow-up Study of 999 Premature Boys Born in Wedlock and of 1,002 Controls." *Acta Paediatrica Scandinavica Supplement 94.*

ANDERSON, E. V. 1964. "Genetics in Mental Retardation." In H. Stevens and R. Heber, eds., *Mental Retardation.* Chicago: University of Chicago Press. Pp. 348–395.

BAROFF, G. S. 1974. *Mental Retardation: Nature, Cause, and Management.* New York: John Wiley.

BAUMEISTER, A. A. 1967. "Learning Abilities of the Mentally Retarded." In A. A. Baumeister, ed., *Mental Retardation: Appraisal, Education and Rehabilitation.* Chicago: Aldine. Pp. 181–211.

BIRCH, H. G., AND J. CRAVIOTO. 1966. "Infection, Nutrition and Environment in Mental Development." In H. V. Eichenwald, ed., *The Prevention of Mental Retardation Through the Control of Infectious Disease.* Public Health Service Publication No. 1692. Washington, D.C.: U.S. Government Printing Office. Pp. 227–248.

BIRCH, H. G., S. A. RICHARDSON, D. BAIRD, G. HOROBIN, AND R. ILLSLEY. 1970. *Mental Subnormality in the Community.* Baltimore: Williams & Wilkins.

CHALLOP, R. S. 1971. "Fact sheet—Estimation of childhood lead poisoning in the United States." *Mental Retardation* 9 (August): 46.

CLARKE, A. M., AND A. D. B. CLARKE. 1976. *Early Experience: Myth and Evidence.* London: Open Books.

COOPER, L. Z. 1968. "Rubella: A Preventable Cause of Birth Defects." D. Bergsma, *Birth Defects* 4 (7): 23–35.

DOBBINS, J. 1974. "The Later Development of the Brain and Its Vulnerability." In J. Davis and J. Dobbins, eds., *The Scientific Foundations of Pediatrics.* London: Heinemann.

DOBZHANSKY, T. 1955. *Evolution, Genetics, and Man.* New York: John Wiley.

DOLL, E. A. 1941. "The Essentials of an Inclusive Concept of Mental Deficiency." *American Journal of Mental Deficiency* 46 (October): 214–219.

FARBER, B. 1968. *Mental Retardation: Its Social Context and Social Consequences.* Boston: Houghton Mifflin.

FRASER, F. C. 1964. "Teratogenesis of the Central Nervous System." In H. Stevens and R. Heber, eds., *Mental Retardation.* Chicago: University of Chicago Press. Pp. 395–429.

GALLAGHER, J. J. 1976. "The Sacred and Profane Uses of Labeling." *Mental Retardation* 14 (December): 3–7.

GATES, R. R. 1946. *Human Genetics,* vol. 1. New York: Macmillan.

GROSSMAN, H., ED. 1973. *Manual on Terminology and Classification in Mental Retardation,* 1973 rev. Washington, D.C.: American Association on Mental Deficiency.

GUINAGH, B., AND I. GORDON. 1976. *School Performance as a Function of Early Stimulation. Final Report.* Grant #NIH-HEW-OCD-09-C-638. Gainesville: University of Florida.

GUSKIN, S. L., AND H. H. SPICKER. 1968. "Educational Research in Mental Retardation." In N. R. Ellis, ed., *International Review of Research in Mental Retardation.* New York: Academic Press. Vol. 3, pp. 217–278.

HEBER, R. F. 1977. "Research on the Prevention of Socio-Cultural Retardation Through Early Prevention." Paper presented to Extraordinary Session of the International Union for Child Welfare Advisory Group on Social Problems of Children and Youth, Ostend, Belgium, November 21–25.

HEBER, R. F., R. B. DEVER, AND J. CONRY. 1968. "The Influence of Environmental and Genetic Variables on Intellectual Development." In H. J. Prehm, L. A. Hamerlynck, and J. E. Crosson, eds., *Behavioral Research in Mental Retardation.* Eugene: University of Oregon.

HEBER, R., AND H. GARBER. 1975. "The Milwaukee Project: A Study of the Use of Family Intervention to Prevent Cultural-Familial Mental Retardation." In B. Friedlander, G. Sterritt, and G. Kirk, eds., *Exceptional Infant.* New York: Brunner/Mazel.

HEBER, R. F., H. GARBER, S. HARRINGTON, C. HOFFMAN, AND C. FALENDER. 1972. *Rehabilitation of Families at Risk for Mental Retardation. Progress Report.* Rehabilitation Research and Training Center in Mental Retardation. Madison: University of Wisconsin.

HSIA, D. Y. 1971. "A Critical Evaluation of PKU Screening." *Hospital Practice* 6(4): 101–112.

HUNT, J. M. 1961. *Intelligence and Experience.* New York: Ronald Press.

ITARD, J. M. G. 1932. *The Wild Boy of Aveyron.* Translated from the French by G. Humphrey and M. Humphrey. New York: Appleton-Century-Crofts.

JERVIS, G. A. 1937. "Phenylpyruvic Oligophrenia: Introductory Study of Fifty Cases of Mental Deficiency Associated with Excretion of Phenylpyruvic Acid." *Archives of Neurology and Psychiatry* 38 (November): 944–963.

KIRK, S. A. 1965. "Diagnostic, Cultural, and Remedial Factors in Mental Retardation." In Sonia F. Osler and R. E. Cooke, eds., *The Biosocial Basis of Mental Retardation.* Baltimore: Johns Hopkins University Press. Pp. 129–145.

KIRK, S. A. 1958. *Early Education of the Mentally Retarded.* Urbana: University of Illinois Press.

LEJEUNE, J., M. GAUTIER, AND R. TURPIN. 1959. *"Etudes des Chromosomes Somatiques de Neuf Enfants."* C. R. Academie Sci. 248: 1721–1722.

LILIENFIELD, A. M. 1969. *Epidemiology of Mongolism.* Baltimore: Johns Hopkins University Press.

LIN-FU, J. S. 1972. "Undue Absorption of Lead Among Children: A New Look at an Old Problem." *New England Journal of Medicine* 286 (March): 702–710.

MACMILLAN, D. L. 1977. *Mental Retardation in School and Society.* Boston: Little, Brown.

MASLAND, R. L., S. B. SARASON, AND T. GLADWIN. 1958. *Mental Subnormality: Biological, Psychological, and Cultural Factors.* New York: Basic Books.

MERCER, J. 1973. "The Myth of 3% Prevalence." In G. Tarjan, R. K. Eyman, and C. E. Meyers, eds., *Sociobehavioral Studies in Mental Retardation: Papers in Honor of Harvey F. Dingman.* Washington, D.C.: Monographs of the American Association on Mental Deficiency, No. 1. Pp. 1–18.

MILUNSKY, A., AND L. ATKINS. 1975. "Prenatal Diagnosis of Genetic Disorders." In A. Milunsky, ed., *The Prevention of Genetic Diseases and Mental Retardation.* Philadelphia: W. B. Saunders. Pp. 221–263.

PASSAMANICK, B. 1959. "Influence of Sociocultural Variables Upon Organic Factors in Mental Retardation." *American Journal of Mental Deficiency* 64 (September): 316–320.

PRESIDENT'S COMMITTEE ON MENTAL RETARDATION. 1975. *The Problem of Mental Retardation.* Washington, D.C.: Department of Health, Education, and Welfare Publication (011D) 75-22003.

PRESIDENT'S COMMITTEE ON MENTAL RETARDATION. 1970. *The Six-Hour Retarded Child.* Washington, D.C.: U.S. Government Printing Office.

RAMEY, C., AND F. CAMPBELL. 1977. "Prevention of Developmental Retardation in High Risk Children." In P. Mittler, ed., *Research to Practice in Mental Retardation,* vol. 1. Baltimore: University Park Press. Pp. 157–164.

SCHREIBER, F. 1939. "Mental Deficiency from Paranatal Asphyxia." *Proceedings and Addresses of the Sixty-third Annual Session of the American Association on Mental Deficiency* 44(1): 95–106.

SKEELS, H. M. 1966. *Adult Status of Children with Contrasting Early Life Experiences.* (Monographs of the Society for Research in Child Development, No. 31.) Chicago: University of Chicago Press.

SKEELS, H. M. 1942. "A Study of the Effects of Differential Stimulation on Mentally Retarded Children: A Follow-up Study." *American Journal of Mental Deficiency* 46 (January): 340–350.

SKEELS, H. M., AND H. B. DYE. 1939. "A Study of the Effects of Differential Stimulation on Mentally Retarded Children." *Proceedings and Addresses of the Sixty-third Annual Session of the American Association on Mental Deficiency* 44(1): 114–130.

SNYDER, L., M. D. SCHONFELD, AND E. M. OFFERMAN. 1945. "The Rh Factor and Feeblemindedness. *Journal of Heredity* 36 (January): 9–10.

SPECIAL EDUCATION FOR HANDICAPPED CHILDREN. 1927–1928. *Annual Report of Superintendent of Public Instruction.* Madison: Wis. Chap. 7.

SWAN, C., A. L. FOSTEVIN, AND G. H. BARHAM-BLACK. 1946. "Final Observations on Congenital Defects in Infants Following Infectious Diseases During

Pregnancy with Special Reference to Rubella." *Medical Journal of Australia* 2 (December): 889–908.

TARJAN, G., S. W. WRIGHT, R. K. EYMAN, AND C. V. KEERAN. 1973. "Natural History of Mental Retardation: Some Aspects of Epidemiology." *American Journal of Mental Deficiency* 77 (January): 369–379.

TREDGOLD, A. F. 1937. *A Textbook of Mental Deficiency,* 6th ed. Baltimore: William Worden.

WAISMAN, H. A., AND T. GERRITSEN. 1964. "Biochemical and Clinical Correlations." In H. Stevens and R. Heber, eds., *Mental Retardation.* Chicago: University of Chicago Press. Pp. 307–348.

WORTIS, J. A. 1961. "Psychiatric Study Tour of the U.S.S.R." *Journal of Mental Science* 107: 119–155.

YANNET, H., AND R. LIEBERMAN. 1944. "The Rh Factor in the Etiology of Mental Deficiency." *American Journal of Mental Deficiency* 49 (October): 133–137.

5

This chapter will discuss the various special educational programs and procedures that have been designed for educable and trainable retarded children described and defined in the previous chapter. The severely handicapped child who is retarded will be discussed in Chapter 12 dealing with multiple handicaps.

Throughout the centuries the human race has had the problem of dealing with those persons who, through inheritance, accident, environment, or disease, were not endowed with the ability to learn and to function in society as well as the majority of people do. Much has been written about the early neglect, mistreatment, and persecution of the mentally retarded, but serious attempts at education and habilitation can be identified as early as 1800.

Historical perspective

A brief history of the management and education of the mentally retarded is presented here to show the changing emphasis and the developmental stages leading to current programs.

EARLY EUROPEAN CONTRIBUTIONS

The history of the treatment of mental retardation in the early nineteenth century is in large measure the history of the work of a series of outstanding physicians imbued with the concept of man's pliability and adaptability. Members of current professions whom we now expect to deal with the mentally retarded, such as speech-language pathologists, psychologists, and special educators, were hardly in existence at that time. The era following the French Revolution was marked by the philosophy that mankind had unlimited possibilities and that education could make a significant difference in the lives and development of citizens. The concept of potential educability was applied in various ways to the problems of the mentally retarded.

That philosophy led Jean Marc Itard, a French physician who was working in an institution for the deaf, to apply techniques similar to those used with deaf children in training a wild boy of 12 who was captured in the forest of Aveyron. Since the story is told in the previous chapter, it is sufficient here to say that in working with Victor, the Wild Boy of Aveyron, Itard was convinced that Victor's intelligence was educable. Itard was the first person to recognize that education must begin with the child's developmental abilities, not, as we would normally expect, with the child's age. In the case of

Victor, this meant starting with simple sensory discriminations between hot and cold, the identification of objects while blindfolded, and the distinction between edible and nonedible substances.

Edward Seguin was first a teacher and later a medical and surgical student under Itard. Seguin's contributions include the organization of a school for idiots in Paris in 1837 and the publication of an influential book entitled *The Moral Treatment, Hygiene, and Education of Idiots and Other Backward Children*. Alarmed by political unrest following the 1848 revolution, Seguin migrated to the United States to continue his work.

In a later book Seguin (1866) described a physiological method of training designed to stimulate the brain through physical activities. He also influenced the development of residential schools in the United States, became a superintendent of one of them, and was chosen in 1876 as the first president of the professional organization now known as the American Association on Mental Deficiency.

Among other European contributors working in the latter part of the nineteenth century was an Italian physician, Maria Montessori. She, like other physicians who worked with mentally retarded children, found that she had no medical treatment for retardation and resorted to the development of educational methods and materials. Montessori found that her methods, apparently successful with the mentally retarded, were also successful with other children. Those methods, which utilize the systematic use and manipulation of concrete objects, are still popular and are the basis of many preschool programs in the United States now bearing the Montessori name.

Another contributor in the early part of the twentieth century was Alfred Binet, a French psychologist. Along with a physician collaborator, Simon, he developed the first individual intelligence test and later organized school classes for the mentally retarded in Paris. Although best known for his attempts to *measure* intelligence, he was in fact committed to the *educability* of intelligence. It is ironic that later versions of the test he originated (the Stanford-Binet Intelligence Scale) were used by later generations of psychologists and educators in the 1920s and 1930s to demonstrate the unchangeability and immutability of intelligence.

Instead of the physiological method of training espoused by Seguin, Binet organized an educational program to train intelligence, which he entitled *mental orthopedics*. He used simple illustrative pictures, three-dimensional objects, pencil and paper, and other common objects and was perhaps the original user of inkblots to demonstrate imagination in perceptual learning.

Binet stressed the direct training of attention and the value of activity and an opportunity to discover (Kirk and Lord, 1974):

All, or almost all, children before given any instruction show a taste for singing, drawing, storytelling, inventing, manipulating objects . . . by grafting education and instruction on these natural activities we benefit from the start already made by nature; nature furnishes the activity, the teachers intervene only to direct it. (pp. 212–213)

The cumulative effect of the works of those men was to provide an instructional base and philosophy that still are influential in special educational programming for the mentally retarded. The work of those early giants was also a great influence on those in the United States who began to concern themselves with similar problems.

EARLY AMERICAN CONTRIBUTIONS

The early history of the United States records no formal program for the education of handicapped children. In the first half of the nineteenth century, handicapped children stayed at home or were stowed away in almshouses or houses of charity. Even as late as 1850, 60 percent of the inmates of poorhouses consisted of the deaf, the blind, the insane, and the mentally retarded.

The first influential person to advocate educational provisions for the retarded in the United States was a physician, Samuel Gridley Howe, who devoted his life to the education of the blind, the deaf, and orphaned children. In 1848 he requested funds from the Massachusetts legislature for a residential school. The legislature appropriated $2,500 for the school, but the bill was vetoed by the governor. Howe attacked the veto in a classic letter to the governor of Massachusetts, advocating the rights of the mentally retarded in a democracy (see Howe, in Kirk and Lord, 1974). The Massachusetts legislature overrode the veto of the governor, and on October 1, 1848, the first institution for the mentally retarded was opened with ten children. For the next fifty years residential schools in the various states became the major, if not the only, educational endeavor for the mentally retarded.

One of the most striking characteristics of the middle to late nineteenth century in the United States was the construction of large residential asylums for the mentally ill and the mentally retarded. The two conditions were viewed similarly in that era, and the special provisions made for them were designed in like fashion.

Residential institutions and colonies, often placed in the rural countryside where agricultural work could be offered, seemed to satisfy two rather different needs of the American culture at that time. First, it provided a viable source of treatment and assistance to those citizens who were in obvious need; second, it had the effect of removing many deviant citizens from sight where they might otherwise be a daily nuisance and problem in the rapidly growing urban culture and society of those times.

The founders of state residential schools had as their goal the education of the mentally retarded and their subsequent return to the community. Baumeister and Butterfield (1970) report that the climate after 1850 was optimistic. Superintendents, echoing Seguin and others that "idiots" were amenable to education and development, tended to exaggerate their claims. "In one report after another, in state after state, the conviction was expressed, often in glowing language, that access has been found to the idiotic brain" (p. 7).

On the other hand, Lazerson (1975) in reviewing the history of that era reported:

> The expectation that the feebleminded could be educated and trained for self-sufficiency soon gave way to custodial practices and a custodial ideology. . . . The founders of asylums for the feebleminded expected to cater to the mildly retarded, but soon found themselves flooded with the most serious cases, individual communities wanted the least contact with. As it became clear that moral treatment would not effect cures among the seriously retarded, and as overcrowding threatened to alter the nature of the treatment, those who ran the asylums protested that their therapeutic programs were being strangled by custodial pressures. (pp. 40–41)

By the end of the nineteenth century the administrators of institutions believed that custodial care for the mentally retarded was desirable. The overoptimism about what could be accomplished through the Seguin physiological method had its inevitable reaction. Educational efforts declined, and another idea gained in ascendancy; namely, that feeblemindedness and criminality were correlated. For the period 1890 to 1920 the feeble-minded were widely regarded as a potential menace to society, and the institutions were the informal prisons that protected society from those "moral imbeciles."

The history of institutions in the United States is filled with evidence of chronic understaffing and limited financing, which, in turn, create conditions of deprivation and neglect that periodically reach the scandalous level (Hansen, 1977).

It is arguable that given proper support and professional staffs, the large institutions could have been, or could even now be, a more effective tool. It is clear that the American public has never agreed to provide the financial support needed to create ideal conditions. The people have turned more and more to the public schools and various other community programs to meet the needs of the mentally retarded.

Public school programs for mentally retarded children did not receive much attention until the end of the nineteenth century. The first special class for the mentally retarded was organized in Providence, Rhode Island, in 1896. The steady growth of such programs characterized the first half of the twentieth century.

The growth and support of such programs usually stemmed from many different factors. One of them was the increasing inability of the institutions to care for all the children with special needs. Other factors in the larger society also played a part. The increasing tendency for more children to attend school longer also had the result of keeping in school many of those who could not learn rather than letting them drop out. That placed more pressures on the public schools to make special adaptations for slow learners. Also the growing popularity and use of intelligence tests by the schools tended to reveal large numbers of children at the lower levels of intellectual development and placed additional pressures on the schools for some additional adaptations.

THE EXPANSION OF SPECIAL CLASSES IN THE PUBLIC SCHOOLS. Between 1920 and 1970 special classes for educable mentally retarded children in public schools were often subsidized by the states and thereby increased at a rapid rate. The greatest expansion occurred after World War II. In 1948, 87,030 children were enrolled in special classes. By 1969, 703,800 children were served, and by 1974, 1,350,000 were enrolled in special education services. The largest increase (Table 1.3) was between 1958 and 1975. This was due probably to increases in state subsidy in more states and in federal aid in the training of professional personnel, which began in 1958 and which increased the supply of specially trained teachers for those classes.

THE ORGANIZATION OF CLASSES FOR TRAINABLE MENTALLY RETARDED CHILDREN. Shortly after World War II parents found that their moderately and severely retarded children were not being admitted to residential schools or institutions because of overcrowding. They were also being told by educators that their children were not eligible for classes for educable mentally retarded children because they could not be expected to profit from the academic program provided (that is, reading and arithmetic).

The frustration of parents seeking help for their handicapped children led them to form parents' groups and to organize and conduct special programs for trainable retarded children in church basements, storefronts, and anywhere they could. Organized parents' groups also placed great pressure on local school boards and state legislatures to provide help for their children. They succeeded in most instances in getting their trainable children included under the special education provisions of the state laws.

THE MOVE TO NORMALIZATION AND LEAST RESTRICTIVE ALTERNATIVES. Since 1970 there has been a strong movement to place retarded citizens in a more normal community setting, if at all possible, and to provide services for all handicapped children, no matter how severely handicapped. Three major factors seem to play an important role in the trend away from segregation of the handicapped from typical life settings and normal peers.

1. An accumulation of research evidence that shows little improvement for the educable retarded child in special classes over what could be accomplished in the regular grades.

2. Strong legal pressures from organized minority groups who are concerned that minority-group children are being mislabeled and shunted off into special education programs inappropriately.

3. A growing emphasis on, and legal attention to, the rights of the individual citizen, particularly the poor and those with special problems. This recommitment to the principle that all should share equally in the opportunities available in the society raised questions as to whether being placed in an institution is to be deprived of individual freedoms and whether being placed in a special class limits the child's educational opportunities.

Special characteristics important for educational planning

It is difficult to describe the abilities, disabilities, and behavioral characteristics of mentally retarded children because of the heterogeneous nature of the group. To organize an educational program for groups, however, it has been necessary for research workers to study the distinctive characteristics of different levels of mentally retarded children. This section will describe briefly the developmental characteristics of the different degrees of mental retardation and the performance of mentally retarded children in (1) physical and motor abilities, (2) intellectual performance, (3) language, (4) reading,

(5) arithmetic, (6) special talents, (7) adjustment in the community, and (8) occupational adjustment.

In reviewing those areas, two points need to be kept in mind. First, the observed characteristics may be a result of how the retarded children have been treated as well as a part of the essential condition. For example, if children are given less opportunity to participate in physical activities and sports, they may appear physically awkward and uncoordinated. In other words, the retardation may be as much a function of the learning environments as a function of the organism.

Second, the descriptions in this section reflect group tendencies. Individual children may well reveal characteristics counter to the group norm. For example, a certain retarded child might be popular with peers although the general trend would be for the retarded to be less popular. One must always be cautious not to ascribe to a particular individual the general characteristics of the group.

THE DEVELOPMENTAL CLASSIFICATIONS

The educational classification of mental retardation based on IQ, adaptive behavior, and educational achievement consists of three levels or degrees, as described in the previous chapter: (1) the educable mentally retarded child, (2) the trainable mentally retarded child, and (3) the severely and profoundly retarded child. The reason for such separate treatment is the different developmental characteristics of each of the groups and the varying educational expectations for each of them.

Special programs are needed to fit the level and age of the retarded child. The classification of the American Association on Mental Deficiency, as indicated in the previous chapter, consists of four degrees: (1) mild, IQs of 55 to 69; (2) moderate, IQs of 40 to 54; (3) severe, IQs of 25 to 39; and (4) profound, IQ less than 24.

A description of the developmental characteristics of the different groups of mentally retarded (Table 5.1) was reported by the President's Committee on Mental Retardation (1975).

THE EDUCABLE MENTALLY RETARDED (AAMD—MILD). It should be recalled that the educable mentally retarded child has been defined as one who has potential for (1) limited educability in the basic academic subjects of the school, (2) social adjustment sufficient to get along independently in the community, and (3) sufficient occupational and social adequacy to support self partially or totally and to manage own personal affairs at the adult level.

Educable mentally retarded children are often not recognized as retarded at the preschool age. Although they are slightly delayed in talking, language development, and sometimes walking, the retardation is not so great as to cause alarm on the part of the parents. Most of the children are not identified as mentally retarded until they enter school and begin to fail in learning the required subject matter.

THE TRAINABLE MENTALLY RETARDED (AAMD—MODERATE). The trainable mentally retarded child has been defined as one who has difficulty in (1) learning academic skills to any functional level, (2) developing total independence in social adjustment at the adult level, and (3) attaining occupational adequacy at the adult level sufficient for total self-support without supervision or help. The trainable person is capable of attaining (1) self-help skills (such as dressing, undressing, using the toilet, and eating), (2) the ability to protect himself from common dangers in the home, school, and neighborhood, (3) social adjustment to the home or neighborhood (learning to share, respect property rights, and cooperate in a family unit and in the neighborhood), and (4) economic usefulness in the home and neighborhood by assisting in chores around the house or in working in a sheltered environment or even in routine jobs under supervision.

TABLE 5.1

Developmental characteristics of mentally retarded persons

Degrees of mental retardation	Preschool age 0–5: maturation and development	School age 6–20: training and education	Adult 21 and over: social and vocational adequacy
Mild	Can develop social and communication skills; minimal retardation in sensorimotor areas; often not distinguished from normal until later age	Can learn academic skills up to approximately sixth-grade level by late teens. Can be guided toward social conformity. "Educable"	Can usually achieve social and vocational skills adequate to minimum self-support but may need guidance and assistance when under unusual social or economic stress
Moderate	Can talk or learn to communicate; poor social awareness; fair motor development; profits from training in self-help; can be managed with moderate supervision	Can profit from training in social and occupational skills; unlikely to progress beyond second-grade level in academic subjects; may learn to travel alone in familiar places	May achieve self-maintenance in unskilled or semiskilled work under sheltered conditions; needs supervision and guidance when under mild social or economic stress
Severe	Poor motor development; speech is minimal; generally unable to profit from training in self-help; little or no communication skills	Can talk or learn to communicate; can be trained in elemental health habits; profits from systematic habit training	May contribute partially to self-maintenance under complete supervision; can develop self-protection skills to a minimal useful level in controlled environment
Profound	Gross retardation; minimal capacity for functioning in sensorimotor areas; needs nursing care	Some motor development present; may respond to minimal or limited training in self-help	Some motor and speech development; may achieve very limited self-care; needs nursing care

Source: President's Committee on Mental Retardation, 1975.

The line between children called educable mentally retarded and those called trainable mentally retarded is of course not clear-cut. Some children diagnosed as trainable learn academic subjects and are reclassified as educable, while some children diagnosed as educable require the program for the trainable.

THE SEVERELY AND PROFOUNDLY MENTALLY RETARDED. Most of these children have multiple handicaps that often interfere with normal instructional procedures. For example, in addition to being mentally retarded, the child may have cerebral palsy and a hearing loss. The goal of training procedures for such seriously handicapped children is limited to establishing some level of adaptation in a controlled environment. Those training issues are not discussed in this chapter but are discussed in Chapter 12 on multiple and severe handicaps.

PHYSICAL AND MOTOR ABILITIES

A few studies have been conducted on the motor proficiency and physical education achievements of the educable retarded. The studies (Francis and Rarick, 1960; Rarick and Widdop, 1970) indicate that in motor proficiency the average scores on physical tests of retarded children are inferior to the average scores for children with average IQs. Studies on the effects of physical education programs in improving motor proficiency have shown positive results (Soloman and Pargle, 1967). In height and weight most educable retarded children are close to normal children. In view of those statements, one should remember that in dealing with an individual child, we cannot generalize from group results to the individual. In height or weight some mentally retarded children are superior to some average children.

Since there is a slight tendency in educable children toward a greater than normal incidence of vision, hearing, and neurologic problems, some tendency to poorer physical and motor abilities would be expected although, as indicated, individual educable retarded children might show outstanding physical and athletic skills. The trainable retarded child almost always reveals neurologic problems that result in generally inferior performance in those skills.

INTELLECTUAL CHARACTERISTICS

Since limited intellectual development defines the category of mental retardation along with adaptive behavior, it is no surprise that retarded children perform less well on the major components of intellectual behavior such as *memory*. However, it is of importance to educators and scientists to probe more deeply to understand more about what the nature of the memory defect means. The observation of poor recall is the beginning of the puzzle, not the end. For example, is the poor memory of the retarded child due to:

1. an inability to attend to objects or ideas in their initial presentation and to understand what is to be retained?
2. an inability to hold information in short-term memory due to language deficiencies (language problems preventing good associative linkages between a new idea and previous information already retained)?
3. an inability to transfer information from short-term memory to long-term memory (an internal process that is important but insufficiently understood, as yet, in normal as well as retarded children)?
4. an inability to use effective retrieval strategies by which to recover the appropriate information from the memory storage?

It would appear from available research information that the inability to attend to objects and ideas and the inability to transfer from short-term to long-term memory are most important. Ellis (1970) thinks that the inability of the retarded child to use rehearsal strategies (to talk to oneself about the material learned) is the key, while Zeaman (1973) suggests that if the retarded child could master and understand the information originally, he could retain it as well as the normal child. With these results in mind, the preferred special education goal with the mentally retarded would be to (1) sharpen and highlight the presentation of stimulus materials and (2) rehearse the information in short-term memory until it is fixed in a more permanent, long-term memory storage.

Other intellectual functions such as reasoning, concept formation, and other cognitive abilities are measured with intelligence tests and are included in language acquisition.

LANGUAGE ACQUISITION

One characteristic commonly regarded as typical of children referred to as mentally retarded is delayed and retarded language. We do not know how much is due to, or how much is a result of, low cognitive abilities.

As with many other problems in mental retardation, the question is: Does the development of language in the retarded follow the same sequence of development as in normal children, but at a slower rate, or are there qualitative differences in the development of language in the mentally retarded?

The position that the mentally retarded develop language in the same sequence as normal children only more slowly is held by many. Graham and Graham (1971) studied the syntactic characteristics of nine trainable mentally retarded children in a residential school. The children were 10 to 18 years old and had mental ages of 3 to 6. They concluded that "retardates develop rules of their language at a different rate but in much the same way as intellectually average children" (p. 623).

Lenneberg, Nicholas, and Rosenberger (1964) studied 61 children with Down's syndrome, ages 3 to 23 years, who were living at home. They found that the trainable retarded children were markedly slower in language development and were arrested at a primitive level, but acquired language in the same sequence as average children.

Other studies have concluded that children at all levels of mental retardation are slower in acquiring language; and the more retarded they are, the slower is the pace of language learning.

Not all researchers agree with the conclusion of "only at a slower pace." Semmel, Barritt, and Bennett (1970) studied institutionalized and noninstitutionalized educable mentally retarded subjects and compared their linguistic performance with two groups of average children. They found that the educable mentally retarded children with average IQ scores of 70 were lower in language skills than normal children even when mental age was taken into account. That is, a mentally retarded child of 10 with a mental age of 7 was still not performing as well as the average 7-year-old. The researchers concluded that there may be not only a difference in rate but a qualitative difference as well.

Cromer (1974) reviewed the studies on receptive language of the mentally retarded and concluded that (1) the retarded develop language at a slower pace, (2) subnormals are more delayed in language age than in mental age, and (3) poor cognitive abilities, such as limited short-term memory span, may be responsible for the linguistic delay.

A clue as to how the issue may be resolved is shown by another study that revealed a rate difference at early ages and a qualitative difference at later ages. Naremore and Dever (1975) collected five-minute speech samples of normal and retarded children at each age level from 6 to 10. The samples were analyzed for such linguistic properties as subject elaboration, subordination index, and relative clause index, as well as for such basic linguistic items as the number of words, sentences, pauses, repeats, and so on.

It appears to be in the ability to use complex clauses and subject elaboration that the retarded child shows the most deficiency. That is an important communication deficit because it limits the kind and amount of information the retarded child can communicate to others, particularly when sequences of activities are called for.

An example of the differences between the oral language of normal children and that of educable retarded children is given in the following as two 10-year-old children describe the same TV program that they saw (Naremore and Dever, 1975).

Normal 10-year-old	*Educable retarded 10-year-old*
Every time he tried to start something they all started to play their instruments and wouldn't do anything so Lucy said that they needed a Christmas tree, a pink one, for the Christmas queen, but when Charlie Brown went out he found that there were lots of them that were pink and green and blue, but there was just one little one.	Charlie Brown didn't seem to have the Christmas spirit *and* so Linus said he should get involved *and* there's this little doctor place *and* Charlie Brown went over there *and* that's what Lucy told him to.

It is clear that the retarded child's production is not only sparser than the normal child's, showing poor content, but is also meager in syntactical form. The retardate depends heavily on *and* as a connective and lacks the ability economically to impose temporal or hierarchical structure on events shown by the normal child.

READING PERFORMANCE

Educable mentally retarded children are usually capable of learning to read somewhere between second- and fifth-grade level and are capable of using reading in their adult life. Trainable mentally retarded children, by definition, probably will not read beyond the first grade but can learn to read words and phrases needed for their own protection, such as *danger, stop, men,* and *women.* Most research on reading has been conducted on the educably mentally retarded. Reviews of reading research have been made by Cegelka and Cegelka (1970) and by Kirk, Kliebhan, and Lerner (1978).

ARITHMETIC PERFORMANCE

Studies on arithmetic achievement indicate that retarded children achieve at about their mental-age grade-expectancy in arithmetic fundamentals but below that expectancy in arithmetic reasoning. It appears that the retarded child is able to achieve at a higher grade level in the more mechanical computational skills. That finding may well be a reflection of the methods of teaching rather than of the basic characteristics of the child. One program that focused on using the inductive method of teaching arithmetic found that primary-age educable retarded children were superior to expectations on both computation and problem solving (Goldstein, Moss, and Jordan, 1965).

Some of the differences that have been found in the processes of arithmetic suggest that retarded children are inferior to average children of the same mental age in (1) solving arithmetic problems presented verbally, (2) establishing mature habits such as eliminating "counting on fingers," (3) decreasing careless mechanical errors and errors in reading, and (4) understanding the abstract terms of mathematics such as *space, time,* and *quantity.*

As in reading studies, research workers have not been able to find a significant difference between the arithmetic abilities of brain-injured retarded children and those of the non-brain-injured of similar mental ages. With the exception of the reports of W. D. Kirk (1968) on the relation of Piaget tasks and arithmetic and of Cawley and Vitello (1972) on an instructional model, there has been a paucity of research on arithmetic abilities of the mentally retarded.

SPECIAL TALENTS

The consensus of most workers is that art and music competence, like achievement in other areas, is related to mental age. The mentally retarded are slower to learn and remain longer at each stage. It is rare to find a mentally retarded child who has exceptional ability in art or music, although there is wide variation among the mentally retarded as a group and considerable overlap with normal children in ability. Occasionally, however, we find someone who is classified and who functions as a mentally retarded child, but who has a special ability.

Kiyoshi Yamashita is such a case. Kiyoshi was rescued from a broken home and placed in a school for retarded children in Japan. His IQ was recorded as 68. Noticing that Kiyoshi had some graphic skills, an instructor in the school encouraged his ability and stimulated him to produce paper collages of high quality. His artistic abilities broadened into the use of oils and developed to a point at which he became, after parole from the institution, a noted artist. The Japanese press referred to him as the Van Gogh of Japan, a wandering genius. Lindsley (1964), who has reviewed the history of this case, rejects the concept of idiot savant and proposes that specific skills in children with other deficits should be sought and developed.

Two other cases of exceptional art talents in so-called idiots savants have been reported by Akira Morishima and Louis Brown (1976; 1977). The first case, Yamamoto, was a hydrocephalic child who was delayed in speech and language development and who was referred to a school for the mentally retarded. There he was trained for fifteen years and developed a special and recognized talent for drawing. Another case, Yamamura, with an IQ of 48 to 53, did not develop expressive language. He, like Yamamoto, obtained intensive instruction in drawing and developed extraordinary talent as a painter of insects. Morishima and Brown explain those special talents with the hypothesis that a narrowing of stimuli tends to lead to the funneling of responses only in cases in which an average residual cognitive function exists.

PERSONAL AND SOCIAL CHARACTERISTICS

Retarded children often show special problems in personal and social characteristics. Such problems relate, in part, to the reactions of others to their condition and also to their history of past failure to reach the level of performance expected by others.

Such characteristics as limited attention span and low frustration tolerance can be ascribed to the previous lack of success attained by the mentally retarded individual. Whether the intellectual limitations of the mentally retarded child and adult also limit their social adjustment is still uncertain.

Weinstein (1969) has presented a theory of interpersonal competence that stresses three major factors:

1. An individual must be able to take the role of another—to assess accurately the other person's definition of a given social situation—what is commonly referred to as *empathy*.
2. A person must possess a repertoire of interpersonal tactics permitting him to control or influence others.
3. A person must be capable of employing those tactics appropriately.

Such characteristics require perceptual skills and even linguistic terms, requirements that put the retarded individual at a disadvantage relative to the average person, even apart from past experience.

The progressive way in which experience influences behavior is summarized by Kauffman and Payne (1975):

1. Mentally retarded individuals typically experience more failure than normal children and therefore develop greater generalized expectancies for failure. The predisposition to expect failure tends to cause retarded children to avoid situations where failure is likely.

2. Retarded children enter novel situations with performances that are usually depressed even below their mental ability.

3. Retarded children have fewer tendencies than normals to increase their output following a mild failure. (p. 164)

Those findings are encouraging to the educator because, if experiences can create the problem, then other experiences can help reduce it. If one can reduce the number of failure experiences, create novel experiences in which the child succeeds, and present successful models of behavior, one can improve the poor attitudes that progressively prevent the retardate from making full use of his or her limited abilities.

FAMILY CHARACTERISTICS

A major difference can be identified in the family backgrounds of educable retarded children as compared with the families of trainable and severely retarded children. Among the educable children many seem to come from family backgrounds that have a rather consistent set of characteristics associated with low income. There is a general assumption that the limited language stimulation and the more chaotic family environment found in low-income homes may be a contributing factor to mild retardation (see Chapter 4).

The trainable child may be found in a wide variety of families and social backgrounds. The wide range of metabolic and genetic accidents that can create such a child do not seem closely related to family income or social status. The family of the trainable retarded child, as a consequence, may often be able to bring more personal and financial resources to bear in aiding their child's program than can the poor family of the educable child.

Farber (1975) has pointed out that families of moderately to severely handicapped children have special problems in that the handicapped child has arrested the normal family cycle and that the difficulties the family faces change over time but do not necessarily ease as the child grows older. The family must face the problem of deciding whether or not to institutionalize the child, the realization that the child may never be self-sufficient, and the worry of what will happen to the child when the parents die.

The full realization of the complex and continuing issues that face the family of a handicapped child has led to much greater emphasis on family counseling and special programming for the family as well as for the child. Those projects will be briefly described later in this chapter.

COMMUNITY AND VOCATIONAL ADJUSTMENT

The ultimate purpose of educating mentally retarded children is to help them at the adult level to adjust to the community as social participants and wage earners. To determine how well the educable mentally retarded adjusts socially and occupationally at the adult level, numerous follow-up studies have been conducted.

One of the first of those was made by Channing (1932). She followed up 1,000 special class graduates in ten large cities in the United States, approximately five years after they had left school. She found that a large proportion of them were employed and earned wages not far below those of their normal peers. Channing pointed out that the subnormal can obtain employment but their employment records are less satisfactory than those for an unselected group.

Kennedy (1948) compared 129 adults of normal IQ with 356 individuals who had been diagnosed as mentally subnormal when they were in school. The two groups were matched for age, sex, and socioeconomic status. Since the study was conducted during a period of high employment, Kennedy found better work records among the retarded than Channing found in the late 1920s. Kennedy pointed out that (1) there were no differences in marriage rate among the two groups, (2) the retarded had a higher divorce rate, and (3) there was a tendency for the retarded to have an unsatisfactory work record but little difference in wages earned. The conclusion was that there were many more similarities between the educable retarded and the normals than there were differences. Some of the adjustment differences noted indicated that the retarded participated less in recreational activities (theater, sports, dancing) and read less. Their jobs were primarily of the unskilled type, while many of the normal adults had office jobs requiring some academic education.

The most extensive long-term follow-up study was conducted by Baller in 1936 and followed up by Charles in 1953. Originally Baller selected 206 individuals who had previously been classified as mentally deficient and enrolled in special classes in Lincoln, Nebraska. He compared their social and economic status with that of a group of adults of the same age who, as children, had been considered normal. He found many more infractions of the law and considerable job instability among the retarded. Fifteen years after Baller's study Charles (1953) was able to find 75 percent of that group of retardates. It should be noted that at the time of Baller's study, the United States was in a depression and there was much unemployment. When Charles made his study, unemployment was at a minimum. His findings were as follows:

1. Eighty percent of the sample found were married.
2. Twenty-one percent of the married group had been divorced. These marriage and divorce rates were lower than the national average.
3. About 80 percent of the married subjects had children; the average number of children per family was 2.03. The national average at that time was 2.62.
4. Their children were, on the whole, making satisfactory progress in school. The average IQ of the 73 children tested was 95, and IQs ranged from 50 to 138.
5. Eighty-three percent of the group located were self-supporting, some living in shacks and some in expensive new homes.
6. Laboring occupations for the males and housekeeping for the females constituted the majority of occupations. A few had managerial positions.
7. Twenty-four of the subjects were retested with the Wechsler-Bellevue Intelligence Scale. The average verbal IQ was 72, the performance IQ was 88, and the total scale was 81. Those scores were considerably higher than the original Binet ratings.
8. Sixty percent of the men had violated the law. Most of the offenses, however, were traffic and civil violations of some kind. None were serious.

Baller, Charles, and Miller (1967) made a second follow-up study thirty years after the original Baller study in 1936. They compared the adjustment of the ex-special-class students with two other groups of children, one of slow learners and one of normal children. They found that:

1. Sixty-five percent of the mentally retarded group returned to, or remained in, their original communities as compared with 40 percent of the other two groups.
2. Unemployment and public assistance were somewhat higher among the retarded.
3. Vocationally successful children in the group of mentally retarded had acquired their work skills early.

The results of the preceding investigations have led to the following conclusions regarding possible occupational adjustment.

1. The educable mentally retarded can learn to do unskilled and semiskilled work at the adult level.
2. Any failure in unskilled occupational tasks is generally related

to personal, social, and interpersonal characteristics rather than to inability to execute the task assigned.

3. Employment records of the educable mentally retarded show that approximately 80 percent eventually adjust to occupations of an unskilled or semiskilled nature and partially or totally support themselves.

4. Trainable mentally retarded children can become economically useful in sheltered workshops or in similar supervised environments.

Educating the educable mentally retarded

The educational programs for the educable mentally retarded differ in some important respects from the educational programs for the trainable mentally retarded. For that reason the special program adaptations for the latter are presented in separate sections.

The purposes of the education of educable mentally retarded children are derived from the definition and needs of the children. It should be recalled that by definition that child is educable in (1) academic subjects, (2) home and community adjustment, and (3) occupational competency. Hence the goals of a program for the educable should be so organized that they

1. develop in the child the basic skills learned in the elementary school including reading, writing, arithmetic, language arts, and manual skills, to the limits of the child's capacity

2. develop in the child habits of physical hygiene through a practical program of health and sex education

3. develop in the child social competence: the ability to get along with the child's peers through programs of social experience

4. develop in the child emotional security and independence in the school and home through a good mental hygiene program and through the organization of instruction that assures success and a positive self-concept

5. develop an ability to become an adequate member of the home and community through a curriculum designed to emphasize home and community membership

6. develop wholesome leisure-time activities through an educational program that teaches enjoyment of recreational and leisure-time pursuits

7. develop occupational competence through prevocational, career, and vocational training and guidance as a part of the

school experience so that the individual may eventually become partially or totally self-supporting in some productive activity

THE LEARNING ENVIRONMENT

One of the persistent problems in the education of the educable mentally retarded is *where* to educate them, as well as *what* or *how* to educate them. As reported in the historical section of this chapter, three learning environments have been advocated at different times in history: (1) the institution, (2) the special class, and (3) the supplemental regular class—mainstreaming.

RESIDENTIAL INSTITUTION. One of the goals of the early residential institution was to provide an educational program for educable retarded children resulting eventually in their rehabilitation in the community. That aspiration has often been defeated by overcrowding and understaffing.

Before World War II about one out of every two children in the large state institutions could be identified as educable. Twenty years later Farber (1968) reported that less than one in every four youngsters in an institution was identified as educable. Eight years later Scheerenberger (1976) reported that only one in every ten youngsters in an institution was classified as mild or borderline. Whenever an educable retarded child was identified and placed in an institution, it was not only because of a low IQ; it was often for other reasons. Henderson (1957) found that such youngsters were committed earlier because of dependency, sexual and criminal delinquencies, chronic truancy, or other behavior disorders that pressured the community to place the youngster in an institution.

The institution also had some built-in limitations in training children for community adaptation. How would they learn that houses are numbered odd and even on opposite sides of the street, that a round-trip ticket may save money, how to shop in a grocery store, or how to have comfortable relationships with the opposite sex (Gunzberg, 1974)?

As the years passed, the institution became less and less an educational center for children who would be rehabilitated into the community and more and more a custodial institution for the moderate to severely handicapped. The organization of special classes in the local community became the major and expected placement for the educable retarded child.

SPECIAL CLASSES. Prior to World War I most of the education of the retarded was taking place in large state institutions. In the 1920s the popularity of the special class began to take hold. The classes expanded rapidly until over 700,000 children were enrolled in special schools and classes and in other programs by 1969. By 1974 there were 1,350,000 enrolled.

Until the 1970s the special class had received broad general acceptance as the appropriate special education provision. It was generally considered a step toward desirable integration since parents no longer had to send their child to a distant institution for special training. Under that strategy exceptional children (such as the blind, deaf, retarded, and disturbed) were identified, placed in special classes with others of similar characteristics, and given a specially trained teacher, special materials, smaller classes, and so on. The basic philosophy of the special class program was generally understood and accepted by both special educator and regular educator. That philosophy briefly stated was:

1. The regular class did not meet the needs of exceptional children. The lessons were too difficult or inappropriate, and the teacher was generally unable to adapt to the special problems of the exceptional child.
2. A special class program, with a trained specialist, could meet the particular needs of the exceptional group.
3. With such a special program exceptional children should achieve in school without the additional social and emotional problems created by an inappropriate school program.
4. Once improvements were made, some mildly handicapped children would be expected to be returned to the regular program.

Since those special class arrangements increased the cost of the education of exceptional children, the state usually accepted some responsibility for reimbursing the local school district for part or all of the additional or excess costs. The manner of such reimbursement from the state often was dependent on the special class model (that is, a state would pay the local district a sum of money based on how many special class units were being operated or on the number of mentally retarded children assigned to special classes).

A number of studies have attempted to determine whether it is better to place retarded children in special classes or to leave them in the regular grades. All of these studies compared children assigned to special classes with children of comparable IQs remaining in the regular grades. The general results of a large number of such experiments indicate that the benefits of special class placement are equivocal. Specifically:

1. Sociometric studies of mentally retarded children in the regular grades indicate that the children tend to be isolated and rejected by their normal peer groups (Johnson, 1950; Johnson and Kirk, 1950). Welch (1967) studied the self-derogation and academic achievement of mentally retarded elementary school children assigned to (a) a segregated special class and (b) an integrated special class in which the children spent a half-day in a regular class. She found that the children in the integrated program made higher achievement scores and decreased in self-derogation over an eight-month period, as compared with the children in the segregated class.

2. Although studies are contradictory, the bulk of research evidence supports the thesis that children in special classes are better adjusted and have a better self-concept and less tension than the mentally retarded children remaining in the regular grades (Guskin and Spicker, 1968; Kirk, 1964).

3. There is some, but no conclusive, evidence that educable mentally retarded children at the lower levels tend to make better educational progress in special classes than in the regular grades, while those at the upper levels (IQs of 75 to 85) tend to make better educational progress in the regular grades than in the special class (Goldstein, Moss, and Jordan, 1965).

4. Children who are placed in special classes and those placed in regular grades at the age of 6 increase equally in IQ. There is no difference in extent of changes in IQ regardless of placement (Goldstein, Moss, and Jordan, 1965).

Starting in the late 1960s and early 1970s there began a significant change in the traditional special education wisdom as to what represented the best learning environment for slow learners and for mildly handicapped children. Renewed attempts were made to keep those children in the normal educational setting. That change came about as a result of a number of different trends and forces:

1. doubt that the beneficial effects of special classes were as great as supposed

2. the tendency for special classes to become the dumping ground for problem children from the regular classes (slow learners, those with behavior disorders, and the learning disabled)

3. the use of special classes for a disguised form of segregation of minority-group children

4. the recognition of the nonreversibility of special education placement, once it was made

One reaction to those criticisms has been the suggestion to abolish all special classes for the mentally retarded and return those children to the regular grades. Dunn (1968) was one of the first special educators to comment on the situation. He stated, "A better education than special class placement is needed for socioculturally deprived children with mild learning problems who have been labeled educable mentally retarded" (p. 5). But he is "not arguing that we do away with our special education programs for the moderately and severely retarded" (p. 61). In an epilogue he states:

> The conscience of special educators needs to rub up against morality. In large measure we have been at the mercy of the general education establishment in that we accept problem pupils who have been referred out of the regular grades. In this way, we contribute to the delinquency of the general educators since we remove the pupils that are problems for them and thus reduce their need to deal with individual differences. (p. 20)

Gallagher (1972) also pointed out that "special education too often was an exclusionary process masquerading as a remedial process" and added that there was precious little evidence that special education was returning a significant number of children to the regular class. Once they were identified and placed as educable retarded, those children were in the special education stream and often were there for the balance of their lives in the educational system.

MAINSTREAMING. The simple procedure of abandoning special classes and returning the children to the regular grades will only raise the same problems that resulted in the original organization of special classes. The concept of mainstreaming does not imply returning children to the regular grades without supporting help. The essence of mainstreaming, as stated by Kaufman et al. (1975), encompasses three major components: (1) *integration*, (2) *educational planning and programming*, and (3) *clarification of responsibility*.

1. Integration refers to educating exceptional children in regular classes to the maximum degree possible. That means that some mentally retarded children will be in the regular class most of the day, while others may be in the regular class a part of the day with the rest of the time spent in a resource room with a special education teacher for special remedial or programmed work.

2. Educational planning refers to an adequate educational assessment and a specified program for each child. It has been referred to as *individual educational programming*.

3. The *responsibility* for the child's program and education is the joint responsibility of the regular class and special class teachers.

The pros and cons of mainstreaming will be discussed in Chapter 13. It is sufficient to state here that at this point in the late 1970s, many special classes for the educable mentally retarded have been abolished and the children returned to the regular grades for a mainstreaming program.

THE CURRICULUM CONTENT

The last section dealt with *where* the educable mentally retarded child is taught. This section deals with *what* he is taught. A curriculum is a set of organized experiences arranged in a developmental sequence designed to attain the educational objectives listed earlier under the purposes of education.

The curriculum for the educable mentally retarded is similar to a curriculum of the elementary school. It includes the teaching of reading, writing, language, arithmetic, science, aesthetics, physical education, recreation, and related topics leading to personal adequacy and social and occupational competence. It is, however, necessary to modify the instructional procedure and curriculum to fit the slower-learning characteristics of the mentally retarded.

ATTAINING THE SKILLS IN THE CURRICULUM

Heiss and Mischio (1972) have identified three strategies for instructional activities for the retarded. They include (1) the unit approach, (2) task analysis, and (3) the social learning approach.

THE UNIT APPROACH. A teaching method of long standing, the unit approach was described many years ago by Christine Ingram (1935). With this approach the classroom program is centered about specific interests, concepts, or experiences through which the child may find a functional use for the skills that are being taught. Such concepts as activities around the home, understanding the city or community, how food is procured and distributed, the post office, and telephone service provide experiences of interest, which give meaning and motivation for using the skills and gaining knowledge of value to the child. Intertwined within each unit are the skill subjects of reading, writing, spelling, arithmetic, industrial education, and social skills. The general idea is to assist the retarded child in seeing interrelationships and applying the skill subjects to a natural situation.

Although this approach is still much in evidence, the lack of a developmental sequence of concepts, the lack of continuity between individual units, and the inconsistency of uniqueness of content for the special problems of the retarded have caused special educators to become less enthusiastic about its value. In a mainstreamed class, however, the retarded child will be assigned tasks within his or her ability to accomplish, while the superior child will be given tasks to accomplish at the child's higher level of attainment.

TASK ANALYSIS. A second approach to skill development is focused on the process of task analysis. In this approach various knowledges or skills are analyzed and broken down into their sequential component parts. Each component part is then taught to the retarded, first in isolation and then in integrated form so that the mastery of an important skills area is obtained. Task analysis is used when a particular skill needs to be broken down into steps to make it easier for the retarded child to learn and progress. It is used extensively in the curriculum for the trainable and severely retarded child.

SOCIAL LEARNING APPROACH. A third curricular approach focuses on the development of those skills necessary to achieve effective adjustment in the life environment of the retarded person. The social learning approach, designed to develop critical thinking and independent actions on the part of the mentally retarded, has been identified mainly with Goldstein (1974). This approach builds lesson experiences around psychological needs such as self-respect and mastery, physical needs such as sensory stimulation, and physical maintenance and social aspects such as dependence and mobility. For example, lesson experiences based on achieving economic security could include these objectives: (1) to choose a job commensurate with skills and interests, (2) to locate and acquire a satisfactory job, (3) to maintain a job, and (4) to manage effectively the financial resources gained from a job.

Goldstein has developed a comprehensive social learning curriculum that encompasses both behavioral and conceptual goals. Like the unit approach, it includes the use of arithmetic, writing, and reading skills. Unlike the unit approach, it orders the concepts and contents. It differs from the task analysis approach in that it provides a larger developmental sequence of behaviors that are related and integrated into terminal behavior. For further details, see Goldstein (1974).

ADAPTATION TO DEVELOPMENTAL LEVEL

The adaptation of the curriculum is needed to fit the level and rate of development of retarded children who are progressing educationally at one-half to three-quarters the rate of the average child. It does not mean that tasks should be made overly simple, but rather they should be within the ability of the child to accomplish with effort but without failure and frustration. They should also be so spaced and broken down into constituent parts that the child can progress step by step toward the desired target.

Kolstoe (1970) has shown how the same general topic can be dealt with for children of varying levels of development. In Table 5.2

he shows what concepts can usually be acquired by children of different developmental levels. The emphasis on successively more complex concepts changes with the developmental level and expected ability of the child.

The following organization of classes constitutes an effort to adapt the curriculum to different levels of ability and interests.

PRESCHOOL EDUCATION. There has been a marked increase in preschool education for all handicapped children. The accelerated development of children who received intervention at an early age (described in Chapter 4) has led to the organization of Head Start and to the Handicapped Children Early Education Act passed by Congress in 1968. Those developments have evolved because of the demonstration that preschool education can minimize further handicapping conditions. Early education of the retarded is now a part of the Head

TABLE 5.2

Instructional objectives for educable mentally retarded children at various levels for money and time

Developmental stage	Money	Time
Preprimary	1. Knows that money buys things 2. Differentiates between a penny, nickel, dime	1. Knows what a clock is 2. Knows the days of the week
Primary	1. Knows the value of coins up to a dollar 2. Knows that five pennies make a nickel, two nickels make a dime, four quarters a dollar	1. Tells time by the half-hour 2. Knows yesterday, tomorrow 3. Differentiates seasons
Intermediate	1. Can make change correctly up to $1.00 2. Understands the relationship of coins 3. Knows what a bank is for	1. Tells time by minutes and quarter-hours 2. Uses clock and calendar correctly 3. Understands *past, to, before, afternoon, midnight, weekend*
Prevocational	1. Understands banking, deposits, withdrawals, and how to write checks 2. Knows how to buy by the dozen, the case, carton, gross, ream	1. Understands being punctual for work 2. Can read timetables and schedules 3. Can apply time to household and work tasks
Vocational	1. Can set up a budget 2. Understands installment buying 3. Understands the value of credit	1. Understands how time is used to compute pay 2. Understands pacing, relating production to time periods. 3. Can budget time

Source: Adapted from O. Kolstoe, *Teaching Educably Mentally Retarded Children* (New York: Holt, Rinehart and Winston, 1970), pp. 92–93.

Start program. It is expected that those programs will aid in the prevention of environmentally determined mental retardation. The emphasis of the curriculum is on language development, motor development, sense training, and perception.

THE PRIMARY AND INTERMEDIATE YEARS. From about 6 to 14 years of age, emphasis is on social adjustment, language, perceptual and motor training, and also the skill subjects of the elementary school—reading, writing, arithmetic, arts and crafts, science, social studies, physical education, and recreation. Student performance is not expected to reach the levels of an average child. For example, reading is conceived as including three levels of competencies: (1) reading for protection, (2) reading for information, and (3) reading for pleasure. For the trainable mentally retarded child, the objective is to teach the child to read words and phrases in his or her environment for protection, words such as *danger, exit, men,* and *women.* The objective for the educable mentally retarded is to teach the child to read for information. Some are able to read for pleasure from books with reduced vocabularies.

The adaptation of the curriculum is keyed to the slow-learning abilities of the children, since the educable mentally retarded progresses educationally at one-half to three-quarters the rate of an average child. Materials are made concrete, and the child is assisted in adapting to a pace slower than that of the rest of the children.

If the child is in a self-contained class, the special education teacher uses the unit of experience, task analysis for some skills, and the social learning approach. If the child is mainstreamed, he or she follows the curriculum of the assigned grade but goes to the resource room for help in academic subjects.

In general, the program tends to emphasize living skills and is directed toward personal and social self-sufficiency at the adult level. The social learning curriculum of Goldstein, mentioned earlier, and the life experience science units such as Meyen (1972) advocates have demonstrated a consistent and integrated approach for the educable mentally retarded child.

PREVOCATIONAL AND VOCATIONAL EDUCATION. In the junior and senior high schools the educable mentally retarded typically obtain prevocational and vocational experiences. In junior high schools they might include occupational exploration, shop and homemaking skills, occupational information, and an introduction of the pupil to the world of work in the school, such as cafeteria and food services, office help, building and ground maintenance, and library work, in addition to academic subjects.

Kolstoe (1970) includes in the program of prevocational and vocational training (1) schoolwork experience, (2) occupational information, (3) physical education and recreation, (4) home economics and shop, (5) social studies, and (6) vocational assignments outside of school. Work-study programs for the educable mentally retarded provide for part- or full-time work in unskilled or semiskilled jobs under supervision of the school. They include jobs in many areas, such as working with copier or mimeograph machines in an office; domestic services in homes, hotels, and hospitals; food services in restaurants; building services (janitor, watchman, elevator operator); and work on farms and grounds maintenance.

Vocational educators are paying more attention to the needs of the retarded in designing their programs. Phelps and Lutz (1977) describe a technique for clustering occupations into various families, doing a task inventory on the cluster to identify the skills to be taught, and then suggesting special instructional adaptations to fit the needs of the mentally retarded.

While learning the skills is important, so are the personal habits needed to hold a job, such as punctuality, responsibility, and personal interactions with fellow employees. Both of these dimensions, skills and work habits, are a part of vocational education for the educable mentally retarded students.

APPLYING LEARNING PRINCIPLES

The primary characteristic of mentally retarded children is that they do not learn as readily as others of the same chronological age. They lack a high level of generalization and are usually unable to learn material incidentally, without instruction, as the average child learns it. Much of the knowledge and skills acquired by the average child is learned without specific instruction by the teacher. But for the retarded child instruction needs to be systematically presented without too much reliance on incidental learning. Learning should be programmed in sequence and presented in such a way that the child will learn at a rate compatible with his or her development. Systematic instruction in every area requires time, planning, and insight, the essentials in a special education program for the educable mentally retarded child.

To implement systematic instruction it is necessary to apply sound principles and techniques that will facilitate learning. Some of the principles that facilitate learning and make teaching more profitable follow.

1. *Let the child experience success.* Organize materials and use

methods that lead the child to the right answer. Provide clues where necessary. Narrow the choices in responding. Lead to the right answer by rewording the question or simplifying the problem. Never leave the child in a failure, but carry him or her along to success.

2. Provide feedback. The child should know when he or she has responded correctly. Learning is facilitated when the child has knowledge of whether the response is correct or not. If the response is incorrect, let the child know it, but let it be only a way station in finding the correct response. Lessons should be so arranged that the child obtains immediate feedback on the correctness of answers. This is one of the principles used in any good programmed learning procedure. If a child is learning to write the word *dog,* for example, he covers the model, writes the word, then compares the response with the model, thus getting feedback.

3. Reinforce correct responses. Reinforcement should be immediate and clear. It can be either tangible, as in providing tokens or food, or it can be in the form of social approval and the satisfaction of winning a game.

4. Find the optimum level at which the child should work. If the material is too easy, the child is not challenged to apply the best effort; if too difficult, he or she faces failure and frustration.

5. Proceed in a systematic way. Lessons should proceed in a step-by-step fashion so that the more basic and necessary knowledge and habits precede more difficult material.

6. Use minimal change from one step to the next to facilitate learning.

7. Provide for positive transfer of knowledge from one situation to another. This is facilitated by helping the child generalize from one situation to another. By having the same concept presented in various settings and in various relationships, the child can transfer the common elements in each. Itard, for example, when training the Wild Boy of Aveyron, noted that the boy learned to select a particular knife from a group of objects in response to the written word *knife* but that when a knife of a different shape was substituted, he could not respond. The child had not generalized the concept of *knife;* he had failed to transfer the understanding of the label to knives in general.

8. Provide sufficient repetition of experiences to develop overlearning. Many teachers have said, "Johnny learns a word one day but forgets it the next day." In such cases Johnny probably had not had enough repetition of the word in varying situations to insure overlearning, that is, learning to the point at which he will not forget it readily. Mentally retarded children seem to require more repetitions of an experience or an association in order to retain it.

9. *Space the repetitions of material over time* rather than massing the experiences in a short duration. When a new concept is presented, come back to it again and again, often in new settings, not as drill but as transfer to a new situation.

10. *Consistently associate a given stimulus or cue with one and only one response in the early stages of learning.* Do not tell the child, "This letter sometimes says *a* and sometimes says *ah.*" Teach one sound at a time until it is overlearned and then teach the other sound as a different configuration in a new setting. If the child has to vacillate between two responses he or she will become confused.

11. *Motivate the child toward greater effort by:* (a) reinforcement and the satisfaction of succeeding, (b) variation in the presentation of material, (c) enthusiasm on the part of the teacher, and (d) optimal length of sessions.

12. *Limit the number of concepts presented in any one period.* Do not confuse the child by trying to have him or her learn too many things at one time. Introduce new material only after older material has become familiar.

13. *Arrange materials with proper cues for attention.* Arrange materials in a way that will direct the pupil's attention so that he or she will learn to attend to the cues in the situation that will facilitate learning, and to disregard those factors in the learning situation that are irrelevant.

14. *Provide success experiences.* Educable mentally retarded children who have faced failure may have developed low frustration tolerance, negative attitudes toward schoolwork, and possibly some compensatory behavior problems that make them socially unpopular. The best way to cope with those problems is to organize a *day-to-day* program presenting the child with short-range as well as long-range tasks in which to succeed. The self-concept and the self-evaluation of the child are dependent on how well he or she succeeds in work assignments. Thus a teacher must be very careful to see not only that the child does not fail but also that he or she experiences positive success and knows success. Although that principle is applicable to all children, it is particularly necessary with children who are retarded. They face enough failures in school and in life without having to repeat them over and over again in a classroom situation.

Educating the trainable mentally retarded

Those children called *trainable retarded* face the special educator with a unique problem. In virtually all other handicapping conditions discussed in this text, the ultimate educational goal is self-sufficiency, and the educational program is geared to that objective. In this instance, the assumption is that complete self-sufficiency will be unlikely for most trainable retarded children. The goal of the program becomes training the child to cope within a state of limited dependency, in self-help and self-care, economic usefulness, and social adjustment in the home and neighborhood or in a sheltered environment. The learning environments of the trainable mentally retarded children can be divided into three major categories: (1) institutions, (2) community facilities, and (3) public schools.

RESIDENTIAL INSTITUTIONS

As discussed earlier, the enrollment at institutions is decreasing, and consequently fewer trainable mentally retarded children are being sent to institutions. That statement does not mean that trainable mentally retarded children have been completely removed from institutions or that some residential care may not be appropriate for some trainable children. Generally, the emphasis of training programs in institutions is on the development of techniques of self-care: dressing, washing, feeding, and using the toilet. Social skills are a part of the formal program objectives.

It is in the area of social skills and economic usefulness that the large, overcrowded institutions with their limited staffs have been most often criticized for inability to accomplish their stated goals for the trainable child. Today there is a belief that some of the atypical behavior often associated with the condition of mental retardation may be caused, in fact, by the special environments of the institution itself.

Suppose one is raised in a bedroom with a hundred other individuals, has a rotating list of adult caretakers (none of whom are present more than eight hours), and never has the experience of going to the store, exploring a neighborhood, or doing many of the things that young children do. The inability of such youngsters to adapt can be partly attributed to the environment rather than to the condition of mental retardation.

One of the most observable characteristics of many retarded individuals, often remarked on by visitors to institutions, is the rather indiscriminate affection and responsiveness shown to casual human contact. As Zigler and Balla (1977) point out, such behavior can be explained as a general behavioral characteristic that is the result of minimal and sporadic positive human contact—such contact as that often found in overcrowded institutions. In addition, there appears to be less opportunity in institutions for the modeling of appropriate behavior, while chronic staff turnover can often lead to a wariness or unwillingness on the part of the retarded individual to establish any permanent social contacts or relationships.

When those disadvantages are added to the widely held view that institutions demand and enforce a conformity that fits the child or adult for institutional living but ill prepares them for any adjustment outside the institution, it is easy to see why institutions are viewed with suspicion and concern.

To match the public school program for trainable retarded children, a program for adults known as *normalization* has been developed. It contends that the life environment of the mentally retarded should be as "culturally normative as possible in order to establish or maintain personal behaviors and characteristics which are culturally normative as possible" (Wolfensberger, 1972, p. 28).

Whether it is *mainstreaming* or *normalization,* it is clear that the current style of providing support for retarded individuals is to work diligently to bring them as close to the normal setting and environment as possible.

COMMUNITY PROGRAMS

It is for these and other reasons that a movement developed in the 1960s to deinstitutionalize and to develop what are now known as community programs for the retarded.

One of the driving forces in changing the emphasis from institutions to community provisions has been the increasing influence of organized groups of parents of retarded children. Beginning in the early 1950s, programs developed by parents for the trainable mentally retarded demonstrated that the trainable child and adult can adapt in the community in a protected environment. In addition to public school classes for children (discussed in the next section), programs for adolescents and adults have been organized in communities. Among the most important are (1) group homes and (2) sheltered workshops.

GROUP HOMES. One alternative to the institution is provided by group homes. In some communities small units have been established that operate as much on the family concept as possible. The purpose of the group home is to create an environment for the mentally retarded adult that is more homelike than that of a large institution, and a setting in which the variety of skills necessary for effective living can be mastered. Permenter (1973) makes available the report of a young student who for one week impersonated a retarded girl in a group home for six girls. While the ethics of such deception are questioned by current-day standards, the report of her experience does provide an interesting description of life in a group home.

After we returned home in the afternoon (from a sheltered workshop) our time was our own. On a typical evening all of us went to our living area to change clothes. We sat around and talked while folding laundry or putting away clothes. Mary was absorbed in soap operas, Pam and Julie played with Robby, the little boy, and with the family dog. Later, Julie, Pam, and I went to help Ann prepare the evening meal while we talked about incidents at work. Soon some of the others came in and set the table or helped with the final stages of the meal. Everyone was together, sometimes in the kitchen, but more frequently in front of the television. While one group did the dishes, the rest managed to get our things ready for the next day. (pp. 20–21)

After a week in the situation, during which neither the house-parents nor the other girls were aware of her true identity, the student observer summed up her experiences.

The members of this cohesive family did a great deal more than just share the same roof, they helped and cared for each other. Conflicts such as those revolving around Mary (a manipulating and disruptive girl) became "family" problems requiring each member to adjust her behavior for the good of the group. The group home became more than just a training ground and residence, it became "home" to the girls. They had a strong sense of belonging—a source of strength when difficulties arose and a contributing factor to their seemingly healthy adjustment. (p. 41)

The group home is one of the settings that is used to encourage deinstitutionalization, bringing retarded adolescents and adults into a semiprotected setting where they can function outside an institution. These homes are financed by the state at a cost sometimes less than that of institutionalization. A description of community homes for the retarded is found in Bergman (1975).

SHELTERED WORKSHOPS. Sheltered workshops have been organized in the larger communities since the majority of trainable retarded citizens are unable to be regularly employed. The workshops enroll adolescent and adult mentally retarded individuals, train them to do routine tasks, contract with industries for piecework or simple assemblies (such as transistor radios), and also develop and make salable products.

In well-established workshops the mentally retarded come to work, or are transported to work, on a full-day basis and are paid wages for their labor. Thus these trainable adults become partially self-supporting. Besides the remuneration that is received from contracts and the sale of products, the sheltered workshops are also supported financially by parents' organizations, foundations, community funds, and donations. In some of the larger cities, the community center working with people at this level of mental retardation may include a diagnositc center, a preschool program, a sheltered workshop, and a recreation center.

PUBLIC SCHOOLS

The public school program for the retarded has been developed and standardized over the past two decades to the point that it is now possible to describe the general characteristics of a public school program. Prior to the enactment of the Education for All Handicapped Children Act (PL 94–142), a series of court cases reaffirmed the rights of retarded children to receive an "appropriate education" in the public schools. Those cases have clearly indicated the responsibilities of the schools. The parents have achieved a remarkable turnaround in public attitudes and responsibilities in a single generation (Gilhool, 1973).

In the early 1950s there was resistance on the part of school boards to organize programs for trainable children in the public schools. Today, after the court cases following Section 504, a basic civil rights provision of Public Law 93–112, and Public Law 94–142, all public schools are required to provide education for all children (see Chapter 13). The organization throughout the country involves special schools and classes, and they are considered least restrictive, compared with institutionalization. Mainstreaming is practiced with young children in Head Start and in kindergarten in public school. Generally, however, school-age trainable children are educated in special schools and classes with contacts with other children when feasible.

THE CURRICULUM CONTENT

In defining an educational program for any group of children, it is necessary to identify the general objectives of the curriculum and then to give the specific elements required in a course of study. The general objectives of the curriculum for a trainable child are inherent in the definition: (1) developing self-care or self-help, (2) aiding the child's social adjustment in the home and neighborhood, and (3) developing economic usefulness in the home or in a sheltered environment. They constitute the broad goals of the educational program for trainable mentally retarded children.

SELF-HELP SKILLS. The major characteristic that differentiates the trainable mentally retarded from the totally dependent mentally retarded is self-care. If a child can (1) learn to dress and undress, (2) eat properly, (3) take care of himself or herself in the bathroom, and (4) follow sleep routines, he or she is not dependent on someone else for personal needs. In a restricted sense the child becomes independent as far as taking care of simple routines is concerned. Although such independence is common among normal children after age 4 or 5, it is necessary to educate the trainable child in those elements of self-care.

SOCIAL ADJUSTMENT IN THE HOME AND NEIGHBORHOOD. It is not expected that trainable mentally retarded children will become independent in the community or be in charge of their affairs outside of the home. They are, however, expected to get along in the home and in their immediate neighborhood. That particular learning achievement includes sharing with others, waiting their turn, obeying, following directions, sensing the feelings of others, and coping with other aspects of interpersonal relationships, especially those concerned with daily associations. Social adjustment is not a subject that is taught like chemistry or physics. It is an intangible type of development that comes about through rewarding group experiences in recreation and play, singing, dramatics, and working and living with others.

ECONOMIC USEFULNESS. The term *economic usefulness* is applied to the trainable mentally retarded child to differentiate that ability from occupational or vocational activities within the capacity of educable children. It is expected that the trainable child will be helpful in the home, the school, or a sheltered environment in either the community or an institution. In the home economic usefulness means helping with housework and yardwork. Those activities can be developed in the classroom through many of the programs requiring care of the room, cooking, washing and wiping dishes, arts and crafts, woodworking, and the ability to complete simple tasks under minimum supervision. That kind of objective is more attainable with older trainable children in school than with younger ones.

In addition to the three major goals preceding, there are basic skills that are offered in every class. Teaching those skills recognizes the equivalent developmental ages in classes for trainable children, which usually range between about 3 and 7 years. At this developmental level the academic program prescribed for the educable mentally retarded or for normal children is not warranted. It would be well here to discuss the expected performance levels for trainable mentally retarded children.

MODIFIED READING. In general, trainable children do not learn to read beyond the first-grade level. Their ability is limited to recognizing their names, isolated words and phrases, common words used for their protection, such as *danger, stop, men,* and *women,* and other signs that they encounter in a community. Some trainable children with special abilities can learn to read at a slightly higher level. Most who learn to read, however, are probably educable mentally retarded children, misdiagnosed as trainable, or children with wide *intra*individual differences.

ARITHMETIC. Trainable children are not taught the formal arithmetic presented in the primary grades. They can learn some quantitative concepts, however, such as more and less, big and little, and the elementary vocabulary of quantitative thinking. They can be taught to count up to ten and to identify quantity in small groupings. The older trainable mentally retarded children can learn to write numbers from one to ten, and some of them can learn time concepts, especially the sequence of activities during the day, telling time by the clock, and possibly an elemental understanding of the calendar. Some can recognize and remember telephone numbers, their own ages, and some simple money concepts. In general, the arithmetic that is taught is related to everyday living.

WRITING. Trainable mentally retarded children can learn to write their own names, addresses, and telephone numbers and certain words that they learn in reading for their own protection.

LANGUAGE. This program includes the development of speech and the understanding and use of verbal concepts. It includes communication skills, such as listening to stories and roll calls, discussing pictures, and other activities familiar to the children in the classroom.

SOCIAL STUDIES. The important area of study is the home and the way it participates in the community. This includes learning about holidays, transportation, and church and knowing the months and days of the week, as well as contributions to home life.

DRAMATIZATION. Classes for trainable children use considerable dramatization such as acting out a story or a song, playing make-believe, shadow play, and using gestures with songs, stories, and rhymes.

ARTS AND CRAFTS. Activities in this area include coloring, drawing, painting, simple woodworking, pasting and cutting, and making simple craft objects. Such activities may help in developing motor coordination, an appreciation of color and form, and the ability to complete a task.

PHYSICAL HYGIENE. The routine of a classroom includes snacks and juice or milk, and discussions about the kinds of food eaten at different meals, the care of the teeth, body cleanliness, clothing, safety, and posture. Health habits usually need to be fostered both in the school and at home.

PRACTICAL ARTS. Under practical arts are included cooking, sewing, dishwashing, cleaning, gardening, setting the table, chores around the classroom, preparing foods, and learning to help with home activities. This program is best limited to older trainable children, although even at a young age, trainable children may be exposed to such activities.

MOTOR DEVELOPMENT. Motor development is best stimulated through games, recreational activities, various manipulative skills, playing, outdoor diversions, and similar activities.

MUSIC. Music is a medium through which trainable children can learn many things. Singing, rhythm bands, musical games, and other activities help release energy and also serve as a form of expression and a socializing influence. Language is sometimes fostered through putting words to music and through group choral experiences. The concepts of sequence and memory can also be developed through music.

STRATEGIES FOR TEACHING SKILLS TO THE TRAINABLE MENTALLY RETARDED

The special problems of the trainable mentally retarded child have stimulated a number of special teaching techniques, including the principles made popular by the American psychologist B. F. Skinner and further developed by Bijou (1966) and by Neisworth and Smith (1973). Those principles have had a multitude of applications in the training of retarded children in the last decade. Since those techniques do not necessarily require language skills or communication in order to work, they are especially valuable for noncommunicative children. The basic principle of operant conditioning, as proposed by Skinner, is that the child's behavior is determined by how the environment responds to it. Behavior that is rewarded will be repeated. Behaviors that do not receive positive reinforcement will gradually drop out of the response repertoire of the child (Skinner, 1953).

The educational strategy is to arrange the environment so that the particular behavior that you wish the child to repeat will occur. When the desired behavior does occur, then it receives a positive reward in terms of food, praise, a token, or some other symbol of recognition. The undesirable, or even actively obnoxious, behavior should go unresponded to, if at all possible.

There is a rather natural tendency to scold the child for whining or clinging to an adult, but the correct response according to Skinnerian theory is to pay no attention to the behavior that you do *not* wish the child to show in the future, while giving attention and other reinforcement to desirable behavior. In most instances, even the disturbed or moderately retarded child begins to respond with more socially constructive behavior if such procedures are followed consistently by the caretaker or teacher.

The applied analysis of behavior (behavior shaping and behavior modification) is used extensively in shaping or modifying habits of self-help. Detailed programs on how to teach toilet training, dressing, undressing, eating, and sleeping have been developed. The teaching of language and other skills for the retarded is developed effectively through the use of behavior modification (operant) techniques. The techniques are available through many publications—by Thompson and Grabowski (1972) for behavior modification in general and by Neisworth and Smith (1973) for the mentally retarded specifically. Teachers and parents of the trainable mentally retarded find such techniques very helpful. Further elaboration of task analysis and behavior modification is made in Chapter 12.

PARENT EDUCATION

In recent years an attempt has been made to bring the parents increasingly into the educational program. Such programs can aid parents in helping the child develop and also in giving the family support through the crises they face during and after the first discovery that their child is seriously handicapped. In that matter, the following are two typical parental statements.

> Some of you know what it's like to look forward to the birth of your first child with eagerness and anticipation, a child with whom to share your world and your life and then be told after the birth that your hopes and expectations have just been shattered by some chromosomal accident. It is a grief process because there is real grief over the loss of the child you expected and grief over the devastation of your dreams and hopes. . . . (Martz, 1964, pp. 34–35)

And from another parent—

> To be told is devastating and all the books on it paint such a bleak picture. It's natural to be scared, afraid of pitying the child. We all have a

fleeting wish that the child will die. It's a normal, healthy reaction. It is fear of the unknown. (Mills, 1974, p. 10)

The parents need counseling and support also as the handicapped child develops, and the family recognizes the continuous care it must provide a child destined to be partially dependent all of his or her life (Farber, 1975).

Rynders and Horrobin (1975) have described a home-training program in which parents were given specific lessons on strengthening the communication skills of their Down's syndrome infants. The mothers in the program spent six weeks with the university staff for instruction and then embarked on a schedule of tutoring their children for one hour a day. In addition, there were semiweekly home visits by the staff to see how the parents were proceeding.

The basis of the program for parents is to specify, in sufficient detail, procedures that the parents can follow to carry out the lessons as games or fun with their child. Too often, parents, in frustration with the slow development of their handicapped child, may give up, and the child then does not even have a chance to develop to the best of his limited capabilities.

The principles listed by the program as fundamental to the activity represent well-accepted ideas.

1. Each activity should engage the child and mother in affectionate, focused, sensory-motor interaction.
2. Each activity should engage mother and child in sensory-motor activity and require, at the same time, that the mother talk with her child about the activities.
3. The program teaches mothers to use a hierarchy of teaching strategies.
4. A child should be exposed systematically to the fact that three-dimensional objects, photographs of the objects, and their printed label have related meaning.
5. When the mother is asked to work with her own child for an hour each day, she may be able to involve normal preschool children in the lesson so as to minimize the risk of jealousy.
6. One of the crucial considerations in a maternal tutoring program is to insure that sufficient structure guides the mother's activity in the execution of curricular principles but at the same time does not stifle her unique maternal style.
7. Capitalize on the reinforcement value of relative novelty by pairing every lesson in all possible level combinations.

The authors reported gains in concept formation and expressive language compared with Down's syndrome children who were not enrolled in the program. This is not to say that those youngsters have

improved to the point of becoming normal or average children. What
it does mean is that there are significant improvements in their attitudes, their learning capabilities, and their approach to the world.
Such improvements prepare them for further training toward self-
sufficiency in adulthood.

Lillie (1974) summarizes the general objectives of working with
parents of moderately to severely handicapped children.

1. *Social and emotional support.* To reduce anxieties caused by guilt
   feelings and feelings of inadequacy in the family, and to provide
   socially stimulating activities which increase positive feelings about
   the family unit as well as the parents' feelings about themselves as
   competent parents.
2. *Exchanging information.* (a) Providing parents with an understanding
   of the rationale, objectives, and activities of the program in which
   their child is enrolled; (b) developing an understanding of the continuous growth and development of the child as they apply to the
   child's interactions in the home; and (c) providing the project personnel with background information on the child to facilitate the effectiveness of the Center program.
3. *Parent participation.* The assumption is that by productively utilizing
   the parents in activities such as being a teacher aide, the parents' feelings of self-worth will be enhanced, their understanding of children
   will increase, and a larger repertoire of experience and activity for the
   parents to draw upon for interaction with their own child will be developed.
4. *Child interactions.* Training parents to become more effective child
   rearers. To facilitate parent-child interaction, your program should
   provide opportunities for parents to develop skills in (a) general child
   rearing practices; (b) promoting and fostering social and emotional
   development; (c) utilizing and optimizing everyday experience; (d)
   fostering and encouraging language growth; and (e) utilizing effectively the community resources available to assist the child in learning activities. (pp. 4–5)

Summary

1. The history of the education of the mentally retarded began
around 1850 when a residential school was developed in 1848. Following that, (a) institutions were developed in many states, (b) special
classes were organized in the public schools 50 years later, around
1900, (c) classes for trainable children were developed around 1950,
again 50 years later, and (d) since then the emphasis has been on deinstitutionalization, community provisions, normalization, and mainstreaming.

2. The educable retarded child develops in mental and educational achievements at about one-half to three-fourths the normal rate but may be expected at maturity, given proper education, to be occupationally, partially, or totally, self-sufficient and socially adequate, having learned academic skills between the first- and the sixth-grade levels.

3. The general characteristics of the educable mentally retarded child that call for special education adaptations are: (a) a limited memory, caused by failure to insert experiences in the memory bank in the first place, and a limited capability for rehearsal of ideas, (b) a lessened capability to use language to describe temporal or causal relationships, (c) special difficulties in arithmetic reasoning, and (d) short attention span and limited frustration tolerance developed, in some measure, from a long history of failure experiences.

4. The families of the educable mentally retarded child are, in most instances, traditionally disadvantaged economically and possess limited resources to aid in the total educational program without special help. The families of the trainable mentally retarded child come from all socioeconomic levels.

5. The philosophy that the handicapped child should be placed in the *least restrictive alternative* (closest to the normal pattern as is feasible) currently guides special education programs of the educable retarded, many of whom are in public schools in regular classes and resource rooms or are in special classes most or part of the time.

6. The usual curriculum for educable mentally retarded children follows the program of the regular grades when mainstreamed, with supporting help in the academic subjects.

7. In the special class the program emphasizes social learning that explicitly teaches life experiences, such as the need for social cooperation, in addition to the academic subjects.

8. The increasing importance of the early environment on the young child has led to the expansion of preschool programs designed for prevention as well as remediation of the retarded.

9. Educational goals for the trainable mentally retarded children include self-care, social skills, and some degree of economic usefulness.

10. A wide variety of placements for trainable mentally retarded children are currently available. They include (a) residential institutions, (b) community-based programs, (c) public school programs, (d) group homes, and (e) sheltered workshops.

11. Specific learning procedures based on task analysis and operant conditioning have been of much value in the teaching of basic skills to trainable mentally retarded children. Breaking down complex tasks into their simplest parts has helped trainable retarded individuals to learn economically useful work.

12. Parents have been included much more frequently in the treatment programs for the trainable mentally retarded through counseling and direct instruction on how to teach their child at home.

References

BALLER, W. 1936. "A Study of the Present Social Status of a Group of Adults Who, When They Were in Elementary Schools, Were Classified as Mentally Deficient." *Genetic Psychology Monographs* 18: 165–244.

BALLER, W., O. CHARLES, AND E. MILLER. 1967. "Midlife Attainment of the Mentally Retarded: A Longitudinal Study." *Genetic Psychology Monographs* 75: 235–329.

BAUMEISTER, A. A., AND E. BUTTERFIELD. 1970. *Residential Facilities for the Mentally Retarded.* Chicago: Aldine Publishing Co.

BERGMAN, J. S., ED. 1975. *Community Homes for the Retarded.* Lexington, Mass.: Lexington Books.

BIJOU, S. W. 1966. "A Functional Analysis of Retarded Development." In N. R. Ellis, ed., *International Review of Research in Mental Retardation,* vol. I. New York: Academic Press. Pp. 1–19.

BLESSING, K. R. 1964. "An Investigation of a Psycholinguistic Deficit in Mentally Retarded Children: Detection, Remediation and Related Variables." Unpublished doctoral dissertation. University of Wisconsin.

CAWLEY, J. F., AND S. J. VITELLO. 1972. "A Model for Arithmetical Programming for Handicapped Children: A Beginning." *Exceptional Children* 39 (October): 101–110.

CEGELKA, P. A., AND W. CEGELKA. 1970. "A Review of Research: Reading and the Educable Mentally Handicapped." *Exceptional Children* 37 (November): 187–200.

CHANNING, A. 1932. *Employment of Mentally Deficient Boys and Girls.* Department of Labor, Bureau Publication No. 210. Washington, D.C.: U.S. Government Printing Office.

CHARLES, D. C. 1953. "Ability and Accomplishment of Persons Earlier Judged Mentally Deficient." *Genetic Psychology Monographs* 47: 3–71.

CROMER, R. F. 1974. "Receptive Language in the Mentally Retarded: Processes and Diagnostic Distinctions." In R. L. Schiefelbusch and L. L. Lloyd, eds., *Language Perspectives—Retardation, Acquisition, and Intervention.* Baltimore: University Park Press. Pp. 237–267.

DUNN, L. 1968. "Special Education for the Mildly Retarded: Is Much of It Justified?" *Exceptional Children* 35 (September): 5–24.

ELLIS, N. R. 1970. "Memory Processes in Retardates and Normals." In N. R. Ellis, ed., *International Review of Research in Mental Retardation,* vol. IV. New York: Academic Press. Pp. 1–32.

FARBER, B. 1975. "Family Adaptation to Severely Mentally Retarded Children." In M. Begab and S. Richardson, eds., *The Mentally Retarded and Society: A Social Science Perspective.* Baltimore: University Park Press. Pp. 247–256.

FARBER, B. 1968. *Mental Retardation: Its Social Context and Social Consequences.* Boston: Houghton Mifflin.

FRANCIS, R. J., AND L. RARICK. 1960. *Motor Characteristics of the Mentally Retarded.* Cooperative Research Monograph No. 1. Washington, D.C.: Department of Health, Education, and Welfare, U.S. Office of Education.

GALLAGHER, J. 1972. "The Special Education Contract for Mildly Handicapped Children." *Exceptional Children.* 38 (March): 527–535.

GILHOOL, T. K. 1973. "Education: An Inalienable Right." *Exceptional Children* 39 (May): 597–609.

GOLD, M. 1974. "Vocational Training." In J. Wortis, ed., *Mental Retardation and Developmental Disabilities,* vol. VII. New York: Brunner/Mazel.

GOLDSTEIN, H. 1974. *The Social Learning Curriculum.* Columbus, Ohio: Charles E. Merrill.

GOLDSTEIN, H. 1957. "Social Aspects of Mental Retardation." Unpublished doctoral dissertation. University of Illinois, Urbana.

GOLDSTEIN, H., J. MOSS, AND L. J. JORDAN. 1965. *The Efficacy of Special Class Training on the Development of Mentally Retarded Children.* Cooperative Research Project No. 619. Washington, D.C.: U.S. Office of Education.

GRAHAM, J. T., AND L. W. GRAHAM. 1971. "Language Behavior of the Mentally Retarded: Syntactic Characteristics." *American Journal of Mental Deficiency* 75 (March): 623–629.

GUNZBERG, H. C. 1974. "The Education of the Mentally Handicapped Child." In A. M. Clarke and A. D. B. Clarke, eds., *Mental Deficiency: The Changing Outlook.* London: Methuen and Company, Ltd. Pp. 653–668.

GUSKIN, S. L., AND H. H. SPICKER. 1968. "Educational Research in Mental Retardation." In N. R. Ellis, ed., *International Review of Research in Mental Retardation,* vol. III. New York: Academic Press. Pp. 217–278.

HANSEN, C. 1977. "Willowbrook." In J. Wortis, ed., *Mental Retardation and Developmental Disabilities.* New York: Brunner/Mazel. Pp. 6–45.

HEISS, W., AND G. MISCHIO. 1972. "Designing Curriculum for the Educably Mentally Retarded." In E. M. Meyen, G. A. Vergason, and R. J. Whelan, eds., *Strategies for Teaching Exceptional Children.* Denver: Love Publishing Co.

HENDERSON, R. A. 1957. "Factors in Commitment of Educable Mentally Handicapped Children to Illinois State Schools." Unpublished doctoral dissertation. University of Illinois, Urbana.

HEWETT, F. M. 1967. "Educational Engineering with Emotionally Disturbed Children." *Exceptional Children* 33 (March): 459–470.

INGRAM, C. P. 1935. *Education of the Slow-Learning Child.* Yonkers, New York: World Book.

ITARD, J. M. G. 1932. *The Wild Boy of Aveyron*. Translated from the French by G. Humphrey and M. Humphrey. New York: Appleton-Century-Crofts.

JOHNSON, G. O. 1950. "A Study of the Social Position of Mentally Handicapped Children in the Regular Grades." *American Journal of Mental Deficiency* 55 (July): 60–89.

JOHNSON, G., AND S. KIRK. 1950. "Are Mentally Handicapped Children Segregated in the Regular Grades?" *Exceptional Children* 17 (December): 65–68.

KARLIN, I. W., AND M. STRAZZULA. 1952. "Speech and Language Problems of Mentally Deficient Children." *Journal of Speech and Hearing Disorders* 17 (September): 286–294.

KAUFFMAN, J., AND J. PAYNE, EDS. 1975. *Mental Retardation: Introduction and Personal Perspectives*. Columbus, Ohio: Charles E. Merrill.

KAUFMAN, M., J. GOTTLIEB, J. AGARD, AND M. KUKIC. 1975. *Mainstreaming: Toward an Explication of the Construct*. Washington, D.C.: U.S. Office of Education.

KENNEDY, R. 1948. *The Social Adjustment of Morons in a Connecticut City*. Hartford, Conn.: Social Service Department, Mansfield-Southbury Training Schools.

KIRK, S. A. 1964. "Research in Education of the Mentally Retarded." In H. Stevens and R. Heber, eds., *Mental Retardation: A Review of Research*. Chicago: University of Chicago Press. Pp. 57–99.

KIRK, S. A., AND G. O. JOHNSON. 1951. *Educating the Retarded Child*. Boston: Houghton Mifflin.

KIRK, S. A., SR. J. M. KLIEBHAN, AND J. LERNER. 1978. *Teaching Reading to Slow and Disabled Learners*. Boston: Houghton Mifflin.

KIRK, S. A., AND F. E. LORD. 1974. *Exceptional Children: Educational Resources and Perspectives*. Boston: Houghton Mifflin.

KIRK, W. D. 1968. "Correlation Between Arithmetic Achievement and Performance on Piaget Tasks." *The Slow Learning Child* 15 (November): 89–101.

KOLSTOE, O. 1970. *Teaching Educably Mentally Retarded Children*. New York: Holt, Rinehart and Winston.

LAZERSON, M. 1975. "Educational Institutions and Mental Subnormality: Notes on Writing a History." In M. Begab and S. Richardson, eds., *The Mentally Retarded and Society: A Social Science Perspective*. Baltimore: University Park Press. Pp. 33–52.

LENNEBERG, E. H., I. A. NICHOLS, AND E. F. ROSENBERGER. 1964. "Primitive Stages of Language Development in Mongolism." In D. McK. Rioch and E. A. Weinstein, eds., *Disorders of Communication*. (Research publications of the Association for Research in Nervous and Mental Diseases, Vol. XLII.) Baltimore: Williams & Wilkins. Pp. 119–137.

LILLIE, D. 1974. "Dimensions in Parent Programs: An Overview." In J. Grim, ed., *Training Parents to Teach*. Chapel Hill: Technical Assistance Development System, University of North Carolina at Chapel Hill. Pp. 1–10.

LINDSLEY, O. R. 1964. "Can Deficiency Produce Specific Superiority: The Challenge of the Idiot-Savant." *Exceptional Children* 31 (December): 225–232.

MARTZ, H. 1974. "We Had Hoped . . ." *United Methodist Today* (January): 34–37.

MEYEN, E. L. 1972. "Preparation of Life Experience Units for Teaching the Educable Mentally Retarded." In E. M. Meyen, G. A. Vergason, and R. J. Whelan, eds., *Strategies for Teaching Exceptional Children*. Denver: Love Publishing Co. Pp. 200–222.

MILLS, D. 1974. "Things Are Looking Up for Down's Syndrome Children." *Seattle Times Magazine*. January 6: 8–10.

MORISHIMA, A., AND L. F. BROWN. 1977. "A Case Report of the Artistic Talent of an Artistic Idiot Savant." *Mental Retardation* 15(2): 32–36.

MORISHIMA, A., AND L. F. BROWN. 1976. "An Idiot Savant Case Report: A Retrospective View." *Mental Retardation* 13(4) 46–47.

MUELLER, M. W., AND J. O. SMITH. 1964. "The Stability of Language Age Modification." *American Journal of Mental Deficiency* 68 (January): 537–539.

NAREMORE, R., AND R. DEVER. 1975. "Language Performance of Educable Mentally Retarded and Normal Children at Five Age Levels." *Journal of Speech and Hearing Research* 18: 82–95.

NEISWORTH, J. T., AND R. M. SMITH. 1973. *Modifying Retarded Behavior*. Boston: Houghton Mifflin.

PERMENTER, N. 1973. "Retardate for a Week." *Journal of Rehabilitation* 39: 18–21, 41.

PHELPS, L., AND R. LUTZ. 1977. *Career Exploration and Preparation for the Special Needs Learner*. Boston: Allyn and Bacon.

PRESIDENT'S COMMITTEE ON MENTAL RETARDATION. 1975. *The Problem of Mental Retardation*. Washington, D.C.: U.S. Department of Health, Education, and Welfare, publication No. (OHO) 75-22003.

RARICK, L., AND J. H. WIDDOP. 1970. "The Physical Fitness and Motor Performance of Educable Mentally Retarded Children." *Exceptional Children* 36 (March): 509–520.

RYNDERS, J., AND J. HORROBIN. 1975. "Project EDGE: The University of Minnesota's Communication Stimulation Program for Down's Syndrome Infants." In J. Hellmuth, ed., *Exceptional Infant*. New York: Brunner/Mazel.

SCHEERENBERGER, R. C. 1976. "A Study of Public Residential Facilities." *Mental Retardation* 14 (February): 32–35.

SCOTTISH COUNCIL FOR RESEARCH IN EDUCATION. 1949. *The Trend of Scottish Intelligence*. London: University of London Press.

SEGUIN, E. 1866. *Idiocy: Its Treatment by the Physiological Method.* Reprinted 1907. New York: Teachers College, Columbia University.

SEMMEL, M. I., L. S. BARRITT, AND S. W. BENNETT. 1970. "Performance of EMR and Non-Retarded Children in a Modified Cloze Task." *American Journal of Mental Deficiency* 74 (March): 681–688.

SKINNER, B. F. 1953. *Science and Human Behavior.* New York: Free Press.

SMITH, J. O. 1962. *Effects of a Group Language Development Program Upon the Psycholinguistic Abilities of Educable Mental Retardates.* (Peabody College Special Education Monograph Series No. 1) Nashville, Tenn.: Peabody College.

SOLOMAN, A., AND R. PARGLE. 1967. "Demonstrating Physical Fitness Impairment in EMR." *Exceptional Children* 34 (November): 163–168.

THOMPSON, T., AND J. GRABOWSKI. 1972. *Behavior Modification of the Mentally Retarded.* New York: Oxford University Press.

WEINSTEIN, E. 1969. "The Development of Interpersonal Competence." In D. Goslin, ed., *Handbook of Socialization Theory and Practice.* Chicago: Rand McNally. Pp. 753–775.

WELCH, E. A. 1967. "The Effects of Segregated and Partially Integrated School Programs on Self-concept and Academic Achievement of Educable Mentally Retarded Children." *Exceptional Children* 34 (October): 93–100.

WOLFENSBERGER, W. 1972. *The Principle of Normalization in Human Services.* Toronto: National Institute on Mental Retardation.

WORLD HEALTH ORGANIZATION. 1968. *Organization of Services for the Mentally Retarded.* Fifteenth report of the WHO Expert Committee on Mental Health. (WHO Tech. Rep. Ser. 392.) Geneva.

ZEAMAN, D. 1973. "One Programmatic Approach to Retardation." In D. K. Routh, ed., *The Experimental Psychology of Mental Retardation.* Chicago: Aldine Publishing Co. Pp. 78–132.

ZIGLER, E., AND D. A. BALLA. 1977. "Impact of Institutional Experience on the Behavior and Development of Retarded Persons." *American Journal of Mental Deficiency* 82 (July): 1–11.

6

Individuals with hearing impairments may have difficulty hearing in one or both ears and in a limited number of cases may not hear at all. Professionals and laymen alike have used various terms: *hard of hearing, deaf, deafened, partially deaf,* and *partially hearing.* Most of those terms came into use as a means of differentiating some hearing-impaired children from others. *Deafened,* for instance, usually refers to someone who once had hearing, developed language and speech, and later became deaf. Such an individual's reactions in the field of learning and communication are quite different from those of a person who was born deaf and never learned to speak spontaneously or to communicate vocally.

As indicated in Chapter 2, the child with a hearing impairment is required to process information partly or totally through other sense channels and in a manner different from that of the child who has intact hearing. The manner of processing information differently and the degree to which such processing is done depend on the extent of hearing loss, the age at onset of the loss, the degree of intelligence, the type of hearing loss, the age at which remedial instruction begins, and the quality of instruction. There have evolved over the years different terms or labels to designate the variables that cause differences in manner and degree of information processing. The following section gives some definitions and classifications that have been found useful.

Definitions and classifications

Educators of hearing-impaired children have tried to classify children with different types of hearing handicaps. One of the classifications that has been used for many years was formulated by the Committee on Nomenclature of the Conference of Executives of American Schools for the Deaf (1938). The committee formulated the following classification:

> *The deaf:* Those in whom the sense of hearing is nonfunctional for the ordinary purposes of life. This general group is made up of two distinct classes based entirely on the time the loss of hearing occurred. These include: (a) *the congenitally deaf*—those who were born deaf, and (b) *the adventitiously deaf*—those who were born with normal hearing but in whom the sense of hearing became nonfunctional later through illness or accident.
> *The hard of hearing:* Those in whom the sense of hearing, although defective, is functional with or without a hearing aid. (p. 2)

Twenty years later Streng et al. (1958) rephrased the definition as follows:

> The child who is born with little or no hearing, or who has suffered the loss early in infancy before speech and language patterns are acquired, is said to be deaf. One who is born with normal hearing and reaches the age where he can produce and comprehend speech but subsequently loses his hearing is described as deafened. The hard of hearing are those with reduced hearing acuity either since birth or acquired at any time during life. (p. 9)

Current reference to the deaf or congenitally deaf and to the deafened or adventitiously deaf is made in these terms: (1) *prelingual deafness,* referring to those who were born deaf or who lost their hearing before speech and language were developed and (2) *postlingual deafness,* referring to those who lost their hearing after spontaneous speech and language had been developed.

In 1973 the Conference of Executives of American Schools for the Deaf appointed an ad hoc committee to redefine *deaf* and *hard of hearing* for educational purposes. Moores (1978) reports that the following definitions were adopted by the conference:

> A "deaf person" is one whose hearing is disabled to an extent (usually 70 dB ISO or greater) that precludes the understanding of speech through the ear alone, without or with the use of a hearing aid.
>
> A "hard of hearing" person is one whose hearing is disabled to an extent (usually 35 to 69 dB ISO) that makes difficult, but does not preclude, the understanding of speech through the ear alone, without or with a hearing aid. (p. 5)

DEGREES OF HEARING LOSS

Hearing loss is generally measured by an audiometer using standards agreed on internationally. The International Standard Organization (ISO), reported by Davis and Krantz (1964), or the American National Standards Institute (ANSI) describes the agreed-on standards. Hearing losses by those standards are measured by decibels (dB) indicating the degree of loss. For educational purposes it is necessary to judge the decibel loss after the child has been fitted with a hearing aid, since many children who have been classified as deaf by the ISO or ANSI standards become hard of hearing when aided by a hearing aid and given adequate training at an early age.

There are many classifications of children with impaired hearing using the decibel loss as a criterion. A practical classification was formulated by the Illinois Commission on Children in 1968; it is similar to the 1965 classification of the Committee on Conservation of

Hearing of the American Academy of Ophthalmology and Oto-

laryngology (Davis, 1970). The classifications of both organizations
are similar, but some of the terms used for each decibel loss are different. The first terms following are from the Illinois Commission
and those in parentheses are from the otolaryngology committee.
The five classifications are:

1. *Slight (mild)* hearing loss refers to losses of 27 to 40 decibels.
Children with such a loss require watching since they *may* have difficulty hearing distant sounds and *may* require preferential seating and
other services.

2. *Mild (moderate)* hearing loss refers to losses of 41 to 55 decibels. These children understand conversational speech at a distance of
3 to 5 feet, may miss some class discussion, and may require hearing
aids and other special educational services such as speech reading (lip
reading) and hearing conservation.

3. *Marked (moderately severe)* hearing loss is a loss of 56 to 70
decibels. These children can understand loud conversation with difficulty. They will require individual hearing aids and special educational services in the form of auditory training and generally some or
all the services required by hard-of-hearing children described later.
Their special needs are assessed by measures other than the audiometer.

4. *Severe (severe)* hearing losses are those of 71 to 90 decibels.
Such children have generally been classified as deaf since they can
only hear loud sounds at close distance. These children require intensive and special educational services in the form of individual hearing
aids, auditory training, language and speech training, lip reading, and
other services described later for hard-of-hearing and deaf children.
With proper special education some of these children become hard of
hearing instead of being deaf, and a part of their education is proc-
essed through the auditory sense. Their special needs are assessed by
other measures and observations.

5. *Extreme or profound (profound)* hearing losses are losses of 91
decibels or more on the ANSI standard. Such children are classified as
deaf although some of them are aware of loud sounds in the form of
vibrations. These children rely on vision rather than hearing for information processing. Speech and language do not develop without
intensive special instruction. The educational program for the deaf
described later is for such children.

The preceding classification by degrees of hearing loss, adapted
from the report of the Illinois Commission on Children (1968, p.
19), is one form of classification that attempts to categorize children
with hearing losses along a continuum of decibel losses (ANSI). Obviously the categories of slight, mild, marked, severe, and extreme

by the decibel criterion alone can only be used as a guideline in deciding on an educational program. The variables of age at onset of hearing loss, intelligence, type of hearing loss, and whether the measurement of loss is aided or unaided must be considered. Like the IQ for mentally retarded children, the decibel loss should be used only as one of several criteria since one child with a 75 decibel loss may converse orally, may use a telephone, and so forth, whereas another child with a similar decibel loss may function like a child with an extreme hearing loss.

CASE ILLUSTRATIONS

To illustrate the differences in development among children with different degrees of hearing loss, three brief case studies will be presented. In Figure 6.1 profiles of three children are shown, Sally, John, and Bill. It will be noticed in the profiles that all three children are 10 years old and that the profiles are similar in shape, but the intraindividual differences increase with the severity of hearing loss and with the age at onset of deafness. Sally is a hard-of-hearing child, John is a postlingual or deafened child, and Bill is a prelingual or deaf child.

SALLY. The upper profile in Figure 6.1 represents Sally, a child with a mild hearing loss of 45 decibels. It will be noticed from her profile that this hard-of-hearing child is 10 years of age and is physically (in terms of height, weight, and motor coordination) average. In mental ability and in social maturity, there appears to be no difference between her and the average child. In speech development Sally is slightly retarded in that she has some difficulty in articulation and requires speech remediation. Her language development and reading are only slightly retarded, while her achievement in arithmetic, spelling, and general information is approximately average. The only difference between Sally and an average child is a slight difficulty in speech development, language development, and reading.

Fortunately, this hard-of-hearing child has been fitted with a hearing aid and has received speech remediation. The only special education Sally has needed is some help in using her hearing aid, in speech remediation, and in speech reading. Otherwise, she is so much like the average child that she has functioned adequately in the regular classroom. An itinerant speech and hearing clinician had given her speech remediation, auditory training, and speech-reading lessons once a week for the first two years of her school career.

JOHN. The middle profile on the chart, labeled John, presents the developmental pattern of a child with a severe hearing loss. This

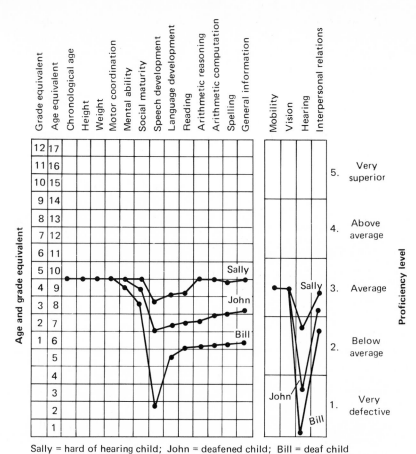

Sally = hard of hearing child; John = deafened child; Bill = deaf child

FIGURE 6.1
*Profiles of three children of
differing degrees of hearing loss*

child was born with normal hearing but at the age of four suffered a serious hearing loss in both ears. He is classified as postlingually deaf. Although he is approximately normal in intelligence, social maturity, and physical ability, his speech and language have not developed normally. On the audiometric test he had a 75 decibel loss even after being fitted with a hearing aid. Fortunately, however, he had learned to talk quite normally before his loss of hearing and had developed considerable language ability, so that now he can still learn through the auditory channel with the help of a hearing aid. His retardation in language results from his not having developed normally in that area since the age of 4. At present his language is below the 7-year (second-grade) level, and his reading and other academic abilities are also around the second-grade level. The hearing loss has interfered considerably with his educational progress, but with the use of hearing aids, speech habilitation, and other specialized techniques, he is progressing satisfactorily, although at an understandably slower rate than Sally.

BILL. The bottom profile is of a child with an extreme hearing loss, which existed at birth. Bill has never heard the spoken word. A hearing aid might alert his attention to environmental sounds but will not help sufficiently in the development of speech and language. Because of the severity of Bill's hearing loss, tested at 90 decibels, it is necessary to place him in a class for the deaf or to offer him intensive tutorial service if he is integrated in a regular class.

In speech development Bill is still quite defective. He does not talk as well as a child of 2½ years, even though he has had some instruction. His language development is at about the 5-year level. In reading and other academic subjects he is at the beginning first-grade level even though he is now 10 years of age. We would consider Bill about four years retarded educationally.

Although the three profiles all represent auditorily impaired children, they differ considerably. They show the progress such children make, depending on the age at onset of deafness, the degree of hearing loss, and the amount of intensive instruction that has been received during the growing stages.

PREVALENCE OF HEARING LOSS

The prevalence of defective hearing is difficult to estimate although many surveys have been made. The rate of occurrence appears to be partly dependent on the method of testing, the criteria used by the investigator, the community, and other factors. For example, Farber (1959) found that in the literature estimates ranged from 1.5 to 5 percent of the school population. Yet in Farber's own study the teachers in Illinois reported only 0.48 percent of the school population as having hearing losses. That figure includes children already placed in classes for the hard of hearing and probably represents the prevalence of moderate and severe hearing losses that are large enough for teachers to recognize. Mild hearing losses are not readily detected by teachers.

According to Silverman (1957) a rough estimate of the prevalence of hearing loss is that 5 percent of school children have a hearing impairment, but about 5 in 1,000 will require special educational attention.

The Illinois Commission on Children (1968), after reviewing studies on prevalence, estimated that 1 to 3 percent of school children have a hearing impairment severe enough to warrant medical or special educational attention. The commission estimated that 1 child in 1,000 is deaf.

Hull et al. (1976) tested 38,568 children in grades one to twelve with a pure-tone audiometer. They stated that the percentage of impairments is only half of the 5 percent, which is most commonly quoted (p. 137). They estimated that 2.6 percent of children with hearing losses amounts to 1,326,000 children in the United States who have hearing impairments of 30 to 100 decibels. In addition, "both sexes showed progressively lower percentages of hearing loss as a function of increasing grade level" (p. 135). The Annual Directory of Services for the Deaf in the United States (Craig and Craig, 1977, p. 138) reported a total of 44,949 children enrolled in residential and day classes for the deaf in the United States in October 1976.

From the preceding figures it should be obvious that only a small proportion of hearing-impaired children are enrolled in residential and day schools and in classes for the deaf. The rest are in regular classrooms being served by speech clinicians and by itinerant and resource teachers for children with minor and moderate hearing losses.

CAUSES OF HEARING IMPAIRMENTS

Hearing impairment is a symptom of a defect in the hearing mechanism. Many of the studies on the causes of deafness have been made on the case records of children admitted to residential schools. Thus we find studies from different residential schools that tend to list the percentage of children in each etiological category. The statistics are for the severe and extreme hearing impairments and generally do not include minor hearing losses.

The Office of Demographic Studies of Gallaudet College has solicited information from the records of 555 educational programs for the deaf (Reis, 1973). It includes statements on the etiology for 41,109 students, approximately 85 percent of the students enrolled in special educational programs. Table 6.1 presents the prenatal and the postnatal causes of hearing losses. It will be noted from the table that: (1) maternal rubella (German measles), heredity, prematurity, and Rh incompatibility are the most commonly reported prenatal causes and (2) the most commonly reported postnatal cause is meningitis.

The etiological factors—heredity, maternal rubella, prematurity, Rh incompatibility, meningitis, other etiologies, and cause unknown—will be discussed briefly.

HEREDITY. Interest in the inheritance of deafness stems from two social questions: (1) Should the deaf intermarry and bear children? (2) Should relatives of the deaf bear children? The data on heredity are obtained from a study of children of deaf parents and also of deaf relatives of deaf children. Vernon (1968b) reported that 5.4 percent of deaf children had both parents who were deaf and 26.4 percent had a deaf relative.

Kloepfer, Laquaite, and McLaurin (1970) estimate that 46 to 60 percent of all cases of severe hearing loss are genetically determined. After surveying the etiological factors in deafness, Moores (1978) concluded that approximately 50 percent of deafness is hereditary.

MATERNAL RUBELLA. German measles (rubella) (also discussed under mental retardation in Chapter 5) afflicting the mother during the first three months of pregnancy often has quite serious effects on the child. In a Johns Hopkins study Hardy (1968) reported on 199 children who were diagnosed as having been subjected to the rubella

TABLE 6.1

Reported causes of deafness for students enrolled in educational programs in the United States, 1970–1971

Causes [1]	Number of students						
	All ages	Under 5 years	5–7 years	8–10 years	11–13 years	14–16 years	17 years and older
	41,109	2,527	10,216	7,529	9,509	6,759	4,569
	Number per 1,000 students [2]						
PRENATAL							
Maternal rubella	147.8	212.1	361.9	57.9	106.2	28.7	44.6
Heredity	74.8	79.1	53.5	81.8	74.6	92.6	82.1
Prematurity	53.7	52.2	45.4	54.7	58.1	66.4	43.3
Rh incompatibility	34.1	34.4	22.6	35.1	34.3	44.1	42.9
Other [1]	79.8	85.0	64.6	89.2	81.2	90.3	76.1
Unknown	188.3	230.3	149.7	196.7	189.5	193.4	227.6
Not reported	112.5	92.2	83.6	121.5	126.4	127.2	122.6
POSTNATAL							
Meningitis	49.1	72.4	40.8	59.1	44.1	45.6	53.6
Other [1]	132.3	83.9	81.5	147.7	141.7	176.2	162.6
Unknown	49.7	37.6	36.9	56.4	53.2	55.9	57.3
Not reported	134.0	79.9	115.0	156.3	144.5	142.5	134.8

Source: Adapted from Reis, 1973, pp. 3–4.

[1] Only etiologies with an incidence of more than 30 per 1,000 (3%) are included. Remaining etiologies are classified in the *other* category.

[2] Each column sums to more than 1,000 because, for about 5% of the students, more than one cause of hearing-impaired loss was reported.

virus prenatally during the 1964–1965 rubella epidemic. The distribution of defects was found to be 50 percent auditory, 20 percent visual, and 35 percent cardiac. The National Communicable Disease Center (Hicks, 1970) reported that the epidemic caused deafness in eight thousand children. Northern and Downs (1974, p. 6) stated that ten to twenty thousand children were affected in the two epidemics of rubella in 1958 and 1964.

In a study on the causes of deafness in students enrolled in educational programs for 1970–1971, Reis (1973) reported that of 1,000 cases of deafness, there were 361.9 cases in children between ages 5 and 7 who were born in 1964–1965 during the rubella epidemic. That is the highest incidence of hearing impairment in any age group shown in Table 6.1. Fortunately since the epidemic, a vaccine has been found which will prevent maternal rubella. It is expected that the incidence of deafness due to maternal rubella will decrease.

PREMATURITY. Children born with birth weights of 5 pounds, 8 ounces or less are usually considered premature. Prematurity has been listed as a cause of deafness in 53.7 out of 1,000 children enrolled in schools for the deaf (Reis, 1973). It has also been listed as a cause of mental retardation and blindness. Some of the children whose deafness was attributed to rubella or to the Rh factor were also reported as being premature. Hence prematurity may occur in conjunction with other etiologies.

Rh INCOMPATIBILITY. Rh incompatibility has been explained in Chapter 5 on mental retardation and is reported by Vernon (1968b) to account for 3.7 percent of cases of deafness. Reis (1973) also reports 3.4 percent of cases result from the condition. There are also other blood incompatibilities that have similar effects on hearing.

MENINGITIS. According to Vernon (1968b), 8.1 percent of deaf children acquired deafness after birth as a result of meningitis. Reis (1973) reports 4.9 percent for this etiology. Of the postnatal or exogenous causes of deafness, meningitis has headed the list. Moores (1978) finds that the percentage of deafness due to meningitis has been decreasing, possibly due to antibiotics and chemotherapy.

CAUSE UNKNOWN AND OTHER ETIOLOGIES. It is surprising that in surveys of causes of deafness, approximately 30 percent are listed as cause unknown. Other etiologies include maternal infections affecting the fetus and childhood diseases such as measles and otitis media.

Identification and measurement of hearing loss

The identification of hearing loss is a technical problem. Whereas severe or extreme loss is rather easily recognized, children with slight or mild hearing loss are hard to identify. Teachers may think that the child just does not pay attention or is mentally handicapped or stubborn.

It is important for a classroom teacher to be aware of some of the symptoms that may be misinterpreted, such as those displayed by the child who (1) ignores, confuses, or does not comply with directions, (2) daydreams a great deal, (3) is educationally retarded, (4) has a slight speech defect, (5) is "lazy," (6) seems dull, or (7) is always asking, "What?"

In fulfilling its responsibilities to hearing-impaired children, the school has to (1) identify those needing help, (2) see that their problems are adequately diagnosed and that whatever medical treatment is necessary is given, and (3) provide an appropriate educational program.

The first problem the school faces is that of locating the children needing help. Often a hearing loss of 40 or 50 decibels is not detected by parents or teachers since the child hears conversational speech and probably learned to talk at an average age. Sometimes deviant behavior is not recognized as related to hearing loss but is attributed to other factors (such as low intelligence, emotional problems, and lack of interest), which may or may not be pertinent. A systematic attempt to find the auditorily handicapped includes a screening test for all children and an individual test for those who fail to pass the screening test.

Screening procedures in schools involve either individual or group testing of children in kindergarten to third grade and periodic examinations in the higher grades. Generally, a sweep-check audiometric test devised for rapid screening of hearing impairments is administered by the school nurse or an audiologist, a hearing specialist. Those suspected of having a hearing loss receive a more complete audiometric test. Such screening procedures are referred to as *identification audiometry* and are utilized in schools to select the 2 to 5 percent of children who should be referred to otologists and audiologists for more exact diagnosis. Many children who indicate a hearing loss on the screening test are found not to have a loss when given the more thorough pure-tone test (threshold testing). Inattention, poor understanding, and other factors sometimes make a child respond poorly to group or individual sweep-check testing.

Children suspected of having a hearing loss are referred to an otologist, who determines the exact nature of the disability and, if possible, administers medical treatment. For example, he may find wax in the ears, infected adenoids or tonsils, or some other abnormality that can be corrected.

The steps in identification diagnosis and services may be summarized as follows:

1. preliminary screening of children
2. threshold testing and, if hearing handicap is found, referral for otological examination
3. otological examination and medical treatment if indicated
4. audiological examination to include special tests and hearing-aid evaluation
5. psychoeducational evaluation and special educational services

The procedure for identification is necessary in preschools and at the school-age level for children with slight and mild hearing losses. For the marked to profound losses, the impairment is detected by the parents at the age at which children learn to respond and talk. The more severe the hearing loss, the earlier it is detected by observation.

Informal tests are used by teachers and psychological examiners to obtain a crude measure of hearing ability. These informal tests include conversation at twenty feet, whisper tests, and watch-tick tests. The most accurate method of testing, however, is with electric audiometers, which produce pure tones of controlled intensity and frequency or present live or recorded speech signals of known intensity.

Types of hearing defects

Because of the complicated structure and functioning of the ear (see Figure 6.2), defects in hearing may occur in many different forms. Basically the defects are of two main types: (1) conductive losses and (2) sensorineural or perceptive losses.

A *conductive hearing loss* is one that reduces the intensity of sound reaching the inner ear, where the auditory nerve begins. To reach the *inner ear,* sound waves in the air must pass through the external canal of the *outer ear* to the eardrum, where the vibrations are picked up by a series of bonelike structures in the *middle ear* and passed on to the *inner ear.* The sequence of vibrations may be blocked anywhere along the line. Wax or malformations may block the external canal; the eardrum may be broken or unable to vibrate; the movement of the bones in the middle ear may be obstructed. Any condition hindering the sequence of vibrations or preventing them from reaching the auditory nerve may cause a conduction loss.

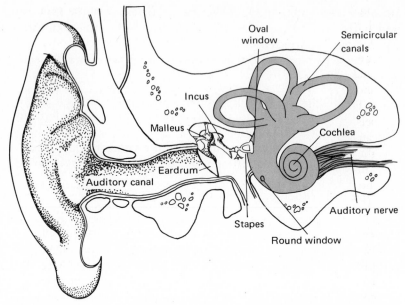

Source: From P. Lindsay and D. Norman, *Human Information Processing* (New York: Academic Press, 1972), p. 221.

Note: The outer ear consists of the auditory canal. The middle ear consists of the eardrum, malleus (hammer), incus (anvil), and stapes (stirrup). The inner ear consists of the round window, the oval window, the semicircular canals, and the cochlea. Any interference in the transmission of sound from the auditory canal to the inner ear causes a conductive hearing loss. When damage has been sustained by the end organ, cochlear hair cells, or the auditory nerve, the hearing loss is considered sensorineural.

That type of defect seldom causes a hearing loss of more than 60 or 70 decibels since the vibrations carried by the bone to the inner ear will still be available. The audiometer has a bone-conduction receiver as well as an air-conduction receiver and can therefore measure the ability of the individual to pick up sound through bone conduction.

These two dimensions—frequency and intensity—are necessary in evaluating a hearing loss. *Frequency* refers to the number of vibrations (or cycles) per second of a given sound wave: the greater the frequency, the higher the pitch. An individual may have difficulty hearing sounds of certain frequencies, whereas those of other frequencies are quite audible to him. For the understanding of speech, the most important frequencies range between 500 and 2,000 hertz (a *hertz* is a unit in measuring vibrations per second). *Intensity,* on the other hand, refers to the relative loudness of a sound.

To determine an individual's level of hearing, it is necessary to know what intensity of sound is needed to cross the threshold of hearing at each of the frequency levels. The frequencies generally tested on audiometric examinations include 125, 250, 500, 1,000, 2,000, 4,000, and 8,000 hertz. Decibel loss refers to a pure-tone average of 500, 1,000, and 2,000 hertz in the better ear. The pure-tone audiometer presents the individual with sounds of known intensity and frequency and asks for a response when he or she hears the tone. The degree of hearing loss is recorded on an audiogram in decibels ranging from −10 to 120. The hearing in each ear is plotted separately. For example, a hearing level of 30 decibels would indicate a slight hearing loss; a level of 91 decibels indicates profound hearing loss. In addition to pure-tone audiometry procedures, audiologists use the speech reception threshold (SRT) and speech discrimination tests (PB Max. %) for the purpose of determining the ability of the child to understand speech.

Routine audiometric procedures cannot be used with infants and young children, but clinical testing of young children can be accomplished by electrodermal and other procedures in audiology clinics, including electroencephalogram audiometry and operant-conditioning audiometry. Those techniques are often used for other hard-to-test individuals such as those severely retarded mentally and the psychotic (Bricker, Bricker, and Larsen, 1968). Often hearing loss in a young child is detected by informal means such as observing behavior and ability to react to sounds in the environment or by the more structured but informal methods described by Di Carlo (1964). Does the child respond to music? to noise? or to voices?

Methods of examining the hearing of young children and of hard-to-test children like the mentally retarded can be found in numerous books such as one by Northern and Downs (1974).

In addition to audiometric testing, children with impaired hearing require formal and informal tests to determine: (1) their intellectual level in tests not using hearing, (2) their level of linguistic and communication development, (3) the level of achievement by school-age children in academic subjects, and (4) social and emotional functioning.

Figure 6.3 shows the audiogram of a child with a conductive hearing loss. On the audiometer the child heard airborne sounds at the −40 to −50 decibel level at all frequencies in the better ear (the left). When using a bone-conduction receiver, however, the child responded within the normal range; the difficulty was a defect or obstruction in the outer or middle ear rather than a defect in the sensory nerve of the inner ear. As might be expected, an audiogram of this type of hearing loss is fairly even at all frequencies.

A *sensorineural* or *perceptive hearing loss* is caused by defects of the

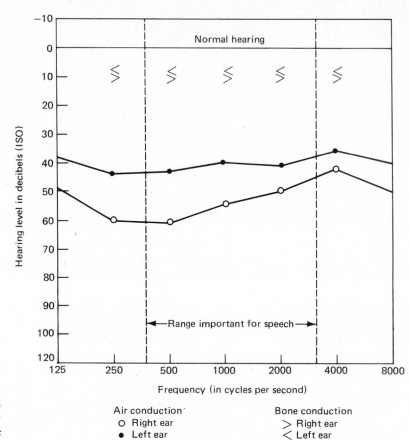

FIGURE 6.3
Audiogram of a child with a
conductive hearing loss

Air conduction
O Right ear
● Left ear

Bone conduction
> Right ear
< Left ear

inner ear or of the auditory nerve transmitting the impulse to the brain. Sensorineural hearing loss may be complete or partial and may affect some frequencies (especially the high ones) more than others. Thus in Figure 6.4 the audiogram shows profound loss at the high frequencies and severe loss at the frequencies below 1,000 cycles. High-frequency loss is often associated with sensorineural deafness. The bone-conduction receiver in this case gave no better reception since the defect was in the nerve, not in the mechanism that carried the vibrations to the nerve.

The proper diagnosis of a hearing defect is a very important and highly technical matter. The treatment, the educational program, and even the selection of a hearing aid are dependent on it. It is obvious, for example, that a bone-conduction hearing aid would not help the child whose audiogram is presented in Figure 6.4, whereas it probably would help the child represented in Figure 6.3.

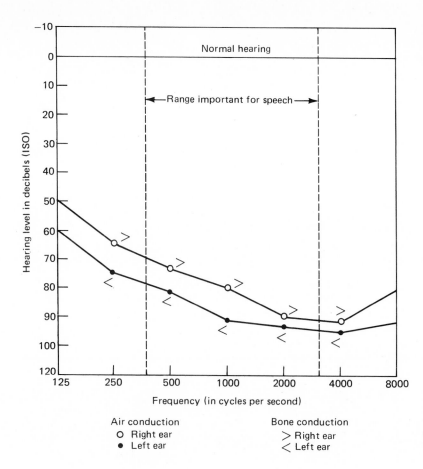

Air conduction
O Right ear
● Left ear

Bone conduction
> Right ear
< Left ear

FIGURE 6.4
Audiogram of a child with a sensorineural or perceptive hearing loss

Social, academic, and occupational adjustment

The inability to hear and the consequent interference with normal communication have effects on interpersonal relations and adjustment. This section will deal with the social, academic, and occupational status and achievements of severely hearing-impaired children and adults.

SOCIAL AND PERSONAL ADJUSTMENT

Studies on the social and personal adjustment of deaf children have dealt with five major dimensions: (1) social maturity, (2) social interaction with peers, (3) self-concept, (4) personality, and (5) extent of emotional disturbance. Meadow (1975) has reviewed the studies on the social and psychological adjustment of deaf children and has formulated some generalizations.

SOCIAL MATURITY. For the social maturity dimension the Vineland Social Maturity Scale has been used by a number of investigators over a period of forty years. They have all concluded (1) that deaf children score lower than hearing children do on the scale and (2) that deaf children of deaf parents score higher than do deaf children of hearing parents. These and other studies have indicated that the immaturity and dependence of deaf children are related to the reduced communicative ability of the child, to child-rearing practices, to dependence fostered by parents of deaf children, and to structured residential life.

SOCIAL INTERACTION. As would be expected from the language and communication handicap, deaf children have fewer social interactions than do hearing children. Although most studies arrive at that conclusion, Van Lieshout (1973) found other results. By a time-sampling technique he observed and compared the peer interactions of thirty-four prelingually deaf and thirty-four hearing children at age 5. He found that in verbal interaction, the hearing children had more social interactions than deaf children had, but deaf children had more physical contacts than hearing children. Meadow concluded that the inability to communicate future plans with peers is the major reason for the reduced social interaction of deaf children.

SELF-CONCEPT. Studies of self-concept and self-image of deaf children indicate that their ideas about themselves are inaccurate. They seem to have inflated ideas about what others think of them and about their capabilities. Deaf children of deaf parents appear to have more positive ideas about themselves than do deaf children of hearing parents. In addition, attendance of deaf children of hearing parents in residential schools seems to enhance their self-concept as compared with that of similar children attending day schools. Meadow interprets those results as suggesting that the opportunities offered deaf children in the protective environment of a residential school enhance positive feelings about themselves.

PERSONALITY. In spite of the difficulty of assessing the personalities of deaf children, numerous studies in this area were reported by Meadow (1975). She found that the many inventories that have been used tended to show more adjustment problems among the deaf. She reported that the deaf have been found to "exhibit characteristics of rigidity, egocentricity, absence of creativity, absence of inner controls, impulsiveness, suggestibility, and lack of empathy" (p. 498).

EMOTIONAL DISTURBANCE. The incidence of severe emotional disturbance and severe behavioral disorders appears to be the same among the deaf population as among hearing individuals. The criterion used by researchers for that conclusion is the incidence of hospitalized patients and of diagnosed schizophrenia in the population. The number of minor behavior problems reported in schools for the deaf, however, appears to be greater than that reported in the general population of children.

In summarizing the general area of social development of deaf children, Meadow (1975) concludes:

> Socialization and social development take place primarily through verbal communication. Rules of behavior, and the reasons for the rules, are transmitted verbally. Children who do not understand what is expected of them, and why, are at a major disadvantage. It is not surprising that they are found to have more than their share of psychological problems. The surprising thing is that the human organism can adapt as well as most deaf children do. (p. 499)

ACADEMIC ACHIEVEMENT

As indicated earlier, the major effect of hearing impairment is on language and related achievements such as reading. The effect the handicap of language has on reading achievement is presented in the numerous surveys that have been made on the deaf child population.

Pugh (1946) studied the reading ability of deaf children in a large number of schools for the deaf by administering the Iowa Silent Reading Test and the Durrell-Sullivan Reading Achievement Test. She found that as a group the deaf are notably retarded at the older ages, less so at the younger ages. That is, they become more and more retarded as the language requirements for understanding increase in complexity. Pugh found a small population of deaf children, however, reading at a high level, exceeding the norms for hearing children of their age.

The Office of Demographic Studies at Gallaudet College annually administers the Stanford Achievement Test to hearing-impaired children. Gentile (1973) reports the results of testing thousands of them in residential and day schools throughout the country. Gentile's results showed that at age 8, the hearing-impaired children scored at about grade two in both reading and arithmetic computation. At age

17, the children scored at about grade four in reading and at grade six in arithmetic computation. Similar to Pugh's results twenty years earlier, his survey shows that the hearing impaired are markedly retarded in reading as compared with normally hearing children of the same chronological age.

Using the Stanford Achievement Test, Jesema (1975) analyzed the scores of 6,873 children, ages 6 to 19 attending special education programs; he found, "in a ten-year period from age 8 to age 18 the average hearing-impaired student increases his vocabulary score only as much as the average normal-hearing student does between the beginning of kindergarten and the latter part of the second grade" (p. 3). In reading comprehension 14-year-old children read at the third-grade level. In arithmetic computation, a subject not entirely dependent on language, 10-year-old deaf children tested at the third-grade-level. Jesema also studied other demographic characteristics and found:

1. When hearing loss occurred after age 3, reading achievement was higher than for those whose hearing loss occurred earlier.

2. Those hearing-impaired students who were reported as having an inherited hearing loss showed superior educational achievement compared with others, with the exception of those whose loss of hearing was attributed to mumps and otitis media. Those latter conditions tend to occur at a later age when some language has been developed.

3. Using the five classifications of hearing losses listed on page 183, it was found that the less severe the hearing loss, the greater the achievement.

Trybus and Karchmer (1977) reported the progress in reading and arithmetic of 1,543 hearing-impaired students over a three-year period. They found: (1) in reading comprehension at age 9, the students tested at the second-grade level, and at age 20 they tested at about the fifth-grade level; (2) they progressed at approximately one-third of a year on the average for each age group in reading comprehension.

In general studies on the academic achievement of hearing-impaired children have not reported much improvement over the years. The majority of deaf children are educationally retarded, with most not exceeding the fourth and fifth grades by the time they reach adulthood. Approximately 10 percent, however, have been able to achieve in academic subjects, including reading at the level of the average hearing child. It appears that, as yet, we have not found the teaching procedures that would assist the hearing-impaired child to reach the level of a Hofsteater (see p. 212) and others like him in reading and in other school subjects.

Deaf adults adjust to virtually any kind of job that does not have as a prerequisite the ability to hear. The deaf are found in professions, in managerial positions, and in skilled, semiskilled, and laboring jobs. The most extensive survey was made during the depression of the 1930s by Elise Martens of the United States Office of Education (1936). Of 3,786 employed men who were profoundly deaf, about one-third (1,173) were operatives in mills or factories, 533 were unskilled laborers, and 330 were typesetters (a trade frequently taught in schools for the deaf). All types of other occupations were represented: shoemaker, teacher, painter, forester, farmer, carpenter, cabinetmaker, and so forth. Engineering, medicine, law, real estate, and the ministry were listed for from one to seven men. Of 1,151 profoundly deaf women, 574 were employed as operatives in mills or factories, 120 as hotel or domestic servants, 75 as teachers, and 65 as dressmakers. One was a real-estate agent, one was a trained nurse, and several were managers, librarians, bookkeepers, and cashiers. The others had positions as cook, typist, waitress, housekeeper, clerk, and welfare worker.

In a later study Lunde and Bigman (1959), in cooperation with the National Association for the Deaf (an association for deaf adults), distributed a questionnaire to deaf individuals throughout the United States. They received 10,101 completed schedules. Of those, 86 percent were from respondents ranging in age from 20 to 59. Of the total group responding, 7,920, or four-fifths, were employed. The rest were housewives, retired persons, and others. The occupational distribution of the employed deaf in that study is shown in Table 6.2.

In a later study Schein and Delk (1974) found a similar distribution of employed deaf. In their study 8.8 percent were in professional

	Employed deaf	In U.S. (1957) population
Professional, technical, and similar workers	6.6%	10.6%
Managers, officials, and proprietors	3.2	15.5
Clerical, sales, and similar workers	7.2	20.7
Craftsmen, supervisors, and similar workers	35.9	13.4
Operatives and similar workers	35.2	20.1
Others—that is, service workers, laborers, etc.	11.9	19.7

TABLE 6.2

Occupational status of deaf adults

Note: It is interesting to note from this distribution of occupations that, as compared to the general population, there were fewer deaf in the professional fields, managerial positions, and clerical and sales positions because of the necessity of communication in these jobs. There were greater numbers of deaf serving as skilled and semiskilled workers and machine operators and in similar jobs.

and technical work, approximately 35 percent were in operative and similar work, and 15.5 percent were in clerical and sales work. In addition Schein and Delk found:

1. Less than 3 percent of deaf males were unemployed as compared with 4.9 percent of the general male population.
2. Approximately 10 percent of deaf females were unemployed as contrasted with 6.6 percent of females in the general population.
3. Nonwhite deaf males had an unemployment rate five times that of white deaf males.
4. Nonwhite deaf females had nearly double the unemployment rate of white deaf females.
5. The income of deaf heads of households was 84 percent of the United States average, with white deaf males obtaining a higher income than white deaf females or nonwhite deaf persons.

In general all the studies confirm the common observation that deaf adults can make a good occupational adjustment despite their handicap.

Factors influencing educational development of hearing-impaired children

As with all children there are many variables that influence individual differences in development among hearing-impaired children. The more tangible and important factors are (1) intelligence and related psychological functions, (2) degree of deafness (severe or extreme), (3) age at onset of deafness, and (4) other handicaps.

INTELLIGENCE AND OTHER PSYCHOLOGICAL CHARACTERISTICS

As we have seen in previous chapters, intelligence scores are not a constant entity but can be dramatically affected by the cumulative experience of the child.

The most relevant experience affecting the performance of deaf children is their relative inability to master language, particularly abstract linguistic concepts such as *irony, furniture,* and *democracy.* That limitation naturally affects performance on tests of verbal intelligence but not on nonverbal intelligence where the experience of deaf children is not substantially different from the average child.

The progress of a hearing-impaired child in school is partially dependent on intelligence and conceptual abilities, such as rate of learning and ability to generalize, draw conclusions, and make use of subtle cues. Some deaf children are superior in intelligence, many are average, and some are mentally retarded. Performance on nonlanguage intelligence tests (when the deaf child's language difficulty is minimized) indicates that deaf children attending school exhibit the same distribution of intelligence as hearing children.

201

FACTORS INFLUENCING
EDUCATIONAL
DEVELOPMENT OF
HEARING-IMPAIRED
CHILDREN

Most of the studies with hearing-impaired children have been concerned with whether or not the intelligence of children with severe or profound hearing losses has been affected because of their difficulties in acquiring language and speech.

Brill (1962) studied the relationship between nonverbal intelligence test scores (Wechsler Intelligence Scale for Children and Wechsler Adult Intelligence Scale) and later academic achievement. He found the distribution for 499 deaf children to be similar to that of a random sample of hearing children, with a mean IQ of 102 and a standard deviation of 17. For the 105 children for whom data were available, the correlation between IQ and Stanford Achievement Test scores was 0.54. IQs were 115.8. For those given an academic diploma, the average IQ was 112, and for those given a vocational diploma, the IQ was 101.7. The certificate group had a mean IQ of 90.1. The academic achievement level of each group showed similar differences. The college group had a mean grade of 9.4, the academic group a mean grade of 7.2, the vocational group a mean grade of 4.9, and the certificate group a mean grade of 3.1.

Of course, these results hold only for nonverbal intelligence tests. Since it is verbal intelligence that is most closely related to school achievement, it is the deaf child's limitations in verbal intelligence that relate to his or her poor school achievement.

Birch, Stuckless, and Birch (1963) studied the relationship between the Leiter International Performance Scale and school achievement eleven years later. They found a significant relationship between the early intelligence rating and educational achievement.

Vernon (1968a) reviewed the research on the intelligence of the deaf and hard of hearing for the past fifty years. He stated that when psychological testing of the deaf was conducted by individuals experienced with deaf children, the results showed the deaf and hard of hearing nearly equal in intelligence. He also concluded that there was no substantial difference in intelligence between the hard of hearing, the deaf, the congenitally deaf, and the adventitiously deaf; or in other words, no major relationship existed between degree of hearing loss and IQ or between age at onset and IQ.

Myklebust (1960) pointed out in his study of deafness and mental development that although the deaf seem to be inferior to hearing children on some intellectual tasks, they are equal or superior on other tasks. For example, he found that the deaf are superior to hearing children on memory for designs, tactile memory, and memory for movement. But they were inferior to hearing children on digit span, picture span, and memory for dots.

Olsson and Furth (1966) administered visual memory span tests to a group of adolescents who were deaf and to a group who had normal hearing. They found that with nonsense forms there was no difference between the deaf and the hearing group but that with digits the deaf were inferior to hearing subjects.

In evaluating the results of intelligence tests Furth (1973) asserted that the deaf succeed "on logical and mathematical tasks" but fail to understand "a sentence that four-year-olds find easy." He felt that "logic is necessary but language is arbitrary" (p. 112). If we measure intelligence on some functions like logic and induction, the deaf perform like hearing individuals. But if we define intelligence in terms of verbal language, they are deficient.

DEGREE OF IMPAIRED HEARING

Children placed in classes and schools for the deaf have either (1) a severe loss of hearing in the speech range (71 to 90 decibel level), (2) an extreme hearing loss at a level of more than 91 decibels, or (3) a marked or profound hearing loss combined with additional handicapping conditions. The severely impaired child has considerable residual hearing and can profit in most instances from a hearing aid. Such a child is sometimes called *educationally deaf;* that is, he or she is not completely deaf but needs the specialized training of a deaf child. In other words, for instructional purposes the child *is* deaf. Without intensive training, hearing aids, special techniques, and individual help, he or she will not develop language and speech. With such help children with that defect usually do develop in language and speech. In some instances and with proper instruction, they can be reclassified as hard of hearing and can move into the program for hard-of-hearing children; that is, they can be placed in a regular class and given additional tutoring by a special teacher part of the day.

The extremely deaf child, however, cannot profit in the same way from a hearing aid and frequently finds it very difficult to acquire speech and language. Such children make slower progress in language, speech, and school subjects than do the severely deaf children.

AGE AT ONSET OF DEAFNESS

It has been emphasized that the age at which a child becomes deaf has a significant influence on language and speech development. If a child does not lose his or her hearing until after acquiring some speech and language, there is at least some concept of the process of communication and a base on which to build more speech and understanding of language. If a child is born deaf or experiences hearing loss before learning to talk, progress is much slower in those areas. Of course, the older the child is when hearing is lost and the more advanced the speech and understanding of language, the easier education will be later. To illustrate this point, Figure 6.5 gives the educational profiles of Carl, who was born with normal hearing, and Ann, who was born deaf.

Carl developed normally until the age of 7. He entered school when he was 6, and his intellectual ability was slightly above average. His school achievement was comparable to that of the average child. At the age of 7, however, he contracted meningitis, and when the disease subsided, Carl was unable to hear. Believing that that was a temporary condition, his parents waited for Carl's hearing to return. But it did not return and he was diagnosed as having a total hearing

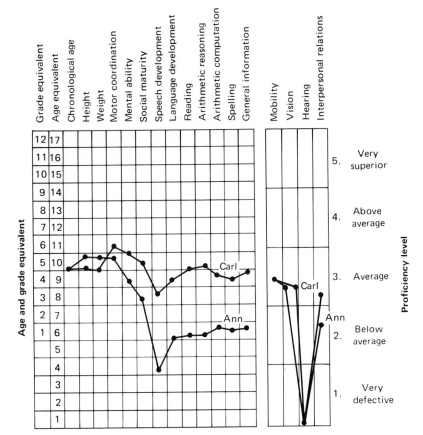

FIGURE 6.5
Profiles of two deaf children: one born with normal hearing, one born deaf

loss of a sensorineural type. There was nothing that could be done for him medically.

At the age of 10 Carl was given a series of physical, educational, and mental tests, the results of which are presented in Figure 6.5. It will be noticed that he was average in height and weight and was slightly above average in motor coordination and mental ability. In social maturity he was average. In speech development his progress had been slowed down by his loss of hearing, and he was considered to have the speech development of a child less than 9 years old. Language development was somewhat better; much of this could be gained from reading, in which, because of a good start in first and second grades, he was able to continue to progress at an average rate. He relied a great deal on reading since this was his best channel for obtaining information. In other school subjects he was also progressing normally. The profile shows that Carl's major difficulty is in speech and language, which, though handicapped by his loss of hearing, were sufficiently well established at the time of his illness to permit him to gain ideas through written language.

Ann's profile reveals a much greater retardation. She was born deaf; the cause of the disability was unknown. It will be seen from the profile that at the age of 10 Ann was slightly above average in height, weight, and motor coordination and was average in intelligence. In social maturity she showed some retardation, but in speech and in language development the retardation was marked.

TABLE 6.3

Relationships of six selected variables to reading achievement level and to three-year gain

Variable	Relationship with reading comprehension level	Relationship with reading comprehension gain
Sex	Females score slightly higher than males	Females gain more than males
Ethnic group	Whites score higher than Spanish-Americans or blacks	No difference among ethnic groups
Degree of hearing loss	Achievement level is inversely related to hearing loss	Students with less than 55 dB loss gain relatively more
Presence of additional handicapping conditions	Students with no additional handicaps score higher than those with one or more	Students with no additional handicaps gain relatively more than those with one or more additional handicaps
Age child began school	Children entering at age 5 score higher than those entering either earlier or later	The younger the child entered school, the greater the relative gain
Parental deafness	Students with 2 deaf parents score higher than those with either 1 deaf parent or 2 normal-hearing parents	Parental hearing status has no relationship to achievement gain

Source: Trybus and Karchmer, 1977, p. 65.

This handicap of course took its toll in other school subjects, so that when she was 10, Ann was doing only first-grade reading and slightly better in other school subjects. Even this ability was due to the fact that she had been fortunate enough to attend nursery school, where she had been taught some speech and speech reading. Had she not had a consistent training program for the deaf, she would probably have learned no speech, no oral language skills, and no reading. The discrepancy between her school achievement and her physical, mental, and social abilities had been decreased because of the educational program.

Figure 6.5 demonstrates the effect of the early loss of hearing. Both children were extremely deaf, with hearing losses of 90 to 100 decibels in each ear due to sensorineural deafness. But Ann, whose educational retardation was very great, had been born deaf, whereas Carl had acquired his deafness after speech and language had had seven years to develop.

OTHER HANDICAPS

Currently, multihandicapped deaf children (such as the mentally retarded deaf and the visually impaired deaf) are being enrolled in residential schools and classes for the deaf. Craig and Craig (1977) report that approximately 25 percent of children enrolled in classes for the deaf are multihandicapped with impaired hearing. Such additional handicaps tend to inhibit more normal educational development.

In an extensive study over a period of three years of the reading achievement of children with impaired hearing, Jesema (1975) found that students with no additional handicaps tend to score higher than children with one or more additional handicaps.

Some variables that affect reading level and reading gains were studied by Trybus and Karchmer (1977). Their study of six selected variables compared each variable with reading achievement and with gains over a three-year period. Trybus and Karchmer formulated the relationships, which are self-explanatory, in Table 6.3.

History of the education of hearing-impaired children

Throughout the centuries there have been heated controversies on the best practices in educating the deaf. Everyone agrees that the major emphasis in education of the deaf is placed on the development of language and communication, since they are the most important vehicles through which the child processes information and expresses himself or herself vocally. All English-speaking educators of the deaf agree that the deaf child must learn the English language and must learn to read and write it.

People concerned with education of the deaf have held sharply differing views on the modes of communication to be emphasized in teaching language to deaf children. The two differing modes of communication are oralism and the combined oral-manual approach. The oral method develops communication through speech and speech reading (lip reading). It is sometimes called the *oral-aural approach* because of its great emphasis on the use of residual hearing. The manual method includes (1) the language of signs, a language system consisting of formalized movements of the hands or arms to express thoughts and (2) finger spelling, using the manual alphabet, in which there is a fixed position of the five fingers for each letter of the alphabet (Figure 6.6). It is a kind of spelling in the air. In communicating manually, deaf persons generally use the two modes together, finger spelling some words and expressing others through the language of signs.

The pioneers in the education of the deaf were Juan Pablo Bonet and Jacob Rodrigues Pereire, Spaniards of the seventeenth century. In Madrid in 1620, according to Moores (1978), Bonet published the first book ever written on teaching deaf children. In that book, *The Reduction of Letters and the Art of Teaching Deaf Mutes to Speak,* he described the manual alphabet for the deaf. It was a major innovation in the field since it gave the deaf a means of communication with those who knew the manual alphabet. Pereire extended Bonet's alphabet and added to it the manual sign language.

But Pereire also expanded a more far-reaching technique known as lip reading or the oral method of teaching the deaf by having them learn to form their own words by acquiring meaning from the movements of other people's lips and facial muscles. According to Wallin (1924), Pereire held to the theory that touch is the primitive sense and that all special senses are modifications of touch. Through teaching the use of the tactile sense, he tried to produce voices in deaf children. Thus, through developing visual apprehension of the movements of the visible speech organs and through the vibrations that could be felt by the deaf child, Pereire introduced the oral method.

Because of his contribution Pereire was awarded a pension by Louis XV, and the oral method received the official commendation of a committee of the Parisian Academy of Science.

Unfortunately Pereire kept his methods of speech, lip reading,

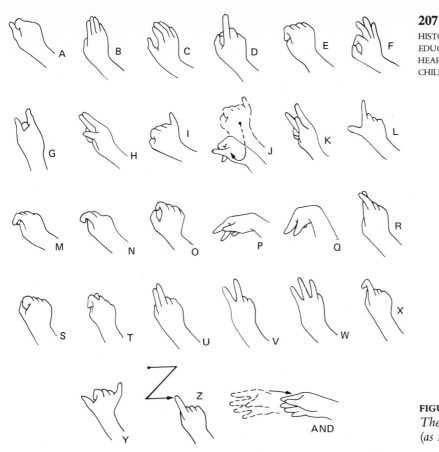

FIGURE 6.6
*The American manual alphabet
(as seen by the finger speller)*

Source: From L. J. Fant, Jr., *Say It with Hands* (Washington, D.C.: Gallaudet College
Centennial Fund Commission, 1964), p. 1. Reproduced with permission.

and other communication a secret, even swearing his students to
secrecy. In describing Pereire's contribution Moores (1978) stated:

> Most of what is known of Pereire's techniques came from a letter
> written by Saboureux de Fontenay, who apparently had little compunc-
> tion about violating his oath. Pereire employed a one-handed manual
> alphabet for the teaching of speech, relied on a natural approach to the
> development of language, developed auditory training procedures for
> those with residual hearing, and utilized special exercises involving sight
> and touch in sense training. (p. 41)

According to Silverman (1960), it was the Abbé Charles Michel
de l'Épée in France and Samuel Heinicke in Germany who advanced
the cause of education of the deaf on the Continent in the eighteenth
century. De l'Épée founded the first public school for the deaf in

1755 in Paris, where he taught by the manual method. Samuel Heinicke, de l'Épée's contemporary, founded the first public school for the deaf in Germany, using the oral method. Thus the two methods of teaching the deaf received impetus at about the same time—de l'Épée favoring signs and manualism; Heinicke advocating speech and speech reading.

The first school for the deaf in the British Isles was opened in Edinburgh in 1760 by Thomas Braidwood, who became well known for his oral methods of teaching deaf children. His reputation spread to the United States and stimulated Thomas Hopkins Gallaudet, a divinity student in Hartford, Connecticut, to go to Scotland to study the oral method. Gallaudet was disappointed with what he obtained there. Braidwood was supposedly getting good results from his use of the oral method with deaf children, but he was secretive about his methods. Gallaudet therefore crossed the Channel to France and studied the manual approach of de l'Épée under Sicard, de l'Épée's successor. After his return to the United States, Gallaudet in 1817 opened at Hartford the first school for the deaf in this country. Education there was by the manual method. Gallaudet was also responsible for bringing Laurent Clerc, who himself was deaf, to Hartford. At the Hartford school, then called the American Asylum for the Education and Instruction of the Deaf and Dumb, Clerc became the first deaf teacher of the deaf in the United States.

Although the Hartford school was supported privately, it soon won public support and became the forerunner of state-supported schools throughout the United States, most of which combine oral and manual methods. Private residential schools such as the Clarke School for the Deaf in Northampton, Massachusetts, the Lexington School for the Deaf in New York, and the Central Institute for the Deaf in St. Louis, Missouri, were organized, and continue to function, as advocates of the oral method. The federally sponsored college for the deaf in Washington, D.C., where the work was carried on by Gallaudet's son, Edward Minor Gallaudet, bears the name of Thomas Hopkins Gallaudet.

In this country Alexander Graham Bell also opened up new channels for teaching speech to the deaf. His method of *visible speech* helped the child understand the placement of the speech organs in producing speech. His invention of the telephone led to the development and use of hearing aids and to greater emphasis on the use of amplification of sound in teaching speech to children with severely defective hearing. Those inventions advanced oral methods of teaching the deaf and made it possible for many children to understand speech and language who previously could not have done so. Bell was also responsible for founding the Volta Bureau, an information agency on deafness.

The oral method has had many advocates in the United States, although advancement of the technique came somewhat later than teaching by the manual method. The first public day school utilizing the oral method was established in Boston in 1869. Horace Mann, who had studied the education of the deaf in Germany, was influential in that undertaking.

For an elaborate summary of the history of the education of the deaf in Europe and the United States, the reader is referred to Moores's *Educating the Deaf: Psychology, Principles and Practices* (1978).

Current communication approaches

History of the education of the deaf has emphasized the ongoing controversy of the oral versus manual or combined methods of instruction, a continuation of de l'Épée's emphasis on the manual method and Heinicke's advocacy of the oral method of instruction. It is also this controversy that made enemies of Gallaudet and Alexander Bell. Actually there are only residual traces of the oral-manual controversy today since no responsible educator of the deaf fails to emphasize oral aspects of instruction. The controversy is over (1) the oral-only method with a prohibition of manual language and (2) a combination of oral-manual instruction. The controversy has subsided considerably since the acceptance of *total communication procedures,* a combination of all methods. The differences are primarily in emphasis. Currently there are four methods used with the severe and the profound (deaf) hearing-impaired child: (1) the oral-aural approach, (2) the Rochester approach, (3) the auditory approach, and (4) the simultaneous or total communication approach.

ORAL-AURAL METHOD

The oral-aural approach is the instructional procedure that uses residual hearing through amplification of sound, speech reading, and speech for developing communication skills. School programs that adhere to this approach do not use or encourage the use of the language of signs or finger spelling on the assumption that manual communication will inhibit the child's learning of language and oral skills and impede adjustment to the hearing world.

ROCHESTER METHOD

The Rochester method was established in the Rochester, New York, School in 1878. It is a combination of the oral method plus finger spelling. It processes information through speech reading, amplification, and finger spelling. The response is through finger spelling and speech. The manual alphabet presented in Figure 6.6 is used by the teacher who spells every letter of every word as it is spoken. This method is similar to neo-oralism practiced in the Soviet Union with very young children. Reading and writing of the alphabet and words are encouraged.

AUDITORY METHOD

The auditory method emphasizes the development of listening skills, especially for children who can profit from auditory training. The procedure is used extensively with children with moderate hearing losses and sometimes with those with severe hearing losses. The auditory method is probably most effective when it is initiated in the early years. Calvert and Silverman (1975) refer to the approach as the *auditory global* method.

TOTAL COMMUNICATION METHOD

The total communication method, sometimes called the simultaneous or combined method, presents finger spelling, signs, speech reading, speech, and auditory amplification at the same time. The Conference of Executives of American Schools for the Deaf (1976) has defined *total communication* as "a philosophy requiring the incorporation of appropriate aural, manual, and oral modes of communication in order to insure effective communication with and among hearing-impaired persons" (p. 358).

COMMUNICATION TRENDS

Jordan, Gustason, and Rosen (1976) investigated the number of classes that use the different modes of communication. In their study they combined the oral and aural (auditory) methods and included a system called cued speech (a system of hand cues used with speech and speech reading). Table 6.4 gives the number of classes reporting the four modes of communication used by 796 programs for children with impaired hearing.

From Table 6.4 it will be noted that (1) total communication is used most frequently and is used almost exclusively at the high school level and (2) the oral-aural method is the next most frequently used. The two procedures together were used by over 90 percent of the schools.

RESEARCH ON COMMUNICATION APPROACHES

The oralists claimed that if a child is permitted to communicate with signs, the child will not make the necessary effort to learn speech. The manualists claimed that language is retarded in children who are not allowed to sign or finger spell and that learning language through speech delays language development. Only recently has research been conducted on the problem.

Morkovin (1960) summarized the research on neo-oralism conducted in the Soviet Union. He reports that they initiated simultaneous finger spelling and speech at an early age (ages 2 and 3) and claim that by age 6 the children had acquired a vocabulary of several thousand words. By age 8, the Russians claim, the children had developed sufficient language (through simultaneous presentation of speech and finger spelling) to abandon finger spelling. Quigley (1969) reviewed the Russian literature on the subject and failed to find definite substantiation of the claims of superiority of neo-oralism over other methods. At the same time Quigley conducted a five-year experiment on the Rochester method (speech and finger spelling) and concluded that: (1) finger spelling plus good oral techniques improves achievement in meaningful language, (2) learning finger spelling is not detrimental to the acquisition of oral skills, (3) finger spelling produces greater benefits with younger rather than with older

TABLE 6.4

Total number of classes reporting primary use of the four modes of communication at different school levels

	Preschool	Elementary	Junior high school	High school
Cued speech	10	14	66	7
Oral-aural	522	1,240	359	249
Rochester method	38	72	33	12
Total communication	689	2,196	688	1,046
Total	1,259	3,522	1,086	1,314

Source: Jordan, Gustason, and Rosen, 1976.

children, and (4) finger spelling is one of a number of useful tools for instructing deaf children. The Russian studies, the reports of observers (Moores, 1972), and a report in England (Education of Deaf Children, 1967) have recreated an interest in the Rochester method.

Stuckless and Birch (1966) compared the language development of a group of deaf children exposed to manual communication, finger spelling, and signs (because they were reared by deaf parents) with a group of children not exposed to early manual communication. They found that the group with early manual communication was superior to the control group in reading, written language, and speech reading. They were equal in speech intelligibility and in psychosocial development. Meadow (1968) conducted a similar experiment in a state school for the deaf, by comparing deaf children raised by deaf parents (manual communication) with a group of deaf children from homes with hearing parents. Meadow found the group of deaf children who had been exposed to early manual communication to be superior in self-concept, academic achievement, and written language. Speech reading and speech ability were similar for both groups.

Vernon (1970) compared the later educational achievement, communication skills, and psychological adjustment of thirty-two children who had received early manual training with the same accomplishments of thirty-two children who had had early oral training. The children who had early manual instruction scored significantly higher on the Stanford Achievement Test than did the early oral-trained group. There was no difference between the groups in communication skills and psychological adjustment.

Brasel and Quigley (1975) compared two groups of deaf children of deaf parents with two groups of deaf children of hearing parents on reading and language. Eighteen children in each group were tested with the Stanford Achievement Test, on six syntactic structures, and on written language. The two groups of children of deaf parents were significantly superior to the two groups of children of hearing parents on every test used.

An example of one who learned finger spelling and who developed excellent language, but who did not learn speech or speech reading, was Howard Hofsteater (1959). Raised by deaf parents, he was taught finger spelling at a young age. He learned to read and thus developed written rather than spoken language, including a high degree of abstract conceptualization. The following is his description of how he developed reading and language:

> As soon as my parents became convinced that I had irretrievably lost my hearing, they were confronted with the question of what next to do with me. . . . Quite normally they argued that if a normal hearing child effortlessly acquires spoken language by hearing it and imitating it, a

deaf child should be able to do exactly the same by seeing it used. They saw no psychological—nor physiological—difference between a baby's using its vocal cords, tongue, and lips to imitate spoken language and a baby's using his hands to imitate movements of finger spelled words. . . .

The idea that whenever they manipulated their fingers in my direction would in some way affect my well-being must have percolated through somehow, for I developed at a rather early age the faculty of "concentrated visual attention"—subject, of course, to my fluctuating desire to listen. (pp. 10–12)

It is obvious from those extracts from Mr. Hofsteater's autobiography that he had developed fluent use of the English language. This conceptual and abstract process was developed by extensive reading throughout his school years and after.

The studies cited tend to favor early manual communication for the development of language. Furthermore, with the restricted samples used, there were no detrimental effects on speech and speech reading. Yet those who deal with the adult deaf see many who rely solely on manual communication, reading, and writing and who do not use speech and speech reading.

With the current emphasis on total communication, the comparisons of oral and manual systems may no longer be relevant since the combined system should include the best of all systems if properly delivered.

Special educational procedures

Whether a hearing-impaired child is placed in a regular class with supporting help, a special class, a day school, a resource room, or a residential school, the child's needs are met by special educational techniques that have been developed over the years to meet the needs of auditorily impaired children. The special educational techniques (those techniques that are unique and not necessarily used with hearing children) are briefly described here. Different techniques or instructional procedures are used with a particular child at a particular stage of development when that procedure is needed. The professional personnel who use these techniques are speech and hearing clinicians and specially trained teachers of the deaf. The special educational procedures are (1) the use of hearing aids, (2) auditory training, (3) speech reading (lip reading), (4) oral speech remediation, (5) speech development, (6) language development, and (7) reading and other school subjects.

INSTRUCTIONS IN THE USE OF HEARING AIDS

Generally an audiologist determines the type of hearing aid to be used by the child and initially instructs the parents and the child in the use and care of the mechanism.

With young children considerable care should be taken in introducing the hearing aid. In the beginning the child should not wear a hearing aid all day. The best procedure is to start using a hearing aid only in the tutoring session and under the supervision of an audiologist. It should be used for short periods of time under instruction, and the periods should be gradually increased so that the child will learn to use the hearing aid profitably.

AUDITORY TRAINING (AURAL)

Training the child to listen to sound clues that are available and to discriminate between different sounds is called auditory training. Before the advent of hearing aids, auditory training involved speaking into the ear or using tubes to amplify sound. Now that the transistor type of hearing aid is available, it is extensively used in auditory training with either individual or group hearing aids.

Modern electronics has vastly improved hearing aids. Specific frequencies can be emphasized, tone quality has been improved to make reproduction more natural and speech more intelligible, adjustments can be made by the wearer, and packaging has become more convenient. With the application of transistors to hearing aids, the size of individual hearing aids has been diminished until now the necessary mechanisms can even be put in an eyeglass frame.

The major aim of auditory training is to help the child at as early an age as possible to learn to discriminate between sounds. That kind of instruction is given to hearing-impaired children by the hearing specialist in school in accordance with the needs of the child. Of great importance for this type of training is home instruction, particularly during the preschool period. Parents can aid a great deal in auditory training, and one of the goals of the hearing specialist is to instruct the parents and obtain their cooperation.

Auditory training is used by speech clinicians in the schools for minor and moderate hearing impairments, but the procedure is also used with the severely impaired at a young age. The method has been called the acoustic method, the acoupedic method, the auditory method, the unisensory method, and the aural method. Calvert and Silverman (1975) termed the procedure the auditory global method.

They described it as including the maximum use of hearing and recommended that it be employed with amplification as early as possible. The emphasis on auditory decoding and corrected speech characterizes the auditory training method by whatever name it is called.

SPEECH READING (LIP READING)

Although we use the auditory sense to understand the spoken word, most of us can hear and understand another person better if we are looking directly at his or her face. Certain facial expressions and movements add meaning to what is said. That is why television, which uses both auditory and visual aids, is more effective than radio. If you turn on your television so that the picture shows clearly, but tune down the voice to the point at which it is only partially audible from where you are sitting, you will experience the cues that a hard-of-hearing person uses. In that situation you will begin to rely on the facial and lip movements of the speaker to supplement the faint voice you hear. If you turn off the visual picture, but leave the faint voice on, you will understand less of what the speaker is saying.

Speech-reading instruction is given to hard-of-hearing and deaf children to sharpen their understanding of what is said to them. By directing their attention to certain cues in lip and facial movements, they can learn to fill in from visual clues the sounds that they do not hear and the words that are indistinct. Many words look much alike to the speech reader—words such as *cup* and *up*. They cannot be discriminated visually. But words like *fish* and *ball* are rather easy to differentiate. It is also fortunate that the vowels, which are harder to tell apart visually, are easier to discriminate auditorily since they belong to the lower-frequency ranges. Some of the consonants, like *s,* are harder to hear because they belong to the high-frequency ranges in speech, where a deficit in sensorineural or perceptive deafness is more common (O'Neill and Oyer, 1961).

Speech reading requires the ability to interpret speech by seeing a few clues to a word or sentence. Those who are able to speech read will fill in or close, so to speak, most of the speech they read. For example, one can see the articulatory movements in sounds such as *th, p,* and *f.* But the articulation of sounds such as *k* and *h* and *g* is not visible. Some sounds such as *n* and *t* cannot be visually differentiated. The vowel sounds of *ee* and *ay* are indistinguishable visually. Hence the speech reader must infer the sounds that cannot be seen from those that can be seen. Likewise, words in a sentence must at times be inferred from the context since words such as *man* and *bat* are not easily distinguishable by sight.

In general, three methods of teaching speech reading have been used. The first emphasizes the analysis of details in a word. It is a phonetic approach to speech reading (Bunger, 1952). A second method, the whole method of teaching speech reading, does not use a phonetic or syllable approach but emphasizes thought units as a whole (Stowell, Samuelson, and Lehman, 1928). A third method, described by Bruhn (1947), is based on the German Mueller-Walle method. In her lessons with children she presents the most visible sounds first and the less visible sounds at a later time. The lessons begin with syllables and move on to sentences.

A combination of various methods is usually used by most teachers of the deaf. When the child is young, the teacher or the parent talks to him or her in whole sentences. Initially the child obtains vague impressions of the idea through the whole or synthetic approach. At first the child may not obtain any clues, but as the parent or teacher repeats the same expression over and over again in the same relationship to something that the child is experiencing—an object or an act or a feeling—the child begins to get an idea of what is being said. At a later stage those vague whole impressions are converted into lessons, which emphasize details. Exercises are given to aid the child in discriminating between different words and between sounds. For example, two pictures may be presented, one of a ball and another of a boat. The child is taught to "point to the ball" or "point to the boat."

Speech reading for auditorily impaired children in special classes for the deaf is used in teaching language, speech, and the regular school subjects. It is not, like arithmetic, taught at certain hours of the day. It permeates the whole class day, whenever the teacher talks to the children. When hearing aids are used, they are combined with auditory training. Programmed self-instructional speech-reading lessons using movie films have been developed to help deaf children gain this technique.

For many years research workers have been wondering why some deaf children become proficient in speech reading while others do not. Variables that might account for success or failure in learning to speech-read include chronological age, length of speech-reading training, intelligence, rate of speech, and concept formation. None of those variables seemed to have a relationship with learning speech reading. Sharp (1972) administered a series of visual closure tests to eighteen good and nineteen poor speech readers in two schools for the deaf. She found that good speech readers were superior to poor ones in visual closure, movement closure, and short-term memory. Those results are consistent with other studies with hard-of-hearing adults, which showed that good speech readers had superior visual synthetic ability (visual closure) over poor speech readers. In a study using speech-reading films to teach speech reading, Evans (1965) found that visual recognition was the best predictor of speech-reading potential.

SPEECH DEVELOPMENT (ORAL)

As the hearing child learns to speak, the observer can recognize a series of stages. At first the child extends gurgling and swallowing into babbling. The child toys with the sounds and experiments with his or her voice, and the babbling child hears himself or herself and sometimes repeats the same sound over and over again. Later the child may repeat the sounds that someone else says if they are in his or her repertoire. That is the stage of imitation that at first is only echoing or imitating the child's own babbling sounds or the sounds the parents make. He or she may say "ma ma ma" or "da da da" just as repetition of sound, without attaching any meaning to it. As "da da da" is repeated over and over again in the father's presence, the child connects the two and moves into a higher stage in learning to talk: associating meaning with certain sounds. When the mother says "da da," the child looks for the father; when the child says "da da," the father comes. By these stages the hearing child turns babbling into meaningful words, and meaningful speech is then well on its way.

But the deaf child cannot hear his or her own babbling, and it soon stops. The child does not hear the words of the parents and hence neither imitates them nor attaches meaning to them. In short, the child does not learn to speak by ordinary channels. If he or she is to learn to speak, it must be by other routes, which are tedious, less efficient, and extremely slow in developing. But it has been found that a totally deaf child can learn to speak if properly taught by skilled parents and teachers. The intonation and expression may not be those of a hearing child, but the child can learn to make himself or herself understood. Vibrations and the sense of touch, visual aids, kinesthetic and proprioceptive cues, and the use of any residual hearing through a hearing aid are all part of the process as the child learns to speak. Although often used together, they will be discussed separately.

SPEECH TRAINING THROUGH VIBRATION AND THE SENSE OF TOUCH. The tactile sense was used intensively by Kate Alcorn (1938) and by Sophia Alcorn (1942) in teaching deaf-blind children and also in teaching deaf-sighted children. With eyes closed the child feels speech vibrations by placing a hand on the teacher's cheek, near the mouth, and so begins to discriminate between sounds, words, and sentences. The child develops comprehension through touch before being required to speak, just as a normal child understands through hearing before he or she speaks. Understanding of ideas precedes expression of ideas.

In all methods of teaching the extremely deaf, the sense of touch is an important factor. Through touch the child feels the teacher's voice when his or her hand is in front of the teacher's mouth when consonants such as *b* and *p* are articulated. The child feels vibrations of some sounds with a hand on the teacher's cheek and other sounds when a hand is on the teacher's throat. With a hand on his or her own cheek, nose, or throat, the child tries to reproduce the same vibrations and gradually learns to pronounce sounds and words in correct order when he or she feels the face of the teacher and then feels his or her own face. Through such tactile cues the deaf child begins to articulate even though he or she does not hear. The steps in developing speech from the beginning stages to more complex phases are highly technical and require a teacher who is thoroughly trained. The process is very different from that used in remediating the speech of a hearing child or a hard-of-hearing child.

SPEECH TRAINING THROUGH THE USE OF VISUAL AIDS. Although deaf-blind children rely primarily on the tactile sense, the deaf-sighted child is taught to use visual cues in addition to tactile cues. The child learns to read other people's speech and, by watching the face of the teacher and using a mirror, learns to reproduce what he or she sees and feels.

Espeseth (1969) found that intensive treatment could significantly improve the visual sequential memory span abilities of the deaf. He concluded that there exists a relationship between visual memory span and reading achievement; therefore, improvement in this ability should have a positive effect on accelerating the communication skills of the deaf.

SPEECH TRAINING THROUGH KINESTHETIC AND PROPRIOCEPTIVE CUES. In addition to vision and touch (both responding to external cues), the child learns to control speech by sensing the muscular movements of his or her own mouth, jaw, tongue, lips, larynx, and so forth. Through practice, use of the kinesthetic cues eventually becomes automatic. Initially, however, the child must be made conscious of the internal cues. The child will eventually learn to control voice and articulation, not because he or she hears them but because the child feels them internally.

SPEECH TRAINING THROUGH AUDITORY STIMULATION. Many deaf children have some residual hearing even though it is not sufficient to understand or learn speech. Through powerful hearing aids their residual hearing can help them to learn rhythm patterns and discriminate differences, and it is used in teaching speech. Residual hearing is a supplementary help in the training of speech, which must utilize the tactile, visual, and kinesthetic methods. Thus hearing aids are used in classes for the deaf, even though extremely deaf children are not able to understand speech by them.

A book by Ling (1976) on the development of speech in the hearing impaired has brought the discreet methods discussed in the preceding into clearer focus. The book discusses the research on multisensory approaches to the development of speech production. It also discusses feedback and "feedforward" mechanisms, the different sense modalities (vision, touch), residual hearing, automaticity, and teaching order. Ling concludes: "These indicate that technological advances, emerging knowledge in speech science, and contributions from related areas are having little, or no, impact on the speech patterns of many children attending our special schools" (p. 17).

Ling presents an integrated model of speech acquisition that is primarily auditory and that develops seven sequential stages of phonetic and phonological levels. Target behaviors are developed at each broad stage before the next speech target is presented. Each stage is systematically evaluated. Teaching strategies to develop speech in hearing-impaired children through an error-free learning situation are described in detail. Ling developed his system based, not on the trial-and-error experience of a teacher, but on a thorough analysis of the research studies and theories that have been described in the literature. The reasons for the development of the system are adequately documented.

Another system that emphasizes speech acquisition for hearing-impaired children is one developed by Leshin (1975) that utilizes phonetic and phonological levels. He also emphasizes auditory aids and the synthesis of the whole-to-part and part-to-whole approach.

SPEECH TRAINING AND IMPROVEMENT THROUGH "VISIBLE SPEECH." By use of an electronic instrument called an oscilloscope, it is possible to display on a screen (like a small TV screen) instantaneous wavelike patterns of light corresponding to varying sound vibrations. Such patterns have been spoken of as *visible speech*. For many years attempts have been made to use such visible displays of speech to develop more adequate speech in deaf children. Potter, Kopp, and Green (1947) published a book describing the possibilities of using visible speech. Later Kopp and Kopp (1963) reported effective results using a cathode-ray translator to train speech. Stark (1968) described the modifications that have been made with the new Bell Telephone Visible Speech Translator. Numerous other studies have been made on the teaching of speech and improving articulation through electronic visual displays of various kinds. An example of one such device is reported by Pronovost (1970). Called the Instantaneous Pitch-Period Indicator (IPPI), it displays the rhythm and intonation patterns of spoken phrases on a five-inch storage oscilloscope screen. The teacher displays his or her voice on the channel so that the student can match the visual display. Matching occurs immediately. The deaf child is able to monitor response and through this feedback learns to control rhythm, intensity, and intonation. Pronovost reports rapid learning with that type of visual analyzer.

SPEECH REMEDIATION. Speech remediation is necessary for many children who are hard of hearing. These children have not heard certain sounds accurately and so have developed speech with sound substitutions and other articulatory defects. In addition, because they sometimes do not hear background noises, they fail to adjust the loudness of their voices to surrounding noises. Some speak too loudly because they cannot hear their own voices, owing to a perceptive loss; others do not speak loudly enough because, having a conductive loss, they can hear their own voices through bone conduction much better than they hear others.

The usual procedure for speech training is first to find out what errors a child makes in speech. Errors can be tabulated in a more formal way by using an articulation test. A child is asked to label or name pictures or objects, and the speech clinician notes whether the child adds or omits sounds and whether distortions or substitutions occur in the initial, medial, or final positions. In addition, the clinician will note the voice quality and any abnormalities in speaking.

Following the detection of specific errors, corrective measures can be initiated. In school it is best for the child to remain in the regular grades for the educational program, while the special teachers help with his or her speaking and hearing problems in an individual situation or in a small group. Most effective results are obtained when such training is integrated with the work of the regular class and when the parents cooperate with the program at home.

THE AMERICAN SIGN LANGUAGE

In addition to finger spelling, a method of communication that has withstood time and is now being used in total communication is the American Sign Language (ASL). This manual system was imported from Europe by Gallaudet in the early 1800s. It is representative of the great emphasis on the manual method as opposed to the oral-only method. The manual communication system includes finger spelling of a word, letter by letter (Figure 6.6), or signing the word—presenting a concept by a system of hand movements. In presenting a word or concept that represents a complete idea through a sign, three elements are used: (1) the position of the hand near the body, (2) the configuration of the hand or hands, and (3) the movement of the hand. Passing the thumb and hand along the face from the head to the chin along the jawbone, for example, represents *girl,* since girls wore strings on bonnets in earlier times. Some signs convey a complete sentence including subject, verb, and objects.

In general, signing is faster than finger spelling and is more frequently used in informal communication. In very formal communication finger spelling is used. Most deaf adults communicate in signs and in finger spelling. Such systems are sometimes called non-verbal communication.

READING AND LANGUAGE DEVELOPMENT

One of the major by-products of deafness is the deficit that results from the inability to hear language spoken by others. Language is one of the most complex of human skills. It involves many facets, including concept formation. It may be easy to teach a child the concept of a ball through lip reading and whether the ball is large or small, or gray or white. But how can one develop the idea of "intangibility" or "the" or "of" or "for"? Concrete objects like a comb and a ball and action verbs such as *sit* and *jump* can be demonstrated, but the more complex forms of language and particularly the different shades of meaning of the same word are difficult to teach. For example, the word *run* has many meanings: "the boy runs," "the river is running," "a road runs in front of the house," and a "run in a stocking."

Reading and language are combined because the deaf child learns language through reading and reading primarily through language. As a matter of fact, deaf children who develop language of a complex nature usually derive their language facility primarily from reading and experience.

There are two major theoretical approaches to teaching language to deaf children. An approach that has been dominant in the past is based on the hypothesis that all children learn the grammatical forms of language through imitation. They hear, speech read, or read words and phrases over and over again, and thus they acquire the syntax of the language.

Another approach to the development of language has been proposed by psycholinguists. They point out that not all grammar (syntax and morphology) is developed through imitation. Hearing children are able to generalize rules for words not encountered in their experience. Thus, a child will answer *wugs* to the statement "This is a wug; these are two ————." In a study by Cooper (1965) it was pointed out that deaf children also apply generalized rules to words, but not to the same extent that hearing children do. Lenneberg (1965) stated that children, deaf or hearing, inherit a predisposition for language in the same way that they inherit a predisposition to stand and to walk. He further stated:

> Language development, or its substitute, is relatively independent of the infant's babbling, or of his ability to hear. The congenitally deaf who will usually fail to develop an intelligible vocal communication system, who either do not babble or to whom babbling is of no avail (the facets have not been reliably reported), will nevertheless learn the intricacies of language and learn to communicate efficiently through writing. Apparently, even under these reduced circumstances of stimulation, the miracle of the development of a feeling for grammar takes place. (p. 589)

Brown and Bellugi (1964) give three processes by which children develop language: (1) by imitation, even though the imitation is an approximation, (2) by expansion in which the parent repeats what the child says ("want milk") in an expanded phrase ("I want some milk"), and (3) by induction in which the child constructs language he or she has not heard ("I sitted," "two mans," for example).

Because of the developmental theories of language advanced by psycholinguists, research teams are currently attempting to develop methods for teaching language to the deaf that implement psycholinguistic theories.

Although language training of deaf children permeates all of their educational activities, numerous and more specific systems for teaching language have been used. They use structured lessons for the purpose of developing English syntax.

The best-known system is the Fitzgerald key (1954). It is used after children have learned some language forms in a natural way, without crutches or mechanical devices. The teacher introduces a series of symbols and structured sentences with questions such as "Who?" "What?" "How many?" and "Where?" in relation to the grammatical structure of their sentences. Those four questions are the key words of the method. By a structured procedure the children gradually develop an understanding of grammar. When it becomes automatic in speech and writing, they have acquired intelligible language.

Such keys are initially crutches, which the child uses to follow some sequence or pattern in language. It is necessary for the child to develop a vocabulary to understand and produce different shades of meaning for words in a sentence and to express relationships. That slow and laborious process cannot be accomplished through speech reading or other activities alone. The greatest aid to the development of language in its higher forms is through the skills of reading and writing.

A common technique is the so-called natural method of teaching language. Groht (1958) is one of the advocates of the method, which uses language in natural situations through speech reading and writing then later presents language principles formally. The method is inductive and is more in harmony with the principles of learning language used by hearing children.

A major researcher in this area is Stephen Quigley of the University of Illinois, who has for some years questioned the methods of teaching language to deaf children by traditional methods. With his students and colleagues he has conducted a series of experiments in linguistics with deaf children (Quigley, Wilbur, and Montanelli, 1976). That research and the research of others have been published by Russell, Quigley, and Power (1976) in a book entitled *Linguistics and Deaf Children.* It was designed to familiarize teachers of the deaf with the field of linguistics and the difficulties encountered by deaf children in the acquisition of Standard English. Students interested in that area are referred to *Linguistics and Deaf Children.* Quigley et al. (1978) have also developed and standardized a criterion reference test of syntactic abilities for deaf children between the ages of 10 and 18. In addition, Alice Streng (1972) has published a volume on transformational grammar, *Syntax, Speech and Hearing,* that teachers can use in teaching language to the deaf. Increasingly, language development curricula, procedures, and materials for the deaf are utilizing concepts and terminology derived from the field of linguistics.

CAPTIONED FILMS FOR THE DEAF

Before the advent of talking films, the deaf were able to enjoy movies since they could read the captions. The invention of sound films deprived the deaf of an earlier medium of educational and cultural enrichment. In order to compensate for that loss, Congress appropriated funds in 1958 for Captioned Films for the Deaf. The program was originally designed to improve and enrich the curriculum for the deaf by providing captioned films for use in educational institutions. The original program of captioned films provided a loan service, and has been expanded to include other services: to provide equipment to be used in homes and schools, to contract for the development of educational media, to train personnel in the use of the educational technology, and to establish a national center for the development of educational media and the use of television for educational purposes, and for the development of technology for programmed learning.

Alternative learning environments

Table 6.5 presents the 1976 summary of schools and classes for hearing-impaired children in the United States. It will be noted in the table that hearing-impaired children are being educated in (1) public and private residential schools, (2) public and private day schools, and (3) public and private day classes. It should be noted from this table that:

1. The total enrollment is 44,949.
2. The largest enrollment is in public day schools and classes (6,094 and 17,120, respectively). The second largest is in public residential schools (18,223).
3. Approximately one-quarter of the enrollment is multi-handicapped (10,859).
4. The preschools are mostly associated with public schools.

TABLE 6.5

Tabular summary of schools and classes in the United States, October 1, 1976

Schools and classes	Program data			Student data — Present enrollment										
	Preschool	*Multi-handcpd. prgm.*	*High school*	*Total enrollment*	*Male*	*Female*	*Residential*	*Day*	*¹Total multi-hndcpd.*	*Deaf-blind*	*Deaf-ment. rtrd.*	*Lrng. disabld., incl. aphasic*	*Soc.-emot. distrbd.*	*Other multi-hndcpd.*
65 Public residential schools	43	46	52	18,223	10,123	8,110	13,378	4,855	4,479	112	793	1,435	747	791
9 Private residential schools	7	3	1	562	314	248	310	252	19	0	2	10	0	1
63 Public day schools	52	36	25	6,094	3,247	2,847	4	6,090	1,600	92	265	781	189	112
29 Private day schools	13	5	1	554	272	282	0	554	146	8	3	68	4	11
403 Public day classes²	262	148	130	17,120	9,056	8,064	113	17,007	2,811	167	799	791	272	376
25 Private day classes³	17	10	3	431	206	225	0	431	97	7	19	30	8	20
30 Multi-handicapped only	15	0	0	638	381	257	213	425	403	105	91	52	11	14
47 Specified handicap facilities	16	0	0	1,317	758	559	1,025	292	1,304	480	637	45	22	18
Total (671) schools and classes	425	248	212	44,949	24,357	20,592	15,043	29,906	10,859	971	2,609	3,212	1,253	1,343

Source: Adapted from Craig and Craig, 1977.

¹Total included in total enrollment figures
²Total itinerant services only, in pub. day cls.: 48
³Total itinerant services only, in priv. day cls.: 1

Education at different developmental levels

Programs for the hearing impaired usually consist of (1) early home training, (2) nursery school and kindergarten training, (3) elementary school training, (4) secondary school training, and (5) postsecondary school training.

EARLY HOME TRAINING

Educators of the deaf emphasize early training in the communication skills as soon as a child is known to be deaf. At first the child learns to communicate at home, partly by facial expressions, gestures, and movements. Those who advocate oralism suggest that the parents not gesture with their hands but rather talk to the child to encourage alertness for clues in facial expression instead of watching hand movements. Those who advocate total communication instruct the parents in finger-spelling and sign language.

Thus even the child in the crib obtains clues from the mother through her manner of handling him or her (tactile and kinesthetic) and through her facial expressions (visual). As the mother says no, she shakes her head; when she says yes, she has a different facial expression and nods. The child soon learns to respond to the lip movements and the facial expression or head movement. Through the tactile sense the child obtains communication clues by feeling the vibrations of the mother's voice as she sings or by feeling her face and throat as she talks.

Parents are generally instructed to use a whole or natural method of communicating with a deaf child rather than a special system. They are asked to talk to the child, even though at first, like hearing babies, he or she does not understand. The child will note in time that lip movements, head movements, facial expressions, vibrations, and signs have some communicative meaning. This sense of meaning develops very slowly, but faster if the parent continues to communicate in a natural way.

Moores (1978) noted that early intervention has been advocated and practiced for several centuries. The recent thrusts have placed more emphasis on (1) early parental involvement, (2) cognitive and academic training, (3) the use of combined oral and manual communication, and (4) greater use of residual hearing. The John Tracy Clinic (1954) in Los Angeles offers a correspondence course for parents, and Northcott (1972) has developed a *Curriculum Guide* for hearing-impaired children from birth to 3 years of age.

THE NURSERY SCHOOL AND KINDERGARTEN

Many schools and programs for the deaf admit children as young as 2½ to 3 years of age. The reason for such early admission is the greater need these children have for opportunities to practice socialization in a group situation and to develop skills in communication. The play activities of the nursery school and kindergarten foster growth in the communication skills through speech reading and in other ways. Although the children cannot hear, rhythm activities use pianos, drums, and other musical instruments, to which they can respond by feeling the vibrations. At a later age speech too will be developed partly through responses to vibration.

In addition, the teacher talks to the children when they are watching his or her face. They learn, for example, to recognize their names; they learn to jump, stop, walk, or dance in response to the verbal and manual request of the teacher. In this way a beginning is made in language as well as a start in speech reading and total communication. At the five-year level the children begin to respond to words and phrases written on flash cards or on the board. That kind of reading is usually initiated earlier with deaf children than with the hearing child. Whereas the latter relies on hearing and speech for communication, the young deaf child has to rely heavily on vision. Hence the emphasis on beginning reading at an earlier age. Ordinarily, the same vocabulary is used in developing speech, speech reading, and reading.

The major purposes of nursery schools and kindergartens for young deaf children between the ages of 3 and 6 are: (1) to give the child experiences with other children in sharing, playing, and taking turns (a socialization process), (2) to develop language and communication ability (oral-aural only or total communication), (3) to help the child take advantage of residual hearing through the use of hearing aids and amplified sounds, (4) to develop in the child elementary number concepts, (5) to develop a readiness for reading words and phrases, and (6) to provide parent education.

THE ELEMENTARY YEARS

The elementary school for deaf children is divided generally into a primary level and an upper elementary level. The primary-level instruction for deaf children is much more highly structured than that in the kindergarten. Training in language and communication permeates all activities and all content subjects. If the child does not learn speech and speech reading at this age level, it is unlikely that he or she will acquire those skills later.

Language, reading, and the content subjects are pursued through total communication in residential schools and day classes. In many residential schools deaf teachers of the deaf are employed for instruction in the manual department. In general, however, the emphasis is on combined forms of communication: finger spelling and speech or sign language and speech.

The upper elementary level in schools for the deaf enrolls children of ages 9 or 10 to 16. Since deaf children are generally retarded educationally from two to six years, the instruction is keyed to the content subjects of the fourth through the eighth grades. The large majority of deaf children consequently do not achieve the educational level of eighth grade.

THE SECONDARY YEARS

Deaf children continue from elementary school into high school in public school systems and residential institutions. In day schools many of them are assigned to regular classes in the high school, rather than to special classes, but have an itinerant teacher who helps them understand what they miss from class discussion. With such assistance some of the severely and extremely deaf are able to complete high school.

Secondary school education is offered in the residential schools for the deaf throughout the country. When the residential school is located in a city, some of the elementary graduates live at the school but attend regular high schools in the city. Some residential schools offer secondary school programs as well as prevocational programs.

Because many hearing-impaired secondary school students are below their age-grade expectancy, they have difficult times coping with college subjects. In 1965 Congress authorized a model secondary school for the deaf to be supported by federal funds. An agreement has been made with Gallaudet College to establish and operate a model secondary school, which also would serve primarily residents of the District of Columbia.

POSTSECONDARY SCHOOL PROGRAMS

In 1864 Congress established Gallaudet College, the only college in the world devoted exclusively to the education of deaf individuals. It has since become an accredited four-year liberal arts college and has added a graduate school, which includes both hearing and deaf students. Gallaudet College also operates the Kendall Demonstration Elementary School.

Not all deaf secondary school graduates who desire a college education attend Gallaudet College. Quigley, Jenne, and Phillips (1968) made a survey of liberal arts colleges and universities in the United States and found 653 deaf individuals who had attended 326 accredited institutions of higher learning in forty-five states.

Another development in higher education was the result of the organization of the National Technical Institute for the Deaf in Rochester, New York, which is also supported by the federal government. The institute was founded in 1967 for the purpose of providing opportunities to deaf adolescents and adults for training in technical and vocational pursuits. In addition to that development and because of the expansion of community colleges, a federally supported project was initiated in 1968–1969 to establish three postsecondary programs for deaf students in community colleges. They have been established in three sections of the country—at Delgado Vocational Technical Junior College, New Orleans, Louisiana; Seattle Community College, Seattle, Washington; and St. Paul Technical Vocational Institute, St. Paul, Minnesota. Career objectives in those community colleges most frequently selected by deaf students were reported by Craig, Craig, and Barrows (1970) to include graphic arts, sheet-metal working, welding and body repair, food services, machine-tool processing, production arts, prosthetics, and electronics.

Stuckless and Delgado (1975) have reported that forty-three other postsecondary schools have been initiated in junior colleges, community colleges and vocational schools, and state colleges.

Those postsecondary developments occurred because, according to Boatner, Stuckless, and Moores (1964) and also to Kronenberg and Blake (1966), the hearing-impaired young adults were more generally unemployed than were the general population, and obtained inferior jobs. Moores, Fisher, and Harlow (1974) evaluated three programs: the Delgado Vocational Technical Junior College, the Seattle Community College, and the St. Paul Technical Vocational Institute. These schools were established and enrolled many hearing individuals but accepted a small group (sixty-five to one hundred) of hearing-impaired young adults. Those authors found that the development of postsecondary vocational programs had positive results. For example, one of their findings was that 75 percent of the graduates of the programs obtained positions in technical, trade, and commercial enterprises as compared with one-third of nontrained individuals who obtained such employment as reported earlier by Boatner, Stuckless, and Moores (1964). In addition, the students and their parents appeared pleased with the new opportunities.

It now appears that within the 1970s higher education for young deaf adults has expanded from liberal arts education at Gallaudet College and at regular colleges and universities to technical schools, junior colleges, community colleges, and vocational schools. This trend is in harmony with the trend for hearing adults in which junior community colleges have mushroomed to accommodate the many young people who are not interested in a liberal arts education or a profession.

Summary

1. Definitions for children with different degrees of hearing impairment or different conditions of hearing loss are (a) the congenitally deaf, or prelingually deaf; those born without hearing; (b) the adventitiously deaf or deafened, or postlingually deaf; those losing their hearing after speech and language is developed; and (c) the hard of hearing; those with reduced hearing acuity.

2. The usual classifications for degrees of hearing loss are (a) slight or mild, (b) mild or moderate, (c) marked or moderately severe, (d) severe, and (e) profound.

3. Two kinds of hearing losses are found in children: (a) conductive hearing losses and (b) sensorineural hearing losses.

4. The prevalence of hearing loss has been estimated from recent studies to be approximately 2.5 percent of the school population or 1.3 million children. Of these, 45,000 are in residential schools and in day schools and classes; the rest are being served in regular grades with supportive help or are not receiving services.

5. The etiology of hearing impairment has been reported as (a) prenatal causes including: (1) maternal rubella, (2) heredity, (3) premature birth, (4) Rh incompatibility, and (5) other complications of pregnancy; and (b) postnatal causes including: (1) meningitis, (2) measles, (3) otitis media, and (4) mumps, fever, trauma, and other causes.

6. Because of the problem of language and communication, the deaf have greater problems in adjustment.

7. Children with severe and profound hearing losses are from two to five years below their chronological age in educational achievements.

8. Deaf adults obtain positions predominantly as operatives, craftsmen, and similar workers and also become members of the professions. There are significantly fewer in management and similar positions as compared with the general population. The income of deaf employed persons is slightly below that of the average hearing person.

9. Factors influencing the linguistic and educational development of hearing-impaired children are (a) age at onset of hearing loss, (b) the degree of hearing loss, (c) the intelligence of the child, and (d) the amount and quality of instruction.

10. The identification and diagnosis of hearing impairment in children include (a) preliminary screening of children through threshold testing, (b) otological and other medical examinations, (c) audiological and hearing-aid evaluation, and (d) psychological and educational assessment.

11. The education of the deaf has a long history characterized by heated controversies concerning the best methods of educating the deaf, the main one being the oral versus the manual method of communication.

12. The current communication approaches include four interrelated methods: (a) the oral-aural method, (b) the Rochester finger-spelling method, (c) the auditory method, and (d) the total communication philosophy.

13. The special educational procedures for children with impaired hearing include (a) instruction in the use of hearing aids, (b) auditory training, (c) speech reading (lip reading), (d) speech remediation, (e) speech development, (f) language development including finger spelling and sign language, and (g) reading and other school subjects.

14. The learning environments that have been organized for the hearing impaired consist of (a) public and private residential schools, (b) public and private day classes, and (c) public and private day schools.

15. The delivery of services for children with impaired hearing consists of (a) early home training by parents and teacher consultants, (b) nursery school and kindergarten programs, (c) elementary and secondary programs, and (d) postsecondary programs, including Gallaudet College, the National Technical Institute for the Deaf, and special provisions for vocational training in community and junior colleges.

References

ALCORN, KATE. 1938. "Speech Developed Through Vibration." *Volta Review* 40 (November): 633–637.

ALCORN, SOPHIA K. 1942. "Development of Speech by the Tadoma Method. *Proceedings of the Thirty-second Meeting of the Convention of American Instructors of the Deaf."* Washington, D.C.: U.S. Government Printing Office. Pp. 241–243.

BIRCH, J. R., E. R. STUCKLESS, AND J. W. BIRCH. 1963. "An Eleven-Year Study of Predicting School Achievement in Young Deaf Children." *American Annals of the Deaf* 108 (May): 236–240.

BOATNER, E., E. STUCKLESS, AND D. MOORES. 1964. *Occupational Status of the Young Deaf Adults of New England and the Need and Demand for a Regional Technical Vocational Training Center.* West Hartford, Conn.: American School for the Deaf.

BRASEL, K., AND S. QUIGLEY. 1975. *The Influence of Early Language and Communication Environments in the Development of Language in Deaf Children.* Urbana: University of Illinois Institute for Research on Exceptional Children.

BRICKER, D. B., W. A. BRICKER, AND L. A. LARSEN. 1968. *Operant Audiometry Manual for Difficult-to-Test Children.* Nashville, Tenn.: IMIRID, George Peabody College.

BRILL, R. G. 1962. "The Relationship of Wechsler IQ's to Academic Achievement Among Deaf Students." *Exceptional Children* 28 (February): 315–321.

BROWN, R. W., AND URSELA BELLUGI. 1964. "Three Processes in the Child's Acquisition of Syntax." *Harvard Educational Review* 34: 133–151.

BRUHN, MARTHA E. 1947. *The Mueller-Walle Method of Lip Reading for the Hard of Hearing.* Boston: M. H. Leavis.

BUNGER, ANNA M. 1952. *Speech Reading: Jena Method,* 2nd ed. Danville, Ill.: The Interstate Press.

CALVERT, D., AND R. SILVERMAN. 1975. *Speech and Deafness.* Washington, D.C.: Alexander Graham Bell Association. Pp. 148–156.

COMMITTEE ON NOMENCLATURE. 1938. Conference of Executives of American Schools for the Deaf. *American Annals of the Deaf* 83.

CONFERENCE OF EXECUTIVES OF AMERICAN SCHOOLS FOR THE DEAF. 1976. *American Annals of the Deaf* 121 (August): 4.

COOPER, R. L. 1965. "The Development of Morphological Habits in Deaf Children." In J. Rosenstein and W. H. Macginitie, eds., *Research Studies on Psycholinguistic Behavior of Deaf Children.* (Research Monograph Series B, No. B02.) Arlington, Va.: Council for Exceptional Children. Pp. 3–11.

CRAIG, W.N., AND HELEN CRAIG, EDS. 1977. *American Annals of the Deaf* 122 (April):2.

CRAIG, W., HELEN CRAIG, AND NONA L. BARROWS. 1970. "A Progress Report: Post Secondary Opportunities for Deaf Students." *Volta Review* 72 (March): 290–295.

DAVIS, H. 1970. "Abnormal Hearing and Deafness." In H. Davis and R. Silverman, eds., *Hearing and Deafness.* New York: Holt, Rinehart and Winston.

DAVIS, H., AND F. W. KRANTZ. 1964. "The International Standard Reference Zero for Pure-Tone Audiometers and Its Relation to the Evaluation of Impairment of Hearing." *Journal of Speech and Hearing Research* 7 (March): 7–16.

DI CARLO, L. M. 1964. *The Deaf.* Englewood Cliffs, N.J.: Prentice-Hall.

Education of Deaf Children: The Possible Place of Fingerspelling and Signing. 1967. London: Department of Education and Science, Her Majesty's Stationery Office.

ESPESETH, V. K. 1969. "An Investigation of Visual-Sequential Memory in Deaf Children." *American Annals of the Deaf* 114 (September): 786–789.

EVANS, L. 1965. "Psychological Factors Related to Lipreading." *Teacher of the Deaf* 63 (May): 131–136.

FANT, L. J., JR. 1964. *Say It with Hands.* Washington, D.C.: Gallaudet College Centennial Fund Commission. P. 1.

FARBER, B. 1959. *The Prevalence of Exceptional Children in Illinois.* (Circular Census 14.) Springfield, Ill.: Office of the Superintendent of Public Instruction.

FITZGERALD, EDITH. 1954. *Straight Language for the Deaf: System of Instruction for Deaf Children,* 2nd ed. Washington, D.C.: The Volta Bureau.

FURTH, H. G. 1973. *Deafness and Learning: A Psychological Approach.* Belmont, Calif.: Wadsworth Publishing Co.

GENTILE, A. 1973. *Further Studies in Achievement Testing, Hearing Impaired Students: 1971.* Annual Survey of Hearing Impaired Children and Youth. (Gallaudet College Office of Demographic Studies, Ser. D, No. 13.) Washington, D.C.: Gallaudet College.

GROHT, MILDRED. 1958. *Natural Language for Deaf Children.* Washington, D.C.: A. G. Bell Association.

HARDY, JANET B. 1968. "The Whole Child: A Plea for a Global Approach to the Child with Auditory Problems." *Education of the Deaf: The Challenge and the Charge.* Washington, D.C.: U.S. Government Printing Office.

HICKS, D. E. 1970. "Comparison Profiles of Rubella and Non-Rubella Deaf Children." *American Annals of the Deaf* 115 (March): 65–74.

HOFSTEATER, H. T. 1959. *An Experiment in Preschool Education: An Autobiographical Case Study.* Bulletin No. 3, Vol. 8. Washington, D.C.: U.S. Government Printing Office. (Reprinted in S. A. Kirk and F. Lord, eds. 1974. *Exceptional Children: Educational Resources and Perspectives.* Boston: Houghton Mifflin, Pp. 263–274.)

HULL, F., P. MIEKEE, JR., J. WILEFORD, AND R. TIMMONS. 1976. *National Speech and Hearing Survey.* Project No. 50978, Bureau of Education for the Handicapped, U.S. Office of Education, Department of Health, Education, and Welfare. Washington, D.C.

ILLINOIS COMMISSION ON CHILDREN. 1968. *A Comprehensive Plan for Hearing Impaired Children in Illinois.* Springfield, Ill.: The Commission.

JESEMA, C. 1975. "The Relationship Between Academic Achievement and the Demographic Characteristics of Hearing Impaired Children and Youth." (Gallaudet College Office of Demographic Studies.) Washington, D.C.: Gallaudet College. Pp. 1–15.

JOHN TRACY CLINIC. 1954. *Correspondence Course for Parents of Little Deaf Children.* Los Angeles: John Tracy Clinic.

JORDAN, I. K., GERILEE GUSTASON, AND ROSLYN ROSEN. 1976. "Current Communication Trends at Programs for the Deaf." *American Annals of the Deaf* 121 (December): 527–536.

KIRK, S. A. 1972. *Educating Exceptional Children,* 2nd ed. Boston: Houghton Mifflin.

KLOEPFER, H. W., JEANNETE LAQUAITE, AND J. W. MC LAURIN. 1970. "Genetic Aspects of Congenital Hearing Loss." *American Annals of the Deaf* 115 (January): 17–22.

KOPP, G. A., AND HARRIET G. KOPP. 1963. *An Investigation to Evaluate the Usefulness of the Visible Speech Cathode Ray Translator as a Supplement to the Oral Method of Teaching Speech to Deaf and Severely Deafened Children.* Washington, D.C.: Vocational Rehabilitation Administration, Department of Health, Education, and Welfare.

KRONENBERG, H., AND G. BLAKE. 1966. *Young Deaf Adults: An Occupational Survey.* Hot Springs, Ark.: Arkansas Rehabilitation Service.

LENNEBERG, E. H. 1965. "The Capacity for Language Acquisition." In J. P. Fodor and J. J. Katz, eds., *The Structure of Language.* Englewood Cliffs, N.J.: Prentice-Hall, Pp. 579–603.

LESHIN, G. 1975. *Speech for the Hearing Impaired Child.* Tucson: University of Arizona Press.

LINDSAY, P. H., AND D. A. NORMAN. 1972. *Human Information Processing.* New York: Academic Press.

LING, D. 1976. *Speech and the Hearing-Impaired Child: Theory and Practice.* Washington, D.C.: Alexander Graham Bell Association for the Deaf.

LUNDE, A., AND S. BIGMAN. 1959. *Occupational Conditions Among the Deaf.* Washington, D.C.: Gallaudet College.

MARTENS, ELISE H. 1936. *The Deaf and Hard of Hearing in the Occupational World.* (Bulletin No. 13.) Washington, D.C.: U.S. Office of Education.

MEADOW, K. P. 1975. "The Development of Deaf Children." In E. Hetherington, ed., *Review of Child Development Research.* Chicago: University of Chicago Press. Pp. 441–507.

MEADOW, K. P. 1968. "Early Communication in Relation to the Deaf Child's Intellectual, Social, and Communicative Functioning." *American Annals of the Deaf* 113 (January): 29–41.

MOORES, D. F. 1978. *Educating the Deaf: Psychology, Principles and Practices.* Boston: Houghton Mifflin.

MOORES, D. F. 1972. Neo-oralism and Education of the Deaf in the Soviet Union. *Exceptional Children* 38 (January): 377–384.

MOORES, D. F., S. FISHER, AND M. HARLOW. 1974. *Post Secondary Programs for the Deaf: Monograph VI: Summary and Guidelines.* (University of Minnesota Research, Development and Demonstration Center in Education of Handicapped Children, Research Report No. 80.) Minneapolis: University of Minnesota.

MORKOVIN, B. V. 1960. "Experiment in Teaching Deaf Preschool Children in the Soviet Union." *Volta Review* 62 (June): 260–268.

MYKLEBUST, H. R. 1960. *The Psychology of Deafness*. New York: Grune & Stratton.

NORTHCOTT, W. H. 1972. *Curriculum Guide: Hearing-Impaired Children—Birth to Three Years—and Their Parents*. Washington, D.C.: Alexander Graham Bell Association for the Deaf.

NORTHERN, J. L., AND M. P. DOWNS. 1974. *Hearing in Children*. Baltimore: Williams & Wilkins.

OLSSON, J. E., AND H. G. FURTH. 1966. "Visual Memory-Span in the Deaf." *American Journal of Psychology* 79 (September): 480–484.

O'NEILL, J. J., AND H. J. OYER. 1961. *Visual Communication for the Hard of Hearing*. Englewood Cliffs, N.J.: Prentice-Hall.

POTTER, R. G., G. A. KOPP, AND HARRIET C. GREEN. 1947. *Visible Speech*. New York: Van Nostrand.

PRONOVOST, W. 1970. "The Instantaneous Pitch-Period Indicator." *Education of the Hearing Impaired* 1 (Spring): 37–39.

PUGH, GLADYS. 1946. "Summaries from Appraisal of the Silent Reading Abilities of Acoustically Handicapped Children." *American Annals of the Deaf* 91 (September): 331–349.

QUIGLEY, S. P. 1969. *The Influence of Finger Spelling on the Development of Language, Communication, and Educative Achievement in Deaf Children*. Urbana, Ill.: Institute for Research on Exceptional Children.

QUIGLEY, S. P., W. C. JENNE, AND SANDRA B. PHILLIPS. 1968. *Deaf Students in Colleges and Universities*. Washington, D.C.: Alexander Graham Bell Association for the Deaf.

QUIGLEY, S. P., M. W. STEINKAMP, D. S. POWERS, AND B. W. JONES. 1978. *Test of Syntactic Abilities*. Beavertown, Ore.: Dormac, Inc.

QUIGLEY, S. P., R. B. WILBUR, AND D. S. MONTANELLI. 1976. "Complement Structures in the Language of Deaf Students." *Journal of Speech and Hearing Research* 19 (September): 448–457.

REIS, P. 1973. *Reported Causes of Hearing Loss for Hearing Impaired Students: 1970–1971*. (Annual Survey of Hearing Impaired Children and Youth, Ser. D, No. 12.) Washington, D.C.: Gallaudet College. P. 12.

RUSSELL, W. K., S. P. QUIGLEY, AND D. J. POWER. 1976. *Linguistics and Deaf Children: Transformational Syntax and Its Applications*. Washington, D.C.: Volta Bureau.

SCHEIN, J. D., AND M. T. DELK, JR. 1974. *The Deaf Population of the United States*. Silver Spring, Md.: National Association of the Deaf.

SHARP, ELIZABETH Y. 1972. "The Relationship of Visual Closure to Speech Reading Among Deaf Children." *Journal of Exceptional Children* 38 (May): 729–734.

SILVERMAN, R. 1957. "Education of the Deaf." In L. E. Travis, ed., *Handbook of Speech Pathology*. New York: Appleton-Century-Crofts.

SILVERMAN, S. R. 1960. "From Aristotle to Bell." In H. Davis and S. R. Silverman, eds., *Hearing and Deafness*. New York: Holt, Rinehart and Winston. Pp. 375–383.

STARK, C. E. 1968. "Preliminary Work with the New Bell Telephone Visible Speech Translator." *American Annals of the Deaf* 113 (March): 205–211.

STOWELL, AGNES, ESTELLE SAMUELSON, AND ANN LEHMAN. 1928. *Lip Reading for the Deafened Child*. New York: Macmillan.

STRENG, ALICE, W. J. FITCH, L. D. HEDGECOCK, J. W. PHILLIPS, AND J. A. CARRELL. 1958. *Hearing Therapy for Children,* 2nd ed. New York: Grune & Stratton.

STRENG, R. 1972. *Syntax, Speech and Hearing*. New York: Grune & Stratton.

STUCKLESS, E. R., AND G. DELGADO. 1973. *A Guide to College Career Programs for Deaf Children*. Washington, D.C.: Gallaudet College.

STUCKLESS, E. R., AND J. W. BIRCH. 1966. The Influence of Early Manual Communication on the Linguistic Development of Deaf Children. *American Annals of the Deaf* 3 (March): 452–460.

TRYBUS, R. J., AND M. A. KARCHMER. 1977. "School Achievement Scores of Hearing Impaired Children: National Data on Achievement Status and Growth Patterns." *American Annals of the Deaf* 122 (April): 62–69.

VAN LIESHOUT, C. F. M. 1973. "The Assessment of Stability and Change in Peer Interaction of Normal Hearing and Deaf Pre-school Children." Paper presented at the 1973 biennial meeting of the International Society for the Study of Behavioral Development, Ann Arbor, Mich., August 21–25.

VERNON, M. 1970. "Early Manual Communication and Deaf Children's Achievement." *American Annals of the Deaf* 115 (September): 527–536.

VERNON, M. 1968a. "Fifty Years of Research on the Intelligence of Deaf and Hard of Hearing Children: A Review of Literature and Discussion of Implications." *Journal of Rehabilitation of the Deaf* 1 (January): 1–12.

VERNON, M. 1968b. "Current Etiological Factors in Deafness." *American Annals of the Deaf* 113 (March): 106–115.

WALLIN, J. E. W. 1924. *The Education of Handicapped Children*. Boston: Houghton Mifflin.

7

Educational activities depend heavily on the sense of vision. Learning colors, watching the hamsters in the cage, observing the expressions on people's faces, using the workbooks and readers, sensing distance perception—all are restricted for children without vision. Their horizons must retract to the immediate vicinity where they can touch and hear stimuli. Walk around blindfolded, or even live behind a clouded glass, and some sense of their restricted environments and limited perceptions will be evident.

This chapter will discuss the characteristics of children who are labeled blind or partially sighted (legally blind, medically blind, occupationally blind, partially sighted, visually impaired, and so forth) and the educational adaptations that must be made for them.

Definitions and classifications

As is true with other handicapping conditions discussed in this text, the definition of the visually impaired is more complicated than the citizen with casual interest might suppose. In general, children with visual impairments are classified in two major groups, (1) the blind and (2) the partially seeing or low-vision children.

The National Society for the Prevention of Blindness Fact Book (1966) developed the following definitions:

> Blindness is generally defined in the United States as visual acuity for distance vision of 20/200 or less in the better eye, with acuity of more than 20/200 if the widest diameter of field of vision subtends an angle no greater than 20 degrees.
>
> The partially seeing are defined as persons with a visual acuity greater than 20/200 but not greater than 20/70 in the better eye with correction. (p. 10)

That definition is a legal-medical classification and requires tests of visual acuity, the most widely used being the Snellen Chart. On the Snellen Chart the rating 20/20 means that the child can distinguish at 20 feet what a normal eye can distinguish at 20 feet. The figure 20/200 means that the child can distinguish at 20 feet what a normal eye can distinguish at 200 feet. The figure 5/200 means that the child can distinguish at 5 feet what a normal eye can distinguish at 200 feet.

Until recently, visually impaired children were grouped in school according to the classification devised for medical and legal purposes. Such groupings provide one program for blind and one for partially seeing youngsters. Research has demonstrated that there is not a one-to-one correspondence between measures of visual acuity and educational performance. Ophthalmologists are also concerned with visual efficiency, and for teachers that factor may be the most important one.

Lowenfeld (1973) notes: "During the past decades, educators have recognized that the functional visual efficiency, the way in which a child utilizes his vision, is more important than his measured visual acuity. Therefore, a functional definition of blindness, rather than the ophthalmological one given above, is being sought" (p. 31).

The terms used by Barraga (1976) to differentiate three types of visually impaired children represent a step in that direction. Barraga considers children *blind* when they have only light perception or have no vision and must learn "through Braille and related media without the use of vision" (p. 14). She considers children as having *low vision* when they "have limitations in distance vision but are able to see objects and materials when they are within a few inches or at a maximum of two feet away" (p. 14). Barraga considers a third group of children with *limited vision*. These children are considered sighted children if their vision can be corrected.

Bateman (1967) defined the blind and partially seeing in terms of the method they use in learning to read. She states, "educationally speaking, *blind* children are those visually handicapped children who use Braille, and *partially seeing* children are those who use print" (p. 258).

Prevalence of visual impairments

The U.S. Office of Education estimated that approximately 0.1 percent of schoolchildren have visual handicaps serious enough even after correction with glasses to warrant special educational provisions. Ashcroft (1963) stated that there are 1 in 500 who are partially sighted (visual acuity 20/70 to 20/200). Hatfield (1975) noted that there are 1 in 2,500 who are legally blind (20/200 and less).

According to *Facts About Blindness* (1976) issued by the American Foundation for the Blind, Inc., there are 1,750,000 persons in the United States who are severely visually impaired. This figure includes 400,000 who have no usable vision. Of these, 4 percent are under age 25, about 33 percent are between the ages of 25 and 64, and over 65 percent are over the age of 65. It is anticipated that the number of blind people over 65 will continue to increase as the average life span increases. On the other hand, the incidence of blindness among preschool children has dropped sharply since the discovery of the cause of retrolental fibroplasia, which accounted for over half of all blindness in preschoolers during the years 1945–1955. The discovery and use of a vaccine for rubella should also decrease the incidence of blindness in preschool children.

The human eye

The human eye is a complex system of interrelated parts (Figure 7.1). Any of the parts may be defective or become nonfunctional through disease, accidents, heredity, and other causes.

The eye has been likened to a camera for the brain. Like a camera, the human eye has a diaphragm, the *iris*. This is the colored

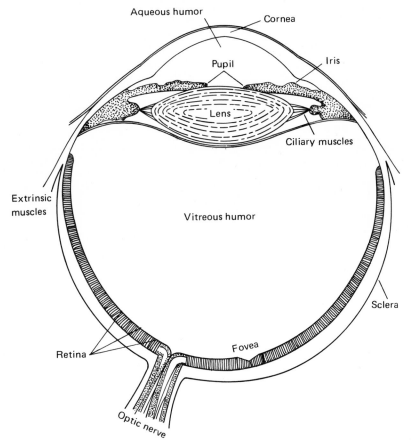

FIGURE 7.1
The human eye

Source: From P. Lindsay and D. Norman, *Human Information Processing* (New York: Academic Press, 1972).

muscular partition that expands and contracts to regulate the amount of light admitted through the central opening, or *pupil*. Behind this is hung the *crystalline lens,* which is an elastic biconvex body that focuses onto the *retina* the light reflected from objects in the line of vision. The retina is the light sensitive, innermost layer of tissue at the back of the eyeball. It contains the neural receptors that translate the physical energy of light into the neural energy that results in the experience of seeing. The process of visual interpretation as summarized by Barraga (1976) is presented in Figure 7.2.

As can be seen in Figure 7.1, there are many other protective and structural elements in the eye that can affect vision. The *cornea* is the transparent anterior portion of the tough outer coat of the eyeball. The *ciliary muscles* control changes in the shape of the *lens* so that the eye can focus on objects at varying distances from the individual. In the normal, mature eye, no muscular effort is necessary to see clearly objects twenty feet or more away. When the eye looks at an object closer than twenty feet, the ciliary muscles increase the convex curvature of the lens so that the closer object will still be focused on the *retina*. This changing of the shape of the lens is called *accommodation*. There are also *external ocular* muscles that control the movement of the *eyeball* in its socket. Those changes made by the external eye muscles are known as *convergence*. Defective functioning of those muscles creates such problems as strabismus (cross-eyedness) and less obvious imbalance of the muscles. Table 7.1 gives a summary of common disorders and anomalies of the eye.

Causes of visual impairments

The major causes of blindness and other visual impairments have been listed in broad categories to include infectious diseases, accidents

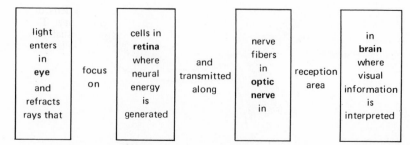

FIGURE 7.2
*Process of
visual interpretation*

Source: Redrawn from *Visual Handicaps and Learning: A Developmental Approach* by Natalie C. Barraga. Copyright © 1976 by Wadsworth Publishing Company, Inc., Belmont, California 94002. Reprinted by permission of the publisher.

TABLE 7.1

Common visual disorders and anomalies

Type of disorder	Description
REFRACTIVE ERRORS	
Hyperopia	Farsightedness; a condition in which rays of light focus behind the retina, forming a blurred and unclear image; a convex lens before the eye increases bending of light rays and brings them to focus
Myopia	Nearsightedness; a condition in which rays of light focus in front of the retina when the eye is at rest and is viewing an object twenty or more feet distant; a concave lens can refocus the image on the retina
Astigmatism	A refractive error resulting from an irregularity in the curvature of the cornea or lens of the eye and causing light rays to be refracted unevenly at different planes so that horizontal and vertical rays are focused at two different points on the retina; usually correctable with proper lenses
DEFECTS OF MUSCLE FUNCTION	
Strabismus	Crossed eyes caused by a lack of coordination of the external eye muscles; the two eyes do not simultaneously focus on the same object; can be constant or intermittent
Heterophoria	Insufficient action of one or more muscles of the eye marked by a tendency for the eyes to deviate from the normal position for binocular fixation; it creates difficulty in fusing the two images from the two eyes into one image; it is not as apparent as strabismus and can sometimes be overcome by extra muscular effort
Nystagmus	Quick, jerky movements of the eyeballs, resulting in marked visual inefficiency
OTHER ANOMALIES	
Albinism	A hereditary, congenital condition characterized by a relative absence of pigment from the skin, hair, choroid coat, and iris. It is often correlated with refractive errors and loss of visual acuity. The lack of color in the iris allows too much light to reach the retina
Cataract	A condition of the eye in which the crystalline lens or its capsule become opaque with loss of visual acuity. Treatment by surgery or other medical processes is usually possible. If the lens is surgically removed, artificial lenses are necessary, and peripheral vision is affected

and injuries, poisonings, tumors, general diseases, and prenatal influences, including heredity. Two of those conditions merit special mention.

RETROLENTAL FIBROPLASIA

An unusual eye disorder, retrolental fibroplasia, appeared suddenly in the 1940s, occurring only in premature babies. In a ten-year period, it increased alarmingly, reaching its peak in 1952–1953 at which time it accounted for well over half of all blindness in preschool children. In some hospitals the disease was striking as many as one of every eight premature babies (Kinsey, 1956). At that time it was discovered that improved incubators for premature babies were so airtight that too much oxygen was administered, causing the eye disorder known as retrolental fibroplasia.

Left in the wake of the problem was a wave of blind children of roughly the same age, requiring special school services that might not be needed after this one generation had passed.

Hatfield (1975) explored the changing causes of blindness in our society by reviewing the causes of blindness in 3,885 students registered with the American Printing House for the Blind. The catastrophic effect of retrolental fibroplasia accounted for approximately 40 percent of blind children. As the specific cause of the disorder was discovered and corrected, its incidence decreased.

Hatfield found that in 1975 there were the following approximate percentages of blind children who had had that short-lived disease:

Children 5 to 9	nearly 0
Children 10 to 14	18 percent
Children 15 to 19	40 percent

Thus, as the age of the group decreases, we find a decreasing percentage of blindness caused by retrolental fibroplasia. The younger ones were born after the cause of the disease was discovered and removed.

Other investigators pointed out that blindness was only one of a number of disastrous conditions occurring with retrolental fibroplasia. Careful neurologic evaluations of children at the age of 10 to 15 who had had retrolental fibroplasia revealed the prevalence of neurologic disorders, behavior disorders reminiscent of autism, and failure to develop normal speech (Bender and Andermann, 1965). The investigators concluded that brain damage, or the symptoms of brain damage, were a result of intrauterine conditions that interfered with normal development and led to premature birth. Silverman (1970) pointed out that the control of oxygen to prevent retrolental fibroplasia has resulted in a greater incidence of cerebral-palsied children among prematurely born babies.

With the wave of retrolental fibroplasia, the special educator was faced with the problem of educating not only a new set of blind children but also with children having a miscellaneous collection of multiple handicaps. This greatly increased educational problems. The special problems of multiply handicapped children will be considered further in Chapter 12.

RUBELLA

Rubella, described in the chapter on mental retardation, commonly produces visual impairments as well as hearing defects, mental retardation, and other disabilities in children. According to Cooper (1969), increases in disabilities and particularly in multiple handicaps occur most frequently during rubella epidemics, which recur unpredictably every seven to ten years. The last major epidemic occurred in 1964 and affected an estimated thirty thousand infants in the United States. Montgomery (1969) studied a small sample of patients referred to a clinic and reported approximately 30 percent infant mortality. From an analysis of 146 rubella survivors in a clinic, he reported 49 percent to have visual handicaps. With the advancement of medical research in isolating the rubella virus and in the development of a rubella vaccine, it is anticipated that this epidemic situation will not recur.

OTHER CAUSES OF BLINDNESS

Other causes of blindness, predominantly hereditary in nature, such as cataracts, optic nerve atrophy, and albinism, remain fairly constant in their appearance across age groups. Hereditary factors remain a much more frequent cause of blindness than do disease and accidents, which seem to be declining due to improved control measures and education.

Many diseases and conditions other than those already mentioned can attack the eyeball, cornea, lens, vitreous humor, retina, and optic nerve and cause marked visual deficiencies or total blindness. Common among these diseases are diabetes, syphilis, glaucoma, and keratitis.

Characteristics of visually impaired children

Various groups of exceptional children, including the blind, have been surveyed extensively with respect to their physical, social, mental, and educational development. Among the visually impaired the research concentration has been primarily with the legally blind, and surprisingly little material has been collected regarding partially sighted children.

In view of the results of those surveys, the major question that arises is whether visual impairments, especially blindness, affect cognitive, affective, and attitudinal characteristics. Scholl and Schur (1976) indicate that researchers have found no specific psychological reactions to visual impairments that are different from the usual reactions to stress or disability. They point out, however, that the visual loss causes (1) some restriction in the range and depth of certain cognitive experiences, since the object world can only be felt if it is small and near, and (2) some restriction of experience because of restricted mobility. In addition, Scholl and Schnur point out that the range of experience is contingent upon whether the child was born blind or became blinded later, or whether blindness was sudden or gradual.

The research on the characteristics of blind children reported in the following pages has several limitations that should be kept in mind.

1. Many of the studies do not distinguish between causes of blindness. If a youngster has been blinded by an accident, there is no reason to believe his or her intelligence has been affected unless the brain has been injured as well. However, in a case of blindness resulting from rubella, which often results in mental retardation also, the chance that intelligence will also have been affected is much greater.

2. Many of the tests used in assessing personality and social adjustment, as well as achievement and intelligence tests, have been designed for and standardized on sighted subjects. The interpretation of scores obtained by blind subjects is, at best, equivocal. (See Scholl and Schnur, 1976.)

3. It is very difficult to know what part of any differences between blind and sighted subjects is due to the visual deficit and what part to differential treatment accorded blind children.

INTELLIGENCE: COGNITIVE ABILITIES

How does blindness or partial sight affect the normal development of cognitive processes? Lowenfeld (1973) has argued that blindness limits perception and cognition in three ways: (1) in the range and variety of experiences, (2) in the ability to get about, and (3) in interaction with the environment and of the self in relation to it.

It has been difficult to assess the usefulness of intelligence tests that were designed and standardized for the sighted child. Samuel Hayes (1941), a pioneer contributor to the measurement of intelligence in blind individuals, administered a modified Stanford-Binet test (the Hayes-Binet) to 2,372 blind children in residential schools and found the mean IQ to be slightly below average (98.8).

The Wechsler Intelligence Scale for Children has also been used to measure the ability of the blind because the verbal section of the test can be administered orally with no vision needed to respond. Using that test, Tillman and Osborne (1969) found differences between blind and sighted children on various subtests. One was the digit span test requiring the repetition of a series of numbers such as 7-4-3-8-2. The blind children were superior to the sighted children on this task, suggesting the presence of good attentive habits and retention for auditory signals.

On the similarities test of the Wechsler scales, which requires the child to tell how two things are alike (for example, rose and potato), the blind performed more poorly than sighted children. That result suggested that lack of experience of the blind children was limiting their ability to link ideas and concepts together.

The responses of blind children to standardized tests may be limited by their narrow range of experiences and interaction with their environment. Kephart, Kephart, and Schwartz (1974) asked thirty-seven normally sighted and forty-nine blind children (5 to 7 years of age) to name the parts that should be included in drawings of a child and of a house. The blind children revealed less knowledge of body parts and house components than did the sighted. Even the 7-year-olds did not mention fingers, ears, or eyes in over 50 percent of the cases.

At that age level the study suggests that the manner in which blind children are processing personal and environmental information appears to result in fragmented and distorted understandings of simple and straightforward concepts. The correct responses of blind children to standard tests may hide their incomplete conceptualization of the immediate world around them.

On the other hand, Tisdall, Blackhurst, and Marks (1967) compared blind children in residential and day schools with sighted children on tests of divergent thinking ability (the ability to give many and diverse answers to questions such as "How many different ways can you use a brick?"). The ability to produce verbally the same associations as sighted children seemed unimpaired, but we do not know if the words used meant the same thing to the blind that they did to the sighted child.

STUDIES OF INTELLECTUAL DEVELOPMENT OF THE PARTIALLY SIGHTED

Livingstone (1958) administered the Stanford-Binet test to sixty children 8 and 9 years old in classes for the partially seeing and found their average IQ to be 98.6. Enlarging the test print did not help them to score any higher than they did on the regular size. Similar results had been found by Pintner, Eisenson, and Stanton (1941). They concluded that although the partially sighted were below normal on visually presented tests, they performed like normal children on reasoning, language development, and abstract generalization.

Bateman (1963) studied the effects of visual handicaps on the reading and psycholinguistic abilities of 131 children enrolled in classes for the partially sighted in public school classes in Illinois. The subjects in the classes were classified by eye condition, that is, degree of measurable loss of acuity. Forty percent were classified as mild (20/70 or better); 40 percent were classified as moderate (20/70 to 20/200); and 20 percent were classified as severe or legally blind (20/200 and less). She found that: (1) the IQs on the Binet or Wechsler scales were normally distributed with an average IQ of 100 and (2) on the experimental edition of the Illinois Test of Psycholinguistic Abilities (Kirk and McCarthy, 1961), those children (a) did not differ from the standardization norms in the auditory-vocal channel subtests but (b) performed significantly less well on visual reception, visual association, motor expression, and visual sequential memory.

The accumulation of research studies on cognitive development suggests that the ability of visually impaired children to hear and be able to communicate orally with others has allowed them to develop their intellectual abilities sufficiently to perform in the normal range on standard tests. There is some concern, however, that the concepts that the blind child has mastered may have less rich conceptual associations than is true with the sighted child.

LANGUAGE DEVELOPMENT

Language of children is studied by aural, oral, written, and reading methods. Cutsforth (1951) tested congenitally blind children with a free-association test by giving them a noun and asking them to name its attributes. He found that they responded with words that were unrealistic to them. For example, to *night,* some of them said *dark, black, blue,* and *yellow,* and only one child out of twenty-six responded *cool.* Cutsforth felt that those verbal responses were in terms of learned, associative visual responses rather than of the children's own tactile or hearing experiences. He explained that the underlying purpose of verbalism was to obtain social approval. The interest in verbalism, defined as excessive use of words not verified by concrete experience, has attracted the attention of workers with the blind because that behavior is related to language and to concept development.

Harley (1963) studied the verbalism of forty children between the ages of 6 and 14 at the Perkins Institute for the Blind and related it to CA, IQ, experience, and social adjustment. He found that (1) verbalism decreases with age, (2) the higher the IQ, the less the verbalism, and (3) the more experience with age, the less verbalism.

Dokecki (1966) reviewed the literature on verbalism in the blind and demonstrated methodological flaws in the procedures. He questioned whether Harley may have been measuring tactile discrimination, which is not really related to verbalism. He questioned the view that verbalism is meaningless and leads to loose thinking. Much of our language is nonsensory, and there is no reason to doubt the word-word nature of meaning.

Sighted individuals are often startled to hear a blind person using terminology that seems unusual, such as "look here" and "now I see the problem." In addition, he or she will employ various kinds of terms requiring visual imagery such as "pure as snow." There is doubt that use of such terms represents understanding. Demott (1972) tested sighted and visually impaired children on their ability to meaningfully associate words and on their understanding of various words. He found that there were no differences between groups in their understanding of ideas and concepts, and concluded that the blind youngster, just like the sighted one, learns many words and their meanings through their use in the language, rather than through direct experience. Those results support Dokecki's proposition that blind children should be encouraged to develop as wide a range of vocabulary as possible and that teachers should not limit the vocabulary of blind children to words that must have a sensory basis for them.

In general, one may conclude that the language of blind children (if we exclude concepts based on visual experience) is not deficient. Since much of language is acquired auditorily, the blind, unlike the deaf, can develop language usage similar to that of seeing individuals.

LISTENING

Since the blind child is denied access to visual information, the ability to gain knowledge from what he or she hears is most important. There is some evidence that listening ability can be improved by training, and the continuing development of procedures for training listening skills is urgently needed.

Talking books for the blind have been used for many years. The books are recorded in different speeds up to 190 words per minute. Efforts have been made to study the comprehension of blind children when the speed of talking is increased. Enc and Stolurow (1960) compared the comprehension of blind children under two speeds of presentation of material: fast (194 to 232 words per minute) and slow (128 to 183 words per minute). They found that the blind comprehended more per unit of listening time when the fast rate was presented. Foulke (1967), summarizing the research on compressed speech, concluded that the procedure of presenting educational materials at faster rates appears promising.

SENSORY PERCEPTION

Research workers have been interested in the question of how other sense functions are affected by visual deficiency. The doctrine of *sensory compensation* holds that if one sense avenue, such as vision, is deficient, other senses will be automatically strengthened. It was believed for some time that the blind have the capacity to hear better and have better memories than do sighted individuals. Yet research has not supported that popular opinion. In a study by Seashore and Ling (1918), it was found that there was no difference between blind and sighted subjects in auditory, tactile, and kinesthetic sensitivity.

Chess (1974) presented the alternative view that damage in one developmental area might have a negative effect on other areas. This means that an incapacity in functioning in one area retards or distorts development in other intact areas.

It remains possible, though, that blind people make better use of their available abilities in other sense fields. A sighted person may tend to disregard sounds in the environment that have, of necessity, become significant to a blind person. It does not follow that the actual hearing abilities of the two individuals differ.

In a comparison of types of imagery experienced in response to oral words or phrases, Schlaegel (1953) found no differences between blind and sighted subjects. Both experienced visual imagery most frequently, then auditory, kinesthetic, tactile-thermal, and olfactory-gustatory in that order. When the blind were subdivided on the basis of amount of remaining vision, however, visual imagery increased with visual acuity to the extent that the subjects who were the *least* blind had *more* visual imagery than the sighted subjects had.

A study by Gottesman (1971) compared the haptic perception of objects—that is, using touch to determine shape—by blind children ages 2 through 8 with a comparable group of sighted children. In comparing the relative ability to identify such things as a key, a comb, scissors, and such geometric shapes as a rectangle and cross, there were no differences found between the blind and sighted groups. Those results suggest that the development through various stages described by Piaget is still being successfully followed by the visually impaired child, when the visual problem is not complicated by the presence of other handicaps such as mental retardation.

The ability of a blind child to utilize various types of imagery is an important consideration in total development and especially in his or her educational program. Much more work is needed in this field, but at present it is known that differences exist in the extent to which blind persons utilize sensory channels and that the extent of visual loss and the age at which the loss occurs are important to educators.

An interesting development has been the discovery that residual vision in blind children can be developed through training. Barraga (1964), believing that the development of the visual process follows a sequential pattern but that training is necessary to develop maximum efficiency, conducted a significant training experiment. She matched ten pairs of blind children on the amount of remaining vision and trained one of each pair, leaving the other as a control. She designed forty-four sequential lessons and taught the experimental group, two children at a time, for thirty days. Testing both groups at the end of the experiment with a reliable visual discrimination test, she found that the experimental group scored significantly higher than did the control group. No increase in near acuity measures was noted in either group. So, while actual visual acuity remained unchanged, visual efficiency was improved.

EDUCATIONAL ACHIEVEMENT

In the 1930s the surveys of Myers (1930) and of Peck (1933) of the educational achievement of partially sighted children indicated that, at all grade levels, the partially sighted scored as well or rated as well as sighted children of the same chronological age.

A more intensive study of reading levels and reading errors made by children in classes for the partially sighted was conducted by

Bateman (1963). Ninety-six partially sighted children, attending public school classes for the partially sighted, grades two to four, were examined on four reading tests, which compose the Monroe Diagnostic Reading Examination. Error types were analyzed to determine whether or not partially sighted children are characterized by any specific kinds of reading errors. Bateman concluded:

1. The reading achievement level of the sample was in general similar to the level of achievement of sighted children.
2. The partially sighted children scored lowest on Gray's Oral Reading Examination (a test that includes a time element) and highest on the silent reading test.
3. The analysis of errors compared with that of a sample of thirty sighted children indicated that the partially sighted group made more reversal errors than did the sighted group sample, and either did not differ or made fewer errors in other areas.

Birch et al. (1966) surveyed the school achievement of 903 partially sighted children in the fifth and sixth grades to determine their level of educational achievement and to establish the appropriateness of the type size of printed material. They found that although the children were of average intelligence, they were overage for grade and two and a half years retarded in academic achievement. Birch et al. also concluded that no one size of type could be considered superior.

In 1967 Goldish estimated that there were 45,000 Braille readers in the United States. Since the educational achievement of the blind is partially dependent on their ability to read Braille, many studies have been conducted on the levels of achievement attained by blind individuals through that medium of instruction and on the methods of teaching Braille.

Nolan (1966) summarized the conclusions from studies on perceptual factors in recognizing Braille words. He concluded that children learn Braille, not as word wholes, but by the integration of the Braille characters. Henderson (1966) trained blind children in grades three to six on the recognition of Braille characters in eighteen daily sessions and found that the training group reduced their errors in character recognition by 85 percent. The training group also increased their rate of reading by twelve words per minute as compared with blind children not receiving this training.

Lowenfeld, Abel, and Hatlen (1967) studied in considerable detail the programs of teaching Braille in the residential and day school programs throughout the United States. By means of a questionnaire they concentrated on blind students in the fourth and eighth grades.

Among other findings their study showed:

1. Braille reading starts in the first grade.
2. Eighty-five percent of the teachers try to teach the children to use both hands in learning Braille.
3. Almost all the teachers taught Braille writing with reading and used a Braille writer.
4. Two-thirds of the teachers emphasized whole-word reading. (This is incongruent with the results of both Nolan and Henderson, previously mentioned.)
5. In comparison with sighted children reading print, the comprehension scores on reading tests showed that fourth-grade blind children were equal in Braille-reading ability to sighted children, while the eighth graders were superior to sighted eighth-grade children. This result was explained by the authors as a result of the higher intelligence ratings of the blind eighth graders, which averaged 110 IQ. Furthermore, the standardized tests administered in Braille allow for two to three times the reading time allowed sighted children!

Some of the studies indicate that the visually handicapped have relatively normal educational achievement. The blind are equal to the sighted child in comprehension of reading when given more time to read the tests. The exception is the study by Birch et al. (1966), who found that in their large sample the "partially seeing" children were several years retarded educationally. Since Bateman (1963) found that the most educationally retarded in her study were children who had the most minor visual handicaps, is it possible that the Birch sample consisted of children who were referred to classes for the visually handicapped because they were educationally retarded *and* also had a minor visual handicap?

SOCIAL ADJUSTMENT AND ACCEPTANCE

The study of personality, social adjustment, and attitudes of peers toward the visually handicapped has been provided by several investigators. This kind of research with children presents some difficult methodological problems. In general, their problems in mobility, the overprotectiveness of adults, and the relationships with peers and sighted individuals have led many to suspect that visually impaired children have problems in personal adjustment, helplessness, and dependency.

Fraiberg (1968) speculates that blind children do not initiate activities because they cannot see the consequences of their own acts. Myerson (1971), in discussing the problems of the partially sighted, points out that their adjustment problems are due to their marginal status (not blind, not sighted). He presents information showing that partially sighted children tend to be less well adjusted than either the blind or the seeing.

Chevigny and Braverman (1950) and Cutsforth (1951) have expressed the feelings of their associates toward them. Chevigny was told, after losing his sight, that his friends and relatives felt the same about him as they had before. He felt, on the other hand, that their attitudes had changed. Cutsforth stated that many of the emotional problems of the blind are induced in the blind person as a result of the attitudes of sighted persons. In reviewing the opinions and studies on the problem, Ashcroft (1963) gave three opinions: (1) social and emotional maladjustment are not necessarily consequences of a visual handicap, (2) when maladjustment occurs, the behavior is not necessarily related to the visual limitations, and (3) negative attitudes toward the visually handicapped and their own negative self-regard may produce more personality problems than are found among the normally seeing.

If the negative attitudes of others affect the blind, it is worthwhile to study the attitudes of sighted people toward the visually handicapped.

Sommers (1944) distributed a questionnaire to seventy-two mothers of blind children. The reactions of the parents fell into five categories: (1) genuine acceptance, (2) denial that either the parents or the child is affected, (3) overprotectiveness and excessive pity, (4) disguised rejection, and (5) overt rejection.

Bateman's study (1962) of 232 sighted children's perceptions of the abilities of blind children found that when sighted children have experience with the blind, their estimate of the blind child's ability is higher than when they had had no experience with blind children.

It is obvious from those selected studies that broad generalizations about the personalities of blind children and their social adjustments are not warranted. There appears to be some evidence of negative attitudes toward the blind, especially by those who have not dealt with them. If association with the blind enhances acceptance by others, it would follow that integrating the blind with the seeing in an educational setting is to be desired.

MOTOR COORDINATION

The research by Buell (1950) on motor performance showed quite clearly the inferiority of the blind to the partially sighted and the inferiority of both to normals. Norris, Spaulding, and Brodie (1957) found a high relationship between blind children's opportunities for learning mobility and their motor performance.

It is highly probable that a group of blind children who had had opportunities to climb trees, roller-skate, and wrestle along with their sighted peers from preschool days would not be found seriously deficient in motor coordination. Similarly, it would be expected that a group of sighted children who had been sedentary and had not taken part in such activities would be somewhat deficient motorically.

Two case studies illustrate the dangers of generalizing in this area. Gesell, Ilg, and Bullis (1950) followed the development of a blind child from infancy through the age of 4 and found the sequence of development to be normally progressing in posture, manipulation, locomotion, exploration, language, and social behavior. On the other hand, Wilson and Halverson (1947) observed another blind child and found general developmental retardation, which was most pronounced in motor areas.

Cratty (1971) has studied aspects of the motor response of blind children and finds that laterality is not as well established in the congenitally blind as in the adventitiously blind (those who had sight before becoming blind), since the former give evidence of lack of left-right tilt while walking, in the absence of auditory cues. Cratty ascribes this turning and veering to perceptual distortions but finds that training can be effective in overcoming the tendency. He suggests that planned stimulation is necessary for the proper development of motor skills in blind children.

MUSIC

It has often been asserted that music is one area in which the blind have exceptional ability and interest. Although music education is often emphasized with the blind, and history provides testimony of some blind individuals who became noted musicians, there is no evidence that the blind in general are superior in musical ability. As Napier (1973) has said: "These children are exposed to music instruction and related experiences from kindergarten on. . . . If normally seeing children were equally saturated with music, more seeing children might demonstrate musical ability, too" (p. 254).

Development of educational programs

This section will discuss (1) the historical development of the education of the blind, (2) the history of the education of the partially sighted, and (3) some recent changes in educational practices.

THE BLIND

The education of the blind has a longer history than that of the partially sighted. It was originally confined to residential schools. According to Farrell (1950), the first school for the blind was organized in Paris in 1785 by Valentin Hauy. In the United States the first residential school for the blind was organized in 1829. It was named The New England Asylum for the Blind, now known as the Perkins Institute and the Massachusetts School for the Blind. Since that date most states have established residential schools for the blind, under private or public auspices.

Historically, it may be pointed out that in the early nineteenth century, when the first schools for the blind were established in this country, the boarding school was considered the most desirable type of educational facility available, as it was so regarded in Europe during that period. Even though institutions provided an opportunity for thorough training, certain disadvantages became apparent—routine, formality, segregation, lack of family life, and so forth.

At that time, however, there were only two alternatives—either (1) send the child to an institution or (2) train him or her at home. In spite of the disadvantages of institutional living, residential schools offered the benefits of socialization, techniques and facilities, and trained teachers. Even today those advantages must be weighed against the disadvantages and viewed in the light of a particular child's needs and alternative opportunities. The child from a small community that does not have specialized facilities for education, the child whose home environment is inadequate to cope with his or her handicap, and the child who has other handicaps as well may find that the advantages of a residential school outweigh the disadvantages.

It is interesting to note that in 1871 Dr. Samuel Gridley Howe foresaw the modern trend toward mainstreaming when he stated:

> With a view of lessening all differences between blind and seeing children, I would have the blind attend the common schools in all cases where it is feasible. . . . Depend on it, one of the future reforms in the education of the blind will be to send blind children to the common schools, to be taught with common children in all those branches not absolutely requiring visible illustrations, as spelling, pronunciation, grammar, arithmetic, vocal music and the like. We shall avail ourselves of the special institutions less, and the common schools more. (Irwin, 1955, p. 128)

That prediction by Dr. Howe was not immediately fulfilled, but the proportion of blind children now being educated with the sighted in the public schools is constantly increasing. (See Figure 7.3, p. 258.)

Since 1900, when the first public school class for the blind was organized in Chicago, special classes for blind children have been established in most of the large cities and in some of the intermediate-sized communities. At the outset all the instruction for the blind was conducted in the special class. Gradually, however, blind children in those classes were assigned for part of the day to regular classes.

THE PARTIALLY SIGHTED

Education of the blind has existed for many centuries, but education of the partially sighted is a twentieth century development. According to Smith (1938), special school classes for partially sighted children originated in England in 1908. Although as far back as 1885 medical examiners in England urged specialized education for those children, it was not until 1908 that Dr. James Kerr and Dr. N. Bishop Harmon were able to persuade the educational authorities to establish the first class at Boundary Lane, England. At that time only nearsighted children were admitted to those so-called myope schools. Soon classes for myopes spread to other schools in England and Scotland.

In the United States the first class for the partially sighted was initiated in Boston in 1913. At first the class was named a "semi-blind class." It was later called a "conservation of eye class," but still later, because that name was somewhat awkward, it was again changed to "sight-saving class" (Smith, 1938).

As other cities heard about the myope classes in England, one was opened in Cleveland, Ohio, in 1913. This class, unlike the Boston class, which was segregated, initiated a program in which the children remained in the regular grades but obtained their close eye work in the special class. It was called a "cooperative class" and resembled what is now known as a resource room.

CHANGES IN EDUCATIONAL PRACTICES

It became obvious that the categories of partial sightedness and legal blindness did not determine the best mode of education for these children and that the performance on visual acuity tests did not accurately predict what the children could learn through the use of their eyes. In the first place, the medical-legal categories, although useful from medical, economic, and legal points of view, were not useful for educational purposes; in the second place, it was difficult to obtain accurate measures of the visual acuity of the children at an early age.

In dealing with exceptional children in general, there has developed a reaction against determining educational procedures on the basis of numerical test scores. The reaction has been most evident in the field of the visually impaired and, in conjunction with educational research following World War II, significantly changed educational practice and programs for the visually impaired. Major changes that occurred may be summarized as follows:

1. In the 1920s and 1930s classes for the partially blind had been called "sight saving" or "sight conservation" classes. The entire educational approach was designed to avoid straining the eyes. Current opinion, on the other hand, holds that the eyes are very rarely damaged through use and that the child should learn to use whatever vision he or she has in as many situations as possible.

2. The common practice was to place children in self-contained classes for the blind and to educate them as blind children through Braille only, even though some of the children had residual vision. Currently, such children are trained to use their eyes whenever possible. Learning print as well as Braille has been possible for many of those children.

3. Instead of placing children in self-contained classes for the blind or partially sighted, current practice is to give similar services to the children in regular classes through access to itinerant teachers or resource rooms.

4. The tests of visual acuity formerly relied on for classification of visually handicapped children are now being supplemented by another criterion, namely, how the child can learn. The concept of intraindividual differences is now the predominating criterion for educational programs.

5. The differentiation of the partially sighted and the legally blind is no longer accepted as the determinant of educational programming. Currently the educational developments apply to all the visually impaired except that the educationally blind learn primarily through the tactile and auditory senses, while others learn primarily through the visual sense.

6. For children with limited vision, the modern approach is to develop more efficient visual perception enhanced through the use of optical aids and educational technology. Evidence to be discussed later indicates that the central process of visual perception in children with residual vision can be developed by training. Although the peripheral vision does not improve with training, the central processes involved in visual perception become more functional.

7. One of the most productive of recent trends in education has been the increased effort toward including the parents of handicapped children in the treatment program. This trend is a recognition that

the home environment is a most important factor in the child's education. One way to capitalize on that fact is to include parents in the educative process by providing them with useful information on how to help their handicapped child. That information includes not only where they might find professional help but how to interact with their child to help the child develop abilities and skills. A recent pamphlet from the American Foundation for the Blind (1975) directed to the parents of blind children gives detailed instructions on how to deal with their child.

Educational patterns and trends

Scientific knowledge about visual impairments has led to current educational practices that will be discussed in this section: (1) the learning environment, (2) instructional adaptations and skills development, (3) specialized materials and equipment, and (4) programming at various age levels.

THE LEARNING ENVIRONMENT

Major changes occurred after 1960 which have had a significant impact on the education of visually impaired children. These trends and changes include (1) changes in enrollment in day and residential schools and (2) changes in type of services offered.

CHANGES IN ENROLLMENT IN DAY AND RESIDENTIAL SCHOOLS. In a survey of the enrollment of visually handicapped children in local and residential schools (Figure 7.3), Jones and Collins (1966) presented the enrollment (1) by year (1949 to 1964), (2) by number of children, and (3) by percentage of enrollment in local and residential schools. (The figures in the graph for 1970 to 1977 were obtained from the American Printing House for the Blind and were not included in Jones and Collins's study of 1966.)

Figure 7.3 shows a substantial increase in the total number of visually impaired children enrolled in public and residential schools, increasing from 5,818 in 1949 to 30,587 in 1977.★ It also shows a year-by-year decline in the percentage of visually impaired children enrolled in residential schools and a year-by-year increase in such

★ *Federal laws providing materials of instruction for the visually handicapped have resulted in the increased registry of such children.*

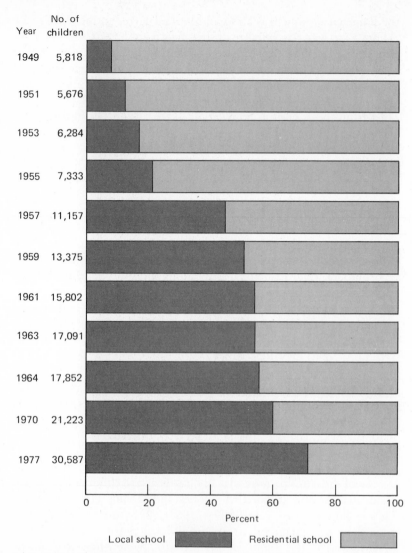

Year	No. of children
1949	5,818
1951	5,676
1953	6,284
1955	7,333
1957	11,157
1959	13,375
1961	15,802
1963	17,091
1964	17,852
1970	21,223
1977	30,587

Local school   Residential school

FIGURE 7.3

Number and percentage of school children registered with the American Printing House for the Blind, by type of school and year; United States: 1949–1977.

Source: Jones and Collins, 1966, p. 2. Data for 1970 and 1977 from American Printing House for the Blind, January 5, 1977.

children in local schools. Whereas in 1949 approximately 5 percent were enrolled in local public schools, in 1977 over 70 percent were enrolled in public schools.

When children were placed in classes according to their level of visual acuity, the very placement determined whether they would be taught to read print or Braille. Currently, *types of classes for the visually handicapped* include (1) classes that enroll children who learn print and children who learn Braille and (2) classes that enroll children who learn only print. The latter class is more common (41 percent) in local school programs. In residential school programs 2 percent learn print.

Whereas previously the *criteria for admission of a child to a program for the visually impaired* were based on type and degree of visual deficit, on normal intelligence, and on relative absence of emotional immaturity, the trend is to accept all children including the multiply handicapped that require service.

The *case load of teachers of the visually impaired* was found by Jones and Collins to be as low as eight children to one teacher in residential school classes with a medium of fifteen students per teacher for a teacher-consultant in local school districts.

Yesterday's teachers were trained to educate either partially sighted children or blind children. Currently teacher-training institutions have but one curriculum for teachers of the visually impaired. Since many programs require the teacher to teach both kinds of children and since there is great overlap in objectives and techniques, *teachers are prepared for diverse programs* including the education of the multiply handicapped. Furthermore, many children classified for legal purposes as blind are in actuality educated as partially sighted. The increased use of residual vision leaves only about 20 percent who are educationally blind and require Braille.

CHANGES IN TYPE OF SERVICES OFFERED. Jones and Collins's extensive survey gathered information from 353 local school programs for the visually impaired and from 54 residential schools in order to determine the educational patterns being used at that time. Their sample constituted 95 percent of local and residential schools in the United States employing a teacher of the visually impaired. They found that there are many patterns and combinations of patterns of service offered visually impaired children. Jones and Collins (1966) defined the five most important patterns as follows:

> *Full-time special class.* A specially staffed and equipped room in which blind and/or partially seeing children receive three-fourths or more of their formal instruction.
> *Cooperative special class.* A specially staffed and equipped room in which blind and/or partially seeing children are enrolled or registered with the special teacher, but receive less than three-fourths of their formal instruction there. The remainder of their school day is spent in regular classrooms.
> *Resource room.* A specially staffed and equipped room to which blind and/or partially seeing children who are enrolled or registered in regular classrooms come at scheduled intervals or as the need arises.

Itinerant teacher. An organizational pattern whereby blind and/or partially seeing children spend most of their school day in regular classrooms but receive special instruction individually or in small groups from itinerant teachers who travel among two or more schools devoting more than half of their time to the instruction of such children.

Teacher-consultant. An organizational pattern whereby special teachers serve as itinerant teachers part of the time but spend 50 percent or more of their time in more general duties, such as consulting with regular school personnel and distributing aids. (pp. 6–7)

While special classes for the visually impaired began as full-time classes, the patterns of organization in school systems have changed dramatically. Prior to 1946 full-time special classes were the most common (60 percent). Gradually the itinerant teacher and resource room became the most common.

INSTRUCTIONAL ADAPTATIONS AND SKILLS DEVELOPMENT

The majority of visually impaired children in local day schools are assigned to a regular grade according to their age and level of academic achievement. They are given special education through the resource rooms, itinerant teachers, or teacher-consultants. The aims and objectives of the regular grade become predominant, even though the techniques (by itinerant and resource room teachers) may be special. In other words, the general goals or objectives of education are the same for visually impaired children as for sighted children, even though the procedures for attaining those goals are achieved by modification of instructional materials and special teaching procedures. The residential schools follow the same curriculum with the exception that the visually impaired children cannot be integrated with sighted children. In residential schools, as in self-contained special classes, the teacher of the visually impaired teaches the whole curriculum, special and regular.

Obviously if visually handicapped children were exposed only to the educational experiences and materials used with sighted children (which are approximately 85 percent visual), they would not achieve their special educational goals. Special methods, materials, and equipment must be employed, utilizing the senses of hearing, touch, smell, residual vision, and even taste.

Lowenfeld (1973) has pointed out three principles to keep in mind in adapting procedures for the visually impaired. They are:

1. Concreteness. The educationally blind child's knowledge is gained primarily through hearing and touch. But if the child is really to understand the surrounding world, it is necessary that he or she be presented with concrete objects that can be touched and manipulated. Through tactile observation of models of objects, the child can learn about their shape, size, weight, hardness, surface qualities, pliability, and temperature.

2. Unifying experiences. Visual experience tends to unify knowledge in its totality. A child entering a grocery store will see the relationships of shelves and objects in space. A visually impaired child cannot obtain this unification unless teachers present him or her with experiences, such as "units of experience" of a farm, post office, and grocery store. It is necessary for the teacher to bring these "wholes" into perspective through actual concrete experience and to attempt to unify them through explanation and sequencing.

Left on their own, educationally blind children live a relatively restricted life. To expand their horizons, to develop imagery, and to orient them to a wider environment, it is necessary to develop those experiences by systematic stimulation.

3. Learning by doing. For a blind child to learn about the environment, it is necessary to initiate self-activity. A blind infant does not reach out for an object because it does not attract him or her. The infant must know of its existence by touch, smell, or hearing. Reaching and contact must be stimulated by deliberately introducing motivating situations like rattles for infants to reach for and games of finding hidden objects with smell or sound.

The visually handicapped child's ability to listen, relate, and remember must be developed to the fullest. He or she needs to learn efficiency and conservation of time because the techniques used to acquire the same information or accomplish the same task are sometimes cumbersome and time consuming. Therefore, the teacher must organize the material better, must be specific in making explanations, and must utilize sound principles of learning.

In the previous discussion we have considered the characteristics that accompany visual handicaps. These characteristics lead to the special adaptations noted in the following discussions.

Visually handicapped children, whether in classes for the blind or in regular classes, differ from each other as much as or more than children in a class for the sighted do. The degrees of blindness, ages, home backgrounds, differences in intelligence, and the special teaching problems that they present require an individualized program for each child. For that reason the size of a class for the blind is generally six to eight pupils, and each child's program must be fitted to his or her particular needs.

Most of the adaptations necessary for visually handicapped children stem from an effort to provide comparable experiences that do not involve the use of sight or that utilize the limited vision available.

That is, the children must be given tactile experiences and verbal explanations.

With the growing emphasis on integrating the blind child into society, much of the instruction of the child is taken up with the learning of skills that are routinely mastered by sighted children without specific instruction. Examples of those routine skills easily mastered by sighted children are cutting meat, handling liquids at the dinner table, identifying coins that are handed to them, and locating objects that have been dropped. Suterko (1973) gives a detailed description of how to help the blind person find a dropped object—not a matter of great concern to the sighted person, but it can be critical if a house key or razor is dropped and one is unable to find it in the dark.

There are a number of special skills that need to be taught blind children in order that they can execute normal tasks, communicate with others, and be independently mobile. The characteristics that accompany visual handicaps lead to the special adaptations noted in the discussions that follow.

VISUAL UTILIZATION. Occasionally a particular piece of research or investigation will trigger an entirely new educational method or direction with regard to exceptional children. Such was the case of the study by Barraga (1964) who investigated the potential for improving the use of vision even in children who were seriously impaired visually and legally blind, since most children labeled legally blind have some residual vision—they can, for example, see light and shadow. She introduced a series of training exercises for ten seriously impaired children that would help them with visual discrimination. Special visual clues were associated with previously experienced stimuli to enhance visual recognition. The children who were trained showed significant improvement in visual discrimination over a similar group of children who did not have the training, and such gains remained when they were all retested five months later.

With those results for encouragement, Barraga (1970) developed visual training exercises for "blind" children with residual vision that are now in substantial use by teachers of the visually handicapped. Thus, instead of avoiding the visual channel, a new educational effort was introduced, using the visual channel to its utmost. For many youngsters with partial sight, such exercises also prove most useful.

SPATIAL COMPREHENSION. One of the areas of educational emphasis is helping the blind child get a feeling for three-dimensional space. The task of map reading is the focus of many educational programs that provide the child with an extensive program of instruction based on relief maps of the community, state, and country. But special maps are not enough, since you first must have some understanding of what it is that the maps represent. Napier (1973) presents the type of careful and comprehensive set of activities that must be planned.

> Just as there must be readiness activities to prepare for the teaching of reading, there must be readiness activities prior to the teaching of map reading. Before the most rudimentary map can be read, children must experience a given area with all its details and cues. Therefore . . . the classroom is the logical place to begin. In this setting, children learn that coats are hung in the closet left of the main door, that the teacher's desk is straight ahead from the door, that the wastebasket is immediately inside the door on the right, etc. (p. 239)

THE USE OF BRAILLE. Braille reading is a system of touch reading. Embossed characters use different combinations of six dots arranged in a cell two dots wide and three dots high. The symbols are embossed on heavy Manila paper in a left-to-right order, and the reader usually "reads" with one hand and keeps the place vertically with the other. An advanced reader may use the second hand to orient himself or herself to the next line while reading the line above and may read as much as a third of the line with the left hand. Music, punctuation, and mathematical and scientific notations are based on the same system.

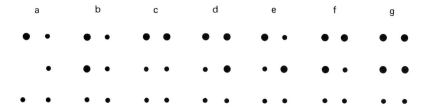

Braille in its original form was developed by Louis Braille, a Frenchman who was himself blind. It was first published in 1829 and further developed five years later. Many other systems have been attempted, including Moon's phonic symbols (modified roman letters), New York Point (using a cell two dots high and varying in width), American Braille, and British Braille. Each system had its advocates and for many years controversies raged. In an attempt to settle them, a study was undertaken in 1932; it concluded that British Braille was superior to any system being used in this country. One hundred years after Louis Braille first presented his scheme, an agreement was reached on a modified system of British Braille now termed Standard English Braille. Even so, that system was not consistently used until about 1950.

Standard English Braille has been developed on several levels of difficulty, which differ in the extent to which contractions are used over and above the basic letters and numerals of Grade 1. It is the standard that serves as a common denominator in English-speaking countries.

Even the most efficient blind reader of Braille shows an average rate of reading about two to three times slower than that of a print reader. In that area alone, one can see how blind students can fall progressively further and further behind in total knowledge when compared with the average reader. Recently attempts have been made to improve the efficiency of Braille reading. Umsted (1972) provided a training program for adolescent blind children to increase their identification and skill in reading the Braille code.

He found that once the young blind child had learned the Braille system, few attempts had been made to improve the efficiency of the youngster's Braille reading when he or she attended a secondary program. The assumption is that the code had been effectively mastered and will remain so. However, Umsted found that almost 10 percent of the Braille code was not correctly identified by blind students and that an intensive, short-term training program designed specifically to help them become more effective with the code increased their reading level from 90 words per minute to 120 words per minute for a medium reading group, and to an average gain of 25 words per minute for the high reading group. That finding suggests that continuing attention to the special skills that the blind have to learn can improve their efficiency in learning. Skills, once learned, can atrophy unless given specific practice and review.

Braille writing is another addition to the curriculum of blind children. It is taught later than Braille reading. There are various devices for writing the symbols, easiest and fastest of which is the Braille typewriter, or Braille-writer machine. It has six keys corresponding to the six dots of the cell. A good Braille typist can type forty to sixty words per minute.

Braille can also be written by hand, using a special slate and stylus. Braille slates, which come in desk and pocket sizes, are boards with a double metal strip, the lower part of which is pitted by cells of six dots each, and the upper punched with corresponding holes. Paper is inserted between the metal strips, and the desired dots are embossed by pressing a dull stylus through the appropriate holes. Since the embossing is to be read from the reverse side of the paper, the work must be done in reverse, beginning at the right margin and working toward the left.

Typing, which is seldom included in the elementary curriculum for sighted children, is very important to blind children if they are to communicate with the sighted world, a very small portion of which can read Braille. Blind children are taught to use a standard print typewriter as soon as possible, usually in the third or fourth grade. Handwriting is usually very difficult and is no longer emphasized to a great extent, except that an effort is made to teach the writing of one's own signature. The inability to write one's own name is often a source of embarrassment, which is why the signature is stressed. The typewriter has all but replaced such devices as wire guidelines, which were needed to help teach handwriting.

MASTERY OF THE ENVIRONMENT. Teaching command of the environment is of special importance to blind children in that both their physical and social independence are involved. The ease with which they can move about, find objects and places, and orient themselves to new or strange physical and social situations will be crucial in determining the role they can assume in peer relations, the types of vocations and avocations that will be open to them as adults, and their own estimation of themselves as individuals.

What can be done to aid the blind child in gaining as much mastery of the environment and of himself or herself in the environment as is possible? From a very early age the child can be helped to avoid unnecessary fear, both of new experiences and of injury. Sighted children skin their knees, bump their shins, fall from trees, and step in holes. Blind children ought to have the same "privilege" if they are to experience freedom for the control of themselves and their environment.

Blind children must be taught to feel the difference in the weight of their forks when they have successfully cornered a few peas and when the fork is still empty. A system of marking clothing and organizing it is essential for both efficiency and good grooming.

The use of models, whether of a room, the Empire State Building, or the child's neighborhood, is generally felt to be helpful in showing the relationship of one place, or size, to another. But this is not to say that models are approved as a substitute for the experience. Rather, they are an extension of experiences and can also help give a perceptual or cognitive map of relations and areas too large to be simultaneously included in direct experience.

ORIENTATION AND MOBILITY. The importance of training blind children and adults to move about in their environment cannot be overestimated. One of the greatest limitations imposed by blindness is mobility. The situations that force dependence and may cause the greatest personality and social problems are very likely to center about mobility. The use of the long cane, the seeing-eye dog, and the sighted guide have been tried with adults. Currently there is an effort to introduce mobility training in the curriculum, not only for secondary school students but also for young blind children.

One of the most important practical questions in helping the blind to move about their environment independently is how to teach the avoidance of obstacles. That is a good example of how research can help the teacher by identifying the relevant area to be emphasized. It has long been observed that many blind persons can avoid obstacles very well. They make turns in hallways, they stop before they run into a door, and so on. But how do they do it? Is it through sensing the change of air pressure on their faces? Is it their using some residual light and dark vision? Is it through the sense of hearing?

Cotzin and Dallenbach (1950) carried out a series of classic experiments designed to find the answer. They asked blind persons to walk down a path and stop when they sensed an obstacle placed there by experimenters. Then systematically the researchers eliminated the various possibilities. They put a velvet hood over the face to eliminate the cues from air pressure, then plugged the ears to eliminate hearing and blindfolded them to rule out residual vision, each in turn.

Out of those experiments came a clear and definitive result. The blind were bothered in their judgment only when their ears were plugged! They were clearly using hearing in a way analogous to that of bats, which use sound to avoid the walls in a cave. Changes in both pitch and loudness seemed to be used as clues.

That information allowed the educational program to focus on enhancing, in natural and artificial ways, the use of hearing for the purpose of effective travel. An example of the development of an artificial device was reported by Juurmaa (1970). He described a research study using an *ultrasonic torch,* a battery-powered device, which is held by the blind person. The torch emits ultrasonic sounds, which then rebound from obstacles and return so that the difference between outgoing and returning sound waves falls within the audio range. In that way the blind person can discern when he or she is approaching targets. Juurmaa reported that in the research study the blind comparison group that did not use the ultrasonic torch also performed surprisingly well. The remaining question is whether the ingeniousness of the device adds that much to the natural skill of the blind to make up for the disadvantages of carrying such a device around. One of the clear alternatives to mechanical intervention is the training of the blind to use more effectively the hearing capabilities they already have.

Hoover (1947) worked with blinded soldiers at Valley Forge Army Hospital and developed a systematic method of travel that employed the use of the long cane. His work has become the basis for instructional programs in orientation and mobility and is still widely followed. Lord (1967) identified the sequential skills that young blind children should be expected to perform. A scale was developed to measure the achievement of children with respect to those tasks. The major tasks included skills in using sensory cues, self-help skills, directions and turns, formal mobility skills, and habitual movement in space.

Additional support for early instruction resulted from a Los Angeles County project (Lord and Blaha, 1968), in which intensive individual instruction in travel was given to youths of high school age. After an average of approximately 108 hours of instruction, the average student acquired skills in the use of the long cane and other skills. In a follow-up study of those youths, it was found that many of them had limited travel needs in relation to the seeing youth of similar age; their parents were protective; their social life was limited; their vocational needs were well ahead of them. They had not grown up with usable travel skills.

Knowles (1969) studied a number of characteristics of the blind in relation to success in vocational rehabilitation. Orientation and mobility led the list of thirteen variables that correlate with success.

The area of personal mobility and independence has a particular significance in adolescence when the child is ready to break away from family restraints and overprotection. In peer relationships, security and comfort in controlling one's self and the environment are most essential to the development of poise and independence and to gaining the respect of others.

In relation to orientation and mobility training, physical education, formerly thought dangerous for the visually impaired, is being stressed as part of the curriculum. In residential schools classes for physical education are now a routine part of the curriculum. In local day schools the visually impaired are encouraged to participate in physical education activities with sighted children whenever possible. Generally, physical education is integrated with the program of orientation and mobility.

LISTENING SKILLS. It is very important that visually handicapped children be more proficient in listening skills than are seeing children. Much of their education is obtained by listening to talking books, tapes, and verbal intercourse. Special teachers have developed techniques for developing listening skills, and the research on compressed speech and its utilization has helped to decrease the time of auditory comprehension earlier considered necessary with talking books. In high school and college blind persons use readers to obtain information and must learn to listen to details.

SOCIAL AND LIVING SKILLS. Part of the job of the blind child's family, teachers, and friends is to help him or her establish patterns of behavior acceptable to others. A sighted child acquires visually much socially useful information that is not accessible to the blind child. A blind girl does not, for instance, know who is in a room as she enters, whether her attire is appropriate and neat, or what visual stimuli may have prompted a burst of laughter from her peers. The skills of successfully determining just what is customary in grooming, eating, etiquette, and the social graces and then of finding ways to implement those customs without visual cues are important to the blind child.

SPECIALIZED MATERIALS AND EQUIPMENT

The recommendations that used to be made concerning adequate lighting and furnishings of classrooms for the visually impaired are now, fortunately, incorporated into the construction of many regular schoolrooms.

Lighting is very important for visually impaired children. Illumination must be free from glare and direct sunlight and be evenly distributed throughout the room. Artificial illumination must be available for use at different times of the day. Other factors to be considered include the amount and height of window space, the adequacy of artificial illumination, and the coloring of walls and ceilings.

CLASSROOM AIDS. In addition to the physical dimensions of the classroom itself, special equipment and aids are required to facilitate instruction and learning for visually impaired children. These include movable and adjustable desks to catch the right angle of light, gray-green chalkboards that reflect more light, typewriters, dictaphones, record players, magnifying lenses, large-type books, three-dimensional maps, and other specially designed teaching-learning aids.

Audio aids are a basic element in a blind child's quest for knowledge, particularly in the upper elementary grades and beyond. Talking books, other records, and often a tape recorder may become part of everyday school life. If the child is in the regular grades, the classroom teacher or itinerant teacher may make special explanations or assignments on tape. Textbooks not available in Braille may be taped or recorded by volunteer workers.

Since Braille reading is done at less than one-fourth to one-third the speed of visual reading and since the books available in Braille are limited, *talking books* have become standard educational media for imparting information to the blind. Those long-playing phonograph records of books read by professional readers are heard at the rate of 160 to 170 words per minute for fiction and of about 150 words per minute for texts. The federal government has appropriated funds for their recording and manufacture, and the Library of Congress distributes them free of charge to libraries on request. Special phonographs are also lent through libraries. Such a system makes talking books available to blind children and adults in all communities.

In general, the talking book has been used for the presentation of fiction rather than of textbooks. Ordinarily school textbooks are made available through the American Printing House for the Blind, the Library of Congress, or privately. Talking books are labeled in Braille with a minimum of Braille words (to save space) and indicate author, title, and reader. The same information is provided in print for the use of librarians.

Arithmetic aids include an arithmetic board, an adaptation of the abacus, and even a *talking calculator.* The Braille writer is also used to compute mathematics. Pins and rubber bands are utilized in constructing geometric designs and graphs of various sorts.

Mental arithmetic, of course, is used a great deal in the education of the blind. But higher levels of arithmetic and mathematics require elaborate machines. Calculators can be adapted for use by Brailling the dials or by giving other tactile cues. Similarly, tape measures, rulers, timepieces, slide rules, compasses, protractors, and so forth have been adapted for use by the blind.

Embossed and relief maps are important in teaching space perception required in understanding geography. Besides Braille maps, relief maps and globes, and audible electric maps, jigsaw puzzles are also used.

One of the reasons for the importance of maps is not only to supplement the study of geography in general but to help orient the blind to their immediate environment. Mobility around the room or the town requires that blind persons have a mental image of the relationship of objects to each other in space. Through sensory cues and the cognitive map they are then able to orient themselves and to move around more freely.

TECHNOLOGICAL AIDS. Much engineering research has been conducted to develop aids for the blind. The following developments were reported at a conference in Los Angeles in 1970 (The Blind in the Age of Technology, 1970).

Developed at Stanford University, the *Optacon* scans print and converts print into 144 tactile pins. These pins, when activated by the print, produce a vibratory image of the letter on the finger of a blind person. As a college student, the blind daughter of Dr. John Linville, one of the inventors, was able to read at sixty to seventy words a minute with the use of the Optacon. The device is still being improved, and a blind person may be able to read regular books and notes not available in Braille. Bliss and Moore (1974) indicate that to learn to read with the Optacon, a child must have high intelligence, must spend long periods in training, and must be highly motivated. Barraga (1976) states that the Optacon is a worthwhile invention since it provides for the reading of print material without modification. At present, the cost of the Optacon is prohibitive for widespread use by blind children.

At the Massachusetts Institute of Technology a *computer automaton* is being developed that will translate ink print into Grade 2 Braille. The procedure is being used extensively at the American Printing House for the Blind.

An expansion of the computer Braille translator, the *MIT Braille Emboss,* is used with a telewriter. A teacher of the blind desiring a Braille output for new materials can request it by phone from a computer center, and it is returned in Braille by means of a teletypewriter.

One way of obtaining more rapid information through records and tapes is to increase their speed. This generally produces a distortion. Another system that has been developed is *compressed speech,* which allows the elimination of one one-hundredth of each second, or one-fiftieth or one-tenth, without causing distortion of voice. This compressor, which is now used at the American Foundation for the Blind, can double the word rate while preserving vocal pitch and quality. A blind person can comprehend recorded voices at 275 words per minute, which is comparable to reading print.

An alternative to compressed speech is available in the *Kurzweil Reading Machine,* which converts printed material into spoken English at normal speech rates. The user places the material to be read face down on the surface of the scanner, which the user activates by means of a separate control unit. The scanning mechanism locates the first line of text and begins scanning the page. Within seconds an electronic voice is heard reading the material. For more information, contact Kurzweil Computer Products, Inc., 68 Rogers St., Cambridge, Mass. 02142.

PROGRAMMING AT VARYING DEVELOPMENTAL LEVELS

One of the strongest trends in special education has been the beginning of the educational process at an early age. Another is paying special attention to the development of positive attitudinal and behavioral characteristics, as well as to the more traditional academic skills such as reading and arithmetic.

The emphasis at the preschool level is to include the parent as a partner, and the educator's work often consists of training the parent to interact more effectively with the handicapped child. As special educators extend their efforts toward earlier and earlier developmental levels, they find themselves working with the developmental building blocks on which later knowledge and skills are based.

More educators have become increasingly sensitive to the importance of the early emotional life of the blind child. Barraga (1976) provides a representative point of view: "With the visually handicapped infant body play must replace eye play to communicate maternal concerns and love—the facilitators of developing a self-concept. More than the usual amount of time should be spent cuddling, holding, touching, stroking and moving the baby" (p. 20).

Table 7.2 shows some major and important emphases in a preschool program for blind children reported by Fraiberg, Smith, and Adelson (1970). In each of the four major areas *human attachment, discovery of objects, prehension,* and *locomotion,* the parents can take specific steps to enhance the development of their child.

It is at the preschool age that parent involvement with the education of the child is most intimate. It is at this age that the parents need most help. Adequate services to the family through the school or other agencies that are knowledgeable in the education of the visually impaired can be very helpful.

Visually impaired children attend regular kindergarten in communities without much difficulty. In the activities of listening to stories, show-and-tell time, and other oral activities, the blind child is not at a disadvantage. In other activities such as painting, playing with three-dimensional crafts, and joining in on other motor activities, minor modifications are made. Teachers allow the blind child to try to participate in as many activities as possible.

Specialized instruction in reading print or Braille for the visually impaired child begins in the first grade. If the local school has a resource room or an itinerant teacher, these personnel will provide the specialized materials and instruction. Materials and aids are brought into the class in which the child is enrolled; regular-print books, large-print books, optical aids, Braille, and so forth are furnished each child. The special teacher gives visual training and any other remedial work necessary to fit the child into the regular classes.

SCIENCE ADAPTATION. Despite the generally acceptable language development of visually impaired children, it is necessary to consider

TABLE 7.2

Special programming for preschool blind children

Developmental areas	Normal child expectation	Special adaptation for blind
I. Human attachment	Vision plays a crucial role in the establishment of human bonds. The response smile to the human face, the discrimination of mother and stranger—the entire sequence of recognitory experience leads to mental representation and evocative memory. Eye-to-eye contact is the matrix of the signal system that evolves between mother and child.	We stressed the importance of "learning to know" through tactile and auditory experience. We encouraged holding and talking to the baby during feeding and also creating "social" times of holding, singing, and playing lap games as the baby's awake times increased. A blind baby, like all babies, has a hunger for experience. As the parents began to satisfy that hunger, the baby, of course, responded with the smiles, the cooing, and the flailing of arms and legs that every parent responds to as the first demonstrations of love.
II. Discovery of objects	Eye-hand coordination in the sighted child forms a nucleus from which many patterns of infant learning and development evolve. We expect the patterns of reach and grasp to develop gradually over the first four to six months in the sighted child when eye and hand become progressively coordinated.	For the totally blind baby there is no adaptive substitution of sound for vision in intentional reaching until the last quarter of the first year. The problem then is to help parents to understand the importance of play experiences in the earliest months before most people expect any baby to know or care about things. We encourage parents to introduce some form of cradle gym or hanging apparatus over the crib of the baby. Such a toy may be lowered over the baby so that random small movements will bring about touch and sound sensations. Between eight months and a year we recommend the use of a play pen for the blind baby. It gives a sense of protection and enclosure. It becomes another place to be explored, a place for finding toys with certainty, and a place for exercise in standing and supporting oneself or for easing oneself down from a standing position.

adaptations of the regular curriculum to eliminate some of its elements that would be unduly difficult for the visually impaired. For example, one of the popular science curricula, the Science Curriculum Improvement Study (SCIS), is a sequential, upgraded program in the physical and life sciences consisting of twelve units for elementary school children. Some of the units depend on the student's observing changes in the color of solutions and on other visual observations that could be extremely difficult for the visually impaired child.

A curriculum effort reported by Linn (1972) involved adapting those SCIS science materials for the blind. It included attempts to redesign the curriculum units to eliminate special content-related problems. Essential scientific concepts can be presented to the vi-

TABLE 7.2 (*cont.*)

Developmental areas	Normal child expectation	Special adaptation for blind
III. Prehension	Prehension—the activity of the baby's hands, their organization, and progressive development—is intimately related to each of the other areas discussed. In the sighted infant the coordination of vision and reaching takes place just under five months with early swiping motions at the object that is seen.	We promote organization of the hands at midline in a number of ways in the early months of life. We ask the mother to place the baby's hands on the bottle. We suggest patty-cake games and other informal, improvised lap games that bring the hands together at midline repeatedly and thus encourage their engagement. The hands exploring the face of the mother unite other sense impressions of the mother with manual tactile experience. Toys that require the child to use them in different ways will afford him or her the first notions of causality and will lead away from stereotypical hand behavior.
IV. Locomotion	It is the reach for the out-of-range object that initiates the pattern for creeping. The sighted baby in the prone position searches with his or her eyes and strains upward in an insatiable need to see. The sighted baby from the earliest weeks will find just looking at the world an absorbing, full-time occupation, which will lead to the struggle to keep his or her head upright and steady.	The delay in creeping is due to the absence of the external stimulus for reaching usually provided by vision. When a baby can demonstrate postural readiness for creeping and reach on a sound cue alone, one can initiate the pattern for creeping by providing a favorite sound toy just beyond reach. We often need to lend support to the parent through periods of fear that the child will be hurt if allowed to try things on his or her own. Such fears easily lead to anxious overprotection that can seriously inhibit the child's spontaneous activity.

Source: After Fraiberg, Smith, and Adelson, 1969.

sually impaired without the special handicaps imposed by the regular curriculum.

SEX EDUCATION. One of the extremely important areas of special instruction necessary for visually limited children is the topic of sexual information and identity. As Barraga (1976) has stated:

> By the time visually impaired youth reach high school and begin to think about relationships (and marriage) with those of the opposite sex, they may have many erroneous ideas or be totally ignorant of the basic facts relating to body parts and sexual functioning. . . . Courses in sex education and preparation for marriage and family life are absolutely necessary for visually impaired children and youth. (p. 70)

MATHEMATICS ADAPTATION. Another example of how specific content has to be designed to help blind children master concepts is provided by Huff and Franks (1973) on the mathematical issue of fractional parts. It is easy enough to provide an intuitive understanding of halves and quarters by visual demonstration, but for the blind such understandings have to be gained tactilely.

Huff and Franks demonstrated that it is possible for blind children at the primary grade levels (K–3) to master those concepts if they are given three-dimensional circles of wood and asked to place them in a form board nest. After placing a whole circle, the child can learn to assemble blocks representing one-third of a circle and put them together in the nest to form the whole.

Given such a tactile experience, the blind children can master the idea of fractional parts and make discriminations between the relative sizes of various fractional parts (halves versus quarters) as well as the sighted child of similar age can.

In the middle grades (fourth through eighth or ninth grades) supplementary materials are furnished visually impaired children to help them absorb the same information learned by sighted children. This is accomplished through talking books, recorded audio lessons, and remedial work if the child needs it.

If the child with visual handicaps is of average intelligence and has learned to use the aids and materials furnished earlier, he or she can enroll in the secondary schools. Blind children are assigned readers to assist them in keeping up with their classmates. Many blind students are found in colleges and universities. With tape recorders, Braille writers, and readers, many blind individuals can graduate from college, and some receive advanced degrees in a variety of fields.

Summary

1. Visually impaired children are classified for educational purposes as (1) the *blind* who have only light perception or have no vision and must learn Braille and related media without the use of vision and (2) the *partially sighted* or those with low vision who have major limitations in distant vision but who can learn to read print and can be educated through the eyes.

2. Retrolental fibroplasia and rubella have been major causes of blindness during the period 1942 to 1965. These conditions are now under preventive control, which should decrease the prevalence of visual impairments in children.

3. It is estimated that 1 to 2 children in 1,000 require special education because of a visual handicap. Approximately 30,000 visually impaired children attend local and residential schools for the visually handicapped.

4. Approximately one-third or more of the visually handicapped children enrolled in special programs have multiple handicaps.

5. Intelligence and achievement tests reveal only slight retardation for the partially sighted or blind children, but there are evidences of subtle intellectual problems in mastering abstract concepts.

6. The majority of visually impaired children are now being educated in local day school classes rather than in residential schools.

7. Enrollments in self-contained classes are being reduced by placing visually impaired children in regular classes whenever possible and by offering the services of resource rooms and itinerant special teachers.

8. The organizational patterns for the education of the visually impaired in communities are: (a) teacher-consultant programs, (b) itinerant teacher programs, (c) resource room programs, (d) cooperative special classes, and (e) full-time special classes.

9. The curriculum for the visually impaired is similar to that for the seeing child with emphasis on concrete learning, unified instruction, and self-activity.

10. Special emphasis is now being placed on parent education to aid the early development of skills and attitudes crucial to later adaptation. The socioemotional area is receiving much greater attention than previously.

11. Special methods of training residual vision have been developed. Children with little or no residual vision acquire knowledge through reading Braille, listening to talking books, and utilizing some of the newer technological aids developed to assist in their education.

12. Orientation and mobility training, earlier confined to adults, are now becoming a part of the curriculum for visually handicapped children in elementary schools.

References

AMERICAN FOUNDATION FOR THE BLIND. 1976. *Facts About Blindness.* New York: American Foundation for the Blind, Inc.

ASHCROFT, S. 1963. "Blind and Partially Seeing Children." In L. M. Dunn, ed., *Exceptional Children in the Schools.* New York: Holt, Rinehart and Winston. Pp. 413–461.

BARRAGA, N. 1976. *Visual Handicaps and Learning.* Belmont, Calif.: Wadsworth Publishing Co.

BARRAGA, N. 1970. *Teacher's Guide for "Utilization" of Low Vision.* (Mimeographed by author.) Austin: University of Texas.

BARRAGA, N. 1964. *Increased Visual Behavior in Low Vision Children.* (Research Series No. 13.) New York: American Foundation for the Blind.

BATEMAN, B. 1967. "Visually Handicapped Children." In N. G. Haring and R. L. Schiefelbusch, eds., *Methods in Special Education.* New York: McGraw-Hill. Pp. 257–301.

BATEMAN, B. 1963. *Reading and Psycholinguistic Processes of Partially Seeing Children.* Arlington, Va.: Council for Exceptional Children.

BATEMAN, B. 1962. "Sighted Children's Perceptions of Blind Children's Abilities." *Exceptional Children* 29 (September): 42–46.

BENDER, L., AND K. ANDERMANN. 1965. "Brain Damage in Blind Children with Retrolental Fibroplasia." *Archives of Neurology* 12 (June): 644–649.

BIRCH, J. W., W. J. TISDALL, R. PEABODY, AND R. STERRETT. 1966. *School Achievement and Effect of Type Size on Reading in Visually Handicapped Children* (Cooperative Research Project No. 1766.) Pittsburgh: University of Pittsburgh.

"Blind in the Age of Technology: A Public Discussion." 1970. *The New Outlook for the Blind* 64 (September): 201–218.

BLISS, J. C., AND M. W. MOORE. 1974. "The Optacon Reading System." *Education of the Visually Handicapped* 6 (December): 98–102.

BUELL, C. 1950. "Motor Performance of Visually Handicapped Children." *Journal of Exceptional Children* 17 (December): 69–72.

CHESS, S. 1974. "The Influence of Defect on Development in Children with Congenital Rubella." *Merrill Palmer Quarterly* 20 (October): 255–274.

CHEVIGNY, H., AND S. BRAVERMAN. 1950. *The Adjustment of the Blind.* New Haven: Yale University Press.

COOPER, L. 1969. "The Child with Rubella Syndrome." *The New Outlook for the Blind* 63 (December): 290–298.

COTZIN, M., AND K. M. DALLENBACH. 1950. " 'Facial Vision': The Role of Pitch and Loudness in the Perception of Obstacles by the Blind." *American Journal of Psychology* 63 (October): 485–515.

CRATTY, B. J. 1971. *Movement and Spatial Awareness in Blind Children and Youth.* Springfield, Ill.: Charles C Thomas.

CUTSFORTH, T. D. 1951. *The Blind in School and Society,* 2nd ed. New York: American Foundation for the Blind.

DEMOTT, R. 1972. "Verbalism and Affective Meaning for Blind, Severely Visually Impaired and Normally Sighted Children." *The New Outlook for the Blind* 66 (January): 1–25.

DOKECKI, P. 1966. "Verbalism and the Blind: A Critical Review of the Concept and the Literature." *Exceptional Children* 32 (April): 525–530.

ENC, M. A., AND L. M. STOLUROW. 1960. "A Comparison of the Effects of the Two Recording Speeds on Learning and Retention." *The New Outlook for the Blind* 54 (February): 39–48.

FARRELL, G. 1950. "Blindness in the United States." In P. A. Zohl, ed., *Blindness*. Princeton: Princeton University Press. Pp. 89–108.

FOULKE, E., ED. 1967. *Proceedings of the Louisville Conference on Time Compressed Speech*. Louisville, Ky.: University of Louisville.

FRAIBERG, S., M. SMITH, AND E. ADELSON. 1969. "An Educational Program for Blind Infants." *Journal of Special Education* 3 (2): 121–141.

FRAIBERG, S. 1968. "Parallel and Divergent Patterns in Blind and Sighted Infants." *Psychoanalytic Study of the Child* 23: 264–300.

GESELL, A., F. L. ILG, AND G. E. BULLIS. 1950. *Vision: Its Development in Infant and Child*. New York: Paul B. Hoeber.

GOLDISH, L. H. 1967. *Braille in the United States: Its Production, Distribution, and Use*. New York: American Foundation for the Blind.

GOTTESMAN, M. 1971. "A Comparative Study of Piaget's Developmental Schema of Sighted Children with That of a Group of Blind Children. *Child Development* (June): 573–580.

HARLEY, R. K. 1963. *Verbalism among Blind Children*. (Research Series No. 10.) New York: American Foundation for the Blind.

HATFIELD, E. 1975. "Why Are They Blind?" *Sight Saving Review* (Spring): 1–22.

HAYES, S. P. 1941. *Contributions to a Psychology of Blindness*. New York: American Foundation for the Blind.

HENDERSON, F. 1966. "The Rate of Braille Character Recognition as a Function of the Reading Process." *American Association of Instructors of the Blind*. (Forty-eighth Biennial Conference.) Washington, D.C.: The Association. Pp. 7–10.

HOOVER, R. E. 1947. *Orientation and Travel Techniques*. Proceedings of the American Association of Workers of the Blind.

HUFF, R., AND F. FRANKS. 1973. "Educational Materials Development in Primary Mathematics: Fractional Parts of Wholes." *Education of the Visually Handicapped* 5 (May): 46–54.

IRWIN, R. B. 1955. *As I Saw It*. New York: American Foundation for the Blind.

JONES, J. W., AND A. P. COLLINS. 1966. *Educational Programs for Visually Handicapped Children*. (Bulletin No. 6, U.S. Office of Education.) Washington, D.C.: U.S. Government Printing Office.

JUURMAA, J. 1970. "On the Accuracy of Obstacle Detection by the Blind." *The New Outlook for the Blind* 64 (April): 104–118.

KEPHART, J., C. KEPHART, AND G. SCHWARTZ. 1974. "A Journey into the World of the Blind Child." *Exceptional Children* 40 (March): 421–429.

KINSEY, V. C. 1956. "Retrolental Fibroplasia: A Cooperative Study of

Retrolental Fibroplasia and Use of Oxygen." *Archives of Opthalmology* 56 (October): 481–543.

KIRK, S. A., AND J. MC CARTHY. 1961. "The Illinois Test of Psycholinguistic Abilities: An Approach to Differential Diagnosis." *American Journal of Mental Deficiencies* 66 (November): 399–412.

KNOWLES, L. 1969. "Successful and Unsuccessful Rehabilitation of the Legally Blind." *The New Outlook for the Blind* 63 (May): 129–169.

LINN, M. C. 1972. "An Experiential Science Curriculum for the Visually Impaired." *Exceptional Children* 39 (September): 37–43.

LIVINGSTONE, J. S. 1958. "Evaluation of Enlarged Test Form Used with the Partially Seeing." *Sight Saving Review* 28 (Spring): 37–39.

LORD, F. E. 1967. *Preliminary Standardization of Scale of Orientation and Mobility Skills of Young Blind Children: Final Report.* (U.S. Office of Education, Bureau of Research, Project No. 6-2464, Grant No. OEG 4-7-062464-0369.) Washington, D.C.: U.S. Government Printing Office.

LORD, F. E., AND L. BLAHA. 1968. *Demonstration of Home and Community Support Needed to Facilitate Mobility Instruction for Blind Youth.* (Report R.D. 1784–5.) Washington D.C.: Rehabilitation Services Administration, Department of Health, Education, and Welfare.

LOWENFELD, B., ED. 1973. *The Visually Handicapped Child in School.* New York: John Day Co.

LOWENFELD, B., G. ABEL, AND P. HATLEN. 1967. *Blind Children Learn to Read.* Springfield, Ill.: Charles C Thomas.

MONTGOMERY, J. R. 1969. Congenital Rubella-Baylor Study. Forty-ninth Biennial Conference, Association for Education of the Visually Handicapped. Pp. 1–7.

MYERS, E. J. 1930. "A Survey of Sight-Saving Classes in the Public Schools of the United States." Publication No. 64. New York: National Society for the Prevention of Blindness. Reprinted from *The Sight-Saving Class Exchange* (April 1930).

MYERSON, L. 1971. "Somatopsychology of Physical Disability." In W. M. Cruickshank, ed., *Psychology of Exceptional Children and Youth,* 3rd ed. Englewood Cliffs, N.J.: Prentice-Hall, Pp. 1–74.

NAPIER, G. D. 1973. "Special Subject Adjustments and Skills." In B. Lowenfeld, ed., *The Visually Handicapped Child in School.* New York: John Day Co.

NOLAN, C. Y. 1966. *Perceptual Factors in Braille Word Recognition.* American Association of Instructors of the Blind, Forty-eighth Biennial Conference. Washington, D.C.: The Association. Pp. 10–14.

NORRIS, M., P. SPAULDING, AND F. BRODIE. 1957. *Blindness in Children.* Chicago: University of Chicago Press.

PECK, O. S. 1933. "Reading Ability of Sight-Saving Class Pupils in Cleveland, Ohio." Publication No. 118. New York: National Society for the Prevention of Blindness. Reprinted from *The Sight-Saving Review* 3 (June 1933).

PINTNER, R., J. EISENSON, AND M. STANTON. 1941. *The Psychology of the Physically Handicapped.* New York: F. S. Crofts.

SCHLAEGEL, T. F., JR. 1953. "The Dominant Method of Imagery in Blind as Compared to Sighted Adolescents." *Journal of Genetic Psychology* 83 (December): 265–277.

SCHOLL, G., AND R. SCHNUR. 1976. *Measures of Psychological, Vocational, and Educational Functioning in the Blind and Visually Handicapped.* New York: American Foundation for the Blind.

SEASHORE, C. E., AND T. L. LING. 1918 "The Comparative Sensitiveness of Blind and Seeing Persons." *Psychological Monographs* 25 (2): 148–158.

SILVERMAN, W. W. 1970. "Prematurity and Retrolental Fibroplasia." *The New Outlook for the Blind* 64 (September): 232–236.

SMITH, H. P. 1938. "Pioneer Work in Sight Saving." *The Sight-Saving Class Exchange* 65 (June): 2–14.

SOMMERS, V. S. 1944. *The Influence of Parental Attitudes and Social Environment on the Personality Development of the Adolescent Blind.* New York: American Foundation for the Blind.

SUTERKO, S. 1973. "Life Adjustment." In B. Lowenfeld, ed., *The Visually Handicapped Child in School.* New York: John Day Co. Pp. 279–318.

TILLMAN, M. H., AND R. T. OSBORNE. 1969. "The Performance of Blind and Sighted Children on the Wechsler Intelligence Scale for Children: Interaction Effects." *Education of the Visually Handicapped* 1 (March): 1–4.

TISDALL, W. J., A. A. BLACKHURST, AND C. MARKS. 1967. *Divergent Thinking in Blind Children.* (U.S.O.E. Project 32-27-0350-6003.) Washington, D.C.: Office of Education.

UMSTED, R. 1972. "Improving Braille Reading." *The New Outlook for the Blind* 66 (May): 169–177.

WILSON, J., AND H. HALVERSON. 1947. "Development of a Young Blind Child." *Journal of Genetic Psychology* 71 (December): 155–175.

8

Educational authorities have recognized for some time that handicapped children do not always fit into neat, well-defined categories with uniform characteristics. Mentally retarded children are not homogeneous in characteristics; not all deaf or blind children learn at the same rate; speech problems are many and varied. One deaf child might learn speech reading, while another unfortunately does not. One child may be classified as cerebral palsied but may also be mentally retarded or emotionally disturbed, while another cerebral-palsied child may learn adequately in school. To make matters worse there are a number of children who are not deaf, not blind, not mentally retarded, but who have difficulty learning under ordinary school instruction. Those among others constitute the group that has been labeled *specific learning disabilities*.

The label *learning disability* has recently evolved to encompass the heterogeneous group of children not fitting neatly into the traditional categories of handicapped children. A substantial number of children show retardation in learning to talk, do not acquire other communication skills, do not develop normal visual or auditory perception, or have great difficulty in learning to read, to spell, to write, or to make arithmetic calculations. Some of them are not receptive to language but are not deaf, some are not able to perceive visually but are not blind, and some cannot learn by ordinary methods of instruction but are not mentally retarded. Although such children form a heterogeneous group and fail to learn for diverse reasons, they have one thing in common: developmental discrepancies in abilities and achievements.

What are specific learning disabilities?

Because of the heterogeneous nature of this group of children, the concept of specific learning disabilities has been hard to define or describe in a few sentences or by a numerical score such as an IQ or by a decibel loss. Furthermore, because the field has been of interest to educators, psychologists, psychiatrists, neurophysiologists, pediatricians, ophthalmologists, optometrists, speech pathologists, and others, the problems have been viewed in each of those disciplines from different perspectives. In general, however, there are two broad aspects of concern in defining or identifying those children: (1) etiology and (2) behavior.

Medical terminology tends to label learning disorders in terms of etiologies (causes) and relates them to abnormalities in the brain. Thus terms such as brain injury, minimal brain damage, minimal cerebral dysfunction, and central nervous system disorders are used to explain deviations in development.

Behavioral terminology attempts to label the disorders according to behavioral or psychological manifestations. Because of those manifestations, terms such as perceptual handicaps, conceptual disorders, reading disabilities, language disorders, and arithmetic disabilities are used, generally referring without reference to biological etiology to the problem the child is having in learning.

BIOLOGICAL DEFINITIONS

An example of a biological definition is presented by Clements (1966):

> The term "minimal brain dysfunction syndrome" refers to children of near average, average, or above average general intelligence with certain learning or behavioral disabilities ranging from mild to severe, which are associated with deviations of function of the central nervous system. These deviations may manifest themselves by various combinations of impairments in perception, conceptualization, language, memory, and control of attention, impulse, or motor function. (pp. 9–10)

Another definition that gives reference to the central nervous system is proposed by Myklebust (1963). He states:

> We use the term "psychoneurological learning disorders" to include deficits in learning, at any age, which are caused by deviations in the central nervous system and which are not due to mental deficiency, sensory impairment, or psychogenicity. The etiology might be disease and accident, or it might be developmental. (p. 27)

Those two definitions and the terms used were designed to emphasize that, although the disability results in behavior aberrations, the cause of the deviant behavior is disordered neurologic functioning. In most instances the brain dysfunction or neurologic disorder is inferred from the behavioral symptoms. This becomes circular. Tom can't read because he is brain damaged, and we know he is brain damaged because he can't read.

BEHAVIORAL DEFINITIONS

In the second category of definitions, stress is laid on behavioral characteristics without reference to brain dysfunction or etiology. The authors of such definitions feel that since all behavior, normal and abnormal, is related to brain function, it is of no benefit educationally to infer brain dysfunction from behavior. It is difficult to find the dysfunction in the brain, and even if it is found, seldom can anything be done about it.

Gallagher (1966) defined children with learning disabilities as: "Children with developmental imbalances are those who reveal a developmental disparity in psychological processes . . ." (p. 28).

In 1968 the National Advisory Committee on the Handicapped of the U.S. Office of Education defined *specific learning disabilities*. Its definition was utilized by Congress in the Learning Disability Act of 1969. With only a few changed words, it was included in the 1975 Education for All Handicapped Children Act as follows:

> The term "children with specific learning disabilities" means those children who have a disorder in one or more of the basic psychological processes involved in understanding or in using language, spoken or written, which disorder may manifest itself in imperfect ability to listen, think, speak, read, write, spell, or to do mathematical calculations. Such disorders include such conditions as perceptual handicaps, brain injury, minimal brain dysfunction, dyslexia, and developmental aphasia. Such term does not include children who have learning problems which are primarily the result of visual, hearing, or motor handicaps, of mental retardation, of emotional disturbance, or of environmental, cultural, or economic disadvantage.

That definition has been accepted by many and criticized by others. One objection was that it could be interpreted to exclude inadvertently children with learning disabilities among the mentally retarded, the disadvantaged, the emotionally disturbed, and those with sensory handicaps. To clarify the misunderstanding, the Professional Advisory Board of the Association for Children with Learning Disabilities amended the definition at the February 1972 meeting of the board of directors, adding a paragraph stating: "Children with specific learning disabilities who also have sensory, motor, intellectual or emotional problems or are environmentally disadvantaged, should be included in this definition, and may require multiple services." *

Following the 1969 Learning Disabilities Act, state after state began to formulate definitions of their own. According to Gillespie, Miller, and Fredler (1975) who reviewed those definitions, most of the states accepted the federal concept or made slight modifications of it. Attempts are continually being made to specify more clearly the exact nature of learning disabilities.

This statement was formulated by the Professional Advisory Board of the Association for Children with Learning Disabilities and approved by the Board of Directors at their annual meeting in Atlantic City, February 5, 1972.

LEARNING DISABILITY CRITERIA

There appear to be three criteria or factors that must exist before we can decide that a child has a specific learning disability. They are (1) a discrepancy between abilities or between potential and achievement, (2) an exclusion factor, and (3) a special education criterion.

THE DISCREPANCY CRITERION. Children with learning disabilities are those who have (1) significant discrepancies in the development of their psychological behavior (perception, seeing relationships, visual-motor ability, attention, memory, and so forth) or (2) unexplained disparity between their academic achievement and their other abilities or achievements. Developmental imbalances in linguistic, social, or visual-motor abilities are generally noted at the preschool level, while discrepancies between general or specialized intellectual development and academic achievement are observable factors at the school-age level. A child, for example, who does not talk at the age of 4 but who has other perceptual, cognitive, and motor abilities that appear normal would be suspected of having a learning disability at the preschool level. When a school-age child gives evidence of relatively average mental ability, has made normal progress in arithmetic computation and other achievement areas, but has not learned to read after three years of adequate schooling, there is an indication of a learning disability in reading.

THE EXCLUSION CRITERION. Most definitions exclude from the learning disability designation those difficulties in learning that can be explained by general mental retardation, auditory or visual impairment, emotional disturbance, or lack of opportunity to learn. The exclusion factor does not mean that children with hearing and vision impairments or children who are diagnosed as mentally retarded cannot *also* have learning disabilities. Those children require multiple services.

THE SPECIAL EDUCATION CRITERION. Children with learning disabilities are those children who require special education for their development. A child who has not had an opportunity to learn and is retarded educationally will learn by ordinary methods of instruction at his or her level of achievement. For example, if a child has not been in school up to the age of 9 or 10 and on examination is found to have normal cognitive and perceptual abilities but has not learned to read or achieve in arithmetic, that child could not be considered to have a learning disability even though there is a discrepancy between ability and achievement. Such a child will learn by developmental methods of instruction and does not need special education. In other words, the addition of the criterion of the need for a special method because of some psychological disorder that has inhibited the child's ability to read is an important criterion and one that sometimes is not included in the criteria for identification. That criterion is necessary since it requires that, following a diagnosis of discrepancy and exclusions, the diagnostician must specify a special remedial program needed by the child. Without that criterion we will just be labeling a child without specifying the individualized educational program needed. Labeling alone is not special education.

A definition of specific learning disabilities in harmony with the three criteria preceding is: *A specific learning disability is a psychological or neurological impediment to spoken or written language or perceptual, cognitive, or motor behavior. The impediment (1) is manifested by discrepancies among specific behaviors and achievements or between evidenced ability and academic achievement, (2) is of such nature and extent that the child does not learn by the instructional methods and materials appropriate for the majority of children and requires specialized procedures for development, and (3) is not primarily due to severe mental retardation, sensory handicaps, emotional problems, or lack of opportunity to learn.*

A historical note

Learning disabilities is an educational term that has derived its heritage from neurology, psychology, speech pathology, ophthalmology, and remedial reading. Wiederholt (1974) has traced the history of the area and has delineated three dimensions of disorders: (1) disorders of spoken language, (2) disorders of written language, and (3) disorders of perceptual and motor behaviors. According to Figure 8.1 there have been three historical phases: (1) the foundation phase (1802–1926), represented primarily by neurologists and ophthalmologists; (2) a transition phase (1926–1963), represented mostly by psychologists, speech pathologists, and educators; and (3) the integration phase (1963–), represented by a number of disciplines but labeled learning disabilities. As with many other areas of special education, the medical profession identifies the severe problems but is unable, in many instances, to cure the disability. Psychologists enter the field to study the behavioral characteristics that need intervention. Educators are then recruited to provide the intervention.

FIGURE 8.1

*A two-dimensional framework in
the study and remediation of learning disabilities*

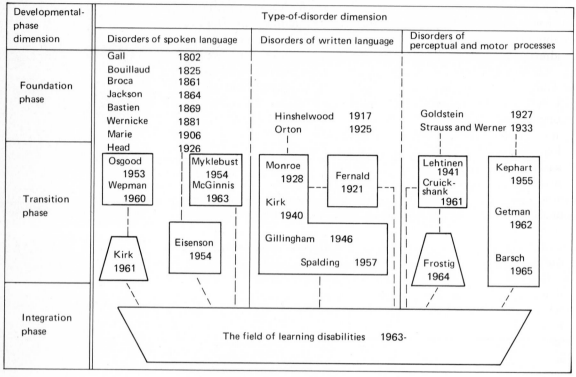

Source: Wiederholt, 1974, p. 105.

Why use the term "learning disability"?

In spite of its current widespread use, the term *specific learning disability* is vulnerable to misunderstanding and misuse. The condition is difficult to define operationally since the designation *learning disability* is an umbrella term for a variety of deviations that are not included in traditional categories of exceptional children. Also it has been confused with general learning problems that are common to some degree in most children. In addition, it has been misused to include educational retardation, which is found in slow-learning children and in children who have not learned because of poor teaching or absence from school. Another vulnerability of the term comes from the difficulty in drawing an explicit line between normal and abnormal. Some allowance must be made for biological and psychological diversity, and considerable variation in abilities is accepted as normal.

Some will ask, "If there are objections to the term *learning disabilities,* why use it? Why not use some other term? Well and good, if a better term can be found. Other terms are either too specific or too broad. *Dyslexia* refers only to severe reading disability and has neurologic implications. *Brain injury* refers to etiology and has little or no educational relevance. *Perceptual handicaps* excludes children with language disorders.

The term *learning disability* became popular when the Association for Children with Learning Disabilities (ACLD) was organized under that name in 1963. During the period just prior to that, parents throughout the United States became concerned because their children who were not learning in school were rejected from special education since they were not mentally retarded, deaf or blind, or otherwise handicapped. Local parent groups were organized. Parent-sponsored schools were initiated. They were called by different names such as schools for the neurologically handicapped, brain-injured, aphasoid, dyslexic, and perceptually handicapped. Parent organizations met in Chicago in 1963 to discuss their mutual problems, one of which was the need for a national organization and an appropriate name.

Discussing the problem and the difficulties of labels for these children, Kirk (1963) explained that sometimes classification labels block our thinking. It is better, he told the conference, to state that a child has not learned to read than to say the child is dyslexic. He continued that it may be more scientific to say "a child has not learned to talk" than to say the child is aphasic or brain injured. He advised that a name should be functional and that if the parents were interested in research on the relation of the brain to behavior, they could use a neurologic term. He suggested further that if they were interested in service to their children, it might be preferable to use a term related to teaching or learning and that a term such as *learning disability* might be preferable to some currently used terms such as *cerebral dysfunction* and *brain injured.*

The term *learning disabilities* struck a receptive chord with the parent groups since it implied teaching and learning and since they were interested primarily in service for their children. They selected the name Association for Children with Learning Disabilities, and from that point on, learning disabilities became a new category of exceptional children and crept into federal, state, and local legislation.

Kinds of learning disabilities

One of the major problems of definition is that a learning disability is not as obvious or homogeneous as blindness or deafness. There are many types of disabilities, each of which may require a unique diagnosis and a remedial method very different from another condition also termed a learning disability. In one school two girls were labeled learning disabled. One had extremely slow visual perception, probably associated with extreme nystagmus, while the other child did not understand language. The child with the visual problem took a long time to recognize and interpret visual objects and pictures. She was diagnosed as legally blind and having very slow "speed of visual perception." She required intensive training in speed of perception via a tachistoscope, which gradually decreased the length of each presentation. During six months of training, she made excellent progress and was able to respond adequately to visual pictures and objects in a life situation. She was no longer considered legally blind.

The other girl in the same class did not talk and did not understand spoken language, even though her hearing was intact. After months of auditory training, she learned to understand language and also learned to talk. These two girls were considered learning disabled, but the problem of one was obviously different from that of the other. That is the reason that we have difficulty in designing one diagnostic or one remedial method for all learning disabilities.

CLASSIFICATIONS OF LEARNING DISABLED CHILDREN

Learning disabilities are of such varied kinds that it is difficult to present a taxonomy or even a specific list of the different types of learning disabilities. During 1964 and 1965 a task force was appointed by the Institute for Neurological Diseases and Blindness to study this problem. Clements (1966), reporting for the task force, delineated five types of minimal brain dysfunctions and listed fifteen categories with ninety-nine symptoms. The symptoms included impairments of perception and concept formation and neurologic indicators such as confused laterality, disorders of speech and communication, disorders of thinking, disorders of attention, academic disabilities, and many others. That type of categorization was not helpful to educators. They prefer to deal primarily with academic learning problems and with the development of language (written and spoken).

After a year of study and discussion during 1977, the Bureau of Education for the Handicapped of the U.S. Office of Education formulated regulations for learning disabilities in the following areas (*Federal Register,* December 29, 1977):

1. oral expression
2. listening comprehension

3. written expression
4. basic reading skills
5. reading comprehension
6. mathematics calculation
7. mathematics reasoning

That federal delineation of the characteristics of learning disabilities in children has reduced the field of learning disabilities to three areas: (1) receptive and expressive language, (2) reading and writing, and (3) mathematics. The formulation differs from the list of characteristics by others. Myers and Hammill (1976), for example, classify the problems as disorders of *memory, attention, symbolization, perception, emotionality,* and *motor activity.* Brutten, Richardson, and Mangel (1973) discuss the major symptom clusters as *activity levels and attention, movement and perceptual development, language and thought development,* and *emotional and social development.* In discussing learning strategies for learning disabled children, Lerner (1976) describes procedures for remediating disabilities in *motor development, perception, memory, listening, speaking, reading, writing, spelling, written expression, arithmetic, reading comprehension, self-concept and emotional attitudes,* and *social skills.* Hammill and Bartel (1975) refer to language development, perceptual-motor processes, and the academic subjects of reading, arithmetic, writing, and spelling.

Thus few if any authorities involved with learning disabilities have confined the field to the restricted areas named in the federal formulation.

It is no wonder that many students, teachers, and parents have become confused about the term *learning disability* and the characteristics of children so labeled. This confusion appears to be international and is illustrated by the remarks of a teacher in Australia who, in testifying to a government committee studying the subject (*Learning Difficulties in Children and Adults,* 1976), stated:

> I find myself asking the following questions: What does the term "learning difficulty" mean? Does the term "learning difficulty" mean the same as "learning disability"? How about the term "dysfunction"? What does the term "minimal brain dysfunction" mean? Do they all mean the same? Certainly, all these labels are not necessary, or are they? Does labelling a child with learning problems create more problems? It all becomes a bit confusing. . . . The terminology changes so often, varies from State to State and from country to country. (p. 3)

Many teachers in the United States have made similar statements. Some have suggested that we abolish the label, merge it with the emotionally disturbed and the educable mentally retarded, and only deal with the child from an instructional point of view by defining the learning tasks so that they can be taught step by step. That approach, we hope, is practiced by regular teachers for the majority of average children defined broadly. For the child with a severe learning disability or for one who is seriously disturbed emotionally, the approach is not sufficient. With deviating children it is necessary to know more than the general, observable problem. Three 5-year-old children may be referred because they do not talk or talk very little. One may be deaf. Another may be severely retarded. The third is neither deaf nor mentally retarded but still does not talk. The individual teaching program will be different for each and will be dependent on the condition of each child to receive stimuli and to respond. With markedly deviant children—those whose deviations are not mild—it is necessary to obtain child analysis as well as task analysis.

ACADEMIC AND DEVELOPMENTAL LEARNING DISABILITIES

For practical purposes it may be well to differentiate specific learning disabilities by dividing them into two broad groups: (1) the academic disabilities and (2) the developmental learning disabilities.

ACADEMIC DISABILITIES. We use the term *academic disabilities* to refer to those school performances that fall below the level reasonably expected of a particular child. These include failure in academic performance in reading, writing, spelling, and arithmetic. These disabilities are readily observed by teachers and parents when a child fails in one or more of the academic subjects.

DEVELOPMENTAL LEARNING DISABILITIES. Some disabilities are not as readily observed as school performance but often underlie the difficulties in the academic subjects. These may be termed *developmental learning disabilities*. In some instances they may be referred to as the lack of prerequisite skills. They include (1) disorders of attention, (2) perceptual and expressive disorders, (3) limited use of the mental operations of memory, seeing relationships, generalizing, associating, and so forth, and (4) language disorders including a limited ability to decode and encode concepts, either verbal or motor.

Although some developmental learning disabilities are often associated with failure in academic subjects, the link between the two is not always clear. Some children who have failed to read have shown disabilities in perceptual-motor functions, although other children who did learn to read also had perceptual-motor disabilities.

There are prerequisite skills that are needed if the child is to achieve in the academic subjects. To learn to write, a child must have developed many prerequisite skills in motor and eye-hand coordination, sequencing, memory, and so forth. To learn to read, a child must have developed optimal visual and auditory discrimination, visual and auditory memory, and other abilities.

One example of a basic ability that most agree is important is *attention,* or the more tangible indicator "attending behavior." Most people will agree that if a child is highly distractible and pays little or no attention to a task, he will not learn.

Selective attention is the ability to select from among numerous competing stimuli—auditory, tactile, visual, kinesthetic—that impinge upon the organism all the time. As described by Ross (1976), selective attention "helps us limit the number of stimuli that we process at any one time" (p. 60). When a child attends and responds to too many stimuli, we consider the child distractible. Ross considers a learning disability to be "the result of delayed development in the capacity to employ and sustain selective attention" (p. 61).

Strauss and Lehtinen (1947), in working with brain-injured children, attempted to help the children in attending to a task by decreasing the external stimuli, by painting the windows of the school to decrease outside stimuli, and by putting children in cubicles so that they would not be distracted by other stimuli. Such environmental controls seem helpful at the beginning of treatment but often become unnecessary as treatment continues. Procedures to develop attending behavior are part of a remedial program for many children with learning disabilities.

Differentiating learning disabilities from other handicapping conditions

In identifying a learning disability, it is necessary to differentiate between learning disabilities, mental retardation, emotional disturbance, and minor educational retardation. The problem of differentiating has risen because many children diagnosed as mentally retarded have later turned out to be children with learning disabilities. In other cases the emotionally disturbed may be confused with disabled learners because of some intraindividual deviations in achievements. An illustration of the first condition, misdiagnosed mental retardation, may clarify some of the confusion.

John did not talk by the age of 4 and was referred for a medical and psychological examination. He was found to have a chromosomal translocation, which is symptomatic of Down's syndrome. He was

291

DIFFERENTIATING
LEARNING DISABILITIES
FROM OTHER
HANDICAPPING
CONDITIONS

untestable on the Binet, and it was estimated that his IQ was below 50. Because of the chromosomal aberration, he was classified as a child with Down's syndrome and was placed in a preschool class for trainable mentally retarded children.

John was later tested on the Illinois Test of Psycholinguistic Abilities (ITPA), a test of twelve abilities including linguistic, perceptual, and memory abilities (see pp. 329–330 for descriptions). Figure 8.2 shows his performance on the twelve subtests of that test. It will be noted that at the age of 4 his performance on the subtests for visual reception and visual association was comparable to that of a 6-year-old child, two years above John's chronological age. He also tested at age 5 on motor expression and visual closure. On tests requiring auditory reception and verbal responses, he tested at the bottom of the norms, ages 2–0 to 2–6. Is this child mentally retarded, or is he superior (above his chronological age) since he tested at the superior level for his age on the visual tests and on motor expression? Here we find a child who has significant discrepancies in developmental functions, a spread of three or four years. He can therefore be considered a child with a learning disability and should be given intensive special education in listening, understanding, and using oral language in real-life experiences.

Figure 8.2 also presents the dotted profile of the performance of another child. Harry was 5 years old and in the same school for trainable children that John was. His IQ was also below 50. His profile, however, shows a child who is equally retarded in all the functions tested. It should be noted that the discrepancies in the psycholinguistic ages are not more than a year or a year and a half from the lowest to the highest age scores and that all the abilities are from two to three years below his chronological age. He is considered a child with retardation in all functions and should be provided with an appropriate general curriculum, rather than with a specific remedial program to help him develop specific abilities.

Here we find two children, both labeled mentally retarded and both placed in a class for trainable mentally retarded children. On further examination we find that one, John, is learning disabled; the other, Harry, is probably correctly classified as mentally retarded.

Prevalence of learning disabilities

How many children with learning disabilities are there in a given population? This is a question that has been raised by school officials and by legislators. Because of the difficulty of defining learning disabilities, most statements of prevalence are based on estimates or even "guesstimates" derived from meager empirical information.

FIGURE 8.2
Profile of abilities

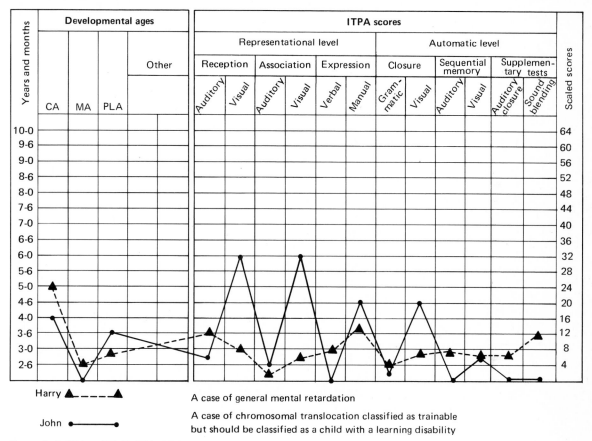

Harry ▲ – – – – ▲   A case of general mental retardation

John ●———●   A case of chromosomal translocation classified as trainable
but should be classified as a child with a learning disability

Source: S. A. Kirk and W. D. Kirk, 1978, p. 71.

Most of the studies that have been made on the prevalence of
learning disabled children tend to include educationally retarded children as well as learning disabled children who require special methods
of instruction for their development (Criterion 3, discussed earlier).
Myklebust and Boshes (1969) estimated that 15 percent of their population were slightly underachieving. When a stricter criterion was
used, 7 percent were considered learning disabled. Likewise Meier
(1971), who studied the prevalence of educational retardation in 2,400
second-grade children, found that 15 percent were considered learning disabled. He stated that slow learners (IQs below 79) and children
with learning disabilities were referred and described by the teachers

in the same way. By using stricter methods of diagnosis, he concluded that 4.7 percent were learning disabled. Wissink, Kass, and Ferrell (1975) found that estimates of learning disability by experts ranged from 2 to 20 percent of their population, with an average of 5 percent. Kirk and Elkins (1975) found that in some federally funded demonstration programs for learning disabilities, the children receiving services ranged from 1 to 26 percent, with an average of 4 percent of the school population from which they were selected.

Recognizing that the concept of learning disabilities can easily be misinterpreted to include all children who are educationally retarded and who have conduct disorders, the National Advisory Committee on Handicapped Children (1968) estimated that 1 to 3 percent of the school population is learning disabled. This estimate was made so that schools would not enroll all children below age-grade level in academic achievement in a learning disabilities program.

Any conclusion from the results of research on prevalence of learning disabilities in the population is as yet unsatisfactory. The prevalence figure is the result of the definition and criteria used by whatever authors conducted the research. A strict criterion including only severe cases brings a small prevalence figure, while a lenient criterion that includes corrective reading cases and slow-learning children results in a high figure. The best guess at this time is that learning disabled children constitute 1 to 3 percent of the school-age population.

Etiology of learning disabilities

From an educational point of view, the etiology of a condition rarely has educational relevance. To know the etiology of Down's syndrome (mongolism) to be a chromosomal aberration does not alter the educational program. Whether or not a teacher knows the etiology of Down's syndrome, he or she uses a developmental curriculum, starting where the child is in behavior and assisting the child in going up the developmental ladder step by step.

When medical treatment is involved, a knowledge of etiology is often very valuable. One teacher, for example, was struggling with a child with a remedial reading problem for several months without success. If it had been known earlier that the child had a brain tumor, the teacher would not have tried to train the child—against odds. A medical diagnosis in that case was eventually helpful and led to an operation for a brain tumor. It is important for a teacher of learning disabled children to know something about etiology in order to aid in diagnosis and remediation and to know if and when such knowledge is applicable. Gaddes (1975) thinks that neuropsychological knowledge aids the diagnosis of a learning disability and that this "more definitive understanding can lead to a more effective remedial prescription" (p. 149).

Researchers have attempted to ferret out factors that inhibit the child's ability to learn. Some of the most common etiological factors will be discussed here briefly. They include (1) brain dysfunctions, (2) genetic factors, (3) biochemical factors, and (4) nutritional and other environmental factors.

BRAIN DYSFUNCTION AND ITS RELATION TO LEARNING DISABILITIES

The brain is the control center of the body. When something goes wrong with the brain, something happens to any or all of the physical, emotional, and mental functions of the organism.

As yet scientists have not been able to specify or precisely locate the functions of the central nervous system sufficiently to explain all behavior on the basis of it. What we have at present is only partial knowledge of the relationship of the central nervous system to behavior and partial knowledge of the relationship of behavior to special disabilities.

Although the term *learning disabilities* is new, the condition in adults and children is as old as humanity. Individuals who had lost the ability to understand language, to speak, or to read as a result of injury to the brain led neurologists to investigate the relationship between brain function and communication.

Hughlings Jackson (Taylor, 1932), although not the first neurologist who contributed to knowledge in this area, is probably the best known. The theory that one hemisphere of the brain is dominant over the other in relation to speech and other behavioral disorders had its true beginning with Jackson. In 1868 Jackson pointed out that there are various degrees of aphasia (loss of the ability to speak) and that aphasia, agraphia (loss of the ability to write), and alexia (loss of the ability to read) are defects in utilizing symbols. He formulated his brain theories on studies of brain-damaged adults and epileptics. His writings and case descriptions had a marked influence on the later work of Henry Head in England and Samuel T. Orton in the United States. Head (1926), following the lead and theories of Hughlings Jackson, published two volumes on aphasia.

Much of the early work on language disorders was done on adults who had lost the ability to speak, read, or write as a result of damage to the brain. Little work had been done with those children who did not develop language ability or who did not learn to read. It was believed that although those children did not have known brain damage similar to that in adult cases, they must have had some early damage before, during, or shortly after birth, hence their inability to learn.

A good example of the inferences drawn from adult brain damage and applied to damage in children is found in the work of Hinshelwood (1917). As an ophthalmologist, Hinshelwood had referred to him for visual examinations children who were having difficulty in learning to read. Teachers in England at that time believed that since reading is accomplished through vision, those who failed to learn must have a visual defect. On examination of the children, Hinshelwood found that very few of those referred to him as reading failures had visual defects. At the time Hinshelwood was pondering this problem, he received a patient who had had a brain concussion, following which he was unable to read. Hinshelwood found that although the man was unable to read, his visual acuity was intact. Hinshelwood diagnosed his problem as *alexia*. Although before the accident the man had been a good reader, he was now unable to recognize words and phrases. An attempt to teach him to recognize words as wholes failed, but he was able to learn isolated letters. Hinshelwood then proceeded to teach him to read successfully by the spelling method.

Several years later the patient contracted pneumonia and died. By previous agreement Hinshelwood was able to procure his brain and to study the extent of the earlier damage. In this patient he found a lesion in the angular gyrus of the left hemisphere. As a result of the case and others, Hinshelwood postulated that the reading center was in the angular gyrus of the left hemisphere and that lesions in that area would produce alexia. He further postulated that children who have difficulty in learning to read must have had an injury or underdevelopment of the left angular gyrus, which produced what he called word blindness. Hinshelwood differentiated between adults who lost the ability to read, "acquired word blindness" (*alexia*), and children who were unable or had difficulty in learning to read, "congenital word blindness," sometimes referred to as *dyslexia*.

In the United States Samuel T. Orton (1928) questioned Hinshelwood's concept of congenital word blindness and the localization of it in the left angular gyrus. He proposed instead a theory of cerebral dominance, which could account for a child's stuttering or inability to read. Orton postulated that when neither of the two cerebral hemispheres was dominant over the other, the child began twisting symbols and seeing *no* as *on* and *saw* as *was*. He called it the theory of *strephosymbolia* (twisted symbols). Orton's associates, Marion Monroe (1932), Gillingham (1936), and others, followed his theories by developing diagnostic procedures and phonic remedial methods for children diagnosed as dyslexics or as having strephosymbolia.

Since the time of Orton and Strauss there has been less emphasis on neurologic factors but greater emphasis on the psychoeducational factors and on methods of remediation. These topics will be discussed in the next chapter on remediation.

GENETICS

Efforts have been made by a large number of people to study the heritability of reading, writing, and language disabilities. Such studies have been made on families that have had many members with reading or language problems. Hallgren (1950) conducted the most extensive family study in Sweden. He examined 276 dyslexic cases and their families. The prevalence of reading, writing, and spelling disabilities in the relatives provided strong evidence that such conditions run in families and are consequently inherited.

Hermann (1959) studied twelve pairs of identical twins, all of whom were dyslexic. He contrasted that group of identical twins with thirty-three pairs of fraternal twins. Only one-third of these fraternal twins showed both children of the pair to be dyslexic. In the other two-thirds of the fraternal twins, only one child of the pair was dyslexic. He presented that kind of evidence to support the hypothesis that reading, spelling, and writing disabilities are inherited since the identical twins had a greater frequency of reading disabilities (dyslexia) than did the fraternal twins.

Critchley (1970), in his book on the dyslexic child, reviewed the studies on the genetics of word blindness and concluded that dyslexia tends to be familial. He cited a publication from Germany in 1936, which recommended sterilization for those suffering from word blindness. Bannatyne (1971) also reviewed the studies on language, reading, and spelling disabilities and concluded that there is good evidence for "genetic dyslexia."

DeFries and McLearn, at the Institute of Behavioral Genetics at the University of Colorado, are conducting an extensive study of the genetics of reading disabilities. Lewitter (1975) has reported an analysis of the first eighty-five cases of the larger study that shows further evidence for a genetic factor in reading disabilities.

ENVIRONMENTAL DEPRIVATION AND NUTRITION

In this area the two problems that have been studied most are (1) the lack of early environmental stimulation and (2) the effects of severe malnutrition at an early age. These two etiological factors are not always independent since, in many circumstances, malnutrition and lack of early psychological stimulation are both operating on the same child.

Cruickshank and Hallahan (1973) reviewed and discussed the studies on environmental deprivation and malnutrition. They summarized the studies conducted on both animals and children and concluded that although a definite relationship between malnutrition and learning disabilities cannot be established, the bulk of the evidence suggests that severe malnutrition at an early age can affect the central nervous system and hence the learning and development of the child.

There are few specific studies on the effects of adverse environment on specific learning disabilities per se other than the studies on intelligence summarized briefly in Chapter 4 on mental retardation. Cravioto and DeLicardie (1975) reviewed and conducted research on environmental and nutritional factors and concluded:

> It is apparent that children who survive a severe episode of malnutrition of sufficient duration early in life are handicapped in learning some of the more fundamental academic skills and are therefore less able to profit from the cumulative knowledge available to the human species in general and to their socioeconomic group in particular. (p. 96)

BIOCHEMICAL FACTORS

There are many children with learning disabilities who are not known to have neurologic problems or any history of genetic or environmental deprivation. It has been hypothesized that there is some unknown biochemical imbalance comparable to phenylketonuria as seen in the mentally retarded.

The use of drugs with hyperactive children with learning disabilities has resulted in considerable controversy. From time to time a report is made that a certain drug can ameliorate learning disabilities, but such reports generally are not substantiated by further research. A related topic is the use of megavitamins. Cott (1975) presented some evidence that megavitamins improve the performance of children with learning disabilities. His clinical observations were questioned by Conner (1975) and others. In summarizing the use of drugs in the treatment of learning disabilities, Conner stated, "I would like to emphasize that drug treatment must be freed from a narrow, dogmatic frame of reference; that it is potentially both powerful and dangerous, depending upon the extent to which a variety of other services and disciplines are integrated with it . . ." (p. 16).

It should be stated that the field of pharmacology along with its relationship to learning disabilities is still in its infancy awaiting scientific studies to determine its value and dangers.

THE RELATIONSHIP OF ETIOLOGY TO EDUCATION

In general, whether the child has had brain damage, lack of cerebral development, genetic deficit, early environmental and nutritional deprivation, or a metabolic imbalance, the task of the teacher is about the same. His or her duty is to remediate the behavioral deficit.

Educators must recognize that although biological factors may inhibit the ability to learn, much of a child's disability is due to the school's inability to adapt instruction to his or her particular needs. If, at an early age, a child avoids those activities that are difficult—perhaps because of a brain dysfunction—the difficulty becomes greater because of the avoidance and disuse of the function. The child who avoids talking because it requires effort may later show a more marked deficiency in language. The deficit may be due partly to the brain dysfunction and partly to behavioral causes, in which case remediation may at least ameliorate the educational disability resulting from earlier avoidance and disuse. But education may do more than just fill in the void resulting from disuse. In 1978 the National Society for the Study of Education produced the book *Education and the Brain.* In commenting on the various essays in the book, Chall and Mirsky (1978) state:

> In essence the neuroscientists writing in this volume are saying to educators that education is central for optimal brain development. Indeed, the more recent findings, the stronger the evidence for the importance of education appears to be . . . over and over again the evidence indicates that practice and stimulation at the right time will foster learning, particularly among those with brain injuries or dysfunctions. (p. 372)

Diagnosis of children with learning disabilities

The major problem in identifying and diagnosing children with specific learning disabilities is to pinpoint the atypical behavior, explain it, differentiate it from similar problems of other handicapped children (differential diagnosis), and determine the remedial program best suited to ameliorate the disability. The problem of identification and diagnosis is somewhat different for preschool than for school-age children. At the school-age level the identification process becomes acute when the child fails in learning to read, to spell, to write, or to calculate. At the preschool level the child is identified through developmental disabilities since he or she has not yet had time to fail in academic subjects.

For the child of any age, however, there are general criteria for making a differential diagnosis. Is the child's atypical behavior a specific disability, and if so, what is the nature of the specific disability that requires remediation? Some of the major determinants are:

1. Does the child have a specific learning disability or is the lack of achievement in language, reading, or other areas the result of some different handicap such as impaired hearing, general mental retardation, lack of instruction, and lack of opportunity to learn? The reason for this differential diagnosis is that the remediation of a child with a specific learning disability is different from the instructional program for children with other handicaps, even though the observable problem, such as a language deficit, may be the same. For example, delayed speech and language in a child may be the result of a marked hearing impairment, severe mental retardation, or an emotional problem. A deaf child is taught to compensate for hearing loss by developing communication through sense avenues other than hearing, whereas a child who does not understand language but who has no hearing loss or general mental retardation is taught primarily to process language through the sense of hearing.

2. If it is decided that the child has a specific learning disability, the next question is "What abilities and disabilities does the child have?" Inherent in the concept of learning disabilities is the concept of intraindividual differences, or discrepancies in the child's own areas of development. If a child has been in school under ordinary instruction for three years and has failed to learn to read, the diagnostician looks for areas in which he or she *has* learned. Is the child's language average? Does he or she have adequate mental ability to learn to read? Has the child learned other school subjects such as arithmetic? If the deficit is in reading while all other abilities and achievements are average or near average for the child's age and mental ability, then the child can be said to have a specific learning disability in reading and will be diagnosed as a child with a learning disability.

3. The third question is how can the child's specific deficit be explained? If mental retardation or sensory deficits are present, the explanation is clear. If emotional or environmental deterrents are present, they should be dealt with. When explanations are not present, the diagnostician asks what inhibiting factor can be found in the child's information processing that can account for the task deficit. If the child does not understand oral language, is the disability the result of a marked deficit in auditory discrimination, in vocabulary, in understanding syntax, or in other factors in auditory processing? The determination of the exact nature of the associated deficit is essential if we desire to organize an appropriate remedial program.

DIAGNOSIS OF PRESCHOOL CHILDREN

As indicated earlier, the referral of preschool children for diagnosis is not based on failure in academic subjects but is more directly related to behavior observed by parents and preschool teachers in relation to tasks and performance typical of the child's agemates. Many deficits can be observed in young children. Among them are (1) failure to understand or respond to meaningful expressions such as oral language or visual symbols, (2) failure to be in tune with the environment or the child's own relationship to it, including poor motor control, body image, and visual and auditory discrimination, and (3) lack of attention and related disorders. Each of those broad areas contains auditory-verbal and visual-motor disabilities.

AUDITORY-VERBAL DISABILITIES. The most common learning disability noted at the preschool level is an auditory-verbal disability. Generally the child is referred because he or she is not talking, is not talking like older brothers or sisters talked at a similar age, or does not respond adequately to directions or verbal statements. Those disabilities have been divided into (1) auditory-receptive disabilities, (2) thinking or association disabilities, and (3) verbal-expressive disabilities. John, the example in Figure 8.2, is a child with an auditory-verbal disability.

1. *Auditory-receptive disabilities* have been referred to in the adult literature as receptive aphasia or sensory aphasia. In the case of a child these terms refer to one who does not understand verbal language or who only partially understands what is told him or her. Many children in this category are thought to have impaired hearing but on examination have been found to have normal hearing, yet are unable to process and understand verbal materials.

2. *Auditory-thinking or association disabilities* have sometimes been referred to as problems in inner language (Myklebust's term), symbolic aphasia, or simply association disability, meaning the inability to relate what is heard to past experience or the inability to generalize or develop concepts in the auditory-verbal modality.

3. *Verbal-expressive disabilities* have sometimes been referred to as expressive aphasia or motor aphasia, but the term *aphasia* is misleading since it technically means the loss of the ability to speak after verbal expression has been acquired. With young children it is not a loss but the inability to acquire verbal-expressive ability. Such a child does

not talk at the ages of 3 and 4 or is delayed in learning to talk. Some prefer to label this disability delayed speech or childhood aphasia.

To diagnose such a child, a psychoeducational examiner does the following:

1. obtains a description of the auditory-verbal behavior as observed by the parent, the preschool teacher, or both
2. peruses the medical record to see whether there are possible explanations from a medical point of view
3. studies the family situation to determine whether there are factors in the home that contribute to the disability
4. examines the child, using formal and informal tests (check lists, criterion-referenced tests, and others) to determine the abilities and disabilities of the child in
   a. understanding language
   b. relating things heard with past experiences
   c. talking (what is the extent of the child's vocabulary and use of syntax?)
5. determines what the child can do and cannot do in a specific area (If, for example, the child functions well in most areas but does not talk, the next step is to find out if he or she understands language. If the child does not understand oral language, the next step is to find out if he or she can discriminate between words, between phonemes, or between common sounds in the environment.)
6. organizes a remedial program at the point at which the child can perform, and moves step by step into areas in which the child could not initially perform (Procedures for remediation of language disorders are discussed in the next chapter.)

VISUAL-MOTOR (NONVERBAL) DISABILITIES. There are *visual* disorders comparable to disabilities in understanding and using *verbal* symbols. Children who are slow to gain meaning from road signs (symbols), danger signals, directional arrows, and words like *men* and *women* or their pictorial equivalents may have a specific difficulty in visual decoding. They may be slow in responding to the meaning of pictures or numbers, in understanding absurdities in funny pictures, and in understanding what they see.

An extreme example of this is a boy of adequate vision who could not recognize his classmates by sight. He could identify them only when he heard their voices or was told their names. He could not attach meaning to things he saw.

Similarly, some individuals cannot express concepts without words, cannot show how a spiral stairway goes up and around, or how a man chops down a tree.

Likewise, there is haptic (tactile and kinesthetic) disability, the inability to identify objects by touch. It is of greatest significance in the blind who must attach meaning to the symbols of Braille. If this ability is intact, it can sometimes be used as an added sense channel to supplement or remediate disabilities in other channels. In evaluating that ability, one must always be aware of the more fundamental ability of haptic discrimination. Can the child recognize differences by touch?

In diagnosing nonverbal disabilities in preschool children, a psychoeducational examiner asks the usual questions about medical and home background and through ratings, interviews, and formal and informal tests attempts to discover the correlated factors and significant manifest difficulties of the child. Some of the questions an examiner tries to answer through the psychoeducational assessment are:

1. Can the child interpret the environment through the significance of what he or she sees (visual decoding or visual reception)?
2. Can the child recognize the whole when only a part is seen (visual closure)?
3. Can the child recognize visual objects and pictures rapidly (speed of perception)?
4. Can a child recognize a specific object embedded in a picture (figure-ground perception)?
5. Can the child express ideas in motor terms (nonverbal) through gestures, dramatics, and writing (motor expression)?

ATTENTIONAL AND OTHER DISABILITIES. Johnson and Myklebust (1967) point out that there are many factors in the environment with which the child cannot cope. These need not be sights and sounds that signify deeper meaning but can include auditory and visual discrimination, awareness of objects in the environment, and especially the child's own relation to them. Left–right orientation, body image, spatial orientation, motor learning, putting jigsaw puzzles together, visual and/or auditory closure, visual and/or auditory memory are important abilities that do not involve the translation of symbols to gain meaning. Their absence is often associated with other disabilities in school and out of school.

Gearhart (1976) gave the title "Nonverbal Disorders" to one of the chapters in *Teaching the Learning Disabled*. He included a discussion of the perceptual-motor theory, which will be discussed later, hyperactivity, and distractibility in children. One must evaluate the effect of the disinhibited child who is always on the move, is distractible, cannot sustain attention long enough to learn, or cannot direct his or her attention purposefully.

The psychoeducational examiner, through observations and formal and informal tests, attempts to answer questions such as the following:

1. Can the child discriminate between two pictures or objects (visual discrimination), between two words or sounds (auditory discrimination), or between two objects touched and felt (haptic discrimination)?
2. Is the child oriented in space? Does he or she have right-left discrimination?
3. Can the child remember immediately what was heard, seen, or felt?
4. Can the child imitate the examiner orally or gesturally? Can the child mimic?
5. Does the child have adequate visual-motor coordination? Is the child clumsy?
6. Can the child sustain attention to oral or visual stimuli?
7. Is the child highly distractible?
8. Does the child persevere?

This list can be expanded indefinitely, but the preceding functions illustrate the questions a psychoeducational examiner has to raise in diagnosing nonverbal disabilities. Diagnosing is done through ratings by teachers and parents, observations and interviews by the examiner, and formal and informal tests.

With preschool children an examiner relies on observations of parents and teachers, rating scales, informal clinical diagnoses, and norm- and criterion-referenced testing. The task of a diagnostician is analogous to that of a detective. Both must gather clues and formulate and discard hypotheses until arriving at the solution that best fits the available evidence.

DIAGNOSIS OF ACADEMIC DISABILITIES

At the school-age level, children are usually referred by teachers because they are failing in basic school subjects (reading, writing, spelling, and arithmetic). After mental retardation, deafness, blindness, lack of opportunity, and lack of motivation are excluded as causes, many learning disability authorities assume that associated developmental disorders are inhibiting the learning of those subjects. Consequently a diagnosis of the academic disability requires an assessment of many variables.

To assess a child's specific learning disability and to organize an appropriate remedial method for the amelioration of the disability, it is necessary to follow a systematic procedure in diagnosis. The diagnostic process generally proceeds in five stages or steps, namely: (1) determining whether the child's learning problem is specific, general, or spurious; (2) analyzing the behavior manifestations that are descriptive of the specific problem; (3) discovering possible physical, environmental, and psychological correlates of the disability; (4) evolving a diagnostic inference (hypothesis) on the basis of the behavior manifestations and the correlates; and (5) organizing a systematic remedial program based on the diagnostic inference.

Those five steps apply to the diagnosis of a child with any academic disability. The five steps in diagnosing a *reading disability,* the most common type of learning disability, will be used for illustration.

Miss Jones, a third-grade teacher, had an 8-year-old boy in her class who was unable to read beyond the primer level. After working with him for four months without success, she decided there was something drastically wrong with the boy because he seemed not to learn readily nor to remember what he had learned from one day to the next. She referred him to a child-study clinic.

1. The first step taken at the clinic was to determine whether the learning problem was specific, general, or spurious. To that end a general intelligence test was administered to find out if the child had the mental capacity necessary to learn to read. If this 8-year-old boy should be found to have an IQ of 50, one would not expect him to be able to read. Miss Jones's boy was found, however, to have an IQ of 104 on the Stanford-Binet Intelligence Scale. He also scored at a second-grade level on an arithmetic computation test, although, as Miss Jones had predicted, he scored at a first-grade level (6 years, 3 months) on a series of reading tests. The psychologist analyzing the problem now had the following information:

Chronological age	8–4
Mental age	8–10
Social maturity age	8–2
Arithmetic computational age	7–8
Reading age	6–3

There was a discrepancy between the chronological age, mental age, social age, and arithmetic achievement age on the one hand and the level of reading on the other hand. The child had attended school with fair regularity, had had adequate teaching for two years, and still had not learned to read. It was clear that a problem did exist and that it was specific, not general. The boy could not read although the apparent capacity was there, as judged by other abilities and achievements.

2. The second step taken at the clinic was to analyze the behavior manifestations that were descriptive of the specific problem. It was necessary to specify the exact nature of the problem, to delineate in greater detail than before just what the child could and could not do in the reading process. It was necessary to know more than the *level* of reading. It was necessary to know *how* the child reads. What faulty habits did he display in reading? How did he attack new words? What kinds of words did he confuse? What kinds of errors did he make? How fast did he try to read? A skilled diagnostician can answer some of those questions by observing the child read, but diagnostic tests are more objective. In the case at hand it was found on diagnostic and criterion-referenced reading tests that the child did not make use of phonics. Although he could tell the sounds of the different letters in isolation, he sounded only the first letter or two of a word. It was also noted that he had had difficulty learning to write his name and found it difficult to reproduce short words from memory. He guessed at many words from context or from interpreting the pictures in the book. He knew a few sight words but often confused similar words such as *that* and *what, the* and *ten, see* and *she.*

3. The next step taken was to discover the physical, environmental, and psychological correlates of the disability. The clinic staff knew that there are many reasons why children fail to learn to read. Did this boy have poor school attendance? Was there an abnormal home background? Was he culturally deprived? An investigation of those factors proved negative. No such conditions were found that could explain his reading retardation. A medical examination revealed no abnormalities. Visual acuity was normal, and on an audiometric test the boy appeared to have normal hearing. His inability to learn to read was therefore not the result of visual or hearing impairment. Should the boy's condition merely be labeled "dyslexia"? Should it be assumed that he must be brain injured? The staff knew that those designations would be of little help to the teacher since they would only be substituting the word *dyslexia,* a medical term, for the term *severe reading disability,* an educational term. To say that the boy was brain injured when the neurologist could find no evidence of brain injury was not very helpful since they would be inferring brain function from behavior observation.

There was one other handicap the clinic had not investigated. Was it possible that the child was so emotionally disturbed that he was unable to concentrate and learn? The teacher reported that he could not concentrate on the reading work books she gave him, that his attention to reading materials was very short, and that he resisted pressure to read. A psychiatric examination did not confirm the hypothesis of emotional disturbance since the boy appeared normal in interpersonal relations and did concentrate on other tasks not involving reading and spelling. His concentration on arithmetic lessons, for example, was adequate. The psychiatrist concluded that the inability to learn to read was not the result of an emotional condition.

In the past much emphasis was placed on finding the cause of a malady, but with learning-disabled children the cause is frequently nebulous, often unknown, and usually irremediable. If a child's aberrant functioning is the result of brain damage (which may or may not show up on an electroencephalogram), it helps little in designing remediation to know that a birth injury affected certain neurons. When the cause is irremediable, it is the behavior that must be remediated.

For that reason the term *correlates* is used instead of *causes*. *Correlates* refers to associated or contributing factors rather than to causes. For example, a sound-blending disability may contribute to poor reading in some children when certain methods of teaching reading (a phonic method) are used. It should not be considered a cause of poor reading since deaf children learn to read and do not have sound-blending ability. Thus the emphasis here will be primarily on educational correlates, or factors relating to the functional behavior of the child. A child who is unable to learn words may have a sound-blending disability. This is considered a correlate of inability to learn to read and leads to a remedial program that will include training the child to blend sounds in relation to teaching him or her to read.

The child can learn to read without sound-blending ability provided he or she has other compensating abilities. But in any case there must be a match between the child and the instructional method. A child with a sound-blending disability can learn to read if the child's visual abilities are matched with a visual (look and say) reading method. But if the child has a sound-blending disability and also a visualization or visual memory disability, the match will not succeed since the child will not be able to compensate through visual channels. An analogy is found with the deaf and blind. We can teach a deaf child to read through a visual approach and a blind child to read through an auditory and haptic approach, but we will need a haptic method for a deaf-blind child. That is what is meant by a match between the child and the instructional method.

The search for correlates of a learning disability is a search for related or contributing factors within the child (physical or psychological) or in the environment, which have been found to occur frequently with the disability under consideration and which need correction or amelioration. These correlates may be (a) physical factors, (b) environmental (including instructional) factors, or (c) psychological factors, such as those on the following list.

Physical correlates	*Environmental correlates*	*Psychological correlates*
Visual defects	Traumatic experiences	Attention disorders; distractibility
Auditory defects	Conditioned avoidance reactions	Poor visual or auditory perception and discrimination
Confused spatial orientation	Undue family pressures	Slow understanding and interpretation of verbal or nonverbal concepts
Mixed laterality	Bilingualism	Poor organizing and generalizing ability
Hyperkinesia	Sensory deprivation	Inability to express concepts vocally or manually
Poor body image	Lack of school experience or instructional inadequacies	Minimal motor and verbal skills
Undernourishment		Defective short-term auditory or visual memory
		Poor closure and sound blending

In the case of Miss Jones's boy, the physical and environmental correlates listed had been ruled out. In the search for correlates that might contribute to the reading difficulty and at the same time be the springboard for remediation, the psychoeducational diagnostician administered tests that might show some developmental correlates. The tests did show marked intraindividual differences in the boy's perceptual abilities and in some of his mental operations. Although functioning at or above his chronological age in most of the tests, this boy was very deficient in visual sequential memory (the ability to remember a sequence of figures or letters), auditory closure, and auditory synthesis (sound blending). Those are deficiencies quite commonly associated (together or in isolation) with poor reading.

4. *The next step taken was to find a diagnostic hypothesis (inference) based on the behavior manifestations and the correlates observed in the second and third steps.* The diagnostic inference is one of the most important factors in diagnosis. It involves specifying the relationship among symptoms and the correlates that have inhibited a child's learning to talk, read, write, or spell. It requires experienced clinicians who can use the relevant tests, select the relevant facts, and put the pieces together in organized form so as to explain the child's inability to

learn. The diagnostic hypothesis must select the relevant variables in the case and pinpoint the specific disabilities on which the remedial program can be organized.

For Miss Jones's boy two working hypotheses evolved from the information at hand. (a) From the observation that the boy did not sound more than the first letter or two of a word although he knew the sounds of all of them in isolation, it was conjectured that he had not learned the skill of sound blending. That conjecture was verified by the child's low score on a sound-blending test. That disability would explain why he had so little success in trying to use phonics in deciphering unknown words. (b) The second inference came from his low score on the visual sequential memory subtest of the ITPA coupled with the fact that the boy had learned very few sight words and showed confusion and uncertainty on many of the ones he thought he knew. The hypothesis was that the boy's inability to remember a sequence of figures made it difficult for him to identify sight words because he had poor memory of what the complete word was supposed to look like. The hypothesis was corroborated by his difficulty in learning to write his name and to reproduce short words from memory. The two handicaps, inability to use a phonic approach in identifying words and inability to use a sight-word approach, gave this boy no usable technique for decoding the printed page.

5. The final step, now required by Public Law 94-142 (Education for All Handicapped Children Act), in any diagnosis is organizing a systematic remedial program—an individualized education program (IEP)—based on the diagnostic hypothesis. The crux of a diagnosis is the effectiveness of the remedial program it generates. The program should be based on the inferences made in the fourth step and should attempt to alleviate the symptoms and, if possible, the correlated factors observed. This IEP must be reviewed annually by a committee and will include "(a) a statement of the child's present level of performance, (b) a statement of annual goals and short term objectives, (c) a statement of specific special education and related services to be provided . . . (d) other needed administrative services." In the present case recommendations were given for improving the visual sequential memory, suggesting particularly the use of a kinesthetic method in learning new words and thereby training the use of visual imagery and visual sequential memory. Likewise, specific suggestions were made for developing sound-blending ability, which in most cases is rather easily acquired once the knack is understood. The remedial program began by teaching the boy words and phrases by the kinesthetic method (to develop visualization ability), and later exercises in sound blending and phonics were introduced. Through this approach the child learned to read.

Summary

1. Learning disabilities afflict a heterogeneous group of children who are not developing or learning normally but who do not fit into the traditional categories of handicapped children. The label incorporates terms for conditions previously called brain injuries, dyslexia, developmental aphasia, and perceptual handicaps, among others.

2. Many attempts have been made to define learning disabilities. The general areas of agreement are that a learning disabled child can be identified by three major criteria: (a) a significant discrepancy exists between developmental areas or between intellectual ability and academic achievement, (b) the disability is not explained by sensory handicap, mental retardation, emotional disturbance, or lack of opportunity to learn, and (c) the child requires specialized instruction in order to develop maximally.

3. Children who are mentally retarded, emotionally disturbed, disabled by sensory handicaps, or disadvantaged can also have learning disabilities and require multiple services.

4. Learning disabled children can be differentiated from mentally retarded children by their significant discrepancies in abilities as distinct from the generalized retardation in all psychological functions of the mentally retarded child.

5. The prevalence of learning disabilities in the general population ranges from 1 percent to 15 percent, depending on the criteria used. Generally, 1 to 3 percent is considered a conservative figure.

6. Authorities have dealt with two kinds of learning disabilities: (a) disabilities in academic subjects and (b) developmental disabilities.

7. The etiology of learning disabilities has been variously believed to be (a) inherited, (b) the result of brain damage, (c) the result of biochemical factors, and (d) the result of environmental deprivation and malnutrition. Research in all of those areas has suggested some evidence in support of each but has provided no conclusive proof.

8. The diagnosis of learning disabilities in preschool children requires an assessment of the developmental behaviors indicating the degree to which the child uses auditory-verbal and visual-motor symbols (words and gestures, oral and written), as well as the attentional and perceptual nonverbal processes.

9. The diagnosis of school-age children requires an assessment of a significant discrepancy between possible potential, as measured by mental tests and performance in other achievements, and achievement in a specific subject; an assessment of symptoms and correlates; a diagnostic hypothesis; and a remedial prescription (IEP).

10. A written statement of an IEP is now required under Public Law 94–142 for all handicapped children assigned for special services.

References

BANNATYNE, A. 1971. *Language, Reading and Learning Disabilities.* Springfield, Ill.: Charles C Thomas.

BRUTTEN, M., S. O. RICHARDSON, AND C. MANGEL. 1973. *Something's Wrong with My Child.* New York: Harcourt Brace Jovanovich.

CHALL, J. S., AND A. F. MIRSKY. 1978. "The Implications for Education." In *Education and the Brain.* The Seventy-seventh Yearbook of the National Society for the Study of Education. Chicago: University of Chicago Press. Pp. 371–378.

CLEMENTS, S. 1966. *Minimal Brain Dysfunction in Children.* Public Health Service Publications, No. 415. Washington, D.C.: Department of Health, Education, and Welfare.

CONNERS, C. K. 1975. "Psychopharmacology." In *Selected Papers on Learning Disabilities, Association for Children with Learning Disabilities, Ninth Annual Conference.* Pittsburgh: Association for Children with Learning Disabilities. Pp. 13–16.

COTT, A. 1975. "Orthomolecular Medicine." In *Selected Papers on Learning Disabilities, Association for Children with Learning Disabilities, Ninth Annual Conference.* Pittsburgh: Association for Children with Learning Disabilities. Pp. 17–22.

CRAVIOTO, J., AND E. DE LICARDIE. 1975. "Environmental and Nutritional Deprivation in Children with Learning Disabilities." In W. M. Cruickshank and D. P. Hallahan, eds., *Psychoeducational Practices.* Perceptual and Learning Disabilities in Children, vol. I. Syracuse, N.Y.: Syracuse University Press.

CRITCHLEY, M. 1970. *The Dyslexic Child,* 2nd ed. London: Heinemann Medical Books.

CRUICKSHANK, W., AND D. HALLAHAN. 1973. *Psychoeducational Foundations of Learning Disabilities.* Englewood Cliffs, N.J.: Prentice-Hall.

Education for All Handicapped Children Act. 1975. Public Law 94–142, Ninety-fourth Congress, November 29, 1975.

FEDERAL REGISTER. 1977. "Procedures for Evaluating Specific Learning Disabilities." 42(250) (December 29): Section 121a.541. Department of Health, Education, and Welfare, Office of Education.

GADDES, W. H. 1975. "Neurological Implications for Learning." In W. Cruickshank and D. Hallahan, eds., *Psychoeducational Practices.* Perceptual and Learning Disabilities in Children, vol. 1. Syracuse, N.Y.: Syracuse University Press. Pp. 149–196.

GALLAGHER, J. 1966. "Children with Developmental Imbalance: A Psycho-educational Definition." In W. Cruickshank, ed., *The Teacher of Brain-Injured Children.* Syracuse, N.Y.: Syracuse University Press. Pp. 23–43.

GEARHEART, B. R. 1976. *Teaching the Learning Disabled: A Combined Task-Process Approach.* St. Louis: C. V. Mosby.

GILLESPIE, P., T. MILLER, AND V. FREDLER. 1975. "Legislative Definitions of Learning Disabilities: Roadblocks to Effective Service." *Journal of Learning Disabilities* 8 (December): 659–666.

GILLINGHAM, A. 1936. *Remedial Work for Reading, Spelling, and Penmanship.* New York: Hackett and Wilhelms.

HALLGREN, B. 1950. "Specific Dyslexia (Congenital Word-Blindness): A Clinical and Genetic Study." *Acta Psychiatrica et Neurologica* 65: 1–287.

HAMMILL, D. D., AND N. R. BARTEL. 1975. *Teaching Children with Learning and Behavior Problems.* Boston: Allyn and Bacon.

HEAD, H. 1926. *Aphasia and Kindred Disorders of Speech,* vols. I, II. New York: Macmillan.

HERMANN, K. 1959. *Reading Disability: A Medical Study of Word-Blindness and Related Handicaps.* Springfield, Ill.: Charles C Thomas.

HINSHELWOOD, J. 1917. *Congenital Word Blindness.* London: H. K. Lewis.

JOHNSON, D. J., AND H. R. MYKLEBUST 1967. *Learning Disabilities: Educational Principles and Practices.* New York: Grune & Stratton.

KIRK, S. A. 1963. "Behavioral Diagnosis and Remediation of Learning Disabilities." In *Proceedings of the Conference on Exploration into the Problems of the Perceptually Handicapped Child.* Chicago: Perceptually Handicapped Children. (Reprinted in J. McCarthy and S. A. Kirk, eds. *Learning Disabilities: Selected ACLD Papers.* Boston: Houghton Mifflin, 1975.)

KIRK, S. A., AND J. ELKINS. 1975. "Characteristics of Children Enrolled in the Child Service Demonstration Centers." *Journal of Learning Disabilities* 8 (December): 630–637.

KIRK, S. A., AND W. D. KIRK. 1978. "Uses and Abuses of the ITPA." *Journal of Speech and Hearing Disorders* 43 (February): 71.

KIRK, S. A., SR. J. M. KLIEBHAN, AND J. W. LERNER. 1978. *Teaching Reading to Slow and Disabled Learners.* Boston: Houghton Mifflin.

Learning Difficulties in Children and Adults. 1976. Report of the House of Representatives Select Committee on Specific Learning Difficulties. Canberra: Australian Government Publishing Service.

LERNER, J. W. 1976. *Children with Learning Disabilities,* 2nd ed. Boston: Houghton Mifflin.

LEWITTER, F. I. 1975. *A Genetic Analysis of Specific Reading Disability.* Master's thesis, Department of Anthropology, University of Colorado, Boulder, Colo.

MEIER, J. 1971. "Prevalence and Characteristics of Learning Disabilities

Found in Second Grade Children." *Journal of Learning Disabilities* 4 (January): 6–19.

MONROE, M. 1932. *Children Who Cannot Read.* Chicago: University of Chicago Press.

MYERS, P. T., AND D. D. HAMMILL. 1976. *Methods for Learning Disabilities,* 2nd ed. New York: John Wiley.

MYKLEBUST, H. 1963. "Psychoneurological Learning Disorders in Children." In S. Kirk and W. Becker, eds., *Conference on Children with Minimal Brain Impairment.* Urbana: University of Illinois.

MYKLEBUST, H. K., AND B. BOSHES. 1969. *Minimal Brain Damage in Children.* Final Report, Contract 108-65-142, Neurological and Sensory Disease Control Program. Washington, D.C.: Department of Health, Education, and Welfare.

NATIONAL ADVISORY COMMITTEE ON HANDICAPPED CHILDREN. 1968. *First Annual Report, Subcommittee on Education of the Committee on Labor and Public Welfare, U.S. Senate.* Washington, D.C.: U.S. Government Printing Office.

ORTON, S. J. 1928. "Specific Reading Disability—Strephosymbolia." *Journal of the American Medical Association* 90: 1095–1099.

QUIRŎS, J. B., AND O. L. SCHRAGER. 1978. *Neuropsychological Fundamentals in Learning Disabilities.* San Rafael, Calif.: Academic Therapy Publications.

ROSS, A. O. 1976. *Psychological Aspects of Learning Disabilities and Reading Disorders.* New York: McGraw-Hill.

STRAUSS, A. A., AND L. LEHTINEN. 1947. *Psychopathology of the Brain-Injured Child.* New York: Grune & Stratton.

TAYLOR, J., ED. 1932. *Selected Writings of Hughlings Jackson.* London: Hodder and Stoughton.

WIEDERHOLT, J. L. 1974. "Historical Perspectives on the Education of the Learning Disabled." In L. Mann and D. A. Sabitino, eds., *The Second Review of Special Education.* Philadelphia: JSE Press. Pp. 103–152.

WISSINK, J., C. KASS, AND W. FERRELL. 1975. "A Bayesian Approach to the Identification of Children with Learning Disabilities." *Journal of Learning Disabilities* 8 (March): 36–44.

9

Anyone attending a professional meeting on exceptional children is impressed by the myriad of exhibits proposing thousands of methods and materials for the remediation of psychological and educational deficits in children. This chapter will discuss (1) three different approaches to remediation, (2) remediation of perceptual-motor disorders, (3) remedial programs based on the Illinois Test of Psycholinguistic Abilities (ITPA) clinical model, (4) remediation of visual perception disorders, and (5) remediation of academic disorders, especially reading disorders.

Different approaches to remediation

As we have seen in the previous chapter, children with learning disabilities compose quite a diverse group. It should be no surprise then to find that the strategies and teaching approaches designed to help those children are also quite diverse. It is possible to cluster the various approaches into three broad educational strategies: (1) task training, in which the emphasis is on the sequencing and simplification of the task to be learned, (2) ability or process training, in which the focus is on the remediation of a specific developmental disability, and (3) ability- or process-task training, in which the first two approaches are combined and integrated into one remedial program.

TASK TRAINING

One of the fundamental strategies that teachers have always used with children who are having difficulty in learning in school is to modify the nature of the task to be learned. In most instances the modification is simplifying the task by breaking up the lessons into component subskills—into smaller and simpler units. Task analysis allows the child to master elements of the task and then synthesize the elements or components into the complex level required by the total task.

In the complex psychomotor skill of swimming, one can note failure by observing the child sinking slowly to the bottom of the pool. The remedial approach in this instance may be to teach the child how to kick his or her legs, how to tread water, how to keep from breathing under water, and so forth. The child is then asked to put each of those skills together through supervised practice until the child demonstrates the ability to complete the complex skill by swimming across the pool.

Similarly in academic subjects such as reading and long division, the task analysis strategy would be to simplify complex tasks so that the components can be mastered independently. The teacher can break up the complex task of reading a paragraph into (1) learning a sentence, (2) learning separate words in the sentence, (3) learning syllables or phonetic elements in a word, and then (4) building up the skills to the point of eventually reading the paragraph.

The task analysis approach does not assume any special learning problem or ability deficit within or intrinsic to the child other than lack of experience and practice with the task.

Ysseldyke and Salvia (1974) have advanced two theoretical models for teaching children with learning disabilities, namely: (1) analyzing the child's abilities and disabilities and (2) analyzing the task and the direct training of the terminal behavior or task. They concluded that the task analysis or behavioral approach is the most parsimonious.

That point of view is supported by the applied behavior analysts who advocate (1) finding out what the child can and cannot do in a particular skill, (2) determining whether or not the child has the behaviors needed to succeed in the task, (3) defining the goals in observable terms, and (4) organizing a systematic remedial program using reinforcement techniques. The applied behavior analysts do not infer processes or abilities that underlie difficulties but rely solely on the child's interactional history and the current behavior and environmental situation. They feel that their approach, which is task oriented and observable, is the most parsimonious approach, and to some it is the only approach needed.

ABILITY OR PROCESS TRAINING

In the second major remedial strategy the teacher or remedial specialist identifies a particular disability in the development of an individual child that, if not corrected, would continue to inhibit the learning processes regardless of how the teacher reconstructs the task. In such case the teaching emphasis becomes focused on remedial attempts to overcome the particular disability that seems to be blocking progress.

In the example of the child who could not swim, we could have diagnosed the problem as the child's having extremely weak upper arm and shoulder muscles. The remediation strategy in that instance may be the successive building up of arm and shoulder strength through particular exercises, weight lifting, and so forth until the child has the minimum ability or skill necessary to allow him or her to perform the tasks required.

Similarly in the case of a severe reading retardation, the child may have a disability or intrinsic deficiency in visual memory or sound blending that interferes with the ability to remember words or to synthesize sounds the child recognizes into a word. Hinshelwood (reported on page 296) described the deficiency of his patient as a deficiency in visualization or word blindness, meaning that the vision was intact but the person could not remember or recall words as wholes.

Those advocating the amelioration of the disability may use task analysis to train sound-blending ability through auditory training, or visual memory through visual training, to improve the ability to remember what was seen—pictures, objects, visual symbols.

Quay (1973) discussed the relative efficacy of task and ability (process) training. He stated that the ability or process dysfunction view postulates a handicap intrinsic to the child. He stated that three approaches to remediation have evolved: (1) remediating a disability so that learning will be facilitated at a later date, (2) training an ability or process for its own sake, and (3) direct training of the task. Having the child creep and crawl at the age of 4 or 5 so that he or she will learn to read later is an example of training an ability (prerequisite skill) so that learning to read will be facilitated at a later date. Learning to listen and understand spoken language is an example of learning an ability (receptive ability) for its own sake. It may be a prerequisite skill or ability needed for reading at a later date, but it is also needed for its own sake. Quay concludes that the direct instruction method (task training) should be tried first and then discarded in favor of other methods if direct instruction is not successful.

THE PROCESS (ABILITY)–TASK APPROACH

Most specialists believe that for the ordinary child with problems evolving from poor teaching or lack of opportunity, the task training approach is adequate and effective. Children with severe disabilities, however, require "child analysis" as well as "task analysis." The resultant remediation will involve ability and task training in the same remedial procedure; that is, teaching the child to utilize a particular process in accomplishing the desired task. We can label this approach as *process-task training* or as *aptitude-task interaction*. It means that we integrate the process and task in remediation. Instead of teaching visual discrimination of abstract, meaningless symbols, we will train visual discrimination of letters and words. The process-task approach integrates remediation of the process dysfunction with the task development as analyzed. That approach is the one generally used by those who analyze the abilities and disabilities of the child and who make a task analysis of the sequence of skills required by the task itself. Those who practice the process-task or aptitude-task-interaction approach are considered diagnostic-prescriptive teachers since they do both child analysis and task analysis and match the instructional materials with the ability of the child to respond.

An example in reading may be given to illustrate the process-task approach to remediation. Tom, who had attended school regularly up to the age of 9, was referred because he was unable to learn to read in spite of his tested IQ of 120 on the WISC. Analysis of the child's information-processing abilities showed a deficit in visual memory. He was unable to reproduce in writing and from memory words presented to him visually. He demonstrated the deficit in visual memory both on norm-referenced tests and on criterion-referenced tests. The procedure for process-task remediation in this case called for a program that would develop visual memory with the words and phrases to be taught. This procedure of training the ability of visual memory on the task itself is process-task training. The Fernald Kinesthetic Method (Fernald, 1943) is a system of training memory for words, not in the abstract—as is done in ability training of memory for digits or objects alone—but directly with the words and phrases needed by the child in learning to read. The Fernald method is a process-task approach since it trains visual memory of words and phrases.

Raschke and Young (1976a; 1976b) support the third approach. They compared the behavior-analysis model with the diagnostic-prescriptive model. They state that neither approach alone has the answer and propose what they call a *dialectic-teaching approach,* which they assert can integrate the two approaches into one system. Essentially the model assesses the abilities and disabilities of the children (intraindividual differences), makes task analyses of the skills to be learned, and prescribes remediation in the functions and skills to be developed. This dialectic system they maintain "permits the teacher to assess, program, instruct, and evaluate the child's psycholinguistic characteristics in the same system as his skill competencies and consequential variables" (1976b, p. 245).

An attempt has been made to present briefly three different strategies of remediation for children with learning disabilities. It should be noted that in some instances the line between one approach and another is not clear-cut. What should be noted, however, is that all three remedial approaches are adequate in different situations and with different children. Each is valuable when used in the appropriate setting. Direct task training is sufficient for minor academic problems in children and for the majority of corrective academic problems. The process remediation approach is suitable in training the ability for its own sake, especially at the preschool level. The process–task approach may be necessary for the severer cases involving a double problem of a specific developmental disability and an academic disability. Dogmatic allegiance to one approach over another is not warranted. Each teacher needs to apply or match the method best suited to the child and his or her needs at a particular stage in development.

Language disorders

Since time immemorial, many societies have had the problem of speech and language disorders in both adults and children. History has it that Demosthenes, the great orator of the fourth century B.C., learned to speak better by putting pebbles in his mouth.

Language can be defined in a number of ways including any form of oral or written communication. This discussion on remediation of language will be confined to auditory-verbal disabilities, which involve (1) receptive language (understanding the spoken word), (2) subvocal thinking (the inner process of manipulating verbal concepts), and (3) expressive language. Further discussion on language and speech development and of language disorders is found in Chapter 10. In this chapter we will note briefly several approaches toward helping children with learning disorders affecting language development.

THE JOHNSON AND MYKLEBUST SYSTEM

Myklebust began his career as a teacher of the deaf, and since deafness presents a major problem in language, he became interested in language defects in the deaf and the language deficits in children whose language disorders resembled those of deaf children even though they were not deaf. Through clinical experience and research Johnson and Myklebust (1967) evolved methods of remediation for what they called *psychoneurological learning disabilities,* one aspect of which is language disorders.

RECEPTIVE LANGUAGE. Johnson and Myklebust agree with most authorities that input and comprehension precede expression. They recommend that for generalized deficiencies in auditory learning, it is necessary, especially in the early stages, for the teacher to teach the child to listen to sounds and words, be aware of sound versus no sound, and respond consistently to auditory stimulation. In addition,

it is necessary for the child to learn to localize sounds and to remember sequences of sounds.

EXPRESSIVE LANGUAGE DISORDERS. Disorders of expressive language consist of three distinguishable types according to Johnson and
Myklebust: (1) defects in reauditorization, (2) defects in auditory-
motor integration, and (3) defects in syntax.

1. Reauditorization involves the inability of the child to recall
words he or she has learned. Here emphasis is placed on exercises and
games that facilitate spontaneous recall of words. Many exercises,
such as sentence completion, use pictures or cues to help recall. In addition, inner language, categorization, and association are developed
through the use of experience, pictures, and completion exercises.
Visual, kinesthetic, and tactile cues are also used. Rapid naming of
objects and pictures is practiced.

2. Deficits in *auditory-motor integration* are found in children who
are unable to imitate words even though they understand the words
(in contrast to children with reauditorization problems who can repeat words but cannot recall them). This condition has been called
apraxia.

To remediate the condition, Johnson and Myklebust suggest: (1)
making an inventory of movements, phonemes, and words that the
child can produce and capitalizing on them to teach new words, (2)
accepting initially a partial response to a word, for example, *ee* for *eat,*
and (3) utilizing visual clues, such as watching the lips, following visual directions, and using motor-kinesthetic aids such as touching or
guiding the child's tongue and lips.

3. Deficiency in syntax is the third type of auditory-expressive
disorder dealt with by Johnson and Myklebust. To remediate this
disorder, they suggest that (a) a planned and programmed presentation be developed to help the child learn the structure of language, (b)
meaningful experiences be arranged either through play activities or
pictures, and (c) the child be presented with simple sentences to teach
noun-verb combinations and then with more complex grammatic
structures.

MCGINNIS ASSOCIATION METHOD

The association method of remediating childhood aphasics was developed by McGinnis (1963) and used with aphasic children at the Central Institute for the Deaf in St. Louis. Mrs. McGinnis was a teacher
of the deaf who also worked with aphasic adults. She noticed a similarity between aphasic adults and children who were referred to the

school for the deaf because of their delay in language and speech development. Such children were found to have relatively normal hearing and intelligence. They were not autistic, yet they did not talk or understand language. McGinnis recognized two general types of language-delayed children: (1) expressive aphasics and (2) receptive aphasics.

In remediation McGinnis believed that inner language had been developed but auditory reception was deficient. To develop both auditory reception and verbal expression, McGinnis began with an elemental approach using a phonetic method of teaching sounds first, next using the learned sounds to form words, and then matching the word with pictures to derive meaning. The teacher enunciates a word, and the child breaks the word into phonemes, writes each sound, and then articulates the whole word and matches it with pictures of objects (nouns) that have been taught. Once the child has learned to understand some words and to express them, he or she begins to add vocabulary from incidental learning.

The McGinnis method, described in detail in her book (1963), explains the program and the stages. The preceding description includes only the first stage or unit, which aims to develop, through phonemes and words, approximately fifty nouns. The second stage is also programmed and includes the development of phrases and sentences with verbs and prepositions. The third stage develops more complex language.

THE MONTEREY PROGRAMMED CONDITIONING FOR THE NONLANGUAGE CHILD

Gray and Ryan (1973) have developed a system of teaching language to nonlanguage children through programmed materials using the principles of operant conditioning. No primary reinforcement is used. The reinforcement schedule of tokens is gradually reduced to zero, but social reinforcement is always given.

The system carries the child step by step through a finite core of basic grammatical forms on the hypothesis that once a minilanguage based on the grammatical forms is acquired, the child will continue to learn new forms and new grammatical rules through his or her own experiences.

For each grammatical form taught, the child proceeds through a sequence of tasks involving the variables of (1) the response required from the child, (2) the stimulus provided, (3) the kind of reinforcement given, (4) the reinforcement schedule, (5) the criteria for proceeding to each next step, and (6) the model that lets the child know what response is expected. Pictures are used in the early stages of each sequence of tasks, next stories (with pictures), and then conversation without pictures.

The system is formalized and highly structured, giving the child great redundancy in hearing and using the critical grammatical forms. The method of presentation is standardized, allowing no variations. Spontaneous language is ignored and receives no reinforcement in order to run the child rapidly through the required sequences. For content, however, the vocabularly used is determined by each teacher (programmer) for each child. The programmer is also responsible for securing appropriate picture content and story content, neither of which has been standardized for the system. When used for small groups, each child's program is individualized, but it is expected that each child will benefit from the incidental learning experience in the group.

The point at which the child enters the program is determined by his or her responses to an initial criterion test involving the same material covered in the system. A branching program is provided for those children who fall below the specified criteria for success at any stage.

Gray and Ryan do not claim that their program is the answer for all those with language problems, but see merit in its use with "expressive, oral language nonusers" (p. 160). It is most applicable to children at age 15 months and over who have problems in form or syntax of oral communication. It does not deal with the content of meaning or vocabulary or with the selective use of language. The effect on comprehension problems is questioned, but no research is available. Advantages in its use include: (1) once organized it reduces preparation time, (2) it can then be used by paraprofessionals, (3) it has a good placement procedure, (4) it provides a nicely ordered developmental sequence, and (5) it can be used with groups.

Perceptual-motor disorders

During the post–World War II period Strauss and Lehtinen generated widespread interest in the problem of specific learning disabilities by focusing attention on brain-injured children. The publication in 1947 of *Psychopathology of the Brain-Injured Child* (Strauss and Lehtinen, 1947) describing their research, theories, and educational methods stimulated national interest in children with learning disabilities.

Strauss's main thesis was that children with brain injuries incurred before, during, or after birth are subject to major disorders in (1) perception, (2) thinking, and (3) behavior, and that these disorders affect the child's ability to learn to read, write, spell, or calculate using arithmetic symbols. The diagnosis of brain injury was reached primarily from the presence of behavioral manifestations or disorders and was not based solely on traditional neurologic diagnosis. Strauss and Lehtinen's educational methods consisted of instructional procedures and environmental changes that would correct or ameliorate the disturbances in perception, thinking, and behavior. Those techniques were integrated with procedures in teaching reading, writing, spelling, and arithmetic.

Although Strauss's concept of brain-damaged children and the procedures in assessment that led to such a diagnosis have been challenged, the educational procedures for remediation of the behavioral symptoms have not been seriously questioned. Many subsequent developments in learning disabilities were stimulated by Strauss and Lehtinen's work. Among these developments are the perceptual-motor approaches of (1) William Cruickshank, (2) Newell Kephart, and (3) Raymond Barsch.

CRUICKSHANK

Cruickshank and his associates working with cerebral-palsied and hyperactive children have adapted and extended the procedures of Strauss and Lehtinen. This group states that the majority of children with known brain damage have the behavioral characteristics pointed out by Strauss, namely: (1) motor disinhibition (inability to refrain from a response), (2) disassociation (the tendency to respond to pieces [elements] of a stimulus), (3) figure-ground disturbance (confusing a figure with its background), (4) perseveration (difficulty in shifting from one psychological task to another), and (5) absence of a well-developed self-concept and body image.

Cruickshank et al. (1961) tested the Strauss hypothesis that a nonstimulating (barren) classroom with specially designed instructional materials would improve the functioning of those children. Forty hyperactive children were divided into four groups of ten each. Two of the groups were given the special nonstimulating classroom program, while the other two groups were placed in special classes with a traditional program.

This experiment by Cruickshank et al., as well as other less extensive experiments (Burnett, 1962; Rost, 1967) did not demonstrate that hyperactive or distractible children can profit more significantly, either intellectually or academically, from a nonstimulating classroom environment than from a special class organized along more traditional lines. The experiment did show, however, that special education with or without the nonstimulating class environment can produce academic progress in such children. It may also be true that for some individual children who are hyperactive, the procedure of decreasing the environmental stimuli is very beneficial. Group results, as previously cited, do not always determine what is most beneficial for a particular child.

KEPHART

Kephart, a well-known contributor to the field of learning disabilities, worked with Strauss, first in research and later as a co-author (Strauss and Kephart, 1955). Kephart (1971) later evolved a system of diagnosis and remediation along somewhat different theoretical lines, relying less on brain dysfunction and more on developmental psychology.

Kephart's basic thesis (1964) is that the child's first encounter with the environment is through motor activities and that this muscular behavior is a prerequisite for later learnings. In normal development the child acquires patterns of movement, namely: (1) posture and the maintenance of balance, (2) contact (reaching, grasping, and releasing), (3) locomotion, and (4) receipt and propulsion (which are dependent primarily on an awareness of self). As the child matures, Kephart postulates, he or she is able to generalize and objectify the relationship of objects in time and space.

Kephart emphasizes the hierarchy of those motor generalizations in developing space and time perception. Thus, through proprioceptive and exteroceptive experiences the child develops a perceptual world that matches his or her motor world. Kephart emphasizes the importance of this perceptual-motor match in which what is perceived must be matched to the child's awareness in order to have meaning. This perceptual-motor match is developed through a feedback system in which the child receives information in response to his or her own output, thereby being able to monitor the correctness or incorrectness of his or her own perceptions and actions.

Kephart's approach to motor pattern development and remediation of the problems attending it attempts to fill in the gaps in the sequence of generalizations that enable the child to integrate and manipulate the information received from the environment, such as an understanding of form, space, and rhythm. Kephart emphasizes process-oriented, rather than task-oriented, procedures; that is, the basic motor generalizations and perceptual-motor skills should be developed before the child can be expected to progress academically. He therefore provides various training activities such as: (1) sensory-motor training using walking boards, trampolines, making "angels in the snow," and various games to teach variations in movement, rhythm, and bilateral as well as unilateral abilities; (2) chalkboard activities designed to develop movement patterns and matching visual perceptions; (3) ocular-motor training to help the child match his or her visual control to the motor and kinesthetic patterns that have been learned; and (4) form perception exercises using pegboards, stick figures, and puzzles, for example.

That approach is applicable to certain children with specific perceptual-motor problems, but its proponents do not claim that the procedures are beneficial for all children with specific learning disabilities. Children who do not have visual-motor perceptual problems but who have retardation in auditory, vocal, and language disorders may require different kinds of remediation.

BARSCH

Barsch (1965; 1967), who also worked with Strauss, has developed what he terms a *movigenic curriculum*. He postulates that man is a moving being in a spatial world. The learning difficulties that children have are deficits in movement efficiency. The movigenic curriculum is therefore designed to facilitate movement efficiency. The program of training movement efficiency is, in a sense, the end in itself. Barsch does not relate this development to deficits in learning to talk or in learning to read—deficits that usually are associated with the concept of learning disabilities.

OTHER PERCEPTUAL-MOTOR APPROACHES

Some of the other perceptual-motor approaches are not direct descendants of Seguin and Strauss. Three of them, the approaches of Delacato, Cratty, and Valett, will be mentioned briefly. The reader is referred to the sources for further information.

DELACATO. Delacato (1963) with Doman, a physiotherapist, has developed a physical therapy program that they believe improves not only the physical abilities of the child but, because of the effects on the brain, also promotes the development of reading, speech, and writing.

This program, established at the Institute for the Achievement of Human Potential at Chestnut Hills, Pennsylvania, has created considerable controversy regarding its effectiveness (Robbins and Glass, 1969).

CRATTY. Cratty (1967; Cratty and Martin, 1969) specialized in physical education and recreation and has used his knowledge in these areas to develop physical education activities that relate to perceptual-motor development. He has developed a screening test in six categories of motor learning that can be administered by the teacher. The categories are body perception, balance, locomotion, agility, throwing, and catching. Cratty describes many activities that develop proficiencies in those six categories.

VALETT. Valett (1967) has developed an eclectic program involving a variety of activities that he considers basic learning abilities for use in developing specific educational programs. He deals with six areas of development and defines operationally and by examples the activities subsumed under each area. The six areas are: (1) gross motor development, (2) sensory-motor integration, (3) perceptual-motor skills, (4) language development, (5) conceptual skills, and (6) social skills.

COMMENT ON PERCEPTUAL-MOTOR TRAINING

The thread of similarity among the preceding approaches is quite apparent. All involve the importance of perceptual-motor diagnosis and subsequent remediation through sensory-motor activities.

It is interesting to note that a century and a third ago Edward Seguin (1846) emphasized sensory-motor training of the mentally retarded. He introduced a physiological method of training the mentally retarded, and his work had some impact on Alfred Strauss. Seguin's work is heavily reflected in the methods of Kephart and Barsch. His treatise on physiological education for the mentally retarded was primarily a sensory-motor one. His aim, like the aims of Strauss and Kephart, was from motor or muscular training to sensory-motor training, and from sensory-motor training to abstract thought. Seguin's use of the trampoline to develop balance, the game of statue to develop attention, and perceptual-motor training to develop cognition is similar in aim and practice to those of the current perceptual-motor emphasis. It is indeed interesting that a system developed in the middle of the nineteenth century for the mentally retarded should crop up in the middle of the twentieth century in somewhat the same form for children with learning disabilities. It is also interesting that Strauss, Barsch, and Kephart developed their theories and procedures with mentally retarded or slow-learning children and then applied them to children with learning disabilities. Is the similarity due to the fact that in the past learning disabled children with those incapacities were often labeled retarded?

Visual perceptual disorders

On the commercial market today there are many materials that have been designed to train some phase of visual perception (visual discrimination, figure-ground discrimination, visual closure, and others). Only two of the more complete systems will be described here as examples of attempts to train children with visual perceptual disorders. Interested readers should go to the source for details of the program.

FROSTIG

Marianne Frostig hypothesized that children with disabilities in visual perception will have difficulty learning in school and that early remediation of these disabilities will prevent future school failures.

Frostig's Developmental Tests of Visual Perception measures performance on various tasks involving visual perception (Frostig et al., 1964). Recognizing that evaluating a single facet of visual perception does not give a complete picture, Frostig developed tests of five different perceptual skills: (1) eye-hand coordination, (2) figure-ground discrimination, (3) sensitivity to constancy of shape, (4) awareness of position in space, and (5) recognition of spatial relations.

The program for remediation developed by Frostig and Horne (1964) consists of work sheets for the children, supplemented by other related remedial techniques together with suggestions for physical exercises and for three-dimensional activities. The exercises are designed to develop skills in the five areas tested by the Developmental Tests of Visual Perception. The materials have been used with kindergarten and first-grade children to develop readiness for later academic achievement as well as with children diagnosed as having visual-motor handicaps.

It should be pointed out that the description of the tests and the remedial procedures of Frostig does not imply that she excludes other approaches. On the contrary, she uses an eclectic method in both diagnosis and remediation. She uses many diagnostic instruments including the Wechsler Intelligence Scale for Children (WISC) and the Illinois Test of Psycholinguistic Abilities (ITPA), as well as her Developmental Tests of Visual Perception. By such analysis she looks for the areas in which the child does not perform well and creates appropriate remedial instruction. In addition to visual perception programs, Frostig and Maslow (1969) developed a program for movement education, the central purpose of which is the "promotion of good health, and a sense of well-being and the development of sensory-motor skills and self-awareness" (p. 6).

Research on the efficacy of the Frostig-Horne program has not provided clear-cut evaluations. In a review of the studies conducted on the materials, Myers and Hammill (1976) report contradictory results. In general, using the Frostig materials with heterogeneous groups of children increases the scores on the Developmental Tests of Visual Perception, but whether or not those children show accelerated reading achievement later is still a question. Similar research on children with marked disabilities in visual perception is not available.

GETMAN

Getman, an optometrist, has long been interested in visual abilities and their relationship to learning disabilities and particularly to reading disabilities. His experience in schools and clinics led him to believe that vision is learned and is important for the development of academic skills.

Getman's program (1965) is divided into five developmental systems: (1) a general-motor system in which the body explores with the eyes, (2) a special-motor system including eye-hand coordination, (3) an ocular-motor system in which vision replaces bodily movement, (4) a speech-motor system in which oral language replaces gesturing, and (5) a visualization system.

On the basis of those developmental systems, Getman, Kane, Halgren, and McKee (1968) prepared a series of developmental exercises for teachers to use at the preschool level.

It should be noted that Getman's system is process oriented and is mainly used at the preschool level. It is directed toward preventing academic failure and is a good example of process training in hopes that success in the process will transfer to academic achievement. There is no substantial research to evaluate the efficacy of the method.

Remedial programs evolving from the ITPA model

After fifteen years of research, Kirk, McCarthy, and Kirk (1968) developed the *Illinois Test of Psycholinguistic Abilities* (ITPA) for the purpose of examining the intraindividual differences in the abilities of young children with verbal or nonverbal disabilities. In 1961 when an experimental edition was developed, the newly coined term *psycholinguistic* was used to refer to the psychological aspects of linguistics.

To cover crucial psychological aspects, the ITPA includes three dimensions and twelve tests. The three dimensions are:

1. *Levels of organization.* These include (a) a representational level that utilizes symbols to carry meaning and (b) an automatic level that is more habitual, is less voluntary, and requires less translation of a symbol into meaning than does the representational level.
2. *Channels of communication.* The ITPA is restricted to (a) the auditory-vocal channel (hearing and talking) and (b) the visual-motor channel (seeing and doing).
3. *Psycholinguistic processes.* These include (a) auditory and visual reception, (b) auditory and visual association, and (c) vocal and manual expression.

The information-processing model of the ITPA was used to develop twelve tests to measure levels, channels, and processes. The model has also been used to develop instructional procedures for preschool and primary-grade children. The instructional and remedial procedures that have been developed were designed to remediate the following:

1. *auditory reception* disability, the inability to listen and to understand what is heard, such as verbal discourse
2. *visual reception* disability, the inability to gain meaning from visual symbols and to interpret them
3. *auditory association* disability, the inability to organize and relate concepts presented orally
4. *visual association* disability, the inability to organize and relate concepts presented visually
5. *verbal expression* disability, the inability to express concepts vocally
6. *manual expression* disability, the inability to express ideas manually
7. *grammatic closure* disability, the inability to make use of redundancies of oral language in acquiring automatic habits for handling syntax and grammatic inflections
8. *visual closure* disability, the inability to identify a common object from the presentation of an incomplete picture of it
9. *auditory sequential memory* disability, the inability to reproduce from memory a sequence of words or phrases of increasing length
10. *visual sequential memory* disability, the inability to reproduce sequences of meaningful or nonmeaningful pictures or figures from memory
11. *auditory closure* disability, the inability to identify a word or phrase from the auditory presentation of incomplete portions of it

12. *sound-blending* disability, the inability to blend sounds presented one at a time

In developing methods and materials for young children, Karnes (1975) explained her concept of the ITPA communication model as follows:

> A much oversimplified description of the ITPA model might go like this. Pretend that a person is a computer. A computer is a machine which receives information (INPUT) which may be stored (MEMORY) for later use or processed in some way (ORGANIZATION). Ultimately, the product of processing is expressed in some way, such as a tape or paper print-out (OUTPUT). People, to continue the analogy, receive information through their senses (RECEPTION). Sometimes this information is merely stored or remembered (MEMORY), but at other times partial information may be in some way completed for better understanding (CLOSURE) or several bits of information may be organized into a new and different whole (ASSOCIATION). Finally, expression is either verbal or gestural or both (VERBAL or MANUAL EXPRESSION). (p. 2)

THE KARNES PROGRAM

The series of kits prepared by Karnes for parents and teachers include the following: The Karnes Early Language Activities (1975) for parents and teachers of children from 18 months to 3 years of age; Learning Language at Home (1977) for parents of children from 18 months to 5 years of age; and Goal: Language Development—Level I, 1972, for children 3 to 6; Level II, 1977, for children in grades two and above.

Those programs are an outcome of Karnes's research with normal and exceptional children of school age and with parents and young children, especially of low-income families. The research with mothers of disadvantaged and handicapped infants (Karnes et al., 1970) led to the preparation of materials for very young children. Karnes, Zehrbach, and Teska (1974) have reported on research showing the efficacy of these programs on disadvantaged children. A follow-up through the third grade showed normal development.

PEABODY LANGUAGE DEVELOPMENT KITS

Using as a base a doctoral dissertation by James Smith (1962) in which it was found that mentally retarded children can profit from language lessons designed from the ITPA model, Dunn and Smith (1967) developed a series of instructional kits to be used for a whole class of children ages 2 to 8. Much emphasis is given to the development of oral language through exercises, games, and lessons. The lessons are arranged in sequence and are designed to develop the psycholinguistic processes of auditory and visual reception, association, and verbal and manual expression. Directions are explicit for the teacher and follow a systematic, well-rounded approach.

MWM PROGRAM FOR DEVELOPING LANGUAGE ABILITIES

The MWM program, developed by Minskoff, Wiseman, and Minskoff (1975), is based on the ITPA model. It is presented on two levels: Level I (1972) for ages 5 to 7 and Level II (1975) for ages 7 to 10. Each level includes three sets of materials: (1) record booklets, (2) a series of manuals for the teacher, and (3) a series of workbooks for the children.

An inventory of observable language behavior is contained in a record booklet used by the teacher in estimating each child's ability in the twelve subtests of the ITPA. The teacher answers a series of questions such as "Does the child have difficulty learning abstract words?" and "Does he or she have difficulty in self-care tasks?"

Explicit directions for the use of materials and workbooks and for developing each task are presented in the teacher's manuals. Each level contains tasks in (1) auditory and visual reception, (2) auditory and visual association, (3) verbal and manual expression, (4) auditory and visual memory, (5) grammatic and visual closure, and (6) auditory closure and sound blending.

OTHER PROGRAMS

A number of informal programs and books outline remedial procedures and suggestions. Bush and Giles's *Aids to Psycholinguistic Teaching* (1969) contains teaching aids for children showing difficulty in the various functions of the model of the ITPA. It also contains suggestions for perceptual-motor activities grouped according to grade level.

Lombardi and Lombardi's *ITPA: Clinical Interpretation and Remediation* (1977) presents a description of clinical and related school behaviors common to children showing difficulty in each of the functions of the ITPA model. Remedial suggestions and activities are provided for helping to overcome specific observable behaviors.

Psycholinguistic Learning Disabilities: Diagnosis and Remediation (Kirk and Kirk, 1971) presents guidelines to help teachers to develop their own remedial procedures based on the individual needs of each child. It provides a breakdown of the functions noted by the ITPA into observable subtasks and further diagnostic clues as to the child's difficulty.

THE EFFECTS OF TRAINING

The attempts to train psycholinguistic functions has aroused a controversy on the effectiveness of such training. Hammill and Larsen (1978) reviewed thirty-eight studies on psycholinguistic training that had been evaluated by the ITPA and concluded "the idea that psycholinguistic constructs, as measured by the ITPA, can be trained by existing techniques remains nonvalidated" (p. 11).

In a re-evaluation of the same studies, Lund, Foster, and McCall-Perez (1978) questioned the conclusions of Hammill and Larsen. The re-evaluation noted that a substantial number of the studies did produce positive results, that many of the studies had been poorly controlled, and that Hammill and Larsen were not justified in their conclusions. In reviewing the criticisms Hammill and Larsen (1978) attempted to justify their earlier conclusions by stating that "the overwhelming consensus of research evidence concerning the effectiveness of psycholinguistic training is that it remains essentially nonvalidated" (p. 412).

We, the authors, hold the opinion that research on the efficacy of any procedure using groups of children labeled learning disabled is very difficult to control since it is impossible to equate the variables of type of deficit, appropriateness of methods, degree of deficit, control of the environment, and teacher competences. It is likely that single-subject research may net more adequate results than group results on a heterogeneous sample.

Academic disabilities

The most common academic disabilities for which teachers refer children are reading, spelling, arithmetic, and writing. Of referrals from teachers, 60 to 80 percent are for reading difficulties. Since space does not permit a discussion of all academic subjects, only reading will be discussed in detail, with brief references to other disabilities.

INDIVIDUALIZED REMEDIAL READING APPROACHES

Many learning disabilities are not detected until the child begins to fail academically in school. Failure in reading is the most common point of detection and one of the most frequent kinds of learning disabilities with which the school is concerned.

Nearly all children are exposed to reading experiences, which sometimes begin at home, sometimes in kindergarten, but most commonly when they are admitted to the first grade. Reading instruction usually begins with developmental reading, but as the child progresses, instruction may proceed on any one of three different levels: (1) developmental reading, (2) corrective reading, or (3) remedial reading.

1. Developmental reading refers to various systems of teaching reading in the classroom and provides a sequential development of the skills of reading.

2. Corrective reading refers to the methods used to change minor incorrect habits or gaps in knowledge acquired in the course of a developmental reading program. Task or skill training is generally employed for corrective reading. In these instances the child may need help in word recognition skills, in vocabulary understanding, in phonics, or in speed of reading. Such help has been called corrective reading since the habits, not the basic processes of the child's thinking, need correcting.

3. Remedial reading refers to the procedure used with children whose reading skills are still not developed after exposure to developmental reading and corrective reading. These children have developmental disabilities within themselves that require remediation before the child will learn to read. These children are said to have learning disabilities and if task or skill training has not succeeded, a process-task approach may be necessary.

A large number of remedial reading methods have been developed for children with learning disabilities. Included in this section will be brief descriptions of (1) the kinesthetic method and (2) phonic methods.

THE KINESTHETIC METHOD. This method was developed by Grace Fernald (1943; Fernald and Keller, 1921), a psychologist who became interested in children who had difficulty in learning to read or spell. Her method involves four developmental stages: (1) In stage one the child traces the form of a known word while saying it, then writes it from memory, comparing each trial with the original model. (2) In stage two he or she just looks at the word or phrase while saying it, then tries to write it from memory, comparing the result with the model until successful. (3) In stage three the child writes the word without vocalizing it until successful. (4) In stage four he or she begins to generalize and to read new words on the basis of experience with previously learned words.

The Fernald kinesthetic method of teaching disabled readers (Fernald and Keller, 1921) has withstood the test of time, since it has been used in various forms by many teachers. Fernald (1943) describes in case studies the progress made by severely disabled readers following training by the kinesthetic method.

Kirk (1933) compared the manual-tracing method with the look-and-say method using six subnormal boys, each serving as his own control. He found no difference between the tracing method and the look-and-say method in number of trials in learning, but retention of the words over a period of twenty-four hours was significantly superior for words learned by the tracing method.

Hirsch (1963) gave a series of visual sequential memory tests to sixteen subjects and trained eight of them on unknown words by the kinesthetic method, teaching the other eight by the look-and-say method. The group that had learned by the kinesthetic method scored higher on the visual memory retests than did the control group, suggesting that the kinesthetic method may train visual sequential memory.

The Fernald kinesthetic method has been beneficial to some children with certain kinds of reading disabilities, probably because the procedure encompasses important variables in learning. First, integrating the visual input with the motor experience strengthens the learning process by the addition of another sensory channel. Second, by writing and using a motor movement, attention is focused on the visual task. Although the method has been called "kinesthetic," its more important function may be that of training visual sequential memory, or visualization ability and attention to detail, since the emphasis of the method is to *write* words from memory. Third, the method has a built-in feedback system. The child can write the word, check it with the original word, and, if it is incorrect, try again to write it from memory. It can be self-correctional. The Fernald method is a good example of the process–task remedial procedure since it remediates the developmental disability (visual memory) in the task of reading.

PHONIC METHODS. Many phonic methods have been developed, but only three of the most commonly used phonic remedial methods will be briefly described here.

The phonic-grapho-vocal method of Hegge, Kirk, and Kirk (1936) was developed while the authors were working with educable mentally retarded children who were also classified as disabled readers. The Hegge, Kirk, and Kirk Remedial Reading Drills are a programmed phonic system that emphasizes sound blending and incorporates much kinesthetic experience.

The procedure begins by giving the child auditory training in sound blending and grapho-vocal practice in writing and vocalizing letter sounds, running them together as he or she sounds them. When sound blending has been achieved, the child is presented with two- and three-letter words in which the child sounds each element separately and then blends the sounds into a word. Supplementary to the printed lessons, the grapho-vocal method is used by asking the child to write words as he or she pronounces the separate components and blends them into a word, thus requiring an analytic as well as a synthetic activity.

The Remedial Reading Drills follow the same principles found valuable in programmed learning: (a) the principle of minimal change, each lesson incorporating only one new sound, (b) overlearning through many repetitions of each new sound in a variety of settings, plus frequent review drills, (c) promptings and confirmation, (d) only one response taught for each symbol, and (e) providing the child with reinforcement through immediate knowledge of his or her success and by social reinforcement given by the tutor.

The *Visual-Auditory-Kinesthetic (VAK) Method* of Gillingham and Stillman (1936; 1965) is a phonic system for the remediation of reading disabilities. In this method children learn both the names of the letters and the sounds of the letters. Sounding is used for reading, but letter names are used for spelling. A systematic procedure is followed in which the child is told the name of a letter and then its sound. The child then says the sound and traces it or writes it from memory. After learning some consonants and vowels, the child is required to sound each letter and blend the sounds into a word. After the child has learned to sound, write, and read three-letter words, those words are made into stories; the child reads them silently and then orally.

The procedures are developed by stages from the names of the letters to the sounds, to the associations, to the reading of words, sentences, and stories, and finally to reading books. The Gillingham-Stillman VAK system is an association system, since the theoretical approach is to integrate visual, kinesthetic, and auditory sense inputs. Many who follow the Gillingham-Stillman method think it produces results with normal children who have been unable to learn by the whole-word method and thus require a more atomistic approach through letter sounds and letter names. Like the Hegge, Kirk, and Kirk Remedial Reading Drills, it has been used for over forty years including the period during which the use of phonics was severely criticized.

Distar was developed by Engelmann and Bruner (1969) who worked with preschool disadvantaged children who did not necessarily show reading disabilities. It is a programmed instructional system that uses a sound-blending technique with words and sentences. It is highly structured and designed to develop the skills needed for word recognition in children who have had little opportunity to read. This system has obtained considerable acceptance in Head Start and first-grade programs in areas dealing with disadvantaged and below-average children. Distar (Direct Instruction Systems for Teaching Arithmetic and Reading) also includes an arithmetic and language program. (See Haring and Bateman, 1977.)

Other phonic and related systems include Spalding and Spalding's Writing Road to Reading (1957), *The Peabody Rebus Reading Program* by Woodcock and Clark (1967), and the *Initial Teaching Alphabet* (ITA) by Pittman (1963).

SPELLING DISABILITIES

Spelling disabilities are often associated with reading disabilities. It is true that poor readers are generally poor spellers, but the reverse is not always true, for some good readers are poor spellers.

Hannah, Hodges, and Hannah (1971) have presented an excellent analysis of spelling. They discuss the structure and strategies that can be used in teaching spelling from kindergarten to eighth grade. In their comprehensive book no mention is made about what to do with the child who fails in the spelling program—in other words, with the child who has a learning disability affecting spelling.

Peters (1975), a British authority on the teaching of spelling, states that children who have difficulty learning to spell tend to be (1) low in intelligence, (2) low in visual perception of word forms, (3) careless, and (4) slow in handwriting.

The first task of a teacher is to determine the present level of spelling skill and that of other academic skills for comparative purposes. Then the teacher needs to determine the method by which the child learns to spell.

From the oral and written spelling of a list of words within the child's level of spelling skill, the examiner or teacher can note the kinds of errors that are made. Examples of some of these errors follow. (1) The child uses primarily a phonic approach, spelling words like *walk* as "wok" and *tough* as "tuf." These errors indicate that he or she has learned phonics and is not using other techniques of spelling. (2) The child writes a word as a whole when the word is known, but does not start when he or she does not know it. This may mean that the child has learned some words visually but has no method of attack to use when unable to recall the word visually. (3) He or she reverses letters in a word spelled orally or written. (4) The child makes errors in some words that indicate an inability to discriminate certain sounds such as in *pin* and *pen*. If the child pronounces words incorrectly, he or she may spell them according to a mispronunciation of them.

For a detailed discussion of procedures for the diagnosis and remediation of spelling difficulties, the reader is referred to Johnson and Myklebust (1967), Hammill and Noone (1975), Lerner (1976), Myers and Hammill (1976), Yee (1966), Persanke and Yee (1966), Arena (1968), and Wallace and McLoughlin (1975).

WRITING DISABILITIES

Writing disabilities are often found in children who have reading and spelling disabilities. They are also found in children who can read and spell orally but who have not learned to express their ideas in writing.

Writing disabilities may include (1) difficulties in handwriting stemming from poor motor coordination, body image, laterality, visual imagery, ocular control, and problems that may affect the ability to copy and/or form letters and words spontaneously and (2) difficulties in organizing concepts and putting them down on paper.

Hammill and Bartel (1975) present an organized list of techniques that are helpful in kindergarten and first grade in developing penmanship, but note that these "are inadequate as comprehensive measures of written expression . . . [or] the child's ability to form letters."

Sometimes basic problems of motor coordination, perceptual-motor difficulties, and left-handedness must be attacked in conjunction with the child's difficulty in handwriting. The left-handed child may need some special help in orienting himself or herself to paper and pencil; the child whose handedness has been changed may need some help in overcoming reversals or misorientation of letters; the child with ocular-motor or perceptual-motor problems may require a sequential program for keeping between the lines on the paper, forming letters, and spacing. Such help should be developmentally programmed, beginning with tracing, then connecting dots, and finishing incomplete letters, words, and finally sentences.

For more detailed help in remediating handwriting, the student is referred to Newland (1932), Hammill and Bartel (1975), and Lerner (1976).

Difficulties in organizing concepts and putting them down on paper involve conceptual problems and are often closely associated with other problems found in reading, spelling, and oral expression.

The child who has difficulty in organizing ideas and in seeing relationships, time sequences, and other such mental operations will have difficulty writing a meaningful sequence of sentences. The child with a poor vocabulary or one who lacks an understanding of word relationships or the inflections of plural and past and future, for example, will have difficulty in writing. Poor written expression and poor oral expression often occur together. Similarly, problems in reading and spelling will usually correspond to problems in written expression. Poor auditory comprehension may also be related to poor written expression. Johnson and Myklebust (1967) note: "Ability to use written language requires many integrities, including adequate auditory language and experience on which to base the written form" (p. 193). The authors have described three types of disorders of written language and provide extensive remedial procedures for each.

1. *Dysgraphia,* or the lack of sufficient visual–motor integration to execute the motor patterns necessary to write what is visualized. A child so afflicted cannot even copy what he or she sees. It is a form of apraxia and may be quite different from the inability to organize and express ideas orally. This child may be able to read and speak but cannot write letters, words, and numbers.

2. *Deficits in revisualization* found in children who can read, speak, and copy but because of a visual memory deficit cannot retrieve the image of the necessary words, numbers, and letters. For these children who can usually recognize words and numbers but cannot recall the visual image, efforts are made to help them to begin with recognition and move through partial recall to total recall.

3. *Disorders of formulation and syntax.* A child so afflicted cannot formulate thoughts into adequate form to communicate in writing. He or she may, however, be able to communicate orally, to copy, and to spell and revisualize words.

DIFFICULTIES WITH LEFT-HANDEDNESS. In addition to, or in combination with, difficulties in writing are found the problems of children whose handedness has been changed and who have tendencies to reverse the position or orientation of their letters in writing.

Left-handed children sometimes have difficulty in learning to write and sometimes tend to write from right to left. Such children should have assistance in adjusting the page and should be allowed to learn to write from the top of the line rather than from the bottom as is normal with right-handed children. Left-handed children need not have difficulty in learning to write if they are initially guided in placing the page in the proper position. (See Plunkett, *A Writing Manual for Teaching the Left-Handed,* 1954.)

PERCEPTUAL-MOTOR PROBLEMS. Many children with perceptual-motor problems have difficulty reproducing letters and words and keeping within two lines as they write. Such children require a sequential program for learning to write, starting with tracing the letters, then connecting dots of incomplete letters, then forming words, and later making sentences. Adequate writing cannot be achieved without extensive practice and adequate reinforcement. Lerner (1975) gives a series of step-by-step procedures including providing windows in cardboard to guide the child in keeping within a line and using tape for guidance for the bottom and the top line. She also describes how to teach the child to hold a pencil.

ARITHMETIC DISABILITIES

Arithmetic disabilities of a severe nature are less frequent than reading disabilities and receive less attention. With the availability of inexpensive electronic calculators, a temporary way out of learning has arrived, but it does not eliminate the value of knowing the fundamental arithmetic skills.

Arithmetic disabilities may be found in children of normal intelligence who are adequate in reading and spelling. Just as children who are doing fifth- and sixth-grade work in arithmetic computation may be reading at the first-grade level, so children who are reading at the fifth- and sixth-grade level may be unable to add or subtract. Such a condition has been labeled *dyscalculia* in the literature.

As with language and reading, that disorder was observed originally in adults as a loss of the ability to calculate after cerebral injuries. Chalfant and Scheffelin (1969) cite the early works of Henschen on brain-injured adults who, on autopsy, were found to have lesions in one or more different areas of the brain (occipital, frontal, parietal, and temporal areas). They also cited the work of Gertsmann and others who found lesions in the parieto-occipital region in the dominant hemisphere. With children it is difficult to determine whether the arithmetic disability is the result of a genetic factor or a cerebral dysfunction acquired before, during, or after birth or whether it is due to poor instruction, to emotional factors, or to lack of early exposure to quantitative thinking.

The diagnosis of arithmetic disabilities is similar to the diagnosis of any learning disability, including (1) determining whether a disability exists by comparing other skills to the level of performance in arithmetic, (2) analyzing types of errors in arithmetic, (3) studying the correlates that are present, (4) evolving a diagnostic hypothesis, and (5) organizing a remedial program. The most important part of the analysis is to study the kinds of errors that are made in arithmetic calculation. The usual procedure is to test the child formally or informally on counting; reading and writing numerals; the four basic operations of addition, subtraction, multiplication, and division; using fractions, decimals, and percentages; and a cognitive understanding of space, time, and quantity.

Remediation of errors in arithmetic is generally successful when the instructional procedures are programmed step by step, beginning at the level on which the child is performing and moving upward only at the rate at which the child can learn successfully. In severe arithmetic disabilities a one-to-one tutoring situation can adapt to the rate of progress and provide adequate reinforcement when needed. If the disability is the result of lack of motivation, poor instruction, or other environmental factors, the remediation of mechanical errors is generally adequate. If, however, the retardation in arithmetic is the result of other factors such as inadequate spatial relations, dysgraphia, lack of verbal ability, deficiencies in inductive thinking, and other correlates, it is necessary to use a process–task approach to remediation by organizing the instruction so as to include the use of the disabling process in relation to the task requirement and by developing an understanding of the errors observed during the operation of the task. Strauss and Lehtinen (1947) have described children with poor visual–spatial organization who had difficulty in discriminating between shapes, sizes, and lengths. Remediation in arithmetic, according to Strauss and Lehtinen, should take those disabilities into consideration in organizing the remedial program.

Kephart (1971) has stressed that some children with learning disabilities show a deficit in body image and spatial awareness, which inhibits the development of arithmetic abilities. They are probably the children for whom the Stern materials and the Cuisenaire Rods are most helpful. The Stern method assumes that it is necessary for a child to develop a space world in order to deal with group phenomena in arithmetic. Spatial knowledge is a premium in developing arithmetic concepts. Kephart's methods of remediation are described in detail in his book *The Slow Learner in the Classroom* (1971).

Cawley and Vitello (1972) have designed a model for teaching arithmetic to handicapped children. It includes (1) an interaction unit between the child and the teacher, (2) a verbal-processing information unit, and (3) a conceptual unit. These are operative within a learning unit that uses types of learning styles and factors that influence learning. Cawley and Goodstein (1972) have developed materials to implement the teaching of arithmetic to handicapped children.

Since the teaching of arithmetic is quite involved, the reader is referred to the following for a description of the various methods of teaching. Bartel (1975) describes the Stern Structural Arithmetic, the Cawley-Goodstein system, the Montessori materials, the Cuisenaire Rods, and other methods and materials. In addition, see Arena (1972), *Building Number Skills in Dyslexic Children;* Bereiter (1968), *Arithmetic and Mathematics;* Johnson and Myklebust (1967); and Lerner (1976).

Learning environments

Children with learning disabilities are an extremely heterogeneous group and hence cannot be educated by one method or by one organizational procedure. Consequently there have arisen a large number of organizational procedures to deal with the different kinds of learning disabilities. Various settings can provide diagnosis and remediation for these children: (1) public schools, (2) private schools and clinics, (3) college and university diagnostic centers, and (4) other programs.

The most common service is found in the public schools, especially after the passage of laws making it mandatory that all children be given appropriate education according to their needs. The most common types of organization within both private and public schools are (1) self-contained classes, (2) resource rooms, (3) itinerant teachers, and (4) consulting or helping teachers. These environmental programs are similar in organization to those described for other groups of exceptional children and need not be repeated here.

The major aim of programs for the delivery of services to children with learning disabilities, as to all children, is to provide appropriate education. The programs for children with specific learning disabilities overlap those for children with speech handicaps, communication disorders, and remedial reading problems. Regardless of the discipline, however, the specialists diagnosing and helping children with specific learning disabilities are learning disability teachers whether their backgrounds are in remedial reading, communication disabilities, or learning disabilities in general.

To the question of which administrative procedure is most effective, only one answer can be given. All can be effective if used with discretion and with the right children. The consultant teacher system is most effective when used for minor problems of educational retardation, especially in problems of reading, spelling, arithmetic, and related school subjects. It would not be effective for severe cases of specific learning disabilities since such children will require considerable individual tutoring by a knowledgeable specialist. One remedial specialist cannot teach more than six or eight children with severe learning disabilities each day, whereas a consultant teacher may serve many children during the same time. Likewise, self-contained classrooms may be managed with eight to twelve children, some of whom have a common disability. Thus the method of organization must take into consideration the kinds of services to be rendered, the degree of severity of the disability, the adequacy of the specialist, the size of the school, and many other factors.

One of the major organizational problems is to determine which children are considered learning disabled for reimbursement purposes. Some school systems select children with minor learning difficulties that require some help, and tend to include 5 to 10 percent of the school population, usually children having difficulty or lacking interest in learning to read up to their grade level. Others restrict the enrollment to the severer disabilities and include 1 to 2 percent of the school population.

All will agree that any child with minor or major difficulties needs some help to achieve at his or her maximum level. State legislators and the Congress have objected to the employment of a large cadre of learning disability specialists for children with minor problems who should be served by the regular teacher. If special reimbursement were to be made for minor problems, the poorest schools, they say, would obtain the most money. They claim that this approach would be subsidizing inefficiency.

Possible solutions to those problems have been suggested by Kirk (1978). He has recommended that, in addition to the improvement of instruction in reading, writing, and arithmetic in the early grades for the prevention of failure, we have two groups of special teachers. One group would be assigned as consultants to the regular teachers to assist them in organizing instruction for the 10 percent in each class who need additional help. Such a consultant might be able to serve twenty to forty such children each year. Another group would consist of highly trained learning disability specialists who would accept children who need more than consultant help and require individual tutoring for at least an hour a day, five days a week. In that way we would be differentiating the children according to the instructional program they need. One would be the responsibility of the regular teacher with consultant help. The other would be the responsibility of the diagnostic-prescriptive specialist for the learning disabled who would tutor the children and assist in their adjustment and participation in the regular class. Such a specialist would not be able to serve more than five or six children in a day.

Summary

1. Since learning disabled children constitute a heterogeneous group with different degrees of disability, three strategies for remediation have been discussed: (a) task training, in which the emphasis is on sequencing and simplification of the task to be learned, (b) process (ability) training, in which the focus is on the remediation of a specific developmental disability or dysfunction, and (c) ability– or process–task training, in which the first two approaches are integrated into one remedial program.

2. Remedial methods for language disorders have been developed by (a) Myklebust and Johnson, who emphasize the remediation of receptive, expressive, and syntax disorders, (b) McGinnis, who developed an association method for childhood aphasics, and (c) Ryan and Gray, who emphasize operant conditioning in the development of language in children.

3. The clinical model of the ITPA has generated a series of remedial methods including (a) the Peabody Language Development Kits, (b) the MWM Program for Developing Language Abilities, (c) the Karnes Game Oriented Activities for Learning (GOAL) and the Karnes Early Language Activities, and (d) other methods. These procedures emphasize the training of developmental dysfunctions at the preschool and primary levels.

4. Remedial programs for perceptual-motor disorders have been developed by Strauss and Lehtinen, Cruickshank, Kephart, Barsch, Doman and Delacato, and Cratty.

5. Among the remedial programs for visual perceptive disorders are the perceptual programs of Frostig and Getman.

6. Remedial programs for severe reading disabilities are variations of a kinesthetic and a phonic method. The individual methods discussed in this chapter include the Fernald kinesthetic method, the Hegge, Kirk, and Kirk grapho-vocal method, and the visual-auditory-kinesthetic method of Gillingham and Stillman. Group methods include the Writing Road to Reading by Spalding and Spalding, Distar, the Initial Teaching Alphabet, and the Peabody Rebus Reading Program.

7. Remediation for spelling, writing, and arithmetic disorders are also discussed.

8. The organization of services for learning disabled children is similar to that for other handicapped children, namely, the self-contained special class, the resource room, the itinerant diagnostic-remedial specialists, and the consultant teacher.

9. Services for learning disabled children are found in public schools, private schools, clinics, and colleges and universities.

References

ARENA, J. I., ED. 1972. *Building Number Skills in Dyslexic Children*. San Rafael, Calif.: Academic Therapy Publications.

ARENA, J. I., ED. 1968. *Building Spelling Skills in Dyslexic Children*. San Rafael, Calif.: Academic Therapy Publications.

BARSCH, R. 1967. *Achieving Perceptual Motor Efficiency: A Space-Oriented Approach to Learning*. Seattle: Special Child Publications.

BARSCH, R. 1965. *A Movigenic Curriculum*. Madison: Wisconsin State Department of Public Instruction.

BARTEL, N. R. 1975. "Problems in Arithmetic Achievement." In D. D. Hammill and N. R. Bartel, eds., *Teaching Children with Learning and Behavior Problems*. Boston: Allyn and Bacon. Pp. 61–88.

BEREITER, C. 1968. *Arithmetic and Mathematics*. San Rafael, Calif.: Dimensions Publishing.

BURNETT, E. 1962. "Influence of Classroom Environment on Word Learning of Retarded with High and Low Activity Level." Unpublished doctoral dissertation. George Peabody College for Teachers.

BUSH, W., AND M. GILES. 1969. *Aids to Psycholinguistic Teaching*. Columbus, Ohio: Charles E. Merrill.

CAWLEY, J. F., AND H. GOODSTEIN. 1972. *A Developmental Program of Quantitative Behavior for Handicapped Children*. Research report to Bureau for Education of the Handicapped. Washington, D.C.: U.S. Office of Education.

CAWLEY, J. F., AND S. J. VITELLO. 1972. "A Model for Arithmetic Programming for Handicapped Children." *Exceptional Children* 39 (October): 101–110.

CHALFANT, J. D., AND M. A. SCHEFFELIN. 1969. *Central Processing Dysfunctions in Children: A Review of Research*. Washington, D.C.: U.S. Department of Health, Education, and Welfare.

CRATTY, B. J. 1967. *Developmental Sequences of Perceptual Motor Tasks: Movement Activities for Neurologically Handicapped and Retarded Youth*. New York: Educational Activities, Inc.

CRATTY, B. J., AND M. M. MARTIN. 1969. *Perceptual Motor Behavior and Educational Processes*. Springfield, Ill.: Charles C Thomas.

CRUICKSHANK, W., F. A. BENTZEN, F. H. RATZEBURG, AND M. TANNHAUSER. 1961. *A Teaching Method for Brain-Injured and Hyperactive Children*. Syracuse, N.Y.: Syracuse University Press.

DELACATO, G. H. 1963. *The Diagnosis and Treatment of Speech and Reading Disorders*. Springfield, Ill.: Charles C Thomas.

DUNN, L. M., AND J. O. SMITH. 1967, 1968, 1969. *Peabody Language Development Kits*. Levels P, I, II, III. Circle Pines, Minn.: American Guidance Service.

ENGELMANN, S., AND E. BRUNER. 1969. *Distar: An Instructional System*. Chicago: Science Research Associates.

FERNALD, G. M. 1943. *Remedial Techniques in Basic School Subjects*. New York: McGraw-Hill.

FERNALD, G. M., AND H. KELLER. 1921. "The Effect of Kinesthetic Factors in the Development of Word Recognition in the Case of Non-Readers." *Journal of Educational Research* 4 (December): 355–377.

FROSTIG, M., AND D. HORNE. 1964. *The Frostig Program for the Development of Visual Perception.* Chicago: Follett Educational Corporation.

FROSTIG, M., AND P. MASLOW. 1969. *Move, Grow, Learn.* Chicago: Follett Educational Corporation.

FROSTIG, M., P. MASLOW, D. LEFEVER, AND J. WHITTLESEY. 1964. *The Marianne Frostig Developmental Tests of Visual Perception,* 1963 Standardization. Palo Alto, Calif.: Consulting Psychologists Press.

GETMAN, G. H. 1965. "The Visuo-Motor Complex in the Acquisition of Learning Skills." In B. Straub and J. Hellmuth, eds., *Learning Disorders,* vol. 1. Seattle: Special Child Publications.

GETMAN, G. H., E. KANE, M. HALGREN, AND G. MC KEE. 1968. *Developing Learning Readiness.* Manchester, Mo.: Webster Division, McGraw-Hill.

GILLINGHAM, A., AND B. STILLMAN. 1965. *Remedial Training for Children with Specific Disability in Reading, Spelling, and Penmanship,* 5th ed. Cambridge, Mass.: Educators Publishing Service.

GILLINGHAM, A., AND B. STILLMAN. 1936. *Remedial Work for Reading, Spelling, and Penmanship.* New York: Hackett and Wilhelms.

GRAY, B., AND B. RYAN. 1973. *A Language Program for the Non-Language Child.* Champaign, Ill.: Research Press.

HAMMILL, D. D., AND N. R. BARTEL. 1975. *Teaching Children with Learning and Behavior Problems.* Boston: Allyn and Bacon.

HAMMILL, D. D., AND S. C. LARSEN. 1978. "The Effectiveness of Psycholinguistic Training: A Reaffirmation of Position." *Exceptional Children* 44 (March): 402–414.

HAMMILL, D. D., AND J. NOONE. 1975. "Improving Spelling Skills." In D. D. Hammill and N. R. Bartel, eds., *Teaching Children with Learning and Behavior Problems.* Boston: Allyn and Bacon. Pp. 89–105.

HANNAH, P., R. HODGES, AND J. HANNAH. 1971. *Spelling: Structure and Strategies.* Boston: Houghton Mifflin.

HARING, N. G., AND B. BATEMAN. 1977. *Teaching the Learning Disabled Child.* Englewood Cliffs. N.J.: Prentice-Hall.

HEGGE, T., S. KIRK, AND W. KIRK. 1936. *Remedial Reading Drills.* Ann Arbor, Mich.: George Wahr.

HIRSCH, E. 1963. "Training of Visualizing Ability by the Kinesthetic Method of Teaching Reading." Unpublished master's thesis. University of Illinois.

JOHNSON, D., AND H. MYKLEBUST. 1967. *Learning Disabilities: Educational Principles and Practices.* New York: Grune & Stratton.

KARNES, M. 1977. *Learning Language at Home.* Reston, Va.: The Council for Exceptional Children.

KARNES, M. 1975. *The Karnes Early Language Activities* (GEM). Champaign, Ill.: Generators of Educational Materials.

KARNES, M. 1972. *GOAL: Language Development.* Springfield, Mass.: Milton Bradley.

KARNES, M., J. TESKA, A. HODGINS, AND E. BADGER. 1970. "Educational Intervention at Home by Mothers of Disadvantaged Infants." *Child Development* 41 (December): 925–935.

KARNES, M., R. ZEHRBACH, AND J. TESKA. 1974. "The Karnes Preschool Program; Rational Curricular Offerings and Followup Data." In S. Ryan, ed., *A Report on Longitudinal Evaluations of Preschool Programs,* vol. I. Office of Child Development, Children's Bureau, DHEW Publication No. (OHD) 77-24 (May): 95–108.

KEPHART, N. 1971. *The Slow Learner in the Classroom,* 2nd ed. Columbus, Ohio: Charles E. Merrill.

KEPHART, N. 1964. "Perceptual-Motor Aspects of Learning Disabilities." *Exceptional Children* 31 (December): 201–206.

KIRK, S. 1933. "The Influence of Manual Tracing on the Learning of Simple Words in the Case of Subnormal Boys." *Journal of Educational Psychology* 24 (October): 525–533.

KIRK, S. 1978. "An Interview with Samuel Kirk." *Academic Therapy* 13 (May): 617–620.

KIRK, S., AND W. KIRK. 1971. *Psycholinguistic Learning Disabilities: Diagnosis and Remediation.* Urbana: University of Illinois Press.

KIRK, S., SR. J. M. KLIEBHAN, AND J. W. LERNER. 1978. *Teaching Reading to Slow and Disabled Learners.* Boston: Houghton Mifflin.

KIRK, S., J. MC CARTHY, AND W. KIRK. 1968. *The Illinois Test of Psycholinguistic Abilities,* rev. ed. Urbana: University of Illinois Press.

LERNER, J. W. 1976. *Children with Learning Disabilities,* 2nd ed. Boston: Houghton Mifflin.

LERNER, J. W. 1975. "Remedial Reading and Learning Disabilities: Are They the Same or Different?" Symposium No. 11. *Journal of Special Education* 9 (Summer): 119–131.

LOMBARDI, T. P., AND E. J. LOMBARDI. 1977. *ITPA: Clinical Interpretation and Remediation.* Seattle: Special Child Publications.

LUND, K., G. FOSTER, AND F. MC CALL-PEREZ. 1978. "The Effectiveness of Psycholinguistic Training, A Reevaluation." *Exceptional Children* 44 (February): 310–321.

MC GINNIS, M. 1963. *Aphasic Children.* Washington, D.C.: Alexander Graham Bell Association for the Deaf.

MINSKOFF, E., D. WISEMAN, AND J. MINSKOFF. 1975. *The MWM Program for Developing Language Abilities.* Ridgefield, N.J.: Educational Performance Associates.

MYERS, P., AND D. HAMMILL. 1976. *Methods for Learning Disabilities,* 2nd ed. New York: John Wiley.

NEWLAND, T. E. 1932. "An Analytical Study of the Development of Illegibilities in Handwriting from the Lower Grades to Adulthood." *Journal of Educational Research* 26 (December): 249–258.

PERSONKE, C., AND A. H. YEE. 1966. "A Model for the Analysis of Spelling Behavior." *Elementary English* 43 (March): 278–284.

PETERS, M. 1975. *Diagnostic and Remedial Spelling Manual*. London: Macmillan Education Ltd.

PITTMAN, J. 1963. "The Future of the Teaching of Reading." Paper presented at the Educational Conference of the Educational Records Bureau, New York City, November 1, 1963.

PLUNKETT, M. B. 1954. *A Writing Manual for Teaching the Left-Handed*. Cambridge, Mass.: Educators Publishing Service.

QUAY, H. C. 1973. "Special Education: Assumptions, Techniques, and Evaluation Criteria." *Exceptional Children* 40 (November): 165–170.

RASCHKE, D., AND A. YOUNG. 1976a. "A Comparative Analysis of the Diagnostic-Prescriptive and Behavioral-Analysis Models in Preparation for the Development of a Dialectic Pedagogical System." *Education and Training of the Mentally Retarded* 11 (April): 135–145.

RASCHKE, D., AND A. YOUNG. 1976b. "The Dialectic Teaching System: A Comprehensive Model Derived from Two Educational Approaches." *Education and Training of the Mentally Retarded* 11 (October): 232–246.

ROBBINS, M. P., AND G. V. GLASS. 1969. "The Doman–Delacato Rationale: A Critical Analysis." In J. Hellmuth, ed., *Educational Therapy*. Seattle: Special Child Publications. Vol. II, pp. 321–378.

ROST, K. 1967. "Academic Achievement of Brain-Injured Children in Isolation." *Exceptional Children* 34 (October): 125–126.

SEGUIN, E. 1846. *Traitement moral, hygiene et education des idiots et des autres enfants arrières*. Paris: J. B. Ballière.

SMITH, J. O. 1962. "Effects of a Group Language Development Program upon Psycholinguistic Abilities of Educable Mentally Retarded Children." *Special Education Monograph* 1. Nashville, Tenn.: George Peabody College for Teachers.

SPALDING, R. B., AND W. T. SPALDING. 1957. *The Writing Road to Reading*. New York: Morrow.

STRAUSS, A. A., AND N. KEPHART. 1955. *Psychopathology and Education of the Brain-Injured Child*, vol. II. New York: Grune & Stratton.

STRAUSS, A. A., AND L. LEHTINEN. 1947. *Psychopathology of the Brain-Injured Child*. New York: Grune & Stratton.

VALETT, R. 1967. *The Remediation of Learning Disabilities*. Palo Alto, Calif.: Fearon Publishers.

WALLACE, G., AND J. A. MC LOUGHLIN. 1975. *Learning Disabilities*. Columbus, Ohio: Charles E. Merrill.

WOODCOCK, R. W., C. R. CLARK, AND C. O. DAVIES. 1967. *The Peabody Rebus Reading Program*. Circle Pines, Minn.: American Guidance Service.

YEE, A. 1966. The Generalization Controversy on Spelling Instruction. *Elementary English* 43 (February): 154–161.

YSSELDYKE, J., AND J. SALVIA. 1974. "Diagnostic-Prescriptive Teaching: Two Models." *Exceptional Children* 4 (November): 181–186.

10

Unlike programs for learning disabilities, communication habilitation programs have existed in the schools since the early part of the twentieth century and in clinics and hospitals even before that time. From time to time the programs have encountered major changes based on research findings, theoretical points of view, and demands for services. As in many other areas of special education, speech and language programs have made major changes and expansions especially since World War II.

The evolution of speech and language habilitation in the schools shows an early emphasis on articulation, voice disorders, and stuttering; later, therapy was included in the regular classroom for the hard-of-hearing child who also had problems of articulation and voice. The expansion of programs for language disorders was stimulated after World War II by the problems of aphasia in veterans. Wepman (1975), in discussing the evolution of speech pathology and audiology, stated that language development was added to the armamentarium because of society's interest in aphasia. This addition expanded into the study of linguistics and psycholinguistics.

Earlier, university departments training specialists in speech disorders were labeled departments of speech pathology. When the speech of the hearing handicapped was included, departments changed their names to departments of speech and hearing, and when language habilitation became popular, some departments changed their names to departments of communication disorders.

Likewise specialists in speech habilitation changed their titles with the changing emphasis. In school systems specialists were called speech improvement teachers or speech correctionists. After World War II when psychotherapy became dominant, the preferred title became speech therapists, following the medical model. In the 1960s the preferred term became speech clinician or speech pathologist, especially in clinics and hospitals. To emphasize the profession's role in language habilitation, the American Speech and Hearing Association (ASHA) at its 1976 meeting adopted the title *speech-language pathologist.* In this chapter the titles *speech and language pathologist, speech and language clinician,* and *speech specialist* will be used synonymously. Likewise the term *communication disorders* will be used synonymously with *language, speech, and hearing* disorders.

Speech and language disorders in children should not be a new subject to the reader. Disorders and delay in the development of speech and language have been mentioned especially in the chapters that deal with the mentally retarded, the hearing impaired, and the learning disabled. The mentally retarded generally have more intensive and severer problems in speech and language than do the other disabled groups. The hearing impaired suffer from articulation, voice, and language problems; a proportion of children with learning disabilities have problems in language development. In addition to those handicaps, children with normal hearing and intellectual abilities also may have speech and language disorders.★

Definition of defective speech and language

Speech and language defects can be defined specifically, in terms of the symptomatic characteristics of the disorder, or in more general terms. A basic definition includes three factors, namely, that speech or language (or both) is considered defective when it (1) draws unfavorable attention to itself, (2) interferes with communication, or (3) affects adversely the speaker or listener. Perkins (1971) defines speech and language disorders by stating that "speech is defective when it is ungrammatical, unintelligible, culturally or personally unsatisfactory, or abusive of the speech mechanism" (p. 4). When some of those characteristics are found, the child is in need of speech remediation.

To be normal, speech should permit the undistracted interchange of verbal language, free from grimaces, phonemic misarticulations, and unnatural and unusual voice qualities, speaking rates, and rhythms. Vocabulary and sound production should be adequate and appropriate for the age level and should be spoken in logical, syntactical order.

In some instances speakers may manifest characteristics of defective speech that may not warrant speech remediation. Among these

★ *The task force of the American Speech and Hearing Association (1977) has formulated definitions to clarify terms such as* language, speech production, communication, *and* language impairment.

Language *is a conventional system of phonological, syntactic, and semantic rules for decoding experience. . . .*

Language impairment *refers to a state in which an individual does not display knowledge of the system of linguistic rules commensurate with the expected norm. Typically, a child is considered to be language impaired when his/her skills in the primary language are deficient relative to expectations for chronological age.*

Speech production *is the vocal-motor channel of language performance and, therefore, is one manifestation of language.*

Communication *is the process of exchanging messages using any system (not confined to language) and various media (e.g., speech, gesture, facial expression).*

A communication problem *occurs when an individual does not use the appropriate set of behaviors that permits transferring information between himself and others.*

are persons with differing accents and regional dialects from various parts of the English-speaking world and from foreign countries. In those instances the speech contains phonemic and intonational peculiarities of the individual's native language or regional dialect. Such speech is not considered defective by most professionals.

Normal development of speech and language

Children normally develop the speech and language of the culture in which they are reared. How speech and language develop in children has been of long-standing interest to psychologists, linguists, and speech-language pathologists. For a time each of those disciplines tended to study different aspects of the phenomenon. The psychologist studied speech and language learning, the linguist studied the properties of natural language, and the speech-language pathologist concentrated on deviations or disorders of speech and language. In recent years the disciplines have attempted to integrate their knowledge into training and service programs that employ research findings from all disciplines.

The process by which a child learns speech and language has been explained by different authorities in different ways. Skinner (1957), a behaviorist psychologist, tended to explain the development of verbal behavior on the basis of principles of learning, that is, stimulus, response, and reinforcement. Some linguists, on the other hand, do not accept the acquisition of speech as wholly learned but tend to explain the development of speech and language on the basis of an inherent disposition similar to that of acquiring the ability to walk.

The maturational cycle for the development of verbal behavior has been described by Berry (1969), as follows:

Prelinguistic vocalization. An infant cries, utters sounds of various kinds.

Babbling. Babbling follows early vocalization. It may not be clearly differentiated from early vocalization and may not relate to later speech. It probably serves as a tuning-up period for the speech organs, which are later used in the production of speech.

Imitation. At this stage, usually between the fourth and sixth months, the child "oohs" and "ahs," imitating his or her own speech production and responding in some vocal fashion to the speech of others.

First words. It is difficult to establish an age level for first intelligible and meaningful words. Nevertheless, by the age of 18 to 20 months most children may be saying "mama" and "daddy" and few or many words.

Two-word sentences. At about 2 years of age most children are using two-word sentences—"more milk," "shoe off," and so forth. At this age level they are communicating in an effort to bring about events. They have a vocabulary of fifty to a hundred words (Eisenson and Ogilvie, 1976).

Development of syntax. After age 2 to 3 the child begins to develop his or her own grammatical system and explores his or her own use of grammar, noun phrases, subject-predicate sentences, and so forth.

The brief outline of the development of speech production and language covers one aspect of speech-language development that has been studied. Another aspect is the acquisition of the sound system (phonemics) of the language code. From the studies made by Templin (1957) and by Ingram (1974), it appears that certain sounds mature later than others. For example, most 3-year-olds produce all the vowels and many consonants, /m/, /w/, /ng/, and so forth. At age 4, the child produces /k/, /j/, /d/, /b/, /r/, and so on and some double and triple consonants. At ages 5 and 6, the child produces more difficult sound clusters like /bl/, /pl/, /cl/, and so forth. Thus a child at a certain stage labels *kitty* as "titi" and *please* as "pease." At one stage a mispronunciation may be average or expected, while at another stage it signifies a speech or language impairment for that age child.

Somewhere along the line a minimum of 2 to 5 percent of the future school population will not reach the level of efficiency in speech and language that is considered normal or adequate for the age level. Some children will not be talking at 4 and 5 years, some will start to speak normally but because of some trauma will stop talking, some will develop their own lingo (prevalent among twin members, who devise their own code), some will have difficulty with sounds for a number of reasons, some will stutter, some will have unintelligible speech, and some will have voice problems.

Prevalence of speech disorders

A persistent question concerns the number and kinds of speech-impaired children in the population who require remediation. To answer that question numerous surveys on different populations have been made, and, as usual, discrepant results have been reported. The percentage of children with speech defects is dependent on the kind of speech defects studied, the ages of the children in the study, the definition of speech defects, the degree of impairment, and other factors.

The traditional estimates of the number of speech-impaired children have been reported repeatedly as 5 percent of the school population. The most commonly quoted prevalence figure of 5 percent is that of the National Institute of Neurological Diseases and Stroke. The Institute's figures for seven speech problems are presented in Table 10.1. It should be noted from the table that functional articulation disorders constitute the largest group with 3 percent, while stuttering is 0.7 percent and voice disorders are 0.2 percent. Language disorders are not included in those estimates.

A recent study of prevalence was conducted by Hull (Hull et al., 1976) in a report known as the National Speech and Hearing Survey. They collected prevalence data on 38,802 public school children.

Table 10.2 gives the prevalence of types of disorders (articulation, voice, and stuttering) for (1) moderate disorders, (2) severe disorders, and (3) combined disorders. It should be noted that the total prevalence of combined disorders is 5.7 percent and is similar to other national figures, but it differs from the estimate in Table 10.1 in that articulation disorders are 1.9 percent, compared to 3.0 percent, and voice disorders are listed as 3.0 percent in contrast with 0.2 percent in Table 10.1. It is obvious from these comparisons that different criteria were used in establishing prevalence rates.

The two tables do not tell the whole story. What is of educational significance is the fact that a large proportion of children with

Types of speech problems	Ages 5–21 years	
	(Percent)	(Number)
Functional articulation	3.0	1,500,000
Stuttering	.7	350,000
Voice	.2	100,000
Cleft-palate speech	.1	50,000
Cerebral-palsy speech	.2	100,000
Retarded speech development	.3	150,000
Impaired hearing (with speech defect)	.5	250,000
Total	5.0	2,500,000

TABLE 10.1

Estimated prevalence of speech defects in the United States

Source: Adapted from National Institute of Neurological Diseases and Stroke, *Human Communication and Its Disorders—An Overview.* Bethesda, Maryland: Public Health Service, 1970, p. 18.

TABLE 10.2

Estimated prevalence of speech disorders (by percent) [1]

	Moderate			Severe			Combined		
Type of disorder	Males	Females	Total	Males	Females	Total	Males	Females	Total
Articulation	1.5	0.8	1.0	1.2	0.7	0.9	2.4	1.5	1.9
Voice	2.8	1.7	2.3	0.9	0.4	0.7	3.7	2.1	3.0
Stuttering	1.2	0.4	0.8	1.2	0.4	0.8	1.2	0.4	0.8
Total	5.5	2.9	4.1	3.3	1.5	2.4	7.3	4.0	5.7

Source: Hull, Mieike, Willeford, and Timmons, 1976, p. 146.

[1] Percent figures are based on a national sample of 38,802 subjects. Males = 19,973; females = 18,829.

voice and articulation problems are found in the first grade. Figure 10.1 shows the rapid decrease in prevalence of extreme articulation deviations for males and females from grades one to twelve.

Figure 10.1 shows that the males had a prevalence rate of 7 percent in the first grade while the females had a prevalence rate of 4.5 percent. This prevalence dropped to 1 percent for males and to about 0.5 percent for females in the third grade, and to 0.5 percent and 0.2

FIGURE 10.1

Extreme articulation deviation. Percent of males and females rated with an extreme articulation deviation at each grade level

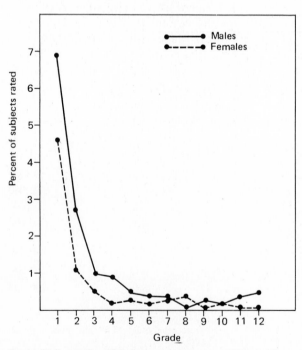

Source: Hull, Mieike, Willeford, and Timmons, 1976, p. 37.

percent in the twelfth grade. No information in the report indicates whether this rapid decrease in rate between the first, second, and third grades is due to remediation, to maturation, or to both remediation and maturation. The problem faced by speech clinicians is to predict whether the child will overcome articulatory, voice, and stuttering problems by maturation or will need intervention.

Identification and diagnosis

In many school systems the procedure in establishing a communication disorder program follows three stages: (1) screening procedures to identify children who require a full diagnostic assessment, (2) diagnosing those selected through the initial screening and from other referrals, and (3) selecting those children who require and can benefit from special speech and language intervention.

SCREENING PROCEDURES

Most school systems have established formal screening programs for vision and hearing. Similarly, the speech and language clinician screens selected grades each year to locate those children who show signs of communication disorders. Which groups are screened each year depends on the specified program of the particular school. Those children who show signs of articulatory, vocal, rhythmic, or linguistic impairment are selected for further diagnosis. In addition, children who are not detected by this formalized procedure are often referred to the clinician by parents or by teachers in classrooms not included in the screening program, when there is concern about performance in speech, language, or hearing.

Children referred by teachers or parents for speech remediation and those identified through the screening procedure require a diagnosis of their specific problems before remediation can be started. The procedure in the diagnosis includes steps similar to those described in the chapter on learning disabilities. These steps are discussed in the following paragraphs.

CASE HISTORY. When a child is referred for a speech, hearing, or language examination, the clinician obtains a history of the child to determine whether the problem is or has been recognized by other persons such as teachers, parents, and physicians. This history furnishes the clinician with background information on the developmental history of the child in terms of the child's age at walking, talking, and so forth. It also may include the medical history of illnesses, information about siblings and other family members with similar problems, the social history, school achievement, and other examinations previously administered, including psychometric tests.

INTELLECTUAL ASSESSMENT. One of the first assessments to be made of a child with a speech or language defect is one of his or her intellectual development. In some cases psychological tests of a performance (nonverbal) type are administered to determine whether or not a child's delay in speech or language is due to mental retardation. Many children referred for communication disorders have a history of normal intellectual development, and psychometric assessments may not be necessary.

ASSESSMENT OF DEFECT. A speech clinician attempts to ascertain the defect or defects by (1) obtaining spontaneous vocal responses from the child through response to pictures, (2) asking the child to repeat after the examiner certain words that will identify an articulation defect, (3) asking the child to repeat sounds in nonsense formation, and (4) obtaining samples of the child's habitual conversation. Each of these procedures—spontaneous speech, imitation, nonsense syllable routine, and habitual conversation—has its place in helping the clinician determine the type of speech defect. From such initial assessment clues are obtained for further diagnosis and recommendations for remediation.

DETERMINING CAUSAL FACTORS AND CORRELATED DEFECTS. If a child has delayed language or a defect in articulation, voice, or rhythm, the next question is "Why?" What factors are responsible for, or associated with, this difficulty? In the examination the speech diagnostician evaluates lip movements and structure, dental alignment, palatal structure and function, and pharyngeal adequacy. A judgment will be made about any structural deviation that may contribute to the speech defect. Factors in the home environment will be explored to see if they may influence the speech problem. Hearing impairment, language delay, cleft palate, and possible brain dysfunction will all be considered. Some observed symptoms or problems may require the speech-language pathologist to refer the child to other specialists such as the audiologist, the otolaryngologist, the plastic surgeon, or the neurologist.

SELECTION OF CHILDREN FOR REMEDIATION. Since the clinician must limit the case load it is necessary to decide which children are in greatest need of help, which ones will respond best, and which ones can await maturational development.

Ordinarily, the diagnosis suggests the initial remedial procedures. Assessment, however, is an ongoing procedure since many aspects of the child's difficulty will come to light during the process of remediation. The major purpose of the diagnosis is to assess the special defects and so to lead to a program for remediation. The speech remediation sessions that may follow will depend heavily on feedback and ongoing assessment to find out what the child is able or unable to do. The remedial tasks may be slightly beyond the base line of what the child is easily able to do, and are programmed for step-by-step development. The tasks presented in these sessions will of course depend on the severity of the defect and the motivational factors involved.

Classifications of speech and language disorders

Various systems of classification of speech disorders depend to some extent on whether the categories are to be used in the public school system, a clinical organization within a hospital, or a speech and hearing clinic. Thus far no one has been successful in developing a classification in which the terminology is consistently logical—that is, one that is totally arranged according to etiology or one that indicates only the phenomenology or behavioral description of the speech or language deficiency.

In recent textbooks on speech disorders, the defects are grouped according to disorders of articulation, voice, rhythm, and language. The American Speech and Hearing Association has defined communication disorders as "impairments in articulation, language, voice, or fluency. Hearing impairment may be classified as a communication disorder when it impedes the development, performance, or maintenance of articulation, language, voice, or fluency" (Comprehensive Assessment and Service (CASE) Information System, 1976, p. 26).

Another classification could relate to etiology, but such a classification is not educationally useful. Etiological categorization, such as cleft-palate speech and cerebral-palsied speech, is avoided because there may be individuals with such disorders who do not have speech problems or do not have the typical problem. Speech disorders may be due to mental retardation, hearing impairment, congenital aphasia, or cerebral dysfunction. It is more accurate to speak of a speech disorder associated with hearing loss, cleft palate, mental retardation, or cerebral palsy than to designate the speech defect as a distinct characteristic of another handicap.

One of the major difficulties in the classification of speech disorders is the overlapping of categories. Articulation problems in which the formation, blending, and pronunciation of sounds may be impaired are often present without an associated problem. However, articulation problems may be associated with cleft palate, cerebral palsy, mental retardation, and other associated handicaps. Voice problems may involve quality disorders (such as hoarseness), lack of sufficient loudness, faulty pitch, and resonance disorders. Voice problems usually exist independent of other associated handicaps but may be part of the symptoms of cleft palate, cerebral palsy, and other organic defects. With those overlapping defects in mind, the subsequent discussions will be organized around (1) articulation disorders, (2) vocal disorders, (3) stuttering, and (4) language disorders.

ARTICULATION DISORDERS

Articulation disorders are those speech deviations that involve substitutions, distortions, omissions, and additions of speech sounds (phonemes). These difficulties may occur at the site of the articulators when the interaction of tongue, lips, teeth, jaws, and palate may be faulty. The oral cavity is modified by the movement of jaw, lips, and tongue producing the various speech sounds. If the movements are faulty or in an improper sequence or are absent, then resulting faulty speech is known as an articulation disorder.

There are a number of factors associated with articulation difficulties. Among them are organic factors, including deviations in the tongue, larynx, pharynx, lips, teeth, hard and soft palate, and the breathing mechanism. Malfunctioning of any of those parts may cause speech difficulty. In the mouth alone, for example, many parts have to function properly. But it should be noted that many persons have malocclusions of the teeth, missing teeth, abnormal tongues, high and narrow hard palates, and various other structural malformations and still have good speech. Even with such deviations, adjustments are possible without any particular effort for many persons and exceedingly difficult for others.

More often there are misarticulations with no apparent structural defect. These disorders of functional origin have been attributed to varied influences, which include impoverished environment, infantile preseveration, bilingualism, emotional problems, slow maturation, and overindulgence in the home. As important as it is for identifying the cause of the misarticulation, most articulation disorders are remediated by directly modifying the problem and *not* by eliminating its cause.

NATURE OF ARTICULATORY DEFECTS. The most common speech errors found among articulatory defects have been classified as (1) substitutions, (2) omissions, (3) distortions, and (4) additions of sounds.

Typical *substitutions* are as follows: *w* for *r,* as in "wight" for *right;* *w* for *l,* as in "yewo" for *yellow;* and *th* for *s,* as in "yeth" for *yes.* This type of error is commonly found among young children with immature speech. Sometimes a sound like *p* is substituted for almost every plosive sound, as *t* or *k,* or for the fricative *f,* as "I peel punny." The substitution may not always be consistent, for a child sometimes will substitute for a sound that he or she is capable of pronouncing perfectly and sometimes uses easily. Often the position of the letter in the word determines whether the child substitutes or not, as at the beginning (initial position) of a word, in the middle (medial position), or at the end (final position).

Omissions, when extensive, may make a child's speech nearly unintelligible. The consonants are most likely to be dropped from the endings of words, though they may be dropped from the beginnings or the middles and sometimes are from all three positions. Occasionally there is a stoppage of air (a glottal stop) between the vowels of successive syllables that substitutes for a consonant.

Distortions show an attempt to approximate the correct sound. Among older children they are relatively more frequent than omissions or substitutions. Whereas a younger child will omit a sound or substitute another, an older child may try to imitate the proper sound but produce a distortion. A distorted *s* sound can have many near approaches to the correct sound, as the sibilant *s* (whistling), the lateral *s* (air emitted at side of tongue), and the dental *s* (tongue thrust against teeth), all of which can be corrected by the modification of the air stream and shift in oral pressures and positions. Studies have suggested that distortions (except for the lateral *s*) are more readily corrected than substitutions and that omissions are the most difficult to correct.

Additions are found in unintelligible speech or jargon, such as in the codes that siblings, especially twin members, have established, and in the speech of deaf children, who may say "sumber" for *summer* or add a vowel between other syllables, as "on-a the table."

In the broadest sense, articulatory difficulties may permeate every kind of speech deviation. Sometimes they exist alone or are associated with a concomitant dysfunction such as stuttering. Sometimes they occur as one of several speech-handicapping factors, as in cerebral palsy, in which vocal factors such as timing, pitch, and quality merge into the articulatory defects.

SPEECH REMEDIATION FOR ARTICULATORY DISORDERS. Speech and language clinicians assigned to schools for the purpose of correcting various types of communication problems in children find that up to 80 percent of their cases may display articulatory deviations or defects. Misarticulations are particularly common in young children, and as noted earlier, articulatory skill increases in efficiency to about age 9. The clinician is therefore not unduly concerned by the kindergarten child who is still unable to make those sounds that many children after age 5 are able to (for example, the *r, s,* or *th* sound). When a child is developing normally, maturation will probably take care of speech development with a little help from the wise teacher and parent. Since the specialist does not have the time to help every minor need, he or she must choose the children most in need of help. Unless the young child has an actual disorder and has difficulty communicating with others, the clinician usually gives time and nature a chance to work. The clinician may assist the parent and teacher in working with the child rather than filling his or her schedule with cases not actually requiring intensive treatment. The major problem for the speech clinician is to be able to predict which child will develop without remediation and which one will need assistance at an early age.

The children selected for speech remediation are scheduled either for individual lessons or for group lessons. The cooperation of the teacher and the parent is solicited in this matter in order to transfer the practice in individual lessons to the home and school situations. Individual speech remediation may use various approaches, such as motor production, ear training, programmed remediation, and general sound stimulation.

Group remediation is utilized successfully by many speech-language pathologists. For example, a developmental speech group may offer the pupil in the primary grades practice in listening to himself or herself and to others, practice in the production of new sounds and words, and practice in social interaction using speech.

In kindergarten and the first and second grades, speech improvement services from the classroom teacher will help every child toward more articulate speech without pointing up those who appear to be different. The speech and language pathologist supervises this type of program, providing the teacher with material and routine procedures. Usually the specialist takes over once a week, and the teacher is responsible for additional sessions during the week.

Bilingual students may profit from group activity more than from individual work, but the group must include some who are not bilingual. The bilinguals need help in listening to others, in identifying objects, and in speaking accurately in situational experiences.

Eisenson and Ogilvie (1976) describe in detail three steps a speech clinician may take in correcting a defective sound (misarticulation): (1) teaching the child to recognize both his or her own misarticulation and the correct target sound, (2) teaching the target sound in isolation, in syllables, and in words, and (3) teaching the child to use the correct sound in everyday speech. Interested readers should refer to Eisenson and Ogilvie's book *Speech Correction in the Schools* (1976) and to other texts for detailed teaching methods and materials.

VOICE DISORDERS

Voice disorders are concerned with problems of (1) voice quality, (2) voice pitch, and (3) voice loudness. Instead of speaking of the formation of sounds, we are now concerned with the production of sound in the larynx and with the selective transmission of that sound including its resonance and loudness. The voice is produced by the outgoing airstream passing between the approximated vocal folds in the larynx. From the larynx the sound travels upward through various cavities of the vocal tract, such as the throat, mouth, and nose. The normal voice should be appropriate to the age and the sex of the child. Ideally, there should be a clear tone (phonation) emitting from the vibrating vocal folds, and this tone should be appropriate in pitch (not too high or too low). The voice should be heard easily, and a person should be able to increase the loudness of it without undue straining. An inflectional speech pattern—rather than a monotone, which is often assumed by adolescents—is important to give meaning to what is said. The three concerns of quality, pitch, and loudness will be discussed separately.

VOCAL QUALITY. The more common defects in vocal quality are found in (1) phonation, or the production of sounds, and (2) resonance, or the direction of the sound in voice placement.

The *phonation,* or the production of sound, originating in the larynx, sometimes exhibits a breathiness, hoarseness, or huskiness. It may be caused by structural aberrations that result in failure of the vocal cords to approximate properly in order to produce the correct vibrations in the air flow. When vocalization is impeded by paralysis of the vocal cords, then the cords cannot meet to allow the proper build-up of air pressure below them. The result is breathiness or huskiness. In every school after an intensive basketball or football schedule, with its accompanying yelling and tension, many students will speak with hoarse and husky voices, sometimes with a whisper (aspirate quality), and sometimes with no voice at all, owing to inflammation of the laryngeal tissue and the vocal cords. If the student continues to abuse his or her voice on the playground or to reflect tensions in the muscles controlling the vocal folds, abnormal changes in voice quality may be evident. Abuse of the voice may lead to vocal nodules on the vocal folds. While small nodules will disappear completely with voice therapy, large nodes that have been there awhile may require surgical removal followed by voice therapy to prevent their recurrence.

Resonance depends on the balance of amplification in the various cavities used for this purpose—the oral cavity, the nasal cavity, the pharyngeal cavity (back of the throat), and the laryngeal cavity (the phonation area). This balance of resonance is affected by the size of the cavities and one's ability to direct the air-sound stream as one chooses.

Two types of difficulty are common: (1) hypernasal speech and (2) denasal speech. In hypernasal speech, sounds that should be emitted through the mouth are emitted instead through the nasal cavity, with the result that the consonants (other than /m/, /n/, and /ng/) and the vowels may have a nasal twang. This often occurs in partial or complete paralysis of the soft palate. The same condition sometimes accompanies cerebral palsy when there is a weakness in muscular coordination and control. An unrepaired cleft palate provides an open passageway into the nasal cavity, which can produce an almost unintelligible hypernasality. Often in children with repaired clefts, there exists tissue insufficiency or musclar incompetence that still permits abnormal misdirection of the air stream.

Denasality is an absence or indequacy of nasal resonance. Some children sound as if they have chronic head colds or enlarged adenoids or as if they were pinching their noses. Insufficient air flows through the nasal cavities and is evident not only on the nasal consonants but also on sounds that are normally emitted through the oral cavity.

VOCAL PITCH. Generally, pitch disturbances can be corrected when the child is older. Because the growing larynx at times develops faster than the rest of the body, pitch may remain at a high level into adolescence. Usually one expects a natural voice change, but there are instances of voice disorders that extend beyond the usual falsetto voice or breaks that generally disappear by the time a boy enters high school. Unusual or deviant adolescent voice characteristics can foster withdrawal behavior and embarrassment and may be symptoms of more serious physical problems. For those reasons a medical examination should be a routine part of the voice examination. After any problem has been properly diagnosed, the speech clinician can work to develop optimum pitch (pitch that is most natural for the vocal mechanism to assume) and can teach the necessary control for maintaining it.

Fairbanks (1960) maintains that each individual voice has a natural pitch level, a level that is maximally comfortable and efficient for that particular individual. The habitual pitch level that is used in speaking should be the natural level for the child's age. Any pitch that is too low or too high may place undue strain on the voice.

LOUDNESS OF VOICE. Intensity of voice means its loudness and softness, the emphasis and stress used to give meaning. There may be many loud voices, especially among children seeking attention or among boys who cannot control the vocal power that comes from laryngeal growth. There may be many soft voices among children who are immature and insecure. If the clinician has time to help those youngsters, it will be time well spent because of their need for adjustment to their peers and because severer vocal problems may be prevented.

REMEDIATION FOR VOICE DISORDERS. The focus of voice remediation by the speech-language pathologist in the schools is to help the child identify any vocal damage he or she might be creating by yelling or throat clearing. Whatever kind of vocal abuse is identified, the clinician works out a program with the child for reducing its occurrence. Efforts are then made to help the child develop the best-sounding voice that can be produced by his or her mechanism. Besides focusing on abuse reduction and developing the best-sounding voice, the effective clinician spends some time in counseling child and parents about conditions that might make the voice better or worse (Boone, 1971).

The child who speaks with a nasal quality, a high-pitched voice, a chronic hoarseness, or a tense monotone has a speech production problem and should be referred to the speech and language clinician for proper diagnosis and correction if indicated. Before voice therapy begins, the child with a voice problem should be examined by an ear-nose-throat specialist to identify or perhaps rule out any organic disorder that may be causing the voice problem.

STUTTERING

Stuttering is a pattern of speaking in which rhythms of speech are disrupted or broken by excessive or inappropriate prolongations, repetitions, hesitations, and/or interjections of sounds, syllables, words, or parts of sentences, usually accompanied by struggle and avoidance behavior. Van Riper (1971) stated that "stuttering behavior consists of a word improperly patterned in time and the speaker's reaction thereto" (p. 15).

West (1958) has summarized some factors relating to stuttering. Those agreed on include (1) stuttering is a phenomenon of childhood, (2) there are three to eight times as many males as females who stutter, and (3) stuttering runs in families.

Webster and Brutten (1974) describe the behavior profile of a stutterer as having several major characteristics such as:

1. failing in fluency of speech by involuntary repetition or prolongation of sounds and syllables
2. having a large proportion of the repetitions and prolongations occurring on the same words
3. having the fluency failures associated with emotional arousal
4. using voluntary efforts to deal with, or cover up, the involuntary occurrences of stuttering by verbal and nonverbal responses, that is, repetition of words and phrases, changes in speaking rate and intensity, eye blinks, lip purses, arm swings, and so forth.

Webster and Brutten explain that involuntary anxiety causes the stuttering, thus motivating the stutterer to engage in behavior that helps to avoid the negative reactions of the listeners.

THEORIES OF STUTTERING. Theories that explain the stuttering phenomenon are numerous but can be categorized in two major groups: (1) organic or constitutional theories and (2) psychological theories, including (a) learned behavior and (b) personality disturbances.

1. Organic or constitutional theories. The theory of cerebral dominance, proposed by Lee Edward Travis (1931), has had its advocates in the past. This theory states that stuttering is the result of lack of cerebral dominance. In most individuals one cerebral hemisphere of the brain controls the flow of speech, while the other hemisphere remains subordinate. Lacking cerebral dominance, so that neither hemisphere takes the lead role or there is an alternation of roles, the individual stutters. For some years Travis and his colleagues based their research on the neurologic theory that cerebral dominance played an important part in causing the stuttering phenomenon. If handedness is shifted to the right in one who is neurologically inclined to be left-handed, confusion in the production of speech results. Research evidence, however, does not substantiate the theory, and at present it has few advocates according to Perkins (1971). Earlier investigators have pointed out other constitutional factors associated with stuttering behavior and have contrasted them with the general population: (1) more left-handedness, (2) more twins, (3) later onset of speech, and (4) higher incidence of illness that might result in damage to the nervous system (Eisenson and Ogilvie, 1976).

   2. Psychological theories. Johnson's *diagnosogenic* theory (1956) states that parents, failing to realize that the very young child is passing through a normal stage of language learning, diagnose the child's normal repetitions and hesitations as stuttering, a label that becomes a stigma, adding fear to anxiety. Then, when the parental responses show concern or are not understanding, the child hastens to get the words out before he or she is reproved, thus continuing the cycle of fear-anxiety-nonfluency. The stuttering of the child, then, is initially something in the mind of the parent. Eventually the child will experience "anticipatory, apprehensive, hypertonic, avoidance reactions" in speech situations, which is another way of saying the child anticipates stuttering, dreads it, becomes tense in trying to avoid it, and so stutters.

   Sheehan (1970) conceives of stuttering not as a speech disorder but as a conflict about self and role, actually an identity problem or a "special instance of self-role conflict." He blends role theory with advances in learning theory and clinical psychology. Van Riper (1970a), who earlier felt that stuttering had a multiple origin involving one's self-concept and one's role, a constitutional predisposition, emotional conflict, or low frustration tolerance, now points out that the trend is to view stuttering as learned behavior, susceptible to unlearning. Consistent with that theory is the fact that some learning psychologists and speech-language pathologists have applied operant-conditioning principles to the amelioration of stuttering.

   Webster and Brutten (1974) present a two-factor learning theory to explain stuttering behavior based on classical conditioning and operant conditioning. Through classical conditioning the individual develops a "conditioned negative emotion," which results in fluency failure, that is, stuttering. To avoid the negative reactions of the listener, the stutterer responds with word changes, lip pursing, and similar avoidance-escape mechanisms. The stuttering is intensified and perpetuated through instrumental learning (operant conditioning). This theory led the authors to procedures for the extinction of the negative emotion and to operant-conditioning procedures to establish more normal fluency of speech. According to Van Riper (1970b), speech-language pathologists have accepted and incorporated behavior modification techniques, with limitations, in practice. In a later publication Van Riper (1971) stated, "Neither classical or operant conditioning nor their combination are completely explanatory. Each of these account for some of the phenomena of stuttering but not for all" (p. 23).

THE MANAGEMENT OF STUTTERING. As indicated earlier, the main concern—the practical concern—of many is to be able to eliminate stuttering or to decrease its effect. When a stutterer asks for help, he or she is asking to stop stuttering and to speak fluently without hesitations, blocks, or repetitions.

Eisenson and Ogilvie (1976) describe the goals for the treatment of stuttering as:

1. A weakening of the forces and pressures with which the individual stuttering is associated.
2. Elimination of the secondary, accessory symptoms of stuttering.
3. Modification of the form of stuttering so that relatively easy, effortless disfluencies replace the specific blocks, marked hesitations, strained prolongations, or repetitions.
4. Modification of the faulty habits directly associated with speaking such as improper breathing, rapid speaking, or excessive tensions of the speech mechanism.
5. Modification of the attitudes of fear, anxiety, or avoidance associated with the need for speaking or that occur after speech is imitated. (p. 369)

Van Riper (1970a) indicates that

contemporary speech therapy for the stutterer seems to aim at several major goals: (1) to improve the general security and morale of the patient; (2) to reduce the situational and phonic anxiety; (3) to weaken the strength of the stereotyped stuttering response; (4) to increase the threshold of discharge; (5) to reduce reinforcement of the stuttering responses by avoidance, repression, and escape-reward (anxiety reduction and frustration release); (6) to give the existing fluency some stimulus value. . . . The trend seems to be away from the use of techniques aimed at modifying the stuttering when it does occur so that the stutterer may stutter and still be fluent. (p. 53)

In a 1974 conference on stuttering therapy, sponsored by the Speech Foundation of America, specific procedures were reviewed for modifying stuttering behavior by direct symptom modification. Transfer and maintenance of more fluent speech plus the feelings and attitudes of the stutterer were all discussed in the publication of the conference entitled *Therapy for Stutterers* (1974).

Two relatively new emphases are developing: (1) treatment through behavior modification techniques and (2) Sheehan's role-conflict theory and treatment. Experts (Sheehan, 1970) have concluded that behavior modification techniques are effective in removing or ameliorating stuttering in some individuals, but the limitations of the approach leave much to the older eclectic methods. Webster and Brutten (1974) outline in detail their method of extinguishing the conditioned emotion, learned through classical conditioning, and also a method of modifying the frequency of stuttering behavior through environmental manipulation so that there is an absence of reinforcement during stuttering behavior. In addition, alternate behaviors are reinforced. The extinction of the involuntary emotional response and the reinforcement of nonstuttering behavior is intertwined at the same time.

Whereas most research in behavior modification uses a positive reinforcement approach, those working with stuttering have sometimes used an aversive stimulus. The experiments by Goldiamond (1968), Martin (1968), and others used punishment in the form of a shock or a blast of air every time the person stuttered. This procedure decreased or eliminated stuttering during the experiment in the laboratories with some carry-over to speech performance outside. Some question this procedure since there is a possibility of side effects.

The reader is reminded that stuttering should not be diagnosed too readily in a young child, since the label and accompanying attitudes of parents may cause a child to stutter. A rhythmic disorder in children often confused with stuttering is *cluttering,* which means (1) speaking rapidly, (2) omitting syllables, (3) pausing in the wrong places in a sentence, and (4) in general appearing to be in a hurry.

DISORDERS OF LANGUAGE

"Language is a code whereby ideas about the world are represented through a conventional system of arbitrary signals for communication" (Bloom and Lahey, 1978, p. 4). If the speaker and the listener understand the same code, the speaker can relay concepts to the listener. How the child learns to use and manipulate a code has been the subject of much controversy. As indicated earlier, Lenneberg (1971), for example, postulates that language develops as a natural human propensity—an inherent disposition found only in *Homo sapiens*—while the behaviorist Skinner (1957) presupposes that language, like other forms of behavior, is purely the product of experience and that its development follows the principles of stimulus-response learning.

Whether language develops as a natural human propensity or as purely the product of experience, it does seem to follow certain typical patterns in a normal environment of social interaction. The formation of concepts in the child through experience (referred to as *inner speech* by Johnson and Myklebust [1967]) precedes the use of verbal symbols to represent those concepts. Such cognition of things in the environment is common to animals other than man, but the use of symbols to represent those concepts is very limited in other species. Certainly the use of the vocal cords, the recognition of the small phonemic differences in speech, and the complexities of grammar and vocabulary mark the greatest difference between man and other animals.

Understanding language precedes meaningful speech. The child learns to associate certain sounds or sequences of sounds with specific objects or situations. The child learns to decode those sound symbols, that is, to understand sounds in the environment that consistently occur in conjunction with other things that he or she knows or is aware of. The child of 8 or 10 months has already learned to attach meaning to many sounds in the environment—both natural sounds and the spoken word. A knock on the door means someone is there; jangling the car keys is a reminder of riding in the car; a sharp "no-no" means cease and desist. In Itard's *Wild Boy of Aveyron,* the child found wandering in the woods had associated the sound of a falling nut with the procurement of food. Although the complexities of spoken language were difficult for him, he could identify the meaning of certain sounds. Such symbolic representation must precede the use of expressive language.

Deviations in the language process have been roughly classified into three related categories: (1) language disorders, (2) delayed speech and language, and (3) developmental and congenital aphasia.

LANGUAGE DEFICIENCY. "The development of language competence in a human occurs only when knowledge of the rules has been acquired" (Task Force on Identifying Children with Language Impairment, American Speech and Hearing Association, 1977). The general category of language deficiency that occurs in minor and moderate forms in children and that may also occur in delayed speech and developmental aphasia is a delay or disruption in the orderly development of understanding and using linguistic characteristics or the special features of a particular language. Children who have not acquired that knowledge have difficulty utilizing, receptively or expressively, one or more of the linguistic characteristics of: (1) phonology, (2) morphology, (3) syntax, and (4) semantics.

Phonologic disorders are those deviations in the use of various features that form the sound patterns of a particular language. Without the ability to discriminate, integrate, and utilize the sound patterns of his or her native language, a child receives only a disorganized chain of sound waves. A discussion of the phonologic development of children is found in Ingram (1976) and in Compton (1976). The latter states that there are roughly forty-five to fifty speech sounds in English, but the actual production of speech by a child far exceeds this number since the sounds of speech do not function independently; they have an intricate, complex relationship with one another.

Morphologic disorders are deviations in the use of morphemes (those smallest sound units of a language that have meaning). Without the ability to cluster the sounds he or she hears into customary units (words, or word stems, prefixes and suffixes, or common inflections of words), the child has difficulty learning sound/symbol relationships.

Syntactic disorders are deviations in the use of meaning derived from the way in which words are put together to form phrases and sentences. Grammar is a code that creates meaning by such formalized structures as word order, word endings, the relationships among words, prefixes, and suffixes. It is widely accepted that all children—regardless of the native language to which they are exposed—construct for themselves a system of grammar or means of expressing and understanding ideas once they recognize that words and morphemes carry meaning.

Slobin (1973) notes that the intricate phenomena underlying that ability are essentially cognitive. In order to construct a grammar, the child must be able (1) to cognize the physical and social events that are encoded in language and (2) to process, organize, and store linguistic information. That is, the cognitive prerequisites for the development of grammar relate to both the *meanings* and the *forms* of utterances (pp. 175–176).

Semantic disorders are those that pertain to the meaning of an utterance as distinct from the language mechanism necessary to express it. This meaning involves not only the lexical meaning of words but the connotations and cognitive bases for the verbal communication—the concept formation preceding an utterance or following the reception of a verbal expression.

According to Moorehead and Ingram (1976), linguistically deviant children do not develop linguistic systems that are qualitatively different from those of normal children but develop their systems at a slower rate. In addition, deviant children do not use the customary linguistic system to produce highly varied utterances.

In a classic treatise on language development, Brown (1973) has presented the first two stages of the five stages he believes children go through with respect to sentence construction and sentence understanding. Those stages are exclusive of pronunciation and the growth of vocabulary.

Bloom and Lahey (1978) have published a scholarly book, *Language Development and Language Disorders*. They contend that language involves the interaction of content, form, and use. *Content* refers to ideas about objects and events in the environment. *Form* refers to the conventional system of rules for comparing sounds and words to form phrases and sentences. *Use* refers to the way in which language is used and the function for which it is used. They describe normal language development as successful interaction among content, form, and use. Disordered language they describe as any disruption within any of those components or in the interaction among the components—content, form, and use.

DELAYED LANGUAGE DEVELOPMENT. Children who show difficulty in understanding or speaking the language code of their peers at a normal age may have difficulty in any one or more of a variety of functions. Most language theorists differentiate between language disorder and delayed language development. Bangs (1968) defines delayed language development as orderly development that progresses at a *slower rate* than normal and is significantly below the appropriate language performance for the child's chronological age. When a child has a language disorder, however, he or she shows a departure from the usual orderly pattern in learning the language code.

Some of the causes of delayed speech and language include hearing loss, mental retardation, emotional disturbance, and environmental deprivation. Pinning down the cause of delayed speech and language sometimes requires diagnostic services from a number of professions in addition to a speech-language pathologist. The neurologist, for example, looks for evidence of cerebral dysfunction, while the school psychologist attempts to rule out mental retardation. The audiologist is responsible for determining hearing abnormalities and level of acuity, and the social worker, psychiatrist, or psychologist explores factors in the home or environment to throw light on possible emotional factors that might have a bearing on the speech or language problems.

Delayed language development is not always a language problem per se. For example, the mentally retarded child shows a retarded symbolic level, but this is not his or her only area of deficiency. The deaf child, on the other hand, often does not develop language because of the inability to hear; he or she may, however, have symbolic language that does not require verbal response. The emotionally disturbed child may reject sound, but that problem is not primarily one of language disturbance.

DEVELOPMENTAL OR CONGENITAL APHASIA. The term *aphasia* has been used to describe in adults and older children the loss of speech and language as a result of a brain injury or trauma. It has been used also with children who failed to learn, not necessarily because of brain injury, but possibly because of a congenital condition, hence the term *developmental or congenital aphasia,* sometimes referred to as "child aphasia."

Eisenson (1971; 1972) emphasizes the difference between congenital aphasia and language retardation or delayed speech and language. He defines a child with delayed speech as "one whose competence (comprehension and/or performance production) is significantly below what we expect on the basis of age, sex, and intelligence" (p. 194). He views congenital or developmental aphasia as "an identifiable syndrome that must be separately considered among the organic causes of language retardation" (p. 197). He insists on definite evidence for "atypical cerebral development" on a congenital basis and has used the term *dyslogia* as a synonym for developmental aphasia.

Kendall (1966) questions the utility of the term *congenital or developmental aphasia.* He states:

> Rather than categorize defects in this complex series by a single static and potentially overworked term, it would contribute more to understanding of the dynamics of the system if it were possible to measure more specifically the integrity and functioning of its main components. Here the approach outlined . . . in the ITPA appears to be potentially fruitful. (p. 296)

The terms *congenital or developmental aphasia* and *delayed speech* are often misapplied to children who show deviant language and speech behavior. The terms *delayed speech* and *aphasia* are difficult to differentiate and may not be necessary. Instead, the evaluation of the child can deal with a learning disability as related to *auditory-vocal disorders.* This method of attack on the problem of perception, speech, and language can lead to specific programs of remediation. The methods of remediation of language disorders in children by Johnson and Myklebust (1967), McGinnis (1963), and Gray and Ryan (1973), along with the remedial methods that have evolved from the ITPA model, have been discussed in Chapter 8 on specific learning disabilities.

Researchers and clinicians have been concerned with a differential diagnosis of language disorders, delayed speech, and developmental aphasia since remediation and prognosis in these areas are believed by some to be slightly different. Delayed speech due to mental retardation leads to efforts to improve the child's vocabulary or semantics. However, if delayed speech is due to a severe hearing loss, the remedial or instructional emphasis is different. Following an initial emphasis on concept formation or cognition, more time may be given to proper syntactic and speech development. The language disorder of a child whose delay is due to environmental factors may differ from that of a child with a brain injury or developmental aphasia.

As indicated earlier under classification, there are conditions with which articulatory, voice, rhythm, and language disorders are often associated. Speech and language disorders are sometimes associated with (1) hearing loss, (2) cleft palate, (3) cerebral palsy, and (4) mental retardation. Although this text includes sections and chapters on those conditions, brief mention should be made here of the speech and language problems often associated with them.

Impairments associated with hearing loss

Children with impaired hearing have been discussed in Chapter 6. Ordinarily children with severe or profound hearing losses are educated in special classes or in residential schools. Children who have mild to moderate hearing impairments (referred to as the hard-of-hearing) tend to remain in the regular grades but require specialized services from a resource or itinerant teacher of the hard-of-hearing or from a speech clinician trained and experienced in speech and hearing. The services include all or some of the following:

1. analyzing the child's type and degree of hearing loss (based on examination by an audiologist and otologist)
2. arranging for the fitting of a hearing aid if advisable
3. training the child, through auditory training, to use the hearing aid appropriately
4. seating the child in an appropriate place in the classroom so he or she can speech-read (lip-read)
5. teaching the child to lip-read
6. correcting articulation errors that are common with the hard-of-hearing child
7. correcting voice problems
8. attempting to alleviate the language difficulties that are frequently associated with impaired hearing
9. counseling with pupils, parents, and teachers

The reader is referred to Chapter 6 for a more complete description and discussion of the diagnoses, characteristics, and educational programs for children with impaired hearing.

Impairments associated with cleft palate

The speech and language disorder with cleft palate and cleft lip is due not to cerebral dysfunction but to structural deficiencies caused by the failure of the bone and tissue of the palate to fuse during the first thirteen weeks of pregnancy. If at that time development is arrested so that fusion does not take place, the child will be born with a cleft in the roof of the mouth and sometimes in the lip (commonly referred to as harelip). A number of studies have indicated that cleft palate and lip may be hereditary but do not explain what factor or combination of factors in the germ plasm may cause the difficulty. The classic study of Fogh-Anderson (1942) reveals that heredity is more likely to be associated with either cleft lip alone or lip and palate than with palate alone. The incidence of cleft palate and/or lip varies in different locales, but there is an accepted ratio of 1 in every 750 to 1,000 live births.

The associated problems of a child with cleft palate and/or lip are related to the cosmetic aspects as well as to speech and hearing involvement. In addition, other conditions may occur: dental irregularities in alignment, supernumerary teeth, a tongue too large and rigid, misplaced tooth buds because of surgery, and respiratory infection affecting the middle ear, causing otitis media and possible hearing impairment. Other anomalies such as webbed fingers, missing ear, hypertelorism, and clubfoot also occur.

In the past, speech case histories were loaded with information about the surgical procedures for the cleft-palate child. They reported children or adults showing irregular lip scars, taut nostrils, and underdeveloped maxilla even after as many as twelve operations. Emphasis was placed on surgical procedures, with speech habilitation accomplished if velopharyngeal closure could be achieved and palatal movement were adequate.

Since 1945 surgical procedures have changed from the goal of closing the cleft to that of speech adequacy. This shift in philosophy was due, no doubt, to the activity of the American Cleft Palate Association, which brought together pediatricians, surgeons, orthodontists, prosthodontists, psychologists, and speech-language pathologists to discuss the problem, not of vegetation, but of improving speech.

It is no longer necessary for child and parents to struggle with the gross deformity and severely distorted nasal speech. Many hospitals maintain a professional team that decides on the time for surgery according to each child's cephalic growth. Through adequate surgery and skin graftings at the appropriate growth stages, the physical and cosmetic deformities can be obliterated.

When surgical procedures are delayed too long, are not deemed advisable, or fail to accomplish the desired effect, all is not lost. Skillful fitting of an obturator or prosthetic device becomes, then, the most satisfactory solution to improving speech. Often a prosthesis is so constructed that it also compensates for dental abnormalities and structural deficiencies in the oral cavity. Those procedures give the speech clinician a more pliable and competent mechanism for speech training. A more thorough discussion of speech problems associated with cleft palate is found in Spreistersbach and Sherman (1968).

Van Hattum (1974) has described four stages in the remedial program for children with cleft-palate speech.

1. The parent provides stimulation for prelinguistic speech from birth until 18 months.
2. From 18 months to 3 years the mother assists a speech clinician in speech and language development and remediation.
3. From 3 to 5 years the emphasis in remediation is placed on correcting or minimizing aberrant speech.
4. From 5 years on, correction and follow-up continue.

Van Hattum includes in the remedial model (1) articulation, (2) voice quality, (3) auditory training, (4) use and direction of air stream, (5) improvement of function of articulation, (6) rate control, and (7) language remediation.

Impairments associated with cerebral palsy

The cerebral-palsied child, discussed in Chapter 12, has a brain dysfunction, which results in a motor handicap. This brain dysfunction is associated with other handicaps in vision, hearing, perception, and behavior as well as in speech defects. The child with cerebral palsy may show a number of defects in almost every aspect of speech. He or she may have speech that varies from jargon to a fairly intelligible effort. The child may stutter and may have articulation defects not associated with the brain dysfunction. In a study of fifty cases of cerebral-palsied children, Wolfe (1950) found that 30 percent had normal articulation while 70 percent had inadequate articulation. Of the group of 70 percent with articulation disorders, 40 percent of them showed causal relationships to the condition of cerebral palsy; in 4 percent the defects were due to other organic factors; and in 26 percent the causes were functional. In addition to speech defects, the cerebral-palsied child's language may be impaired as a result of the neurologic involvement or because the motor handicap interferes with the ability to have the same experiences, to understand the same visual and motor relationships, and to practice in the same way with language that the nonhandicapped child does.

SPEECH CHARACTERISTICS OF CEREBRAL-PALSIED CHILDREN

The most common categories of cerebral palsy are the spastic, athetoid, and ataxic types. Differential generalizations can be made on the speech characteristics of these three types consistent with the motor characteristics representative of each.

1. The speech of the spastic child will show greater articulatory deviations than the speech of the other types. Speech will be labored and indistinct, and sounds will be omitted, slurred, or distorted, especially consonant blends like /sk/ or /tsh/. Pitch changes will be uncontrolled and abrupt rather than gradual and continuous. Vocal quality may be husky, guttural, and tense and may show hypernasality of vowels. Saliva is likely to be excessive in sound formation.

2. The speech of the athetoid child usually is slurring in rhythm and constantly changing in pitch, inflection, effort, and emphasis, not unlike the postural balance characteristic of the athetoid type. Sounds are distorted inconsistently because of the continuous involuntary movements. The voice may be lacking in force owing to respiratory disturbances and excessive movement. It may be unintelligible because of the irregular movements to which the speech musculature is subjected. If there is an effort at voluntary control, the resulting coordination is much like that of the spastic—hence the term *tension athetoid*.

3. The ataxic child will talk with the same rhythm shown in walking and bodily movements. He or she may give the impression of walking on stilts or of a mechanical doll that has been wound up for motor performance. Speech sounds are mechanically motivated also and exhibit spasmodic breaks and pauses rather than slurring and scanning rhythm. At times the child's speech seems to fade away as if the mechanism needs to be wound up again. Assimilation of sounds and intonational patterns appear to be most difficult.

SPEECH REMEDIATION FOR THE CEREBRAL-PALSIED CHILD

The remediation of speech impairments in the cerebral-palsied child does not differ greatly from that for other children. Six major areas require attention.

1. Because of the cerebral-palsied child's physical difficulties in walking, chewing, and swallowing, the parents tend to overprotect or do too much for him or her. Sometimes the speech is delayed or

inadequate, partly because the parents do not give the child the opportunity to try to exercise vocal musculature. When that situation prevails, it is necessary to solicit the cooperation of the parents and to motivate speech through experience and exercise.

2. Sometimes the speech clinician must alleviate as soon as possible the stigmata generally associated with cerebral palsy; they include drooling and the protruding tongue hanging from an open mouth. Effort should be made to teach the child to swallow acceptably and to close the mouth and enclose the tongue in its habitat. Again the cooperation of the parents is required since they are in hourly or daily contact with the child. Conscientious parents will remind the child to swallow prior to the accumulation of saliva and so prevent drooling.

3. The use of mirrors should depend on the speech specialist's clinical judgment. It is sometimes thought that seeing his or her own reactions creates greater muscular tension in the child. It is considered by others an acceptable technique. With some children, being readied by what they see in the mirror will help them learn to live with their handicap and to profit from the use of a mirror. They can thus be prepared for control in speech as well as in social living.

4. Language is aided by exploration, experience, and the need for verbal expression. The severely palsied child is restricted in movement and does not have normal opportunities to move about and explore the environment. He or she needs experiences in motor activities. Since speech is a motor activity, it is necessary to use what speech specialists call a multiple-sense modality approach: the use of auditory, visual, and kinesthetic senses in the production of speech. At times speech remediation is conducted in collaboration with physiotherapy.

5. Children do not speak unless they are motivated to speak. One of the problems with cerebral-palsied children is creating a need in them for improving their speech. Their own efforts in correcting inappropriate tongue and jaw movements and in breathing properly require concentrated attention. How to supply the necessary motivation is one of the major concerns of a speech clinician.

6. Finally, it will be necessary for a speech clinician to help the child manage his or her tongue movements, control the synergetic movements of swallowing, control facial movements (grimaces, tics), and control breathing, inflection, and intonations of voice.

Impairments associated with mental retardation

A major diagnostic characteristic of mentally retarded children is the observed delay in the development of speech and language. Numerous studies on the speech and language of the mentally retarded have been completed over the years. In 1930 Kennedy found a large percentage of speech defects among the mentally retarded. Of the mildly retarded group, 42.6 percent had speech defects, while 96.9 percent of the severe were so afflicted. Similar percentages were later found by Sirkins and Lyons (1941), Schlanger and Gottsleben (1957), and others in studies of the institutionalized mentally retarded.

Batza (1956) studied the speech and language development of mentally retarded children in the Chicago public schools. He found that the higher the IQ, the better the child was in articulation, oral language, auditory discrimination, motor coordination, and memory span. A similar study was made in the New York public schools by Donovan (1957). She found that of the 2,000 children studied with IQs between 50 and 75, a large majority had some developmental speech and language problem. Eight percent had severe speech defects.

It is obvious from the review of the research on speech handicaps with the mentally retarded that (1) speech defects are more prevalent among all levels of the mentally retarded than among normal children, (2) the greater the degree of mental retardation, the greater the prevalence of speech defects, and (3) the effects of speech remediation have not been adequately determined.

Studies on the language behavior of the mentally retarded have also indicated quite clearly that language development is correlated with mental age and IQ, possibly because most tests of intelligence are verbal tests.

Cromer (1974) also reviewed the studies on the speech and language of the mentally retarded. Since mentally retarded children are not a homogeneous group, it is not surprising that a generalization for all the mentally retarded is not possible. A few generalizations, however, can be made.

1. The acquisition of language by some retarded children is basically the same as that by children with average intelligence but is at a slower pace, hence delayed language development.
2. Some retarded children do not seem to be able to generalize the rules of grammar as readily as do normal children.
3. The language processes of mentally retarded children appear to be different from those of normal children, and their products are below those expected of their mental age.
4. There is some evidence that deficits in certain cognitive abilities, such as short-term memory, may explain the lag in comprehension and production.

Lillywhite and Bradley (1969) in their book *Communication Problems of the Mentally Retarded* discuss the causes, characteristics, and treatment of communication problems with mentally retarded children. They found that the children studied functioned in speech and language below others of the same chronological age and even below the average child of the same mental age.

A more crucial problem is whether or not language in the mentally retarded can be trained. Lyle (1960) studied the effects of institutionalization on the development of language. He randomly removed sixteen imbeciles from a state hospital and developed a language program for them. Another sixteen remained in the hospital as controls. After twelve months of training, the experimental group showed significant gains over the control group on intelligence tests and on language and speech tests. The experimental group retained the gains for eighteen months on follow-up tests. Language training was included in other studies on the long-term effects of training of the mentally retarded, which are reported in Chapter 4, "Children with Low Intelligence."

School services

Language, speech, and hearing services are offered by speech-language pathologists in hospitals and clinics, in public and private schools, in university speech clinics, and through private practice. This section will describe briefly the options for delivery of services to the schools.

Speech remediation in schools has been in existence since the beginning of the century. It is among the earliest special education programs that have been organized and accepted in the schools. It is also one of the programs that has attempted to maintain high standards of training for speech clinicians. Through the efforts of the American Speech and Hearing Association during the last fifty years, much progress has been made.

There are over two million speech- and language-impaired children in the United States. According to Table 1.3 in Chapter 1, speech services are the most common type of special education, and approximately 88 percent of speech-handicapped children were enrolled in some such service program as of 1975–1976. The number of children enrolled has been gradually increasing due to the passage of mandatory legislation in most states.

CHANGES IN SCHOOL SERVICES

Remediation of speech and language problems in the schools has changed considerably over the last two decades. Earlier, speech clinicians devoted 80 percent of their time to articulatory disorders in the kindergarten, first, and second grades in school. The rest of their time was devoted to hearing therapy and voice disorders, with little time being devoted to language disorders, delayed speech, and stuttering.

During the last decade emphasis has shifted to the broader field of communication disorders in general, rather than remaining concentrated in the area of articulatory disorders. It was found that many articulatory defects disappeared without speech remediation as the child matured. Also it has been found that to be more effective a speech-language clinician must not only work with the child but must integrate the work with the regular teacher and the parents and also broaden the field to include language development and language disorders. Some departments of speech and hearing have changed their names to departments of communication disorders. As a consequence, the training of speech clinicians has been broadened to include the study of language, linguistics, language disorders, and learning disabilities, in addition to the traditional areas of articulation, voice, and stuttering. The title of such workers has recently been changed to speech-language pathologist.

Van Hattum (1976) suggests that the remediation of articulatory disorders should continue but that visual aids and taped programs could be used for a majority of the children under the supervision of a speech clinician. That move would free the speech clinician to become a supervisor, an administrator, a master clinician, a consultant, and a counselor. Van Hattum recommends that the duties of speech clinicians should emphasize the supervision of aides: "early case selection, . . . language (studies), more services to special groups, extension of services to new areas, . . . prevention, and improved methods of accountability" (p. 61).

OPTIONS IN SERVICE DELIVERY

The organization of programs for language, speech, and hearing disorders in the schools is varied and dependent on the situation and the expertise of the clinician. The following section presents some of the more common delivery services.

ITINERANT SERVICE. In the past the most common delivery system has been the itinerant model in which a clinician travels from school to school to give direct service to children enrolled in the regular classrooms. This model is most applicable to areas with small schools or to rural and semirural areas. In small schools in sparsely settled areas there may not be a sufficient number of children in one school to maintain the services of one clinician on a full-time basis.

THE RESOURCE ROOM. The resource room stations a clinician in a room that accepts, individually or in small groups, children with language, speech, or hearing problems. In this model the child is enrolled in a regular classroom, as in the itinerant model, but receives direct service in the resource room at scheduled periods. The model is applicable generally to large schools that have a sufficient number of children to warrant the full-time services of a speech-language pathologist. A modification of this model is to have one speech clinician spend only one-half day in one school and either serve as a resource teacher in another school for half a day or serve as an itinerant teacher in several schools.

CONSULTATIVE SERVICES. This model provides a school system, not with the direct services of a clinician, but with a speech consultant, that is, a speech-language clinician who serves as a consultant to regular classroom teachers, special class teachers, aides, administrators, parents, and curriculum specialists in organizing a speech and language development program. The clinician in this capacity provides specialized materials and procedures, in-service education, demonstration sessions, and other activities designed to improve the communication skills of children in natural settings—the classroom and the home.

SELF-CONTAINED SPECIAL CLASSROOM. This type of delivery system is used infrequently and is for children with severe disabilities that cannot be managed in the regular classroom with supportive help. Such classes are organized for children with delayed speech, developmental aphasia, or related disorders. Children can be grouped for instruction in a small special class in which individualized, as well as group, instruction is practiced. Classes for so-called aphasic children are examples of self-contained special classes.

THE SPECIAL SCHOOL. This model is sometimes common in private schools where the whole school is devoted to children with communication disorders. In such schools the classes are small, and the children are grouped according to level or type of disorder.

HOME AND HOSPITAL SERVICES. Language, speech, and hearing services are provided for children confined to hospitals or to homes when they are unable to attend school.

RESIDENTIAL SCHOOLS. For children who require residential care as well as educational services, there are residential schools that handle severe disorders. In such schools are found cerebral-palsied children with speech and language defects, severe cases of developmental aphasia, and similar problems.

PARENT AND PRESCHOOL SERVICES. For young children who are actually or potentially language and speech handicapped, consultant help from a clinician is given to parents and preschool teachers who are in a position to help the child. Although not common in the past, this model is becoming more popular as early childhood education for the handicapped increases. The growth of early childhood education has necessitated the recruitment of speech clinicians for this work.

DIAGNOSTIC CENTERS. This model provides an interdisciplinary team for the diagnosis and temporary remediation of children assigned to these centers. The procedure provides a more thorough diagnosis of the problem and initial experimentation with effective procedures for remediation. Such centers are sometimes found in hospitals and in university departments of speech and hearing sciences.

PARAPROFESSIONAL SERVICES. Speech education programs, especially for severe handicaps, have utilized paraprofessional personnel (aides) to help the speech-language clinician. The Committee on Supportive Personnel of ASHA (1970) has studied the use of paraprofessional personnel for speech- and language-handicapped children and has recommended the use of communication aides in schools and clinics. On the basis of the committee's report, ASHA recognized this category of personnel and established guidelines for the training and supervision of communication aides. The procedure is necessary to free the clinician for more intense work with seriously handicapped children and at the same time to provide more services for more children.

The role of the speech-language pathologist

From the variety of settings and options for delivery of services to language-, speech-, and hearing-handicapped children, it is obvious that a speech and language clinician must be able to serve in more than one capacity. An itinerant or resource speech clinician must be prepared to deal with a large variety of speech-, language-, and hearing-handicapped children. He or she must deal with all the types of handicaps discussed earlier—articulation problems, voice problems, stuttering, language disorders—as well as with problems found among the hearing handicapped, cleft palated, and mentally retarded.

Although speech clinicians sometimes specialize and work primarily with one area (with language and speech disorders or with the hearing handicapped), it is necessary that they be competent in a number of areas. It is for that reason that the training of speech-language pathologists has been extended in those three hundred or so universities and colleges developing these specialists. Sixty hours of undergraduate and graduate work in speech, hearing, and language are generally required for the master's degree. State departments of education in most states have these same requirements for certification, based on the recommendations of the American Speech and Hearing Association, which is the professional organization representing this field.

The general duties that can be performed by speech-language clinicians in the schools have been suggested in a publication entitled *Project Upgrade* (1973). Their duties include the following:

1. Supervision and administration of programs for children with communication disorders. For every ten to twenty-nine speech clinicians in the school system, a supervisor is required to organize and supervise the program and personnel. Such an individual should not only be certified but should have broad experience with all communication disorders.

2. Identification and diagnosis. In other areas of special education, the diagnostician may be a psychologist or a physician who refers the child to a teacher for education. In speech pathology, the diagnostician assesses the child and also provides the necessary remediation. This procedure may be the preferred one, since diagnosis by others sometimes leads to classification but not to remediation when the two functions of diagnosis and remediation are accomplished by two or more individuals.

3. Consultation. Speech clinicians can devote all their time to professional consultation such as (1) demonstrating procedures, (2) providing in-service training of regular and special teachers to serve children with minor problems, (3) training and supervising communication aides, (4) disseminating information to teachers and administrators, and (5) serving as a consultant to parents and preschool teachers.

4. Direct services. The large majority of speech and language clinicians devote their full time to the identification of children with communicative disorders and to direct remedial services for the children selected. In this capacity they serve children who stutter, children who have voice problems, hearing, handicaps, articulation defects, and language-learning disabilities, and children with communicative disorders associated with cerebral palsy, mental retardation, emotional disturbances, and developmental aphasia. Services are also provided to preschool children and infants.

5. Recording and reporting.   Speech clinicians are required to keep records and reports on all children with communicative handicaps. The report is part of the school record and is treated by the school as such. The case record includes a statement of the problem, the assessment, the remediation and assignment, and the termination.

Summary

1. Speech and language habilitation has been a part of public school programs since the beginning of the twentieth century.

2. A speech and language disorder is defined as speech or language that (a) draws unfavorable attention to itself, (b) interferes with communication, or (c) affects adversely the speaker or listener.

3. Research on the prevalence of articulation, voice, and stuttering disorders in the school population shows a rate of 4 to 6 percent for moderate and severe disorders.

4. Most disorders in school children are found in the first and second grades. The prevalence drops markedly by the third and fourth grades as a result of maturation, treatment, or both.

5. Identification of children with communication handicaps includes (a) screening to identify children who require full diagnostic assessment, (b) diagnosing those selected through the initial screening and from other referrals, and (c) selecting for remediation those who require and will probably benefit from special speech or language remediation.

6. Speech disorders can be classified as disorders of (a) articulation, (b) voice, (c) fluency (stuttering), and (d) language.

7. Language and speech impairments are commonly associated with children who have (a) cerebral palsy, (b) hearing loss, (c) cleft palate, and (d) mental retardation.

8. There are a number of models for the delivery of language, speech, and hearing services in the schools. The most common are itinerant teachers, resource rooms, and consultative services. In addition there are self-contained classrooms, special schools, residential schools, and home and hospital services, as well as public and private clinics.

9. A speech and language pathologist (clinician) serves in many capacities including (a) supervision, (b) identification and diagnosis,

(c) consultation, (d) direct services with children, and (e) recording and reporting.

10. Speech, language, and hearing clinicians are prepared for their work in over three hundred colleges and universities and are required to have a master's degree or the equivalent of sixty semester hours of professional training.

References

BANGS, T. 1968. *Language and Learning Disorders of the Pre-Academic Child with Curriculum Guide.* New York: Appleton-Century-Crofts.

BATZA, E. 1956. "Investigation of the Speech and Oral Language Behavior of Educable Mentally Handicapped Children." *Dissertation Abstracts* 17 (February): 299.

BERRY, MILDRED F. 1969. *Language Disorders of Children: The Basis and Diagnosis.* New York: Appleton-Century-Crofts.

BLOOM, L., AND M. LAHEY. 1978. *Language Development and Language Disorders.* New York: John Wiley.

BOONE, D. 1971. *The Voice and Voice Therapy.* Englewood Cliffs, N.J.: Prentice-Hall.

BROWN, R. 1973. *A First Language—The Early Stages.* Cambridge: Harvard University Press.

COMMITTEE ON SUPPORTIVE PERSONNEL. 1970. "Guidelines on the Role, Training and Supervision of the Communication Aide." *ASHA* 10: 781.

Comprehensive Assessment and Service (CASE) *Information System.* 1976. Washington, D.C.: American Speech and Hearing Association.

COMPTON, A. 1976. "Generative Studies of Children's Phonological Disorders." In D. M. Morehead and A. E. Morehead, eds., *Normal and Deficient Child Language.* Baltimore: University Park Press, Pp. 61–96.

CROMER, R. 1974. "Receptive Language in the Mentally Retarded: Processes and Diagnostic Distinctions." In R. Schiefelbusch and L. Lloyd, eds., *Language Acquisition, Retardation, and Intervention.* Baltimore: University Park Press. Pp. 237–267.

DONOVAN, H. 1957. "Organization and Development of a Speech Program for the Mentally Retarded Children in New York City Public Schools." *American Journal of Mental Deficiency* 62:455–459.

EISENSON, J. 1972. *Aphasia in Children.* New York: Harper & Row.

EISENSON, J. 1971. "The Nature of Defective Speech." In W. Cruickshank, ed., *Psychology of Exceptional Children and Youth,* 3rd ed. Englewood Cliffs, N.J.: Prentice-Hall.

EISENSON, J., AND M. OGILVIE. 1976. *Speech Correction in the Schools,* 4th ed. New York: Macmillan.

FAIRBANKS, G. 1960. *Voice and Articulation Drillbook,* 2nd ed. New York: Harper & Row.

FOGH-ANDERSON, P. 1942. *Inheritance of Harelip and Cleft Palate.* Copenhagen: Nyt Nordisk Forlag, Arnold Busck.

GOLDIAMOND, I. 1968. "Stuttering and Fluency as Manipulative Operant Response Classes." In H. Sloan and B. Macauley, eds., *Operant Procedures in Remedial Speech and Language Training.* Boston: Houghton Mifflin. Pp. 348–407.

GRAY, B., AND B. RYAN. 1973. *A Language Program for the Non-Language Child.* Champaign, Ill.: Research Press.

HULL., F., P. MIEIKE, JR., J. WILLEFORD, AND R. TIMMONS. 1976. *National Speech and Hearing Survey.* Project No. 50978, Bureau of Education for the Handicapped, U.S. Office of Education. Washington, D.C.: Department of Health, Education, and Welfare.

INGRAM, D. 1976. "Current Issues in Child Phonology." In D. M. Morehead and A. E. Morehead, eds., *Normal and Deficient Child Language.* Baltimore: University Park Press. Pp. 3–27.

INGRAM, D. 1974. "Phonological Rules in Young Children." *Journal of Child Language* 1 (May): 97–106.

ITARD, J. M. G. 1932. *The Wild Boy of Aveyron.* Translated from the French by G. Humphrey and M. Humphrey. New York: Appleton-Century-Crofts.

JOHNSON, D. J., AND H. MYKLEBUST. 1967. *Learning Disabilities: Educational Principles and Practices.* New York: Grune & Stratton.

JOHNSON, W. 1956. *Speech Handicapped School Children.* New York: Harper & Brothers.

KENDALL, D. C. 1966. "Language Problems in Children." In R. Rieber and R. Brubaker, eds., *Speech Pathology.* Philadelphia: J. B. Lippincott, Pp. 285–298.

KENNEDY, L. 1930. "Studies in the Speech of the Feebleminded." Unpublished doctoral dissertation. University of Wisconsin.

LENNEBERG, E. 1971. "Of Language Knowledge, Apes and Brains." *Journal of Psycholinguistic Research* 1(1): 1–29.

LILLYWHITE, H. S., AND D. BRADLEY. 1969. *Communication Problems in Mental Retardation.* New York: Harper & Row.

LYLE, J. 1960. "The Effect of an Institutional Environment upon Verbal Development of Imbecile Children. III: The Booklands Residential Family Unit." *Journal of Mental Deficiency Research* 4 (September): 14–23.

MARTIN, R. 1968. "The Experimental Manipulation of Stuttering Behaviors." In H. Sloan and B. Macauley, eds., *Operant Procedures in Remedial Speech and Language Training.* Boston: Houghton Mifflin. Pp. 325–334.

MC GINNIS, M. 1963. *Aphasic Children*. Washington, D.C.: Volta Review.

MOREHEAD, D. M., AND D. INGRAM. 1976. "The Development of Base Syntax in Linguistically Normal and Linguistically Deviant Children." In D. M. Morehead and A. E. Morehead, eds., *Normal and Deficient Child Language*. Baltimore: University Park Press.

NATIONAL INSTITUTE OF NEUROLOGICAL DISEASES AND STROKE. 1969. *Human Communication and Its Disorders—An Overview*. Bethesda, Md.: Public Health Service.

PERKINS, W. 1971. *Speech Pathology*. St. Louis: C. V. Mosby.

PROJECT UPGRADE. 1973. *Model Regulations for School Language, Speech and Hearing Programs and Services*. Washington, D.C.: American Speech and Hearing Association.

SCHLANGER, B. B., AND R. H. GOTTSLEBEN. 1957. "Analysis of Speech Defects Among the Institutionalized Mentally Retarded." *Journal of Speech and Hearing Disorders* 22 (March): 98–103.

SHEEHAN, J. G., ED. 1970. *Stuttering Research and Therapy*. New York: Harper & Row.

SIRKINS, J., AND W. F. LYONS. 1941. "A Study of Speech Defects in Mental Deficiency." *American Journal of Mental Deficiency* 46: 74–80.

SKINNER, B. F. 1957. *Verbal Behavior*. New York: Appleton-Century-Crofts.

SLOBIN, D. 1973. "Cognitive Prerequisites for the Development of Grammar." In C. Ferguson and D. Slobin, eds., *Studies of Child Language Development*. New York: Holt, Rinehart and Winston. Pp. 175–208.

SPREISTERSBACH, D., AND D. SHERMAN. 1968. *Cleft Palate and Communication*. New York: Academic Press.

Task Force on Identifying Children with Language Impairment. 1977. Washington, D.C.: American Speech and Hearing Association.

TEMPLIN, M. 1957. *Certain Language Skills in Children*. Minneapolis: University of Minnesota Press.

Therapy for Stutterers. 1974. Memphis, Tenn.: Speech Foundation of America.

TRAVIS, L. E., ED. 1957. *Handbook of Speech Pathology*. New York: Appleton-Century-Crofts.

VAN HATTUM, R. 1976. "Services of the Speech Clinician in Schools: Progress and Prospects." *ASHA* 18: 59–63.

VAN HATTUM, R. 1974. "Communication Problems Associated with Cleft Palate." In S. Dickinson, ed., *Communication Disorders, Remedial Principles and Practices*. Glenview, Ill.: Scott, Foresman. Pp. 296–355.

VAN RIPER, C. 1971. *The Nature of Stuttering*. Englewood Cliffs, N.J.: Prentice-Hall.

VAN RIPER, C. 1970a. "Historical Approaches." In J. Sheehan, ed., *Stuttering Research and Therapy*. New York: Harper & Row.

VAN RIPER, C. 1970b. *Behavior Modification: An Overview in Conditioning Stuttering Therapy.* Memphis, Tenn.: Speech Foundation of America.

WEBSTER, L., AND G. BRUTTEN. 1974. "The Modification of Stuttering and Associated Behaviors." In S. Dickinson, ed., *Communication Disorders, Remedial Principles and Practices.* Glenview, Ill.: Scott, Foresman.

WEPMAN, J. 1975. "New and Wider Horizons for Speech and Hearing Specialists." *ASHA* 17: 9–10.

WEST, R. 1958. "An Agnostic Speculation About Stuttering." In J. Eisenson, ed., *Stuttering: A Symposium.* New York: Harper & Brothers.

WOLFE, W. G. 1950. "A Comprehensive Evaluation of Fifty Cases of Cerebral Palsy." *Journal of Speech and Hearing Disorders* 15 (September): 234–251.

11

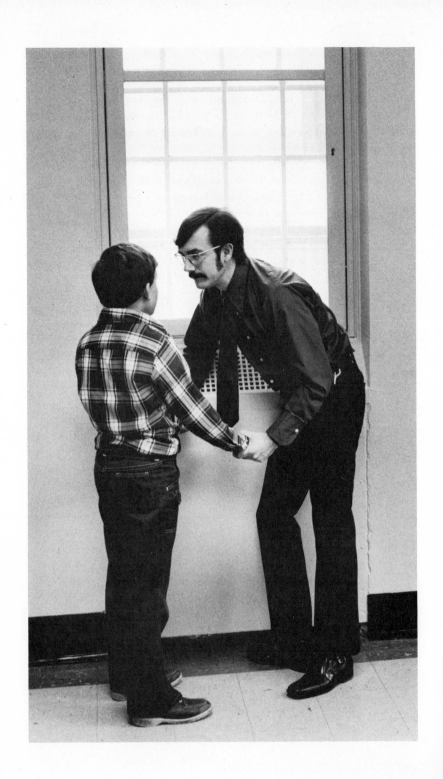

There are few experiences quite so disturbing to sensitive and alert teachers as children who seem chronically unhappy or distressed or who seem to be driven to aggressive and antisocial behavior that can only lead the child into greater and greater social difficulties. Sometimes the teacher may view such problems as if from a far mountain, watching a car about to crash on a distant highway, knowing there will be great damage, but being unable to do anything about it. One teacher's report will give the flavor.

> I can't stop worrying about one little girl in my first grade. She behaves so peculiarly. She doesn't talk most of the time, though she can talk. She answers the other children and me with animal sounds. She hides under chairs like a dog and barks at people. . . . She has been on a clinic waiting list for six months, and I've had the child up for Special Service to test her for three months. In the meantime, the class all laugh at her, and she just gets worse, and I don't know what to do. (Long and Newman, 1976, pp. 286–287)

Behavioral disorders can be defined in terms of personality dynamics or in terms of the effect of a child's behavior on himself or herself or on other people. For purposes of this chapter a *behavioral disorder* is defined as a marked deviation from age-appropriate behavior that significantly interferes with (1) the child's own development, (2) the lives of others, or (3) both.

A child who is extremely withdrawn and fearful, who does not relate to other people, and who does not seem to respond to the environment (notwithstanding average intelligence) is one whose behavior is interfering with his or her own development. Such children have been termed *withdrawn, neurotic, autistic,* and *schizophrenic.*

Children of another type behave in ways that create repeated conflict with siblings, parents, classmates, teachers, and community. They disturb by directly interfering with the lives of other people. Neighbors call them "bad boys" or "bad girls." Teachers call them "conduct problems." Social workers say they are "socially maladjusted." Psychiatrists and psychologists say they are "emotionally disturbed." If they come in conflict with the law, the judge may call them "delinquent."

Behavioral disorders are of interest to workers in many professions: social work, psychology, psychiatry, sociology, neurology, education, and related disciplines. Education has traditionally dealt only with the mild behavioral disorders, leaving the severer disorders to psychiatry; however, the field of mental health has gradually moved away from a medical or psychoanalytical approach toward a behavioral, educational approach (Glasser, 1965; Hewett, 1968; Ullmann and Krasner, 1965; Wood, 1975). Education, meanwhile, has

CHILDREN WITH BEHAVIORAL AND EMOTIONAL DIFFERENCES

taken increased responsibility not only for prevention but also for the treatment of many of the severer behavioral disorders (Hewett, 1968; Hobbs, 1970; Rhodes and Sabin, 1974).

Types of behavioral disorders

There appears to be an almost infinite variety of deviant actions that can cause a child or adult to be called "behaviorally disordered." Attaching such a label to a child in the absence of definitive treatment may well do more harm than good (Hobbs, 1975).

Despite the diversity of behavior that can be observed, a number of research studies have revealed a constant set of only two or three major syndromes (clusters of symptoms that occur together) that can be identified for purposes of differentiated programming.

One such classification was made by Jenkins and Hewitt (1944), who analyzed five hundred cases of maladjusted children referred to child guidance clinics. By statistical means they related the patterns of maladjustment to home situations. Three patterns of maladjustment were found, each being associated with a different home situation. From these relationships Jenkins and Hewitt defined three types of behavioral disorders:

1. The unsocialized aggressive child is one who defies authority, is hostile toward authority figures (police officers, teachers, and so forth), is cruel, malicious, and assaultive, and has no guilt feelings. Children of this type come from homes where they receive no love or attention in infancy. They have developed no attachments to anyone or to any group. In psychoanalytical terms they did not develop a superego or conscience.

2. The socialized aggressive child has the same characteristics or behavioral problems as the unsocialized aggressive but is socialized within his or her peer group, usually the gang or companions, in misdemeanor and crime. Unlike the unsocialized aggressive child, this child had some security with the mother or mother figure in infancy but was later rejected.

3. The overinhibited child is shy, timid, withdrawn, seclusive, sensitive, and submissive. He or she is overdependent and easily depressed. Such children in the study come mostly from overprotective families in the higher socioeconomic levels.

In terms of the behavior observed (though not the motivations behind it), it will be noted that Types 1 and 2 in the preceding classification are identical. Both the socialized aggressive and unsocialized aggressive children display the kind of behavior that is unacceptable to society. Type 3 represents the personality problems of children who are overinhibited, sensitive, and shy. In other words, from an observation of behavior, Jenkins and Hewitt's three types boil down to the traditional dichotomy of (1) aggressive behavior (including delinquency) and (2) withdrawn behavior.

Quay, Morse, and Cutler (1966) have identified similar categories that describe the behavior of three groups of children. They conducted a factor analysis of teacher ratings of 441 children in classes for the emotionally disturbed, using a Behavior Rating Check List developed originally by Peterson (1961). The sample consisted of 80 percent boys and 20 percent girls. They found three patterns of behavior clusters as follows:

1. *Conduct disorders,* sometimes referred to as unsocialized aggressive or psychopathic behavior. Included in this dimension is such behavior as defiance, disobedience, impertinence, uncooperativeness, irritability, boisterousness, attention seeking, bullying, temper tantrums, hyperactiveness, restlessness, and negativism. These maladaptive behaviors are similar to those described by Jenkins and Hewitt (1944) and labeled socialized aggressive and unsocialized aggressive.

2. *Personality problem dimension,* sometimes referred to as neurotic or overinhibited. These children were rated as being hypersensitive, shy, having feelings of inferiority, lacking in self-confidence, self-conscious, easily flustered, fearful, and anxious. Jenkins and Hewitt (1944) referred to such children as overinhibited. They lacked close friendships and were overdependent and easily depressed.

3. *The inadequate-immature dimension.* This dimension refers to children who were rated as inattentive, sluggish, lacking interest in school, lazy, preoccupied, daydreamers, drowsy, and reticent. They resemble children sometimes labeled autistic or prepsychotic. They appear to be less able to function in the regular classroom than do children who are labeled neurotic or children with conduct disorders.

Spivack, Swift, and Prewitt (1972) tried to identify specific syndromes of disturbed classroom behavior by examining ratings from thirty-two teachers in elementary schools. A total of 809 children were rated by using a behavioral check list that allowed for statements describing the intensity of a characteristic or behavior as well as its presence or absence. The investigators found similar clusters of behaviors at all grade levels.

One symptom cluster was labeled *impulsive.* In this syndrome are clustered extremes of classroom disturbance, impatience, disrespect-defiance, external blame mixed with inattentiveness, and irrelevant responsiveness. It is not surprising that most of the youngsters rated in this fashion were boys.

Another major cluster represented *internalized disturbance* and was characterized by extremely high reliance on the teacher for appropriate direction, high inattentiveness mixed with low comprehension, and low creative initiative. These children seem unable to make productive use of the classroom without being taken by the hand. There are approximately twice as many boys as girls in this group.

A third cluster exhibits a high level of *classroom disturbance, irrelevant responses,* and *tendency to externalize blame.* In some respects this cluster seems to be a less intense version of the first. As in most of these studies, the deviant behavior seems to divide into two major groups: a cluster of anxiety and fearfulness on one hand and impulsiveness, aggression, and a lack of behavioral control on the other.

Prevalence of behavioral disorders in school

Any line drawn between "normal" children and children with behavioral and emotional disorders is obviously going to be difficult to define. All children show aggressive and antisocial behavior at one time or another, and all children show fearful behavior. The difference between children identified as special problems will be in *how often, how strong or intense,* and *how appropriate to the situation.*

The studies on prevalence show a great disparity in the frequency of behavioral disorders and emotional disturbance in schoolchildren. Estimates vary from around 2 percent (Froomkin, 1972) to 8 percent (Ullmann, 1952) to 10.5 percent (Bower, 1960) to 20–24 percent (Kelly, Bullock, and Dykes, 1977; Salvia, Schultz, and Chapin, 1974). While some of these differences may be due to different judges using different levels of problem intensity as yardsticks or criteria, Wood and Zabel (1978) have another explanation. Most of the identification procedures require teachers to rate children in their classrooms *at that point in time* as being behavioral problems.

There are apparently many children who will manifest behavioral problems at one time or another in the school program, and a one-time screening will identify them. Wood and Zabel believe that the low incidence figures of 2 to 3 percent generally refer to those students who have such serious, recurrent, or persistent problems in adjusting to school as to need special programming over an extended period of time.

The large number of children who show sufficiently active transient behavioral problems to justify their being identified by teachers on a one-time basis also make apparent the need to provide teachers with help in coping with these stressful situations and in promoting healthy social development for these children.

There is general agreement that the percentage of children who need intensive and consistent special education programming as a result of their problems is rather small (1 to 2 percent of the general population). However, the same behavioral and emotional symptoms at a lesser level of intensity are obviously present in much larger numbers of youngsters. No matter how stringently we raise the identification standards (and no one has suggested it is less than 1 to 2 percent), there are at least a million children of school age in serious behavioral difficulties requiring specific help.

Characteristics of children with behavioral disorders

As noted in the previous section, the two major clusters of factors identified in previous work involve (1) hyperactive-aggressive children and (2) fearful, withdrawn, and autistic children. The characteristics of the two groups are naturally quite different and will be considered separately.

HYPERACTIVE-AGGRESSIVE CHILDREN

Whatever the basic cause of the problem, there is little question that hyperactive-aggressive children are a serious problem in a school setting. They show a marked inability to persist in a task, often disrupt the class, and are distractible and a constant irritation to the teacher because of their inability to follow directions and maintain a learning set. Bell, Weller, and Waldrop (1971) developed an analysis of the elements of hyperactivity and withdrawal that can be used in rating scales. The six elements making up the pattern of hyperactivity are *emotional aggression, inability to delay gratification, spilling and throwing, nomadic play, frenetic play,* and *requiring teacher intervention.* It is not hard to see why such a collection of symptoms will set on edge teachers, parents, and neighbors.

As education has become more directly involved with behaviorally disturbed children, increasing concern has been evidenced about their academic status.

The developmental history of hyperactive behavior reveals that the more manifest elements of that syndrome disappear over time. Douglas (1972) reported that hyperactivity decreased over the preadolescent age range, *but* impulsiveness and the inability to attend remained a serious problem. These youngsters are apparently unable to keep their impulses under control in order to cope with the situations in which care, concentrated attention, and organized planning are required. They tend to react to the first idea that occurs to them, or to those aspects of the situation that are the most obvious or compelling. Douglas stated that they have a marked inability to "stop, look, and listen."

A behaviorally disturbed child has more problems than just the behavioral disturbance itself. In most cases there also is a serious academic problem accompanying the emotional or behavioral discrepancy. Glavin and Annesley (1971) compared a group of 130 behavior problem children, identified by means of a behavioral check list, with 90 normal boys of the same age and IQ level. Among the behavior problem boys 81 percent were identified as underachieving in reading and 72 percent in math. The underachievement was determined by contrasting expected academic achievement levels with actual performance on achievement tests. When compared with the normal group, behaviorally disturbed youngsters showed 40 percent underachievement in reading and 20 percent in math. Similar achievement results have been replicated by Werry (1968) and by Graubard (1964) who found extreme underachievement in the disturbed youngsters in residential treatment centers.

Keogh (1971) summarized the literature on the relationship between hyperactivity and learning disorders and concluded that a wide variety of studies have substantiated that some hyperactive children have learning problems and are poor achievers in school. Both clinical and educational observers have noted that hyperactive children are variable in learning performance, sometimes doing excellent work and sometimes failing miserably. Keogh discussed three possible reasons for the cause of learning problems in hyperactive children.

1. Excessive extraneous movement especially in the head and eyes appears with learning difficulties, and heightened motor activity may disrupt learning by interfering with the accurate intake of information, particularly through the visual channels.

2. Hyperactive children have a different approach to problems because of their general condition. They tend to make decisions impulsively and might be considered extreme examples of the "impulsive" child syndrome described by Kagan, Moss, and Sigel (1963), who concluded that impulsive children have difficulty in solving problems because they react to the first reasonable inference and fail to evaluate the quality of the choice or to consider other possibilities.

3. Hyperactivity may be merely one symptom of neural impairment.

In a later publication Keogh (1977) discussed the importance of attention in learning and behavioral disorders. Special attention is paid to hyperactivity and impulsive characteristics since these characteristics seem linked to later delinquency. One of the characteristic responses identified with delinquent children is their impulsiveness and the inability to delay gratification. The label *delinquency* is a legal term reserved for those youngsters whose behavior results in arrest and court action. The youngsters who were earlier described as "socialized aggressive" and "unsocialized aggressive" frequently display behavior that brings them in contact with the law and results in their being labeled "delinquent."

Delinquency has become a serious problem in the United States. According to Murray (1976):

> Youth arrests for all crimes rose 138 percent during the fifteen years from 1960 through 1974, while arrests of people 18 years of age and over were increased by only 16 percent. . . . These increases in serious offenses far outstrip increases in the youth population. The youth population aged 9 through 17 increased only 27 percent during the same period. (p. 2)

WITHDRAWN CHILDREN—AUTISTIC

Children show many degrees of anxiety, fearfulness, and regression. Relatively few children, however, show the extreme withdrawn behavior referred to as *infantile autism* or *childhood schizophrenia*. These children seem literally to be walking around in a plastic envelope that prevents them from communicating with others; they show (1) an inability to relate themselves to people or situations, (2) retardation in expressive language and in comprehension, and (3) ritualistic behavior with an obsessive demand for sameness. Even the most casual observer of these children knows immediately that there is something seriously wrong.

Schopler and Reichler (1970) conducted a unique study on the mothers of autistic children. Other studies had indicated that these mothers have a cool and detached attitude toward their children. Schopler and Reichler, in comparing the behavior of the mothers of autistic children with mothers of more normal children, found that the behavior of the mothers of autistic children was significantly more disturbed. However, Schopler and Reichler also studied the behavior of these mothers of autistic children when interacting with the normal siblings of the autistic child. In these relationships the mothers appeared to behave normally. This finding raises the possibility, at least, that some of the abnormal parental behavior may be a reaction to an abnormal child rather than the cause of the abnormal child's behavior.

The work of Farber (1959) describing the family crisis created by the presence of a handicapped child reinforces the concept of interaction between handicapping conditions and parental behavior.

Rutter (1968) claimed that the primary problem of autistic children is one of language coding and auditory comprehension, rather than social relationships, the most obvious of the problems. Rutter found that more boys than girls were autistic and that often only one child in a family was afflicted with the disturbance. Such a finding argues against a simple environmental explanation, such as maternal-child relationships.

The basic causes of childhood schizophrenia or autism have not been clearly delineated. According to Rutter and Bartak (1971) the basic cause of the cognitive/language defect is unknown but the high rate of fits in intellectually retarded autistic children suggests the existence of an organic brain disorder. It is also possible that in some cases autism may be the result of a maturational disorder or a genetically determined condition. Fortunately, there are some remedial techniques that can be used with those conditions even if we remain in essential ignorance of the basic causes.

Adult behavior of children previously diagnosed as disturbed

One of the major reasons for our concern about behaviorally disturbed children is the assumption that such characteristics will continue into adulthood if no significant intervention or special program is provided. Do withdrawn, fearful, and disturbed children grow up to be adult psychiatric patients? Do behavior problem, aggressive, impulsive children grow up to be adult criminals? The evidence is not as clear as one might assume.

One follow-up study by Robins (1966) analyzed the adult performance of over five hundred children who had been seen in a child guidance clinic thirty years previously. The basic question that this study attempted to answer was whether or not youngsters identified as "sociopathic" turned out to be adult "sociopathic" cases. The term *sociopathic* in this regard is used to describe a pattern of behavior characterized by gross, repetitive failure to conform to societal norms in many areas of life, in the absence of thought disturbances suggesting psychosis.

A structured interview was given to 524 persons who had been seen for various problems thirty years previously in a child guidance clinic of a major metropolitan area. The elements used to diagnose adult sociopathic personality were work history, marital history, drug use, alcohol use, arrest, belligerence, unusual sexual behavior, suicide attempts, impulsiveness, truancy combined with other school problems, financial dependence, performance in the armed forces, vagrancy, somatic complaints, pathological lying, maintenance of social relationships, lack of guilt, and wild behavior in late adolescence.

A control sample of 100 children from the same neighborhood and school district was identified and given the same structured interview as were the graduates of the child guidance clinic.

Children who had been in the clinic were more maladjusted as adults than were the comparison subjects, particularly regarding antisocial behavior. Only 4 percent of the control subjects had shown five or more adult antisocial symptoms, while 45 percent of the clinic group had that many antisocial characteristics. It was not the stigmatization of being a "problem child" that led to later problems but was rather the *nature* and *severity* of the childhood behavior occasioning the referral in the first place. It was the adults who as children had been referred to the clinic for *antisocial behavior* who showed the most difficult adult adjustment. Those who as children had been referred for the miscellaneous problems of temper tantrums, learning problems, speech difficulties, and so forth did not show major antisocial tendencies in adulthood.

The one hundred adults with sociopathic personality from Robins's total group, so diagnosed by psychiatrists on the basis of written materials and structured interviews, had had a chaotic and disturbed childhood. Their childhood histories showed "juvenile theft, incorrigibility, running away from home, truancy, associating with bad companions, sexual activities, staying out late, etc." Most of them were discipline problems in school and had been held back at least one grade by the time they appeared in the clinic. Most of them never even graduated from elementary school. More often than any other type of patient in the child guidance clinic, they were described as aggressive, reckless, impulsive, enuretic, lacking guilt, and lying without cause. It is impulsive, antisocial behavior, rather than fearful and shy behavior, that appears to be the symptom with the most ominous prediction for adult problems.

One of the most distressing elements in the development of behaviorally disturbed children is that their problems seem to carry over from one generation to another. Figure 11.1 shows the scope of family problems reported by a group of sociopathic adults in comparison with a group of average citizens. As studied by Robins (1966) in the thirty-year follow-up, the sociopathic child grows up into unproductive and asocial adult patterns. In their own families 78 percent of this group have already been divorced with a record of high rates of desertion and unfaithfulness in comparison with control samples.

Perhaps more significant are the figures on the level of behavioral problems in the spouse. The spouse in the partnership showed a high incidence of neglect, alcoholism, and desertion relative to the comparison sample, suggesting that unstable and asocial persons tend to pick similar persons to marry. It is also no surprise to see that the problems of the children born into such families are much greater than those found in a comparable control group.

Therefore the problems of asocial and antisocial behavior, unless met vigorously in a child, may well result in the child's growing up

FIGURE 11.1
Family problems of sociopathic adults first seen as sociopathic children

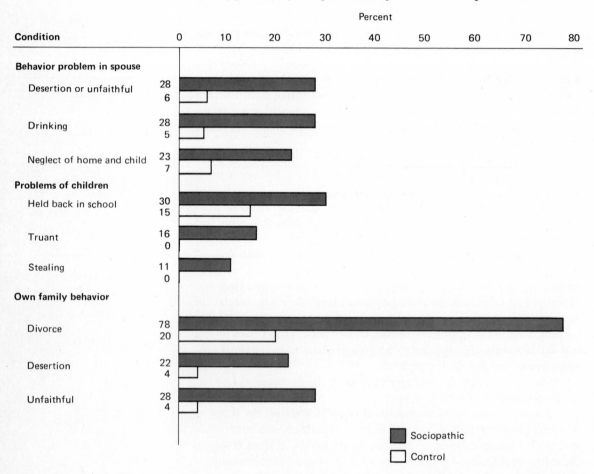

into an antisocial adult who in turn may create a family atmosphere leading to a new generation of antisocial children, and so the cycle will continue.

If the child shows early symptoms of hyperactivity and distractibility, will he or she continue in that vein? Thomas, Chess, and Birch (1968) studied 141 children through the preschool years. Forty-two of those children were seen for behavioral disturbances. Their parents were also counseled. The temperamental traits in the children of either low or high activity, nonadaptability, high intensity, and so forth were consistent over time despite efforts at parental counseling. Children with such disturbances will improve with maturity but, relative to their peer group, will still appear more distractible.

Factors contributing to behavioral disorders

As with many functional disorders, it is difficult to discover "a cause" of a deviant behavioral reaction. We tend to discuss correlates or factors that seem to be occurring consistently with deviant behavior. Two general factors are discussed: (1) physiological factors and (2) environmental factors.

PHYSIOLOGICAL FACTORS IN BEHAVIORAL DISORDERS

Neither psychological factors nor psychosocial factors explain all forms of behavioral deviations. Central nervous system dysfunction is considered by many to be another cause (Wender, 1971). There is probably no question about the role of cerebral dysfunction in some cases of behavioral deviations. In addition to brain dysfunction, many physiological conditions may exist which are not detected and corrected. Physiological factors have sometimes been noted to relate to irritability, lack of school progress, and other conduct disorders.

We have heard a great deal about the term *psychosomatic disturbances,* meaning the effect of the mind on the body. Because of considerable discussion and literature from psychoanalysis, we tend sometimes to forget that there is also a somatopsychological factor—that is, the effect of the body on the mind and the emotions.

Do physiological variables influence behavioral patterns of young children? The complex interactive nature of the child's internal environment and the external world is evident in a study by Waldrop, Pedersen, and Bell (1968). They examined a group of seventy-four intellectually normal children between 2 and 3 years of age who had a set of minor physical symptoms associated with Down's syndrome (mongolism). The number of symptoms was not, however, sufficient to justify a diagnosis of Down's syndrome. Nevertheless, these children showed strong tendencies toward a pattern of hyperactivity. The more symptoms the child showed, the more likely it was that he or she would be aggressive, hyperkinetic, and intractable. So part of this pattern of aggressive behavior traditionally linked to environmental causes or parental handling was clearly associated with physiological factors.

If the parents of such an aggressive child become counteraggressive toward the child in an attempt to control the behavior, an observer could easily reach the conclusion that it was the parental aggressiveness that caused the child's aggressiveness, when it may be just the reverse. Caution is called for before any sizable leap is made to a conclusion, based on observational data alone, as to *what* is causing *what*.

PSYCHOSOCIAL FACTORS RELATED TO BEHAVIORAL DISORDERS

What are the environmental factors that influence the development of deviant patterns of behavior? There are two major, and to some extent opposing, ideas about the basic causes. One school of thought puts the major emphasis on the internal thought processes of the children who have misperceived their problems and their environment and who need help in more accurately assessing themselves and how they influence their sociopsychological environment.

The second major school of thought is that deviant behavior emerges primarily from a social environment that is pathological and creates so few positive options for the child, and so many negative opportunities, that the child is predetermined to emerge with disturbed patterns.

It has been pointed out by some observers (Caplan and Nelson, 1973; Ryan, 1971) that the label *delinquent* in itself focuses the problem on the individual. If the problem lies within the individual, then extensive programs of psychotherapy, behavior modification, and other individual remediation efforts would be the treatment of choice.

If, on the other hand, delinquency is seen as a somewhat normal reaction to a pathological environment, then the treatment of choice would be such strategies as slum clearance and guaranteed annual income, strategies designed to recast the social environment in which the child develops.

Most social scientists and special educators take a somewhat middle view. A poor social environment creates a situation in which the experiences to which the child is exposed are less constructive, and the range of responses that the child has available to him is less extensive. A poor social environment creates a predisposition toward an individual nonadaptive response. Even within highly destructive social situations, however, there are many youngsters who are performing in a socially acceptable fashion and showing that individual patterns of development and response can sometimes overcome an unfavorable social situation.

It is one level of wisdom to say that the social environment influences deviant behavior. It is much more helpful, however, to determine what it is about that environment that is causing such negative influences. We have some clues about possible answers to that question.

One of the dimensions that seems to be influential in shaping the behavioral patterns of children is the phenomenon of modeling or imitating the behavior of others. Bandura (1969) and his associates have conducted a decade of research on the issue of what factors cause children to imitate behavior that they observe, either in person or on TV or in movies. Some of the most relevant conclusions from a series of research studies are:

1. Children who watch aggressive models who are rewarded for their aggressiveness tend to be more aggressive themselves.

2. Children tend to identify with the successful aggressor and find reasons why those who are aggressed against deserve their fate.

3. Children who see models who set high standards and reward themselves sparingly behave in like manner. The behavior of the models is influential in the development of self-control.

4. There is no evidence that viewing violence dissipates aggressive drives and makes a person more healthy (the catharsis hypothesis). Instead a frustrated TV viewer watching violence is more likely to act out violent impulses.

Those findings seem to confirm the work of Whiting (1963) who studied the behavior of children in many different cultures around the world. He concluded that *status envy* is a prime force in the development of personality. A child most envies the person who can withhold the resources he or she values most highly, and the child tries to identify with that person.

When we consider the implications of those results for a social setting that is chaotic, has few positive models, and tends to reward the aggressor, then it seems understandable that such areas as urban slums will produce many children who are aggressive and antisocial and who have little interest in delayed gratification that children from the more traditional middle-class culture can accept. Also, when one is a member of a social minority group and feels that that group is an outcast in the more general society, then predictable feelings of alienation develop.

Seeman (1967) describes the elements of alienation, or seeing oneself as apart from the general society. Such feelings predominate in minority groups who feel little loyalty or attachment to the general culture that they perceive has exploited them. Such feelings nourish many of the social delinquents described previously by Jenkins and Hewett.

1. Powerlessness. The person who experiences a sense of powerlessness expects outside forces to control personal and social rewards. Such a person has little expectancy that his or her own behavior can be useful in gaining those rewards.

2. Meaninglessness. The individual regards social affairs as incomprehensible and has little hope of ever being able to predict the outcome of social events.

3. Normlessness. The individual believes that he or she is not bound by conventional standards of conduct in the pursuit of goals. Normlessness implies a high expectancy that socially unapproved means must be used to achieve those goals.

4. Value isolation. The individual rejects the values of society and assigns low value to the goals and behavior highly valued by most other members of society.

5. Self-estrangement. The individual is continuously engaged in activities that he or she does not value highly (that is, school or a boring job).

Any child or adolescent growing up with that cluster of feelings is a fine candidate for behavioral deviation as that term is defined by the majority culture, which always sets the rules and expectations for that society.

FACTORS CONTRIBUTING TO FEARFUL-WITHDRAWN CHILDREN

The reasons for the emergence of the chronically fearful and unhappy child are less apparent than the origins of aggression. Aggression is more easily understood in terms of the type of frustration-aggression hypothesis originally presented by Miller and Dollard (1941); that is, the more frustrating the circumstances in which the individual is placed, the greater the chance for aggression. Two major theoretical positions, not totally different from one another, concerning the origin of the fearful or withdrawn child can be considered.

One explanation that has received general acceptance adopts the conditioning model presented by Pavlov (1928), Skinner (1953), Hull

(1947), and others. In this model the withdrawn child has received no reinforcement to any attempt to react to a given stimulus. No matter what the reaction of the fearful child has been, there has been unsatisfactory and painful reaction from the surrounding environment. Faced with a frustrating situation (for example, a strange animal), a child might first try to attack the frustrating object without success, might then cry and receive no response nor even punishment from parents, and might try to run away and be restrained and shamed. In short, the child uses up the repertoire of responses and finds none of them effective or useful. It is predictable from this theory that such unpleasant stimuli reinforce the tendency to withdraw from interaction or contact with the environment, thus continuing a state of anxiety about what will happen next.

One of the key elements in that theory is that once substantially unpleasant stimuli have been perceived in conjunction with certain interrelationships (let us say experiences with authority figures), there is a tendency to withdraw from those relationships. This withdrawal may effectively keep the child from testing similar experiences again and thus from ever knowing that the current authority figures (teachers) are not as fearful as the original one on which the withdrawal response was based (parents). Thus, for example, an early catastrophic experience with men (say, an unfortunate relationship with father) will cause some girls to avoid all men and never be able to differentiate one man from another ("all men are alike" approach).

A different answer to the origin of fearfulness emerges from the Freudian theory, which assumes that the child passes through a variety of stages of development on the way to maturity. If there are breakdowns in the essential family relationships necessary to progress through these stages, then conditions are generated for the creation of neurotic symptoms that can prevent the child from maturing into a healthy adult. For example, the male child is supposed to progress through the stage at which he wishes to replace the father (the Oedipus complex) to a stage of identification with, and acquisition of, the characteristics of the feared and respected adult of the same sex. If there is an especially brutal or cruel relationship between father and son, the boy can never really adopt the characteristics of the father but must live in fear that the father will take revenge on him for his unacceptable impulses to replace the father in relationship to the mother.

Non-Freudian therapists place less emphasis on psychosexual development and more on general interactions with the social environment as the basis for emotional problems (see Erickson, 1950; Sullivan, 1953). The emphasis on progression through stages remains, however, as does the language of psychoanalysis. For example, *regression* is the retreat to an earlier state of development; *fixation* is remaining at a given stage beyond the time expected. Those terms suggest that there have been psychic or emotional barriers that have arrested the normal progress of the child.

The psychiatric perspectives supplied by those two terms suppose a breakdown in the normal relationships expected of the child and seem to be supported by research evidence. For example, Jenkins (1966) studied five hundred cases from the Michigan Child Guidance Institute. He related clusters of behaviors to certain types of home environments. The shy, seclusive, inhibited child tended to come from a family in which both parents were present, there was little feeling of rejection, and the mother was not hostile toward the child. In the neurotic, overanxious group many of the mothers were considered neurotic. The aggressive delinquents tended to come from neglected homes and poor neighborhoods.

Maccoby and Masters (1970) in reviewing the vast literature on the relationship of parental behavior to child behavior concluded: "There is evidence that dependency is associated not with warmth but with its polar opposite, rejection or hostility" (p. 140).

The parent who withdraws love and affection creates panic in the child; the child reacts in the way that has got affection in the past; the child becomes dependent. Thus the strategy of being cold and distant that the parent adopts to try to "cure" the child of dependency actually increases the likelihood that dependency behavior will occur.

Historical perspectives

Over the past century and a half we have undergone striking changes in our views of emotionally disturbed children. Hoffman (1972) reported four separate stages of societal viewpoint and action toward the emotionally disturbed. The pioneering efforts of Dorothea Dix in Massachusetts in the 1840s led to the building of institutions for the severely emotionally disturbed and delinquent children. In a period of optimism stimulated by the early work of Seguin and Howe, there was a feeling that proper care could *cure* these difficult problems. However, limitations in budget and staff soon turned the schools for delinquents into punitive institutions and the reform schools into detention centers.

At the turn of the century compulsory attendance laws brought into the public schools, and kept in the schools, many youngsters who previously would have been expelled or allowed to drop out. That situation led to a major effort to develop special classes and special schools for the disturbed child.

One of the first examples of a special school was the New Haven

Ungraded School for Mischievous and Disruptive Children, established in 1871. It was followed by similar programs in a large number of urban centers. There remains a major question as to whether the disruptive children were removed in order to provide them with a constructive program or whether their removal was mainly stimulated by the desire to get them out of the regular program so that the nondisruptive children could then learn with less distraction and disturbance.

The third major development followed World War I. It was the origin of the multidisciplinary team approach to children with emotional or social maladjustment. Such organizations as the Bureau for Child Guidance in New York City were created and brought together the professional skills of school psychologists, social workers, psychiatrists, and guidance personnel. There was a gradual increase in special class programs for disturbed and maladjusted children, but the classes existed in only one-third of the states. They were often known as disciplinary classes, and among the prime requisites of a teacher in such a program were the physical build and attitude of a professional football player.

Following World War II, another substantial increase in programs for emotionally disturbed children was noted in the public schools. In the 1960s federal legislation resulted in a sharp increase in well-trained personnel, in model programs, and in research to find the best and most constructive learning environment for disturbed and impulsive children.

We are now entering into yet another era in which the emphasis is on integration of the child with normal children for a major part of the school day (mainstreaming) and on the provision of special services in the form of itinerant, resource room, or crisis teachers.

Educational strategies

Although at one time the preferred treatment for children with behavioral and emotional difficulty (CBED) was psychiatric, there has been a shift in emphasis and responsibility from psychiatry to education. Several conditions have influenced this change. In the first place, only a small proportion of the children who need help can be treated by psychiatrists, psychologists, or social workers. In the second place, the results of treatment in clinics and residential institutions led many within the psychiatric profession to call on the schools to assume the major responsibility. As a result, the bulk of responsibility has shifted from (1) the medical or mental health professions as the responsible agents for treatment, using teachers as ancillary personnel, to (2) the schools as the responsible agents for treatment, with the ancillary assistance of psychiatrists, psychologists, and social workers.

As the schools increased their responsibility for the education and treatment of children with behavioral disorders, it was necessary to modify or develop strategies for the organization of programs and teaching procedures for the heterogenous group of children variously labeled as behaviorally disordered, emotionally disturbed, socially maladjusted, and maladapted.

A wide variety of curricular changes, teaching techniques, and environmental variations have been tried with CBED. Some of the major educational strategies that have developed are described briefly in the following paragraphs.

PSYCHODYNAMIC STRATEGIES

The basic philosophy of the psychodynamic approach is "know the truth and it shall set you free." The prime objective is to help children become aware of their own needs, desires, and fears. Long, Morse, and Newman (1971) explain the psychodynamic approach as follows:

> Freud's theory might be called an education theory. The therapist is a teacher. His subject matter is the patient himself; his curriculum is the patient's past experience, present world and unconscious feelings. The methods used to help the patient gain awareness, insight, and consequent change, while set down by Freud in specific terms for treating adult neurotics have been modified or altered according to the empirical or convictional information gained by treating not only neurotic adults but also psychotics and criminals, as well as children suffering from emotional illnesses. (p. 158)

Anna Freud (1954), the daughter of Sigmund Freud, did much to popularize the use of psychoanalytic techniques with children. She devoted her own career as a child psychiatrist to extending her father's basic concepts into this area.

Proponents of the psychodynamic or medical model place heavy emphasis on psychiatric procedures such as diagnosis, treatment, decision making, and evaluation, which place the educator in an ancillary role. Maladaptive behavior is viewed as symptomatic of intrapsychic conflict involving the id, the ego, and the superego. The focus of treatment is to remove the "underlying cause" for the behavior. It is believed that the removal of a symptom, for example, aggressive behavior, without alleviating the cause will result in the substitution of another symptom, perhaps one more maladaptive than the first.

The underlying causes are said to originate in traumatic childhood events and conflicts, which are subsequently repressed. Sexual feelings and conflict are considered to be particular sources of difficulty. Treatment focuses on analysis of the unconscious and the interpretation of symptoms and dreams in an effort on the part of the patient to develop insight. Insight along with a positive transference relationship with the therapist is considered essential for the type of personality reorganization that takes place during psychotherapy.

The major emphasis is on treatment through psychotherapy with educational aspects as secondary, although acceptance by the child and the establishment of a positive interpersonal relationship between the pupil and teacher are considered essential (Berkowitz and Rothman, 1960).

Some of the later adaptations of the Freudian approach have focused more on relationship therapy, the basic attention being applied not on past but on current feelings and on the consequences of the reactions of the child within his or her environment. These neoanalytic approaches still employ professional personnel other than the teacher (that is, psychiatrists) as the key treatment source.

During the past decade the psychoanalytic approach has lost popularity as a preferred method of dealing with CBED. It is so expensive in cost and personnel, requiring extraordinarily well-trained professionals, that its continued use would be made desirable only by its clearly demonstrated superiority. Sagor (1974) reports that there is only one psychiatrist for every 18,000 citizens in this country.

PSYCHOEDUCATIONAL STRATEGY

The focus of the psychoeducational approach is on the educational setting and the child's reaction and performance within that setting, as opposed to therapy that takes place when the child is removed from that setting.

In the psychoeducational strategy the child is viewed as possessing an innate biological potential, which, in combination with early experiences, determines the child's self-concept, aspirations, and the manner in which he or she copes with reality and tension. On entering school the child is expected to possess certain social and readiness skills that will allow him or her to perform in a prescribed manner acceptable to school, home, and society.

Failure of the child to meet certain externally imposed demands will result in internal anxiety and frustration, which lead directly to maladaptive behavior. If the teacher, peers, or both counter with hostile, rejecting responses, anxiety and frustration are increased, leading eventually to a school crisis.

Long (1974) presents a conflict cycle to introduce those concepts to the teacher.

1. A child in conflict views the classroom through the eyes of his life history.
2. A child in conflict has learned to be vulnerable to specific school tasks (i.e., competition, separation, etc.).
3. Acceptance of positive and negative feelings within and between children is normal, healthy and necessary to a fulfilling life.
4. Each child has been socialized to process feelings by direct expression, defense mechanisms, or coping techniques.
5. Under severe stress, a child in conflict will regress from coping techniques, to defensive techniques, and to primitive expressions of feelings.
6. The problem behavior of a child in conflict represents his present solution to stress, although it may cause difficulties with adults, peers, learning, rules, and self.
7. A child in conflict creates feelings and behaviors in others (peers and adults) which almost always perpetuate his problem.
8. The child's awareness and skills in perpetuating negative environmental reaction to his behavior justifies his conviction that it is not safe to change his view of the world or himself. In other words, he has been successful in maintaining his self-fulfillment prophecy of himself and his world. (p. 182)

The goal of intervention is to interrupt that cycle. Some of the factors that should be examined in an attempt to reach the goal include: (1) the nature of the demands and pressures placed on the child, (2) the ability of the child to meet those demands, (3) peer group relations, (4) pupil-teacher relations, (5) the youngster's motivation for the behavior, and (6) the child's self-concept. For example, the task in which the child is involved may contain the seeds of acute frustration. The child who feels inferior in academic pursuits may try to compensate by exhibiting his or her fighting ability. To ignore those factors may result in improper handling and increased frustration for the child (Morse, 1965).

On the other hand, the child must be taught to maintain behavior within acceptable limits. Long and Newman (1976) have described four alternatives to behavior that may be used by the teacher.

1. *Preventive planning.* The creation of a hygienic environment will allow the child to bring his or her behavior under control.
2. *Permitting.* Certain types of behavior should be sanctioned by the teacher at times, such as running and shouting on the playground.
3. *Tolerating.* The teacher should tolerate the behavior because

it is temporarily beyond the child's ability to control; but it is explained to the child that improvement is expected.

4. *Interrupting.* The teacher should interfere with a behavior sequence for the protection of the child, for the protection of others in the class, or for the protection of ongoing classroom activities.

Coping skills that the child lacks can also be taught by proper handling and the skillful use of the life-space interview (Redl, 1971). The life-space interview is designed to deal with the child's feelings while he or she is in the midst of a crisis (for example, attacking another child), pointing out what influence his or her behavior is having on the situation. This immediate attempt to help the child gain insight is more likely to be effective than would be a discussion of the incident in a therapy session a week later when the incident is a memory and the child's rationalizations have solidified.

Proponents of the psychoeducational approach view acceptance of the child (but not the deviant behavior) and positive, interpersonal adult-child relationships as essential for effective treatment.

An advantage of the psychoeducational model is that it can be organized and implemented within the scope of the school's responsibility. The teacher is not left on the sidelines as an observer but is considered an integral part of a team with much decision-making responsibility.

Some suggested changes in the instructional materials are also called for with CBED, with major criteria for selection being enrichment, interest, and achievement flexibility (McNeil, 1972). On the assumption that problems of impulsiveness and overreaction are due to past failures, the tasks should be designed to be short with success easily identified, as with jigsaw puzzles. High-interest and low-vocabulary readers are other examples of devices to stir motivation, whereas task flexibility allows the teacher to come up quickly with something that will interest the child and be closely linked to the child's current skill level.

BEHAVIOR MODIFICATION STRATEGY

The proponents of behavior modification view all behavior, maladaptive as well as adaptive, as learned. Unlike the psychodynamic workers who see behavioral disorders as symptoms of intrapsychic conflict that must be uncovered, analyzed, and treated, the behaviorist views the manifest behavior as the problem that must be dealt with. While the behaviorists admit that complex historical events determine behavior, they do not believe the reconstruction of the past is necessary to effect successfully a change in behavior. Wolpe, Salter, and Renya (1965) have described the different kinds of therapies that have been used by applying the principles of *respondent* and *operant conditioning.*

According to Bijou (1976), *respondent* behaviors are those behaviors that are sensitive to preceding stimulus events and insensitive to consequences such as an eye blink. Respondent conditioning, which pairs a neutral stimulus with eliciting stimulus, is classical conditioning. The classical experiments illustrating respondent conditioning of fear in a child paired a rabbit with a loud noise, which the child already fears. After these stimuli are presented together a number of times, the child begins to show a fear reaction when only the rabbit is presented *without* the loud noise.

The treatment of fears, phobias, and other emotional reactions is accomplished by extinguishing the fear response through pairing the rabbit, for example, with a pleasant stimulus, such as candy, to which the child responds positively (without crying). This is done gradually with the rabbit at a distance at first, gradually bringing it closer until the child may be petting it. This is called *respondent extinction.*

Operants, on the other hand, function through controlling the stimuli that *follow* the responses. For example, a child sucks his or her thumb when watching television. The mother arranges to press a button that will turn off the television when the thumb is in the mouth and turn on the television when it is not. Soon the child learns not to indulge in thumb sucking in order to keep the television on.

In that situation the operant (thumb sucking) is controlled by the stimulus (television off) that follows. Operant conditioning is based on the principle that behavior is a function of its consequence. The application of a positive stimulus (television on) immediately following a response is called positive reinforcement; the withdrawal of a positive stimulus (television off) constitutes punishment.

The principles of operant conditioning have been applied extensively to the control of the behavior of children with behavioral disorders. This is accomplished by first making a functional analysis of behavior, or specifying what behaviors are to be changed. One common behavior of concern to teachers is a child's failure to work on lessons because he or she is constantly jumping up, bothering others, and running around the room on one excuse or another. To shape the behavior in a classroom would require the teacher to provide step-by-step lessons the child can do seated and then to reinforce that acceptable behavior.

Ordinarily teachers pay attention to children when they are out of their seats disrupting others, and ignore them when they are working quietly. Such teacher behavior may actually reinforce disruptive student behavior. To change such a situation the teacher must positively reinforce the child for doing lessons and staying seated.

Sometimes social approval by the teacher for appropriate behavior is sufficient. She praises the child for working at his or her seat and ignores the child when out of the seat. If that tactic does not work, a tangible reward (candy or something else desirable) is given every time the child is seated and working. Marks or tokens given for the completion of a particular task or for other appropriate behavior may be cashed in at a later time for some reward. The teacher may also openly praise another child for staying seated and disregard the problem child's wandering around the classroom.

The use of behavior modification techniques with special behavioral problems is often objected to on the basis of the techniques' being too mechanistic, treating the child like a slot machine (insert the token, get good behavior) and, as a result, having little impact on the child's basic personality. Such criticisms are more than a little unfair. Although some of the original techniques do assume a simple conditioning model, the educational objective is to create a positive response in the child that can be expanded and used for better overall social adjustment.

For example, Gallagher (1972) described an attempt to develop better social interaction skills in a group of emotionally disturbed children.

> Six emotionally disturbed children received frequent reinforcement during their first hour of scheduled short work periods. If one hour of work was completed the children also received orange juice and vanilla wafers. Initially the children ate vigorously and talked simultaneously . . . as the school months elapsed the children ate smaller portions of the snack and monitored their own conversations. . . . Several months later all the students were participating very appropriately in conversation and generally refusing the food. . . . The extrinsic consequence, food, gradually shifted into a very natural consequence, the enjoyment of conversation with friends. (p. 307)

In other words, the token or food rewards are designed as a bridge to encourage responses that, when established, make the extrinsic rewards unnecessary.

The usual procedure in behavior modification or shaping in the classroom is to establish goals and organize the tasks in small steps so that the child can experience continuous success. This procedure is referred to as *task analysis*. The child can then receive positive reinforcement for each step or part of the total task as it is completed (arithmetic, reading, or spelling, for example). School assignments are presented to the child programmed in easy steps. As the child completes a task that can be accomplished successfully in a specified period of time, the teacher checks the work, praises the child (social reinforcement), and gives him or her a mark, a grade, a token, or some other tangible reinforcement. In that way the child is able to work at assignments for longer and longer periods and to accept increasingly more difficult ones.

Programmed learning materials and teaching machines utilize operant-conditioning techniques and rely heavily on positive reinforcement through knowledge of results. The children are helped to succeed at each step by prompting and confirmation. The main responsibilities of a teacher as a behavior modifier are (1) to delineate specifically the behavior or behaviors that are considered maladaptive, (2) to determine the situations or environmental events that are sustaining or reinforcing this maladaptive behavior, and (3) to restructure the environment of the child to modify, change, or alter the maladaptive behavior.

Figure 11.2 shows the type of record keeping that is an essential part of the behavior modification technique (Kroth, Whelan, and Stables, 1972). The child's program is divided into before, during, and after intervention phases. The teacher first establishes a base line, the performance of the child before treatment is begun. In this case the child completed only about four of twenty problems assigned over a ten-day period. The teacher, having previously noticed that the child liked to play with a puppet in free time, made a contract with the child providing that if the problems were completed during the allotted time, the child would have twenty minutes of free time to play with the puppet.

Figure 11.2 shows the dramatic change in constructive behavior that followed the establishment of the contract. On day 23 the teacher decided to test the stability of the new pattern of behavior and collected seven days of data on what happened after the reward of the puppet play was no longer used.

The results shown in the figure are fairly typical. The rate of performance decreased somewhat but did not fall back to the previous base line performance. In other words, the treatment maintained much of its effect, probably strengthened by the increased self-concept of the child for the demonstrably improved performance. If the intervention period was maintained somewhat longer, then the reduction in performance after intervention would likely be somewhat less. This technique can clearly be utilized by regular or special classroom teachers with a little additional effort and planning and can provide the tangible record of improvement so important to both the student and teacher.

Axelrod (1971) has reported on a variety of studies using token reinforcement, the use of marks or poker chips to be exchanged later for tangible rewards such as candy. The studies were almost unanimous in suggesting that token reinforcement does produce clearly favorable changes in the behavior of children within the classroom.

Hewett (1968) is the principal advocate of the developmental strategy
for the education of children with behavior disorders. He has established an educational program that is primarily a behavior modification procedure with a developmental sequence of seven educational
goals. These developmental sequences are (1) attention, (2) response,

FIGURE 11.2

*Effects of a child-teacher contract for completion of arithmetic skill problems.
Contract specified that child could earn time to play with a puppet if problems
were completed within thirty minutes.*

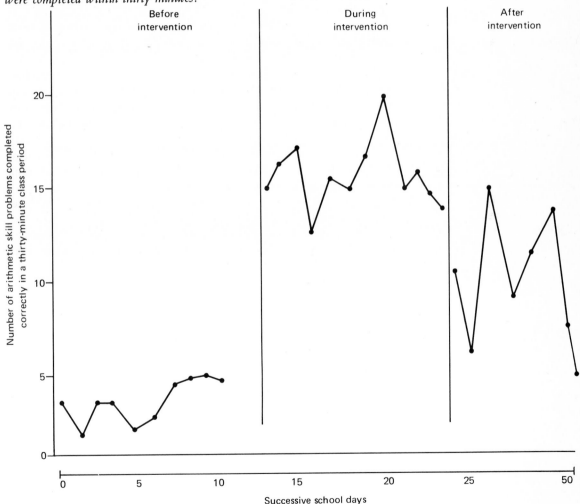

Source: From Kroth, Whelan, and Stables, 1972.

(3) order, (4) exploratory, (5) social, (6) mastery, and (7) achievement. In Hewett's own words (1967), the developmental strategy

> hypothesizes that in order for successful living to occur, the child must pay attention, respond, follow directions, freely and accurately explore the environment, and function appropriately in relation to others. It further hypothesizes that the learning of these behaviors occurs during the normal course of development from infancy to school age, and failure to learn any or all of them may preclude the child's being ready for school. For such a child they constitute the "somethings" he must learn in the process of getting ready for school while he is actually there. (p. 42)

To assist the teacher in moving the child up the hierarchy from attention to achievement, Hewett (1967) has organized what he considers to be the three essential ingredients for effective teaching: (1) selection of a suitable task, (2) selection of a meaningful reward following accomplishment of that task, and (3) maintenance of a degree of structure under the control of the teacher.

Hewett has implemented his approach in what he calls the "engineered classroom." The engineered classroom is divided into work sections corresponding to levels on the developmental hierarchy. There are three areas in the classroom: (1) the mastery center, (2) the order center, and (3) the exploratory center.

The mastery center is designed for mastery and achievement tasks primarily in academic fields. The order center is designed to train children to follow directions, complete assignments, and control their behavior. The exploratory center is used for science, art, and communication activities.

The role of the teacher in Hewett's engineered class is to assign the child to the appropriate center and give tasks he or she needs to learn, is ready to learn, and can successfully complete. The teacher rewards the child by the use of a check-mark system. The child receives two check marks for starting the assigned task or activity, three for completion of the task, and up to five for "being a student." One child may receive check marks for writing his or her name and another for writing an essay. Rewards are individualized for each child, depending on particular abilities. The teacher gives the marks with an explanation: "You get two marks because you completed four arithmetic problems," "because you paid attention," and so forth.

It is at that point that Hewett departs from the strict behavior modification strategy. Being reinforced for being "a student" is quite different from being reinforced for progress toward some specific goal behavior. In Hewett's model reinforcement continues even if the child has a bad day and regresses somewhat. The child is not penalized for maladaptive behavior on one level if he or she can stabilize behavior on another. For that reason assignments are quickly changed at the first sign of maladaptive behavior on any assigned task.

Proponents of a strict behavior modification model would contend that removing a child from a demanding task and assigning him or her to a less demanding one while continuing to reward behavior would actually constitute rewarding inappropriate behavior. They suggest that children may misbehave in an attempt to be assigned to more rewarding, less frustrating activity. Hewett (1967) contends that this phenomenon has seldom occurred because teachers anticipate such problems and attempt to control them by limiting the amount of mastery work given and by assigning the child to alternate centers before behavior becomes disruptive.

Hewett (1968) compared engineered classrooms with classrooms using the same materials and schedule but not on a behavior modification check-mark system. Although the results slightly favored the developmental behavior modification classes, Hewett concluded that "the engineered classroom design appears basically a launching technique for initiating learning with children who often fail to 'get off the ground' in school. It does not appear to be essential in its present form for more than one semester with many children" (p. 333).

Hewett (1974) has presented an advanced version of his engineered classroom, which he labeled the Madison Plan after the school system that adopted it. In this plan the child with behavior problems starts in the original engineered classroom and graduates through two different settings before continuing into the regular classroom. After responding to the engineered classroom, the child progresses to a small teacher group setting emphasizing social and language training and then finally to a large teacher class setting with emphasis on the mastery level.

This gradual progression is typical of the special education strategy that small and gradual steps are the best strategy to insure that a successful movement back to the regular class will be made. A leap from the engineered class directly to the regular class would often be too sudden and sharp a change, and the child could easily regress to past inadequate adaptive habits.

THE LEARNING DISABILITY STRATEGY

The proponents of this strategy maintain that a specific learning disability creates a discrepancy between the capacity of the individual to behave and the requirements of the school environment, or between the child's ability in one area and what the child and others expect because of his or her ability in other areas. The discrepancy results in frustration, conduct and personality problems, and sometimes in school truancy and delinquency. The child might strike out against the situation by becoming hostile and aggressive or might withdraw. As indicated in Chapter 8, the correlates of a specific learning disability are physical, environmental, psychological, or a combination of these.

Research reviewed earlier has indicated that a sizable portion of the children in schools and classes for the emotionally disturbed are retarded educationally and that a number of them can be classified as learning disabled. How many of the emotional problems can be ascribed to the learning disability or how much of the learning disability can be ascribed to the emotional problems in an individual case is difficult to determine. Generally it is a vicious circle in which one affects the other.

The learning disability strategy is employed as an attempt to remove or modify the objectionable behavior through establishing a better self-concept by successful experience in academic subjects through the remediation of the disability.

The link between learning disabilities and delinquency has been assumed by many. Mauser (1974) has reviewed the literature and has pointed out similarities such as (1) both the learning disabled and the juvenile delinquent evidence negative self-concept and low frustration tolerance, (2) males outnumber females in both learning disabilities and delinquency four to one, (3) there is some evidence of the greater occurrence of brain dysfunction in both groups than in the general population, and (4) both groups have difficulty in school beginning in the first grade.

Murray (1976), in an extensive survey for the Law Enforcement Assistance Administration, found that adjudicated delinquents are significantly retarded educationally. On the basis of the discrepancy between ability and achievement, many of them could be classified as learning disabled. The link between delinquency and learning disabilities continues to be questionable. To quote Murray's conclusion: "As of the end of 1975: The existence of a causal relationship between learning disabilities and delinquency has not been established; the evidence for a causal link is feeble" (p. 65).

The learning disability strategy has been used with CBED and bears directly on the remediation of the specific disability: language, reading, writing, spelling, thinking, perceiving, and others. Effective remediation tends to decrease conduct and personality problems by assisting the child in decreasing the discrepancy between capacity to perform and the requirements of society (Kirk, 1934).

The reader is referred to Chapter 8 for a discussion of learning disabilities and the strategies used for the diagnosis and remediation of them. Suffice it to say that classes and programs for children with learning disabilities contain many children with emotional problems and that many classes for the CBED contain children with learning disabilities. Most programs for emotionally disturbed children, using any of the other strategies discussed, include provisions for remediation of learning disabilities.

The relationship of learning disabilities and behavioral disorders tends to be combined in current books. For example, Stephens (1977) entitled his book *Teaching Skills to Children with Learning and Behavior Disorders;* Shea (1978) entitled his book *Teaching Children and Youth with Behavior Disorders* but devoted most of it to learning disabilities and their diagnosis and treatment as a teaching method for behavioral disorders.

THE ECOLOGICAL STRATEGY

Proponents of the ecological strategy believe that a total redefinition of the nature of social pathology is required. Rhodes (1967) states:

> In this alternative view of disturbance it is suggested that the nucleus of the problem lies in the content of behavioral prohibitions and sanctions in the culture. Any behavior which departs significantly from this lore upsets those who have carefully patterned their behavior according to cultural specifications. The subsequent agitated exchange between *culture violator* and *culture bearer* creates a disturbance in the environment. It is this reciprocal product which engages attention and leads to subsequent action. (p. 449)

The proponents of the ecological model are critical of those interventions that deal with the child alone, assuming that the behavioral disorders are the exclusive property of the child. Psychotherapy and behavior modification assume that the target is the child, and it is the child who must change or adjust to the environment. The ecological model, on the other hand, proposes that human problems result from an agitated transaction between the excitor (the child) and the responder (the environment—family, siblings, teachers, children, and others). The behavior disorder is a point of misfit between the child and his or her environment.

Culture-violating behavior becomes upsetting to surrounding individuals when its message is received and recognized under the overlay of sanctions and prohibitions that the responding individuals have acquired from the storehouse of the culture (Rhodes, 1967).

THE RE-ED PROGRAM. Hobbs (1970) and his colleagues have implemented the ecological strategy with programs for emotionally disturbed children called *Re-Ed* (a project for the re-education of emotionally disturbed children). As indicated earlier, the ecological approach rejects reliance on psychotherapy and assumes that "the child is an inseparable part of a small social system, of an ecological unit made up of the child, his family, his school, his neighborhood and community."

Two residential schools in the Re-Ed program were organized to house approximately forty children each, ages 6 to 12. The plan was to re-educate these children for a short period of time (four to six months) and at the same time, through a liaison teacher, to modify the attitudes of the home, the school, and the community. The entire program was oriented toward re-establishing the child as quickly as possible in his or her own home, school, and community. The general program of re-education follows a number of principles, explained by Hobbs as follows:

1. *Life is to be lived now.* This was accomplished by occupying children every hour of the day in purposeful activities, and in activities in which they could succeed.
2. *Time is an ally.* Some children improve with the passage of time. But a child should not remain in a residential setting for long periods since this length of time may estrange him from his family. Six months in the residential center was the stated goal of Re-Ed.
3. *Trust is essential.* Trust, according to Hobbs, is not learned in college courses, but some of those working with emotionally disturbed children "know, without knowing they know, the way to inspire trust in children."
4. *Competence makes a difference.* The arrangement of the environment and learning tasks must be so structured that the child is able to obtain confidence and self-respect from his successes.
5. *Symptoms can and should be controlled.* The treatment of symptoms instead of attempting to use the medical model of treating causes is emphasized.
6. *Cognitive control can be taught.* This is accomplished by immediate experience, by the moment-to-moment know-how, and day-to-day relationship between the teacher and the child.
7. *Feelings should be nurtured.* Situations are arranged with animals and people to allow the child to show affection or other feelings.
8. *The group is important to the children.* Children in Re-Ed are organized in groups of eight with two counselor-teachers for each group. Discussions of difficulties or sharing experiences develop the kind of human relations to which these children are unaccustomed.
9. *Ceremony and ritual give order, stability, and confidence.* Rituals and ceremonies, like a nightly backrub or being a member of a club, or a Christmas pageant, serve a major purpose.
10. *The body is the armature of the self.* This is accomplished through the physical activities of swimming, climbing, clay modeling, etc.

11. *Communities are important.* Activities to give the child a sense of responsibility to the community such as trips to fire departments, etc., are provided by Re-Ed. In addition, a liaison teacher could prepare the family, school, and community for the return of the child to the community.

12. *Finally, a child should know joy.* In Re-Ed the counselor-teacher arranges for each child to recognize joy each day and to anticipate joy the next day. (p. 302)

A comprehensive follow-up evaluation of a special program has been conducted on Project Re-Ed by Weinstein (1974). The progress of these children was compared with the progress of children who had comparable emotional problems but were not in the Re-Ed program, and with a group of "normal" children of similar age and background.

The comparison of the three groups of children six months and eighteen months after they had been through the residential education treatment program showed that the treated children had more positive self-concepts and greater confidence in their ability to control their own situations than did the untreated children. The Re-Ed children were judged by their teachers to be better adjusted than the untreated children both academically and socially. Although the Re-Ed students were doing better than the disturbed children who were not treated, the Re-Ed graduates continued to show more maladjustment on all measures than the group of children designated as normal.

In other words, the treatment program did not create normal children out of disturbed children but merely reduced the level of their disturbance by a significant degree. It is always worthwhile to be cautious about the effects of treatment and not to give the impression that treatment, even when clearly superior, will completely transform the exceptional child to a normal child.

OPEN EDUCATION PROGRAM. Knoblock (1973) presented an open education therapeutic setting for emotionally disturbed children. The open education program with its freedom and flexibility provides a setting in which the child can act out feelings and the trained teacher can immediately react to them. Children who have conflict with authority and who have a continuing battle with a structured program can work out their feelings with an adult who is nonauthoritarian in an environment that does not create a constant excuse for battles with authority.

Knoblock points out that the open education program requires decisions on the part of the child and also allows the child to exert a degree of control over his or her own environment. Both features, in turn, provide a more constructive ego development since disturbed

children have negative self-concepts and feelings of inadequacy. Knoblock appears to be addressing the problems of the withdrawn child rather than the behaviorally disruptive child in recommending this particular setting.

One general rule that might stand the test of application is that withdrawn and inhibited children need the opportunity to expand and express themselves and to try out new behavior styles. Behaviorally disruptive children need to have environmental controls so that their own impulsive behavior does not carry them away and create a large variety of secondary problems.

The use of drugs

One of the most recent developments in the treatment of emotionally disturbed children has been the use of drugs designed to modify the impulsive or inattentive behavior typical of emotionally disturbed children. Wender (1971) and Haslam and Valletutti (1975), in summarizing studies on the use of drugs, state that the most common drugs used with hyperactive children are Dexedrine and Ritalin and that 60 to 80 percent of children using them have favorable responses in relation to attention span, reduction of hyperactivity, and temperament.

In one study (Sprague, Barnes, and Werry, 1970), twelve preadolescent children in a special education class for disturbed children were used in a comparison of drug effectiveness. A stimulant (methylphenidate) and a tranquilizer (thioridazine) were given children who had previously been observed under conditions of no drug administration. In laboratory learning tasks the methylphenidate improved learning performance on the part of the children, while thioridazine decreased learning performance.

These children were also observed in the classroom. Observations corroborated the findings from the laboratory that methylphenidate, the stimulant, increased attention to schoolwork and improved the quality of the child's behavior that day as rated by the teacher. Attention can apparently be improved by the addition of a stimulant.

Millichap (1977) has summarized the medication used for hyperactivity, which he includes under learning disabilities, and concludes:

1. Certain medications, particularly the central nervous system stimulants, are of proven value in the management of a high percentage of children with learning disabilities.

2. Drugs should be employed as adjuncts to remedial education and not solely for the control of hyperactive and impulsive behavior.
3. The response to drug therapy should be monitored by objective perceptual tests in addition to teacher and parent questionnaires.
4. The dosage should be kept to the minimum required to facilitate learning and adjusted to the needs of the individual child.

Treatment for seriously disturbed children

The treatment of seriously disturbed children such as autistic and schizophrenic children is likely to take place in a special school or hospital setting. As the condition improves, it would be expected that most such children could adjust in a special class program in the public schools or exist for a part of the day in the regular program with help and assistance from the resource teacher.

Providing an effective remedial program for an autistic child who neither receives communication nor gives it is a special challenge. Autistic children have serious memory problems, auditory perception problems, no developed language, and minimum social skills. If they show interest in anything at all, it is in things such as rock collections and mechanical gadgets rather than in people. Hargrove and Swisher (1975) found, for example, that autistic children gave a consistently higher percentage of correct verbal responses when pictures had been paired with a machine that provides a voice stimulus than when paired with a live voice. Autistic children's obsession with order (having toys in just the same place every day) has frequently been noted by a number of observers. Such children may have temper tantrums if toys and bedclothes, for example, have been rearranged in any way.

Those are the raw materials with which therapy must begin. Prior to the emergence of behavior modification or operant-conditioning techniques, therapy was not very effective since other therapies are based on the willingness or ability of the child to communicate or respond in some way with the therapist.

Most treatment programs are based on the proposition that the first task is to develop a response repertoire that allows the child to begin to interact with his or her environment. As Wing and Wing (1966) state:

> It is possible to teach an autistic child to hug his father when he comes home from work, to kiss his mother, to form his mouth into a smile, to say "please" and "thank you," to have reasonable table manners, and not steal packets of detergent from the supermarket without

the child understanding why he has to behave in such ways. This, of course, is how a normal child learns to behave socially, except that much of it happens spontaneously by imitation at an earlier age. (p. 194)

Hewett (1965) developed a step-by-step procedure for treating autistic children starting at the most primitive level and gradually progressing. He used food rewards to condition the youngsters to *eye contact* with another human being. Following that basic achievement, he then moved to a phase of *social imitation* in which the child would imitate gestures and hand movements. He then moved to the use of *expressive language* to obtain food reinforcement and finally to *transfer these expressive skills* to other social situations. In that way Hewett demonstrated how to work with a mute 5-year-old to build a thirty-two-word working vocabulary for the child. Other attempts have utilized sign language, similar to that used by deaf children, as an alternative communication route for mute autistic children (Miller and Miller, 1973).

The use of parents as aides in carrying out such treatment plans has been reported favorably by Oral and Wiegerink (1970) and by Schopler and Reichler (1970). The treatment of seriously disturbed children is always slow paced with small gains achieved over a long time, but if the treatment program is sufficiently detailed and intensive and if the tasks to be learned are broken into manageable component parts, then some meaningful gains can be made.

Learning environments: educational organization

There have been many variations or modifications of environments for CBED. Only recently has special attention been paid, however, to the specific design of that environment *as a part of the therapy* rather than as just a physical place where the remediation or therapy is carried out.

Children with behavioral and emotional differences vary widely in their needs for special services, depending on the severity and the types of the disorders. In Chapter 1 the cascade model of Reynolds was presented with the philosophy that the exceptional child should be removed from the normal setting only as far as needed. The same philosophy holds for the CBED.

REGULAR CLASSES

The regular classroom is the setting for the largest number of children with behavioral and emotional differences. Three alternative procedures have been used in the regular classroom, depending on the needs of the children:

1. The regular classroom teacher assumes sole responsibility for minor problems.

2. The regular classroom teacher obtains consultative help from psychologists, social workers, counselors, principals, and others as needed. The consultants provide the teacher with a better understanding of the child and suggestions for treatment. The major treatment responsibility remains with the classroom teacher.

3. The third alternative is to enroll the child in the regular classroom but with special services from itinerant teachers. The itinerant teacher can tutor such children in their academic subjects when needed, and can assist them in adjustment to the regular class and to other children. Itinerant teachers include speech clinicians, remedial reading teachers, and child therapists.

CRISIS TEACHER

One of the variations on the theme of the resource teacher or itinerant teacher is the proposal by Morse (1976) who introduced the concept of *crisis teacher* in the public schools. The *crisis teacher* would be available to help disturbed children over periods of specific crises or tension in the regular classroom. Many disturbed children cannot remain in the regular class program without a major explosion when they are under conditions of severe stress.

The objective of the crisis teacher is to make it possible for the child to be temporarily removed from the regular class and allowed to work on an individual basis with the crisis teacher until the nature of the immediate upset or crisis is resolved. In this way a child who has periodic but temporary outbursts or overwhelming anxiety can utilize the crisis teacher as a special means of getting over the problem without creating secondary problems in the regular class program.

REGULAR AND SPECIAL CLASSES

Similar to other types of classes for exceptional children discussed in the preceding chapters, the organization of programs includes: (1) regular class plus resource room, (2) part-time special class, (3) full-time special class, and (4) special day school. These variations comply with the philosophy of "the least restrictive environment," depending on the kinds and severity of the behavioral disturbance.

MENTAL HEALTH CLINICS

The community mental health clinics also play a role in the treatment of children with behavioral disorders. Such a clinic can provide (1) consultative services to regular and special class teachers, (2) itinerant personnel to the school to assist regular and special class teachers, (3) a resource room in the clinic where the child can attend on a part-time basis, and (4) an all-day class for children with behavioral disorders.

THE RESIDENTIAL SCHOOL

The residential school is reserved for those children whose needs are not met in their home community and for those who require around-the-clock education, management, and supervision. The Re-Ed program described earlier is such a residential school. Many of its children are removed from the community and home for various reasons, including the effect of the child on siblings, the inability of the parents to manage the child, and in some instances the fact that the child has no home or the home is unsuitable for aid in rehabilitation.

Children who are in trouble, especially those whose homes cannot manage them, may be placed in detention homes, usually under the supervision of the juvenile court. Education is offered these children in small groups or individually while they are awaiting examination and court action. Ordinarily the children are in a detention home for short periods ranging from a week to six or eight weeks. The program is utilized in this setting partly for educational purposes but mostly for therapeutic benefits.

Residential schools have been established for delinquent children or youths who are unable to be at large in society or whose home is of such a nature that the child cannot live there and attend a day school. In some of the larger cities such as New York and Chicago, these schools are operated twenty-four hours a day and are administered by the public school board of education. The schools are for the severer delinquents who are not profiting from a special class or a day school.

By far the most common type of residential school is the state-operated "correctional" institution that is used for children committed by the courts for serious crimes and offenses; the type of security and freedom given the children varies from one such institution to another.

The psychiatric hospital is planned for the very severely emotionally disturbed children who require consistent medical and psychiatric supervision. Some psychiatric hospitals now have residential schools on the grounds. If at all possible, children in residence attend a hospital school where education is provided in a program designed by the teachers and psychiatric personnel. Some children in hospitals are so severely disordered that they are unable to attend the hospital school and must obtain education in the wards.

Summary

1. Children with behavioral and emotional difficulty (CBED) are those who deviate in age-appropriate behavior in ways that significantly interfere with the child's own growth and development or the lives of others.

2. There are two major personality patterns consistently identified in this grouping. The first is an impulsive, hyperactive, antisocial pattern that, at its most extreme, becomes dangerous to others and is labeled delinquent behavior. The second pattern is of a fearful, withdrawn, unhappy child with many vague concerns and anxieties. The more extreme version of that pattern is the autistic or schizophrenic child.

3. Since the definition of behavioral disturbance involves the amount and intensity of behavior that is manifest by large numbers of these children, its prevalence depends on where the line is drawn between what is normal and what is abnormal and in need of assistance. Figures from 2 to 22 percent are used to describe the prevalence of this population, indicating no general professional agreement on the boundary line between disturbance and normality.

4. Factors relating to the causes of behavioral disturbance have been identified in specific family patterns, in the social environment, and also in the physiological characteristics of the child.

5. There has been a distinct shift in the responsibility for treatment of emotionally disturbed children from mental health professionals to the schools.

6. Strategies to modify the educational program for behaviorally disturbed children include different approaches labeled as psychodynamic, psychoeducational, behavior modification, learning disabled, and ecological.

7. Behavior modification techniques have shown special consistency in achieving the limited objectives stated for them.

8. Drug therapy carefully applied under competent supervision also appears to modify hyperactive behavior, as do ecologically designed experiences.

9. Even when treatment is effective, it does not appear to move children with behavioral and emotional difficulty completely into the normal range but merely moves them a significant distance in that direction. Even after specific successful treatment, it is likely that observers will still differentiate the behaviorally disturbed child from the normal.

10. There is a major movement to allow educational and paraeducational personnel, including parents, to play a larger and larger role in the implementation of treatment programs, with a correspondingly lower emphasis on highly trained and scarce psychiatric specialists.

References

AXELROD, S. 1971. "Token Reinforcement Programs in Special Classes." *Exceptional Children* 27 (January): 371–379.

BANDURA, A. 1969. *Principles of Behavior Modification*. New York: Holt, Rinehart and Winston.

BELL, R. Q., G. M. WELLER, AND M. F. WALDROP. 1971. "Newborn and Preschooler: Organization of Behavior and Relations Between Periods." *Monographs of the Society for Research in Child Development* 36 (Nos. 1–2, Serial No. 142). Chicago: University of Chicago Press.

BERKOWITZ, PEARL, AND ESTHER ROTHMAN. 1960. *The Disturbed Child: Recognition and Psychoeducational Theory in the Classroom*. New York: New York University Press.

BIJOU, S. W. 1976. *Child Development: The Basic Stages of Early Child Development*. Englewood Cliffs, N.J.: Prentice-Hall.

BOWER, E. M. 1960. *Early Identification of Emotionally Handicapped Children in School*. Springfield, Ill.: Charles C Thomas.

CAPLAN, N., AND S. NELSON. 1973. "On Being Useful: The Nature and Consequences of Psychological Research on Social Problems." *American Psychologist* 28 (March): 199–211.

DOUGLAS, V. 1972. "Stop, Look, and Listen: The Problem of Sustained Attention and Impulse Control in Hyperactive and Normal Children." *Canadian Journal of Behavioral Science* 4 (October): 259–282.

ERICKSON, E. H. 1950. *Childhood and Society*. New York: W. W. Norton.

FARBER, B. 1959. "Effects of a Severely Mentally Retarded Child on Family Integration." *Monographs of the Society for Research in Child Development* 24 (No. 2, Serial No. 71): 5–112.

FREUD, ANNA. 1954. *Psychoanalysis for Teachers and Parents.* New York: Emerson Books.

FROOMKIN, J. 1972. *Estimates and Projections of Special Target Group Populations in Elementary and Secondary Schools.* Report prepared for the President's Commission on School Finance, Washington, D.C.

GALLAGHER, P. 1972. "Structuring Academic Tasks for Emotionally Disturbed Boys." *Exceptional Children* 38 (September).

GLASSER, W. 1965. *Reality Therapy.* New York: Harper & Row.

GLAVIN, J. P., AND F. R. ANNESLEY. 1971. "Reading and Arithmetic Correlates of Conduct-Problem and Withdrawn Children." *Journal of Special Education* 5 (Fall): 213–219.

GRAUBARD, P. S. 1964. "The Extent of Academic Retardation in a Residential Treatment Center." *Journal of Educational Research* 58 (October): 78–80.

HARGROVE, E., AND L. SWISHER. 1975. "Modifying the Verbal Expression of a Child with Autistic Behaviors." *Journal of Autism and Childhood Schizophrenia* 5 (June): 147–154.

HASLAM, R. H. A., AND P. J. VALLETUTTI. 1975. *Medical Problems in the Classroom.* Baltimore: University Park Press.

HEWETT, F. 1974. "Frank M. Hewett." In J. Kauffmann and C. Lewis, eds., *Teaching Children with Behavior Disorders: Personal Perspectives.* Columbus, Ohio: Charles E. Merrill.

HEWETT, F. 1968. *The Emotionally Disturbed Child in the Classroom.* Boston: Allyn and Bacon.

HEWETT, F. 1967. "Educational Engineering with Emotionally Disturbed Children." *Exceptional Children* 33 (March): 459–470.

HEWETT, F. M. 1965. "Teaching Speech to an Autistic Child Through Operant Conditioning." *American Journal of Orthopsychiatry* 35 (October): 927–936.

HOBBS, N. 1975. *The Futures of Children.* San Francisco: Jossey-Bass.

HOBBS, N. 1970. "Project Re-Ed: New Ways of Helping Emotionally Disturbed Children." In Joint Commission on Mental Health of Children, *Crisis in Child Mental Health: Challenge for the 1970's.* New York: Harper and Row.

HOFFMAN, E. 1972. *The Treatment of Deviance by the Education System.* Ann Arbor, Mich.: Institute for the Study of Mental Retardation and Related Disabilities.

HULL, C. 1947. *Principles of Behavior.* New York: Appleton-Century-Crofts.

JENKINS, R. 1966. "Psychiatric Syndromes in Children and Their Relation to Family Background." *American Journal of Orthopsychiatry* 36 (April): 450–457.

JENKINS, R. L., AND L. HEWITT. 1944. "Types of Personality Structure Encountered in Child Guidance Clinics." *American Journal of Orthopsychiatry* 14 (January): 83–94.

KAGAN, J., H. A. MOSS, AND I. SIGEL. 1963. "Psychological Significance of Styles of Conceptualization." In J. C. Wright and J. Kagan, eds., "Basic Cognitive Processes in Children." *Monographs of the Society for Research in Child Development* 28 (No. 2, Serial No. 86): 73–112.

KELLY, T. J., L. M. BULLOCK, AND M. K. DYKES. 1977. "Behavioral Disorders: Teachers' Perceptions." *Exceptional Children* 43 (February): 316–318.

KEOGH, B. 1977. "Current Issues in Educational Methods." In J. Millichap, ed., *Learning Disabilities and Related Disorders*. Chicago: Year Book Medical Publishers. Pp. 65–72.

KEOGH, B. 1971. "Hyperactive and Learning Disorders: Review and Speculation." *Exceptional Children* 38 (September): 101–109.

KIRK, S. A. 1934. "The Effects of Remedial Reading on the Educational Progress and Personality Adjustment of High-Grade Mentally Deficient Children: Ten Case Studies." *Journal of Juvenile Research* 44 (July): 140–162.

KNOBLOCK, P. 1973. "Open Education for Emotionally Disturbed Children." *Exceptional Children* 39 (February): 358–365.

KROTH, R. L., R. J. WHELAN, AND J. M. STABLES. 1972. "Teacher Application of Behavior Principles in Home and Classroom Environments." In E. L. Meyen, G. A. Vergason, and R. J. Whelan, eds., *Strategies for Teaching Exceptional Children*. Denver: Love Publishing Co.

LONG, N. J. 1974. "Nicholas J. Long." In J. Kauffmann and C. Lewis, eds., *Teaching Children with Behavior Disorders: Personal Perspectives*. Columbus, Ohio: Charles E. Merrill.

LONG, N. J., W. C. MORSE, AND R. C. NEWMAN. 1976. *Conflict in the Classroom*, 3rd ed. Belmont, Calif.: Wadsworth Publishing Co.

LONG, N. J., AND R. C. NEWMAN. 1976. "The Teacher and His Mental Health." In N. J. Long, W. C. Morse, and R. C. Newman, eds., *Conflict in the Classroom,* 3rd ed. Belmont, Calif.: Wadsworth Publishing Co. Pp. 281–292.

MACCOBY, E., AND J. MASTERS. 1970. "Attachment and Dependency." In P. Mussen, ed., *Carmichael's Manual of Child Psychology,* vol. II. New York: John Wiley.

MAUSER, A. J. 1974. "Learning Disability and Delinquent Youth." *Academic Therapy* 9(6) (Summer): 389–402.

MC NEIL, D. C. 1972. "Developing Instructional Materials for Emotionally Disturbed Children." In E. L. Meyen, G. A. Vergason, and R. J. Whelan, eds., *Strategies for Teaching Exceptional Children*. Denver: Love Publishing Co. Pp. 283–296.

MILLER, A., AND E. MILLER. 1973. "Cognitive-Developmental Training with Elevated Boards and Sign Language." *Journal of Autism and Childhood Schizophrenia* 3 (January–March): 65–82.

MILLER, N., AND J. DOLLARD. 1941. *Social Learning and Imitation*. New Haven, Conn.: Yale University Press.

MILLICHAP, J. G. 1977. "Medications as Aids to Education in Children with Minimal Brain Dysfunction." In J. G. Millichap, ed., *Learning Disabilities and Related Disorders*. Chicago: Year Book Medical Publishers. Pp. 111–115.

MORSE, W. 1976. "The Helping Teacher/Crisis Teacher Concept." *Focus on Exceptional Children* 8 (September): 1–11.

MORSE, W. C. 1965. "Intervention Techniques for the Classroom Teacher of the Emotionally Disturbed." In P. Knoblock, ed., *Educational Programming for Emotionally Disturbed Children: The Decade Ahead*. Syracuse, N.Y.: Syracuse University Press. Pp. 29–41.

MURRAY, C. A. 1976. *The Link Between Learning Disabilities and Juvenile Delinquency: Current Theory and Knowledge*. Washington, D.C.: American Institutes for Research.

ORAL, J., AND R. WIEGERINK. 1970. *Regional Intervention Project for Parents and Children*. Bureau of Education for the Handicapped, Progress Report. Washington, D.C.: U.S. Office of Education.

PAVLOV, I. P. 1928. *Lectures on Conditioned Reflexes*. Translated by W. H. Gantt. New York: International.

PETERSON, D. R. 1961. "Behavior Problems of Middle Childhood." *Journal of Consulting Psychology* 25 (June): 205–209.

QUAY, H. C., W. MORSE, AND R. L. CUTLER. 1966. "Personality Patterns of Pupils in Special Classes for the Emotionally Disturbed." *Exceptional Children* 32 (January): 297–301.

REDL, F. 1971. "The Concept of the Life-Space Interview." In N. J. Long, W. C. Morse, and R. G. Newman, eds., *Conflict in the Classroom*. Belmont, Calif.: Wadsworth Publishing Co. Pp. 363–371.

RHODES, W. C. 1967. "The Disturbing Child: A Problem of Ecological Management." *Exceptional Children* 33 (March): 449–455.

RHODES, W. C., AND H. SABIN. 1974. *Service Delivery Systems*. A Study of Child Variance, vol. 3. Ann Arbor: University of Michigan.

ROBINS, LEE. 1966. *Deviant Children Grown Up*. Baltimore: Williams & Wilkins.

RUTTER, M. 1968. "Concepts of Autism: A Review of Research." *Journal of Child Psychology and Psychiatry* 9 (October): 1–25.

RUTTER, M., AND L. BARTAK. 1971. "Causes of Infantile Autism: Some Consideration from Recent Research." *Journal of Autism and Childhood Schizophrenia* 1 (January–March): 20–32.

RYAN, W. 1971. *Blaming the Victim*. New York: Random House.

SAGOR, M. 1974. "Treatment of Deviance by the Mental Health System Structure." In W. C. Rhodes and H. Sabin, *Service Delivery System*. A Study of Child Variance, vol. 3. Ann Arbor: University of Michigan.

SALVIA, J., E. W. SCHULTZ, AND N. CHAPIN. 1974. "Reliability of Bower Scale for Screening of Children with Emotional Handicaps." *Exceptional Children* 41 (October): 117–118.

SCHOPLER, E., AND R. REICHLER. 1970. "Developmental Therapy by Parents with Their Own Autistic Child." In M. Rutter, ed., *Colloquium on Infantile Autism.* London: Ciba Foundation.

SEEMAN, M. 1967. "Powerlessness and Knowledge: A Comparative Study of Alienation and Learning." *Sociometry* 30 (June): 105–123.

SHEA, T. M. 1978. *Teaching Children and Youth with Behavior Disorders.* St. Louis: C. V. Mosby.

SKINNER, B. F. 1953. *Science and Human Behavior.* New York: Macmillan.

SPIVACK, G., M. SWIFT, AND J. PREWITT. 1971. "Syndromes of Disturbed Classroom Behavior: A Behavioral Diagnostic System for Elementary Schools." *Journal of Special Education* 5 (Fall): 269–292.

SPRAGUE, R., K. BARNES, AND J. WERRY. 1970. "Methylphenidate and Thioridazine: Learning Reaction Time, Activity and Classroom Behavior in Disturbed Children." *American Journal of Orthopsychiatry* 40 (July): 615–628.

STEPHENS, T. M. 1977. *Teaching Skills to Children with Learning and Behavior Disorders.* Columbus, Ohio: Charles E. Merrill.

SULLIVAN, H. S. 1953. *The Interpersonal Theory of Psychiatry.* New York: W. W. Norton.

THOMAS, A., S. CHESS, AND H. BIRCH. 1968. *Temperament and Behavior Disorders in Children.* New York: New York University Press.

ULLMANN, C. E. 1952. *Identification of Maladjusted School Children.* Public Health Monograph No. 7. Washington, D.C.: U.S. Government Printing Office.

ULLMANN, L., AND L. KRASNER. 1965. *Case Studies in Behavior Modification.* New York: Holt, Rinehart, and Winston.

VACE, N. A. 1968. "A Study of Emotionally Disturbed Children in Regular and Special Classes." *Exceptional Children* 35 (November): 197–204.

WALDROP, M., F. PEDERSEN, AND R. BELL. 1968. "Minor Physical Anomalies and Behavior in Preschool Children." *Child Development* 39 (June): 391–400.

WEINSTEIN, LAURA. 1974. *Evaluation of a Program for Re-Educating Disturbed Children: A Follow-up Comparison with Untreated Children.* Final Report, Project Nos. 6-2974 and 522023. Nashville, Tenn.: George Peabody College for Teachers.

WENDER, P. H. 1971. *Minimal Brain Dysfunctions in Children.* New York: Wiley-Interscience.

WERRY, J. S. 1968. "The Diagnosis, Etiology, and Treatment of Hyperactivity in Children." In J. Hellmuth, ed., *Learning Disorders,* vol. 3. Seattle: Special Child Publications. Pp. 171–190.

WHITING, B. B. 1963. *Six Cultures—Studies of Child Rearing.* New York: John Wiley.

WING, J., AND L. WING. 1966. "A Clinical Interpretation of Remedial Teaching." In J. Wing, ed., *Early Childhood Autism.* New York: Pergamon Press.

WOLPE, J. A., A. SALTER, AND L. RENYA, EDS. 1965. *The Conditioning Therapies*. New York: Holt, Rinehart and Winston.

WOOD, F. H. 1975. "Children with Social and Emotional Problems." In J. Gallagher, ed., *The Applications of Child Development Research to Exceptional Children*. Reston, Va.: Council for Exceptional Children. Pp. 318–332.

WOOD, F. W., AND R. H. ZABEL. 1978. *Making Sense of Reports on the Incidence of Behavior Disorders/Emotional Disturbance in School Populations*. (Mimeographed.) Minneapolis: University of Minnesota. In press.

12

Throughout this text reference has been made to the fact that handicapped children do not always fit into neat, well-defined categories with uniform characteristics. There are not only individual differences among the hearing, visually, mentally, and socially impaired, but there are children who have more than one impairment and children who are severely handicapped. Since the child who has two or more impairments and the child who is profoundly retarded require very special education, this chapter will describe children with multiple and severe impairments and the provisions that society makes for their maximum development.

It is difficult to define the multiply and severely handicapped as a group since those children vary widely in superficial characteristics. We can, however, define their educational needs, which are homogeneous. Sontag, Smith, and Sailor (1977) offer a "basic skills" definition, stating essentially that multiply and severely handicapped children are those whose primary educational needs are the establishment and development of basic skills in social, self-help, and communication areas. Those basic skills are the behaviors that normal children typically acquire within the first five years of life.

In the past many multiply and severely handicapped children were excluded from public schools and, in some instances, assigned to residential schools. Multiply handicapped children also tended to be excluded from public schools because they did not fit into programs provided for either handicap. If a child was deaf and mentally retarded, he or she was assigned to the residential institution for the more severe and supposedly the least remedial of his or her handicaps—in this case, a residential institution for the mentally retarded. Frequently, in such residential institutions, there were no facilities or personnel capable of providing special education for the hearing impaired.

Because of litigation under the Civil Rights Act and the 1975 federal legislation entitled Education for All Handicapped Children Act (PL 94-142), it is now mandatory for public schools to educate *all* children. The law reads: "It is the purpose of this Act to assure that all handicapped children have available to them, within the time periods specified, a free, appropriate public education which emphasizes special education and related services designed to meet their unique needs" (Sec. 3, a).

In brief, the courts and the federal law have stated that if schools are operated at public expense, it is mandatory that *all,* not *some,* children be given adequate service. This means that the public schools must now organize for the multiply handicapped and for the most severely handicapped children within a public school system.

CHILDREN WITH MULTIPLE AND SEVERE HANDICAPS

Nature and extent of the problem

Advances of medical science have produced an ironic situation. Inroads have been made on specific problems, and many children survive difficult health and physical conditions from which they would have perished only a few years before. They survive, however, with a variety of handicapping conditions. The result is fewer children with a single, uncomplicated disability and more children with development complicated by a number of handicaps.

Table 12.1 shows the range of agents that can produce multiply handicapped children and their consequences. Those listed are only examples of many more conditions, which, fortunately, do not occur with high incidence.

Rawlings and Gentile (1970) studied the number and rate of additional handicaps among hearing-impaired students enrolled in residential and day school programs for the deaf. They found that out of a population of approximately nine thousand pupils, about 25 percent were multiply handicapped. Table 12.2 shows Rawlings and Gentile's statistics on the kinds of multiply handicapped hearing-impaired children. It will be noted from the table that we need to consider not

TABLE 12.1

Sample conditions leading to multiply handicapped children

Time of injury	Affecting agent	Agent activity	Typical result
Conception	Translocation of chromosome pairs at birth	Serious changes in embryo and fetus, often fatal	Certain chromosomal regroupings can lead to Down's syndrome (mongolism) and mental retardation
	Inborn errors of metabolism such as phenylketonuria	Inability to carry out normal chemical and metabolic processes; injures fetal development	Results in severe retardation and other complications; can be reversed partially by early diagnosis and special diet
Prenatal	Drugs such as thalidomide	Drug used as a sedative for mother; can arrest normal development of embryo	A markedly deformed child with serious anomalies of heart, eye, ear, limbs, and others
Natal	Anoxia. (sustained lack of oxygen to fetus during birth process)	Prolonged lack of oxygen can cause irreversible destruction of brain cells	Cerebral-palsied child who may or may not have mental retardation and other defects affecting vision and hearing
Postnatal	Encephalitis and meningitis	Infectious diseases (measles, whooping cough, and others) can lead to inflammation of brain and destruction of brain cells	Can lead to a variety of problems such as lack of attention and hyperactivity; causes epilepsy, mental retardation, and behavioral problems

only hearing impairment but, for one out of four hearing-impaired children, an adaptation of the educational program for the additional handicaps of cleft palate and lip and of visual, mental, emotional, perceptual, neurologic, and other health impairments. It should also be noted that emotional and behavioral problems, mental retardation, and perceptual-motor learning disabilities constitute numerically the largest group.

Another study illustrating those problems is reported by Cohen (1966). He followed the progress of fifty-seven visually handicapped children in their adjustment to school over a twelve-year span. Eighty-five percent of those cases were due to *retrolental fibroplasia,* a condition caused by excessive oxygen given to prematurely born babies. In addition to their inability to see, there was a much higher than usual incidence of other physical handicaps, including a substantial number of brain wave abnormalities. A number of the children also had epileptic seizures or cerebral palsy.

In following those children into their educational programs, Cohen found that the majority were not testing in the normal intellectual range and were not making a satisfactory educational adjustment. Within this general conclusion, however, Cohen remarked that

TABLE 12.2

Number and rate of additional handicapping conditions among hearing-impaired students enrolled in participating special educational programs: United States 1968–1969 school year

Additional handicapping conditions	Total number of reported conditions	Number of conditions per 1,000 students	Number of times condition reported as the only additional handicap	Number of times condition reported in combination with other handicapping conditions
Cleft lip or palate	153	7.2	95	58
Severe visual impairment	883	41.8	458	425
Mental retardation	1,700	80.5	1,004	696
Emotional problems	1,403	66.4	563	840
Behavioral problems	1,225	58.0	475	750
Perceptual motor disorders	1,169	55.3	544	625
Cerebral palsy	708		414	294
Heart disorders	186	8.8	100	86
Other	1,444	68.3	967	477
Total	8,871	419.8	4,620	4,251

Source: Rawlings and Gentile, 1970, Table G, p. 6.

some children with gross multiple handicaps were making good academic progress and developing normal personalities.

The 1950s were characterized by a decisive increase in the number of visually handicapped children with additional handicapping conditions. This was due at first to *retrolental fibroplasia* (see Chapter 7) and later to the effects of an epidemic of maternal rubella (German measles) (Lowenfeld, 1973). The rubella epidemic of 1964–1965 created a number of handicapped children. In the space of two years, an epidemic of rubella swept across the United States and left in its wake an estimated thirty thousand children born with one or more handicaps: visual impairments, hearing impairments, mental retardation, other physical disabilities, and a combination of these handicaps.

The emergence of that group of multiply and severely handicapped children also revealed the absence of organized and institutional services for such children and their families. While the number of those children is large from a national standpoint, very few of them would be found in any one community, and the attempt to organize services for them at the local level has not always been successful.

The innumerable combinations of multiple handicaps in children shown in Table 12.2 shows associated conditions for only one kind of handicap, deafness. It is not known from the statistics in the table how severe the other handicaps are. In the following sections we will discuss the best known and most studied groups of multiply handicapped conditions.

The multiply handicapped hearing impaired

As shown in Table 12.2, there are many multiply handicapped deaf children. Only three combinations will be discussed here: (1) the deaf-blind, (2) the deaf mentally retarded, and (3) the deaf emotionally disturbed.

THE DEAF-BLIND CHILD

One of the most difficult combinations of handicaps for parents and special educators to cope with is the loss of both of the primary sensory avenues—hearing and vision. With these avenues closed, how does a message get into the information-processing system? How can a child so afflicted learn speech and language when he or she can neither hear nor see? It is testimony to the resilient human spirit of both the handicapped and those who work with the handicapped that even such seemingly insuperable handicaps can be partially overcome.

Whenever the deaf-blind are discussed, the first name to come to mind is that of Helen Keller, who has become a symbol of what devoted teaching can do against great odds. With the help of her constant companion, this deaf-blind child with a keen mind achieved speech and other ways of communicating and a high level of academic accomplishment. The popular play and movie *The Miracle Worker* is based on Helen Keller's early discovery of the world around her with the help of her tutor Anne Sullivan. The problem for educators is how to make Helen Kellers out of more of the three thousand deaf-blind children in the United States.

The deaf-blind child is defined by the Bureau of Education for the Handicapped (1969) as:

> a child who has both auditory and visual impairments, the combination of which cause such severe communication and other developmental and educational problems that he cannot properly be accommodated in special education programs either for the hearing handicapped child or for the visually handicapped child. (p. 1)

In a survey by the U.S. Office of Education in April 1970, it was estimated that there were 2,461 deaf-blind children in the United States between birth and 20 years of age. In spite of their small numbers compared with other handicaps, the problem is great. These children are scattered throughout the fifty states, and it is difficult to arrange for specialized educational facilities in their local communities.

In the past the education of the deaf-blind had been largely conducted in private residential schools for children of parents who could afford such education. To deal with the problem nationally, the federal government passed legislation in 1968 to establish ten model centers for deaf-blind children. These centers were each given responsibility for a wide geographic area; it was now possible for families of these multiply handicapped children to receive some degree of help wherever their children resided in the United States. This program, begun in 1969, has provided a wide variety of family counseling services, medical and educational diagnoses, and itinerant home services, as well as teacher-training opportunities and full-time educational programs for almost three thousand deaf-blind children. As Dantona (1976) stated:

> These centers also conduct a program for helping state educational departments and other responsible agencies develop appropriate state plans assuring the provision of meaningful relevant and continuous services throughout the lifetime of the deaf/blind person; and each center collects and disseminates information about practices found effective in working with deaf/blind children and their families. (p. 173)

It is fortunate for the special educator that the term *deaf-blind* is something of a misnomer, implying the complete loss of both sensory avenues. In actual practice most of such children have some residual vision or residual hearing that can be used to aid in educating the child. Other senses, such as touch, are also used in the almost exclusively tutorial approach that must be used to meet the special and idiosyncratic needs of the deaf-blind child (Wolf and Anderson, 1969).

THE HEARING-IMPAIRED MENTALLY RETARDED

It is difficult to educate a deaf child whose intelligence is intact. It is doubly difficult to educate a deaf child who is also a slow learner. In the past the mentally retarded deaf were assigned usually to residential schools for the mentally retarded. Actually, nine out of ten such persons were confined in public institutions for the mentally retarded (Task Force Report on the Mentally Retarded-Deaf, 1973).

Healey and Karp-Nortman (1975), summarizing other studies on the prevalence of the hearing-impaired mentally retarded (HIMR), estimated that 10 to 15 percent of children and adults in residential institutions for the mentally retarded have hearing losses and that a similar number of children in schools for the deaf are mentally retarded. Regardless of the accuracy of those figures, it is still a fact that there are many HIMR children who require educational services and that their placement in residential schools organized for the mentally retarded or for the deaf is not necessarily meeting their needs.

In a review of this problem for the American Speech and Hearing Association, Healey and Karp-Nortman (1975) report that HIMR individuals are those "who have hearing impairments, subaverage general intellectual functioning, and deficits in adaptive behavior. The combination of these three factors requires services beyond those traditionally needed by persons with either mental retardation or hearing impairment" (p. 9).

THE HEARING-IMPAIRED EMOTIONALLY DISTURBED

As in many areas of handicapping conditions, there is no accurate estimate of the number of emotionally disturbed hearing-impaired children. The number depends on the criteria of emotional disturbance and the degree of hearing loss considered. Altshuler (1975), a psychiatrist who has specialized in the treatment of emotionally disturbed deaf children, reviewed the literature and concluded that "the *eight percent* [of deaf children who are emotionally disturbed] estimate nationwide is a marked underrepresentation." He estimated that one to three out of ten deaf students present significant emotional problems that warrant attention. At one end are deaf children with mild emotional problems, and at the other end are children with severe emotional problems who are denied admission to any school and are placed in custodial institutions.

Workers with emotionally disturbed deaf tend to classify those children as *mild, moderate,* and *severe.* The latter have been, in some instances, removed from schools for the deaf because their teachers were unable to cope with the bizarre behavior of the group. About these children, Ranier (1975) stated:

> It is my strong feeling on the basis of our two decades of experience in the psychiatric care of the deaf, as well as the reports of others, that there is a significant core of deaf children who cannot be treated on an outpatient basis, cannot remain in regular classes and cannot be educated or managed even in special classes without a total therapeutic milieu under psychiatric direction. Temporary separation of the child from his environment and placement in a controlled therapeutic setting is essential to help the child develop better controls, better socialization and better identification. Drug and behavior therapies as well as recreation, art and occupational skills need to be furnished. At the same time, special teachers can provide continuing education on an individual basis. (p. 19)

Ranier indicated that following that type of program, the child can be returned to the special class and to the home.

Mild and moderately emotionally disturbed deaf children are often enrolled in residential and day schools for the deaf. In such classes teachers tend to emphasize pupil adjustment, success in tasks assigned, and, in general, a more structured program. Emphasis on parent education and parent cooperation with the school is a major effort.

As yet, standard programs for emotionally maladjusted hearing-impaired children have not been highly developed. The group is so heterogeneous that, to an extent greater than that with many other handicapped children, each child will need an individualized educational program to fit his or her specific needs.

The multiply handicapped cerebral palsied

Since *cerebral* refers to the brain and *palsy* to motor disability, *cerebral palsy* refers to a motor disability caused by brain damage. A neurologic involvement can result in many handicaps, not only of the motor system, but also of any or all the information-processing system. A neurologic deficiency may make it difficult for the child to direct and sustain attention. It may distort perception, hinder meaningful reception, and inhibit various mental operations and expressive behaviors. It may interfere with the child's awareness of feedback information and with his or her ability to use effective judgment by taking all factors into account in decision making. Of all handicapped children the cerebral-palsied child shows the greatest variety of multiple handicaps. Thus cerebral damage may cause none, one, or a number of psychological deviations, intellectual defects, and/or deficiencies in vision, hearing, speech, and visual-motor perception. Capute (1975) has stated: "Cerebral palsy is no longer considered a condition with a pure motor component but rather as a multidimensional disorder in which the type and distribution of the motor disability has become a neurodevelopmental marker for underlying associated neurologic, cognitive, and perceptual impairments" (p. 149).

Cerebral palsy is not a disease but is a neurologic consequence of a wide variety of prenatal, natal, and postnatal conditions that affect the central nervous system. The term *cerebral palsy* was coined by Winthrop Phelps, orthopedic surgeon and pioneer in work with the cerebral palsied in the United States. In describing cerebral palsy a diagnostic team tends to indicate (1) the general condition, cerebral palsy; (2) the parts of the body affected; (3) the degree of involvement, such as mild or severe; and (4) associated disabilities of vision, hearing, intelligence, speech, and learning. Cerebral palsy is often further delineated as to the different forms of neuromuscular involvement. These include: (1) spasticity, (2) athetosis, (3) ataxia, (4) tremor, and (5) rigidity. The first two, the spastic and athetoid groups, comprise about 75 to 80 percent of cerebral-palsied individuals.

SPASTICITY. Spastic children make up the largest group of the cerebral palsied, constituting 40 to 60 percent of the total. Spasticity can occur in one or more limbs with hemiplegia (one side of the body affected) being the most common locus of involvement.

In mild cases the spastic child may extend his or her arms for balance in controlling a somewhat awkward gait. In moderate cases the child may hold both arms close to the body, bent at the elbow, with the hand bent toward the body; the legs are rotated inwardly and flexed at the knees, by which a "scissoring gait" results. In severe cases the child may have poor bodily control and be unable to sit, stand, and walk without the support of braces, crutches, a walking frame, and other supports.

ATHETOSIS. Athetoid children make up the second largest group in cereral palsy—about 15 to 20 percent of the total. Athetosis is characterized by a fluctuating tone and uncontrollable, jerky, irregular, twisting movements. The head is frequently drawn back, the neck extended and tense, with the mouth held open and the tongue protruding; drooling often occurring. Children with athetosis walk in a lurching, writhing, and stumbly manner. Their movements are not rhythmical and do not seem to follow any sequence. Their postural attitude is uncontrolled, and many of them writhe and wriggle in variable fashion.

The athetoid individual is able to put hand to mouth but in so doing goes through various uncontrollable movements, in the extreme case showing squirming gestures and marked facial grimaces. During sleep, however, the athetoid does not writhe or squirm. Those movements occur only in the conscious state. As conscious effort and emotionality increase, the athetosic movements become intensified.

ATAXIA. This particular condition, less prevalent than spasticity and athetosis, is due to a lesion in the cerebellum, which normally controls balance and muscle coordination. The ataxic child is unsteady in his or her movements, walks with a high step, and falls easily. Sometimes the eyes are uncoordinated, and nystagmus (jerky movements of the eye) is common. Ordinarily, ataxia is not detected at birth but is apparent when grasping and walking begin. As in spasticity and athetosis, there are varying degrees of ataxia, from mild (barely detectable) to very severe, depending on the extent of damage in the cerebellum.

TREMOR AND RIGIDITY. Tremor and rigidity are also, like athetosis, the result of injury to the extrapyramidal system. They occur in a small proportion of cerebral-palsied children. Tremor cerebral palsy is sometimes detected at an early age when the whole body shows involuntary vibrating movements of an irregular nature. Those movements result from an interference in the normal balance between antagonistic muscle groups. The child is generally consistent and more predictable than is the athetoid or spastic. Rigidity refers to interference with postural tone and diminishes motion rather than causing abnormal motions.

Although different kinds of cerebral palsy can be identified and classified, many cerebral palsy cases are mixed types, with some characteristics of spasticity and athetosis, spasticity and ataxia, or other combinations.

ETIOLOGY. The causes of cerebral palsy appear to be very similar to the causes of some types of mental retardation discussed in Chapter 4. The lack of oxygen at birth (anoxia), traumatic infections such as meningitis and encephalitis, and a wide variety of metabolic disorders in utero are among many factors that can produce cerebral palsy. Cerebral palsy, like some other conditions, may be caused by factors operative before birth (prenatal), during birth (natal or perinatal), or after birth (postnatal), but there appears to be little agreement as to the role played by genetics in the etiology of cerebral palsy (Denhoff, 1976).

CEREBRAL PALSY WITH MENTAL RETARDATION

The association of mental retardation with cerebral palsy has been studied earlier by identifying intellectual subnormality with tests of intelligence. These tests have sometimes led to overestimates of mental retardation among the cerebral-palsied group. Using the IQ as a criterion of mental retardation, Hohman and Freedheim (1958) tested 1,003 cases referred to a medical clinic and found that 58.8 percent of the cerebral-palsied children obtained IQ scores below 70. Schonell (1956) evaluated the intelligence of 354 cerebral-palsied children in England and found 45 percent had IQs below 70. Similarly, Hopkins, Bice, and Colton (1954) tested 992 cerebral-palsied children on the Stanford-Binet scale and found that 49 percent had IQs below 70. In reviewing the literature on mental retardation and cerebral palsy, Stephen and Hawks (1974) estimated that 40 to 60 percent of the cerebral palsied are mentally retarded.

With cerebral-palsied children it is hard to justify making a diagnosis of mental retardation based on an intelligence test that was standardized on children with adequate speech, language, and motor abilities. Since many cerebral-palsied children have expressive problems in both the speech and psychomotor areas, test results are often questionable. All we can conclude from the preceding data on the intelligence of the cerebral palsied is that when we assess cerebral-palsied children on tests standardized on other populations, about one-half of cerebral-palsied children will test under an IQ of 70. Is this an adequate criterion for diagnosis of mental retardation? The discussion on the criteria for mental retardation in Chapter 4 would indicate that it is not.

Often poor speech and the uncontrolled writhing or spastic movements of cerebral-palsied children give the layperson an unwarranted impression of mental retardation. There is actually little direct relation between intelligence and degree of physical impairment in cerebral palsy. An individual with severe writhing or uncontrolled spasticity may be intellectually gifted, while one with mild, almost unnoticed physical involvement may be severely retarded mentally.

Suffice it to say, the assessment of mental retardation in cerebral-palsied children is extremely difficult and generally must await the results of intensive instruction. If, after prolonged appropriate instruction, the child does not make relatively average progress in most areas, the assessment of mental retardation may be more valid.

PERCEPTUAL AND PSYCHOLINGUISTIC HANDICAPS IN CEREBRAL-PALSIED CHILDREN

Considerable research has been conducted to find what kinds of perceptions and psycholinguistic functions become distorted as a result of the cerebral dysfunction. Cruickshank, Bice, and Wallen (1957) reviewed the literature in this area and concluded that both spastics and athetoids show poorer performance on visual perception and visual-motor tasks than non-cerebral-palsied children. Meyers (1963) tested twenty-four athetoids, sixty-eight spastics, and thirty-two normal children ages 4–0 to 9–0 with the Illinois Test of Psycholinguistic Abilities (Experimental Edition). Figure 12.1 gives the comparison profiles. From that profile it should be noted that: (1) both the athetoids and spastics were inferior to the normal groups, (2) the athetoid group was superior to the spastic group in tests at the *representational* level, where symbols must be translated into meaning, but (3) the spastic group was superior to the athetoid group at the automatic level (grammatic closure, auditory and visual memory).

VISION AND HEARING DEFECTS IN THE CEREBRAL PALSIED

Studies have also shown that there is an excess of visual anomalies and impaired hearing in cerebral-palsied children. Hopkins, Bice, and Colton (1954) pointed out that in a sample of 1,297 cases, 72 percent had normal vision while 28 percent had defective or questionable vision. Of the children with visual disabilities, 42.7 percent were ataxic, 27.3 percent were spastic, and 20.4 percent were athetoid.

According to Denhoff and Robinault (1960), "various authors agree that over 50 percent of the cerebral-palsied children have oculomotor defects and 25 percent or more have subnormal vision" (p. 63). Since hearing does not have motor functions comparable to those of the eye muscles, hearing defects should be less frequent. Actually, research has found that hearing defects among cerebral-palsied children are not as common as are visual problems.

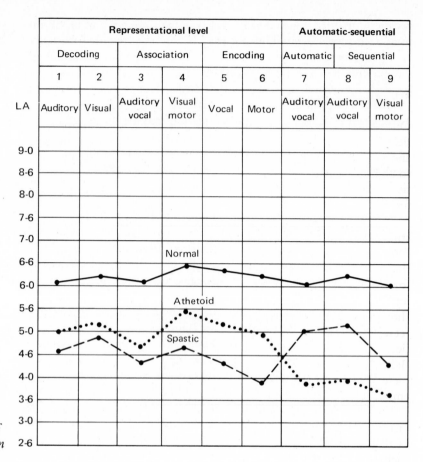

FIGURE 12.1

*Comparison profiles of
cerebral-palsied children*

Hopkins, Bice, and Colton (1954) also reported that 13.3 percent of 1,121 cases had hearing defects. Of this group the athetoids comprised 22.6 percent and the spastics only 7.2 percent. In a survey from England, Fish (1955) found that 20 percent of the cerebral-palsied children had hearing losses.

It would appear from those studies that hearing losses among the cerebral palsied, especially among the athetoid group, are greater than among children who are not cerebral palsied but are not as marked as are visual problems.

The multiply handicapped mentally retarded

In previous sections hearing-impaired and cerebral-palsied mentally retarded children have been discussed. This section will discuss the

mentally retarded emotionally disturbed and severely multiply handicapped mentally retarded children.

THE BEHAVIORALLY DISTURBED MENTALLY RETARDED CHILD

One of the most frequent combinations of multiple handicaps in the
field of exceptional children is the merging of emotional disturbance
and mental retardation. The difficulties that this combination presents
to educators are clearly evident. The retardation part of the combination affects the ability to learn, while the emotional disturbance interferes with attending behavior and with learning.

While the extent to which these two conditions occur together is
still uncertain, it is generally agreed that there is a substantial overlap.
Balthazar and Stevens (1975) summarize a variety of research studies
that indicate that a substantial percentage of youngsters in institutions
for the mentally retarded show neurotic or psychotic behavioral patterns. Also many persons hospitalized for emotional disturbance
show indications of mental retardation. In addition, other disturbed-
retarded youngsters and youth can be found in state prisons, correctional facilities for delinquents, orphanages, and other institutions.
Balthazar and Stevens conclude that "the knowledge is certain that
there is a relatively high predisposition for emotional disturbance
among the mentally retarded" (p. 9).

While there appears to be a range of emotional and behavioral
disturbance that can be identified with mental retardation, these types
of disturbance do not often include sophisticated neurotic defenses
such as sublimation and reaction formation, behaviors that require a
high degree of language development and intellectual sophistication.
Robinson and Robinson (1976), after reviewing the studies on personality with the mentally retarded, state:

> We have seen, for example, that as a group the retarded tend to be
> more anxious than nonretarded children; that both their positive and
> their negative reaction tendencies toward adults tend to be heightened;
> that many have come to expect failure as a way of life and have learned
> to defend themselves against it; . . . their self-concepts may be more
> negative and certainly are more defensive than those of nonretarded
> children. (p. 195)

THE MULTIPLY HANDICAPPED SEVERELY RETARDED

Among the multiply handicapped severely retarded, rarely do we
find a so-called single handicap of mental retardation in an otherwise

normally functioning individual. The severely and profoundly retarded child has one or more additional handicaps—motor, speech and language, emotional, visual, or auditory.

It is possible to identify three major strategies that have been tried in an effort to provide specific help in improving the status of emotionally disturbed and severely and profoundly handicapped mentally retarded individuals. These are drug therapy, psychotherapy, and applied behavioral analysis.

The most common of the drugs used are the *phenothiazines,* tranquilizers or antipsychotic agents; *diphenhydramine,* which seems effective with highly anxious children, particularly with young children; and the *amphetamines,* which have been useful in reducing hyperkinetic (distractible) behavior. Like all powerful therapies, drugs need to be used with care and with full knowledge of their limitations. The temptation to use drugs as a management device in an overcrowded and understaffed institution is great.

Of the two techniques *psychotherapy* and *applied behavioral analysis,* there is a clear choice in favor of applied behavioral analysis for multiply and severely handicapped youngsters. The choice is because psychotherapy requires a degree of language sophistication that is often beyond the capabilities of the disturbed and severely retarded child. Also, psychotherapy requires a sophisticated professional staff to apply it appropriately.

In contrast, the principles of applied behavioral analysis can be used by a relatively untrained staff with limited educational background if the supervision of a competent behavioral therapist is provided. Some basic principles of behavioral analysis focus on: (1) observing responses that are already available in the child, (2) ignoring undesirable behavior and reinforcing desirable behavior, (3) insuring that the reinforcement is immediate and is given whenever the desired response occurs, and (4) task analyzing the target behaviors. All of these principles are well within the operational capabilities of daycare workers and attendants in institutions. As a result there has been an increasing tendency to use task analysis and operant-conditioning principles as a standard for both daily management and for dealing with specific behavioral responses.

Roos and Oliver (1969) compared the progress of three groups of severely and profoundly retarded institutionalized children under conditions of (1) operant conditioning, (2) special attention but not operant conditioning, and (3) no special attention. On the basis of independent ratings by attendants and teachers, Roos and Oliver concluded that the group trained through operant-conditioning procedures showed significantly greater improvement than did either the control or *placebo* group. Both the formal and informal experiences with these operant procedures have encouraged their extension and application in increasing numbers of settings.

Educational programs

Educational programs for the multiply and severely retarded children are relatively new. According to Sontag, Smith, and Sailor (1977), the emphasis on the education of this group of multiply and severely handicapped children is only about eight years old, beginning seriously in about 1970. They felt that the inclusion of this difficult group into public education will lead the way to the goal of the education of *all* handicapped children.

Visitors to residential institutions for the mentally retarded often will find severely and multiply handicapped children sitting on floors, rocking in a stereotyped manner, and neglected because of an overworked and understaffed organization. With the help of federal grants that provide more personnel, attempts have been made to provide training in self-care and independence for these youngsters. While it is important to try to help the residential schools that have been overcrowded and understaffed, there is a parallel goal today to deinstitutionalize children and adults from the residential schools. With proper training and supervision some of these children and adults have the potential to adapt to community facilities. (See Chapter 5.)

To emphasize deinstitutionalization and normalization, Brown, Nietupski, and Hamre–Nietupski (1976) have advocated that "severely handicapped students should be placed in self-contained classes in public schools. . . . They have the right to be visible, functioning citizens integrated into everyday life of complex public communities" (p. 3).

COMPONENTS OF A COMPREHENSIVE SYSTEM

Haring and Bricker (1976) describe the necessary components for a comprehensive system of education for most types of multiply and severely handicapped children, regardless of the type of handicap. The six components are discussed in the following paragraphs.

1. A developmental framework. The developmental approach accepts three basic ideas. First, that growth or changes in behavior follow a developmental hierarchy (for example, children vocalize before uttering words); second, behavior acquisition moves from simple to more complex responses (that is, children focus their eyes before learning to read); and third, more complex behavior is the result of coordinating or modifying simpler component response forms. Most developmental education will follow those basic principles. Since the developmental model assures that the simpler forms of behavior serve as building blocks for complex responses, it is therefore important to start with those simpler building blocks.

2. Early and continuous intervention. Early intervention reduces the possibility of the child's developing inappropriate responses and brings important support to the primary care-givers, the parents, at a time most needed.

3. Systematic instructional procedures. Once the developmental theory fixes on which behavior should be taught and in what sequence others follow, specific procedures should match the stages of learning a particular skill. These stages can be divided into five distinct phases: (a) acquiring, (b) strengthening, (c) maintaining, (d) generalizing, and (e) applying the new skill.

4. Appropriate curricula. Specific curriculum materials must often be developed to meet the special needs of the severely handicapped. The criteria for selecting these materials should be that (a) they are flexible and can be used in a variety of settings since we wish to help children acquire skills that can be adapted to a variety of situations; (b) the training materials must include precise behavioral descriptions of objectives, the procedures for reaching these objectives, and the criteria for determining when the objectives have been met; and (c) there must be a direct link between the curriculum materials and objective measures of progress.

5. Adjunctive services. Severely multiply handicapped persons have a wide variety of disorders—physical, sensory, and psychological, as well as educational—and therefore require that a diverse group of disciplines be available to provide treatment. Children with chronic health problems need consultative medical supervision. Children with muscular problems must have attention from specially trained individuals who can work directly with teachers and parents. Other children will need the services of nutritionists, physical therapists, and other specialists. One of the increasingly important roles played by all of these adjunctive services is the providing of specific training and instruction to the parents themselves, since the parents are the primary care-givers and the most highly motivated persons to help the child develop on a consistent basis.

6. Objective evaluation. One of the most difficult jobs facing educators is the development of evaluation systems that will allow for the assessment of programs on a daily, weekly, and yearly basis. This issue can partially be dealt with by developing curricula that have evaluation or assessment built into the programs themselves.

As indicated earlier, programs for the mild and moderately hand-icapped child have been developed. Only recently, however, since about 1970, have programs for the multiply and severely handicapped attracted the attention of professionals. As Sherr (1976) has stated, the most adequate programs will have to be developed in the public schools, since it is in this setting that a full-service program can be offered at reasonable cost to the public. The mandate that public schools are required to educate all children (PL 94-142) has created a demand for organized curricula for the severe and multiply handicapped child. The essentials of a curricula for this group of children include: (1) self-help skills, (2) gross and fine motor skills, (3) communication skills, (4) socialization, (5) occupational training, (6) functional academics, and (7) cognitive skills. The essentials will be described briefly.

Self-help skills include training in dressing and undressing, using the toilet, eating, and personal hygiene.

Gross and fine motor skills include programs to overcome or compensate for motor deficits. They include sensory-motor activities, manipulation, movement, and posture.

Communication includes receptive and expressive language and, for the nonverbal child, sign language.

Socialization includes assisting the child in social interaction with peers and adults and decreasing the tendency of severe and multiply handicapped children to withdraw or to have bursts of physical aggression.

Occupational training includes training in manipulative skills and in sheltered workshops for routine tasks.

Academic skills include the acquisition of reading some words, writing their own names and addresses, and the elements of quantitative thinking.

Cognitive skills include music, art, general information, and knowledge of the environment.

The curricula that have been developed for the severely and profoundly handicapped and their implementation and instruction have been influenced by the new behaviorism, by task analysis and operant conditioning. An example of such a curriculum is *The Teaching Research Curriculum for the Moderately and Severely Handicapped* by Fredericks and others at the Teaching Research Infant and Child Center in Oregon (1977). This curriculum was developed over the years by teachers of preschool handicapped children and includes task analysis of the behaviors to be taught with detailed steps in teaching the target behaviors. The curriculum consists of teaching:

1. self-help skills, including the areas of dressing, undressing, eating, using the toilet, and personal hygiene
2. receptive language, including attending and listening
3. expressive language, including verbal and nonverbal expression
4. writing skills
5. reading skills
6. motor skills, including gross and fine motor skills and recreation
7. cognitive skills

According to Fredericks, each of the preceding areas has three possible subcomponents: (1) skills, (2) phases, and (3) steps. A skill is a complex behavior requiring the acquisition of a number of subordinate behaviors before it is acquired. A phase is a breakdown of the skill into parts or units, and a step is a minute breakdown of the phase. An example of a self-help area is dressing (a skill). A phase of dressing could be putting on pants. The seven steps in teaching a child to put on pants to develop that aspect of dressing are described as:

Step 1. Child puts on pants when pulled to thighs.
Step 2. Child puts on pants when pulled to knees.
Step 3. Child puts on pants with both feet in to ankles.
Step 4. Child puts on pants with one foot in and other started in.
Step 5. Child puts on pants with one foot started in.
Step 6. Child puts on pants when placed in front of him.
Step 7. Child unfolds pants and puts them on (Fredericks et al., 1977, p. 7).

Similar task analysis and steps are made for other self-help areas including the skills of: removing socks, removing pants, removing jacket, removing shirt, removing shoes, putting on socks, putting on pants, putting on jacket, putting on shirt, untying shoes, and other skills.

In the area of receptive language one of the skills to be developed is eye contact. This skill is divided into the following phases, and the steps are in time frames of seconds.

Phase I   Child's face is held in position for eye contact by an adult as he or she calls the child's name.

Phase II   Child will, when name is called, look to flashlight held in front of adult's face.

Phase III   Child will, when name is called, look at doll held in front of adult's face.

Phase IV   Child will, when name is called and he or she is
            asked to look at adult's eyes, maintain eye contact
            with adult.

Phase V   Child will, when name is called, maintain eye contact
            with adult.

Phase VI   Child will, when asked to look, maintain eye contact.

For any one of those phases, the steps are as follows:

Step 1. 1 second
Step 2. 2 second
Step 3. 3 seconds
Step 4. 4 seconds
Step 5. 5 seconds (Fredericks et al., 1977, p. 8)

In some other behaviors, such as teaching a child to walk, the steps may break down into distances of feet or yards.

Other curricula that have been developed consist of three volumes by Bender, Valletutti, and Bender (1976). These volumes deal with: I, *Behavior, Self-Care, and Gross and Fine Motor Skills;* II, *Communication, Socialization, Safety, and Leisure Time Skills;* and III, *Functional Academics for the Mildly and Moderately Handicapped.* Students interested in these and in other task analysis procedures should refer to Biggs and O'Donnell (1976), who have also written in detail on procedures to be used with the severely and multiply handicapped child. Billingsley and Neafsey (1978) have reviewed twenty-six curriculum training guides relating to instructional programs for the multiply and severely handicapped.

STRATEGIES

The general strategy by which programs are planned for the multiply and severely handicapped are noted as follows:

1. isolating the necessary behavior components to reach a specified terminal state
2. sequencing those components according to the best information available on normal acquisition patterns
3. generating a variety of activities to train each of the necessary steps in the developmental hierarchy (Bricker and Iacino, 1977, p. 170)

Figure 12.2 indicates a developmental hierarchy map in the area of motor development. Starting from birth, this map indicates the

FIGURE 12.2
Motor training lattice

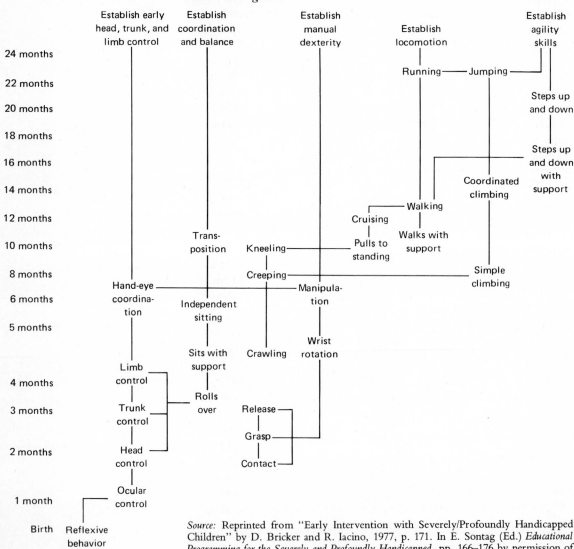

Source: Reprinted from "Early Intervention with Severely/Profoundly Handicapped Children" by D. Bricker and R. Iacino, 1977, p. 171. In E. Sontag (Ed.) *Educational Programming for the Severely and Profoundly Handicapped,* pp. 166–176 by permission of the Division on Mental Retardation/Council for Exceptional Children. Copyright 1977 by the Division on Mental Retardation/Council for Exceptional Children, 1920 Association Drive, Reston, Virginia 22091.

expected sequence of motor development for the first two years. A youngster who has cerebral palsy and is much delayed in motor development as a consequence can be placed on this map in terms of his or her present development, and the teacher will know what is the next expected skill to begin working on.

One outstanding feature of the current training emphases on early development is the extensive detailing of basic skills usually thought too routine or basic to be a part of an instructional program. For example, Greg, a 6-year-old quadriplegic youngster with very limited motor skills, can still be approached through exercises designed to help him develop his visual attention.

Attending	Given the command "Greg, look at me," he will look at the teacher so that eye contact is made for 3 seconds on eighteen of twenty trials conducted on two consecutive days.
Turning head to right	With Greg placed supine on a mat, his head positioned by the teacher so that his right cheek is flush against the mat, Greg will hold his head in this position independently for a 2-minute period.
Eye tracking	Placed in a prone position on the table with a bolster under the armpits, Greg will track horizontally and vertically for a total of 3 minutes out of a 5-minute block of time, as judged acceptable by the teacher and one independent observer.
Shifting gaze	Properly supported in his wheelchair so that his head is free to turn to the left and right when two toys are held 18 inches apart and alternately squeaked or rattled, Greg will shift his gaze from one toy to another within 5 seconds of the sound on 80 percent of the trials on three of four consecutive days (McKenzie et al., 1977, p. 106).

The more handicapped the child, the more detailed and precise must be the analysis of the skills to be taught. Even the simplest task can turn into a marvel of complexity once one breaks down every single component of the task itself. Figure 12.3 gives a framework for tying one's shoes. As one can see, such a task analysis reveals the full range of a complex sequence of simple behaviors necessary for the

FIGURE 12.3
Lattice for "shoes tied"

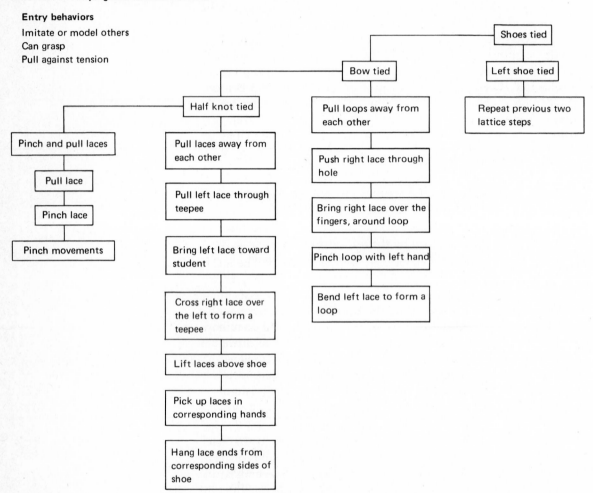

Model for developing instructional materials

Entry behaviors
Imitate or model others
Can grasp
Pull against tension

			Shoes tied
		Bow tied	Left shoe tied
	Half knot tied	Pull loops away from each other	Repeat previous two lattice steps
Pinch and pull laces	Pull laces away from each other	Push right lace through hole	
Pull lace	Pull left lace through teepee	Bring right lace over the fingers, around loop	
Pinch lace	Bring left lace toward student	Pinch loop with left hand	
Pinch movements	Cross right lace over the left to form a teepee	Bend left lace to form a loop	
	Lift laces above shoe		
	Pick up laces in corresponding hands		
	Hang lace ends from corresponding sides of shoe		

Source: Smith, Smith, and Edgar, 1976, p. 167.

final act to be successful. It also provides a basis for step-by-step instruction so that one can identify the point at which the child is having trouble and at which specific instructions should be given.

The recent interest in the multiply and severely handicapped has stimulated the organization of a new association under the name of the American Association for the Education of the Severely / Profoundly Handicapped. This association has sponsored meetings, conferences, and publications including several volumes applying behavior principles to the teaching of these children (Haring and Bricker, 1976; Haring, 1977). In addition to these publications readers are referred to a compilation of contributions edited by Snell (1978), *Systematic Instruction of the Moderately and Severely Handicapped*. These articles describe in detail lattices, programs, and teaching strategies for broad curricula for the severely handicapped.

COMMUNICATION

Of all the problems faced by the multiply handicapped child, perhaps the most serious is the interference with communication. The major communication problems of the multiply handicapped may be revealed in receiving, transmitting, or both; they require special educational tools to aid the communication process. "As the severity of the language deficit increases, the educational system uses more tutorial and individual instruction. Language, either spoken, written, or signed, is our most common means of sharing private experiences with other people" (Withrow and Nygren, 1976, p. 2).

In addition to training in oral receptive and expressive language, for those not able to acquire oral language, manual signing systems are used. Stremel-Campbell, Cantrell, and Halle (1977) have described in detail methods of communication used with nonverbal severely handicapped children. They used a manual signing system similar to that used with deaf children since this communication system did not require spelling, reading, or elaborate formal syntax. Although they were able to teach communication through the manual sign system, they found that some physically handicapped children could not express themselves adequately by signing and gesturing because of their motor handicap. Nevertheless, different systems of signing are being tried with the nonverbal severely handicapped child.

Guess, Sailor, and Baer (1977) report the use of a *communication board* on which cards are placed with common words that the child may use. The child communicates with others by pointing to the words on the board. Complex messages require the child to point to words in sequence and to begin to grasp the various components of language.

With the increase of resources for research and development activities over the past two decades, there has emerged a collection of ingenious devices and equipment to aid in the communication process. These include:

1. the Optacon, which translates the printed word into a tactile form
2. the Cybertype machine, which transforms the typewriter into a seven- or fourteen-key system for children with severe physical handicaps (Kafafian, 1968)
3. the Kurzweil Reading Machine, which converts printed words into synthetic speech (See p. 270.)
4. the captioning of films and TV programs for hearing-handicapped individuals (Withrow and Nygren, 1975)

EVALUATION

The programs for the severely handicapped have not been operating long enough to be subjected to an evaluation of their efficacy. Clinical reports indicate that many children thought to be educationally hopeless have responded to stimulation and programming. One such attempt (Fredericks et al., 1975) described a preschool setting where six moderately to severely handicapped children were integrated into a day-care program with over thirty normal children. The handicapped children were a year or two older than the nonhandicapped children whose ages were 3 to 6 years.

A well-organized and structured program designed to facilitate social behavior and language development was carried out at the day-care center. In social behavior the special educators tried first to draw the handicapped youngsters from unoccupied behavior to independent play with toys and objects. A second stage in socialization was to help the handicapped children play in parallel activity with the normal children. Finally, the environment was arranged by the adults to facilitate associative play with the normal peers, who were encouraged and rewarded for their interacting with the handicapped children.

In language behavior there were attempts to reinforce and reward all verbal and nonverbal communication attempted by the handicapped children and to create situations that required verbalization on the part of the handicapped children to other peers and adults.

This carefully designed program reported meaningful gains in drawing the handicapped children from isolation into social interaction with their peers and in a small but meaningful improvement in language expression. What this program illustrates is the benefit accruing from a carefully structured program and trained personnel. Merely placing handicapped children in the same physical environment as normal children without such measures is unlikely to produce major results. The Head Start program currently mandates that 10 percent of the youngsters selected for that program be handicapped. Unless that placement is accompanied by appropriate program design and personnel training, it is unlikely that the goals of integration will be met. Fredericks et al. (1975) commented:

> But it is critical to emphasize that, for moderately and severely handicapped children to benefit from placement in day care, Head Start, or any other preschool environment, the type and extent of training that must be provided to the staff is complex and of long duration. Specifically, it has been suggested here that carefully structured procedures are probably necessary to facilitate the child's improvement of social play and language interactions and to generate interactive behaviors with nonhandicapped children. (p. 205)

PROVISIONS FOR ORTHOPEDIC AND OTHER HEALTH-IMPAIRED CHILDREN

A variety of children have been previously considered *exceptional* because of their special physical condition. These physical conditions tended to interfere with mobility and periodically might force the child out of the normal learning setting. Often the educational environment was unintentionally hostile to such children, requiring crippled children to negotiate steps and other barriers that prevented many children from gaining easy access to the school.

Increasing advances in biomedical science have sharply reduced or eliminated many of these conditions as serious educational problems, though their health implications may continue. The incidence of polio has been substantially reduced by the development and use of polio vaccine. Epilepsy, a condition in which the convulsive seizures of children had impaired their learning opportunities and social development, has been dramatically improved by the development of appropriate medication that controls the majority of seizures.

Rheumatic fever, diabetes, cystic fibrosis, and asthma are other conditions now essentially under medical control. When a condition is so severe that it still cannot be totally handled through medical treatment, each child is planned for on an individual basis with the teacher providing special lessons as required to help the child stay even with other children in the classroom.

In previous years special rooms had been set aside for orthopedically handicapped children. These rooms would use a variety of devices to help youngsters with special mobility problems and might even provide special physical therapy opportunities. Now the vast majority of orthopedically handicapped children are found in the regular classroom under the *mainstreaming* philosophy.

These orthopedically and health-impaired children are dramatic examples of the continuing changing nature of special education. As we gain in knowledge in medical, psychological, and educational areas, some children no longer need to be considered *exceptional* in the educational sense. Conversely, as we have seen in the first part of the chapter, our increasing knowledge sometimes results in the creation of more or different kinds of youngsters, such as the multiply handicapped children who have become of much greater concern to special educators.

SPECIAL ADAPTATIONS AND MODIFICATIONS

Because of the heterogeneity of severely and multiple handicapping conditions, it is difficult to describe facilities for all the children. One child may be deformed in one arm, may be severely retarded, or have other handicapping impairments. One is mobile in the classroom, another is mobile on crutches, and still another is confined to a wheelchair. One has some verbal language, another one only gestures. With these differences in physical and mental abilities in mind, it becomes obvious that we can consider here only the more general types of modification.

SCHOOL HOUSING. One of the most notable of the changes brought by Public Law 94–142 and its companion, Section 504 of the Vocational Rehabilitation Act of 1973 (PL 93–112), is that the physical environment in the schools has been made more hospitable to the severely and multiply handicapped child as a part of normal expectations, not as an unusual innovation. We thus see ramps for wheelchairs, guardrails in toilets, nonskid surfaces, and other environmental modifications that encourage independence. Section 504 provides the basis for those changes with the following statement: "No otherwise qualified handicapped individual in the United States . . . which solely by reason of handicap [will] be excluded in the participation in, be denied the benefit of, or be subjected to discrimination under any program or activity receiving Federal financial assistance" (Abeson and Zettel, 1977, p. 127).

TRANSPORTATION. The transportation phase of the program for these impaired children is expensive. Most of them will require transportation to and from school. They may be scattered in many areas of the city and will have to be transported for some distance. This means providing facilities for loading some of the children into the bus and arranging their seating for safety and comfort, especially if they have severe handicaps.

SPECIAL EQUIPMENT. In some schools special rooms for physical and occupational therapy are equipped with the necessary materials used in the treatment of muscle disabilities and in improving motor coordination. Special chairs and cutout tables, which will support a child as he or she sits or stands, are common classroom equipment. Sometimes such equipment has to be made to specifications for a particular child if the physician in charge recommends special supports in a chair or table.

In addition to the modifications necessary in the gross physical environment, the teacher will utilize numerous aids and devices for instructional use. All of these pieces of equipment have special purposes: book racks for children who cannot hold books, ceiling projectors for children in bed in hospitals or at home, electric typewriters with remote control devices for children in bed, cots for special rest periods, and so on. What is actually needed in a particular class depends on the children in the class. The child who has to have support to stand needs a standing table. The child who cannot use his or her hands to turn pages needs an automatic page turner. The child who cannot follow a line or hold a pencil firmly needs a pencil holder or guides in writing. Special equipment is usually obtained only when there is a specific requirement for it since it is just an aid and has to be selected on an individual rather than on a group basis.

MEDICAL SUPERVISION. School authorities are responsible for the total program of the child, which includes not only classroom instruction but also the child's health program. The physician may recommend special care and specifically prescribe that the child is to have rest periods and not become fatigued, that child's diet is to be controlled according to physical needs, or that a particular postural aid is to be used to correct certain deformities.

INDIVIDUALIZED INSTRUCTION. Because of the heterogeneous nature of the group of children and because of the wide range of adaptations necessary for varying abilities and achievements, much of the work is individualized. Since many severely and multiply handicapped children have limited firsthand experiences about their community or about the world, secondary experiences are necessary, especially through the use of visual aids, field trips, and particularly appropriate educational films and television.

The attitude of the teacher toward each child's personality and adjustment is of utmost importance. He or she must not only understand the physical problems and their requirements but also help motivate the child who is depressed and withdrawn, dampen the tantrums that sometimes follow frustration, and in general promote the personal and emotional adjustment of these children.

EDUCATIONAL FACILITIES

To provide for the wide range and combinations of intellectual and physical disabilities found among the physically handicapped, different kinds of educational provisions have evolved. The following types of facilities have been organized for the physically impaired child.

REGULAR SCHOOL CLASSES. A large majority of children with mild or moderate physical handicaps attend regular classes with non-handicapped children. Adaptations to their physical condition are made in the regular class.

HOME INSTRUCTION. Home instruction is provided for children who are physically disabled to the extent that they cannot attend a school or who live where a school suitable for them is unavailable.

HOSPITAL SCHOOLS. Hospital schools generally enroll physically handicapped children during short-term diagnostic and treatment periods. Children with severe physical handicaps are usually admitted to such hospital schools.

SHELTERED–CARE FACILITIES. Children with severe physical handicaps who cannot be taken care of at home are provided with sheltered-care (residential) facilities and are offered education in these centers.

SPECIAL SCHOOLS OR CLASSES. Special schools or special classes in regular schools are one type of facility for the multiply and severely handicapped child. Such facilities are found in separate schools or in a class or section of a regular school. For some activities and for some children integration with ordinary children for part of the day is practical. Such mainstreaming is practiced more widely with preschool children.

grade and the program is mainstreamed, resource rooms and itinerant services are furnished for those children who need supporting help. Medical services in the form of physical therapy, speech remediation, and occupational therapy are also provided.

Summary

1. Children considered in this chapter are those who have severe and multiple handicaps that interfere with their normal functioning in a regular classroom and who require basic skills instruction in the social, self-help, and communication areas.

2. In the United States it is now mandated by federal law that all children, regardless of the severity of their handicap, are entitled to an appropriate public education. Such legal mandates have stimulated increased attention to the special educational needs of such children.

3. Advances in medical science and in prenatal, natal, and postnatal care have resulted in saving many children who would have died in an earlier era but who now survive with multiple or severe handicaps requiring special education.

4. Among the more common groups of multiply handicapped children who require special planning are:

 a. the hearing-impaired child who is also visually impaired (the deaf-blind child), mentally retarded, or emotionally disturbed
 b. the cerebral-palsied child who is also mentally retarded, is visually or auditorily impaired, has specific learning and perceptual problems, or is emotionally disturbed
 c. the mentally retarded child who is emotionally disturbed
 d. the severely and multiply handicapped mentally retarded child

5. The special educational principles found necessary for educating the multiply and severely handicapped are (a) a developmental framework, (b) early and continuous intervention, (c) systematic instructional procedures, (d) appropriate curricula, (e) the use of adjunctive services, and (f) an objective evaluation.

6. Of the educational strategies in use, behavior modification methods including task analysis and operant conditioning seem to aid the more severely impaired children to gain necessary self-help, communication, and social skills.

7. Multiply handicapped children have widely varying needs and problems and require careful individual diagnosis as part of their educational plan.

8. Because of advances in the biomedical sciences, orthopedic and general health problems have become less of a problem for special education.

9. Parent education has become an increasingly important part of special education plans for both the multiply and severely handicapped children.

References

ABESON, A., AND J. ZETTEL. 1977. "The End of the Quiet Revolution: The Education for All Handicapped Children Act of 1975." *Exceptional Children* 44 (October): 114–130.

ALTSHULER, K. Z. 1975. "Identifying and Programming for the Emotionally Handicapped Deaf Child." In D. W. Naiman, ed., *Needs of Emotionally Disturbed Hearing Impaired Children.* New York: New York University School of Education.

BALTHAZAR, E., AND H. STEVENS. 1975. *The Emotionally Disturbed, Mentally Retarded.* Englewood Cliffs, N.J.: Prentice-Hall.

BENDER, M., P. J. VALLETUTTI, AND R. BENDER. 1976. Teaching the Moderately and Severely Handicapped: Curriculum Objectives, Strategies and Activities. vol. I, *Behavior, Self-Care, and Gross and Fine Motor Skills;* vol. II, *Communication, Socialization, Safety and Leisure Time Skills;* vol. III, *Functional Academics for the Mildly and Moderately Handicapped.* Baltimore: University Park Press.

BIGGS, J., AND P. O'DONNELL. 1976. *Teaching Individuals with Physical and Mental Disabilities.* Columbus, Ohio: Charles E. Merrill.

BILLINGSLEY, F. F., AND S. S. NEAFSEY. 1978. "Curriculum Training Guides: A Survey of Content and Evaluation Procedures." *AAESPH Review* 3 (March): 42–57.

BRICKER, D., AND R. IACINO. 1977. "Early Intervention with Severely/Profoundly Handicapped Children." In E. Sontag, ed., *Educational Programming for the Severely and Profoundly Handicapped.* Reston, Va.: Council for Exceptional Children. Pp. 166–176.

BROWN, L., J. NIETUPSKI, AND S. HAMRE–NIETUPSKI. 1976. "Criterion of Ultimate Functioning." In M. A. Thomas, ed., *Hey, Don't Forget About Me.* Reston, Va.: Council for Exceptional Children. Pp. 2–15.

CAPUTE, A. J. 1975. "Cerebral Palsy and Associated Dysfunctions." In R. H. A. Haslam and P. J. Valletutti, ed., *Medical Problems in the Classroom.* Baltimore: University Park Press.

COHEN, J. 1966. "The Effects of Blindness on Children's Development." *New Outlook for the Blind* 60 (May): 150–154.

CRUICKSHANK, W., H. BICE, AND N. WALLEN. 1957. *Perception and Cerebral Palsy.* Syracuse, N.Y.: Syracuse University Press.

DENHOFF, E. 1976. "Medical Aspects." In W. M. Cruickshank, ed., *Cerebral Palsy: A Developmental Disability,* 3rd ed. Syracuse, N.Y.: Syracuse University Press.

DENHOFF, E., AND I. ROBINAULT. 1960. *Cerebral Palsy and Related Disorders.* New York: McGraw-Hill.

DANTONA, R. 1976. "Services for Deaf-blind Children." *Exceptional Children* 43 (November): 172–174.

FISH, L. 1955. "Deafness in Cerebral Palsied School Children." *Lancet* 2 (August 20): 370–371.

FREDERICKS, H., V. JORDAN, M. GAGE, L. LEVAK, G. ALRICH, AND M. WADLOW. 1975. *A Data-Based Classroom for the Moderately and Severely Handicapped.* Monmouth, Ore.: Instructional Development Corp.

FREDERICKS, H., C. RIGGS, T. FUREY, D. GROVE, W. MOORE, J. MC DONNELL, E. JORDAN, W. HANSON, V. BALDWIN, AND M. WADLOW. 1977. *The Teaching Research Curriculum for the Moderately and Severely Handicapped.* Springfield, Ill.: Charles C Thomas.

GUESS, D., W. SAILOR, AND D. M. BAER. 1977. "A Behavioral-Remedial Approach to Language Training for the Severely Handicapped." In E. Sontag, ed., *Educational Programming for the Severely and Profoundly Handicapped.* Reston, Va.: Council for Exceptional Children. Pp. 360–376.

HARING, N., ED. 1977. *Developing Effective Individualized Education Programs for Severely Handicapped Children and Youth.* Washington, D.C.: Bureau of Education for the Handicapped.

HARING, N., AND D. BRICKER. 1976. "Overview of Comprehensive Services for the Severely/Profoundly Handicapped." In N. Haring and L. Brown, eds., *Teaching the Severely Handicapped.* New York: Grune & Stratton. Vol. I, pp. 17–32.

HEALEY, W., AND D. KARP-NORTMAN. 1975. *The Hearing Impaired, Mentally Retarded: Recommendations for Action.* Washington, D.C.: American Speech and Hearing Association.

HOHMAN, L., AND D. FREEDHEIM. 1958. "Further Studies on Intelligence Levels in Cerebral Palsied Children." *American Journal of Physical Medicine* 37 (April): 90–97.

HOPKINS, T., H. BICE, AND K. COLTON. 1954. *Evaluation and Education of the Cerebral Palsied Child.* Arlington, Va.: International Council for Exceptional Children.

KAFAFIAN, H. 1968. *Study of Man-Machine Communication Systems for the Handicapped.* Washington, D.C.: Cybernetics Research Institute.

LOWENFELD, B., ED. 1973. *The Visually Handicapped Child in School.* New York: John Day Co.

MC KENZIE, H. S., M. G. HILL, S. D. SOUSIE, R. YORK, AND K. BAKER. 1977. "Special Education Training to Facilitate Rural, Community-Based Programs for the Severely Handicapped." In E. Sontag, ed., *Educational Programming for the Severely or Profoundly Handicapped.* Reston, Va.: Council for Exceptional Children. Pp. 96–110.

MEYERS, P. 1963. "A Comparison of Language Disabilities of Young Spastic and Athetoid Children." Unpublished doctoral dissertation. University of Texas.

RANIER, J. D. 1975. "Severely Emotionally Handicapped Hearing Impaired Children." In D. W. Naiman, ed., *Needs of Emotionally Disturbed Hearing Impaired Children.* New York: New York University School of Education.

RAWLINGS, B., AND A. GENTILE. 1970. *Additional Handicapping Conditions, Age at Onset of Hearing Loss and Other Characteristics of Hearing Impaired Students.* Washington, D.C.: Gallaudet College Office of Demographic Studies.

ROBINSON, H., AND N. ROBINSON. 1976. *The Mentally Retarded Child,* 2nd ed. New York: McGraw-Hill.

ROOS, P., AND M. OLIVER. 1969. "Evaluation of Operant Conditioning with Institutionalized Retarded Children." *American Journal of Mental Deficiency* 74 (November): 325–330.

SCHONELL, F. 1956. *Educating Spastic Children.* Edinburgh, Scotland: Oliver and Boyd.

SHERR, R. D. 1976. "Public School Programs." In M. A. Thomas, ed., *Hey, Don't Forget About Me.* Reston, Va.: Council for Exceptional Children. Pp. 98–107.

SMITH, D., J. SMITH, AND E. EDGAR. 1976. "Prototype Models for the Development of Instructional Material." In N. Haring and L. Brown, eds., *Teaching the Severely Handicapped,* vol. 1. New York: Grune & Stratton. Pp. 155–176.

SNELL, M. E., ED. 1978. *Systematic Instruction of the Moderately and Severely Handicapped.* Columbus, Ohio: Charles E. Merrill.

SONTAG, E., ED. 1977. *Educational Programming for the Severely and Profoundly Handicapped.* Reston, Va.: Council for Exceptional Children.

SONTAG, E., J. SMITH, AND W. SAILOR. 1977. "The Severely/Profoundly Handicapped: Who Are They? Where Are We?" *Journal of Special Education* 11(1):5–11.

STEPHEN, E., AND G. HAWKS. 1974. "Cerebral Palsy and Mental Subnormality." In A. M. Clarke and D. B. Clarke, eds., *Mental Deficiency: The Changing Outlook,* 3rd ed. New York: The Free Press. Pp. 482–523.

STREMEL-CAMPBELL, K., D. CANTRELL, AND J. HALLE. 1977. "Manual Signing as a Language System and as a Speech Initiator for the Nonverbal, Severely

Handicapped Student." In E. Sontag, ed., *Educational Programming for the Severely and Profoundly Handicapped*. Reston, Va.: Council for Exceptional Children. Pp. 335–347.

TASK FORCE REPORT ON THE MENTALLY RETARDED-DEAF. 1973. Washington, D.C.: Office of the Assistant Secretary for Human Development, Office of Mental Retardation Coordination, November.

WITHROW, F., AND C. NYGREN. 1975. *Language, Materials, and Curriculum Management for the Handicapped Learner*. Columbus, Ohio: Charles E. Merrill.

WOLF, J. M., AND R. M. ANDERSON. 1969. *The Multiply Handicapped Child*. Springfield, Ill.: Charles C Thomas.

13

Public and professional views of exceptional children and their needs have changed dramatically over the past two decades. The special education programs designed to meet the needs of exceptional children have shown a comparable change. Some major trends and social forces that are responsible for or accompany these changes can be identified. The end results or consequences of these trends are hard to evaluate since we are still in the midst of their influence. While we have not yet felt all their implications, it is important for the student to grasp where we are headed and what factors are at work changing us from the way we are now to something new and different in the future.

We have chosen to discuss six of the most important forces now at work in terms of their impact and future consequences. These are as follows: (1) the changing role of parents, (2) the impact of state and federal legislation, (3) the role of the courts, (4) the move to least-restrictive alternatives and mainstreaming, (5) the move to reduce the detrimental effects of labels, and (6) the movement to early education.

The changing role of parents

During the past twenty years the increase of parent and citizen action in behalf of the handicapped and disadvantaged child sometimes leaves the impression that parent education and participation began only recently. Actually, parents began meaningful participation before the turn of the century in the child-study movement initiated by the noted psychologist G. Stanley Hall. The emergence of the Parent-Teacher Association prior to World War I was another step forward in parent activism. The post–World-War-I era when parent education became established as a part of school policy and the influential writings of Dewey and Watson, which featured the pliability of the young child, also added to the parent movement (Schlossman, 1976).

Nevertheless, the importance of the more recent parents' movement in the field of exceptional children cannot be overestimated. In many respects the other changes—the legislation, additional professional resources, and the court actions—are merely consequences of the forces put into motion by the organized parents' movement. The parents have gone through a number of phases and roles which may be referred to as: (1) parents as scapegoats, (2) parents as program organizers, (3) parents as political activists, and (4) parents as program participants and partners.

467

PARENTS AS SCAPEGOATS

In the 1940s and 1950s, the parent was often identified as a cause of the problems of the exceptional child and in many cases became the scapegoat for most of the problems. Particularly in cases such as emotional disturbance, it was the parent who was identified by professionals as the basic cause of the problem. Such identification led to an attitude of suspicion and distrust on the part of the professional and to an attitude of guarded defensiveness on the part of parents who sensed the professional's disapproval of their performance as parents.

The roles of the professionals and the parents of handicapped children have been the topic for much discussion. Many professionals have been concerned about what was then a prevailing professional attitude that regarded parents as a barrier to the child's development. Gallagher (1956) objected to the term *rejecting parents* to describe parents who experience understandable stress in trying to deal with one of life's major crises. He commented:

> What parent could be completely happy or positively oriented to a child who is quadriplegic, or blind, or severely mentally retarded, or, for that matter, completely normal in every respect?
>
> It might be useful in considering this problem for the reader to picture in his mind the most emotionally mature individual he knows. Should we expect him or her to accept totally a child with these handicaps and accompanying problems with merely a calm smile or philosophical shrug of the shoulders? The I-like-to-suffer-because-it-makes-me-feel-so-good-and-noble philosophy occurs quite frequently in soap operas, but fortunately does not turn up too often in real life situations. Parents are entitled to a little negative outpouring without having their human response labelled as something psychologically revolting. (p. 273)

Such problems have diminished over the past decades but have not been eliminated, as can be noted by a recent example of soul searching by conscientious professionals. Cansler, Martin, and Valand (1975) stated:

> Have we as professionals working in a field that traditionally has been child-centered unwittingly cast parents into the role of adversary, object of pity, inhibitor of growth, or automatic misfit, while expecting them to perform in a way expected of no other parents? Have we been too quick to focus on weakness and too slow to recognize the normality of the behaviors we see? (p. 9)

Many parents had attempted to encourage the local education authorities to provide some program to aid their handicapped children. Failing in the effort they formed local programs of their own in church basements, in vacant stores, in any place that would house them. These makeshift arrangements at least provided some type of organized care and experience for their handicapped children and demonstrated the feasibility of these programs for the local schools.

Those local organizations, loosely formed by parents around the common needs of their children, often provided important informal help and assistance to new parents entering into the problem of finding aid for their handicapped children. It has been found in other settings that those who have had actual experience with a problem (such as alcoholism or emotional disturbance) are often the best counselors for persons with a similar problem since literally they have been there (for example, Alcoholics Anonymous). In many respects the parents who counsel other parents provide a base of confidence that the problem can be dealt with and that other people understand and share the anxieties and worries that often accompany the discovery that one's child has special problems.

Such local organizations also helped parents meet the general public, which is not the easiest of their tasks. Marcus (1977) has observed that "For all families, dealing with the public means confronting ignorance or callousness, having to explain inexplicable behavior, suppressing anger or shame, and eventually developing a 'thick skin,' a sense of humor, or a casual indifference" (p. 392).

PARENTS AS POLITICAL ACTIVISTS

The logical next step in the process of parental activity was in the formation of larger and more politically active organizations of parents. The parents quickly realized that fundamental changes were needed in the allocation of resources at local, state, and federal levels. No casual or haphazard approach was going to provide much permanent assistance for them or their exceptional children. Accordingly, in the 1940s and 1950s, they were able to form large parent groups as exemplified by the National Association of Retarded Citizens, the United Cerebral Palsy Foundation, and the Association for Children with Learning Disabilities.

In these organizations parents were able to make an impact directly on state legislators and to effect the passage of legislation that provided state programs and state support for handicapped children. State laws generally took the form of providing financial help that encouraged local school systems to take more responsibility for programming in this area. The parent organizations also were successful in obtaining legislation that provided for additional trained personnel, for needed research, and for a variety of other programs that brought the handicapped to the attention of the general public and also attracted more qualified people into the field to provide a stronger professional base (Cain, 1976). This activism took another form in initiating the various legal suits that brought the cause of exceptional children into the courts, a trend to be noted in more detail later in this chapter.

PARENTS AS PROGRAM PARTICIPANTS

Another major step in the changing role of parents took place when the parents themselves began to participate meaningfully in the programs. Such participation grew as more information was gained regarding the role that parents can play in the early development of the disadvantaged child (Levenstein, 1971). In several reviews by Bronfenbrenner (1975) and by Ryan (1974), the positive roles that parents can play by actively participating in the program for their children were confirmed. It became more and more appropriate, therefore, for parents to become members of the treatment team rather than unwanted and suspected outsiders as they had been only a quarter of a century earlier.

Turnbull and Turnbull (1978) list several reasons why there has been movement toward a parent-professional partnership based on mutual respect and decision making:

1. the experimental evidence that parents can positively influence the development of their children through teaching them at home
2. the encouraging results of early intervention in ameliorating some of the developmental deficits associated with moderate and severe handicaps
3. the success of parents in bringing litigation to establish the educational rights of their children
4. federal legislation, notably Public Law, 94–142, that sets forth clear standards for parental involvement in the educational process

One of the most recent steps was to certify the rights of parents as full-fledged and active participants in the programs provided for in

Public Law 94–142, the Education for All Handicapped Children Act. In a quarter of a century, the parents of handicapped children have evolved from being suspect to becoming partners with the professionals in treatment, and have made that transformation largely through their own individual and collective efforts. As will be explained later under legislation, Public Law 94–142 specifies that parents or guardians must be consulted and that schools must provide appropriate education for all handicapped children at no cost to the parent or guardian.

The impact of state and federal legislation

Ever since the turn of the century, states have been involved in a limited way in subsidizing programs in public schools for the severer handicaps—the blind, the deaf, the physically impaired. Some states helped local school systems organize and support classes for the mentally retarded and the behaviorally disordered.

It was not until after World War II that a major thrust was made by states to support financially special classes and services for all types of handicapped children in local schools. This expansion created an emergency in the late 1940s and early 1950s because of the short supply of professional educators and the lack of knowledge about the education of exceptional children.

Although traditionally education is a local matter, the need for knowledge and personnel was a federal matter. After much debate, the federal government between 1957 and 1963 acceded to supporting limited research and limited training for the preparation of professional personnel.

Only since the passage of the Elementary and Secondary Education Act in 1965 did the federal government become involved in public education in a significant way. It still contributes less than 10 percent of the total cost of education, while the state and local governments contribute over 90 percent of the cost of public education from kindergarten through grade twelve.

Federal legislation in support of handicapped children was not easy to obtain. Parents groups had organized and with the aid of other interested citizens convinced Congress that they needed help. The arguments that they used were compelling, as was the intensity of feeling that accompanied it. Why should handicapped children and their parents be penalized through the accident of birth in a particular state or a particular region of a state? Were not American citizens (in this case the parents of handicapped children) entitled to equal treatment anywhere in the United States? Should they, in addition to the special burdens of having a handicapped child, be forced to move their family to another community where special education resources were available, or to send their child to some institution far away from home and family because no local resources existed? The manifest unfairness of the situation called out for special attention.

The United States Congress was responsive, but the reaction was at first fragmentary and limited in nature. Table 13.1 details the legislation passed from 1957 to 1967. The Congress first passed a variety of special legislation to improve the research and training efforts to help the deaf and mentally retarded. The 1963 passage of Public Law 88-164 represented the first major expansion applying training and research funds to a broader group of handicapped children. While the list of federal laws is long and impressive, we will limit our discussion to two of the more comprehensive pieces of legislation that illustrate the important role legislation has played at the federal level in changing the status of handicapped children.

The year after the landmark Elementary and Secondary Education Act was passed by the Congress, it was amended to include a major collection of legislative authority for the handicapped contained in earlier legislation. These included:

> special grants to states to encourage new programs for handicapped children
>
> the support of research and demonstration projects to seek better ways to educate the handicapped
>
> establishment of regional resource centers to help teachers develop specific educational programs and strategies
>
> extension of provisions for training leadership personnel to head training programs and administer programs for the handicapped
>
> establishment of a nationwide set of centers for deaf-blind children to aid multiply handicapped children
>
> insurance that some funds for innovative programs in general education were reserved for special projects for the handicapped
>
> establishment of a major Bureau of Education for the Handicapped within the Office of Education to administer these and other provisions for the handicapped

That flood of provisions served notice that the federal government was beginning to accept responsibilities to provide support resources for the handicapped and to encourage and aid the states in carrying out their basic responsibilities.

Ten years after this initiative, programs for the handicapped had dramatically increased across the country. States began putting a

TABLE 13.1

Basic federal legislation for education of the handicapped, 1957–1967

Year	Authority	Purpose
1957	PL 83-531, cooperative research	Action of the Appropriation Committee earmarked for the retarded approximately two-thirds of the $1 million appropriated
1958	PL 85-905, captioned films	A program of captioning films for cultural enrichment and recreation of deaf persons
	PL 85-926, professional personnel	Grants for training leadership personnel in education of the mentally retarded
1961	PL 87-276, teachers of the deaf	Grants for training basic instructional personnel in education of the deaf
1963	PL 88-164, Section 301, professional personnel	Expanded authority to train personnel for handicapping conditions not previously covered; "hard of hearing, speech impaired, visually handicapped, seriously emotionally disturbed, crippled, or other health impaired" were added to mentally retarded and deaf
	PL 88-164, Section 302, research and demonstration	Grants for research and demonstration projects in the area of education of the handicapped
1965	PL 89-36, National Technical Institute for the Deaf	Created a new source for higher education for the deaf
	PL 89-313, state schools	Amended Title I, ESEA, to provide grants to states for children in state-operated or state-supported schools for the handicapped
1966	PL 89-694, model secondary school for the deaf	Created a model high school in Washington, D.C.
	PL 89-750, education of handicapped children (Title VI, ESEA)	Grants to states for preschool, elementary, and secondary school children; National Advisory Committee; Bureau of Education for the Handicapped
1967	PL 90-170, mental retardation amendments of 1967	Extended basic training authority, added new authority for training personnel and for research in area of physical education and recreation for handicapped children
	PL 90-247, amendments to Title VI, ESEA	Regional resource centers; centers for deaf-blind children; expansion of media services; grants for recruitment and information dissemination; earmarking 15 percent of Title III, ESEA, for handicapped children; intramural research and contracts for research

Source: Adapted from Martin, 1968, p. 497.

much greater share of their educational dollars into educating the handicapped, increasing their contributions by almost 300 percent (Gallagher et al., 1975).

One major area of continued dissatisfaction was that some states were still not assuming responsibility for providing services for many of their handicapped children. This led to the next major legislative initiative: Public Law 94-142, the Education for All Handicapped Children Act, passed in 1975 to take effect in 1977.

The purpose of the act was to make certain that needed services reached all handicapped children. To that end the federal government authorized the spending of up to $3 billion by 1982, much larger sums of money to aid the states than had previously been provided from the federal level. In return for this aid, states were required to provide evidence that they were doing their utmost to help handicapped children receive needed services.

The stated purpose of the Education for All Handicapped Children Act was as follows:

> To assure that all handicapped children have available to them . . . a free, appropriate public education which emphasizes special education and related services to meet their unique needs, . . . to assist states and localities to provide for the education of all handicapped children, and to assess and assure the effectiveness of efforts to educate handicapped children. (Pelosi and Hocutt, 1977, p. 3)

Some of the specific requirements placed on the states were as follows:

1. Each state must submit a state plan to the commissioner of education, and each local education agency must submit an application to the state.
2. The state plan must guarantee:
   a. assurance of a goal of full educational opportunity for all handicapped children and a detailed timetable for accomplishing that goal
   b. assurance of an individualized education plan (IEP) for all handicapped children
   c. assurance that special education is being provided to all handicapped children in the *least restrictive environment*
   d. maintenance and use of programs and procedures for a system of comprehensive personnel development—in-service training
   e. provision for an annual evaluation of the effectiveness of programs in meeting the educational needs of handicapped children

The implications of this broad-ranging legislation are many, not the least of which is the changing of the balance of power and authority in education away from the states and toward the federal government.

Another important change has been the increased interest the law has stirred up in the educational problems of moderately to severely handicapped children. This increased interest stems from two elements of the legislation. First, the emphasis on *all* children means that some children previously excluded from public school programs by the severity of their handicap must now be considered.

Second, there is the emphasis in the legislation on placing the child in the *least restrictive alternative,* or the most normal education setting possible. In this view the special class is preferable to the institution, the resource room preferable to the special class, and the regular classroom preferable to the resource room, *if the capabilities of the child permit.* Abeson and Zettel (1977) explain that it was never intended that this legislation would force all handicapped children to be educated in the regular classroom. For many moderately to severely impaired children and multiply handicapped children, the normal classroom would clearly be inappropriate, but many such youngsters were brought back into the orbit of the public schools, requiring attention that was previously denied them.

Although individualization of instruction has long been one of the key concepts in special education, the design and formalization of the individualized education plan (IEP) has been a new and complicated experience. The law itself specifies in some detail that the IEP should include:

1. a statement of the present levels of educational performance of each child
2. a statement of annual goals, including short-term instructional objectives
3. a statement of the specific educational services to be provided to each child and the extent to which such child will be able to participate in regular educational programs
4. the projected date for initiation and anticipated duration of such services and appropriate objective criteria and evaluation procedures for determining . . . whether instructional objectives are being achieved

In two decades the federal government has moved from a position of little concern or involvement to become a major partner with the local and state public education programs for the handicapped. By 1978 the total federal investment approached $1 billion and encompassed all the support areas that undergird successful educational programs—research, development, training, demonstration, technical assistance—plus a major service supplement to the states. Special areas of federal emphasis have included early childhood, the multiply handicapped, and the development of special media products to instruct the handicapped. Each of those priorities has had a clearly discernible impact on increasing needed services. The federal programs supporting training and research have provided trained leadership personnel and scientists to guide the expanding programs and new ideas to supplement the local and state service programs. Legislation also includes monitoring and evaluation roles through which the federal government has become a force in setting standards and urging compliance with those standards.

Gifted children, alone among the exceptional children, are not included in this cornucopia of legislation and remain without meaningful assistance from federal sources, though some small beginnings have been made. The federal government in 1977–1978 expended $2.56 million on special education programs for the gifted student, less than 1 percent of that spent on those children with handicapping conditions.

The trends seem to suggest more federal financial support and probably more control of program directions as well. In this area, as in others, those who provide money want to have a say in how it is spent.

The role of the courts

Since World War II individuals and groups interested in the education of handicapped children have appealed to governmental sources at the local, state, and federal levels to gain help and assistance. It has only been since the early 1970s, however, that there has been a sustained effort to use the courts as a device to bring additional resources to these children and their families.

PHILOSOPHICAL BASES FOR COURT ACTION

As our society has matured enough to reject the option of physically removing the handicapped from view (out of sight, out of mind), many persons have begun to review the legal status of the handicapped in the society itself. If handicapped persons are citizens, are they not entitled to all the rights and privileges of ordinary citizens? It is out of this type of self-examination that another major trend has emerged, namely: the deliberate attempt to translate these abstract rights into tangible societal actions.

The use of the courts to establish the rights of individuals has been a common device used by minority groups beginning with the classic school desegregation case of Brown vs. the Board of Education in 1954. Since that time, courts have reaffirmed the rights of minority citizens in a wide variety of settings. It is clear that those interested in the rights of the handicapped have watched these cases with some interest and have seen that a similar situation applies to the handicapped whose rights as citizens need to be reaffirmed.

One of the most vigorous of those actions has been the seeking of court decisions to support the rights of the handicapped to an appropriate education. Most state constitutions have statements in them to the effect that "every child has a right to a free public education." Seizing on the phrase *all children have a right to education,* various interested groups have brought legal suits against states to compel them to provide special education that would fulfill the stated promise.

An example of the early promise to educate all children at public expense is found in Article X, Section [1] of the Wisconsin Constitution adopted March 13, 1848, which stated: "The legislature shall provide by law for the establishment of district schools which shall be free to all children between the ages of four and twenty years" (Melcher, 1976).

The use of *class action* law suits has been influential in changing the status of handicapped children in the United States. A class action suit provides that legal action taken as part of a suit applies not only to the individual who brought the particular case to the courts but applies equally well to all members of the particular class to which that individual belongs. Thus the rights of all mentally retarded children and emotionally disturbed children can be reaffirmed by one case involving one exceptional child.

SOME EXAMPLES OF COURT ACTION

A wide variety of court cases have laid the groundwork for the rights of handicapped children. Some of the major ones are noted below:

Case	Judgment
Brown vs. Board of Education, 1954	Education in separate facilities is inherently unequal
Pennsylvania Association for Retarded Children vs. Commonwealth of Pennsylvania, 1971	Acknowledged the right of all handicapped children to a free public education

Case	*Judgment*
Hobson vs. Hansen, 1967	Education in separate ability tracks in the same school is inherently unequal
Wyatt vs. Stickney, 1972	Individuals placed in state institutions have a right to appropriate treatment programs in such institutions
Mills vs. District of Columbia, 1972	Lack of funds is not an acceptable excuse for excluding handicapped children from public school

Gilhool (1976) has summarized the major outcomes of the first and subsequent court cases on education for the handicapped. In describing the landmark Pennsylvania court case, he noted three major outcomes of the decision of the federal court:

1. The court ordered "zero reject" education—that is, access to free public schools for all retarded children whatever the degree of retardation or associated handicaps. Of the fifteen thousand children previously out of school but admitted to the public schools as a consequence of the decree, over 50 percent were only mildly or moderately retarded.

2. Education and training provided to all children must be based on programs appropriate to the needs and capacities of each child. The language of "appropriateness" and the obligation to provide an appropriate program to each child were borrowed from Pennsylvania's education code, which purported to guarantee a proper program of education and training to *all* Pennsylvania's exceptional children.

3. The appropriateness of the program for each child is to be determined within the confines of a presumption in favor of the most integrated, most normalized program; that is, a regular class with a resource room is preferable to a special class. This order for integration was the courts' response to the problem of stigmatic labeling and classification.

IMPLEMENTING COURT ACTION

In previous encounters with the school, the parent of the handicapped child often depended on the educator to be moved by compassion or by professional challenge to take on the difficult issue of educating handicapped children. The court decisions have changed that. It is now not merely through the generosity of the educator that special help for the handicapped is provided; instead it is the fundamental right of the child to an education, and it is the responsibility of the educator to provide it. These court decisions create an expectation that something will be done, but do not guarantee it. Just as laws have to be enforced, and money promised has to be appropriated, so court decisions once made have to be executed. The class action suits that affect large numbers of citizens have been implemented very slowly.

It is now clear that merely passing a law or getting a court decision is no guarantee that something will be done. Kirp, Kurloff, and Buss (1975) in reviewing the results of the court decisions and their implementation concluded:

1. Legal mandates do not fulfill themselves; they must rely on others for implementation.
2. The mandates most readily implemented are those that require a minimum amount of organizational change.
3. Resistance to such mandates comes not so much from resentfulness and malevolence as from a perceived threat to the current institutional and social structure and to the people who are functioning comfortably within that structure.

Hobbs (1975) concluded that full implementation of the laws and court decisions requires (1) intense and lasting pressure together with systematic incentives, (2) court-appointed overseers to help direct and encourage implementation to completion, (3) the provision of some additional resources to pay for what has been mandated, and (4) the strong commitment of institutional administrators (that is, school superintendents, state education officials, and others).

The financial and psychic cost of closing down state institutions, of reorganizing the public schools, or of providing special services to every handicapped child does amount to substantial change and markedly increased financial investment. It is still up to the American culture, as a whole, to determine the degree to which they wish to live up to the theoretical ideas of equality that were placed in laws and constitutions many years ago.

There is evidence that the court decisions and legislation related to the handicapped can be linked together. The series of court decisions that reaffirmed the states' responsibility to provide education for all handicapped children caused great dismay among many state executive and legislative leaders who wondered aloud where the additional money would be found.

Mainstreaming and least restrictive alternatives

In the 1970s there has arisen an accelerated movement to teach handicapped children together with normal peers whenever possible. This program is called *mainstreaming*. It is an effort to provide special services for these children in the least restrictive environment. By mainstreaming is meant that the exceptional child (1) will be placed with his or her normal peers, (2) will receive special services in the regular classes (not special classes), and (3) will interact as much as possible with his or her normal peers in a least restrictive environment. To understand this movement it is necessary to trace its development and to analyze the social forces leading to its implementation.

RESTRICTIVE ENVIRONMENTS—SEGREGATION

The early provision for the education of exceptional children was the organization of residential schools—in 1817 for the deaf, in 1848 for the mentally retarded. Such provisions took the children out of the home and out of the community, segregating them full time in state or private residential schools. The residential schools or institutions are now considered the most restrictive of environments.

PARTIAL INTEGRATION

Beginning in the latter part of the nineteenth century and in the early part of the twentieth century, a movement developed to integrate handicapped children in the home and community by oganizing special schools and special classes in public schools. This movement obtained its impetus on the assumption that if handicapped adults are to live in the community, it is important that they not be segregated during childhood but that they should be integrated in the community by remaining at home, in the community, and in the public schools. This approach was considered integration, a rejection of segregation for the mildly handicapped. Following this movement, special schools and special classes were organized in public school systems for the mildly handicapped.

EARLY ATTEMPTS AT MAINSTREAMING

The current concept of mainstreaming is not new. In 1913 a "sight saving class" was organized in Cleveland and called a "cooperative class." The children spent a portion of the day in a regular grade with normal peers and a part of the day in a special class for close eye work. Today these classes are called "resource rooms." When classes for the hearing impaired were organized in the public schools, it was found that many of the children were not deaf but hard of hearing. With the advent of improved hearing aids, it was found that hard-of-hearing children could be educated in the regular grades with the help of itinerant speech clinicians. Following that development, classes for the hard-of-hearing began to disappear in school systems. Only children with severe hearing impairments—the deaf—remained in special schools and classes.

Following World War II special classes for many types of handicaps expanded at an accelerated rate in the public schools. With the expansion came the cry for deinstitutionalization and for more adequate provisions in the local schools. As indicated in previous chapters, the enrollment of the educable mentally retarded decreased in residential schools as special classes for the mentally retarded increased in the public schools. The same trends are found with the other kinds of exceptional children.

IMPETUS TO CURRENT MAINSTREAMING EMPHASIS

One may ask, "If mainstreaming was developing gradually, why the current surge for least restrictive alternatives and mainstreaming in legislation, the press, and popular magazines, as well as among professionals?" A simple answer could be a reaction against the use and misuse of labeling children and placing them in special classes, especially the mentally retarded and the emotionally disturbed. The following criticisms of special classes have been given.

1. Many children were misclassified as mentally retarded. From the 1920s to the 1940s, special classes for the mentally retarded were organized for the obviously retarded children who were unable to learn in the regular grades. In Wisconsin, for example, the state regulation for special classes in 1927–1928 stated "the intelligence quotient of these children for whom state aid is drawn shall range from fifty to seventy inclusive" (Report of the Superintendent of Public Instruction, Madison, Wisconsin, 1927–1928, p. 61).

Following World War II when other states began to subsidize special classes for the mentally retarded in public schools, the IQs required for enrollment began to rise to 75, to 80, and in a few instances even to 84. The American Association on Mental Deficiency, as indicated in Chapter 4, defined mental retardation psychometrically as minus one standard deviation, or an IQ below 84 to 85, as mentally retarded. Special schools and classes for the mentally retarded increased in enrollment from 87,000 in 1948 to 1,350,000 in 1975. (See Table 1.3.) When reaction set in against classifying a disproportionate number of minority and bilingual children as mentally retarded based on intelligence tests standardized on white children, the AAMD in 1973 redefined mental retardation psychometrically as minus two standard deviations, or an IQ below 70.

It appears that our society has gone the full circle in the concept of mental retardation; that is, from using an IQ below 70 from 1915 (when Goddard defined a "moron" as one whose IQ is 69 and below) to using an IQ of 84 and below in 1962 (as defined by AAMD) and back to an IQ below 70 in current use. If we have mislabeled children as mentally retarded, we are now mainstreaming those children who should never have been assigned to special classes for the mentally retarded. In other words, a partial reason for mainstreaming is to correct the mistake of mislabeling and misclassifying children who should never have been assigned to special classes for the mentally retarded.

2. Many minority children were misclassified as mentally retarded. As indicated earlier, the diagnosis of mental retardation was often based on a score from intelligence tests that had been standardized on whites. This caused the assignment of a disproportionate number of minority-group children to special classes. In the larger cities the special classes enrolled a disproportionate number of blacks, Puerto Ricans, Mexican-Americans, and Indians. In San Francisco in 1973, for example, black children were found in classes for the educable retarded at twice (53 percent) their proportion in the population which was 27 percent. In Riverside, California, there were 300 percent more Mexican-Americans and 50 percent more blacks in the special classes than their rate in the community (Mercer, 1972, 1973).

When this fact was added to the inappropriate use of intelligence tests, such as administering verbal intelligence tests in English to Spanish-speaking children, there was widespread suspicion that special education was being used as a means of getting troublesome minority-group children out of the regular education program (Jones, 1976).

If one adds the potential stigma of labeling a child mentally retarded or emotionally distured, as one had to do to place the child in a special program, and the possible insignificant results obtained from that placement, it is easy to see why there were strong efforts made to break down the special class organization so familiar in the public schools and to return such children to the regular educational program (Hobbs, 1975).

3. Special classes showed few beneficial results. Research on the efficacy of special class placement by Blatt and Garfunkel (1969), by

Goldstein, Moss, and Jordon (1965), and by Kirk (1964) showed fewer beneficial effects than was expected. These results eroded confidence in one of the fundamental assumptions in special education, that is, that a specially trained teacher working with small groups of exceptional children could make a significant difference in academic achievement.

4. *Special classes for the mentally retarded became classes for problem children.* A further concern of special educators was that the special class program was becoming involved in educational politics in ways never conceived of by their originators. The standards for placement of educable retarded children in special classes in many school systems was often such (that is, an IQ score under 80) that 10 percent or more of a school population could theoretically be eligible for placement. Since few school programs would place more than 2 percent of children in such special education classes, which 2 percent were being placed? In many school systems it was that 2 percent who caused the most active trouble for the regular classroom teacher! A number of special educators began to raise the issue of what the real goal of such placement was. Was it to provide special education services for the child in question, or merely to remove a troublesome child from the regular educational program?

THE CHANGE TO MAINSTREAMING

Dunn (1968) was one of the first of the special educators to comment on this situation. He urged special educators to stop being pressured into "a continuing and expanding special education program (special classes) that we know now to be undesirable for many of the children we are dedicated to serve" (p. 5).

Gallagher (1972) pointed out that "special education too often was an exclusionary process masquerading as a remedial process" and added that there was precious little evidence that special education was returning a significant number of children to the regular class. His comments were particularly true of the educable retarded. Once they were identified and placed as *educable retarded,* such children were often in the special education stream for the balance of their school careers.

All the forces just mentioned have come together to create a powerful surge within the public schools toward abandoning special class programs for exceptional children and replacing them with regular class programs, which would be supplemented by special remedial or special educational services provided by a resource or itinerant teacher (Reynolds and Birch, 1977).

WHAT MAINSTREAMING SHOULD PROVIDE

The essential elements of mainstreaming provide that the exceptional child

1. will spend more time in school with his or her normal peers
2. will receive coordinated special and regular educational services
3. will have the time and opportunity to interact socially with normal peers (Kaufman et al., 1975)

Unless the program in question has at least the following characteristics, it probably should not be called mainstreaming:

1. The regular teacher can identify the exceptional children and state what special program modifications are being planned for each of them.
2. There are special education personnel available to work actively with the regular teacher.
3. There is an educational administrator whose major responsibility is to oversee the program for exceptional children.

As special educators broaden program objectives from the cognitive to other dimensions, such as social development, the case for mainstreaming becomes even more important. If children learn much of their patterns of behavior from observation and imitation, then to what advantage is it to place an emotionally disturbed child in a special class with other emotionally disturbed children, all of whom are behaving bizarrely? Where will that child see the proper behavior to emulate? Obviously it is important for them to have some time in the presence of children whose behavior and social interaction patterns are those you wish the child in question to adopt.

Hartup (1978) summarized the position as follows:

> Peer interaction contains numerous elements through which it contributes to the socialization of the child. Such contributions are unique in that aggressive socialization, sex-role learning, and moral development would be seriously impeded if children did not have contact with other children in their formative years . . . Usually family and school values tend to reinforce values emanating from the peer culture and vice versa. (pp. 47–48)

Table 13.2 shows the projected advantages and disadvantages of the two major alternative educational environments and strategies currently being used: special class and mainstreaming.

TABLE 13.2

Two alternative models for educating exceptional children

Mainstreaming	*Special class*
DESCRIPTION The exceptional children stay in the regular classroom for most of the day. Although they receive some special help from resource teachers or specialists, they are considered a part of the regular program.	DESCRIPTION The exceptional children are placed in a small group with a specially trained teacher. In most instances they will remain with that group for the better part of the day and sometimes will stay with the same teacher for two or three years.
RATIONALE The exceptional children will best be able to cope in a normal world by learning to adapt in as normal a school environment as possible. Their lessons will not be too easy and thus not fail to challenge as in some special classes. Special instruction will be available when needed.	RATIONALE The exceptional children will not be frustrated, humiliated, and discouraged by constant failure or inappropriate requirements they experience in the regular program. The special teacher should be able to teach the child at his or her level and restore self-confidence and enthusiasm.
IMPLEMENTATION PROBLEM Handicapped children can get lost in the shuffle and will always be at or near the bottom of the class no matter what is done. Individualized instruction will be limited by the shortage of special resource teachers.	IMPLEMENTATION PROBLEM Special classes are often used as dumping ground for behavioral problems or difficult children. Once in this class, it is very hard to get out. Often treated as "dummy class." The teacher may be too impressed by children's mental or emotional limitations and fail to challenge them.

EVALUATION OF MAINSTREAMING

Does mainstreaming work? Does it provide for a more effective social and educational environment for exceptional children to develop in than any of the alternatives? The answers to these questions will have to await more definitive evidence than is now available. If history is any judge, we shall find that mainstreaming will work in some instances, in some communities, at some ages, and not in others. The real question is "Can we define and reproduce the conditions under which mainstreaming has been a success?"

Merely placing a handicapped child with normal peers can hardly be expected to create educational miracles for the child nor to transform the attitudes of his or her normal peers. There is some research evidence on this point.

Positive results of mainstreaming have been reported by a number of investigations at the preschool and first-grade level. Fredericks (1978) reported favorable results with preschool moderately retarded children (see Chapter 12).

Cantrell and Cantrell (1976) reported the effects of mainstreaming on first graders in twenty schools in Tennessee. Two elementary experimental schools and two elementary control schools from each of five districts in Tennessee participated in the project. In the experimental schools the first-grade teachers had trained support teachers working with them to solve the problems of any child about whom a teacher was concerned. Children referred for help went through a systematic analysis of their needs, and a specific program was planned for them. Children with a variety of specific handicaps (intellectual, perceptual, physical, emotional) were included in the program.

The results of achievement tests given to both sets of schools revealed significantly greater achievement gains for the exceptional students in the regular program at all levels of intellectual functioning. Those results suggest that mainstreaming at the primary-grade level can be effective, at least for mild and borderline handicapped children, if properly trained support personnel are available. Much more evidence is needed to delineate the elements necessary for successful mainstreaming for more severe handicaps.

Shotel, Iano, and McGettigan (1972) studied the attitude of elementary teachers associated with a mainstreaming and resource room program. They found that at the beginning of the study the elementary teachers expressed optimism concerning the retarded child's adjustment. At the end of the study, the elementary teachers found retarded children were not achieving academically and were not accepted by the other children. The elementary teachers were more positive in their attitude toward the learning disabled child than toward the emotionally disturbed and retarded child.

The Bureau for the Education of Handicapped Children has sponsored in Texas an extensive study on mainstreaming known as Project PRIME. This study has not been fully reported, but several preliminary studies have been published. Gottlieb and Baker (1975) analyzed the social acceptance of 291 educable mentally retarded children in relation to the amount of time spent in the regular grades. Seven thousand nonhandicapped children in grades three, four, and five furnished the sociometric data. Gottlieb and Baker found that when the children spent 25 percent of their time in the regular grades, they were more socially accepted by their peers than when they spent 75 percent or more of their time in the regular grades. In studying the reading activities of educable mentally retarded children assigned to regular grades, Gottlieb and associates (1976) cast doubt on the ability of the regular grades to cope with the academic instruction of educable mentally retarded children.

Kaufman et al. (1978) reported the results for children in the third- to fifth-grade age range. In Texas, in one of the largest studies conducted on this subject, 356 educable mentally retarded students were placed in a regular class program with special professional help. They were compared with the same number of normal peers who were their classmates and with 273 retarded children who remained in special class programs. Data were collected on a wide variety of achievement, social-behavior, and learner-behavior characteristics, and over 400 teachers were involved in the project.

The results indicated that the mainstreamed retarded youngsters did not seem to learn significantly more than those retarded students who remained in the special classes. In addition, their teachers rated them lower than the nonmainstreamed children on characteristics of social and personal behaviors, such as expressiveness and outgoingness. Furthermore, they participated in fewer interactions with their teachers.

Although the mainstreamed children were rated as significantly less socially accepted, their attitude toward school was not significantly different from either the normal or the special class students. The results must be analyzed more carefully to identify those factors related to superior performance in all these settings, but the data seem to indicate clearly that there is no easy road to an effective or positive educational adjustment for the retarded child, either in the special class or in a mainstreamed program.

A review of other studies on mainstreaming shows equivocal results. Tentatively one may state that mainstreaming of the mildly handicapped appears feasible with preschool and primary-age children, with those with mild orthopedic, visual, and auditory impairments, and with the gifted. The questionable group is that of the intermediate-age mentally retarded, the seriously emotionally disturbed, and the severely handicapped.

Reynolds and Birch (1977) report other complications. These issues are the attitudes of teachers' associations and teachers' unions regarding mainstreaming. They report that some teacher organizations have requested (1) a moratorium on mainstreaming and a return to programs of self-contained special classes or (2) a reduction in the size of the class by five children for every handicapped child assigned to the regular grades.

The final resolution of how and in what way the exceptional child should fit into the public educational programs in the United States will be a source of study and debate for many years to come and probably will be determined by values in vogue at the time.

The use of labels

In recent years there has been an attempt by some to abolish the labels and categories we use with exceptional children. The major reason for the rejection of labels is that a label has little educational relevance. Telling a teacher that a child is dyslexic, brain injured, or mentally retarded does not help the teacher to organize an instructional program. When a label is given to a child, it is sometimes used in the place of the more important assessment of educational needs.

Another reason given for decreasing the emphasis on labels and categories is that many children are mislabeled and miscategorized. To call a hard-of-hearing child "deaf" is to mislabel, or to call a child blind or legally blind when he has some vision is to mislabel. Many attacks on categories and labels cite errors like those but should instead be directed toward the *mis*labeling.

One troublesome issue intruding on these decisions is the potential effect of labeling on the exceptional child. In the process of providing special assistance, it is likely that the child must be given, under current procedures, a classification and label. For example, if a state will give additional money to a local school district that agrees to establish a program for the mentally retarded, then it will clearly wish the local school district to demonstrate that the child in question is, in fact, mentally retarded. In the process the child acquires a label.

In 1972 the question of "to label or not to label" became acute. The Secretary of Health, Education, and Welfare appointed a task force to study the issue. The task force, reported by Hobbs (1975), discussed the advantages and disadvantages of labeling. Their arguments as well as those of Gallagher (1976) on the relative merits of labeling are included in the following.

SUPPOSED ADVANTAGES OF LABELING

Proponents of labeling note the following:

1. It tends to identify the child and thereby serves as a basis for further diagnosis and treatment.
2. It serves as a basis for further research into etiology, prevention, and treatment.
3. It serves as a basis for differentiated treatment, often opening up opportunities that children might not experience in other programs.
4. It allows local schools to establish eligibility for additional resources through state and federal legislation.
5. It serves as a rallying point for volunteer groups that espouse

one group or another and are often influential in securing financial and other assistance.

6. It facilitates passage of legislation.
7. It serves as a rational structure for governmental administration.
8. It serves as a shorthand for communication, making it possible to focus on one relevant characteristic.

SUPPOSED DISADVANTAGES OF LABELING

Opponents of labeling note the following:

1. Labeling may tranquilize diagnosticians into reaching closure by applying labels (such as *autism* or *minimal brain dysfunction*) rather than outlining differentiated programs of treatment.
2. It allows misdiagnosis of minority-group children who show superficial abnormalities resulting from lack of experience.
3. It delays needed social reform by focusing on the individual rather than on social and ecological conditions.
4. It allows practices and policies to deprecate individuality and diverse cultural backgrounds.
5. It serves as a means of social control by eliminating undesirables from the mainstream. It has been used as "an exclusionary process disguised as a remedial process" (Gallagher, 1973).
6. Once labeled, a child often remains in an inappropriate program in spite of changing conditions.
7. It blinds people to the rapid and irregular growth patterns of childhood and may allow a child to remain in a program that he or she has outgrown.
8. It denies many children the normal experiences of childhood and wholesome community life.
9. It allows some children to be placed in inadequate, uncaring programs that "legitimize mistreatment" (Hobbs, 1975, p. 8), such as poorly staffed institutions.
10. In communication, it allows bias and stereotyping because of the incompleteness of the label.

THE MIDDLE GROUND

Because of the inherent dangers in labeling and the possibilities for damaging children's personalities and self-concepts, it is vital that certain precautions be taken if labeling is to be used. Although the

Hobbs report did not recommend the abolition of labels, it recommended a reduction of the harmful effects of their use by "(1) improvements in the classification system, (2) some constraints on the use of psychological tests, (3) improvements in procedures for early identification of children of developmental risk, (4) some safeguards in the use of records, and (5) attention to due process of law in classifying and placing exceptional children" (pp. 232–233).

The United States is not alone in its efforts to decrease the harmful effects of labeling. The Warnok Committee appointed by the British Parliament spent three years studying the problems of special education in the British Isles before issuing its report (Warnok, 1978). The problem of labels and categories caused members of the committee considerable concern. They preferred to describe handicapped children in terms of their educational needs but found this approach also difficult. In the end they accepted some of the categories (the blind, the deaf, the maladjusted) as a "serviceable form of description" (p. 44), but they changed the label *educationally subnormal* to *children with learning difficulties* with subcategories of *mild, moderate,* and *severe*. In this description they included other children who needed remedial services.

THE RESEARCH EVIDENCE

Since the proposed disadvantages are serious indeed, it is important to review what we know that would support those claims. It is clearly not enough to show that there is negative feeling toward the handicapped child. That feeling might be present, label or no. What must be demonstrated is some linkage between the label and the attitudes and actions of others. Some of the available evidence may be summarized in the following discussion.

Johnson (1950) found that retarded students seem to be isolated and rejected in sociometric studies in the regular classroom even when they are not identified and labeled. Goodman, Gottlieb, and Harmon (1972) found similar results when retarded children are identified, labeled, and placed in a regular grade under a mainstream program. Smith and Greenberg (1975) found that teachers tended to accept a diagnosis of mental retardation in hypothetical cases if the child was from a low-income family.

Gottlieb (1974) studied the attitude of peers in a fourth grade toward children labeled retarded. He concluded that the judgment of the children about a retarded child was based on their academic achievement and not on the label.

In a review of the literature by MacMillan, Jones, and Aloia (1974), it was concluded: "Few studies were found in which labeling was isolated, thus enabling differences between labeled and unlabeled groups to be attributed to the label use. The evidence uncovered failed to provide support for the notion that labeling has long lasting and devastating effects on those labeled" (p. 241).

In an experimental study of the impact of labeling on the rejection of the mentally ill, Kirk (1974) found that "there is little evidence that labelling the mentally ill makes a significant difference in how people react to them" (p. 108).

Early education for the handicapped

The final trend to be noted is the movement toward establishing programs for younger and younger handicapped children. This trend, like the others noted in this chapter, stems from many different forces: research evidence on child development, models of successful performance, and the observations of lay persons and experts.

The implementation of the general principle "the younger we start, the better" is not easy primarily because there is no single social institution, like the schools, through which programs can be directed.

The importance of early intervention to provide a proper developmental start for exceptional children has been known for many years. Leadership for such programs can be found in the field of the deaf where such children need assistance to develop communication systems from the earliest age possible. Other exceptionalities such as cerebral palsy are quickly brought to the attention of professionals at, or shortly after, birth. They receive attention from multidisciplinary teams who plan multifaceted treatment programs in such dimensions as physical therapy, speech and communication, and cognitive development at the earliest time in the child's life.

It has not been lack of awareness of the importance of early childhood that has been a problem but rather securing the resources to support the programs and the commitment of such social institutions as the public schools to take the responsibility for implementing programs for these children. Also, the condition of mildly handicapped children (learning disabled, educably retarded, behaviorally disturbed, or delayed development) is often overlooked by parents and community until they reach the public schools. The schools apply standards of expected development that are rarely expected by parents or neighbors at this age. Only then do these problems of developmental delay or inappropriate social adaptability reveal themselves.

RESEARCH EVIDENCE

The studies of Skeels, Kirk, and Heber on the mentally retarded reported in Chapter 4 and Hunt's influential review of what was known about the relationship of intelligence and experience (1961), among many others, led the way to an acceptance of the rich possibilities of early intervention. Hunt commented, "The assumption that intelligence is fixed and that its development is predetermined by the genes is no longer tenable" (p. 342). "It might be feasible to discover ways to govern the encounters that children have with their environments especially during the early years of their development, to achieve a substantially faster rate of intellectual capacity" (p. 363).

Karnes and Teska (1975) reviewed the growing literature on the effect of intervention programs on young children and reached the following conclusions:

> Can the developmental status of children be changed through deliberate programming? The answer to that from the available research is "yes." It is possible to move groups of children from one-half to one standard deviation higher on measures of intellectual ability. There is substantial evidence that many children will lose the temporary gain in intellectual ability as measured by standard tests, but will keep achievement and motivational gains for a longer period of time. There is substantial evidence to support the general principle, "the earlier the instructional program is begun, the better." While all studies did not show age differentials, those that did invariably showed the younger children in the program to be responding at a greater rate of gain than those who were older. (p. 219)

Stedman (1977) reviewed over forty longitudinal intervention research programs for children "at risk" for developmental problems and concluded:

> The manner in which a child is reared, and the environment into which he is born have a major impact on what he will become. The family's method of establishing social roles leaves little doubt that early family environment has a significant impact on the child's development before he reaches his second birthday. Where access to children can be gained in the early years, preferably during the language emergent years (one to two years of age), intervention programs will be more effective than those begun at later ages. There is evidence that the effects of early intervention programs for children are strengthened by the involvement of the child's parents. (pp. 2–3)

FEDERAL STIMULATION

One of the priorities of the Bureau of Education for the Handicapped in the U.S. Office of Education has been the stimulation of greater action to provide services to preschool handicapped children. This has been done by encouraging the states to use federal money to establish programs for the preschool handicapped, by encouraging and financing universities to begin personnel preparation programs to educate preschool handicapped, by establishing research programs in early education to provide more knowledge for the special programs for the preschool handicapped, and by establishing a set of over one hundred and fifty demonstration centers across the country to illustrate the best of current practices in preschool education for a wide variety of handicapping conditions.

This demonstration program began in a separate bill passed by the Congress (the Handicapped Children's Early Education Act) and received initial support of less than $1 million in 1968. The program had grown to $22 million by 1977 and was then serving over eight thousand handicapped children and their parents, as well as encouraging professionals to venture into areas not well covered under traditional programming.

> There has been a particular concentration on those projects involving children from birth to age 3, projects serving sparsely populated areas, projects using a variety of staffing patterns, projects for bilingual or multilingual groups, projects serving handicapped native American children and projects for children who are both handicapped and gifted. (DeWeerd and Cole, 1976, p. 156)

The development of special education programs for the preschool handicapped has resulted in many program changes from the traditional special education program, changes that are having their influence on the issue of how to aid exceptional children. Some of the more important of these changes are discussed in the following paragraphs.

LESS EMPHASIS ON CLASSIFICATION. The child with developmental problems at the preschool level is likely to have a wide variety of difficulties. The categorization of such children, or pigeonholing them, by use of such well-defined terms as *mentally retarded and speech handicapped* becomes less important than the need to identify the child's developmental problems and to take special action on them. Differential diagnosis of problems, except when the diagnosis is essential to special treatment as with language training for the deaf, becomes much less important at early ages.

MORE EMPHASIS ON MULTIDISCIPLINARY APPROACHES. The problems of the young handicapped child are likely to include the domains of health, education, and social psychological issues. No single profession could lay claim to all the expertise necessary to provide all the help that the child and his or her family will require. This has resulted in the bringing together of many different disciplines to work together in a single setting so that the family can have the range of expertise needed to develop a comprehensive treatment program. Table 13.3 shows the variety of disciplines that will often bring their skills to bear in a standard diagnostic evaluation of the child and family.

PARENT EDUCATION. The parent remains the primary caretaker of the child at the preschool age. Most programs at this level include the parents in the total treatment program, as noted earlier in this chapter.

TABLE 13.3

Typical areas of investigation in diagnosis

Areas of investigation	Personnel involved	Type of information obtained
(1) Social history	Social worker	Information relative to the functioning of the total family unit; note what the child's problem means to the family
(2) Physical examination	Pediatrician	Child's general health at present; review the child's medical history; note any physical defects that may be present
(3) Neurological examination	Neurologist	Specific information of any central nervous system impairment if brain damage is suspected; run an EEG to detect possibility of seizures or other malfunctioning
(4) Psychological examination	Psychologist	Data from the administration of psychometric techniques; use diagnostic tests to measure child's performance against normative standards and projective tests to determine nature of child's emotional responses
(5) Hearing examination	Audiologist or public health worker	Data from the application of audiometric procedures to determine any type of hearing impairment
(6) Vision examination	Ophthalmologist or public health worker	Detection of any visual impairment
(7) Speech examination	Speech pathologist	Child's ability to understand and/or use words, phrases, concepts
(8) Educational examination	Special education/early childhood	Diagnostic instruction to determine child's learning style and abilities (general here; more specific within the area of Assessment)

Source: From the book *Identifying Handicapped Children* by Lee Cross and Kenneth Goin. Copyright© 1977 by The University of North Carolina at Chapel Hill. By permission of the publisher, Walker and Company.

While parents often leave much of the care and education of their child to the schools when the child reaches 5 or 6, they are quite often prepared and ready to take responsibility for some of the training program for their child before that age. Many parents also appreciate the opportunity to do something constructive with their child who has often been a puzzlement and a source of great frustration to them. The professional community finds itself using more and more of its time and effort teaching parents rather than providing the service to the preschool handicapped child directly.

CHILD FIND. Quite often the handicapped child at school age identifies himself or herself through inadequate adaptation to the expectations and demands of the school program. The necessity for embarking on a major search for such children is not often a key school objective unless forced to it by governmental requirements. At the preschool level, however, it becomes important to search out those children in need of help, whose problems may be hidden or not realized until the child reaches the schoolhouse door. A substantial effort has been made to develop means for screening children to find those in need of special help. This means developing more sophisticated measures for evaluating or assessing the child's progress during that period.

IDENTIFYING HANDICAPS IN YOUNG CHILDREN

The search for young children with handicapping conditions so that they could be given necessary services early in life was given formal mandate in the 1967 amendment to the Social Security Act, which required the early and periodic screening, diagnosis, and treatment (EPSDT) of all children on Medicaid. The group included approximately twelve million individuals between birth and 21 years of age.

Frankenburg (1977) presented important criteria for using screening as a technique, since it obviously was beyond professional capabilities to screen all children for all conditions.

1. The condition should be treatable or controllable.
2. Early treatment should help more than later treatment.
3. Screening should be done while distinctive treatment is still possible.
4. A firm diagnosis should be possible in the screened child to differentiate that child from a nondiseased or nonhandicapped individual.
5. The condition sought should be relatively prevalent.
6. The condition should be serious or potentially so.

Using these criteria we should screen for potential mental retardation, hearing problems, and emotional problems since they fit the criterion, but not for phenylketonuria (too rare and treatment must be done in first few weeks of life to be effective), sickle cell anemia (since we cannot do anything about it now), and mild articulation deviations (since the condition is not serious).

In addition to the new concepts, there have been substantial additions to the standard issues, such as *mainstreaming,* in the preschool programs. The *mainstreaming* philosophy of bringing handicapped children into contact with normal children has been carried over into the preschool years through the Head Start program. That program, which focuses primarily on the educational and social needs of low-income children, is required by federal law to draw at least 10 percent of its total enrollment from among handicapped children. Data★ from the 1975–1976 program indicated that 12.2 percent of the children enrolled in the Head Start program across the country could be identified as handicapped.

However, children with speech handicaps were found to dominate the type of handicapped child being served, making up almost half of the total handicapped group and being three times as frequent as any other type of handicap. The more serious handicapping conditions such as emotional disturbance, mental retardation, and sensory handicaps were found quite infrequently in Head Start programs. For example, while mentally retarded children comprise about 20 percent of the total handicapped group under normal circumstances, they made up only 5.8 percent of the Head Start handicapped group (Enscher, Blatt, and Winschel, 1977).

BARRIERS TO IMPLEMENTATION

Despite all of these efforts, the trend toward preschool education for handicapped children has not snowballed as fast as expected, and the majority of preschool handicapped children still receive no special service. Hensley, Jones, and Cain (1975) have reported that over 70 percent of the states, through legislation, allow early education to be offered to handicapped children younger than the legislated school age for normal children. From 40 to 45 percent of the state legislation

★*Preschool Handicapped Children: Data compiled from the survey of Head Start handicapped efforts 1975–1976 for use by researchers, educators, and planners. Washington, D.C., Administration for Children, Youth, and Families, Department of Health, Education, and Welfare, 1977.*

on preschool education is of a mandatory nature; that is, it is supposed to be done as a standard and expected procedure by school systems in that state. However, there has always been a major gap between that which is permitted and that which is done. Until financial support is provided from the states or the federal government, such mandates have the effect of promissory notes to be cashed in at some indefinite time in the future.

Special educators, faced with problems of transforming their programs to fit the philosophy of *least restrictive alternative* and of retraining regular educators to work with the handicapped, have tended to postpone the program development needs of the preschool handicapped for the time being. For example, well-qualified personnel are the hallmark of any successful educational program, and the special education community has been slow in implementing the mandate of the Education for All Handicapped Children Act to educate all children ages 3 through 18. States that do not have provisions in their own laws for the preschool handicapped do not have to provide services by the federal law, either. Only twelve states have certification for teachers of the preschool handicapped. Hirshoren and Umansky (1977) commented, "It is apparent that few states currently have or are concerned about developing separate certification standards for teachers of preschool handicapped children . . . this leaves some questions as to the future status of staffing mandated programs for these children" (p. 191).

The movement to provide special services for all exceptional children who need it from birth on still has many roads to travel before fulfillment, yet it remains one of the most significant trends of the last two decades.

Summary

The major changes that are occurring in our society in relation to the education of exceptional children include the following:

1. Parents are becoming partners with schools in organizing programs for their handicapped children.

2. Federal legislation beginning in 1957 has now culminated in a bill that will assure the education of *all* handicapped children in the public schools. No longer can schools reject children because of the severity of their handicap.

3. The courts have become a major force in decreeing the rights of all handicapped children to an appropriate and free education.

4. The tradition of educating handicapped children in institutions has moved, first, toward integration in the home, community, and special schools and classes in the public schools and, second, toward educating the children in the least restrictive environment with as much interaction with their normal peers as possible. This movement is termed mainstreaming.

5. Labeling and categorizing children may have some advantages in communication and legislation, but it has been abused by mislabeling many children. In addition, a label has little educational relevance since it does not assist a teacher in organizing an educational program. Attempts are now being made to de-emphasize labels.

6. Early education of the handicapped has been demonstrated to accelerate the development of handicapped children. The assistance of the federal government in organizing demonstration projects and in including handicapped children in Head Start has been of great help in the expansion of programs for young handicapped children.

References

ABESON, A., AND J. ZETTEL. 1977. "The End of the Quiet Revolution: The Education of All Handicapped Children Act of 1975." *Exceptional Children* 44 (October): 114–130.

BLATT, B., AND F. GARFUNKEL. 1969. *The Educability of Intelligence.* Washington, D.C.: Council for Exceptional Children.

BRONFENBRENNER, U. 1975. "Is Early Intervention Effective?" In M. Guttentag and E. Streuning, eds., *Handbook of Evaluation Research,* vol. II. Beverly Hills, Calif.: Sage Publications. Pp. 519–603.

CAIN, L. 1976. "Parent Groups: Their Role in a Better Life for the Handicapped." *Exceptional Children* 42 (May): 432–437.

CANSLER, D., G. MARTIN, AND M. VALAND. 1975. *Working with Families.* Winston-Salem, N.C.: Kaplan School Supply.

CANTRELL, R. P., AND M. L. CANTRELL. 1976. "Preventive Mainstreaming: Impact of a Supportive Services Program on Pupils." *Exceptional Children* 42 (April): 381–386.

DE WEERD, J., AND A. COLE. 1976. "Handicapped Children's Early Education Program." *Exceptional Children* (November): 155–157.

DUNN, L. M. 1968. "Special Education for the Mildly Retarded—Is Much of It Justified?" *Exceptional Children* 35 (January): 5–24.

ENSCHER, G., B. BLATT, AND J. WINSCHEL. 1977. "Head Start for the Handicapped: Congressional Mandate Audit." *Exceptional Children* 43 (January): 202–210.

FRANKENBURG, W. 1977. "Considerations for Screening." In N. Ellis and L. Cross, eds., *Planning Programs for Early Education of the Handicapped.* New York: Walker & Co.

FREDERICKS, H., V. BALDWIN, D. GROVE, W. MOORE, C. RIGGS, AND B. LYONS. 1978. "Integrating the Moderately and Severely Handicapped Preschool Child into a Normal Day Care Setting." In M. Guralnick, ed., *Early Intervention and the Integration of Handicapped and Nonhandicapped Children.* Baltimore: University Park Press. Pp. 191–206.

GALLAGHER, J. 1976. "The Sacred and Profane Uses of Labeling." *Mental Retardation* 14 (December): 3–7.

GALLAGHER, J. 1972. *The Search for the Educational System That Doesn't Exist.* Reston, Va.: Council for Exceptional Children.

GALLAGHER, J. 1956. "Rejecting Parents?" *Exceptional Children* 22 (April): 273–276, 294–295.

GALLAGHER, J., P. FORSYTHE, D. RINGELHEIM, AND F. WEINTRAUB. 1975. "Federal and State Funding Patterns for Programs for the Handicapped." In N. Hobbs, ed., *Issues in the Classification of Children: A Handbook on Categories, Labels, and Their Consequences.* San Francisco: Jossey-Bass.

GILHOOL, T. 1976. "Changing Public Policies in the Individualization of Instruction: Roots and Forces." *Education and Training of the Mentally Retarded* 11 (April): 180–188.

GOLDSTEIN, H., J. MOSS, AND L. JORDAN. 1965. "The Efficacy of Special Class Training on the Development of Mentally Retarded Children." Cooperative Research Project No. 619. Washington, D.C.: U.S. Office of Education, Department of Health, Education, and Welfare.

GOODMAN, H., J. GOTTLIEB, AND R. HARRISON. 1972. "Social Acceptance of EMR's Integrated into a Nongraded Elementary School." *American Journal of Mental Deficiency* 76 (January): 412–417.

GOTTLIEB, J. 1974. "Attitudes Toward Retarded Children: Effects of Labeling and Academic Performance." *American Journal of Mental Deficiency* 79 (November): 268–273.

GOTTLIEB, J., J. AGARD, M. KAUFMAN, AND M. SEMMEL. 1976. "Retarded Children Mainstreamed: Practices as They Affect Minority Group Children." In R. L. Jones, ed., *Mainstreaming and the Minority Child.* Reston, Va.: Council for Exceptional Children.

GOTTLIEB, J., AND J. BAKER. 1975. "Socio-Emotional Characteristics of Mainstreamed Children. Report at CEC." *The Relationship between Amount of Integration and the Sociometric Status of Retarded Children.* Report at A.E.R.A.

HARTUP, W. 1978. "Peer Interaction and the Process of Integration." In M. Guralnick, ed., *Early Intervention and the Integration of Handicapped and Nonhandicapped Children.* Baltimore: University Park Press.

HENSLEY, G., C. JONES, AND N. CAIN. 1975. *Questions and Answers: The Education of Exceptional Children.* Denver: Education Commission of the States.

HIRSHOREN, A., AND W. UMANSKY. 1977. "Certification of Teachers of Preschool Handicapped Children." *Exceptional Children* 44 (November): 191–196.

HOBBS, N. 1975. *The Futures of Children.* San Francisco: Jossey–Bass.

HUNT, J. MC V. 1961. *Intelligence and Experience.* New York: Ronald Press.

JOHNSON, G. O. 1950. "A Study of the Social Position of Mentally Handicapped Children in the Regular Grades." *American Journal of Mental Defiency* 55 (July): 60–89.

JONES, R. L., ED. 1976. *Mainstreaming and the Minority Child.* Reston, Va.: Council for Exceptional Children.

KARNES, M., AND J. TESKA. 1975. "Children's Response to Intervention Programs." In J. Gallagher, ed., *The Application of Child Development Research to Exceptional Children.* Reston, Va.: Council for Exceptional Children. Pp. 196–243.

KAUFMAN, M., J. AGARD, AND M. SEMMEL. (1978). *Mainstreaming: Learners and Their Environment.* Baltimore: University Park Press.

KAUFMAN, M., J. GOTTLIEB, J. AGARD, AND M. KUKIC. 1975. "Mainstreaming: Toward an Explication of the Construct." In E. L. Meyen, G. A. Vergason, and R. J. Whelan, eds., *Alternatives for Teaching Exceptional Children.* Denver: Love Publishing Co. Pp. 35–54.

KIRK, S. A. 1974. "The Impact of Labelling on Rejection of the Mentally Ill." *Journal of Health and Social Behavior* 15 (June): 108–117.

KIRK, S. A. 1964. "Research in the Education of the Mentally Retarded." In H. Stevens and R. Heber, eds., *Mental Retardation: A Review of Research.* Chicago: University of Chicago Press. Pp. 57–99.

KIRP, D., P. KURLOFF, AND W. BUSS. 1975. "Legal Mandates and Organizational Change." In N. Hobbs, ed., *Issues in the Classification of Children,* vol. II. San Francisco: Jossey-Bass.

LEVENSTEIN, P. 1971. *Verbal Interaction Project: Aiding Cognitive Growth in Disadvantaged Preschoolers through the Mother-Child Home Program, July 1, 1967–August 31, 1970.* Final Report of Child Welfare, Research and Demonstration Project R-300 to the Children's Bureau, Office of Child Development, Department of Health, Education, and Welfare, Washington, D.C.

MAC MILLAN, D., R. JONES, AND G. ALOIA. 1974. "The Mentally Retarded Label: A Review of Research and Theoretical Analysis." *American Journal of Mental Deficiency* 79 (November): 241–261.

MARCUS, L. 1977. "Patterns of Coping in Families of Psychotic Children." *American Journal of Orthopsychiatry* 47 (July): 388–399.

MARTIN, E. 1968. "Breakthrough for the Handicapped: Legislative History." *Exceptional Children* 34 (March): 493–504.

MELCHER, J. 1976. "Law, Litigation, and Handicapped Children." *Exceptional Children* 43 (November): 126–130.

MERCER, J. 1973. *Labelling the Mentally Retarded.* Riverside: University of California Press.

MERCER, J. 1972. "Discussion of Alternative Value Frames for Classification of Exceptional Children." Manuscript prepared for the National Advisory Committee on Classification of Exceptional Children.

PELOSI, J., AND A. HOCUTT. 1977. *The Education for All Handicapped Children Act: Issues and Implications.* Chapel Hill: Frank Porter Graham Child Development Center, University of North Carolina at Chapel Hill.

REYNOLDS, M. C., AND J. W. BIRCH. 1977. *Teaching Exceptional Children in All America's Schools.* Reston, Va.: Council for Exceptional Children.

RYAN, S., ED. 1974. *A Report on Longitudinal Evaluation of Preschool Programs,* vol. I. Office of Child Development, Department of Health, Education, and Welfare. Publication No. (OHD) 74-24. Washington, D.C..

SCHLOSSMAN, S. 1976. "Before Head Start: Notes Toward a History of Parent Education in America, 1897–1929." *Harvard Educational Review* 46: 436–467.

SHOTE, J., R. IANO, AND J. MC GETTIGAN. 1972. "Teacher Attitudes Associated with the Integration of Handicapped Children." *Exceptional Children* 38 (May): 677–683.

SMITH, I., AND S. GREENBERG. 1975. "Teacher Attitudes and the Labelling Process." *Exceptional Children* 41 (February): 319–324.

STEDMAN, D. 1977. "Early Childhood Intervention Programs." In B. Caldwell and D. Stedman, eds., *Infant Education: A Guide for Helping Handicapped Children in the First Three Years.* New York: Walker & Co. Pp. 1–12.

TURNBULL, H., AND A. TURNBULL, EDS. 1978. *Parents Speak Out: Views from the Other Side of a Two Way Mirror.* Columbus, Ohio: Charles E. Merrill.

WARNOCK, H. M. 1978. *Special Educational Needs: Report of the Committee of Enquiry into the Education of Handicapped Children and Young People.* London: Her Majesty's Stationery Office.

ADJUNCTIVE SERVICES Services that supplement or support the basic educational program. Also various diagnostic procedures, medical consultation, paraprofessional aides, and the use of mechanical aids in vision and hearing.

ADVENTITIOUS Acquired accidentally in contrast to congenital or inherent causes.

AGRAPHIA Impairment in the ability to write.

ALBINISM Hereditary lack of pigment in the iris, skin, and hair.

ALEXIA Loss of the ability to read written or printed language.

AMINO ACID One of a group of acids that are both basic and acid and are obtained from protein by hydrolysis.

AMNIOCENTESIS A procedure for analyzing the amniotic fluid (a watery liquid in which the embryo is suspended) of the pregnant woman to determine any genetic deficits in the unborn child.

ANGULAR GYRUS A cerebral convolution that forms the back part of the lower parietal region of the brain.

ANTICONVULSANT MEDICATION Medication employed to inhibit or prevent the onset of epileptic or other convulsive seizures.

APHASIA Loss or impairment of the ability to communicate by language, spoken or written, or by signs.

ASPHYXIA Loss of consciousness as a result of too little oxygen. Considered as one possible cause of brain damage at birth.

ASPIRATE To pronounce a vowel, a consonant, or a word with an initial *h* sound.

ASTHMA A disease marked by recurrent attacks of wheezing coughs, labored breathing (particularly on expiration of air), and a sense of constriction due to spasmodic contraction of the bronchi.

ATAXIA A form of cerebral palsy marked by incoordination in voluntary muscular movements.

ATHETOSIS A form of cerebral palsy marked by slow, recurring, weaving movements of arms and legs, and by facial grimaces.

AUDIOGRAM A graphic record of hearing acuity at selected intensities throughout the normal range of audibility, recorded from a pure-tone audiometer.

AUDIOMETER An instrument for testing acuity of hearing.

AUDITORY ASSOCIATION Ability to relate concepts presented orally.

AUDITORY CLOSURE The ability to recognize the whole word or phrase from the presentation of a partial auditory stimulus.

AUDITORY RECEPTION The ability to derive meaning from orally presented material.

AUDITORY SEQUENTIAL MEMORY The ability to remember a sequence of auditory stimuli.

AURA, EPILEPTIC A subjective sensation that precedes and marks the onset of an epileptic attack.

AUTISM   A childhood disorder rendering the child noncommunicative and showing ritualistic behavior or obsession with sameness.

AVERSIVE STIMULUS   A stimulus that a subject will avoid if possible.

BEHAVIOR MODIFICATION   Applied behavior analysis, using behavior concepts and laws to deal with problems of education and other life adjustments.

BILINGUAL   Using or able to use two languages.

BRONCHIECTASIS   A chronic dilation of one of the two main branches of the windpipe or their subdivisions.

CARBOHYDRATE   Any of various neutral compounds as sugars, starches, and cellulose that constitute a major part of human foods.

CATARACT   A condition in which the crystalline lens of the eye, its capsule, or both become opaque with consequent dimming of vision.

CATASTROPHIC REACTION   Response to a shock or a threatening situation with which an individual is unprepared to cope. Behavior is inadequate, vacillating, inconsistent, and generally retarded.

CENTRAL NERVOUS SYSTEM (CNS)   That part of the nervous system to which sensory impulses are transmitted and from which motor impulses originate; in vertebrates, the brain and spinal cord.

CEPHALIC   Pertaining to the head.

CEREBRAL DOMINANCE   An assumption that one cerebral hemisphere generally dominates the other in control of bodily movements. In most individuals the left side of the brain controls language and is considered the dominant hemisphere.

CEREBRAL DYSFUNCTION   Refers to a specific learning disability in mental functioning where the suspected cause is in physiological or neurologic operation of the brain.

CEREBRAL PALSY   Any of a number of abnormal conditions affecting control of the motor system due to brain lesions.

CEREBROSPINAL FLUID   The fluid that circulates in certain spaces within the brain and down the central canal of the spinal cord.

CHROMOSOME   One of the minute bodies in the nucleus of a cell that contains the genes or hereditary factors.

CLEFT PALATE   Congenital fissure of the roof of the mouth, often associated with cleft lip (harelip).

CLONIC   Pertaining to a spasm (clonus) in which rigidity and relaxation alternate in rapid succession.

CLONUS   Involuntary rapid contractions and relaxations of a muscle.

CONDUCTIVE HEARING LOSS   A condition that reduces the intensity of the sound vibrations reaching the auditory nerve in the inner ear.

CONGENITAL   Present in an individual at birth.

CONSERVATION   The ability to retain a concept of area, mass, length, and other features when superficial changes are made in the appearance of an object or scene.

CONTROL GROUP   A group of subjects who are similar to those used in an experiment but who do not receive the experimental treatment.

CRITERION REFERENCE TEST   A test designed to measure a child's development in terms of absolute levels of mastery, as opposed to the child's status relative to other children, as in a norm reference test.

CYSTIC FIBROSIS   A hereditary disease due to a generalized dysfunction of the pancreas.

DECIBEL   A unit of measure of the relative loudness of sound, from the faintest sound that can be heard to a sound that is painful. It is used in measuring the degree of hearing loss.

DIABETES MELLITUS   A disorder of carbohydrate metabolism, characterized by insulin deficiency and an excessive amount of glucose (sugar) in the urine and in the blood.

DIAGNOSTIC PRESCRIPTIVE TEACHING   An educational strategy of delineating a child's strengths and weaknesses and then of designing a specific program for teaching on the basis of those findings.

DIPLEGIA   Bilateral paralysis affecting like parts on both sides of the body.

DISINHIBITION   Lack of ability to refrain from response to what is perceived, often resulting in hyperactivity and distractibility.

DYSARTHRIA   Difficulty in the articulation of words due to involvement of the central nervous system.

DYSCALCULIA   Inability to perform mathematical functions.

DYSGRAPHIA   Inability to produce the motor movements required for handwriting.

DYSLEXIA   Impairment of the ability to read.

EDEMA   The presence of abnormally large amounts of fluid in the intercellular tissue spaces of the body.

ELECTROENCEPHALOGRAPH   An instrument for graphically recording electrical brain waves.

EMBRYO   The human organism from conception up to the third month of pregnancy.

ENCEPHALITIS LETHARGICA   An infectious inflammation of the brain (sleeping sickness).

ENDOGENOUS   Originating from within. A term used to characterize a constitutional condition. Compare *exogenous.*

EPICANTHIC FOLD   A congenital formation of the eyelid consisting of a vertical fold of skin on either side of the nose.

EPILEPSY   A group of nervous diseases marked primarily by convulsions of varying forms and degrees.

ETIOLOGY   The study of causes or origins of a disease or condition.

EXAPHORIA   Insufficient action of certain muscles of the eye so that one eye tends to deviate outward but can be controlled by extra muscular effort.

EXOGENOUS   Derived or developed from external causes.

EXPERIMENTAL GROUP   A group participating in an experiment that is subjected to whatever is being tested or evaluated.

FAMILIAL   Occurring in members of the same family, as a familial disease.

FEEBLEMINDED   An outmoded term used to refer to the entire range of mentally retarded individuals. In England it referred to the higher levels of the mentally retarded.

FETUS   The unborn child from the third month of pregnancy until birth.

FIGURE-GROUND DISTURBANCE   The inability to discriminate a figure from its background.

FINGER AGNOSIA   The inability to recognize or identify the individual fingers of one's own hand when stimulated by touch.

GALACTOSEMIA   An inherited condition of mental retardation caused by an error in the metabolism of the galactose in milk.

GLAUCOMA   A disease characterized by increased pressure inside the eyeball caused by accumulation of fluid in the front portion.

GONORRHEA   An infectious disease of the genitourinary tract, transmitted chiefly by sexual intercourse.

GRAMMATIC CLOSURE   Ability to make use of the redundancies of oral language in acquiring automatic habits for handling syntax and grammatical inflections.

GRAND MAL   An epileptic seizure in which the convulsions are severe and widespread with rather prolonged loss of awareness.

HAPTIC   Pertaining to the sense of touch and kinesthesis.

HEMIPLEGIA   Paralysis of one side of the body.

HEMOPHILIA   A hereditary condition characterized by delayed clotting of the blood with consequent difficulty in checking hemorrhage.

HYDROCEPHALUS   A condition of excess cerebrospinal fluid within the ventricular and subarachnoid spaces in the brain.

HYPERACTIVITY   Excessive movement or motor restlessness.

HYPERKINESIS   Pathologically excessive motion.

HYPERTONICITY   Excessive tension in the condition of a muscle not at work.

HYPOACTIVE   Showing diminished motor function or activity.

IDIOT   An outdated term referring to the most severely retarded for whom total dependency throughout life was expected.

IMBECILE   An outmoded term used to refer to the moderately retarded (IQ range 25–50), who are roughly equivalent to the subgroup referred to as trainable retarded children.

INCUS   The central one of three small bones in the middle ear that transmit sound to the inner ear.

INDIVIDUAL EDUCATION PLAN (IEP)   A formal statement of short-term and long-term objectives and educational services to meet the unique needs of a particular handicapped child.

INSULIN   A protein hormone produced by the pancreas and secreted into the blood where it regulates carbohydrate (sugar) metabolism.

INTERINDIVIDUAL   Pertaining to a comparison of one person with another or of one person with a group of individuals.

INTONATION   Rise and fall in pitch of the voice in speech.

INTRAINDIVIDUAL   Pertaining to a comparison of different characteristics within an individual.

IN UTERO   In the uterus; the period of time in a baby's life from conception until birth.

KERATITIS   Inflammation of the cornea.

KINESTHESIS   Sensations from nerve endings in the muscles, joints, and tendons that are stimulated by bodily movements and tensions.

LATERALITY   Awareness of the two sides of the body and the ability to identify left and right. Often used to mean preferential use of one side of the body.

LEAST RESTRICTIVE ALTERNATIVE   The philosophy, supported in some legislation, of bringing the handicapped as close to the normal social setting as possible.

LIPIDS   Any one of numerous fats and fatlike materials that, together with carbohydrates and proteins, form the principal structural components of living cells.

MAINSTREAMING   An administrative procedure for keeping exceptional children in the normal classroom for the majority of the school day.

MALLEUS   The largest and outermost of the three small bones in the middle ear that carry sound to the inner ear.

MALOCCLUSION   Abnormality in the coming together of the teeth.

MASTOIDECTOMY   Surgical removal of the mastoid cells surrounding the temporal bone.

MEGAVITAMIN THERAPY   A treatment program that features an unusually heavy dosage of selected vitamins to modify behavioral and emotional disturbances.

MENINGITIS   Inflammation of the meninges (the membranes covering the brain and spinal cord), sometimes affecting vision, hearing, and/or intelligence.

METABOLISM   The conversion of digested nutrients into building material for living tissue or energy to meet the body's needs.

MINIMUM BRAIN DYSFUNCTION   A poorly defined syndrome often including hyperactivity, distractibility, perseveration, and disorders of perception, body image, laterality, and sometimes symbolization.

MONOPLEGIA   Paralysis of one body part.

MORON   A term not in current use that referred to the upper range of mentally retarded individuals capable of self-sufficiency under favorable environmental conditions. Roughly equivalent to the group referred to as "educable."

MOSAICISM   A form of Down's syndrome (mongolism) in which adjacent cells will be found to contain different numbers of chromosomes.

MUSCULAR DYSTROPHY   One of the more common primary diseases of muscle. It is characterized by weakness and atrophy of the skeletal muscles with increasing disability and deformity as the disease progresses.

MYOPIA   Nearsightedness in which the rays from distant objects are brought to a focus before they reach the retina.

NEPHROSIS   A noninflammatory, degenerative condition of the kidney.

NEUROLOGIC   Pertaining to the normal and abnormal functions of the nervous system.

NEUROPHYSIOLOGICAL   Pertaining to the physiology of the nervous system.

NORMALIZATION   A philosophy encouraging environmental design as much like the norm as possible. Even in institutionalized settings it is possible to create more normal living arrangements to aid eventual adaptive behavior.

OBTURATOR   Any organic structure or prosthetic device in the body (e.g., the soft palate) that closes or stops an opening.

OPEN CLASSROOM   A classroom providing learning centers in open space, allowing children of various levels of ability some freedom of choice, interests, and creativity.

OPHTHALMIA NEONATORUM   Gonorrheal inflammation of, and discharge from, the conjunctiva of the eye of the newborn baby under two weeks.

OPHTHALMOLOGIST   A physician who specializes in the diagnosis and treatment of defects and diseases of the eye.

OPTOMETRIST   A person who examines, measures, and treats certain eye defects by methods requiring no physician's license.

OSTEOMYELITIS   Inflammation of bone that begins with a hematogenous abcess and, if not checked, may spread through the bone to involve the marrow and other parts.

OTITIS MEDIA   An inflammation of the middle ear.

OTOLARYNGOSCOPIC   Referring to an examination of the ear, nose, and throat.

OTOSCLEROSIS   The formation of spongy bone in the capsule bone in the ear.

PARAPLEGIA   Paralysis of both legs and the lower part of the body; motion and sensation are affected.

PERINATAL   The period of time closely surrounding the time of birth.

PERSEVERATION   Continuation of an activity after cessation of the causative stimulus.

PETIT MAL   Epileptic seizure in which there may be only a momentary dizziness or blackout or some automatic action of which the patient has no knowledge.

PHARYNX   That part of the throat that leads from mouth and nose to the larynx.

PHENYLKETONURIA (PKU)   An inherited error of metabolism resulting in a lack of the necessary enzyme for oxydizing phenylalanine which in turn promotes accumulation of phenylpyruvic acid and mental retardation.

PHONATION   The production of speech sounds.

PHONEME   A speech sound or closely related variants commonly regarded as being the same sound.

POLIOMYELITIS   An acute viral disease characterized by involvement of the central nervous system, sometimes resulting in paralysis.

POSTNATAL   After birth.

PRENATAL   Occurring or existing before birth.

PROPRIOCEPTIVE   Pertaining to stimulations from the muscles, tendons, and labyrinth which give information concerning the position and movement of the body and its members.

PROSTHESIS   An artificial substitute for an absent part of the body.

PROSTHODONTICS   Making dental substitutes such as crowns, bridges, and dentures.

PSYCHOLINGUISTICS   The study of the process whereby the intentions of speakers are transformed into signals and whereby those signals are transformed into interpretations by hearers.

PSYCHOMOTOR EPILEPSY   A form of epilepsy in which the seizures consist of purposeful but inappropriate acts; a difficult form to diagnose and control.

PSYCHOPATHOLOGY   The study of the causes and nature of mental disease.

PSYCHOTROPIC DRUG   A medication used primarily for its behavioral effects; used with children particularly for its influence on attention and hyperactivity.

RECESSIVE TRAIT   A trait, controlled by heredity, that remains latent or subordinate to a dominant characteristic.

REINFORCEMENT   A procedure to strengthen a response by the administration of immediate rewards (positive reinforcement).

RESONANCE   The vibrating quality of a sound.

RESPONSE   The activity of an organism or an organ, or the inhibition of previous activity resulting from stimulation.

RETINA   A layer of light-sensitive cells at the back of the eyeball. These cells receive the visual image formed by the lens and carry the message to the brain via the optic nerve.

RETROLENTAL FIBROPLASIA   A disease of the retina in which a mass of scar tissue forms in back of the lens of the eye. Both eyes are usually affected, and it occurs chiefly in infants born prematurely who received excessive oxygen.

RHEUMATOID ARTHRITIS   A systemic disease characterized by inflammation of the joints and a broad spectrum of manifestations often involving destruction of the joints with resultant deformity.

RH INCOMPATIBILITY   The combination of an Rh-negative mother and an Rh-positive father can produce antibodies that can cause serious consequences for the fetus unless the condition is identified and blood transfer procedures are instituted immediately after birth.

RUBELLA   German measles.

SCHEMA   A number of ideas or concepts combined into a coherent plan; a model that displays the essential or important relations between concepts.

SCHIZOPHRENIA   A group of psychotic reactions characterized by fundamental disturbances in reality relationships, by a conceptual world determined excessively by feeling, and by marked affective, intellectual, and overt behavioral disturbances.

SENSORIMOTOR   Referring to an act whose nature is primarily dependent on the combined or integrated functioning of sense organs and motor mechanisms.

SENSORY-NEURAL HEARING LOSS   A defect of the inner ear or the auditory nerve in transmitting impulses to the brain.

SOUND BLENDING   Ability to synthesize the separate parts of a word and produce an integrated whole.

SPASTICITY   Excessive tension of the muscles and heightened resistance to flexion or extension, as in cerebral palsy.

SPHINCTER   A ringlike muscle that closes a natural orifice.

SPINA BIFIDA   A defect of closure in the posterior bony wall of the spinal canal without associated abnormality of the spinal cord or meninges.

STAPES   A small stirrup-shaped bone, the inner-most of a chain of three bones in the middle ear transmitting sound to the inner ear.

STILL'S DISEASE   Juvenile rheumatoid arthritis.

STIMULUS   The physical, chemical, biological, and social events that act on the individual.

STREPHOSYMBOLIA   Reversal in perception of left-right order especially in letter or word order; "twisted symbols."

STUTTERING   A pattern of speaking in which the even flow of words is interrupted by hesitations, rapid repetition of speech elements, and/or spasms of breathing.

SYNERGIC   Acting together or in cooperation.

SYNTAX   That part of a grammar system that deals with the arrangement of word forms to show their mutual relations in a sentence.

SYNTHESIS   Process of putting together to form a whole.

SYPHILIS   A contagious venereal disease.

TACHISTOSCOPE   A machine that exposes visual material for a variable period of time.

TACTILE (tactual)   Having to do with the sense of touch.

TASK ANALYSIS   A procedure of reducing complex tasks to their simpler components so that they can be taught more easily.

TAXONOMY   The science of classification of objects or events into natural or related groups based on some factor common to each.

TONIC   Characterized by contraction of a muscle sufficient to keep the muscle taut but not sufficient to cause movement.

TOTAL COMMUNICATION   The incorporation of appropriate aural, manual, and oral methods of communication to ensure effective communication with and among hearing-impaired persons.

TRANSLOCATION   A type of chromosomal aberration, found in some cases of Down's syndrome (mongolism), in which a chromosome has broken and become fused to another chromosome.

TRAUMA   Any experience that inflicts serious damage to the organism. It may be a psychological as well as a physiological insult.

TRIPLEGIA   Paralysis of three of the body's limbs.

TRISOMY 21   Mongolism caused by having three instead of a pair of chromosome 21.

UVULA   The pendent fleshy lobe suspended from the soft palate, above the back of the tongue.

VERBAL EXPRESSION   Ability to express one's own concepts verbally in a discrete, relevant, and approximately factual manner.

VISUAL ASSOCIATION   Seeing relationships among concepts presented visually.

VISUAL CLOSURE   Ability to identify a visual stimulus from an incomplete visual presentation.

VISUAL FUSION   The coordination of the separate images in the two eyes into one image.

VISUAL RECEPTION   Ability to gain meaning from visual symbols.

VISUAL SEQUENTIAL MEMORY   Ability to reproduce sequences of visual items from memory.

Education (cont.)

and psychoeducational approach, 407–409

and re-education (Re-Ed program), 417–419, 421 (see also Emotional disturbance)

"special" defined, 12–14, 24 (see also Special services)

U.S., influences on and philosophy of, 3, 6, 23, 60, 96–97

vocational and prevocational
for hearing impaired, 228, 230
for mentally retarded, 160–161

See also Individualized instruction; Learning environment(s); Schools; Teachers; Teaching/educational strategies

Education, U.S. Office of, 8, 61, 199, 238, 283, 288, 437, 472, 492

Education and the Brain (National Society for the Study of Education), 299

Education for All Handicapped Children Act, see Laws and legislation

Egalitarianism, see Equality of opportunity

Einstein, Albert, 70–71

Elementary and Secondary Education Act (1956), 471, 472. See also Laws and legislation

Emotional disturbance: and behavioral disorders, 389, 416 (see also Behavioral disorders)

and communication disorders, 300, 370

drug therapy for, 420–421, 426

feedback utilization and, 53

the hearing impaired and, 197

and labeling, 482, 491

and learning disabilities, 416–417

memory and, 48

mental retardation and, 445

and multiple handicaps
cerebral palsy, 461
hearing impairment, 197, 438–439, 461
mental retardation, 445, 461
visual impairment, 242

prevalence of, 8, 9, 435

screening for, 496

social attitude toward, 418, 486

and special services for the disturbed, 8, 9, 17, 405

vs. "mainstreaming," 487

open education program, 419–420

psychiatric hospital, 425

Re-Ed program, 417–419, 421

Employment, see Vocational status and employment

Encephalitis, 120–121, 434, 442

"Engineered classroom," 414–415

England, see Great Britain

Enrollment: public school, see Schools in special services, see Special services

Environment: adaptability to, see Adaptability

the blind's mastery of, 265–267, 269, 275

classroom, and hyperactivity, 323–324

and environmental intervention, 122–128, 129 (see also Institutionalization)

learning, see Learning environment(s)

and nature-nuture controversy, 122, 128 (see also Genetics)

physical, handicapped children and, 457, 458

social, and behavioral disorders, 400–402, 425

social, of learning disabled, 297–298, 310, 370, 372

See also Community

Epilepsy, 435, 457. See also Health

EPSDT (early and periodic screening, diagnosis, and treatment), 495. See also Diagnosis; Education; Tests and testing

Equality of opportunity, 3, 27, 60, 96

Europe: education in, 5, 6, 59–60, 135–136

ethnic groups from, compared, 78

Evaluation: of acceleration effects, 94

of gifted child and of programs for, 94–96, 98

in information processing, 48, 49–50, 53–54

by intellectually subnormal, 105

of "mainstreaming," 485–487

of programs for multiply/severely handicapped children, 456–457, 461

as thinking process, 86, 88–89 (see also Thinking abilities/strategies)

See also Diagnosis; Tests and testing

Exceptional children: classification of, 21–23 (see also Classification/categorization)

defined, 3–4, 23–24, 457, 458

and extremes of exceptionality, 53

identification of, 14, 23, 484 (see also Diagnosis)

prevalence of, 7–9